Oxford Start P9-DHF-869 ry

Second edition

Also available from Oxford University Press

Oxford Take off in German
Language learning pack with almost 5 hours of audio
Book and 4 × 75 minute cassettes 0–19–860275–8
Book and 4 × 75 minute CDs 0–19–860294–4
Book only 0–19–860295–2

Oxford Take off in German Dictionary
0–19–860332–0
(available in the UK only)

The Oxford Colour German Dictionary
Colour headwords throughout
0–19–860188–3
0–19–860189–1 (US edition)

The Pocket Oxford German Dictionary
Ideal for intermediate learners
0–19–860280–4

Oxford German Grammar
0–19–860342–8

Oxford German Wordpack
0–19–860336–3

Oxford German Verbpack
0–19–860339–8

The Oxford Starter German Dictionary

Second edition

Edited by
Neil and Roswitha Morris

Revised introduction
Graham Bishop
Mary O'Neill

C 2/

OXFORD
UNIVERSITY PRESS

Great Clarendon Street, Oxford OX2 6DP

Oxford University Press is a department of the University of Oxford.
It furthers the University's objective of excellence in research, scholarship,
and education by publishing worldwide in

Oxford New York
Athens Auckland Bangkok Bogotá Buenos Aires Calcutta
Cape Town Chennai Dar es Salaam Delhi Florence Hong Kong Istanbul
Karachi Kuala Lumpur Madrid Melbourne Mexico City Mumbai
Nairobi Paris São Paulo Singapore Taipei Tokyo Toronto Warsaw

with associated companies in Berlin Ibadan

Oxford is a registered trade mark of Oxford University Press
in the UK and in certain other countries

Published in the United States
by Oxford University Press Inc., New York

British Library Cataloguing in Publication Data
Data available

Library of Congress Cataloging in Publication Data
Data available

ISBN 0-19-860329-0
ISBN 0-19-968014-0 (educational edition)

10 9 8 7 6 5 4 3 2

Typeset in Swift and Arial by Latimer Trend & Company Ltd.
Printed in Italy

Contents

Proprietary terms

This dictionary contains some words which are, or
are asserted to be, proprietary names or trade marks.
Their inclusion does not imply that they have
acquired for legal purposes a non-proprietary or
general significance, nor is any other judgement
implied concerning their legal status. In cases where
the editors have some evidence that a word is used as
a proprietary name or trade mark, this is indicated
by the symbol ®, but no judgement concerning the
legal status of such words is made or implied thereby.

Introduction

A fresh approach

Created to meet the specific needs of English speakers who are starting to learn German, the *Oxford Starter German Dictionary* takes a completely fresh approach to helping you make sense of the new language. We have changed the design of the entries to make them different from entries in traditional dictionaries. What exactly is it that makes the entries so different?

* they have a new, clearer layout
* they are designed to provide the information you need in a helpful, readable way with the minimum of clutter
* since you will be using the English–German and the German–English sides of the dictionary for different tasks, each side works differently and it shows in the way the information is presented.

Because of these major changes, you will find that the *Oxford Starter German Dictionary* is a far more efficient language-learning tool for you as a beginner. Finding the right information quickly and easily will make German more satisfying to learn.

A clearer layout

Each page of the dictionary presents the information you will need in entries which are well-spaced, easy to read, and which have a consistent layout both in English and German. The main features of the new design are:

* bullet points and numbers to indicate the various uses of each word
* different typefaces as well as the symbol = to indicate the switch from one language to the other
* use of the symbol ! to indicate important grammar points
* use of the symbol ✹ to indicate INFORMAL or colloquial words
* use of the symbol ☞ to indicate words which should be used with care.

More helpful and easy to use

The entries have been designed so that you can find the information you need quickly. Many of the conventions in traditional dictionaries which you may find confusing or off-putting have been avoided, so:

* PARTS OF SPEECH and grammatical terms are written out in full for you. A separate section explains all the terms used if you should need to find out more about them.
* Explanations of specific grammar points and notes on how a word is actually used are provided in short paragraphs at appropriate places in the dictionary text.
* Groups of words which behave in a similar way, or which present similar difficulties, are treated in a consistent manner which you will quickly come to recognize. You will also find handy language notes which deal with such concepts as colours, countries, and dates.

Words in capital letters are found in the glossary

- The language used in the examples and in the signposts to the right translation has been carefully chosen to ensure that it is clear and up to date.
- At the back of the dictionary, the basics of German grammar are explained in relation to all the important PARTS OF SPEECH that are referred to in the text.

This dictionary, with its precise and lively examples, contains all the words you will need as a beginner and includes plenty of examples of British as well as American English in both the English–German and German–English texts.

Using the two sides of the dictionary to do different things

Each side of the dictionary has been separately designed to take account of the different ways in which you will use it.

The English–German side is longer. Since you are moving from your own language into German, you will need more detailed guidance. We have provided regular reminders about essential grammar rules. The signposts which pinpoint the precise context in which a word is used are there to help you choose the right translation. These 'sense indicators' are also supported with a wide selection of useful examples.

The German–English side makes the most of what you already know about your own language. The presentation of translations from German is therefore more streamlined. There is detailed treatment of the more irregular and unpredictable features of German which you may come across in newspapers and magazines, for example. A particularly useful feature is that the variations in spelling of IRREGULAR VERBS, ADJECTIVES and PLURAL NOUNS are all listed as separate entries in the word list. These words then send you to the main dictionary form where you will find the translation you are looking for.

New German spelling

In 1996 changes to the spelling of some German words were agreed by the governments of Germany, Austria, and Switzerland. These changes took some time to be adopted in German-speaking countries, but the aim is that new spellings will be used in all written texts by 2005. Until then, you may come across both old and new spellings.

This dictionary generally uses new spellings, but German headwords also list old spellings in brackets. A special symbol ⓄⓁⒹ is used to make this clear. Where necessary, the old spelling is cross-referred to the new spelling.

Words in capital letters are found in the glossary

How to use the dictionary

Where to look for a word

Bilingual dictionaries are divided into two sections.

- The first section gives you a list of German words followed by their English equivalents as well as information about the contexts in which they are used.

- The second section gives you a list of English words followed by the German words which match their exact meaning according to the contexts in which they are used.

    Decide first which section you need to look at.

German–English

Every dictionary entry tells you whether that particular word is a VERB, an ADJECTIVE, a PREPOSITION, or another PART OF SPEECH. If you need help to find out what any PART OF SPEECH means, look it up in the glossary of grammatical terms on pages xiii to xiv. NOUNS are preceded in the German wordlist by the DEFINITE ARTICLE to show their GENDER: *der* for MASCULINE, *die* for FEMININE and *das* for NEUTER nouns. This is followed by the NOUN'S PLURAL form, if it has one, and then the translation:

> die **Gabel**, *plural* Gabeln
>   = fork

VERBS are marked if they are irregular, and you will find a list of IRREGULAR VERBS and their forms on page 361. A note tells you if a VERB takes *sein* in the PERFECT TENSE, and SEPARABLE VERBS are marked with a vertical bar after the PREFIX:

> **ab|fahren** *irregular verb* (**!** *sein*)
>   = to leave

If there is more than one PART OF SPEECH within an entry, numbers are used to separate them. Within each PART OF SPEECH, different senses are given after bullet points (•):

> **sicher**
> **1** *adjective*
>   = safe
>   = certain, = sure
> **2** *adverb*
>   = safely
>   = certainly, = surely
>   sicher! = certainly!

Cross-references are marked with a ▶. These are specially useful for VERB forms that you might not otherwise recognize:

> **bog** ▶ biegen

Words in capital letters are found in the glossary

English–German

The English–German entries tend to be longer, so it is a good idea to scan the whole entry to find the sense which is closest to the one you need. Remember, different senses are marked with a •. In examples, different words with which a PHRASE can be used are put in square brackets. This means that it is possible to substitute another word for the alternatives given in the dictionary:

> **as** [intelligent | rich | strong ...] **as** = so
> [intelligent | reich | stark ...] wie

On this side, you will again find additional information on points of basic German grammar such as the use of *sein* when forming the PERFECT TENSE of certain VERBS and the CASE of NOUNS following PREPOSITIONS. Additional notes in entries are there to help with special points of grammar and usage:

> **along** *preposition*
> = entlang (+ *accusative*)
>> ! *Note that* entlang *is usually put after the noun, which is in the accusative. When* entlang *is used with a verb, it forms a new, compound verb.*
>
> **along the street** = die Straße entlang
> **to run along** = entlanglaufen (! *sein*)

In relevant entries, a number refers you to the page with a boxed note:

> **seven** *adjective*
> = sieben ▶**Numbers p. 282**

Getting to know your dictionary

In the central section of this dictionary—pages 165 to 172—you will find a short section of games and exercises which will help you get to know your dictionary better and to use it more effectively. Your dictionary is a very important study aid which can greatly help you to find out how the German language works and how to expand your vocabulary.

Words in capital letters are found in the glossary

How German–English entries work

headword	**ab**
numbers indicating different PARTS OF SPEECH	**1** *preposition* (+ *dative*) = from
	2 *adverb* = off
	ab und zu = now and again
translation clearly indicated by =	
superior numbers show different words with the same spelling	die **Bank**¹, *plural* Banken = bank
PLURAL given for every NOUN that has one	
	die **Bank²**, *plural* Bänke = bench
	decken *verb*
PART OF SPEECH	
bullet points indicating separate senses of the headword	• = to cover
	den Tisch decken = to lay the table
example	
	• **jemanden decken** = to cover up for someone, (*in sport*) = to mark someone
special meaning indicated	
GENDER	die **EU**
	(*Europäische Union*) = EU
ABBREVIATION	
what ABBREVIATION stands for	
	fährt ▶ fahren
cross-reference to headword	
division of a SEPARABLE VERB shown by a vertical bar	**hinaus|gehen** *irregular verb* (**!** *sein*)
	• = to go out
	• **das Zimmer geht nach Westen hinaus** = the room faces west
IRREGULAR VERB indicated (see **gehen** in list of IRREGULAR VERBS)	
MASCULINE/FEMININE/ NEUTER forms of a headword are given where necessary	**jener/jene/jenes**
	1 *adjective* = that, (*plural*) = those
	2 *pronoun* = that one, (*plural*) = those
	das **Klo×** *plural* Klos = loo
symbol drawing attention to a German word used only in informal situations	
possible SUBJECTS used with the VERB, giving different translations	**los|gehen** *irregular verb* (**!** *sein*)
	• = to set off, = to start
	• = (*of a button*) = to come off
	• = (*of a bomb*) = to go off
note that this verb takes **sein** in the PERFECT TENSE	
REFLEXIVE VERB shown in full	**nähern: sich nähern** *verb* = to approach
MASCULINE and FEMININE forms of NOUNS shown as separate headwords	der **Sänger**, *plural* Sänger = singer
	die **Sängerin**, *plural* Sängerinnen = singer
old spelling	die **Walnuss** (**Walnuß**⊙ᴸᴰ), *plural* Walnüsse = walnut

Words in capital letters are found in the glossary

How English–German entries work

headword ········· **adventure** *noun*
= (das) Abenteuer

GENDER of German
NOUNS given in
brackets

benefit
numbers indicating ········· **1** *noun*
different PARTS OF
SPEECH
(*advantage*) = (der) Vorteil
it will be to your benefit = das wird zu
deinem Vorteil sein
2 *verb* = nützen (+ *dative*) ································· information on the
CASE taken by a
German VERB

superior numbers ·········
show different
words with the
same spelling
case¹ *noun*
= (der) Fall
in case = falls

case² *noun* ································ PART OF SPEECH
bullet points ·········· • (*suitcase*) = (der) Koffer
indicating separate
senses of the
headword
• (*for spectacles*) = (das) Etui
• (*crate*) = (die) Kiste

dentist *noun*
MASCULINE and ·········· (der) Zahnarzt / (die) Zahnärztin
FEMININE forms of
NOUNS given with
GENDERS
▶ Professions p. 298 ································ cross-reference to a
boxed usage note
with its page
number

kick
1 *verb*
to kick someone = jemandem einen Tritt
geben
to kick the ball = den Ball schießen ·········· translation clearly
indicated by =
2 *noun* = (der) Tritt

PHRASAL VERBS ·········· **kick off**
appear separately in
blue at the end of a
VERB entry
= anstoßen
kick out
to kick someone out = jemanden
rausschmeißen✶ ································ symbol drawing
attention to a
German word used
only in INFORMAL
situations

lack
1 *noun* = (der) Mangel
example showing ·········· **lack of** [money|interest|tact ...] = Mangel an
alternative uses of a
PHRASE
[Geld |Interesse|Takt ...]
2 *verb* = fehlen an (+ *dative*) ································ information on the
CASE taken by a
German PREPOSITION
he lacks confidence = ihm fehlt es an
Selbstvertrauen

melt *verb*
= schmelzen (! *sein*) ································ note that this VERB
takes sein in the
PERFECT TENSE

such
information on ·········· **1** *adjective* = solcher/solche/solches
grammatical usage
**! Note that solcher, solche and solches
change their endings in the same way as
der/die/das.**
such a thing should not have happened =
so etwas hätte nicht passieren dürfen
2 *adverb*
example ·········· **they have such a lot of money** = sie haben
so viel Geld

Words in capital letters are found in the glossary

Glossary of grammatical terms

Abbreviation A shortened form of a word or phrase: etc. = **usw.**

Accusative The case of a direct object; some prepositions take the accusative.

Adjective A word describing a noun: a *red* pencil = **ein *roter* Bleistift.**

Adverb A word that describes or changes the meaning of a verb, an adjective or another adverb: she sings *beautifully* = **sie singt *schön.***

Article The definite article, the = **der/die/das,** and indefinite article, a/an = **ein/eine/ein,** used in front of a noun.

Auxiliary verb One of the verbs—**haben, sein, werden**—used to form the perfect or future tense: I will help = **ich *werde* helfen.**

Case The form of a noun, pronoun, adjective or article that shows the part it plays in a sentence; there are four cases—nominative, accusative, genitive and dative.

Clause A self-contained section of a sentence that contains a subject and a verb.

Comparative The form of an adjective or adverb that makes it 'more': smaller = **kleiner,** more clearly = **klarer.**

Compound noun A noun formed from two or more separate words: **der Flughafen** = airport.

Compound verb A verb formed by adding a prefix to a simple verb; in German, some compound verbs are separable (**anfangen**), and some are inseparable (**verlassen**).

Conditional tense A verb tense that expresses what might happen if something else occurred: he would go = **er würde gehen.**

Conjunction A word used to join clauses together: and = **und,** because = **weil.**

Consonant A letter representing a sound that can only be used together with a vowel, such as b, c, d; see vowel.

Dative The case of an indirect object; many prepositions take the dative.

Definite article the = **der/die/das.**

Direct object The noun or pronoun directly affected by the verb: he caught *the ball* = **er fing *den Ball.***

Ending Letters added to the stem of verbs, as well as to nouns and adjectives, according to tense, case, etc.

Feminine One of the three noun genders: **die Frau** = the woman.

Future tense The tense of a verb that refers to something that will happen in the future: I will go = **ich werde gehen.**

Gender One of the three groups of nouns: masculine, feminine or neuter.

Genitive The case that shows possession; some prepositions take the genitive.

Imperfect tense The tense of a verb that refers to something that happened in the past: I went = **ich ging.**

Indefinite article a/an = **ein/eine/ein.**

Indefinite pronoun A pronoun that does not identify a specific person or object: one = **man,** something = **etwas.**

Indirect object The noun or pronoun indirectly affected by the verb, at which the direct object is aimed: I gave *him* the book = **ich gab *ihm* das Buch.**

Infinitive The basic part of a verb: to play = **spielen.**

Informal Informal language is used in everyday conversation. Informal German is marked with a **✱** in the dictionary.

Inseparable verb A verb with a prefix that can never be separated from it: **verstehen, ich verstehe.**

Interjection A sound, word or remark expressing a strong feeling such as anger, fear or joy: oh! = **ach!**

Interrogative pronoun A pronoun that asks a question: who? = **wer?**

Intonation The pattern of sounds made in a sentence as the speaker's voice rises and falls.

Inverted commas The quotation marks put around direct speech: "Yes," he said = **"Ja", sagte er.**

Irregular verb A verb that does not follow one of the set patterns and has its own individual forms; see pages 361 to 364 for a list.

Masculine One of the three noun genders: **der Mann** = the man.

Neuter One of the three noun genders: **das Buch** = the book.

Nominative The case of the subject of a sentence; in sentences with **sein** and

werden the noun after the verb is in the nominative: that is my car = **das ist mein Wagen**.

Noun A word that names a person or thing: apple = **Apfel**.

Number The state of being either singular or plural.

Part of speech A grammatical term for the function of a word; noun, verb, adjective, etc., are parts of speech.

Passive In the passive form the subject of the verb experiences the action rather than performs it: he was asked = **er wurde gefragt**.

Past participle The part of a verb used to form past tenses: made = **gemacht**.

Perfect tense The tense of a verb that refers to something that happened in the past: I have said = **ich habe gesagt**.

Personal pronoun A pronoun that refers to a person or thing: he/she/it = **er/sie/es**.

Phrasal verb A verb combined with a preposition or an adverb to have a particular meaning: to run away = **weglaufen**.

Phrase A self-contained section of a sentence that does not contain a full verb.

Plural Of nouns, etc., referring to more than one: the trees = **die Bäume**.

Possessive pronoun A pronoun that shows possession, belonging to someone or something: mine = **meiner/meine/meins**.

Prefix A syllable or word added to the beginning of another word; in German, the prefix can move from separable verbs (**anfangen**), but stay fixed to inseparable verbs (**verlassen**).

Preposition A word that stands in front of a noun or pronoun, relating it to the rest of the sentence; with = **mit**, for = **für**.

Present participle The part of a verb that in English ends in -ing, and in German adds -d to the infinitive: asking = **fragend**.

Present tense The tense of a verb that refers to something happening now: I make = **ich mache**.

Pronoun A word that stands instead of a noun: he = **er**, she = **sie**, mine = **meiner/meine/meins**, etc.

Pronunciation The way of pronouncing, or speaking, words.

Reflexive pronoun A pronoun that goes with a reflexive verb: **mich, dich, sich, uns, euch, sich**. The reflexive pronouns of some verbs are in the dative.

Reflexive verb A verb whose object is the same as its subject; in German, it is used with a reflexive pronoun, for example **sich waschen**.

Regular verb A verb that follows a set pattern in its different forms.

Relative pronoun A pronoun that introduces a subordinate clause, relating to a person or thing mentioned in the main clause: the man *who* visited us = **der Mann, *der* uns besucht hat**.

Sentence A sequence of words, with a subject and a verb, that can stand on their own to make a statement, as a question or to give a command.

Separable verb A verb with a prefix that can be separated from it in some tenses: **anfangen, ich fange an**.

Singular Of nouns, etc., referring to just one: the tree = **der Baum**.

Stem The part of a verb to which endings are added; **fahr-** is the stem of **fahren**.

Subject In a clause or sentence, the noun or pronoun that causes the action of the verb: *he* caught the ball = **er fing den Ball**.

Subjunctive A verb form that is used to express doubt or unlikelihood: it could be true = **es könnte wahr sein**.

Superlative The form of an adjective or adverb that makes it 'most': the *smallest* house = **das *kleinste* Haus**, most clearly = **am klarsten**.

Syllable Part of a word that forms a spoken unit, usually a vowel sound with consonants before or after: **an-ge-ben**.

Tense The form of a verb that tells when the action takes place: present, future, perfect.

Umlaut Two dots over a vowel—ä, ö, ü—to show a change in pronunciation.

Verb A word or group of words that describes an action: the children *are playing* = **die Kinder *spielen***.

Vowel A letter representing a sound that can be spoken by itself; in German a, ä, e, i, o, ö, u, ü, y.

Pronunciation guide

The following are general guidelines to the way in which German is pronounced. Some of the German sounds can be imitated quite well by using English equivalents, but remember that these are close rather than exact imitations. You will need to listen to native German speakers, perhaps on tape or on the radio, and then imitate their pronunciation, particularly of the vowels a, o and u.

Listening and imitating will also help you with German intonation, the pattern of sounds made in a sentence as the speaker's voice rises and falls.

Vowel sounds

Here there is a major difference between German and English. German vowels are pure sounds, whereas in English vowels usually have one sound quickly followed by another.

In German, each vowel has a long and a short form: for example, an a can be long, as in **Bahn**, or short, as in **hat**. These are given separately in the following list, along with the nearest English equivalent. As a general rule, vowels are long when followed by h (**Bahn**) or by one consonant (**bar**) and short when followed by two consonants (**lassen**).

When they follow consonants, vowels are not normally run on as they are in English. For example, **ein Apfel** is pronounced as two separate words, whereas *an apple* might be run together as if it were one word, *'anapple'*.

Particular care must be taken with the umlaut sounds—ä, ö and ü—which do not exist in English.

German vowel	long or short	German example	nearest English equivalent
a	short	**hat**	vowel sound between hat and hut
a	long	**Bahn**	barn
ä	short	**Geschäft**	left
ä	long	**Käse**	between pair and pace
ai	long	**Kaiser**	fine
au	long	**aus**	cow
äu	long	**Häuser**	boy
e	short	**essen**	lesson
e	long	**geben**	gate
e	short, in unstressed syllables	**Nase**	ago
ei	long	**weit**	right
eu	long	**Heu**	boy
ey	long	**Meyer**	fire
i	short	**billig**	bit
i	long	**ihn**	ease
ie	long	**viel**	feel
o	short	**Post**	lost
o	long	**Monat**	bone (pronounced without moving tongue or lips)
ö	short	**können**	fur (with short u)
ö	long	**böse**	burn (with long u)
u	short	**Nuss**	put
u	long	**Hut**	moon
ü	short, like the French tu	**Müll**	round your lips and try to say ee
ü	long, like the French tu	**über**	round your lips and try to say longer ee
y	long, like the French tu	**typisch**	round your lips and try to say longer ee

Consonants

Some German consonants change pronunciation according to their position in a word. For example, at the end of a word or syllable, b, d and g are pronounced p, t and k respectively.

German consonant	notes	German example	nearest English equivalent
b	at the beginning of a word	**Ball**	ball
b	at the end of a word or syllable	**ab**	up
c	hard, before a, o, u	**Comic**	café
c	soft, before e, i	**Celsius**	bits
ch	after a, o, u	**Loch**	loch, pronounced in the Scottish way
ch	after e, i	**ich**	similar to the first sound in huge
ch	hard	**Charakter**	car
chs		**sechs**	six
d	at the beginning of a word	**dann**	done
d	at the end of a word or syllable	**Bad**	dart
dt		**Stadt**	rat
f		**Fuß**	fat
g	at the beginning of a word	**Gast**	guest
g	at the end of a word	**Tag**	park
g	-ig, at the end of a word	**billig**	similar to the first sound in huge
h		**hat**	hat
h	at the end of a syllable	**sah, sehen**	not pronounced, and makes the previous vowel long
j		**ja**	yet
k		**kalt**	kit
l		**Last**	lot
m		**Mast**	mast
n		**Name**	name
p		**Person**	person
qu		**Quatsch**	pronounced kv (to make 'kvatsh')
r	rolled, usually at the back of the mouth	**rasten**	rest
s	hissing ss sound	**es**	set
s	before a vowel, z sound	**Hase**	zoo
s	before p or t at the beginning of a syllable, sh sound	**Stunde**	ship
sch	like English sh	**Schule**	shut
ß	same as ss	**heiß**	press
t		**Tal**	tip
tsch	like English ch	**deutsch**	chin
v	like English f	**vier**	fat
v	in most foreign words	**Vene**	vase
w	like English v	**was**	van
x		**Taxi**	taxi
z	like English ts	**Zahl**	hits

German–English

ab
1 *preposition* (+ *dative*) = from
2 *adverb* = off
ab und zu = now and again

die **Abbildung**, *plural* Abbildungen
= illustration

der **Abend**, *plural* Abende
= evening

das **Abendessen**, *plural* Abendessen
= dinner

abends *adverb*
= in the evening

das **Abenteuer**, *plural* Abenteuer
= adventure

aber *conjunction*
= but

abergläubisch *adjective*
= superstitious

ab|fahren *irregular verb* (**!** *sein*)
= to leave

die **Abfahrt**, *plural* Abfahrten
• = departure
• (*on a motorway*) = exit
• (*ski slope*) = run

der **Abfall**, *plural* Abfälle
= rubbish, = garbage

der **Abflug**, *plural* Abflüge
= departure

ab|geben *irregular verb*
• = to hand in
• jemandem etwas abgeben = to give
  someone something

der/die **Abgeordnete**, *plural* Abgeordneten
= member of parliament

ab|hängen *irregular verb*
abhängen von = to depend on

ab|heben *irregular verb*
• = to lift off
• (*take out money*) = to withdraw

ab|holen *verb*
= to collect

das **Abitur**
≈ A levels

das **Abkommen**, *plural* Abkommen
= agreement

ab|kürzen *verb*
= to abbreviate

die **Abkürzung**, *plural* Abkürzungen
• = abbreviation
• = short cut

ab|legen *verb*
= to take off
abgelegte Kleidung = cast-offs

ab|lehnen *verb*
• = to refuse
• = to reject

ab|lenken *verb*
= to divert
= to distract

ab|machen *verb*
• (*remove*) = to take off
• (*make arrangements*) = to fix

die **Abmachung**, *plural* Abmachungen
= agreement

ab|melden: sich abmelden *verb*
• (*notify authorities*) = to report that one is
  leaving
• = to check out

ab|nehmen *irregular verb*
• (*remove*) = to take off
  den Hörer abnehmen = to pick up the
  phone
• = to lose weight

das **Abonnement**, *plural* Abonnements
= subscription

ab|raten *irregular verb*
jemandem von etwas abraten = to advise
someone against something

ab|räumen *verb*
= to clear away

die **Abrechnung**, *plural* Abrechnungen
= settlement of accounts

die **Abreise**
= departure

ab|reisen *verb* (**!** *sein*)
= to leave

ab|reißen *irregular verb*
• = to tear down
• (**!** *sein*) = to break off

ab|sagen *verb*
= to cancel

der **Absatz**, *plural* Absätze
• (*of a shoe*) = heel
• (*in text*) = paragraph

der **Abschied**, *plural* Abschiede
• = farewell
• (*separation*) = parting

ab|schließen *irregular verb*
= to lock

ab|schneiden *irregular verb*
= to cut off
gut abschneiden = to do well

ab|schreiben *irregular verb*
= to copy

abseits *adverb*
- = far away
- (*in soccer*) = offside

der **Absender**, *plural* Absender
= sender

ab|setzen *verb*
- = to take off
- = to put down
wir setzen dich am Bahnhof ab = we'll drop you at the station

die **Absicht**, *plural* Absichten
= intention

absichtlich *adverb*
= intentionally, = on purpose

der **Abstand**, *plural* Abstände
- = distance
- = interval

ab|stellen *verb*
- = to turn off
- (*if it's a vehicle*) = to park

die **Abstimmung**, *plural* Abstimmungen
= vote

ab|stürzen *verb* (**!** *sein*)
= to crash

das **Abteil**, *plural* Abteile
= compartment

die **Abteilung**, *plural* Abteilungen
= department

die **Abtreibung**, *plural* Abtreibungen
= abortion

ab|trocknen *verb*
= to dry up

ab|wägen *irregular verb*
= to weigh up

ab|waschen *irregular verb*
= to wash up

die **Abwechslung**, *plural* Abwechslungen
= change

abwesend *adjective*
= absent

ab|wischen *verb*
= to wipe

das **Abzeichen**, *plural* Abzeichen
= badge

ab|ziehen *irregular verb*
- = to take off
die Betten abziehen = to strip the beds

✻ in informal situations

- = to take away
= to deduct
- (**!** *sein*) (*of smoke, steam*) = to escape

ab|zielen *verb*
abzielen auf = to be aimed at

ach *interjection*
= oh!

acht *adjective*
= eight

das **Achtel**, *plural* Achtel
= eighth

achten *verb*
- = to respect
- achten auf = to pay attention to
(*mind*) = to look after

achter/achte/achtes *adjective*
= eighth

die **Achterbahn**, *plural* Achterbahnen
= roller coaster

die **Achtung**
1 *noun* = respect
2 *interjection*
Achtung! = look out!

achtzehn *adjective*
= eighteen

achtzig *adjective*
= eighty

der **Acker**, *plural* Äcker
= field

die **Ader**, *plural* Adern
= vein

der **Adler**, *plural* Adler
= eagle

adoptieren *verb*
= to adopt

die **Adresse**, *plural* Adressen
= address

der **Affe**, *plural* Affen
= monkey
= ape

(das) **Afrika**
= Africa

der **Afrikaner**, *plural* Afrikaner
= African

(das) **Ägypten**
= Egypt

ähneln *verb*
= to resemble

ähnlich *adjective*
= similar
er sieht seinem Vater ähnlich = he looks like his father

die **Ähnlichkeit**, *plural* Ähnlichkeiten
= similarity

die **Ahnung**
= idea

das **Aids**
= Aids

die **Akte**, *plural* Akten
= file

die **Aktentasche**, *plural* Aktentaschen
= briefcase

die **Aktie**, *plural* Aktien
= share

die **Aktivität**, *plural* Aktivitäten
= activity

aktuell *adjective*
= topical
= current

der **Akzent**, *plural* Akzente
= accent

alarmieren *verb*
• = to alert
• = to alarm

der **Albtraum**, *plural* Albträume ▶ Alptraum

der **Alkohol**
= alcohol

alle ▶ aller

allein *adverb*
• = alone
• (*automatically*) = on one's own

der/die **Alleinerziehende**, *plural*
Alleinerziehenden
= single parent

aller/alle/alles
1 *pronoun*
• = all
• = every
alle Tage = every day
• alle (*plural*) = all
alle miteinander = all together
alle beide = both
• alles = everything, = all
alles aussteigen! = all change!
alles Gute! = all the best!
vor allem = above all
2 *adjective*
alle sein✱ = to be all gone

die **Allergie**, *plural* Allergien
= allergy

allergisch *adjective*
= allergic

alles ▶ aller

allgemein *adverb*
= generally
im Allgemeinen = in general

allmählich
1 *adjective* = gradual
2 *adverb* = gradually

alltäglich *adjective*
= everyday

alltags *adverb*
= on weekdays

Alpen (*plural*)
die Alpen = the Alps

das **Alphabet**, *plural* Alphabete
= alphabet

der **Alptraum**, *plural* Alpträume
= nightmare

als *conjunction*
• = when
erst als = only when
• (*as comparison*) = than
• = as
als Frau = as a woman

also
1 *adverb* = so
2 *conjunction* = so
also gut = all right then

alt *adjective*
= old

das **Alter**
= age

älter *adjective*
• = older
• = elderly

altern *verb* (**!** sein)
= to age

das **Altersheim**, *plural* Altersheime
= old people's home

ältester/älteste/ältestes
adjective
= oldest

altmodisch *adjective*
= old-fashioned

am = an dem
am Sonntag = on Sunday
am Abend = in the evening
am meisten = (the) most

die **Ameise**, *plural* Ameisen
= ant

(das) **Amerika**
= America

der **Amerikaner**, *plural* Amerikaner
= American

die **Amerikanerin**, *plural*
Amerikanerinnen
= American

amerikanisch *adjective*
= American

die **Ampel**, *plural* Ampeln
= traffic lights

amtlich *adjective*
= official

amüsant *adjective*
= amusing

an
1 *preposition* (+ *dative or accusative*)
* = at
  = against
  (*attached to*) = on
* = to
  einen Brief an jemanden schicken = to
  send a letter to someone
* (*when talking about time*) = on
2 *adverb*
  das Licht ist an = the light is on
  von heute an = from today

die **Ananas** *plural* Ananas
  = pineapple

an|bieten *irregular verb*
  = to offer

das **Andenken**, *plural* Andenken
  = souvenir

anderer/andere/anderes
1 *adjective*
* = other
* = different
2 *pronoun*
  der/die/das andere = the other one
  die anderen = the others
  ein anderer/eine andere/ein anderes
  (*thing*) = a different one, (*person*) =
  someone else
  kein anderer = no one else
  unter anderem = among other things

andererseits *adverb*
  = on the other hand

ändern *verb*
  = to change

anders *adverb*
  = differently
  niemand anders = no one else

anderthalb *adjective*
  = one and a half

der **Anfall**, *plural* Anfälle
  = fit, = attack

der **Anfang**, *plural* Anfänge
  = beginning, = start

an|fangen *irregular verb*
  = to begin, = to start

der **Anfänger**, *plural* Anfänger
  = beginner

die **Anfängerin**, *plural* Anfängerinnen
  = beginner

an|fassen *verb*
  = to touch

an|geben *irregular verb*
* = to give
* = to show off

das **Angebot**, *plural* Angebote
  = offer

die **Angel**, *plural* Angeln
  = fishing rod

die **Angelegenheit**, *plural*
  Angelegenheiten
  = matter
  = business

angenehm
1 *adjective* = pleasant
2 *interjection*
  (*when being introduced*) = pleased to
  meet you

der/die **Angestellte**, *plural* Angestellten
  = employee

die **Angewohnheit**, *plural*
  Angewohnheiten
  = habit

an|greifen *irregular verb*
  = to attack

der **Angriff**, *plural* Angriffe
  = attack

die **Angst**, *plural* Ängste
  = fear
  Angst haben = to be afraid
  jemandem Angst machen = to frighten
  someone

ängstlich *adjective*
* = nervous
* = frightened
* = anxious

an|halten *irregular verb*
  = to stop

der **Anhalter**, *plural* Anhalter
  = hitchhiker
  per Anhalter fahren = to hitchhike

die **Anhalterin**, *plural* Anhalterinnen
  = hitchhiker

der **Anhänger**, *plural* Anhänger
* = supporter
* = trailer
* = pendant

der **Anker**, *plural* Anker
  = anchor

an|klicken *verb*
  = to click on

an|kommen *irregular verb* (**!** *sein*)
* = to arrive
* ankommen auf = to depend on
  das kommt darauf an = it depends

die **Ankunft**
  = arrival

an|machen *verb*
  = to turn on

an|melden *verb*
* = to register
* sich anmelden = to register, (*for an
  appointment*) = to make an
  appointment

die **Anmeldung**, *plural* Anmeldungen
- = registration
- = appointment

die **Annahme**, *plural* Annahmen
= assumption

an|nehmen *irregular verb*
- = to accept
- = to assume
= to suppose

an|passen: sich anpassen *verb*
= to adapt

anpassungsfähig *adjective*
= adaptable

der **Anruf**, *plural* Anrufe
= (phone) call

der **Anrufbeantworter**, *plural*
Anrufbeantworter
= answering machine

an|rufen *irregular verb*
= to ring, = to call

ans = an das
ans Telefon gehen = to answer the phone

die **Ansage**, *plural* Ansagen
= announcement

an|schlagen *irregular verb*
- = to put up
- = to knock
- = to chip, = to crack

an|schließen *irregular verb*
- = to connect
- sich einer Gruppe anschließen = to join a group

der **Anschluss** (**Anschluß**ⓞⓛⓓ), *plural*
Anschlüsse
= connection

an|schnallen: sich anschnallen
verb
= to fasten one's seatbelt

die **Anschrift**, *plural* Anschriften
= address

die **Anschuldigung**, *plural*
Anschuldigungen
= accusation

die **Ansicht**, *plural* Ansichten
= view

der **Anspruch**, *plural* Ansprüche
= claim

anstatt
1 *preposition* (+ *genitive*) = instead of
2 *conjunction*
anstatt zu schlafen = instead of sleeping

an|stellen *verb*
- = to employ
- = to turn on

- sich anstellen = to queue, = to stand in line

die **Anstrengung**, *plural* Anstrengungen
= effort

die **Antenne**, *plural* Antennen
= aerial

das **Antibiotikum**, *plural* Antibiotika
= antibiotic

der **Antrag**, *plural* Anträge
= application

die **Antwort**, *plural* Antworten
= answer, = reply

antworten *verb*
= to answer, = to reply

anwesend *adjective*
= present

die **Anzahl**
= number

die **Anzahlung**, *plural* Anzahlungen
= deposit

die **Anzeige**, *plural* Anzeigen
- = advertisement
- (*to the police*) = report

an|zeigen *verb*
- = to report
- = to show

an|ziehen *irregular verb*
- = to attract
- (*dress*) = to put on
- sich anziehen = to get dressed

der **Anzug**, *plural* Anzüge
= suit

an|zünden *verb*
= to light

der **Apfel**, *plural* Äpfel
= apple

die **Apfelsine**, *plural* Apfelsinen
= orange

die **Apotheke**, *plural* Apotheken
= chemist's, = pharmacy

der **Apotheker**, *plural* Apotheker
= chemist, = pharmacist

die **Apothekerin**, *plural* Apothekerinnen
= chemist, = pharmacist

der **Apparat**, *plural* Apparate
- (*TV, radio*) = set
- = camera
- = telephone
am Apparat! = speaking!

das **Appartement**, *plural* Appartements
= apartment

der **Appetit**
= appetite
guten Appetit! = enjoy your meal!

die **Aprikose**, *plural* Aprikosen
= apricot

der **April**
= April

der **Äquator**
= equator

die **Arbeit**, *plural* Arbeiten
- = work
- = job
- (*at school*) = test

arbeiten *verb*
= to work

der **Arbeiter**, *plural* Arbeiter
= worker

die **Arbeiterin**, *plural* Arbeiterinnen
= worker

der **Arbeitgeber**, *plural* Arbeitgeber
= employer

arbeitslos *adjective*
= unemployed

der **Ärger**
- = annoyance
- (*problems*) = trouble

ärgerlich *adjective*
- = annoyed
- = annoying

ärgern *verb*
- = to annoy
- sich ärgern = to get annoyed

arm *adjective*
= poor

der **Arm**, *plural* Arme
= arm

das **Armband**, *plural* Armbänder
= bracelet

die **Armbanduhr**, *plural* Armbanduhren
= wrist-watch

der **Ärmel**, *plural* Ärmel
= sleeve

der **Ärmelkanal**
= (English) Channel

arrangieren *verb*
- = to arrange
- sich arrangieren = to come to an arrangement

der **Arsch**⚫, *plural* Ärsche
= arse, = ass

die **Art**, *plural* Arten
- = way, = manner
- = kind, = sort

artig *adjective*
= good, = well-behaved

⚫ considered offensive

der **Arzt**, *plural* Ärzte
= doctor

die **Ärztin**, *plural* Ärztinnen
= doctor

ärztlich *adjective*
= medical

der **Aschenbecher**, *plural* Aschenbecher
= ashtray

der **Asiat**, *plural* Asiaten
= Asian

die **Asiatin**, *plural* Asiatinnen
= Asian

asiatisch *adjective*
= Asian

(das) **Asien**
= Asia

aß ▶essen

der **Assistent**, *plural* Assistenten
= assistant

die **Assistentin**, *plural* Assistentinnen
= assistant

der **Ast**, *plural* Äste
= branch

der **Asylant**, *plural* Asylanten
= asylum-seeker

der **Atem**
= breath

atemlos *adjective*
= breathless

der **Athlet**, *plural* Athleten
= athlete

die **Athletin**, *plural* Athletinnen
= athlete

der **Atlantik**
= the Atlantic

der **Atlas**, *plural* Atlanten
= atlas

atmen *verb*
= to breathe

die **Atmosphäre**, *plural* Atmosphären
= atmosphere

attraktiv *adjective*
= attractive

au *interjection*
= ouch!

auch *adverb*
= also, = too
nicht nur . . . sondern auch . . . = not only . . . but also . . .
auch wenn = even if
wann|was|wer|wo auch = whenever | whatever | whoever | wherever

auf
1 *preposition*
- (*+ dative*) (*indicating position*) = on
  auf der Party = at the party
- (*+ accusative*) (*moving in the direction of*) = on, = onto
- auf Deutsch = in German
- (*indicating time*) = for
  etwas auf morgen verschieben = to put something off until tomorrow
  auf Wiedersehen! = goodbye!
2 *adverb* = open
  auf und ab = up and down

aufeinander *adverb*
- = one on top of the other
- = one after the other
- aufeinander warten = to wait for each other

der **Aufenthalt**, *plural* Aufenthalte
- = stay
- (*pause in a journey*) = stop

die **Aufgabe**, *plural* Aufgaben
- = task
- (*at school*) = exercise, = assignment
  Aufgaben = homework

auf|geben *irregular verb*
- = to give up
- = to post
- Hausaufgaben aufgeben = to set homework

auf|halten *irregular verb*
- = to hold
- = to hold open
- sich aufhalten = to stay

auf|heben *irregular verb*
- (*from the ground*) = to pick up
- (*preserve*) = to keep

auf|hören *verb*
= to stop

der **Aufkleber**, *plural* Aufkleber
= sticker

auf|legen *verb*
- = to put on
- = to publish
- (*when phoning*) = to hang up

auf|machen *verb*
= to open
jemandem aufmachen = to open the door to someone

aufmerksam *adjective*
= attentive
er machte sie auf einen Fehler aufmerksam = he drew her attention to a mistake

die **Aufnahme**, *plural* Aufnahmen
- = photograph, = shot
- = recording
- (*to hospital, club*) = admission

auf|nehmen *irregular verb*
- = to receive
  (*into hospital, club*) = to admit
- = to record
- (*with a camera*) = to film
  = to photograph

auf|passen *verb*
= to pay attention
aufpassen auf = to look after, = to look out for

auf|räumen *verb*
= to tidy up

auf|regen *verb*
- = to excite
- = to annoy
- sich aufregen = to get worked up

die **Aufregung**, *plural* Aufregungen
= excitement

aufrichtig *adjective*
= sincere

der **Aufsatz**, *plural* Aufsätze
= essay

auf|schließen *irregular verb*
= to unlock

der **Aufschnitt**
= sliced cold meat and cheese

auf|schreiben *irregular verb*
= to write down

die **Aufsicht**
- = supervision
- (*person*) = supervisor

auf|stehen *irregular verb* (! *sein*)
= to get up

der **Auftrag**, *plural* Aufträge
- = job
- (*in business*) = order

auf|wachen *verb* (! *sein*)
= to wake up

auf|wachsen *irregular verb* (! *sein*)
= to grow up

auf|wecken *verb*
= to wake up

auf|ziehen *irregular verb*
= to wind up

der **Aufzug**, *plural* Aufzüge
= lift, = elevator

das **Auge**, *plural* Augen
= eye
unter vier Augen = in private

der **Augenblick**, *plural* Augenblicke
= moment

die **Augenbraue**, *plural* Augenbrauen
= eyebrow

das **Augenlid**, *plural* Augenlider
= eyelid

der **August**
= August

aus
1 *preposition* (+ *dative*)
- (*indicating direction*) = out of
- (*originating from*) = from
　aus welchem Grund? = for what reason?
- (*consisting of*) = made of
　aus Spaß = for fun
2 *adverb* = out
　das Licht ist aus = the light is off
　von mir aus = as far as I'm concerned

aus|beuten *verb*
= to exploit

die **Ausbildung**
= education
= training

der **Ausdruck**, *plural* Ausdrücke
= expression

aus|drücken *verb*
- = to squeeze
- = to express
- sich ausdrücken = to express oneself

auseinander *adverb*
= apart

die **Ausfahrt**, *plural* Ausfahrten
= exit
　'Ausfahrt freihalten' = 'keep clear'

der **Ausflug**, *plural* Ausflüge
= trip

aus|füllen *verb*
= to fill in

die **Ausgabe**, *plural* Ausgaben
- = edition
- Ausgaben = expenditure

der **Ausgang**, *plural* Ausgänge
= exit, = way out

aus|geben *irregular verb*
= to spend

aus|gehen *irregular verb* (**!** *sein*)
= to go out
　gut ausgehen = to end well

ausgezeichnet *adjective*
= excellent

aus|halten *irregular verb*
= to stand

die **Aushilfe**, *plural* Aushilfen
= temporary assistant, = temp

die **Auskunft**, *plural* Auskünfte
= information
　(*when telephoning*) = inquiries

das **Ausland**
　im Ausland = abroad
　ins Ausland reisen = to travel abroad

der **Ausländer**, *plural* Ausländer
= foreigner

die **Ausländerin**, *plural* Ausländerinnen
= foreigner

aus|machen *verb*
- = to put out
- = to turn off
- = to arrange
　das macht mir nichts aus = I don't mind

die **Ausnahme**, *plural* Ausnahmen
= exception

aus|nutzen *verb*
= to use
= to take advantage of

aus|packen *verb*
= to unpack

der **Auspuff**, *plural* Auspuffe
= exhaust

die **Ausrede**, *plural* Ausreden
= excuse

das **Ausrufezeichen**, *plural*
Ausrufezeichen
= exclamation mark

aus|ruhen: sich ausruhen *verb*
= to have a rest

die **Ausrüstung**
= equipment

aus|schalten *verb*
- = to switch off
- = to eliminate

aus|schneiden *irregular verb*
= to cut out

der **Ausschuss** (**Ausschuß**ⓄⓁⒹ), *plural*
Ausschüsse
= committee
= board

aus|sehen *irregular verb*
= to look

außen *adverb*
= outside
　nach außen = outwards

der **Außenminister**, *plural* Außenminister
= Foreign Secretary, = Foreign Minister

außer
1 *preposition* (+ *dative*) = except (for)
= apart from
　alle außer ihr = everyone except (for) her
2 *conjunction* = except
　außer wenn = unless

außerdem *adverb*
- = as well
- = moreover

äußerer/äußere/äußeres *adjective*
= external

ⓄⓁⒹ = old spelling

außerhalb *preposition* (+ *genitive*)
= outside

äußerlich *adjective*
= external

außerordentlich *adjective*
= extraordinary

äußerst *adverb*
= extremely

die **Aussicht**, *plural* Aussichten
• (*from a window*) = view
• = prospect

die **Aussprache**, *plural* Aussprachen
= pronunciation

aus|sprechen *irregular verb*
• = to pronounce
• = to express

aus|steigen *irregular verb* (**!** *sein*)
= to get out

aus|stellen *verb*
• (*in a shop, museum*) = to display
= to exhibit
• (*write*) = to make out
= to issue

die **Ausstellung**, *plural* Ausstellungen
= exhibition

aus|suchen *verb*
• = to choose
• sich etwas aussuchen = to choose
  something

der **Austausch**
= exchange

(das) **Australien**
= Australia

der **Australier**, *plural* Australier
= Australian

die **Australierin**, *plural* Australierinnen
= Australian

australisch *adjective*
= Australian

aus|trinken *irregular verb*
= to drink up

der **Ausverkauf**
= sale

die **Auswahl**, *plural* Auswahlen
= choice

aus|wandern *verb* (**!** *sein*)
= to emigrate

der **Ausweis**, *plural* Ausweise
= identity card

auswendig *adverb*
= by heart

aus|wirken: sich auswirken *verb*
sich auf etwas auswirken = to affect
something

aus|ziehen *irregular verb*
• = to take off
= to undress
• sich ausziehen = to get undressed
• (**!** *sein*) (*move house*) = to move out

das **Auto**, *plural* Autos
= car

die **Autobahn**, *plural* Autobahnen
= motorway, = freeway

der **Autobus**, *plural* Autobusse
= bus

das **Autogramm**, *plural* Autogramme
= autograph

der **Automat**, *plural* Automaten
= machine

die **Autonummer**, *plural* Autonummern
= registration number

der **Autor**, *plural* Autoren
= author

die **Autorin**, *plural* Autorinnen
= authoress

die **Autorität**
= authority

die **Axt**, *plural* Äxte
= axe, = ax

der **Bach**, *plural* Bäche
= stream

die **Backe**, *plural* Backen
= cheek

backen *irregular verb*
= to bake

der **Bäcker**, *plural* Bäcker
= baker

die **Bäckerei**, *plural* Bäckereien
= baker's (shop), = bakery

die **Backpflaume**, *plural* Backpflaumen
= prune

das **Bad**, *plural* Bäder
• = bath
• = bathroom
• (*for swimming*) = pool

der **Badeanzug**, *plural* Badeanzüge
= bathing costume, = swimsuit

die **Badehose**, *plural* Badehosen
= swimming trunks

baden verb
- = to have a bath
- = to bathe
- (wash someone) = to bath

die **Badewanne**, plural Badewannen
= bath-tub
= bath

das **Badezimmer**, plural Badezimmer
= bathroom

die **Bahn**, plural Bahnen
- = train
- = tram, = streetcar
- (in sport) = track
- (single) = lane

der **Bahnhof**, plural Bahnhöfe
= (railway) station

der **Bahnsteig**, plural Bahnsteige
= platform

der **Bahnübergang**, plural
Bahnübergänge
= level crossing, = grade crossing

bald adverb
= soon

der **Balkon**, plural Balkons
= balcony

der **Ball**, plural Bälle
= ball

das **Ballett**, plural Ballette
= ballet

die **Banane**, plural Bananen
= banana

das **Band**¹ plural Bänder
- = ribbon
- (for recording) = tape
- am laufenden Band = non-stop

der **Band**² plural Bände
= volume

die **Band**³ plural Bands
(group) = band

die **Bande**, plural Banden
= gang

die **Bank**¹ plural Banken
= bank

die **Bank**² plural Bänke
= bench

bankrott adjective
= bankrupt

bar adverb
= (in) cash

der **Bär**, plural Bären
= bear

barfuß adverb
= barefoot

das **Bargeld**
= cash

der **Barren**, plural Barren
- = bar
- (in gymnastics) = parallel bars

der **Bart**, plural Bärte
= beard

bärtig adjective
= bearded

basta interjection
= and that's that!

basteln verb
= to make
sie bastelt gerne = she likes making
things

bat ▶bitten

der **Bauch**, plural Bäuche
= stomach

Bauchschmerzen (plural)
= stomach-ache

bauen verb
= to build

der **Bauer**, plural Bauern
= farmer

die **Bäuerin**, plural Bäuerinnen
= farmer's wife

der **Bauernhof**, plural Bauernhöfe
= farm

der **Baum**, plural Bäume
= tree

die **Baumwolle**
= cotton

die **Bausparkasse**, plural Bausparkassen
= building society

die **Baustelle**, plural Baustellen
= building site

(das) **Bayern**
= Bavaria

beabsichtigen verb
= to intend

beachten verb
- = to take notice of
- = to observe
- = to follow

der **Beamte**, plural Beamten
= civil servant
= official

die **Beamtin**, plural Beamtinnen
= civil servant
= official

die **Beanstandung**, plural
Beanstandungen
= complaint

beantragen *verb*
= to apply for

beantworten *verb*
= to answer

beaufsichtigen *verb*
= to supervise

beauftragen *verb*
= to instruct
= to commission

der **Becher**, *plural* Becher
= beaker, = mug
= pot, = carton

das **Becken**, *plural* Becken
• (*for washing*) = basin
• (*for swimming*) = pool
• (*part of the body*) = pelvis

bedanken: sich bedanken *verb*
= to say thank you
ich habe mich bei ihm bedankt = I
thanked him

der **Bedarf**
= need
bei Bedarf = if required

bedauerlicherweise *adverb*
= unfortunately

bedauern *verb*
• = to regret
• jemanden bedauern = to feel sorry for
someone

bedecken *verb*
= to cover

bedeckt *adjective*
= overcast

bedenken *irregular verb*
= to consider

das **Bedenken**, *plural* Bedenken
= reservation
ohne Bedenken = without hesitation

bedenklich *adjective*
• (*serious*) = worrying
• = dubious

bedeuten *verb*
= to mean

die **Bedeutung**, *plural* Bedeutungen
• = meaning
• = importance

bedienen *verb*
• (*help*) = to serve
• = to operate
• sich bedienen = to help oneself

die **Bedienung**, *plural* Bedienungen
• = service
Bedienung inbegriffen = service included
• (*person*) = waiter/waitress
• (*of a machine*) = operation

die **Bedingung**, *plural* Bedingungen
= condition

bedingungslos *adjective*
= unconditional

die **Bedrohung** *plural* Bedrohungen
= threat

bedürftig *adjective*
= needy

beeilen: sich beeilen *verb*
= to hurry (up)

beeindrucken *verb*
= to impress

die **Beerdigung**, *plural* Beerdigungen
= funeral

die **Beere**, *plural* Beeren
= berry

das **Beet**, *plural* Beete
(*of flowers*) = bed
(*of vegetables*) = patch

befahl ▶ befehlen

der **Befehl**, *plural* Befehle
= order

befehlen *irregular verb*
jemandem etwas befehlen = to order
someone to do something

befestigen *verb*
= to fasten, = to attach

befinden: sich befinden *irregular
verb*
= to be

befördern *verb*
• (*by lorry, train*) = to transport
• (*in a job*) = to promote

die **Befreiung**
= liberation

befreunden: sich befreunden
verb
= to make friends
befreundet sein = to be friends

befriedigen *verb*
= to satisfy

die **Befugnis**, *plural* Befugnisse
= authority

begabt *adjective*
= gifted

die **Begabung**
= gift, = talent

begann ▶ beginnen

begegnen *verb* (! sein)
• jemandem begegnen = to meet someone
• sich begegnen = to meet (each other)

begehen *irregular verb*
= to commit

begeistert *adjective*
= enthusiastic

die **Begeisterung**
= enthusiasm

der **Beginn**
= beginning

beginnen *irregular verb*
= to begin, = to start

begleiten *verb*
= to accompany

beglückwünschen *verb*
= to congratulate

begnadigen *verb*
= to pardon

begraben *irregular verb*
= to bury

begreifen *irregular verb*
= to understand

der **Begriff**, *plural* Begriffe
• = concept
• (*expression*) = term

die **Begründung**, *plural* Begründungen
= reason

begrüßen *verb*
= to greet
= to welcome

begünstigen *verb*
= to favour

behalten *irregular verb*
• = to keep
• = to remember

der **Behälter**, *plural* Behälter
= container

die **Behandlung**, *plural* Behandlungen
= treatment

behaupten *verb*
• = to claim
• sich behaupten = to assert oneself

die **Behauptung**, *plural* Behauptungen
= claim, = assertion

beherrschen *verb*
• = to rule over
• = to know
• sich berherrschen = to control oneself

behilflich *adjective*
jemandem behilflich sein = to help
   someone

behindern *verb*
= to obstruct

behindert *adjective*
= disabled, = handicapped

der/die **Behinderte**, *plural* Behinderten
= disabled person, = handicapped person

die **Behörde**, *plural* Behörden
= authority

behüten *verb*
= to protect

bei *preposition* (+ *dative*)
• = near, = by
   nimm ihn bei der Hand = take him by the
      hand
• (*indicating a place, time*) = at
   bei mir = at my place
   bei uns in der Firma = in our company
   bei Schmidt = c/o Schmidt
   bei Regen = when *or* if it rains
• (*indicating cause*) = with
   bei der hohen Miete = (what) with the
      high rent

bei|bringen *irregular verb*
jemandem etwas beibringen = to teach
   someone something

beide
1 *adjective* = both
   die beiden Schwestern = the two sisters
2 *pronoun* = both
   ihr beide = both of you, = you two
   (*in tennis*) dreißig beide = thirty all

der **Beifall**
= applause

beiläufig *adjective*
= casual

beim = bei dem
beim Lesen sein = to be reading

das **Bein**, *plural* Beine
= leg

beinah(e) *adverb*
= almost

beiseite *adverb*
= aside

das **Beispiel**, *plural* Beispiele
= example
zum Beispiel = for example

beißen *irregular verb*
= to bite

der **Beitrag**, *plural* Beiträge
• = contribution
• (*in a newspaper*) = article
• (*members'*) = subscription

bekam ▶bekommen

bekämpfen *verb*
= to fight, = to combat

bekannt *adjective*
• = well-known
   = familiar
• etwas bekannt machen = to announce
   something
• jemanden bekannt machen = to
   introduce someone

B

der/die **Bekannte**, *plural* Bekannten
= acquaintance

die **Bekanntschaft**, *plural*
Bekanntschaften
= acquaintance
(*group of people*) = acquaintances

beklagen: sich beklagen *verb*
= to complain

die **Bekleidung**
= clothes

bekommen *irregular verb*
• = to get
• = to catch
• es bekommt mir gut (**!** *sein*) (*of the
climate*) = it is good for me, (*of food*) =
it agrees with me

der **Belag**, *plural* Beläge
= covering, = coating

belästigen *verb*
• = to bother
• (*sexually*) = to harass

belegt *adjective*
• = occupied
• ein belegtes Brot = an open sandwich

beleidigen *verb*
= to insult

die **Beleidigung**, *plural* Beleidigungen
= insult

die **Beleuchtung**
= lighting

(das) **Belgien**
= Belgium

der **Belgier**, *plural* Belgier
= Belgian

die **Belgierin**, *plural* Belgierinnen
= Belgian

belgisch *adjective*
= Belgian

belichten *verb*
(*in photography*) = to expose

beliebig
1 *adjective* = any
2 *adverb*
beliebig [oft | lange | viele …] = as [often |
long | many …] as one likes

beliebt *adjective*
= popular

bellen *verb*
= to bark

belohnen *verb*
= to reward

bemerkbar *adjective*
sich bemerkbar machen (*of a person*) =
to attract attention, (*of a thing*) = to
become noticeable

bemerken *verb*
• = to notice
• (*utter*) = to remark
nebenbei bemerkt = by the way

die **Bemerkung**, *plural* Bemerkungen
= remark

bemühen: sich bemühen *verb*
= to try
sich um eine Stelle bemühen = to try to
get a job

die **Bemühung**, *plural* Bemühungen
= effort

benachrichtigen *verb*
= to inform
(*officially*) = to notify

benehmen: sich benehmen
irregular verb
= to behave

das **Benehmen**
= behaviour, behavior

beneiden *verb*
= to envy

benutzen, benützen *verb*
= to use

das **Benzin**
= petrol, = gas

beobachten *verb*
= to observe, = to watch

bequem *adjective*
• = comfortable
• = lazy

beraten *irregular verb*
• = to advise
• = to discuss
• sich über etwas beraten = to discuss
something

der **Berater**, *plural* Berater
= adviser

die **Beratung**, *plural* Beratungen
• = advice
• = discussion
• (*with a doctor*) = consultation

der **Bereich**, *plural* Bereiche
= area

bereit *adjective*
= ready

bereits *adverb*
= already

bereuen *verb*
= to regret

der **Berg**, *plural* Berge
= mountain

bergab *adverb*
= downhill

der **Bergarbeiter**, *plural* Bergarbeiter
  = miner

bergauf *adverb*
  = uphill

bergen *irregular verb*
  = to rescue

der **Bergsteiger**, *plural* Bergsteiger
  = climber, = mountaineer

die **Bergwacht**
  = mountain rescue (service)

das **Bergwerk**, *plural* Bergwerke
  = mine

der **Bericht**, *plural* Berichte
  = report

berichten *verb*
  = to report

berücksichtigen *verb*
  = to take into account

der **Beruf**, *plural* Berufe
  = occupation
  = profession
  = trade
  was sind Sie von Beruf? = what do you
    do for a living?

beruflich
  1 *adjective* = professional
  = vocational
  2 *adverb* = professionally

die **Berufsberatung**
  = careers advice

berufstätig *adjective*
  = working

beruhigen *verb*
  = to calm (down)

berühmt *adjective*
  = famous

berühren *verb*
  • = to touch
  • sich berühren = to touch

besaß ▶besitzen

beschädigen *verb*
  = to damage

beschäftigen *verb*
  • (*keep busy*) = to occupy
  beschäftigt sein = to be busy
  • (*in a job*) = to employ
  • sich beschäftigen = to occupy oneself

die **Beschäftigung**, *plural*
  Beschäftigungen
  • (*work*) = occupation
  • (*hobby*) = activity

der **Bescheid**
  = information
  jemandem Bescheid sagen = to let
    someone know

bescheiden *adjective*
  = modest

die **Bescheinigung**, *plural*
  Bescheinigungen
  • = (written) confirmation
  • = certificate

die **Bescherung**, *plural* Bescherungen
  = giving out of Christmas presents

beschimpfen *verb*
  = to abuse

beschlagnahmen *verb*
  = to confiscate

beschleunigen *verb*
  = to speed up
  = to accelerate

beschließen *irregular verb*
  = to decide

beschreiben *irregular verb*
  = to describe

die **Beschreibung**, *plural* Beschreibungen
  = description

beschuldigen *verb*
  = to accuse

beschützen *verb*
  = to protect

die **Beschwerde**, *plural* Beschwerden
  = complaint

beschweren: sich beschweren
  verb
  = to complain

beschwipst* *adjective*
  = tipsy

beseitigen *verb*
  = to remove

der **Besen**, *plural* Besen
  = broom

besetzt *adjective*
  = occupied
  besetzt sein (*of a phone, toilet*) = to be
    engaged, (*of a seat*) = to be taken, (*of a
    train, bus*) = to be full (up)

besichtigen *verb*
  = to look round
  = to see

die **Besichtigung**, *plural* Besichtigungen
  = visit

besinnungslos *adjective*
  = unconscious

der **Besitz**
  = property

*** in informal situations

besitzen *irregular verb*
= to own

der **Besitzer**, *plural* Besitzer
= owner

die **Besitzerin**, *plural* Besitzerinnen
= owner

besonderer/besondere/ besonderes *adjective*
• = special
• = particular

besonders *adverb*
= particularly

besorgen *verb*
= to get

besorgt *adjective*
= worried

besprechen *irregular verb*
• = to discuss
• (*write article on*) = to review

die **Besprechung**, *plural* Besprechungen
• = discussion
• (*of a film, play*) = review
• (*conference*) = meeting

besser
1 *adjective* = better
2 *adverb* = better
alles besser wissen = to know better

die **Besserung**
= improvement
gute Besserung! = get well soon!

beständig *adjective*
• = constant
• (*of the weather*) = settled

bestätigen *verb*
= to confirm

die **Bestätigung**, *plural* Bestätigungen
= confirmation

beste ▶bester

die **Bestechung**, *plural* Bestechungen
= bribery

das **Besteck**, *plural* Bestecke
= (set of) cutlery

bestehen *irregular verb*
• = to exist
es besteht die Gefahr, dass . . . = there is a danger that . . .
• eine Prüfung bestehen = to pass an exam
• auf etwas bestehen = to insist on something
• aus etwas bestehen = to consist of something, = to be made of something

bestellen *verb*
• (*in a restaurant, factory*) = to order
• (*reserve*) = to book

• = to tell
bestell ihr schöne Grüße = give her my regards

die **Bestellung**, *plural* Bestellungen
(*for goods*) = order
(*of tickets*) = reservation

bester/beste/bestes
1 *adjective* = best
besten Dank = many thanks
2 *adverb*
am besten = best

bestimmen *verb*
• (*arrange*) = to fix
etwas allein bestimmen = to decide (on) something on one's own
• für jemanden bestimmt sein = to be meant for someone
• = to be in charge

bestimmt
1 *adjective* = definite, = certain
2 *adverb* = definitely, = certainly

die **Bestimmung**, *plural* Bestimmungen
= regulation

bestrafen *verb*
= to punish

bestreiten *irregular verb*
• = to deny
• = to dispute
• = to pay for

bestürzt *adjective*
= dismayed

der **Besuch**, *plural* Besuche
= visit

besuchen *verb*
= to visit
= to go to, = to attend

der **Besucher**, *plural* Besucher
= visitor

die **Besucherin**, *plural* Besucherinnen
= visitor

die **Betäubung**
= anaesthesia
örtliche Betäubung = local anaesthetic

beteiligen *verb*
• = to give a share to
• sich an etwas beteiligen = to take part in something

beten *verb*
= to pray

der **Beton**
= concrete

betonen *verb*
= to stress

der **Betrag**, *plural* Beträge
= amount

betragen *irregular verb*
- = to amount to
- sich betragen = to behave

betreffen *irregular verb*
= to concern
was mich betrifft = as far as I'm concerned

betreten *irregular verb*
- = to step on
- (*go into*) = to enter

der **Betrieb**, *plural* Betriebe
- = business
- = activity
außer Betrieb = not in use, (*broken*) = out of order

betrinken: sich betrinken
irregular verb
= to get drunk

betrog ▶ betrügen

der **Betrug**
= deception, = fraud

betrügen *irregular verb*
= to cheat
= to be unfaithful to

betrunken *adjective*
= drunk

das **Bett**, *plural* Betten
= bed

betteln *verb*
= to beg

der **Bettler**, *plural* Bettler
= beggar

die **Bettlerin**, *plural* Bettlerinnen
= beggar

die **Bettwäsche**
= bed linen

beugen *verb*
- = to bend
- (*in grammar*) = to decline
= to conjugate

die **Beule**, *plural* Beulen
- = bump
= lump
- = dent

beurteilen *verb*
= to judge

der **Beutel**, *plural* Beutel
= bag

die **Bevölkerung**, *plural* Bevölkerungen
= population

bevor *conjunction*
= before
bevor nicht = until

bevorzugen *verb*
= to prefer

bewachen *verb*
= to guard

bewährt *adjective*
= reliable

bewegen *verb*
- = to move
- sich bewegen = to move

die **Bewegung**, *plural* Bewegungen
= movement
körperliche Bewegung = physical exercise

der **Beweis**, *plural* Beweise
= proof
= evidence

beweisen *irregular verb*
- = to prove
- = to show

bewerben: sich bewerben
irregular verb
= to apply
sich um einen Job bewerben = to apply for a job

die **Bewerbung**, *plural* Bewerbungen
= application

bewilligen *verb*
= to grant

der **Bewohner**, *plural* Bewohner
- (*of a house*) = resident, = occupant
- (*of a region*) = inhabitant

die **Bewohnerin**, *plural* Bewohnerinnen
- (*of a house*) = resident, = occupant
- (*of a region*) = inhabitant

bewundern *verb*
= to admire

bewusst (**bewußt** ⓞⓛⓓ) *adjective*
- = conscious
- = deliberate

bewusstlos (**bewußtlos** ⓞⓛⓓ)
adjective
= unconscious

das **Bewusstsein** (**Bewußtsein** ⓞⓛⓓ)
= consciousness
bei vollem Bewusstsein sein = to be fully conscious

bezahlen *verb*
= to pay
= to pay for

die **Bezahlung**
= payment

beziehen *irregular verb*
- = to cover
- ein Haus beziehen = to move into a house
- (*receive goods*) = to get
- sich auf jemanden beziehen = to refer to someone

� in informal situations   ⓞⓛⓓ = old spelling

die **Beziehung**, *plural* Beziehungen
- = connection
- = relationship

beziehungsweise *conjunction*
- = or rather
- = respectively

der **Bezirk**, *plural* Bezirke
= district

bezweifeln *verb*
= to doubt

der **BH**, *plural* BHs
= bra

die **Bibel**, *plural* Bibeln
= Bible

die **Bibliothek**, *plural* Bibliotheken
= library

biegen *irregular verb*
- = to bend
- (**!** *sein*) = to turn
- sich biegen = to bend

die **Biene**, *plural* Bienen
= bee

das **Bier**, *plural* Biere
= beer

bieten *irregular verb*
- = to offer
- (*at auction*) = to bid

das **Bild**, *plural* Bilder
= picture

bilden *verb*
- = to form
- sich bilden = to form
  (*gain knowledge*) = to educate oneself

der **Bildschirm**, *plural* Bildschirme
= screen

die **Bildung**
- = formation
- (*knowledge*) = education

billig *adjective*
= cheap

die **Billion**, *plural* Billionen
(*million million*) = billion

bin ▶sein

die **Binde**, *plural* Binden
- = bandage
- = sanitary towel

binden *irregular verb*
- = to tie
- = to bind
- (*in cooking*) = to thicken
- sich binden = to commit oneself

der **Bindestrich**, *plural* Bindestriche
= hyphen

der **Bindfaden**, *plural* Bindfäden
= (piece of) string

die **Bindung**, *plural* Bindungen
- = tie
- = relationship
- (*on a ski*) = binding

die **Biokost**
= health food

die **Biologie**
= biology

die **Birne**, *plural* Birnen
- = pear
- = (light) bulb

bis
1 *preposition* (+ *accusative*)
- (*with a place*) = as far as, = to
- (*indicating limit*) = up to
  bis auf = except for, (*including*) = down to
- (*with time*) = until, = till
  bis bald! = see you soon!
- (*at the latest*) = by
- = to
  drei bis vier Tage = three to four days
2 *conjunction* = until

der **Bischof**, *plural* Bischöfe
= bishop

bisher *adverb*
= so far

biss (**biß** ⓞⓛⓓ) ▶beißen

bisschen (**bißchen** ⓞⓛⓓ) *pronoun*
ein bisschen = a bit, = a little
kein bisschen = not a bit

bist ▶sein

bitte *adverb*
- = please
- (*in reply to thanks*) = you're welcome
  (*in response to a knock at the door*) =
  come in
- (*in a shop*) bitte? = yes, please?
  wie bitte? = sorry?

die **Bitte**, *plural* Bitten
= request

bitten *irregular verb*
= to ask

bitter *adjective*
= bitter

blamieren *verb*
= to disgrace

die **Blase**, *plural* Blasen
- = bubble
- = blister
- (*part of the body*) = bladder

blasen *irregular verb*
= to blow

blass (**blaß** ⓞⓛⓓ) *adjective*
= pale

das **Blatt**, *plural* Blätter
- = leaf

- (*piece of paper*) = sheet
  (*in a book*) = page
- = (news)paper

blau *adjective*
- = blue
  ein blaues Auge = a black eye
- blau sein✶ (*be drunk*) = to be tight

das **Blech**, *plural* Bleche
- = tin
- = baking tray
- (*in music*) = brass

das **Blei**
= lead

bleiben *irregular verb* (**!** *sein*)
- = to stay, = to remain
  bleiben Sie am Apparat = hold the line
- (*of remains*) = to be left

bleifrei *adjective*
= unleaded

der **Bleistift**, *plural* Bleistifte
= pencil

der **Bleistiftspitzer**, *plural* Bleistiftspitzer
= pencil sharpener

blenden *verb*
- = to dazzle
- = to blind

der **Blick**, *plural* Blicke
- = look
- = view

blieb ▶ bleiben

blies ▶ blasen

blind *adjective*
= blind

der **Blinddarm**, *plural* Blinddärme
= appendix

der/die **Blinde**, *plural* Blinden
= blind person, = blind man/woman

blinken *verb*
- = to flash
- (*of a car*) = to indicate

der **Blinker**, *plural* Blinker
(*on a car*) = indicator

der **Blitz**, *plural* Blitze
- (flash of) lightning
- flash

blitzen *verb*
= to flash
es hat geblitzt = there was a flash of
lightning

der **Block**, *plural* Blocks *or* Blöcke
- (*for writing*) = pad
- (*of apartments*) = block

die **Blockflöte**, *plural* Blockflöten
= recorder

blöd *adjective*
= stupid, = silly

der **Blödsinn**
= nonsense

die **Blondine**, *plural* Blondinen
= blonde

bloß *adverb*
= only, = just

blühen *verb*
- (*of a plant*) = to blossom, = to flower
- (*of a business*) = to flourish

die **Blume**, *plural* Blumen
= flower

der **Blumenkohl**
= cauliflower

die **Bluse**, *plural* Blusen
= blouse

das **Blut**
= blood

bluten *verb*
= to bleed

der **Bock**, *plural* Böcke
(*deer, rabbit*) = buck
(*goat*) = billy-goat
(*sheep*) = ram

der **Boden**, *plural* Böden
- = ground
  (*in a room*) = floor
  (*of a container*) = bottom
- = loft, = attic

der **Bodensee**
= Lake Constance

bog ▶ biegen

der **Bogen**, *plural* Bögen
- = curve
- = arch
- (*in skiing*) = turn

die **Bohne**, *plural* Bohnen
= bean

bohren *verb*
= to drill

der **Bohrer**, *plural* Bohrer
= drill

der **Bolzen**, *plural* Bolzen
= bolt

der *or* das **Bonbon**, *plural* Bonbons
= sweet

das **Boot**, *plural* Boote
= boat

die **Bordkarte**, *plural* Bordkarten
= boarding pass

borgen *verb*
- = to borrow

- sich etwas borgen = to borrow something
- jemandem etwas borgen = to lend someone something

die **Börse**, *plural* Börsen
= stock exchange

böse *adjective*
- = bad
= evil
- (*of a child*) = naughty
- = angry
ich bin ihm böse = I am angry with him

boshaft *adjective*
= malicious

bot ▶bieten

der **Bote**, *plural* Boten
= messenger

die **Botin**, *plural* Botinnen
= messenger

die **Botschaft**, *plural* Botschaften
- = message
- = embassy

der **Botschafter**, *plural* Botschafter
= ambassador

die **Botschafterin**, *plural* Botschafterinnen
= ambassador

die **Bowle**, *plural* Bowlen
(*drink*) = punch

boxen *verb*
- = to box
- = to punch

brach ▶brechen

brachte ▶bringen

die **Branche**, *plural* Branchen
= (line of) business

das **Branchenverzeichnis**, *plural* Branchenverzeichnisse
= classified directory

die **Brandung**
= surf

brannte ▶brennen

(das) **Brasilien**
= Brazil

braten *irregular verb*
- = to fry
- = to roast

die **Bratpfanne**, *plural* Bratpfannen
= frying pan

der **Brauch**, *plural* Bräuche
= custom

brauchen *verb*
= to need

die **Brauerei**, *plural* Brauereien
= brewery

braun *adjective*
= brown

die **Bräune**
= tan

die **Brause**, *plural* Brausen
= fizzy drink

die **Braut**, *plural* Bräute
= bride

der **Bräutigam**, *plural* Bräutigame
= bridegroom

brav *adjective*
= good

die **BRD**
(*Bundesrepublik Deutschland*) = FRG

brechen *irregular verb*
- = to break
er hat sich den Arm gebrochen = he broke his arm
- = to vomit

breit *adjective*
= wide
= broad

die **Breite**, *plural* Breiten
= width

die **Bremse**, *plural* Bremsen
- (*of a car, bike*) = brake
- = horsefly

bremsen *verb*
= to brake
= to slow down

brennen *irregular verb*
- = to burn
- (*of a light*) = to be on

die **Brennnessel** (**Brennessel**ⓞⓛⓓ), *plural* Brennnesseln
= stinging nettle

der **Brennpunkt**, *plural* Brennpunkte
= focus

das **Brett**, *plural* Bretter
- = board
- = plank
- = shelf

bricht ▶brechen

der **Brief**, *plural* Briefe
= letter

der **Brieffreund**, *plural* Brieffreunde
= pen friend

die **Brieffreundin**, *plural* Brieffreundinnen
= pen friend

der **Briefkasten**, *plural* Briefkästen
- = letterbox
- = postbox, = mailbox

die **Briefmarke**, *plural* Briefmarken
= stamp

die **Brieftasche**, *plural* Brieftaschen
= wallet

der **Briefträger**, *plural* Briefträger
= postman, = mailman

der **Briefumschlag**, *plural*
Briefumschläge
= envelope

briet ▶ braten

der **Brillant**, *plural* Brillanten
= diamond

die **Brille**, *plural* Brillen
= glasses, = spectacles

bringen *irregular verb*
• = to bring
(*bring away*) = to take
ich bringe dich nach Hause = I'll take you home
• (*in a cinema*) = to show

die **Brise**, *plural* Brisen
= breeze

der **Brite**, *plural* Briten
= Briton
die Briten = the British

die **Britin**, *plural* Britinnen
= Briton

britisch *adjective*
= British

die **Brombeere**, *plural* Brombeeren
= blackberry

die **Brosche**, *plural* Broschen
= brooch

die **Broschüre**, *plural* Broschüren
= brochure

das **Brot**, *plural* Brote
= bread
ein Brot = a loaf of bread *or* a slice of bread

das **Brötchen**, *plural* Brötchen
= roll

der **Bruch**, *plural* Brüche
• = break
(*of a bone*) = fracture
• (*in maths*) = fraction

der **Bruchteil**, *plural* Bruchteile
= fraction

die **Brücke**, *plural* Brücken
= bridge

der **Bruder**, *plural* Brüder
= brother

die **Brühe**, *plural* Brühen
= broth
(*for cooking*) = stock

brüllen *verb*
= to roar

brummen *verb*
= to buzz
(*of an animal*) = to growl
(*of an engine*) = to hum

der **Brunnen**, *plural* Brunnen
• = well
• = fountain

die **Brust**, *plural* Brüste
= chest
= breast

brutto *adverb*
= gross

das **Buch**, *plural* Bücher
= book

buchen *verb*
= to book

die **Bücherei**, *plural* Büchereien
= library

der **Buchhalter**, *plural* Buchhalter
= accountant, = bookkeeper

die **Buchhalterin**, *plural* Buchhalterinnen
= accountant, = bookkeeper

die **Buchhandlung**, *plural*
Buchhandlungen
= bookshop

die **Büchse**, *plural* Büchsen
= tin, = can

der **Buchstabe**, *plural* Buchstaben
= letter
ein großer Buchstabe = a capital letter
ein kleiner Buchstabe = a small letter

buchstabieren *verb*
= to spell

die **Bucht**, *plural* Buchten
= bay

bücken: sich bücken *verb*
= to bend down

die **Bude**, *plural* Buden
• = hut
• (*in a market*) = stall
• **seine Bude** ✱= his room

das **Bügeleisen**, *plural* Bügeleisen
= iron

bügeln *verb*
= to iron

die **Bühne**, *plural* Bühnen
= stage

der **Bulle**, *plural* Bullen
= bull

✱ in informal situations

bummeln *verb*
- (**!** *sein*) (*around town*) = to stroll
- (*be slow*) = to dawdle

der **Bundesrat**
= Upper House (*of the German Parliament*)

die **Bundesrepublik**
= federal republic

der **Bundestag**
= Lower House (*of the German Parliament*)

die **Bundeswehr**
= army

bunt *adjective*
= colourful, = colorful

der **Buntstift**, *plural* Buntstifte
= coloured pencil, = crayon

die **Burg**, *plural* Burgen
= castle

bürgen *verb*
bürgen für = to vouch for

der **Bürger**, *plural* Bürger
= citizen

die **Bürgerin**, *plural* Bürgerinnen
= citizen

bürgerlich *adjective*
- = civil
- = middle-class

der **Bürgermeister**, *plural* Bürgermeister
= mayor

der **Bürgersteig**, *plural* Bürgersteige
= pavement, = sidewalk

das **Büro**, *plural* Büros
= office

die **Büroklammer**, *plural* Büroklammern
= paper clip

die **Bürokratie**, *plural* Bürokratien
= bureaucracy

die **Bürste**, *plural* Bürsten
= brush

bürsten *verb*
= to brush

der **Bus**, *plural* Busse
= bus

der **Busch**, *plural* Büsche
= bush

der **Busen**, *plural* Busen
= bosom

der **Büstenhalter**, *plural* Büstenhalter
= bra

das **Butterbrot**, *plural* Butterbrote
= sandwich

bzw. ▶beziehungsweise

Cc

ca. *abbreviation*
(*circa*) = approx.

der **Campingplatz**, *plural* Campingplätze
= campsite

die **CD**, *plural* CDs
= CD

der **CD-Spieler**, *plural* CD-Spieler
= CD player

Celsius *adjective*
= Celsius, = centigrade

der **Champignon**, *plural* Champignons
= mushroom

die **Chance**, *plural* Chancen
= chance

der **Charakter**, *plural* Charaktere
= character

charakteristisch *adjective*
= characteristic

charmant *adjective*
= charming

der **Chef**, *plural* Chefs
= boss

die **Chefin**, *plural* Chefinnen
= boss

die **Chemie**
= chemistry

der **Chemiker**, *plural* Chemiker
= chemist

die **Chemikerin**, *plural* Chemikerinnen
= chemist

chemisch *adjective*
= chemical
chemische Reinigung = dry-cleaning

chinesisch *adjective*
= Chinese

Chips (*plural*)
= crisps, = chips

der **Chirurg**, *plural* Chirurgen
= surgeon

die **Chirurgin**, *plural* Chirurginnen
= surgeon

der **Chor**, *plural* Chöre
= choir

der **Christ**, *plural* Christen
= Christian

das **Christentum**
= Christianity

die **Christin**, *plural* Christinnen
= Christian

der **Christus**
= Christ

circa *adverb*
= approximately

der **Clown**, *plural* Clowns
= clown

der **Club**, *plural* Clubs
= club

die or das **Cola**®, *plural* Colas *or* Cola
= Coke®

der **Comic**, *plural* Comics
= cartoon

das **Comicheft**, *plural* Comichefte
= comic

der **Computer**, *plural* Computer
= computer

der **Container**, *plural* Container
* = container
* = skip

der **Cordsamt**
= corduroy

die **Couch**, *plural* Couchs
= sofa

die **Creme**, *plural* Cremes
= cream

Dd

da
1 *adverb*
* = there
  da unten = down there
* (*indicating time*) = then
  von da an = from then on
* (*for that reason*) = so
  der Zug war weg, da habe ich den Bus
  genommen = the train had gone, so I
  took the bus
* da sein = to be there/here
  sind alle da? = is everyone here?
  ich bin gleich wieder da = I'll be right
  back
  ist noch Brot da? = is there any bread
  left?
2 *conjunction*
= as, = since

dabei *adverb*
* (*next to, included*) = with it
  dicht dabei = close by
* (*referring to something previously
  mentioned*) = about it
  wichtig dabei ist, dass . . . = the
  important thing about it is that . . .
  da ist doch nichts dabei = there's nothing
  to it
* = at the same time
  = during this
* (*although*) = and yet
* dabei sein (*be present*) = to be there
* dabei sein (*take part*) = to be involved
  dabei sein, etwas zu tun = to be just
  doing something

das **Dach**, *plural* Dächer
= roof

der **Dachboden**, *plural* Dachböden
= loft, = attic

dachte ▶ denken

der **Dackel**, *plural* Dackel
= dachshund

dadurch *adverb*
* = through it/them
* (*for that reason*) = because of that
* dadurch, dass = because

dafür *adverb*
* = for it/them
  dafür kriegst du nicht viel = you won't get
  much for it/them
* = instead
* (*to even things out*) = but then
* dafür, dass = considering (that)

dagegen *adverb*
* = against it/them
* (*when swapping*) = for it/them
* (*showing the opposite*) = by comparison

daheim *adverb*
= at home

daher *adverb*
* = from there
* (*for that reason*) = that's why

dahin *adverb*
= there
bis dahin = until then, (*in the future*) = by
then

dahinter *adverb*
* = behind it/them
* dahinter kommen = to find out

da|lassen *irregular verb*
= to leave there

damals *adverb*
= at that time

die **Dame**, *plural* Damen
* = lady
* (*in chess, cards*) = queen
* (*game*) = draughts, = checkers

D

damit
1 *adverb*
* = with it/them
  hör auf damit = stop it
* (*thus*) = therefore
2 *conjunction* = so that
  schreib es auf, damit du es nicht vergisst
    = write it down so that you don't forget

der **Damm**, *plural* Dämme
* = dam
* = embankment

dämmern *verb*
  es dämmert (*in the morning*) = it is
    getting light, (*in the evening*) = it is
    getting dark

die **Dämmerung**
* = dawn
* = dusk

der **Dampf**, *plural* Dämpfe
  = steam

dampfen *verb*
  = to steam

dämpfen *verb*
* (*in cooking*) = to steam
* = to muffle
* (*reduce*) = to dampen

danach *adverb*
* = after it/them
  danach suchen = to search for it/them
  danach riechen = to smell of it/them
  es sieht danach aus = it looks like it
* = according to it/them
* = afterwards

daneben *adverb*
* = next to it/them
* = in addition
* = by comparison

(das) **Dänemark**
  = Denmark

der **Dank**
  = thanks
  vielen Dank = thank you very much

dankbar *adjective*
  = grateful

danke *interjection*
  = thank you, = thanks
  danke schön = thank you very much

danken *verb*
  = to thank
  nichts zu danken = don't mention it

dann *adverb*
  = then

daran *adverb*
* = on it/them, = at it/them
* daran denken = to think of it/them
* nahe daran sein, etwas zu tun = to be on
  the point of doing something

darauf *adverb*
* = on it/them
* darauf warten = to wait for it
* darauf antworten = to reply to it
* = after that

daraufhin *adverb*
  = as a result

daraus *adverb*
* (*from a container*) = out of it/them
* (*from material*) = from it/them
* was ist daraus geworden? = what has
  become of it?

darf, darfst ▶dürfen

das **Darlehen**, *plural* Darlehen
  = loan

der **Darm**, *plural* Därme
  = intestine(s)

dar|stellen *verb*
* = to represent
* = to portray
* = to describe
* (*in the theatre*) = to play

der **Darsteller**, *plural* Darsteller
  = actor

die **Darstellerin**, *plural* Darstellerinnen
  = actress

die **Darstellung**, *plural* Darstellungen
* = representation
* = portrayal
* = description
* = interpretation

darüber *adverb*
* = over it/them
* (*higher up*) = above it/them
* darüber lachen = to laugh about it

darum *adverb*
* = round it/them
* darum kämpfen = to fight for it
* (*for that reason*) = that's why
* darum, weil = because

darunter *adverb*
* = under it/them
  (*lower*) = below it/them
* = less
  fünfzig Mark oder sogar darunter = 50
    marks or even less

das
1 *article* (*neuter*) = the
2 *pronoun*
* (*object*) = which
  (*person*) = who
  das Kind, das weint = the child who is
    crying
* that
  das da = that one
  das geht = that's all right

da sein = **dasein**ⓄⓁⒹ ▶da

das **Dasein**
  = existence

dass (**daß** ⓄⓁⒹ) *conjunction*
= that
ich bin froh, dass . . . = I'm glad that . . .

dasselbe *pronoun*
= the same, = the same one

die **Datei**, *plural* Dateien
= (data) file

Daten (*plural*)
= data

die **Datenverarbeitung**
= data processing

datieren *verb*
= to date

das **Datum**, *plural* Daten
= date

die **Dauer**
= duration, = length
auf die Dauer = in the long run

der **Dauerauftrag**, *plural* Daueraufträge
= standing order

die **Dauerkarte**, *plural* Dauerkarten
= season ticket

dauern *verb*
= to last

dauernd *adjective*
= constant

die **Dauerwelle**, *plural* Dauerwellen
= perm

der **Daumen**, *plural* Daumen
= thumb

die **Daunendecke**, *plural* Daunendecken
= duvet, = continental quilt

davon *adverb*
• = from it/them
• = about it/them
• die Hälfte davon = half of of it/them

davor *adverb*
• = in front of it/them
• Angst davor haben = to be frightened of
  it
• = beforehand

dazu *adverb*
• = to it/them
• = in addition, = with it/them
  noch dazu = in addition to it
• = for it
  ich habe keine Lust dazu = I don't feel
  like it
• jemanden dazu bringen, etwas zu tun =
  to get someone to do something
  er kam nicht dazu = he didn't get round
  to it

dazu|geben *irregular verb*
= to add

dazu|gehören *verb*
• = to belong to it/them
• (*of accessories*) = to go with it/them

dazu|kommen *irregular verb* (❗ *sein*)
• = to arrive
• = to be added
  kommt noch etwas dazu? = would you
  like anything else?

dazwischen *adverb*
= in between

dazwischen|kommen *irregular verb*
(❗ *sein*)
= to crop up

die **Debatte**, *plural* Debatten
= debate

die **Decke**, *plural* Decken
• (*on a bed*) = blanket, = cover
• (*on a table*) = cloth
• = ceiling

der **Deckel**, *plural* Deckel
= lid
(*on a bottle*) = top

decken *verb*
• = to cover
  den Tisch decken = to lay the table
• jemanden decken = to cover up for
  someone, (*in sport*) = to mark someone

die **Deckung**
• = cover
  in Deckung gehen = to take cover
• (*in sport*) = marking, = defence

das **Defizit**, *plural* Defizite
= deficit

der **Degen**, *plural* Degen
= sword
(*in fencing*) = épée

dehnbar *adjective*
= elastic

dehnen *verb*
= to stretch

der **Deich**, *plural* Deiche
= dike

dein *adjective*
= your

deiner/deine/deins *pronoun*
= yours

der **Delfin**, *plural* Delfine ▶ Delphin
= dent

die **Delle**, *plural* Dellen
= dent

der **Delphin**, *plural* Delphine
= dolphin

dem
1 *article* = (to) the
2 *pronoun*
• (*person*) = to him
  (*object*) = to it, = to that one
• (*person*) = to whom

(*object*) = to which
der Junge, dem der Ball gehört = the boy to whom the ball belongs

demnächst *adverb*
= shortly

die **Demokratie**, *plural* Demokratien
= democracy

demokratisch *adjective*
= democratic

der **Demonstrant**, *plural* Demonstranten
= demonstrator
= protester

den
1 *article* = the
2 *pronoun*
• (*person*) = him
 (*object*) = it, = that one
• (*person*) = whom
 (*object*) = which
 der Rock, den ich gekauft habe = the skirt I bought

denen *pronoun*
• = (to) them
• (*person*) = to whom
 (*object*) = to which
 die Zuschauer, denen der Film gezeigt wurde = the audience to whom the film was shown

denken *irregular verb*
= to think
das kann ich mir denken = I can imagine

das **Denkmal**, *plural* Denkmäler
= monument

denn
1 *conjunction* = for
2 *adverb*
 warum denn nicht? = why ever not?
 es sei denn = unless

dennoch *adverb*
= nevertheless

deprimieren *verb*
= to depress

der
1 *article*
• (*masculine*) = the
• (*genitive of die*) = of the
 das Kleid der Frau = the woman's dress
 (*dative of die*) = (to) the
 sie gab es der Frau = she gave it to the woman
2 *pronoun*
• (*person*) = who
 (*object*) = which
 der Arzt, der mir geholfen hat = the doctor who helped me
• (*person*) = he, = him
 (*object*) = that (one)

deren *pronoun*
• = their

• (*person*) = whose
 (*object*) = of which

derselbe *pronoun*
= the same, = the same one

des *article*
= of the
die Mütze des Jungen = the boy's cap

D

deshalb *adverb*
= therefore

desinfizieren *verb*
= to disinfect

dessen *pronoun*
• (*person*) = his
 (*object*) = its
• (*person*) = whose
 (*object*) = of which
 der Junge, dessen Hund bellt = the boy whose dog is barking

desto *adverb*
= the
je mehr, desto besser = the more the better

deswegen *adverb*
= therefore

der **Detektiv**, *plural* Detektive
= detective

deutlich *adjective*
= clear

deutsch *adjective*
= German
auf Deutsch = in German

das **Deutsch**
= German

der/die **Deutsche**, *plural* Deutschen
= German

(das) **Deutschland**
= Germany

Devisen (*plural*)
= foreign currency

der **Dezember**
= December

d.h. *abbreviation*
(*das heißt*) = i.e.

das **Dia**, *plural* Dias
= slide

der **Dialekt**, *plural* Dialekte
= dialect

der **Diamant**, *plural* Diamanten
= diamond

die **Diät**, *plural* Diäten
= diet

dich *pronoun*
• = you
• (*reflexive*) = yourself

dicht *adjective*
- = thick, = dense
- = airtight
- = watertight

der **Dichter**, *plural* Dichter
= poet

die **Dichterin**, *plural* Dichterinnen
= poetess

die **Dichtung**, *plural* Dichtungen
- = poetry
- = seal, = washer

dick *adjective*
- = thick
  = swollen
- (*of person*) = fat

die
1 *article*
- (*feminine singular*) = the
- (*plural of the articles der, die and das*) =
  the
2 *pronoun*
- (*person*) = who
  (*object*) = which
  die Frau, die ich gesehen habe = the
  woman I saw
- (*plural of the pronouns der, die and das*)
  **die [Kinder | Sachen | Städte ...], die ich
  gesehen habe** = the [children | things |
  towns ...] I saw
- (*person*) = she, = her, (*plural*) = them
  (*object*) = that (one), (*plural*) = those

der **Dieb**, *plural* Diebe
= thief

die **Diebin**, *plural* Diebinnen
= thief

der **Diebstahl**, *plural* Diebstähle
= theft

die **Diele**, *plural* Dielen
- = hall
- = floorboard

dienen *verb*
= to serve

der **Dienst**, *plural* Dienste
= service
Dienst haben = to work, (*of a soldier or
doctor*) = to be on duty

der **Dienstag**
= Tuesday

dienstags *adverb*
= on Tuesdays

dienstfrei *adjective*
= free
ein dienstfreier Tag = a day off

dienstlich *adverb*
= on business

die **Dienstreise**, *plural* Dienstreisen
= business trip

dies *pronoun*
= this

dieselbe *pronoun*
= the same, = the same one

dieser/diese/dieses
1 *adjective* = this, (*plural*) = these
2 *pronoun* = this one, (*plural*) = these

diesmal *adverb*
= this time

die **Digitaluhr**, *plural* Digitaluhren
= digital watch
= digital clock

das **Diktat**, *plural* Diktate
= dictation

die **Diktatur**, *plural* Diktaturen
= dictatorship

das **Ding**, *plural* Dinge
= thing

der/die/das **Dings**
= thingamy

das **Diplom**, *plural* Diplome
= diploma, = degree

dir *pronoun*
- = (to) you
- (*reflexive*) = yourself

direkt *adjective*
= direct

der **Direktor**, *plural* Direktoren
= director
(*of a bank*) = manager
(*of a school*) = headmaster, = principal
(*of a prison*) = governor

die **Direktorin**, *plural* Direktorinnen
= director
(*of a bank*) = manager
(*of a school*) = headmistress, = principal
(*of a prison*) = governor

der **Dirigent**, *plural* Dirigenten
= conductor

die **Diskette**, *plural* Disketten
= (floppy) disk

die **Diskussion**, *plural* Diskussionen
= discussion

diskutieren *verb*
= to discuss

die **Disziplin**, *plural* Disziplinen
= discipline

DM *abbreviation*
(*Deutsche Mark*) = DM, = Deutschmark

die **D-Mark**, *plural* D-Mark
= German mark, = Deutschmark

✕ in informal situations

doch
1 *adverb*
• = yes
  das stimmt nicht—doch! = that's not
  right—yes it is!
• = after all
2 *conjunction* = but

der **Doktor**, *plural* Doktoren
  = doctor

das **Dokument**, *plural* Dokumente
  = document

der **Dokumentarfilm**, *plural*
  Dokumentarfilme
  = documentary (film)

dolmetschen *verb*
  = to interpret

der **Dolmetscher**, *plural* Dolmetscher
  = interpreter

die **Dolmetscherin**, *plural*
  Dolmetscherinnen
  = interpreter

der **Dom**, *plural* Dome
  = cathedral

die **Donau**
  = Danube

der **Donner**
  = thunder

donnern *verb*
  = to thunder

der **Donnerstag**
  = Thursday

donnerstags *adverb*
  = on Thursdays

doof✘ *adjective*
  = stupid

das **Doppel**, *plural* Doppel
• = duplicate
• (*in sport*) = doubles

der **Doppelpunkt**, *plural* Doppelpunkte
  = colon

doppelt
1 *adjective* = double
2 *adverb* = twice
  doppelt so viel = twice as much

das **Dorf**, *plural* Dörfer
  = village

der **Dorn**, *plural* Dornen
  = thorn

dort *adverb*
  = there

die **Dose**, *plural* Dosen
  = tin, = can

der **Dosenöffner**, *plural* Dosenöffner
  = tin opener, = can opener

die **Dosis**, *plural* Dosen
  = dose

der **Dozent**, *plural* Dozenten
  = lecturer

die **Dozentin**, *plural* Dozentinnen
  = lecturer

der **Drache**, *plural* Drachen
  = dragon

der **Drachen**, *plural* Drachen
  = kite

das **Drachenfliegen**
  = hang-gliding

der **Draht**, *plural* Drähte
  = wire

dran✘ ▶daran
  ich bin dran = it's my turn

drängen *verb*
• = to push
• (*persuade*) = to press

dran|kommen✘ *irregular verb* (**!** *sein*)
  = to have one's turn
  wer kommt dran? = whose turn is it?

drauf✘ ▶darauf
  gut drauf sein = to be in a good mood

draußen *adverb*
  = outside

der **Dreck**
  = dirt

dreckig *adjective*
  = dirty
  = filthy

das **Drehbuch**, *plural* Drehbücher
  = screenplay
  = script

drehen *verb*
• = to turn
• (*make a film*) = to shoot
• sich drehen = to turn
  es dreht sich um unsere Ferien = it is
  about our holidays

drei *adjective*
  = three

das **Dreieck**, *plural* Dreiecke
  = triangle

dreifach *adjective*
  = triple

dreißig *adjective*
  = thirty

drei viertel (**dreiviertel**ⓞⓛⓓ) *adverb*
  = three-quarters

die **Dreiviertelstunde**, *plural*
  Dreiviertelstunden
  = three-quarters of an hour

dreizehn *adjective*
= thirteen

dressieren *verb*
= to train

dringend *adjective*
= urgent

drinnen *adverb*
= inside
= indoors

dritt *adverb*
wir sind zu dritt = there are three of us

dritte ▶ dritter

das **Drittel**, *plural* Drittel
= third

drittens *adverb*
= thirdly

dritter/dritte/drittes *adjective*
= third

die **Droge**, *plural* Drogen
= drug

drogensüchtig *adjective*
= addicted to drugs

der/die **Drogensüchtige**, *plural*
Drogensüchtigen
= drug addict

die **Drogerie**, *plural* Drogerien
= chemist's, = drugstore

drohen *verb*
= to threaten

die **Drohung**, *plural* Drohungen
= threat

drüben *adverb*
= over there

der **Druck**¹
= pressure

der **Druck**² *plural* Drucke
= print

drucken *verb*
= to print

drücken *verb*
• = to press
= to push
• = to hug
• (*of shoes*) = to pinch

der **Drucker**, *plural* Drucker
= printer

die **Drucksache**, *plural* Drucksachen
= printed matter

die **Druckschrift**, *plural* Druckschriften
• = type
• = block letters
• = pamphlet

der **Dschungel**, *plural* Dschungel
= jungle

du *pronoun*
= you

der **Duft**, *plural* Düfte
= fragrance, = scent

duften *verb*
nach etwas duften = to smell of
something

dumm *adjective*
= stupid

dunkel *adjective*
• = dark
im Dunkeln = in the dark
• eine dunkle Stimme = a deep voice

die **Dunkelheit**
= darkness

dünn *adjective*
= thin
(*watery*) = weak

das **Duo**, *plural* Duos
= duet

durch
1 *preposition* (+ *accusative*)
• = through
• (*with the help of*) = by
• (*because of*) = as a result of
2 *adverb* = through
die Nacht durch = throughout the night

durchaus *adverb*
= absolutely

durch|brechen *irregular verb*
• = to snap
• (**!** *sein*) das Brett ist durchgebrochen =
the board has snapped

durcheinander *adverb*
durcheinander sein (*of a room*) = to be in
a mess, (*of a person*) = to be confused

das **Durcheinander**
= muddle, = chaos

der **Durchfall**
= diarrhoea

durch|fallen *irregular verb* (**!** *sein*)
• = to fall through
• (*in an exam*) = to fail

durch|führen *verb*
= to carry out

der **Durchgang**, *plural* Durchgänge
• = passage
• (*in sport*) = round

der **Durchgangsverkehr**
= through traffic

durch|gehen *irregular verb* (**!** *sein*)
• = to go through
• (*escape*) = to run away

durch|halten *irregular verb*
- (*in a battle*) = to hold out
- = to keep up, = to stand

durch|kommen *irregular verb* (**!** *sein*)
- = to come through
- (*on the phone, in an exam*) = to get through
- (*beat illness*) = to pull through

durch|lassen *irregular verb*
- = to let through
- = to let in

der **Durchmesser**, *plural* Durchmesser
= diameter

die **Durchsage**, *plural* Durchsagen
= announcement

der **Durchschnitt**, *plural* Durchschnitte
= average

durchschnittlich
1 *adjective* = average
2 *adverb* = on average

durch|setzen *verb*
- = to carry through
- **sich durchsetzen** (*of a person*) = to assert oneself, (*of an idea*) = to catch on

durchsichtig *adjective*
= transparent

durch|streichen *irregular verb*
= to cross out

durch|wählen *verb*
= to dial direct

der **Durchzug**
= draught

dürfen *irregular verb*
- = to be allowed
  er darf nicht auf der Straße spielen = he is not allowed to play in the street
- (*in questions*) **darf ich?** = may I?
- **das darf er nicht sehen** = he must not see it
- **das dürfte genügen** = that should be enough

durfte, durften. durftest, durftet ▶ dürfen

die **Dürre**, *plural* Dürren
= drought

der **Durst**
= thirst

durstig *adjective*
= thirsty

die **Dusche**, *plural* Duschen
= shower

duschen *verb*
- = to have a shower
- **sich duschen** = to have a shower

das **Düsenflugzeug**, *plural* Düsenflugzeuge
= jet (aircraft)

düster *adjective*
= gloomy

das **Dutzend**, *plural* Dutzende
= dozen

duzen *verb*
jemanden duzen (*use the familiar form of 'you'*) = to call someone 'du'

der **D-Zug**, *plural* D-Züge
= fast train, = express

Ee

die **Ebbe**, *plural* Ebben
= low tide

eben
1 *adjective* = level, = flat
2 *adverb*
- = just
  er war eben hier = he was just here
- **eben!** = exactly!

die **Ebene**, *plural* Ebenen
- (*in geography*) = plain
- (*in geometry*) = plane
- = level

ebenso *adverb*
= just as

echt *adjective*
= genuine, = real

der **Eckball**, *plural* Eckbälle
= corner (kick)

die **Ecke**, *plural* Ecken
= corner

eckig *adjective*
= square
= angular

der **Edelstein**, *plural* Edelsteine
= precious stone

der **Efeu**, *plural* Efeus
= ivy

die **EG**
(*Europäische Gemeinschaft*) = EC

egal *adjective*
das ist mir egal = it's all the same to me, = I don't care
egal, wie groß = no matter how big

egoistisch *adjective*
= selfish

ehe *conjunction*
= before

die **Ehe**, *plural* Ehen
= marriage

die **Ehefrau**, *plural* Ehefrauen
= wife

ehemalig *adjective*
= former

der **Ehemann**, *plural* Ehemänner
= husband

das **Ehepaar**, *plural* Ehepaare
= married couple

eher *adverb*
• = earlier, = sooner
• = rather
er ist eher faul als dumm = he's lazy
rather than stupid

die **Ehre**, *plural* Ehren
= honour

der **Ehrgeiz**
= ambition

ehrgeizig *adjective*
= ambitious

ehrlich *adjective*
= honest
ehrlich gesagt = to be honest

das **Ei**, *plural* Eier
= egg

die **Eiche**, *plural* Eichen
= oak

das **Eichhörnchen**, *plural* Eichhörnchen
= squirrel

der **Eid**, *plural* Eide
= oath

die **Eidechse**, *plural* Eidechsen
= lizard

der **Eifer**
= eagerness

eifersüchtig *adjective*
= jealous

eigen *adjective*
= own

eigenartig *adjective*
= peculiar

die **Eigenschaft**, *plural* Eigenschaften
• = quality
• = characteristic

eigentlich
1 *adjective* = actual
2 *adverb* = actually

---

das **Eigentum**
= property

der **Eigentümer**, *plural* Eigentümer
= owner

eignen: sich eignen *verb*
= to be suitable

die **Eile**
= hurry

eilen *verb* (**!** sein)
= to hurry

eilig
1 *adjective*
• = urgent
• = hurried
2 *adverb*
= hurriedly
es eilig haben = to be in a hurry

der **Eimer**, *plural* Eimer
= bucket

ein
1 *article* = a, = an
2 *adjective* = one
eines Tages = one day
einer Meinung sein = to be of the same
opinion
3 *adverb*
(*on appliances*) ein-aus = on-off
ein und aus gehen = to come and go

einander *pronoun*
= each other, = one another

die **Einbahnstraße**, *plural*
Einbahnstraßen
= one-way street

der **Einband**, *plural* Einbände
= cover

ein|bauen *verb*
= to fit
= to install

die **Einbauküche**, *plural* Einbauküchen
= fitted kitchen

ein|biegen *irregular verb* (**!** sein)
= to turn

ein|bilden: sich einbilden *verb*
= to imagine

ein|brechen *irregular verb* (**!** sein)
= to break in

der **Einbrecher**, *plural* Einbrecher
= burglar

eindeutig *adjective*
= clear
= obvious
= definite

der **Eindruck**, *plural* Eindrücke
= impression

eine ▶ einer

eineinhalb *adjective*
= one and a half

einer/eine/eins *pronoun*
• = one
• = someone
  kaum einer = hardly anyone
• das macht einen müde = it makes you
  tired

einerseits *adverb*
= on the one hand

einfach
1 *adjective*
• = simple, = easy
• (*of a ticket*) = single
2 *adverb* = simply

die **Einfahrt**, *plural* Einfahrten
• = entrance
• (*of a train*) = arrival
• (*on a motorway*) = slip road

der **Einfall**, *plural* Einfälle
= idea

ein|fallen *irregular verb* (**!** *sein*)
  jemandem einfallen = to occur to
    someone
  sein Name fällt mir nicht ein = I can't
    think of his name

der **Einfluss** (**Einfluß**ⓄⓁⒹ), *plural* Einflüsse
= influence

ein|frieren *irregular verb* (**!** *sein*)
= to freeze

die **Einfuhr**, *plural* Einfuhren
= import

ein|führen *verb*
• = to introduce
• = to import

die **Einführung**, *plural* Einführungen
= introduction

der **Eingang**, *plural* Eingänge
= entrance, = way in
  kein Eingang = no entry

ein|geben *irregular verb*
• = to hand in
• (*in computing*) = to input

eingebildet *adjective*
• = imaginary
• = conceited

der/die **Eingeborene**, *plural* Eingeborenen
= native

ein|gehen *irregular verb* (**!** *sein*)
• (*arrive*) = to come in
• (*of clothes*) = to shrink
• (*of plants*) = to die
• auf einen Plan eingehen = to agree to a
    plan
  ein Risiko eingehen = to take a risk

ein|gießen *irregular verb*
= to pour

der **Eingriff**, *plural* Eingriffe
• = intervention
• (*medical*) = operation

einheimisch *adjective*
• = native
• = local

die **Einheit**, *plural* Einheiten
• = unity
• (*measure*) = unit

einheitlich *adjective*
= uniform

der **Einheitspreis**, *plural* Einheitspreise
• = standard price
• = flat fare

einhundert *adjective*
= one hundred

einige ▶ einiger

einigen *verb*
• = to unite
• sich einigen = to come to an agreement

einiger/einige/einiges
1 *adjective*
  = some
  = quite a lot of
  vor einiger Zeit = some time ago
2 *pronoun*
• einige (*plural*) = some
  (*more*) = several
  (*even more*) = quite a lot
  nur einige waren noch da = there were
    only a few left
• einiges = some things

einigermaßen *adverb*
  = fairly
  = fairly well

einiges ▶ einiger

der **Einkauf**, *plural* Einkäufe
• = shopping
• (*single item*) = purchase
  Einkäufe machen = to do some shopping

ein|kaufen *verb*
• = to buy
• = to shop
  einkaufen gehen = to go shopping

das **Einkaufszentrum**, *plural*
  Einkaufszentren
  = shopping centre, = shopping mall

das **Einkommen**, *plural* Einkommen
  = income

die **Einkommenssteuer**, *plural*
  Einkommenssteuern
  = income tax

ein|laden *irregular verb*
• = to invite
• = to load

die **Einladung**, *plural* Einladungen
= invitation

die **Einleitung**, *plural* Einleitungen
= introduction

ein|lösen *verb*
= to cash

einmal *adverb*
* (*in the past*) = once
  (*in the future*) = one day
* (*other uses*)
  auf einmal = suddenly, (*at once*) = at the
  same time
  nicht einmal = not even

einmalig *adjective*
* = unique
* einmalig!✖ = fantastic!

ein|mischen: sich einmischen
verb
= to interfere

ein|ordnen *verb*
* = to put in order
* sich einordnen (*when driving*) = to get in
  lane

ein|packen *verb*
* = to pack
* = to wrap

ein|reichen *verb*
= to hand in

die **Einreise**
= entry

ein|richten *verb*
* = to furnish
* sich einrichten = to furnish one's home

die **Einrichtung**, *plural* Einrichtungen
* = furnishing
  (*furniture*) = furnishings
* = institution

eins
1 *adjective* = one
2 *pronoun* ▶einer

einsam *adjective*
= lonely

der **Einsatz**, *plural* Einsätze
* = use
* (*bet*) = stake

ein|schalten *verb*
* = to switch on
* sich einschalten = to intervene

ein|schicken *verb*
= to send in

ein|schlafen *irregular verb* (**!** sein)
= to go to sleep

ein|schließen *irregular verb*
* = to lock in

* = to include
  Bedienung eingeschlossen = service
  included

einschließlich
1 *preposition* (+ *genitive*) = including
2 *adverb* = inclusive

ein|schränken *verb*
* = to restrict
* = to cut back
* sich einschränken = to economize

das **Einschreiben**, *plural* Einschreiben
= registered letter *or* parcel
per Einschreiben = by registered post, =
registered

ein|sehen *irregular verb*
= to realize

einseitig
1 *adjective* = one-sided
2 *adverb* = on one side

ein|senden *irregular verb*
= to send in

ein|setzen *verb*
* = to use
* (*when betting*) = to stake
* = to insert
* sich für jemanden einsetzen = to support
  someone

die **Einsicht**
* = insight
* = sense

ein|sperren *verb*
= to lock up

der **Einspruch**, *plural* Einsprüche
= objection

einspurig *adjective*
= single-lane

einst *adverb*
* = once
* (*in the future*) = one day

ein|steigen *irregular verb* (**!** sein)
= to get in
(*if it's a bus, train*) = to get on

ein|stellen *verb*
* (*in a job*) = to employ
* (*if it's a machine*) = to adjust
  (*if it's a programme, station*) = to tune
  into
* = to stop
  (*if it's a strike, search*) = to call off

die **Einstellung**, *plural* Einstellungen
* (*of workers*) = employment
* (*of machines*) = adjustment
* (*of a station*) = tuning
* = stopping
  (*of strike, search*) = calling off
* = attitude, = view

einstöckig *adjective*
= single-storey

ein|stürzen *verb* (**!** *sein*)
= to collapse

einstweilen *adverb*
• = for the time being
• = meanwhile

eintausend *adjective*
= one thousand

ein|teilen *verb*
• = to divide up
• = to organize

der **Eintopf**, *plural* Eintöpfe
= stew

der **Eintrag**, *plural* Einträge
= entry

ein|tragen *irregular verb*
• (*in a list*) = to enter
• sich eintragen = to register, = to put your name down

ein|treten *irregular verb* (**!** *sein*)
= to enter
in einen Klub eintreten = to join a club

der **Eintritt**
= entrance, = entry
= admission

die **Eintrittskarte**, *plural* Eintrittskarten
= (admission) ticket

der **Eintrittspreis**, *plural* Eintrittspreise
= admission charge

einverstanden *adjective*
einverstanden sein = to agree
mit jemandem einverstanden sein = to approve of someone

der **Einwand**, *plural* Einwände
= objection

der **Einwanderer**, *plural* Einwanderer
= immigrant

die **Einwanderin**, *plural* Einwanderinnen
= immigrant

einwandfrei *adjective*
= perfect

die **Einwegflasche**, *plural* Einwegflaschen
= non-returnable bottle

ein|weichen *verb*
= to soak

ein|weisen *irregular verb*
(*to hospital*) = to admit

ein|werfen *irregular verb*
• = to post, = to mail
(*if it's a coin*) = to put in
• (*in soccer*) = to throw in

ein|wickeln *verb*
= to wrap (up)

ein|willigen *verb*
= to agree

der **Einwohner**, *plural* Einwohner
= inhabitant

der **Einwurf**, *plural* Einwürfe
• (*for coins*) = slot
• (*comment*) = objection
• (*in soccer*) = throw-in

die **Einzahl**
= singular

ein|zahlen *verb*
= to pay in

das **Einzel**, *plural* Einzel
(*in sport*) = singles

der **Einzelhandel**
= retail trade

die **Einzelheit**, *plural* Einzelheiten
= detail

das **Einzelkind**, *plural* Einzelkinder
= only child

einzeln
1 *adjective*
• = single
= individual
• (*not matching*) = odd
2 *adverb*
• = individually
• (*one after another*) = separately

der/die/das **Einzelne**, *plural* Einzelnen
• der/die Einzelne = the individual
• ein Einzelner/eine Einzelne/ein Einzelnes = a single one
jeder/jede Einzelne = every single one
Einzelne (*plural*) = some
• ins Einzelne gehen = to go into detail

das **Einzelzimmer**, *plural* Einzelzimmer
= single room

ein|ziehen *irregular verb*
• (*if it's a payment*) = to collect
• (*if it's feelers, claws*) = to draw in
den Kopf einziehen = to duck
• = to breathe in
• (**!** *sein*) (*into a house*) = to move in
(*be absorbed*) = to soak in

einzig *adjective*
= only
ein einziges Mal = only once

der/die/das **Einzige**, *plural* Einzigen
• = the only one
kein Einziger/keine Einzige/kein Einziges = not a single one
• das Einzige, was mich stört = the only thing that bothers me

das **Eis**
• = ice
• = ice cream

E

die **Eisbahn**, *plural* Eisbahnen
= skating rink

das **Eisen**, *plural* Eisen
= iron

die **Eisenbahn**, *plural* Eisenbahnen
= railway, = railroad

eisig *adjective*
= icy, = freezing

das **Eislaufen**
= ice-skating

der **Eiszapfen**, *plural* Eiszapfen
= icicle

die **Eiszeit**, *plural* Eiszeiten
= ice age

eitel *adjective*
= vain

der **Eiter**
= pus

das **Eiweiß**, *plural* Eiweiße
• = egg-white
• = protein

der **Ekel**
= disgust

ekeln: sich ekeln *verb*
sich vor etwas ekeln = to find something
disgusting

eklig *adjective*
= disgusting

der **Elefant**, *plural* Elefanten
= elephant

der **Elektriker**, *plural* Elektriker
= electrician

elektrisch *adjective*
= electrical

die **Elektrizität**
= electricity

die **Elektronik**
= electronics

elektronisch *adjective*
= electronic

das **Elend**
= misery

elf *adjective*
= eleven

die **Elfe**, *plural* Elfen
= fairy

der **Elfmeter**, *plural* Elfmeter
(*in soccer*) = penalty

der **Ellbogen**, *plural* Ellbogen
= elbow

ⓄⓁⒹ = old spelling

Eltern (*plural*)
= parents

die **E-Mail**, *plural* E-Mails
= e-mail

das **Email**, *plural* Emails
= enamel

die **Emanzipation**, *plural* Emanzipationen
= emancipation

empfahl ▶empfehlen

der **Empfang**, *plural* Empfänge
• (*party*) = reception
• = receipt

empfangen *irregular verb*
= to receive

der **Empfänger**, *plural* Empfänger
• = recipient
(*of a letter*) = addressee
• (*TV, radio*) = receiver

die **Empfängnisverhütung**
= contraception

empfehlen *irregular verb*
= to recommend

empfindlich *adjective*
• = delicate
• = sensitive

empfing ▶empfangen

empört *adjective*
= indignant

das **Ende**, *plural* Enden
= end
(*of a film, novel*) = ending
zu Ende sein = to be finished

enden *verb*
= to end

endgültig
1 *adjective* = final
2 *adverb* = finally
sich endgültig trennen = to separate for
good

endlich *adverb*
= at last, = finally

die **Endstation**, *plural* Endstationen
= terminus

die **Energie**
= energy

energisch *adjective*
= energetic

eng *adjective*
• = narrow
= tight
• (*of friendship*) = close
eng befreundet sein = to be close friends

der **Engel**, *plural* Engel
= angel

der **Engländer**, plural Engländer
= Englishman

die **Engländerin**, plural Engländerinnen
= Englishwoman

englisch adjective
= English
auf Englisch = in English

der **Enkel**, plural Enkel
= grandson

die **Enkelin**, plural Enkelinnen
= granddaughter

das **Enkelkind**, plural Enkelkinder
= grandchild

entdecken verb
= to discover

die **Entdeckung**, plural Entdeckungen
= discovery

die **Ente**, plural Enten
= duck

entfernen verb
= to remove

entfernt
1 adjective = distant
fünf Kilometer entfernt = 5 kilometres
away
2 adverb
entfernt verwandt = distantly related

die **Entfernung**, plural Entfernungen
• = distance
• (of stains) = removal

entführen verb
• = to kidnap
• = to hijack

entgegengesetzt adjective
• = opposite
• (of views) = opposing

entgegenkommend adjective
• = obliging
• (of traffic) = oncoming

das **Entgelt**
= payment

das **Enthaarungsmittel**, plural
Enthaarungsmittel
= hair remover

enthalten irregular verb
• = to contain
im Preis enthalten = included in the price
• sich der Stimme enthalten = to abstain

entkommen irregular verb (! sein)
= to escape

entlang preposition (+ accusative)
= along
die Straße entlang = along the road

entlang|gehen irregular verb (! sein)
= to walk along

entlang|laufen irregular verb (! sein)
= to run along

entlassen irregular verb
• (from a job) = to dismiss
• (from hospital) = to discharge
(from prison) = to release

die **Entlassung**, plural Entlassungen
• = dismissal
• = discharge
• = release

die **Entschädigung**, plural
Entschädigungen
= compensation

entscheiden irregular verb
• = to decide (on)
• sich entscheiden = to decide

die **Entscheidung**, plural Entscheidungen
= decision

entschließen: sich
entschließen irregular verb
= to decide
sich anders entschließen = to change
one's mind

entschlossen adjective
= determined

der **Entschluss** (**Entschluß**⓪ᴸᴰ), plural
Entschlüsse
= decision

entschuldigen verb
• = to excuse
entschuldigen Sie bitte = excuse me
• sich bei jemandem entschuldigen = to
apologize to someone

die **Entschuldigung**, plural
Entschuldigungen
• = apology
Entschuldigung! = sorry!, (following a
question) = excuse me?
• = excuse

das **Entsetzen**
= horror

entsetzlich adjective
= horrible
= terrible

entspannen: sich entspannen
verb
= to relax

die **Entspannung**
= relaxation

entsprechend
1 adjective
• = corresponding
• = appropriate
2 preposition (+ dative) = in accordance
with

entstehen irregular verb (! sein)
• = to develop
• (of a building) = to be built
• (of damage) = to result

enttäuschen *verb*
= to disappoint

die **Enttäuschung**, *plural* Enttäuschungen
= disappointment

entweder *conjunction*
= either

entwerten *verb*
• = to devalue
• (*in a ticket machine*) = to cancel

der **Entwerter**, *plural* Entwerter
= ticket-cancelling machine

entwickeln *verb*
• = to develop
• sich entwickeln = to develop

die **Entwicklung**, *plural* Entwicklungen
= development
= developing

das **Entwicklungsland**, *plural*
Entwicklungsländer
= developing country

der **Entwurf**, *plural* Entwürfe
• = design
• = draft

entzünden *verb*
• = to light
• sich entzünden = to ignite, (*of a wound*)
= to become inflamed

die **Entzündung**, *plural* Entzündungen
= inflammation

der **Enzian**, *plural* Enziane
= gentian

er *pronoun*
= he
(*thing*) = it

der **Erbe**¹ *plural* Erben
= heir

das **Erbe**²
= inheritance

erben *verb*
= to inherit

die **Erbin**, *plural* Erbinnen
= heiress

erblich *adjective*
= hereditary

die **Erbschaft**, *plural* Erbschaften
= inheritance

die **Erbse**, *plural* Erbsen
= pea

das **Erdbeben**, *plural* Erdbeben
= earthquake

die **Erdbeere**, *plural* Erdbeeren
= strawberry

die **Erde**, *plural* Erden
• = earth, = soil
• = ground
• (*planet*) = Earth
• (*for electrical circuit*) = earth, = ground

das **Erdgeschoss** (**Erdgeschoß**ⓞⓛⓓ),
plural Erdgeschosse
= ground floor, (*US*) = first floor

die **Erdkunde**
= geography

die **Erdnuss** (**Erdnuß**ⓞⓛⓓ), *plural*
Erdnüsse
= peanut

ereignen: sich ereignen *verb*
= to happen

das **Ereignis**, *plural* Ereignisse
= event

erfahren
1 *irregular verb* = to learn
2 *adjective* = experienced

die **Erfahrung**, *plural* Erfahrungen
= experience

erfinden *irregular verb*
= to invent

die **Erfindung**, *plural* Erfindungen
= invention

der **Erfolg**, *plural* Erfolge
= success
= hit
viel Erfolg! = good luck!

erfolglos *adjective*
= unsuccessful

erfolgreich *adjective*
= successful

erforderlich *adjective*
= necessary

erforschen *verb*
= to explore
= to investigate

die **Erfrischung**, *plural* Erfrischungen
= refreshment

erfüllen *verb*
• = to fulfil
• sich erfüllen = to come true

das **Ergebnis**, *plural* Ergebnisse
= result

erhalten *irregular verb*
• = to receive
• = to preserve

erhältlich *adjective*
= obtainable, = available

erheben *irregular verb*
• = to raise
• eine Gebühr erheben = to charge a fee
• sich erheben = to rise (up)

---

erheblich *adjective*
= considerable

erhöhen *verb*
• = to increase
• sich erhöhen = to rise

die **Erhöhung**, *plural* Erhöhungen
= increase

erholen: sich erholen *verb*
• = to rest
• sich von einer Krankheit erholen = to recover from an illness

erholsam *adjective*
= restful

die **Erholung**
• = rest
• = recovery

erinnern *verb*
• = to remind
• sich erinnern = to remember

die **Erinnerung**, *plural* Erinnerungen
• = memory
• = souvenir

erkälten: sich erkälten *verb*
= to catch a cold
erkältet sein = to have a cold

die **Erkältung**, *plural* Erkältungen
= cold

erkennen *irregular verb*
• = to recognize
• = to realize

erklären *verb*
• = to explain
• = to declare

die **Erklärung**, *plural* Erklärungen
• = explanation
• = declaration

erkundigen: sich erkundigen
verb
= to inquire, = to ask about

die **Erkundigung**, *plural* Erkundigungen
= inquiry

erlauben *verb*
= to allow

die **Erlaubnis**, *plural* Erlaubnisse
= permission

erleben *verb*
= to experience
eine Überraschung erleben = to have a surprise

das **Erlebnis**, *plural* Erlebnisse
= experience

erledigen *verb*
= to deal with
= to settle

erledigt *adjective*
(*of a matter*) = settled
ich bin erledigt✶ = I'm worn out

der **Erlös**
= proceeds

die **Ermäßigung**, *plural* Ermäßigungen
= reduction

ermorden *verb*
= to murder
= to assassinate

ermutigen *verb*
= to encourage

ernähren *verb*
• = to feed
• sich von Bananen ernähren = to live on bananas

die **Ernährung**
= nutrition
= diet

erneut
1 *adjective* = renewed
2 *adverb* = once again

ernst *adjective*
= serious

der **Ernst**
= seriousness

ernstlich *adjective*
= serious

die **Ernte**, *plural* Ernten
= harvest

ernten *verb*
= to harvest

erobern *verb*
= to conquer

die **Eroberung**, *plural* Eroberungen
= conquest

eröffnen *verb*
= to open

die **Eröffnung**, *plural* Eröffnungen
= opening

erpressen *verb*
= to blackmail

der **Erreger**, *plural* Erreger
= germ

erreichbar *adjective*
= reachable

erreichen *verb*
• = to reach
• (*be in time for*) = to catch
• = to achieve

erröten *verb* (**!** *sein*)
= to blush

der **Ersatz**
= replacement, = substitute

das **Ersatzteil**, plural Ersatzteile
= spare part

erscheinen irregular verb (**!** sein)
= to appear
(of a book) = to be published

erschöpft adjective
= exhausted

erschrecken verb
• = to scare
• irregular (**!** sein) = to get a fright

ersetzen verb
= to replace
einen Schaden ersetzen = to compensate
for damages

erst adverb
• = first
• = only
eben erst = only just
erst nächste Woche = not until next
week

erstaunlich adjective
= astonishing

erste ▶erster

der/die/das **Erste**
• der/die Erste = the first one
das Erste = the first thing
der Erste, der gekommen ist = the first
one who came
als Erstes = first of all
• fürs Erste = for the time being
• = the best
sie war die Erste in Latein = she was top
in Latin

erstens adverb
= firstly

erster/erste/erstes adjective
= first
der erste April = the first of April
das erste Mal = the first time
erste Hilfe = first aid

erteilen verb
= to give

der **Ertrag**, plural Erträge
= yield

ertragen irregular verb
= to bear, = to endure

ertrinken irregular verb (**!** sein)
= to drown

erwachsen adjective
= grown-up

der/die **Erwachsene**, plural Erwachsenen
= adult, = grown-up

erwähnen verb
= to mention

erwarten verb
= to expect

die **Erwartung**, plural Erwartungen
= expectation

erzählen verb
= to tell

die **Erzählung**, plural Erzählungen
= story

das **Erzeugnis**, plural Erzeugnisse
= product

erziehen irregular verb
• = to bring up
• = to educate

die **Erziehung**
• = upbringing
• = education

erzogen adjective
gut erzogen = well brought up

es pronoun
= it
(female person) = she, (accusative) = her
(male person) = he, (accusative) = him
es gibt = there is/there are
ich hoffe es = I hope so

der **Esel**, plural Esel
= donkey

essbar (**eßbar**⃝ᴸᴰ) adjective
= edible

essen irregular verb
= to eat

das **Essen**, plural Essen
• = meal
• = food

der **Essig**, plural Essige
= vinegar

das **Esszimmer** (**Eßzimmer**⃝ᴸᴰ), plural
Esszimmer
= dining room

die **Etage**, plural Etagen
= floor, = storey

das **Etikett**, plural Etikette
= label

das **Etui**, plural Etuis
= case

etwa adverb
• = about
etwa so = roughly like this
• = for example

etwas pronoun
• = something
(in questions and with negatives) =
anything
• = some
(in questions and with negatives) = any
• = a little

⃝ᴸᴰ = old spelling

die **EU**
(*Europäische Union*) = EU

euch *pronoun*
= (to) you
(*reflexive*) = yourselves

euer *adjective*
= your

die **Eule**, *plural* Eulen
= owl

eurer/eure/eures *pronoun*
= yours

der **Euro**, *plural* Euros
= euro

(das) **Europa**
= Europe

der **Europäer**, *plural* Europäer
= European

die **Europäerin**, *plural* Europäerinnen
= European

europäisch *adjective*
= European

eventuell
1 *adjective* = possible
2 *adverb* = possibly

ewig
1 *adjective* = eternal
2 *adverb* = forever

das **Examen**, *plural* Examen
= examination

das **Exemplar**, *plural* Exemplare
= copy
= specimen

existieren *verb*
= to exist

explodieren *verb* (**!** *sein*)
= to explode

extra *adverb*
• = separately
• = extra
• = specially

extrem *adjective*
= extreme

Ff

die **Fabel**, *plural* Fabeln
= fable

fabelhaft *adjective*
= fantastic

die **Fabrik**, *plural* Fabriken
= factory

das **Fach**, *plural* Fächer
• = compartment
• (*at school*) = subject

der **Fächer**, *plural* Fächer
= fan

der **Fachmann**, *plural* Fachleute
= expert

die **Fachschule**, *plural* Fachschulen
= technical college

der **Faden**, *plural* Fäden
= thread

fähig *adjective*
• = able
• = capable

die **Fahndung**, *plural* Fahndungen
= search

die **Fahne**, *plural* Fahnen
= flag

die **Fahrbahn**, *plural* Fahrbahnen
= road

die **Fähre**, *plural* Fähren
= ferry

fahren *irregular verb* (**!** *sein*)
(*in a vehicle*) = to go
(*of a motorist*) = to drive
(*of a cyclist*) = to ride
(*of a train*) = to run
mit dem [Auto | Zug | Bus ...] **fahren** = to go
by [car | train | bus ...]
wann fahrt ihr? = when are you leaving?

der **Fahrer**, *plural* Fahrer
= driver

die **Fahrerin**, *plural* Fahrerinnen
= (woman) driver

der **Fahrgast**, *plural* Fahrgäste
= passenger

das **Fahrgeld**, *plural* Fahrgelder
= fare

die **Fahrkarte**, *plural* Fahrkarten
= ticket

der **Fahrplan**, *plural* Fahrpläne
= timetable

fahrplanmäßig *adjective*
= scheduled

der **Fahrpreis**, *plural* Fahrpreise
= fare

die **Fahrprüfung**, *plural* Fahrprüfungen
= driving test

das **Fahrrad**, *plural* Fahrräder
= bicycle

die **Fahrradspur**, *plural* Fahrradspuren
= cycle lane

F

der **Fahrschein**, *plural* Fahrscheine
= ticket

die **Fahrschule**, *plural* Fahrschulen
= driving school

der **Fahrstuhl**, *plural* Fahrstühle
= lift, = elevator

die **Fahrt**, *plural* Fahrten
• = journey
  (*in a car*) = drive
• in voller Fahrt = at full speed

fährt ▶fahren

das **Fahrzeug**, *plural* Fahrzeuge
= vehicle

der **Fall**, *plural* Fälle
• = fall
• = case
  auf jeden Fall = in any case
  auf keinen Fall = on no account

die **Falle**, *plural* Fallen
= trap

fallen *irregular verb* (**!** *sein*)
• = to fall
• etwas fallen lassen = to drop something
  sie haben den Plan fallen lassen = they
    dropped the idea
• im Krieg fallen = to die in the war

fällig *adjective*
= due

falls *conjunction*
• = if
• = in case

der **Fallschirm**, *plural* Fallschirme
= parachute

falsch *adjective*
• = wrong
• = false
• = forged

fälschen *verb*
= to forge

die **Fälschung**, *plural* Fälschungen
= fake
= forgery

die **Falte**, *plural* Falten
• = crease
  = fold
  = pleat
• = line, = wrinkle

falten *verb*
= to fold

die **Familie**, *plural* Familien
= family

der **Familienname**, *plural* Familiennamen
= surname

fand ▶finden

fangen *irregular verb*
• = to catch
• sich fangen = to get caught

die **Fantasie**, *plural* Fantasien
▶Phantasie

fantastisch ▶phantastisch

die **Farbe**, *plural* Farben
• = colour, = color
• = paint
  = dye
• (*playing cards*) = suit

farbecht *adjective*
= colour-fast, = color-fast

färben *verb*
= to colour, = to color
sich die Haare färben = to dye one's hair

der **Farbfilm**, *plural* Farbfilme
= colour film, = color film

farbig *adjective*
= coloured, = colored

der **Farbstoff**, *plural* Farbstoffe
• = dye
• (*for food*) = colouring, = coloring

der **Fasching**, *plural* Faschinge
= carnival

die **Faser**, *plural* Fasern
= fibre, = fiber

das **Fass** (**Faß** ⓞⓛⒹ), *plural* Fässer
= barrel
Bier vom Fass = draught beer

fassen *verb*
• (*with one's hands, understand*) = to
    grasp
  einen Dieb fassen = to catch a thief
  nicht zu fassen = unbelievable
• (*of a container*) = to hold
• sich fassen = to compose oneself

die **Fassung**, *plural* Fassungen
• = version
• = composure
  jemanden aus der Fassung bringen = to
    upset someone
• (*for gems*) = setting

fast *adverb*
= almost, = nearly
fast nie = hardly ever

die **Fastnacht**, *plural* Fastnächte
= carnival

faszinieren *verb*
= to fascinate

faul *adjective*
• = lazy
• (*of fruit*) = bad, = rotten

faulenzen *verb*
= to laze about

die **Faust**, plural Fäuste
= fist
auf eigene Faust = off one's own bat

das **Fax**, plural Fax or Faxe
= fax

faxen verb
= to fax

der **Februar**
= February

fechten irregular verb
= to fence

die **Feder**, plural Federn
• = feather
• (on a pen) = nib
• = spring

der **Federball**
= badminton

das **Federmäppchen**, plural
Federmäppchen
= pencil case

die **Federung**, plural Federungen
= suspension

die **Fee**, plural Feen
= fairy

fegen verb
= to sweep (up)

fehl adverb
fehl am Platz = out of place

fehlen verb
• = to be missing
• = to be lacking
es fehlt an Lehrern = there is a shortage
of teachers
was fehlt dir? = what's the matter?
sie fehlt mir sehr = I miss her very much

der **Fehler**, plural Fehler
• = mistake, = error
• = fault

fehl|schlagen irregular verb (! sein)
= to fail

die **Feier**, plural Feiern
= party
= celebration

der **Feierabend**
= finishing time
nach Feierabend = after work

feierlich adjective
= ceremonial
= formal

feiern verb
= to celebrate

der **Feiertag**, plural Feiertage
= holiday
= festival
ein gesetzlicher Feiertag = a public
holiday, = a bank holiday

feiertags adverb
= on public holidays

feige adjective
= cowardly
feige sein = to be a coward

die **Feige**, plural Feigen
= fig

der **Feigling**, plural Feiglinge
= coward

die **Feile**, plural Feilen
= file

fein adjective
• = fine, = delicate
sich fein machen = to dress up
• = great

der **Feind**, plural Feinde
= enemy

die **Feindin**, plural Feindinnen
= enemy

feindlich adjective
= hostile

das **Feinkostgeschäft**, plural
Feinkostgeschäfte
= delicatessen

das **Feld**, plural Felder
• = field
= pitch
• (on a form) = box
(on a board game) = space, = square

das **Fell**, plural Felle
= fur
= skin

der **Fels**, plural Felsen
= rock

der **Felsen**, plural Felsen
= rock
= cliff

feministisch adjective
= feminist

das **Fenster**, plural Fenster
= window

Ferien (plural)
= holidays, = vacation

fern
1 adjective = distant
2 adverb = far away

die **Fernbedienung**
= remote control

die **Ferne**
= distance
in weiter Ferne = far away

das **Ferngespräch**, plural Ferngespräche
= long-distance call

ferngesteuert adjective
= remote-controlled

F

das **Fernglas**, *plural* Ferngläser
= binoculars

das **Fernrohr**, *plural* Fernrohre
= telescope

das **Fernschreiben**, *plural* Fernschreiben
= telex

der **Fernsehapparat**, *plural* Fernsehapparate
= television set

fern|sehen *irregular verb*
= to watch television

das **Fernsehen**
= television

der **Fernseher**, *plural* Fernseher
= television

der **Fernsprecher**, *plural* Fernsprecher
= telephone

die **Ferse**, *plural* Fersen
= heel

fertig
adjective
- = finished
  fertig sein✱ = to be worn out
- = ready
- etwas fertig machen = to finish something
  fertig essen = to finish eating
- etwas fertig machen = to get something ready
- sich fertig machen =to get ready
- jemanden fertig machen✱ = to wear someone out

fesseln *verb*
- = to tie up
- = to fascinate

fest
1 *adjective*
- = solid
- = firm, = tight
- (*of a salary, address*) = fixed
- (*of a job*) = permanent

2 *adverb*
fest schlafen = to be fast asleep

das **Fest**, *plural* Feste
- = party
  = celebration
- = festival

fest|binden *irregular verb*
= to tie (up)

fest|halten *irregular verb*
- = to hold on to
- sich an etwas festhalten = to hold on to something

fest|legen *verb*
- = to fix
- sich auf etwas festlegen = to commit oneself to something

fest|machen *verb*
= to fix
= to fasten

fest|nehmen *irregular verb*
= to arrest

fest|stehen *irregular verb*
= to be certain

fest|stellen *verb*
= to establish

die **Festung**, *plural* Festungen
= fortress

das **Fett**, *plural* Fette
= fat
= grease

fett *adjective*
= fatty
ein fetter Alter✱ = a fat old man
fette Haare = greasy hair

fettarm *adjective*
= low-fat

fettig *adjective*
= greasy

feucht *adjective*
= damp

die **Feuchtigkeit**
= damp

das **Feuer**, *plural* Feuer
= fire
jemandem Feuer geben = to give someone a light

feuergefährlich *adjective*
= flammable, = inflammable

der **Feuerlöscher**, *plural* Feuerlöscher
= fire extinguisher

die **Feuerwache**, *plural* Feuerwachen
= fire station

die **Feuerwehr**, *plural* Feuerwehren
= fire brigade

das **Feuerwerk**
= fireworks

das **Feuerzeug**, *plural* Feuerzeuge
= lighter

das **Fieber**
= (high) temperature
= fever
Fieber haben = to have a temperature

fiel ▶fallen

die **Figur**, *plural* Figuren
- = figure
- = character

die **Filiale**, *plural* Filialen
= branch

✱ in informal situations

der **Film**, *plural* Filme
= film, = movie

der **Filz**, *plural* Filze
= felt

der **Filzstift**, *plural* Filzstifte
= felt pen

finanziell *adjective*
= financial

finanzieren *verb*
= to finance

finden *irregular verb*
• = to find
• = to think
findest du? = do you think so?

der **Finderlohn**, *plural* Finderlöhne
= reward

fing ▶ fangen

der **Finger**, *plural* Finger
= finger

(das) **Finnland**
= Finland

finster *adjective*
• = dark
im Finstern = in the dark
• = sinister

die **Firma**, *plural* Firmen
= firm, = company

das **Firmenzeichen**, *plural* Firmenzeichen
= trade mark

der **Fisch**, *plural* Fische
• = fish
• Fische = Pisces

der **Fischer**, *plural* Fischer
= fisherman

fix *adjective*
= quick
eine fixe Idee = an obsession
fix und fertig✱ = all finished,
(*exhausted*) = shattered

flach *adjective*
• = flat, = level
• = low
• = shallow

die **Fläche**, *plural* Flächen
• = surface
• = area

flackern *verb*
= to flicker

die **Flagge**, *plural* Flaggen
= flag

die **Flamme**, *plural* Flammen
= flame

die **Flasche**, *plural* Flaschen
= bottle

flechten *irregular verb*
= to weave
= to plait

der **Fleck**, *plural* Flecke
= stain, = spot
ein blauer Fleck = a bruise

die **Fledermaus**, *plural* Fledermäuse
= bat

das **Fleisch**
• = flesh
• = meat

der **Fleischer**, *plural* Fleischer
= butcher

fleißig *adjective*
= hard-working

flicken *verb*
= to mend

die **Fliege**, *plural* Fliegen
• = fly
• = bow tie

fliegen *irregular verb* (**!** *sein*)
• = to fly
• er ist geflogen✱ = he's been fired

fliehen *irregular verb* (**!** *sein*)
= to flee, = to escape

die **Fliese**, *plural* Fliesen
= tile

das **Fließband**, *plural* Fließbänder
= conveyor belt

fließen *irregular verb* (**!** *sein*)
= to flow

fließend *adjective*
• = running
(*of traffic*) = moving
• fließendes Deutsch = fluent German

flirten *verb*
= to flirt

Flitterwochen (*plural*)
= honeymoon

die **Flocke**, *plural* Flocken
= flake

flog ▶ fliegen

der **Floh**, *plural* Flöhe
= flea

die **Flosse**, *plural* Flossen
• = fin
• = flipper

die **Flöte**, *plural* Flöten
= flute

die **Flotte**, *plural* Flotten
= fleet

der **Fluch**, *plural* Flüche
= curse

F

fluchen verb
= to curse, = to swear

flüchten verb (**!** sein)
• to flee
• sich flüchten (**!** haben) = to take refuge

der **Flüchtling**, plural Flüchtlinge
= refugee

der **Flug**, plural Flüge
= flight

der **Flügel**, plural Flügel
• = wing
• = grand piano

der **Fluggast**, plural Fluggäste
= (air) passenger

der **Flughafen**, plural Flughäfen
= airport

der **Flugplatz**, plural Flugplätze
= airport, = airfield

der **Flugschein**, plural Flugscheine
= (air) ticket

der **Flugsteig**, plural Flugsteige
= gate

das **Flugzeug**, plural Flugzeuge
= aeroplane, = airplane

der **Flur**, plural Flure
= hall

der **Fluss** (**Fluß** ⓞⓛⓓ), plural Flüsse
= river

flüssig adjective
= liquid

die **Flüssigkeit**, plural Flüssigkeiten
= liquid

flüstern verb
= to whisper

die **Flut**, plural Fluten
= high tide

der **Föhn**, plural Föhne
= hair-dryer

föhnen verb
= to (blow-) dry

die **Folge**, plural Folgen
• = consequence
• = episode

folgen verb (**!** sein)
= to follow

folgend adjective
= following
Folgendes = the following

folglich adverb
= consequently

---

die **Folie**, plural Folien
= foil
= film

der **Fön** ⓞⓛⓓ® plural Föne
▶Föhn

fönen ⓞⓛⓓ ▶föhnen

fordern verb
= to demand

fördern verb
• = to promote
• (financially) = to support
• Kohle fördern = to mine coal

die **Forderung**, plural Forderungen
• = demand
• = claim

die **Forelle**, plural Forellen
= trout

die **Form**, plural Formen
• = form
in Form sein = to be in good form
• = shape
• (for baking) = tin

formen verb
• = to form
= to shape
• sich formen = to take shape

förmlich adjective
= formal

das **Formular**, plural Formulare
= form

der **Forscher**, plural Forscher
• = researcher
• = explorer

die **Forschung**, plural Forschungen
= research

der **Förster**, plural Förster
= forester

fort adverb
= away
und so fort = and so on

fort|bewegen verb
• = to move
• sich fortbewegen = to move

die **Fortbildung**
= further education

fortgeschritten adjective
= advanced

der/die **Fortgeschrittene**, plural
Fortgeschrittenen
= advanced student

die **Fortpflanzung**
= reproduction

der **Fortschritt**, plural Fortschritte
= progress

fort|setzen *verb*
- = to continue
- sich fortsetzen = to continue

die **Fortsetzung**, *plural* Fortsetzungen
- = continuation
- = instalment

das **Foto**, *plural* Fotos
= photo

der **Fotoapparat**, *plural* Fotoapparate
= camera

der **Fotograf**, *plural* Fotografen
= photographer

die **Fotografie**, *plural* Fotografien
- = photography
- = photograph

fotografieren *verb*
= to photograph
= to take photographs

die **Fotografin**, *plural* Fotografinnen
= photographer

die **Fracht**, *plural* Frachten
= freight
= cargo

der **Frack**, *plural* Fräcke
(*evening dress*) = tails

die **Frage**, *plural* Fragen
= question

der **Fragebogen**, *plural* Fragebogen
= questionnaire

fragen *verb*
- = to ask
- sich fragen = to wonder

das **Fragezeichen**, *plural* Fragezeichen
= question mark

(das) **Frankreich**
= France

der **Franzose**, *plural* Franzosen
= Frenchman

die **Französin**, *plural* Französinnen
= Frenchwoman

französisch *adjective*
= French

die **Frau**, *plural* Frauen
- = woman
- = wife
- (*with a name*) = Mrs, = Ms

das **Frauenhaus**, *plural* Frauenhäuser
= women's refuge

das **Fräulein**, *plural* Fräulein
- = single woman
- = young lady
- (*with a name*) = Miss

frech *adjective*
= cheeky

die **Frechheit**, *plural* Frechheiten
- = cheek
- = cheeky remark

frei *adjective*
- = free
  sich frei nehmen = to take time off
- = freelance
- = vacant
  ist dieser Platz frei? = is this seat taken?
  'Zimmer frei' = 'vacancies'

das **Freibad**, *plural* Freibäder
= open-air swimming pool

das **Freie**
im Freien = in the open air

frei|haben *irregular verb*
= to have time off
eine Stunde freihaben (*at school*) = to
have a free period

die **Freiheit**, *plural* Freiheiten
= freedom, = liberty

frei|machen *verb*
- = to take time off
- = to frank
- sich freimachen = to take time off

frei|sprechen *irregular verb*
= to acquit

der **Freispruch**, *plural* Freisprüche
= acquittal

der **Freistoß**, *plural* Freistöße
= free kick

der **Freitag**
= Friday

freitags *adverb*
= on Fridays

freiwillig *adjective*
= voluntary

die **Freizeit**
= spare time
= leisure

fremd *adjective*
- = foreign
- = strange
  fremde Leute = strangers
  ich bin hier fremd = I'm a stranger here

der/die **Fremde**, *plural* Fremden
- = foreigner
- = stranger

der **Fremdenführer**, *plural* Fremdenführer
= tourist guide

der **Fremdenverkehr**
= tourism

das **Fremdenverkehrsbüro**, *plural*
Fremdenverkehrsbüros
= tourist office

die **Fremdsprache**, plural
Fremdsprachen
= foreign language

fressen irregular verb
• (of an animal) = to eat
• fressen✶ (of a person) = to guzzle

die **Freude**, plural Freuden
= joy, = pleasure

freuen verb
• = to please
es freut mich = I'm pleased
• sich über etwas freuen = to be pleased
about something
sich auf etwas freuen = to look forward
to something

der **Freund**, plural Freunde
= friend
= boyfriend

die **Freundin**, plural Freundinnen
= friend
= girlfriend

freundlich adjective
= friendly
= kind

die **Freundschaft**, plural Freundschaften
= friendship
mit jemandem Freundschaft schließen =
to make friends with someone

der **Frieden**
= peace

der **Friedhof**, plural Friedhöfe
= cemetery

frieren irregular verb
• = to be cold
• (! sein) = to freeze

frisch
1 adjective = fresh
sich frisch machen = to freshen up
2 adverb = freshly
'frisch gestrichen' = 'wet paint'

der **Friseur**, plural Friseure
= hairdresser

die **Friseuse**, plural Friseusen
= hairdresser

frisieren verb
• jemanden frisieren = to do someone's hair
• sich frisieren = to do one's hair

die **Frisur**, plural Frisuren
= hairstyle

froh adjective
• = happy
• über etwas froh sein = to be pleased
about something

fröhlich adjective
= cheerful

fromm adjective
= devout

fror ▶frieren

der **Frosch**, plural Frösche
= frog

das **Frottee**, plural Frottees
= towelling

die **Frucht**, plural Früchte
= fruit

fruchtbar adjective
= fertile

früh
1 adjective = early
2 adverb = early
heute früh = this morning

die **Frühe**
in aller Frühe = at the crack of dawn

früher
1 adjective
• = earlier
• = former
2 adverb = formerly
ich wohnte früher in München = I used to
live in Munich
früher oder später = sooner or later

frühestens adverb
= at the earliest

der **Frühling**, plural Frühlinge
= spring

das **Frühstück**, plural Frühstücke
= breakfast

frühstücken verb
= to have breakfast

der **Fuchs**, plural Füchse
= fox

fühlen verb
• = to feel
• sich krank fühlen = to feel ill

fuhr ▶fahren

führen verb
• = to lead
• = to show round
• (be in charge of) = to run
• ein Tagebuch führen = to keep a diary

der **Führer**, plural Führer
• = leader
• = guide

der **Führerschein**, plural Führerscheine
= driving licence, = driver's license
den Führerschein machen = to take one's
driving test

die **Führung**, plural Führungen
• = leadership
• = guided tour
• in Führung = in the lead

✶ in informal situations   ✦ considered offensive

füllen *verb*
- = to fill
  (*in cooking*) = to stuff
- sich füllen = to fill (up)

der **Füller**, *plural* Füller
= fountain pen

das **Fundament**, *plural* Fundamente
= foundations

das **Fundbüro**, *plural* Fundbüros
= lost property office

fünf *adjective*
= five

das **Fünftel**, *plural* Fünftel
= fifth

fünfter/fünfte/fünftes *adjective*
= fifth

fünfzehn *adjective*
= fifteen

fünfzig *adjective*
= fifty

der **Funk**
= radio

der **Funke**, *plural* Funken
= spark

funkeln *verb*
= to sparkle
(*of a star*) = to twinkle

die **Funkstreife**, *plural* Funkstreifen
= radio patrol

funktionieren *verb*
= to work

für *preposition* (+ *accusative*)
= for
für sich = by oneself/itself

die **Furcht**
= fear

furchtbar *adjective*
= terrible

fürchten *verb*
- = to fear
- sich vor jemandem fürchten = to be afraid of someone

fürchterlich *adjective*
= dreadful

die **Fürsorge**
- = care
- = welfare
- = social security

furzen *verb*
= to fart

der **Fuß**, *plural* Füße
= foot

der **Fußball**, *plural* Fußbälle
= football

der **Fußboden**, *plural* Fußböden
= floor

der **Fußgänger**, *plural* Fußgänger
= pedestrian

die **Fußgängerzone**, *plural* Fußgängerzonen
= pedestrian precinct

der **Fußweg**, *plural* Fußwege
= footpath

das **Futter**
- = feed
- = lining

füttern *verb*
- = to feed
- = to line

Gg

gab ▶geben

die **Gabel**, *plural* Gabeln
= fork

gähnen *verb*
= to yawn

die **Galerie**, *plural* Galerien
= gallery

der **Galgen**, *plural* Galgen
= gallows

galoppieren *verb* (**!** *sein*)
= to gallop

der **Gammler**, *plural* Gammler
= drop-out

die **Gammlerin**, *plural* Gammlerinnen
= drop-out

der **Gang**, *plural* Gänge
- = walk
  in Gang setzen = to get going
  im Gange = in progress
- = errand
- = corridor
- (*part of a meal*) = course
- (*of a car*) = gear

gängig *adjective*
- = common
- = popular

die **Gangschaltung**, *plural* Gangschaltungen
= gear change

die **Gans**, *plural* Gänse
= goose

das **Gänseblümchen**, plural
Gänseblümchen
= daisy

ganz
1 adjective
• = whole
eine ganze Menge = quite a lot
ganz Deutschland = the whole of
Germany
im Großen und Ganzen = on the whole
• = all
die ganzen Leute = all the people
• = intact
etwas wieder ganz machen = to mend
something
2 adverb = quite
ganz und gar = completely

ganztägig adjective
= all-day, = full-time

ganztags adverb
= all day, = full time

gar
1 adjective = done, = cooked
2 adverb
gar [nichts | keiner | nicht …] = [nothing | no
one | not …] at all

die **Garantie**, plural Garantien
= guarantee

garantieren verb
= to guarantee

garantiert adverb
er kommt garantiert zu spät✶ = he's bound
or sure to be late

die **Garderobe**, plural Garderoben
= cloakroom, = checkroom

die **Gardine**, plural Gardinen
= curtain, = drape

das **Garn**, plural Garne
= thread

die **Garnele**, plural Garnelen
= shrimp
= prawn

der **Garten**, plural Gärten
= garden

der **Gärtner**, plural Gärtner
= gardener

die **Gärtnerei**, plural Gärtnereien
= nursery

die **Gärtnerin**, plural Gärtnerinnen
= gardener

das **Gas**, plural Gase
• = gas
• = petrol, = gas
Gas geben = to accelerate

die **Gasse**, plural Gassen
= lane

der **Gast**, plural Gäste
= guest
= visitor

der **Gastarbeiter**, plural Gastarbeiter
= foreign worker, = guest worker

das **Gästezimmer**, plural Gästezimmer
• (in a hotel) = room
• (in a house) = spare room

gastfreundlich adjective
= hospitable

die **Gastfreundschaft**
= hospitality

der **Gastgeber**, plural Gastgeber
= host

die **Gastgeberin**, plural Gastgeberinnen
= hostess

das **Gasthaus**, plural Gasthäuser
= inn

der **Gasthof**, plural Gasthöfe
= inn

die **Gaststätte**, plural Gaststätten
= restaurant

der **Gastwirt**, plural Gastwirte
= landlord

die **Gastwirtin**, plural Gastwirtinnen
= landlady

der **Gaumen**, plural Gaumen
= palate

der **Gauner**, plural Gauner
= crook

das **Gebäck**
= pastries
= biscuits

das **Gebäude**, plural Gebäude
= building

geben irregular verb
• = to give
(on the phone) geben Sie mir bitte Herrn
Braun = please put me through to Mr
Braun
etwas in die Reinigung geben = to have
something cleaned
• (when playing cards) = to deal
• (at school) = to teach
• sich geben = to wear off, = to get better
sich natürlich geben = to act naturally
• es gibt = there is/there are
was gibt es im Kino? = what's on at the
cinema?

das **Gebet**, plural Gebete
= prayer

gebeten ▶ bitten

das **Gebiet**, *plural* Gebiete
- • = area
- • (*subject*) = field

gebildet *adjective*
= educated

das **Gebirge**, *plural* Gebirge
= mountain range
im Gebirge = in the mountains

gebirgig *adjective*
= mountainous

das **Gebiss** (**Gebiß**ⓄⓁⒹ), *plural* Gebisse
- • = teeth
- • = false teeth, = dentures
- • (*for a horse*) = bit

geboren *adjective*
= born
Frau Petra Schmidt geborene Meyer =
Mrs Petra Schmidt née Meyer

der **Gebrauch**, *plural* Gebräuche
- • = use
- • = custom

gebrauchen *verb*
= to use

die **Gebrauchsanweisung**, *plural*
Gebrauchsanweisungen
= instructions (for use)

gebraucht *adjective*
= used, = second-hand

gebrochen
1 *adjective* = broken
2 *adverb*
gebrochen Deutsch sprechen = to speak
broken German

die **Gebühr**, *plural* Gebühren
= charge, = fee

gebührenfrei *adjective*
= free (of charge)

gebührenpflichtig *adjective*
= subject to a charge
eine gebührenpflichtige Straße = a toll
road

die **Geburt**, *plural* Geburten
= birth

die **Geburtenregelung**
= birth control

das **Geburtsdatum**, *plural* Geburtsdaten
= date of birth

der **Geburtsort**
= place of birth

der **Geburtstag**, *plural* Geburtstage
= birthday

die **Geburtsurkunde**, *plural*
Geburtsurkunden
= birth certificate

das **Gedächtnis**, *plural* Gedächtnisse
= memory

der **Gedanke**, *plural* Gedanken
= thought
sich über jemanden Gedanken machen =
to worry about someone

gedankenlos
1 *adjective* = thoughtless
2 *adverb* = without thinking

das **Gedeck**, *plural* Gedecke
- • = place setting
- • = set meal

das **Gedicht**, *plural* Gedichte
= poem

die **Geduld**
= patience

geduldig *adjective*
= patient

gedurft ▶ dürfen

geehrt *adjective*
= honoured, = honored
Sehr geehrter Herr Roth = Dear Mr Roth

geeignet *adjective*
= suitable
= right

die **Gefahr**, *plural* Gefahren
= danger
= risk

gefährlich *adjective*
= dangerous

gefallen *irregular verb*
- • = to please
  es gefällt mir = I like it
- • sich etwas gefallen lassen = to put up
  with something

der **Gefallen**¹ *plural* Gefallen
= favour, = favor

das **Gefallen**²
= pleasure
dir zu Gefallen = to please you

der/die **Gefangene**, *plural* Gefangenen
= prisoner

das **Gefängnis**, *plural* Gefängnisse
= prison, = jail

das **Gefäß**, *plural* Gefäße
= container

gefasst (**gefaßt**ⓄⓁⒹ) *adjective*
- • = calm, = composed
- • auf etwas gefasst sein = to be prepared
  for something

gefiel ▶ gefallen

das **Geflügel**
= poultry

gefrieren *irregular verb* (**!** sein)
= to freeze

G

das **Gefrierfach**, *plural* Gefrierfächer
= freezer (compartment)

der **Gefrierschrank**, *plural*
Gefrierschränke
= freezer

das **Gefühl**, *plural* Gefühle
= feeling
= emotion

gefüllt *adjective*
• = filled, = full
• (*in cooking*) = stuffed

gefunden ▶ finden

gefüttert *adjective*
= lined

gegangen ▶ gehen

gegebenenfalls *adverb*
= if need be

gegen
1 *preposition* (+ *accusative*)
• = against
ein Mittel gegen Kopfschmerzen = a
remedy for headaches
• (*in direction*) = towards
• (*in time*) = around
gegen Abend = towards evening
• (*in sport*) = versus
• = compared with
2 *adverb*
gegen fünfzig Leute = about 50 people

die **Gegend**, *plural* Gegenden
• = area
• = district

gegeneinander *adverb*
= against each other, = against one
another

die **Gegenfahrbahn**, *plural*
Gegenfahrbahnen
= opposite carriageway

das **Gegenmittel**, *plural* Gegenmittel
• = remedy
• = antidote

die **Gegenrichtung**, *plural*
Gegenrichtungen
= opposite direction

der **Gegensatz**, *plural* Gegensätze
• = contrast
• = opposite

gegenseitig
1 *adjective* = mutual
2 *adverb*
sich gegenseitig helfen = to help each
other *or* one another

der **Gegenstand**, *plural* Gegenstände
• = object
• (*theme*) = subject

das **Gegenteil**
= opposite
im Gegenteil = on the contrary

gegenüber
1 *preposition* (+ *dative*)
• = opposite
• = compared with
• jemandem gegenüber freundlich sein = to
be kind to *or* friendly towards someone
2 *adverb* = opposite

der **Gegenverkehr**
= oncoming traffic

die **Gegenwart**
• = present
• = presence

gegessen ▶ essen

der **Gegner**, *plural* Gegner
= opponent

gehabt ▶ haben

das **Gehalt**, *plural* Gehälter
= salary

geheim *adjective*
= secret

das **Geheimnis**, *plural* Geheimnisse
= secret

geheimnisvoll *adjective*
= mysterious

gehen *irregular verb* (**!** *sein*)
• = to go
• = to walk
über die Straße gehen = to cross the road
• = to work
meine Uhr geht falsch = my watch is
wrong
• (*other uses*)
es geht = it's not too bad
das geht nicht = that's impossible
wie geht es dir? = how are you?
worum geht es hier? = what is all this
about?

das **Gehirn**, *plural* Gehirne
= brain

die **Gehirnerschütterung**, *plural*
Gehirnerschütterungen
= concussion

geholfen ▶ helfen

das **Gehör**
= hearing

gehorchen *verb*
= to obey

gehören *verb*
• = to belong
dazu gehört Mut = that takes courage
zu den Besten gehören = to be one of the
best
• sich gehören = to be fitting
es gehört sich nicht = it isn't done

gehorsam *adjective*
= obedient

die **Geige**, *plural* Geigen
= violin

die **Geisel**, *plural* Geiseln
= hostage

der **Geist**, *plural* Geister
* = mind
* = wit
* = ghost

die **Geisteskrankheit**, *plural* Geisteskrankheiten
= mental illness

Geisteswissenschaften (*plural*)
= arts, = humanities

geistig *adjective*
= mental

der **Geistliche**, *plural* Geistlichen
= clergyman

geizig *adjective*
= mean

gekonnt ▶ können

das **Gelächter**, *plural* Gelächter
= laughter

gelähmt *adjective*
= paralysed

das **Geländer**, *plural* Geländer
* = banisters
* = railings
* = parapet

gelassen *adjective*
= calm, = composed

gelaunt *adjective*
gut gelaunt sein = to be in a good mood

gelb *adjective*
= yellow

das **Geld**, *plural* Gelder
= money

der **Geldautomat**, *plural* Geldautomaten
= cash dispenser

die **Geldbörse**, *plural* Geldbörsen
= purse

der **Geldschein**, *plural* Geldscheine
= banknote, = bill

die **Geldstrafe**, *plural* Geldstrafen
= fine

die **Gelegenheit**, *plural* Gelegenheiten
* = opportunity
* = occasion

gelegentlich *adverb*
= occasionally

das **Gelenk**, *plural* Gelenke
= joint

der/die **Geliebte**, *plural* Geliebten
= lover

gelingen *irregular verb* (**!** *sein*)
= to succeed
es ist mir gelungen = I succeeded

gelten *irregular verb*
* = to be valid
das gilt nicht = that doesn't count
* (*of a rule*) = to apply
* als etwas gelten = to be regarded as something
[viel | wenig | mehr ...] **gelten** = to be worth [a lot | little | more ...]

das **Gemälde**, *plural* Gemälde
= painting

gemäß *preposition* (+ *dative*)
= in accordance with

gemein *adjective*
= mean

die **Gemeinde**, *plural* Gemeinden
* = community
* = parish
* (*in a church*) = congregation

gemeinsam
1 *adjective* = common
2 *adverb* = together

die **Gemeinschaft**, *plural* Gemeinschaften
= community

gemocht ▶ mögen

das **Gemüse**, *plural* Gemüse
= vegetables

der **Gemüsehändler**, *plural* Gemüsehändler
= greengrocer

gemusst (**gemußt**ⓞⓛⓓ) ▶ müssen

gemustert *adjective*
= patterned

gemütlich *adjective*
= cosy
es sich gemütlich machen = to make oneself comfortable

genau
1 *adjective*
* = exact, = precise
* = meticulous
2 *adverb* = exactly

genauso *adverb*
= just the same
genauso viel = just as much, = just as many

die **Genehmigung**, *plural* Genehmigungen
* = permission
* = permit
= licence, = license

G

die **Generation**, *plural* Generationen
= generation

generell *adjective*
= general

(das) **Genf**
= Geneva

der **Genfer See**
= Lake Geneva

genial *adjective*
= brilliant

das **Genick**, *plural* Genicke
= (back of the) neck

das **Genie**, *plural* Genies
= genius

genießen *irregular verb*
= to enjoy

genommen ▶ nehmen

genug *adverb*
= enough

genügend *adjective*
= enough

der **Genuss** (**Genuß**⊙ᴸᴰ), *plural* Genüsse
• = enjoyment
• = consumption

geöffnet *adjective*
= open

das **Gepäck**
= luggage, = baggage

die **Gepäckaufbewahrung**, *plural*
Gepäckaufbewahrungen
= left-luggage office, = check room

der **Gepäckschein**, *plural* Gepäckscheine
= luggage ticket, = baggage check

der **Gepäckträger**, *plural* Gepäckträger
• = porter
• (*on a car*) = roof rack
• (*on a bike*) = carrier

gerade
1 *adjective*
• = straight
• = upright
• eine gerade Zahl = an even number
2 *adverb*
• = just
gerade erst = only just
• = directly
gerade an dem Tag = on that very day
nicht gerade billig = not exactly cheap

geradeaus *adverb*
= straight ahead

das **Gerät**, *plural* Geräte
= appliance, = piece of equipment
(*TV, radio*) = set

(*for gardening*) = tool
(*for cooking*) = utensil

geraten *irregular verb* (**!** *sein*)
= to get
schlecht geraten = to turn out badly
nach jemandem geraten = to take after
someone

geräumig *adjective*
= spacious

das **Geräusch**, *plural* Geräusche
= noise

gerecht *adjective*
= just, = fair

die **Gerechtigkeit**
= justice

das **Gericht**, *plural* Gerichte
• = court
• = dish

gering *adjective*
• = small
= low
• = slight

das **Gerippe**, *plural* Gerippe
= skeleton

gerissen *adjective*
= crafty

gern(e) *adverb*
= gladly
etwas gern(e) tun = to like doing
something
jemanden gern(e) haben = to like
someone
das glaube ich gern(e) = I can well
believe that

der **Geruch**, *plural* Gerüche
= smell

das **Gerücht**, *plural* Gerüchte
= rumour, = rumor

das **Gerüst**, *plural* Gerüste
= scaffolding

gesamt *adjective*
= whole, = entire

die **Gesamtschule**, *plural*
Gesamtschulen
= comprehensive school

das **Geschäft**, *plural* Geschäfte
• = business
• = deal
• = shop, = store

der **Geschäftsführer**, *plural*
Geschäftsführer
= manager

Geschäftszeiten (*plural*)
= business hours

geschehen *irregular verb* (**!** *sein*)
= to happen

⊙ᴸᴰ = old spelling

gescheit *adjective*
= clever

das **Geschenk**, *plural* Geschenke
= present, = gift

die **Geschichte**, *plural* Geschichten
* = history
* = story

das **Geschick**
* = skill
* = fate

geschickt *adjective*
* = skilful
* = clever

geschieden *adjective*
= divorced

das **Geschirr**, *plural* Geschirre
* = crockery
  = dishes
* = harness

die **Geschirrspülmaschine**, *plural*
Geschirrspülmaschinen
= dishwasher

das **Geschirrtuch**, *plural* Geschirrtücher
= tea towel, = dish towel

das **Geschlecht**, *plural* Geschlechter
* = sex
* = gender

geschlossen ▶ schließen

der **Geschmack**, *plural* Geschmäcke
= taste

geschrieben ▶ schreiben

die **Geschwindigkeit**, *plural*
Geschwindigkeiten
= speed

die **Geschwindigkeitsbeschränkung**, *plural*
Geschwindigkeitsbeschränkungen
= speed limit

Geschwister (*plural*)
= brother(s) and sister(s), = siblings

geschwommen ▶ schwimmen

der/die **Geschworene**, *plural*
Geschworenen
= juror

gesellig *adjective*
= sociable

die **Gesellschaft**, *plural* Gesellschaften
* = society
* = party
* = company
  jemandem Gesellschaft leisten = to keep
  someone company

gesessen ▶ sitzen

das **Gesetz**, *plural* Gesetze
= law

gesetzlich *adjective*
= legal, = lawful

das **Gesicht**, *plural* Gesichter
= face

gesollt ▶ sollen

gespannt *adjective*
* = eager
  auf etwas gespannt sein = to look
  forward eagerly to something
  ich bin gespannt, ob … = I am keen to
  know whether …
* = tense

das **Gespenst**, *plural* Gespenster
= ghost

das **Gespräch**, *plural* Gespräche
= conversation
(*on the phone*) = call

gesprochen ▶ sprechen

die **Gestalt**, *plural* Gestalten
* = figure, = character
* = form

gestanden ▶ stehen

gestatten *verb*
= to permit, = to allow
gestatten Sie? = may I?
nicht gestattet = prohibited

gestern *adverb*
= yesterday

gestorben ▶ sterben

gestreift *adjective*
= striped

gesund *adjective*
= healthy
Obst ist gesund = fruit is good for you

die **Gesundheit**
= health
(*said after a sneeze*) Gesundheit! = bless
you!

gesungen ▶ singen

getan ▶ tun

das **Getränk**, *plural* Getränke
= drink

die **Getränkekarte**, *plural*
Getränkekarten
= wine list

das **Getreide**
= grain

das **Getriebe**, *plural* Getriebe
= gearbox

getroffen ▶ treffen

getrunken ▶ trinken

das **Getue**
= fuss

G

die **Gewalt**, plural Gewalten
- = power
- = force
- = violence

gewalttätig adjective
= violent

gewann ▶ gewinnen

das **Gewehr**, plural Gewehre
= rifle, = gun

die **Gewerkschaft**, plural Gewerkschaften
= trade union

gewesen ▶ sein

das **Gewicht**, plural Gewichte
= weight

der **Gewinn**, plural Gewinne
- = profit
- = prize, = winnings
- = win

gewinnen irregular verb
= to win
Zeit gewinnen = to gain time

gewiss (**gewiß**ⓄⓁⒹ)
1 adjective = certain
2 adverb = certainly

das **Gewissen**, plural Gewissen
= conscience

gewissenhaft adjective
= conscientious

das **Gewitter**, plural Gewitter
= thunderstorm

gewöhnen verb
- jemanden an etwas gewöhnen = to get someone used to something
- sich an etwas gewöhnen = to get used to something

die **Gewohnheit**, plural Gewohnheiten
= habit

gewöhnlich
1 adjective
- = ordinary
- = usual
- = common
2 adverb = usually
wie gewöhnlich = as usual

gewohnt adjective
= usual
etwas gewohnt sein = to be used to something

gewollt ▶ wollen

gewonnen ▶ gewinnen

geworden ▶ werden

geworfen ▶ werfen

das **Gewürz**, plural Gewürze
= spice

Gezeiten (plural)
= tides

gezwungen ▶ zwingen

gibt ▶ geben

gierig adjective
= greedy

gießen irregular verb
- = to pour
- = to water

das **Gift**, plural Gifte
= poison

giftig adjective
= poisonous
= toxic

ging ▶ gehen

der **Gipfel**, plural Gipfel
= peak, = summit

der **Gips**, plural Gipse
= plaster

das **Girokonto**, plural Girokonten
= current account

die **Gitarre**, plural Gitarren
= guitar

das **Gitter**, plural Gitter
= bars

der **Glanz**
- = shine
  (on paper, colour) = gloss
- = splendour, = splendor

glänzen verb
= to shine

glänzend adjective
- = shining, = shiny
- = brilliant

das **Glas**, plural Gläser
- = glass
- = jar

die **Glasscheibe**, plural Glasscheiben
= pane (of glass)

glatt
1 adjective
- = smooth
  = slippery
- eine glatte Absage = a flat refusal
2 adverb
- = smoothly

ⓄⓁⒹ = old spelling

- **das ist glatt gelogen** = that's a downright lie
- **das habe ich glatt vergessen** = it completely slipped my mind

das **Glatteis**
= (black) ice

die **Glatze**, *plural* Glatzen
= bald patch
eine Glatze haben = to be bald

der **Glaube**
= belief, = faith

glauben *verb*
= to believe, = to think
das ist nicht zu glauben = that's incredible

gleich
1 *adjective*
= same
das ist mir gleich = it's all the same to me
ganz gleich, wer = no matter who
2 *adverb*
- = the same
- = equally
- = immediately

gleichberechtigt *adjective*
= equal

die **Gleichberechtigung**
= equality
= equal rights

gleichen *irregular verb*
- = to be like
- **sich gleichen** = to be alike

gleichfalls *adverb*
= also, = likewise
danke gleichfalls! = (thanks and) the same to you!

das **Gleichgewicht**
= balance

gleichgültig *adjective*
= indifferent

gleichmäßig *adjective*
= regular, = even

die **Gleichung**, *plural* Gleichungen
= equation

gleichzeitig
1 *adjective* = simultaneous
2 *adverb* = at the same time

das **Gleis**, *plural* Gleise
- = track
- = platform

das **Glied**, *plural* Glieder
- = limb
- = link

die **Glocke**, *plural* Glocken
= bell

das **Glück**

- = luck
  zum Glück = luckily
- = happiness

glücklich *adjective*
- = lucky
- = happy

glücklicherweise *adverb*
= luckily, = fortunately

der **Glückwunsch**, *plural* Glückwünsche
= congratulations
herzlichen Glückwunsch zum Geburtstag! = happy birthday!

die **Glühbirne**, *plural* Glühbirnen
= light bulb

glühen *verb*
= to glow

die **Glut**
- = embers
- = passion

die **Gnade**
- = mercy
- (*in religion*) = grace

das **Gold**
= gold

der **Golf¹** *plural* Golfe
= gulf

das **Golf²**
= golf

goss (**goß** ⓞⓛⓓ) ▶gießen

der **Gott**, *plural* Götter
= god

der **Gottesdienst**, *plural* Gottesdienste
= service

die **Göttin**, *plural* Göttinnen
= goddess

das **Grab**, *plural* Gräber
= grave

graben *irregular verb*
= to dig

der **Grad**, *plural* Grade
= degree

der **Graf**, *plural* Grafen
= count
= earl

die **Gräfin**, *plural* Gräfinnen
= countess

das **Gramm**, *plural* Gramme
= gram

die **Grammatik**, *plural* Grammatiken
= grammar

grantig *adjective*
= grumpy

G

das **Gras**, *plural* Gräser
= grass

grässlich (**gräßlich**⟨OLD⟩) *adjective*
= horrible

die **Gräte**, *plural* Gräten
= (fish)bone

die **Gratifikation**, *plural* Gratifikationen
= bonus

gratis *adverb*
= free (of charge)

gratulieren *verb*
= to congratulate
ich gratuliere! = congratulations!

grau *adjective*
= grey, = gray

grausam *adjective*
= cruel

greifen *irregular verb*
• = to take hold of, = to grasp
• = to catch
• = to reach

grell *adjective*
• = glaring
• = garish
• = shrill

die **Grenze**, *plural* Grenzen
• = border
= frontier
• = limit

grenzen *verb*
an etwas grenzen = to border on
something

der **Grieche**, *plural* Griechen
= Greek

(das) **Griechenland**
= Greece

die **Griechin**, *plural* Griechinnen
= Greek

griechisch *adjective*
= Greek

griff ▶ greifen

der **Griff**, *plural* Griffe
• = grasp, = hold
• = handle

griffbereit *adjective*
= handy

der **Grill**, *plural* Grills
= grill
= barbecue

die **Grille**, *plural* Grillen
• = cricket
• (*idea*) = whim

grillen *verb*
• = to grill
• = to barbecue, = to have a barbecue

das **Grillfest**, *plural* Grillfeste
= barbecue

grinsen *verb*
= to grin

die **Grippe**, *plural* Grippen
= flu

grob *adjective*
• = coarse
• = rough
• = rude
• ein grober Fehler = a bad mistake

groß *adjective*
• = big, = large
im Großen und Ganzen = on the whole
groß werden = to grow up
• = great
• = tall
• ein großer Buchstabe = a capital letter

großartig *adjective*
= great, = magnificent

(das) **Großbritannien**
= Great Britain

die **Größe**, *plural* Größen
• = size
• = height
• = greatness

Großeltern (*plural*)
= grandparents

der **Großmarkt**, *plural* Großmärkte
= hypermarket

die **Großmutter**, *plural* Großmütter
= grandmother

groß|schreiben *irregular verb*
ein Wort großschreiben = to write a word
with a capital

die **Großstadt**, *plural* Großstädte
= city

der **Großvater**, *plural* Großväter
= grandfather

großzügig *adjective*
= generous

grün *adjective*
= green

der **Grund**, *plural* Gründe
• = ground
• = bottom
im Grunde genommen = basically
• = reason

gründen *verb*
• = to found, = to set up
• = to base
• sich auf etwas gründen = to be based on
something

✖ in informal situations ⟨OLD⟩ = old spelling

die **Grundlage**, *plural* Grundlagen
= basis, = foundation

gründlich *adjective*
= thorough

grundsätzlich *adjective*
= fundamental, = basic

die **Grundschule**, *plural* Grundschulen
= primary school, = grade school

das **Grundstück**, *plural* Grundstücke
= plot (of land)

die **Gruppe**, *plural* Gruppen
= group

der **Gruß**, *plural* Grüße
* = greeting
einen schönen Gruß an Emma = give my
regards to Emma
mit herzlichen Grüßen = with best wishes
* = salute

grüßen *verb*
* = to greet
grüße deine Eltern von mir = give your
parents my regards
* = to say hello
grüß Gott! = hello
* = to salute

gucken *verb*
= to look

gültig *adjective*
= valid

der **Gummi**, *plural* Gummis
= rubber

das **Gummiband**, *plural* Gummibänder
= rubber band

der **Gummistiefel**, *plural* Gummistiefel
= rubber boot, = wellington

günstig *adjective*
= favourable, = favorable
= convenient

die **Gurke**, *plural* Gurken
* = cucumber
* = gherkin

der **Gurt**, *plural* Gurte
* = strap
* = belt

der **Gürtel**, *plural* Gürtel
= belt

die **Gürteltasche**, *plural* Gürteltaschen
= bum bag, = fanny pack

gut
1 *adjective* = good
2 *adverb* = well
* **es gut haben** = to be well off, = to be
lucky
* **der Laden geht gut** = the shop is doing
well
es geht mir gut = I am well

die **Güte**
= goodness
= quality

der **Güterzug**, *plural* Güterzüge
= goods train, = freight train

gutgehen⊙ᴸᴰ ▸ gut

der **Gutschein**, *plural* Gutscheine
= voucher
= coupon

das **Gymnasium**, *plural* Gymnasien
= grammar school

die **Gymnastik**
= gymnastics
= exercises

Hh

das **Haar**, *plural* Haare
= hair

der **Haarschnitt**, *plural* Haarschnitte
= haircut

haben *irregular verb*
* = to have
[Angst | Hunger | Durst …] haben = to be
[frightened | hungry | thirsty …]
heute haben wir Montag = it's Monday
today
was hat er? = what's the matter with
him?
* (*forming the perfect tense*)
er hat es gewusst = he knew it
* **sich haben✱** = to make a fuss

hacken *verb*
* = to chop
* = to peck
* (*in computing*) = to hack

das **Hackfleisch**
= minced meat, = ground meat

der **Hafen**, *plural* Häfen
= harbour, = port

Haferflocken (*plural*)
= (porridge) oats

haften *verb*
* = to stick, = to cling
* **für etwas haften** = to be responsible for
something

die **Haftung**
= liability

der **Hagel**
= hail

hageln *verb*
= to hail

der **Hahn**, *plural* Hähne
• = cock
• = tap, = faucet

der **Hai**, *plural* Haie
= shark

häkeln *verb*
= to crochet

der **Haken**, *plural* Haken
• = hook
• (*mark*) = tick
• der Haken dran✶ = the catch, = the snag

halb
1 *adjective* = half
halb eins = half past twelve
2 *adverb* = half

halbfett *adjective*
= low-fat, = semi-skimmed

halbieren *verb*
= to halve

die **Halbinsel**, *plural* Halbinseln
= peninsula

der **Halbkreis**, *plural* Halbkreise
= semicircle

halbtags *adverb*
= part-time

halbwegs *adverb*
• = half-way
• = more or less

die **Halbzeit**, *plural* Halbzeiten
• = half
• = half-time

half ▶helfen

die **Hälfte**, *plural* Hälften
= half

die **Halle**, *plural* Hallen
• = hall
• = foyer

das **Hallenbad**, *plural* Hallenbäder
= indoor swimming pool

hallo *interjection*
• = hey!
• = hello!

der **Hals**, *plural* Hälse
= neck
= throat

das **Halsband**, *plural* Halsbänder
= collar

Halsschmerzen (*plural*)
= sore throat

---

halt *interjection*
= stop!

der **Halt**
• = hold
• = stop
Halt machen = to stop

haltbar *adjective*
• = hard-wearing
• mindestens haltbar bis . . . = best before . . .

halten *irregular verb*
• = to hold
• = to keep
zu jemandem halten = to be loyal to someone
viel von jemandem halten = to think a lot of someone
• = to stop
• (*in soccer*) = to save
• (*subscribe to*) = to take
• eine Rede halten = to give a talk
• sich halten = to keep, = to last
sich gut halten = to do well

die **Haltestelle**, *plural* Haltestellen
= stop

das **Halteverbot**
'Halteverbot' = 'no stopping'

haltmachenᴼᴸᴰ ▶Halt

die **Haltung**, *plural* Haltungen
• = posture
• = attitude
• = composure

das **Hammelfleisch**
= mutton

der **Hammer**, *plural* Hämmer
= hammer

hämmern *verb*
= to hammer

die **Hand**, *plural* Hände
= hand

die **Handarbeit**, *plural* Handarbeiten
• = handicraft
• = hand-made article

der **Handel**
= trade

handeln *verb*
• = to trade, = to deal
= to haggle
• = to act
• es handelt sich um . . . = it's about . . .
von etwas handeln = to be about something

die **Handelsschule**, *plural* Handelsschulen
= business school, = vocational college

die **Handfläche**, *plural* Handflächen
= palm

das **Handgelenk**, *plural* Handgelenke
= wrist

das **Handgepäck**
= hand luggage

handhaben *verb*
= to handle

der **Händler**, *plural* Händler
= trader, = dealer

die **Handlung**, *plural* Handlungen
• = act
• = action
• = plot

die **Handschrift**, *plural* Handschriften
= handwriting

der **Handschuh**, *plural* Handschuhe
= glove

die **Handtasche**, *plural* Handtaschen
= handbag, = pocketbook

das **Handtuch**, *plural* Handtücher
= towel

der **Handwerker**, *plural* Handwerker
= craftsman

das **Handwerkszeug**
= tools

das **Handy**, *plural* Handys
= mobile (phone)

die **Hängematte**, *plural* Hängematten
= hammock

hängen *irregular verb*
= to hang

der **Happen**, *plural* Happen
= mouthful

die **Harfe**, *plural* Harfen
= harp

die **Harke**, *plural* Harken
= rake

harmlos *adjective*
• = harmless
• = innocent

hart *adjective*
• = hard
• = harsh

die **Härte**, *plural* Härten
• = hardness
• = harshness

der **Hase**, *plural* Hasen
= hare

die **Haselnuss** (**Haselnuß**⊙ᴸᴰ), *plural*
Haselnüsse
= hazelnut

der **Hass** (**Haß**⊙ᴸᴰ)
= hatred

hassen *verb*
= to hate

hässlich (**häßlich**⊙ᴸᴰ) *adjective*
• = ugly
• = nasty

hast ▶ haben

hastig *adjective*
= hasty, = hurried

**hat, hatte, hatten, hattest,
hattet** ▶ haben

die **Haube**, *plural* Hauben
• = bonnet
= cap
• (*of a car*) = bonnet, = hood

hauen *verb*
• = to beat
• = to thump, = to bang
• sich hauen = to fight, = to have a punch-
up

der **Haufen**, *plural* Haufen
• = heap, = pile
• (*of people*) = crowd

häufig *adjective*
= frequent

der **Hauptbahnhof**, *plural* Hauptbahnhöfe
= main station

die **Hauptrolle**, *plural* Hauptrollen
(*in a film*) = lead

die **Hauptsache**, *plural* Hauptsachen
= main thing

hauptsächlich
1 *adjective* = main
2 *adverb* = mainly

die **Hauptstadt**, *plural* Hauptstädte
= capital

die **Hauptstraße**, *plural* Hauptstraßen
= main road

das **Haus**, *plural* Häuser
= house
nach Hause = home
zu Hause = at home

die **Hausarbeit**, *plural* Hausarbeiten
• = housework
• = homework

Hausaufgaben (*plural*)
= homework

der **Haushalt**, *plural* Haushalte
• = household
den Haushalt machen = to do the
housework
• = budget

das **Haushaltswarengeschäft**, *plural* Haushaltswarengeschäfte
= hardware shop *or* store

der **Hausmeister**, *plural* Hausmeister
= caretaker, = porter

der **Hausschlüssel**, *plural* Hausschlüssel
= front-door key

der **Hausschuh**, *plural* Hausschuhe
= slipper

das **Haustier**, *plural* Haustiere
= pet

die **Haustür**, *plural* Haustüren
= front door

die **Haut**, *plural* Häute
= skin
aus der Haut fahren✶ = to go up the wall

die **Hebamme**, *plural* Hebammen
= midwife

der **Hebel**, *plural* Hebel
= lever

heben *irregular verb*
• = to lift, = to raise
• **sich heben** = to rise

die **Hecke**, *plural* Hecken
= hedge

das **Heer**, *plural* Heere
= army

die **Hefe**, *plural* Hefen
= yeast

das **Heft**, *plural* Hefte
• = exercise book
• (*magazine*) = issue

heften *verb*
• = to pin, = to clip
• = to staple
• = to stick
• (*in sewing*) = to tack

heftig *adjective*
• = violent
• = heavy

die **Heftklammer**, *plural* Heftklammern
= staple

die **Heftzwecke**, *plural* Heftzwecken
= drawing pin, = thumbtack

heil *adjective*
• = intact
• = unhurt

heilen *verb*
• = to cure
• = to heal

heilig *adjective*
= holy
= sacred

der **Heiligabend**
= Christmas Eve

der/die **Heilige**, *plural* Heiligen
= saint

das **Heim**, *plural* Heime
= home

die **Heimat**, *plural* Heimaten
• = home
• = native land

die **Heimfahrt**, *plural* Heimfahrten
= journey home
= drive home

heimlich *adjective*
= secret

der **Heimweg**, *plural* Heimwege
= way home

das **Heimweh**
= homesickness
Heimweh haben = to be homesick

die **Heirat**, *plural* Heiraten
= marriage

heiraten *verb*
= to marry
= to get married

heiser *adjective*
= hoarse

heiß *adjective*
= hot

heißen *irregular verb*
• = to be called
ich heiße Emma = my name is Emma
• = to mean
das heißt = that is

heiter *adjective*
• = bright
• = cheerful

heizen *verb*
• = to heat
• = to have the heating on

die **Heizung**, *plural* Heizungen
• = heating
• = radiator

der **Held**, *plural* Helden
= hero

helfen *irregular verb*
• = to help
es hilft nichts = it's no good
• **sich zu helfen wissen** = to know what to do

der **Helfer**, *plural* Helfer
= helper, = assistant

die **Helferin**, *plural* Helferinnen
= helper, = assistant

hell *adjective*
• = light

✶ in informal situations

- = bright
- eine helle Stimme = a clear voice
- heller Wahnsinn✱ = sheer madness

hellwach *adjective*
= wide awake

der **Helm**, *plural* Helme
= helmet

das **Hemd**, *plural* Hemden
- = shirt
- = vest, = undershirt

der **Hengst**, *plural* Hengste
= stallion

der **Henkel**, *plural* Henkel
= handle

die **Henne**, *plural* Hennen
= hen

her *adverb*
- = here
  komm her = come here
  her mit dem Geld✱ = give me the money
  von der Farbe her = as far as the colour is concerned
- = ago
  von ihrer Kindheit her = since childhood

herab *adverb*
= down (here)

herab|setzen *verb*
- = to reduce, = to cut
- = to belittle

heran
= near
bis an die Wand heran = up to the wall

heran|kommen *irregular verb* (! *sein*)
= to come near, = to approach

herauf *adverb*
= up (here)

herauf|kommen *irregular verb* (! *sein*)
= to come up

heraus *adverb*
= out

heraus|finden *irregular verb*
- = to find out
- = to find one's way out

heraus|geben *irregular verb*
- = to hand over, = to give
- = to bring out

heraus|kommen *irregular verb* (! *sein*)
= to come out

heraus|stellen *verb*
- = to put out
- sich herausstellen = to turn out

die **Herberge**, *plural* Herbergen
= hostel

her|bringen *irregular verb*
= to bring (here)

der **Herbst**, *plural* Herbste
= autumn, = fall

der **Herd**, *plural* Herde
= cooker

die **Herde**, *plural* Herden
= herd
= flock

herein *adverb*
= in (here)
herein! = come in!

herein|fallen *irregular verb* (! *sein*)
= to be taken in

herein|kommen *irregular verb* (! *sein*)
= to come in

herein|lassen *irregular verb*
= to let in

die **Herfahrt**
= journey here
= drive here

her|geben *irregular verb*
- = to hand over
- = to give away

her|kommen *irregular verb* (! *sein*)
= to come here

die **Herkunft**, *plural* Herkünfte
= origin
(*of a person*) = background

der **Herr**, *plural* Herren
- = gentleman
- = master
- (*with a name*) = Mr
  Sehr geehrte Herren = Dear Sirs

her|richten *verb*
= to get ready, = to prepare

herrlich *adjective*
= marvellous

herrschen *verb*
= to rule
es herrschte Stille = there was silence

her|stellen *verb*
= to produce, = to manufacture
in Deutschland hergestellt = made in Germany

die **Herstellung**, *plural* Herstellungen
= production, = manufacture

herüber *adverb*
= over (here)

herum|drehen *verb*
- = to turn (over)
- sich herumdrehen = to turn round

herum|gehen *irregular verb* (! *sein*)
- = to go round
- (*of time*) = to pass

herunter adverb
= down (here)

herunter|fallen irregular verb (**!** sein)
= to fall down, = to fall off

herunter|kommen irregular verb
(**!** sein)
= to come down

herunter|lassen irregular verb
= to let down, = to lower

hervor adverb
= out

hervorragend
1 adjective = outstanding
2 adverb = outstandingly well

das **Herz**, plural Herzen
* = heart
* (playing cards) = hearts

der **Herzanfall**, plural Herzanfälle
= heart attack

herzlich adjective
* = warm
* = kind
* = sincere
herzlichen Dank = many thanks

herzlos adjective
= heartless

der **Herzog**, plural Herzöge
= duke

die **Herzogin**, plural Herzoginnen
= duchess

der **Herzschlag**, plural Herzschläge
* = heartbeat
* = heart failure

hetzen verb
* = to rush
* sich hetzen = to rush

das **Heu**
= hay

heulen verb
= to howl

die **Heuschrecke**, plural Heuschrecken
= grasshopper

heute adverb
= today

heutig adjective
= today's
in der heutigen Zeit = nowadays

heutzutage adverb
= nowadays

die **Hexe**, plural Hexen
= witch

---

hielt ▶ halten

hier adverb
= here

hierher adverb
= here

hierhin adverb
= here

hieß ▶ heißen

die **Hilfe**, plural Hilfen
= help, = aid

hilflos adjective
= helpless

hilfsbereit adjective
= helpful

hilft ▶ helfen

die **Himbeere**, plural Himbeeren
= raspberry

der **Himmel**, plural Himmel
* = sky
* = heaven

hin adverb
* = there
einmal Köln hin und zurück = a return to
Cologne
hin und her = back and forth
* hin und wieder = now and again

hinauf adverb
= up (there)

hinaus adverb
= out (there)
zur Tür hinaus = out of the door

hinaus|gehen irregular verb (**!** sein)
* = to go out
* das Zimmer geht nach Westen hinaus =
the room faces west

hindern verb
* = to stop, = to prevent
* = to hinder

das **Hindernis**, plural Hindernisse
= obstacle

hindurch adverb
= through it/them
das ganze Jahr hindurch = throughout
the year

hinein adverb
= in (there)
in etwas hinein = into something

hinein|gehen irregular verb (**!** sein)
= to go in
in etwas hineingehen = to go into
something

hin|fahren irregular verb (**!** sein)
= to go there, = to drive there

die **Hinfahrt**
    = journey there
    = drive there

hin|fallen *irregular verb* (**!** *sein*)
    = to fall over

hing ▶hängen

hin|gehen *irregular verb* (**!** *sein*)
*   = to go (there)
*   (*of time*) = to go by

hinken *verb*
    = to limp

hin|kommen *irregular verb* (**!** *sein*)
*   = to get there
*   (*belong somewhere*) = to go
*   mit etwas hinkommen✗ = to manage
    (with something)

hin|legen *verb*
*   = to put down
*   sich hinlegen = to lie down

die **Hinreise**, *plural* Hinreisen
    = journey there

hin|setzen *verb*
*   = to put down
*   sich hinsetzen = to sit down

hinten *adverb*
    = at the back
    von hinten = from behind

hinter *preposition* (+ *dative or*
    accusative)
    = behind
    hinter jemandem herlaufen = to run after
        someone
    etwas hinter sich bringen = to get
        something over with

hintere ▶hinterer

hintereinander *adverb*
*   = one behind the other
*   = one after another
    dreimal hintereinander = three times in a
        row

hinterer/hintere/hinteres
    adjective
    = back, = rear

der **Hintergrund**, *plural* Hintergründe
    = background

hinterlistig *adjective*
    = deceitful

der **Hintern✗**, *plural* Hintern
    = bottom

hinüber *adverb*
    = over (there), = across (there)

hinunter *adverb*
    = down (there)

der **Hinweg**, *plural* Hinwege
    = way there

der **Hinweis**, *plural* Hinweise
*   = hint
*   unter Hinweis auf = with reference to

hin|weisen *irregular verb*
    = to point
    jemanden auf etwas hinweisen = to point
        something out to someone

hinzu *adverb*
    = in addition

hinzu|kommen *irregular verb* (**!** *sein*)
*   = to come along, = to arrive
*   = to be added

das **Hirn**, *plural* Hirne
    = brain

der **Hirsch**, *plural* Hirsche
*   = deer
*   (*male*) = stag
*   (*as food*) = venison

der **Hirte**, *plural* Hirten
    = shepherd

die **Hitze**
    = heat

hoch
    1 *adjective*
*   = high
*   (*of a tree*) = tall
*   (*of snow*) = deep
*   (*of age, weight*) = great
*   (*of damage*) = severe
    2 *adverb*
*   = high
*   = highly
*   die Treppe hoch = up the stairs

das **Hoch**, *plural* Hochs
*   = cheer
*   (*weather system*) = high

hochachtungsvoll *adverb*
    (*ending a letter*) = yours faithfully

das **Hochhaus**, *plural* Hochhäuser
    = high-rise building
    = tower block

hoch|heben *irregular verb*
    = to lift up, = to raise

die **Hochschule**, *plural* Hochschulen
    = college
    = university

höchst *adverb*
    = extremely, = most

höchster/höchste/höchstes
    adjective
    = highest
    es ist höchste Zeit = it is high time

die **Hochzeit**, *plural* Hochzeiten
    = wedding

der **Hochzeitstag**, *plural* Hochzeitstage
*   = wedding day
*   = wedding anniversary

H

hocken verb
= to squat

der **Hocker**, plural Hocker
= stool

der **Hof**, plural Höfe
* = courtyard
* (at school) = playground
* = court
* = farm

hoffen verb
= to hope

hoffentlich adverb
= hopefully
= I hope so
hoffentlich nicht = I hope not

die **Hoffnung**, plural Hoffnungen
= hope

hoffnungslos adjective
= hopeless

höflich adjective
= polite

die **Höflichkeit**, plural Höflichkeiten
= politeness, = courtesy

die **Höhe**, plural Höhen
= height
= altitude
das ist die Höhe!✖ = that's the limit!

hoher/hohe/hohes ▶ hoch

hohl adjective
= hollow

die **Höhle**, plural Höhlen
* = cave
* = den

holen verb
* = to fetch, = to get
* sich etwas holen = to get or catch something

der **Holländer**, plural Holländer
= Dutchman

die **Holländerin**, plural Holländerinnen
= Dutchwoman

holländisch adjective
= Dutch

die **Hölle**, die, plural Höllen
= hell

das **Holz**, plural Hölzer
= wood

der **Honig**, plural Honige
= honey

das **Honorar**, plural Honorare
= fee

horchen verb
* = to listen
* = to eavesdrop

hören verb
= to hear
= to listen (to)

der **Hörer**, plural Hörer
* = listener
* (of phone) = receiver

die **Hörerin**, plural Hörerinnen
= listener

der **Horizont**, plural Horizonte
= horizon

die **Hose**, plural Hosen
= trousers, = pants

das **Hotel**, plural Hotels
= hotel

hübsch adjective
= pretty
= nice

der **Hubschrauber**, plural Hubschrauber
= helicopter

der **Huf**, plural Hufe
= hoof

das **Hufeisen**, plural Hufeisen
= horseshoe

die **Hüfte**, plural Hüften
= hip

der **Hügel**, plural Hügel
= hill

das **Huhn**, plural Hühner
= chicken
= hen

die **Hülle**, plural Hüllen
= cover
= wrapping

die **Hummel**, plural Hummeln
= bumble-bee

der **Hummer**, plural Hummer
= lobster

der **Humor**
= humour, = humor
Humor haben = to have a sense of humour

humpeln verb (! sein)
= to hobble

der **Hund**, plural Hunde
= dog

die **Hundehütte**, plural Hundehütten
= kennel, = doghouse

hundert adjective
= a hundred, = one hundred

der **Hunger**
= hunger

die **Hungersnot**, *plural* Hungersnöte
= famine

hungrig *adjective*
= hungry

die **Hupe**, *plural* Hupen
= horn

hupen *verb*
= to beep

hüpfen *verb* (**!** *sein*)
= to hop

hurra *interjection*
= hurray!

husten *verb*
= to cough

der **Husten**, *plural* Husten
= cough

der **Hut**, *plural* Hüte
= hat

hüten *verb*
• = to look after
• sich hüten = to be on one's guard

die **Hütte**, *plural* Hütten
• = hut
• = iron and steel works

die **Hyäne**, *plural* Hyänen
= hyena

hypnotisieren *verb*
= to hypnotize

die **Hypothek**, *plural* Hypotheken
= mortgage

hysterisch *adjective*
= hysterical

I i

ich *pronoun*
= I

der **IC-Zug**, *plural* IC-Züge
(*Intercity-Zug*) = intercity train

die **Idee**, *plural* Ideen
= idea

identifizieren *verb*
= to identify

identisch *adjective*
= identical

der **Idiot**, *plural* Idioten
= idiot

idiotisch *adjective*
= idiotic

der **Igel**, *plural* Igel
= hedgehog

ihm *pronoun*
= (to) him
(*thing*) = (to) it

ihn *pronoun*
= him
(*thing*) = it

ihnen *pronoun*
= (to) them

Ihnen *pronoun*
= (to) you

ihr
1 *pronoun*
• (*plural*) = you
• = (to) her
(*thing*) = (to) it
2 *adjective* = her
(*thing*) = its
(*plural*) = their

Ihr *adjective*
= your

ihrer/ihre/ihrs *pronoun*
= hers
(*plural*) = theirs

Ihrer/Ihre/Ihrs *pronoun*
= yours

die **Illustrierte**, *plural* Illustrierten
= magazine

im = in dem
im Juni = in June
im Kino = at the cinema

der **Imbiss** (**Imbiß**ⓞⓛⓓ), *plural* Imbisse
• = snack
• = snack bar

imitieren *verb*
= to imitate

immer *adverb*
= always
immer wieder = again and again
für immer = for ever
immer noch = still
wo/wer/wann immer =
wherever/whoever/whenever

immerzu *adverb*
= all the time, = the whole time

impfen *verb*
= to vaccinate, = to inoculate

imprägniert *adjective*
= waterproof

imstande *adverb*
= able

in *preposition*
* (+ *dative*) = in
in diesem Monat = this month
* (+ *accusative*) = into, = in
in die Stadt gehen = to go to town

inbegriffen *adjective*
= included
Essen ist inbegriffen = food is included

indem *conjunction*
* = while
* indem man etwas tut = by doing
something

der **Inder**, *plural* Inder
= Indian

die **Inderin**, *plural* Inderinnen
= Indian

der **Indianer**, *plural* Indianer
= (American) Indian

die **Indianerin**, *plural* Indianerinnen
= (American) Indian

(das) **Indien**
= India

indisch *adjective*
= Indian

die **Industrie**, *plural* Industrien
= industry

die **Infektion**, *plural* Infektionen
= infection

infizieren *verb*
* = to infect
* sich bei jemandem infizieren = to be
infected by someone

infolge *preposition* (+ *genitive*)
= as a result of

die **Informatik**
= information technology
= computer studies

die **Information**, *plural* Informationen
= (piece of) information

informieren *verb*
* = to inform
informiert sein = to be aware
* sich über etwas informieren = to find out
about something

der **Ingenieur**, *plural* Ingenieure
= engineer

der **Ingwer**
= ginger

der **Inhaber**, *plural* Inhaber
* (*of an office*) = holder
* (*of a shop*) = owner

die **Inhaberin**, *plural* Inhaberinnen
* (*of an office*) = holder

* (*of a shop*) = owner

der **Inhalt**, *plural* Inhalte
* = contents
* (*of a story*) = content
* (*of a rectangle*) = area
* (*of a cylinder*) = volume

das **Inhaltsverzeichnis**, *plural*
Inhaltsverzeichnisse
= contents list

innen *adverb*
= inside
nach innen = inwards

die **Innenstadt**, *plural* Innenstädte
* = inner city
* = city centre, = town centre

das **Innere**
= inside
= interior

innerer/innere/inneres *adjective*
* = inner
* = inside
* (*in medicine*) = internal

innerhalb
1 *preposition* (+ *genitive*) = within
2 *adverb*
innerhalb von = within

innerlich
1 *adjective* = inner
2 *adverb* = inwardly

ins = in das
ins Kino gehen = to go to the cinema

das **Insekt**, *plural* Insekten
= insect

die **Insel**, *plural* Inseln
= island

das **Inserat**, *plural* Inserate
= advertisement

inserieren *verb*
= to advertise

insgesamt *adverb*
= in all, = all in all

der **Installateur**, *plural* Installateure
* = fitter
* = plumber

der **Instinkt**, *plural* Instinkte
= instinct

die **Intelligenz**
= intelligence

interessant *adjective*
= interesting

das **Interesse**, *plural* Interessen
= interest

interessieren *verb*
* = to interest

✗ in informal situations   OLD = old spelling

• sich für etwas interessieren = to be
 interested in something

das **Internat**, plural Internate
 = boarding school

das **Internet**
 = Internet

das **Interview**, plural Interviews
 = interview

 inzwischen adverb
 = in the meantime
 = meanwhile

der **Ire**, plural Iren
 = Irishman
 die Iren = the Irish

 irgend adverb
 = at all
 wenn irgend möglich = if at all possible

 irgendein article
 = some, = any
 irgendein anderer = someone or anyone
 else

 **irgendeiner/irgendeine/
 irgendeins** pronoun
 = someone, = somebody
 (in questions and negatives) = anyone,
 = anybody

 irgendetwas pronoun
 = something
 (in questions and negatives)
 = anything

 irgendjemand pronoun
 = someone, = somebody
 (in questions and negatives) = anyone,
 = anybody

 irgendwann adverb
 = (at) some time, = (at) any time

 irgendwas* pronoun
 = something, = anything

 irgendwie adverb
 = somehow

 irgendwo adverb
 = somewhere, = anywhere

die **Irin**, plural Irinnen
 = Irishwoman

 irisch adjective
 = Irish

(das) **Irland**
 = Ireland

 ironisch adjective
 = ironic

 irre
 1 adjective
 = mad, = crazy
 2 adverb
 irre gut* = incredibly good

 irren verb
 • = to be wrong, = to be mistaken
 • (**!** sein) (when lost) = to wander
 • sich irren = to be wrong, = to be mistaken

der **Irrtum**, plural Irrtümer
 = mistake

 isolieren verb
 • = to isolate
 • = to insulate

 isst (**ißt**⟨OLD⟩) ▶ essen

 ist ▶ sein

(das) **Italien**
 = Italy

der **Italiener**, plural Italiener
 = Italian

die **Italienerin**, plural Italienerinnen
 = Italian

 italienisch adjective
 = Italian

Jj

 ja adverb
 = yes
 ich glaube ja = I think so

die **Jacht**, plural Jachten
 = yacht

die **Jacke**, plural Jacken
 • = jacket
 • = cardigan

das **Jackett**, plural Jacketts
 = jacket

die **Jagd**, plural Jagden
 = hunt
 auf die Jagd gehen = to go hunting

 jagen verb
 • = to hunt
 • = to chase

der **Jäger**, plural Jäger
 • = hunter
 • (plane) = fighter

das **Jahr**, plural Jahre
 = year

der **Jahrestag**, plural Jahrestage
 = anniversary

die **Jahreszeit**, plural Jahreszeiten
 = season

der **Jahrgang**, plural Jahrgänge
 = year
 = vintage

das **Jahrhundert**, *plural* Jahrhunderte
= century

die **Jahrhundertwende**
= turn of the century

jährlich
1 *adjective*
= annual, = yearly
2 *adverb*
= annually, = yearly
zweimal jährlich = twice a year

der **Jahrmarkt**, *plural* Jahrmärkte
= fair

das **Jahrtausend**, *plural* Jahrtausende
= millennium

das **Jahrzehnt**, *plural* Jahrzehnte
= decade

jähzornig *adjective*
= hot-tempered

jammern *verb*
= to moan

der **Januar**
= January

der **Japaner**, *plural* Japaner
= Japanese

die **Japanerin**, *plural* Japanerinnen
= Japanese

japanisch *adjective*
= Japanese

jawohl *adverb*
= yes
= certainly

je
1 *adverb*
• = ever
• = each
2 *preposition* (+ *accusative*) = per
3 *conjunction*
je mehr, desto besser = the more the
better

jede ▶jeder

jedenfalls *adverb*
= in any case

jeder/jede/jedes
1 *adjective*
• = every
jedes Mal = every time
jedes Mal wenn = whenever
• = each
• = any
2 *pronoun*
• = everyone
• = each one
• = anyone

jederzeit *adverb*
= (at) any time

jedes ▶jeder

jedesmal⃝ᴸᴰ ▶jeder

jedoch *adverb*
= however

jemand *pronoun*
= someone, = somebody
(*in questions and negatives*) = anyone, =
anybody

jener/jene/jenes
1 *adjective* = that, (*plural*) = those
2 *pronoun* = that one, (*plural*) = those

jenseits
1 *preposition* (+ *genitive*)
= (on) the other side of
= beyond
2 *adverb* = (on) the other side

jetzt *adverb*
= now

jobben✶ *verb*
= to work

joggen *verb* (! *sein*)
= to jog

der or das **Joghurt**, *plural* Joghurts
= yoghurt

die **Johannisbeere**, *plural*
Johannisbeeren
rote Johannisbeeren = redcurrants
schwarze Johannisbeeren =
blackcurrants

der **Journalist**, *plural* Journalisten
= journalist

die **Journalistin**, *plural* Journalistinnen
= journalist

jubeln *verb*
= to cheer

das **Jubiläum**, *plural* Jubiläen
• = jubilee
• = anniversary

jucken *verb*
• = to itch
• sich jucken = to scratch

der **Jude**, *plural* Juden
= Jew

die **Jüdin**, *plural* Jüdinnen
= Jewess

jüdisch *adjective*
= Jewish

die **Jugend**
= youth

die **Jugendherberge**, *plural*
Jugendherbergen
= youth hostel

✶ in informal situations   ⃝ᴸᴰ = old spelling

der/die **Jugendliche**, *plural* Jugendlichen
= young person
= youth

(das) **Jugoslawien**
= Yugoslavia

der **Juli**
= July

jung *adjective*
= young

der **Junge**, *plural* Jungen
= boy

die **Jungfrau**, *plural* Jungfrauen
• = virgin
• = Virgo

der **Junggeselle**, *plural* Junggesellen
= bachelor

jüngster/jüngste/jüngstes
adjective
= youngest
in jüngster Zeit = recently

der **Juni**
= June

Jura (*plural*)
= law

die **Jury**, *plural* Jurys
• = jury
• (*in sport*) = judges

das **Kabarett**, *plural* Kabaretts
= cabaret

das **Kabel**, *plural* Kabel
= cable

der **Kabeljau**, *plural* Kabeljaus
= cod

die **Kabine**, *plural* Kabinen
• = cabin
• (*for changing*) = cubicle
• (*of cable car*) = car

das **Kabrio**, *plural* Kabrios
= convertible

die **Kachel**, *plural* Kacheln
= tile

der **Käfer**, *plural* Käfer
= beetle

der **Kaffee**, *plural* Kaffees
= coffee

der **Käfig**, *plural* Käfige
= cage

kahl *adjective*
• = bald
• = bare

der **Kai**, *plural* Kais
= quay

der **Kaiser**, *plural* Kaiser
= emperor

die **Kaiserin**, *plural* Kaiserinnen
= empress

die **Kajüte**, *plural* Kajüten
= cabin

der **Kakao**, *plural* Kakaos
= cocoa

der **Kakerlak**, *plural* Kakerlaken
= cockroach

der **Kaktus**, *plural* Kakteen
= cactus

das **Kalb**, *plural* Kälber
= calf

das **Kalbfleisch**
= veal

der **Kalender**, *plural* Kalender
• = calendar
• = diary

der **Kalk**, *plural* Kalke
• = lime
• = limescale
• = calcium

die **Kalorie**, *plural* Kalorien
= calorie

kalorienarm *adjective*
= low-calorie

kalt *adjective*
= cold

die **Kälte**
• = cold
zehn Grad Kälte = 10 degrees below zero
• (*emotional*) = coldness

kam ▶ kommen

das **Kamel**, *plural* Kamele
= camel

die **Kamera**, *plural* Kameras
= camera

der **Kamin**, *plural* Kamine
= fireplace

der **Kamm**, *plural* Kämme
• = comb
• = ridge

kämmen *verb*
• = to comb
• sich die Haare kämmen = to comb one's
hair

K

die **Kammer**, *plural* Kammern
* = store room
* = chamber

der **Kampf**, *plural* Kämpfe
* = battle
* = fight
* (*in sport*) = contest

kämpfen *verb*
= to fight

der **Kämpfer**, *plural* Kämpfer
= fighter

die **Kämpferin**, *plural* Kämpferinnen
= fighter

(das) **Kanada**
= Canada

der **Kanadier**, *plural* Kanadier
= Canadian

die **Kanadierin**, *plural* Kanadierinnen
= Canadian

kanadisch *adjective*
= Canadian

der **Kanal**, *plural* Kanäle
* = canal
* = channel
  der Kanal = the (English) Channel
* = sewer

die **Kanalisation**
= sewers
= drains

der **Kandidat**, *plural* Kandidaten
= candidate

das **Känguru** (**Känguruh**ⓞⓛⒹ), *plural* Kängurus
= kangaroo

das **Kaninchen**, *plural* Kaninchen
= rabbit

kann ▶können

das **Kännchen**, *plural* Kännchen
* = pot
  ein Kännchen Kaffee bitte = a pot of coffee please
* = jug

die **Kanne**, *plural* Kannen
* (*for water*) = jug
* (*for coffee, tea*) = pot
* (*for oil*) = can
* (*for milk*) = churn

kannst ▶können

kannte ▶kennen

die **Kante**, *plural* Kanten
= edge

die **Kantine**, *plural* Kantinen
= canteen

das **Kanu**, *plural* Kanus
= canoe

der **Kanzler**, *plural* Kanzler
= chancellor

die **Kapelle**, *plural* Kapellen
* = chapel
* = band

kapieren✱ *verb*
= to understand, = to get

das **Kapital**
= capital

der **Kapitän**, *plural* Kapitäne
= captain

das **Kapitel**, *plural* Kapitel
= chapter

die **Kappe**, *plural* Kappen
= cap

kaputt *adjective*
= broken
ich bin kaputt✱ = I'm shattered

kaputt|gehen✱ *irregular verb* (❗ *sein*)
= to break, = to pack up

kaputt|machen✱ *verb*
* = to break
* sich kaputtmachen = to wear oneself out

die **Kapuze**, *plural* Kapuzen
= hood

der **Karfreitag**
= Good Friday

kariert *adjective*
* = check
* (*of paper*) = squared

der **Karneval**, *plural* Karnevale
= carnival

das **Karo**
(*playing cards*) = diamonds

die **Karotte**, *plural* Karotten
= carrot

die **Karte**, *plural* Karten
* = card
* = ticket
* = menu
* = map

die **Kartoffel**, *plural* Kartoffeln
= potato

der **Kartoffelbrei**
= mashed potatoes

der **Karton**, *plural* Kartons
* = cardboard
* = cardboard box, = carton

das **Karussell**, *plural* Karussells
= merry-go-round

✱ in informal situations   ⓞⓛⒹ = old spelling

der **Käse**
  = cheese

die **Kasse**, *plural* Kassen
  • = till
  • (*in a supermarket*) = checkout
  • (*in a bank*) = cash desk
  • (*in a theatre*) = box-office
  • knapp bei Kasse sein = to be short of money

die **Kassette**, *plural* Kassetten
  • = cassette
  • = box

kassieren *verb*
  • = to collect
  • = to collect the money
  darf ich bei Ihnen kassieren? = would you like your bill?

die **Kastanie**, *plural* Kastanien
  = chestnut

der **Kasten**, *plural* Kästen
  • = box
  • (*for bottles*) = crate
  • (*for bread*) = bin

der **Katalog**, *plural* Kataloge
  = catalogue

der **Katalysator**, *plural* Katalysatoren
  • = catalyst
  • = catalytic converter

die **Katastrophe**, *plural* Katastrophen
  = catastrophe

der **Kater**, *plural* Kater
  • = tom-cat
  • einen Kater haben✶ = to have a hangover

die **Kathedrale**, *plural* Kathedralen
  = cathedral

katholisch *adjective*
  = Catholic

die **Katze**, *plural* Katzen
  = cat

kauen *verb*
  = to chew

der **Kauf**, *plural* Käufe
  • = purchase
  • etwas in Kauf nehmen = to put up with something

kaufen *verb*
  = to buy

der **Käufer**, *plural* Käufer
  = buyer

die **Käuferin**, *plural* Käuferinnen
  = buyer

die **Kauffrau**, *plural* Kauffrauen
  = businesswoman

das **Kaufhaus**, *plural* Kaufhäuser
  = department store

der **Kaufmann**, *plural* Kaufleute
  = businessman

der **Kaugummi**, *plural* Kaugummis
  = chewing gum

kaum *adverb*
  = hardly, = scarcely

die **Kaution**, *plural* Kautionen
  • = deposit
  • = bail

der **Kegel**, *plural* Kegel
  • = cone
  • = skittle

kehren *verb*
  • = to turn
  • = to sweep

kein *adjective*
  = no
  keine fünf Minuten = less than five minutes

keiner/keine/keins *pronoun*
  = no one, = nobody
  (*thing*) = none, = not one

keinmal *adverb*
  = not once

keins ▶ keiner

der **Keks**, *plural* Kekse
  = biscuit, = cookie

der **Keller**, *plural* Keller
  = cellar

das **Kellergeschoss** (**Kellergeschoß**ⓄⓁⒹ), *plural* Kellergeschosse
  = basement

der **Kellner**, *plural* Kellner
  = waiter

die **Kellnerin**, *plural* Kellnerinnen
  = waitress

kennen *irregular verb*
  • = to know
  kennen lernen = to get to know, = to meet
  ich habe sie in London kennen gelernt = I met her in London
  • sich kennen lernen = to get to know each other, = to meet

Kenntnisse (*plural*)
  = knowledge

das **Kennzeichen**, *plural* Kennzeichen
  • = distinguishing mark
    = characteristic
  • (*of a vehicle*) = registration number

der **Kerl**, *plural* Kerle
  = fellow, = bloke

der **Kern**, *plural* Kerne
  • = pip

K

(*in an apricot, peach*) = stone
(*in a nut*) = kernel
* = core
* der Kern der Sache = the heart of the matter

die **Kernenergie**
= nuclear power

das **Kernkraftwerk**, *plural* Kernkraftwerke
= nuclear power station

die **Kerze**, *plural* Kerzen
= candle

der **Kessel**, *plural* Kessel
= kettle

die **Kette**, *plural* Ketten
* = chain
* = necklace

keuchen *verb*
= to pant

der **Keuchhusten**
= whooping cough

kichern *verb*
= to giggle

der **Kiefer**[1] *plural* Kiefer
= jaw

die **Kiefer**[2] *plural* Kiefern
= pine (tree)

der **Kieselstein**, *plural* Kieselsteine
= pebble

das **Kilo**, *plural* Kilo *or* Kilos
= kilo

der **Kilometer**, *plural* Kilometer
= kilometre, = kilometer

das **Kind**, *plural* Kinder
= child

der **Kindergarten**, *plural* Kindergärten
= nursery school

die **Kindertagesstätte**, *plural*
Kindertagesstätten
= day nursery

der **Kinderwagen**, *plural* Kinderwagen
= pram, = baby carriage

die **Kindheit**, *plural* Kindheiten
= childhood

kindisch *adjective*
= childish

das **Kinn**, *plural* Kinne
= chin

das **Kino**, *plural* Kinos
= cinema, = movie theater

kippen *verb*
= to tip (up)

die **Kirche**, *plural* Kirchen
= church

die **Kirsche**, *plural* Kirschen
= cherry

das **Kissen**, *plural* Kissen
* = cushion
* = pillow

die **Kiste**, *plural* Kisten
= box, = crate

kitschig *adjective*
= kitsch

das **Kitz**, *plural* Kitze
(*goat*) = kid
(*deer*) = fawn

kitzeln *verb*
= to tickle

die **Klage**, *plural* Klagen
= complaint

klagen *verb*
= to complain

die **Klammer**, *plural* Klammern
* (*for washing*) = peg
* (*for hair*) = grip
* (*in text*) = bracket

der **Klang**, *plural* Klänge
* = sound
* = tone

die **Klappe**, *plural* Klappen
* = flap
* = clapperboard
* halt die Klappe!✖ = shut up!

klappen *verb*
* nach vorne klappen = to tilt forward
nach oben/unten klappen = to lift up/put down
* klappen✖ = to work out

klar
1 *adjective*
* = clear
* = definite
* sich über etwas im Klaren sein = to realize something
* klar werden = to become clear
sich über etwas klar werden = to realize something
2 *adverb*
* = clearly
* = of course

klären *verb*
* = to clarify
= to sort out
* sich klären = to clear

die **Klarinette**, *plural* Klarinetten
= clarinet

klarwerden⊙ᴸᴰ ▶ klar

die **Klasse**, *plural* Klassen
= class

die **Klassenarbeit**, *plural* Klassenarbeiten
= (written) test

das **Klassenzimmer**, *plural*
Klassenzimmer
= classroom

klassisch *adjective*
= classical

der **Klatsch**
= gossip

klatschen *verb*
• = to clap
• = to splash
• = to gossip

klauen✻ *verb*
= to pinch

das **Klavier**, *plural* Klaviere
= piano

kleben *verb*
= to stick
= to glue

klebrig *adjective*
= sticky

der **Klebstoff**, *plural* Klebstoffe
= adhesive, = glue

der **Klebstreifen**, *plural* Klebstreifen
= sticky tape

der **Klecks**, *plural* Kleckse
= stain
= spot

das **Kleid**, *plural* Kleider
• = dress
• Kleider (*plural*) = clothes

der **Kleiderbügel**, *plural* Kleiderbügel
= clothes-hanger

der **Kleiderschrank**, *plural*
Kleiderschränke
= wardrobe

die **Kleidung**
= clothes, = clothing

klein *adjective*
• = small, = little
• = short

das **Kleingeld**
= change

die **Kleinigkeit**, *plural* Kleinigkeiten
= trifle, = small thing
eine Kleinigkeit essen = to have a bite to
eat

kleinlich *adjective*
= petty

klemmen *verb*
• = to stick, = to jam
• sich den Finger klemmen = to get one's
finger caught

klettern *verb* (**!** *sein*)
= to climb

das **Klima**, *plural* Klimas
= climate

die **Klimaanlage**, *plural* Klimaanlagen
= air-conditioning

die **Klinge**, *plural* Klingen
= blade

die **Klingel**, *plural* Klingeln
= bell

klingeln *verb*
= to ring
es klingelt = there's a ring at the door

klingen *irregular verb*
= to sound

die **Klinik**, *plural* Kliniken
= clinic

die **Klinke**, *plural* Klinken
= handle

die **Klippe**, *plural* Klippen
= rock

das **Klo✻**, *plural* Klos
= loo

klopfen *verb*
• = to knock
• = to beat

das **Klosett**, *plural* Klosetts
= lavatory

das **Kloster**, *plural* Klöster
• = monastery
• = convent

der **Klotz**, *plural* Klötze
= block
= log

der **Klub**, *plural* Klubs
= club

klug *adjective*
= clever
aus etwas nicht klug werden = to not
understand something

der **Klumpen**, *plural* Klumpen
= lump

knabbern *verb*
= to nibble

der **Knall**, *plural* Knalle
= bang

knallen *verb*
• = to go bang
• (*of a whip*) = to crack
• (*of a cork*) = to pop
• (*of a door*) = to slam

K

knapp *adjective*
* = scarce
  mit etwas knapp sein = to be short of something
  mit knapper Mehrheit = by a narrow majority
* = tight
  eine knappe Stunde = just under an hour
  das war knapp✗ = that was a close shave

knarren *verb*
= to creak

knautschen *verb*
* = to crease
* = to crumple

kneifen *irregular verb*
* = to pinch
* kneifen✗ = to chicken out

die **Kneipe✗**, *plural* Kneipen
= pub, = bar

kneten *verb*
* (*in baking*) = to knead
* (*in pottery*) = to mould

knicken *verb*
* = to bend
* = to fold

das **Knie**, *plural* Knie
= knee

knien *verb*
* = to kneel
* sich knien = to kneel (down)

knipsen *verb*
* (*photograph*) = to snap
* (*make a hole in*) = to punch

der **Knoblauch**
= garlic

der **Knöchel**, *plural* Knöchel
* = ankle
* = knuckle

der **Knochen**, *plural* Knochen
= bone

der **Knopf**, *plural* Knöpfe
* = button
* = knob

die **Knospe**, *plural* Knospen
= bud

der **Knoten**, *plural* Knoten
* = knot
* (*hairstyle*) = bun

knurren *verb*
* = to growl
* = to rumble
* = to grumble

knusprig *adjective*
= crisp, = crunchy

der **Koch**, *plural* Köche
= cook
= chef

kochen *verb*
* = to cook
* (*of water*) = to boil
* Kaffee kochen = to make coffee

die **Köchin**, *plural* Köchinnen
= cook

der **Kochtopf**, *plural* Kochtöpfe
= saucepan

der **Koffer**, *plural* Koffer
= (suit)case

der **Kofferkuli**, *plural* Kofferkulis
= luggage trolley

der **Kofferraum**, *plural* Kofferräume
= boot, = trunk

der **Kohl**
= cabbage

die **Koje**, *plural* Kojen
* = berth
* = bunk

die **Kokosnuss** (**Kokosnuß**ⓄⓁⒹ), *plural* Kokosnüsse
= coconut

der **Kollege**, *plural* Kollegen
= colleague

die **Kollegin**, *plural* Kolleginnen
= colleague

(das) **Köln**
= Cologne

die **Kombination**, *plural* Kombinationen
* = combination
* (*clothing*) = suit

komisch *adjective*
= funny

das **Komma**, *plural* Kommas
* = comma
* = decimal point
  eins Komma fünf = one point five

kommen *irregular verb* (**!** *sein*)
= to come
etwas kommen lassen = to send for something
hinter etwas kommen = to find out about something
wie kommt das? = why is that?
wer kommt zuerst? = who's first?

der **Kommissar**, *plural* Kommissare
= superintendent

die **Kommode**, *plural* Kommoden
= chest of drawers

die **Komödie**, *plural* Komödien
= comedy

ⓄⓁⒹ = old spelling

der **Kompass** (**Kompaß**(OLD)), *plural* Kompasse
= compass

komplett *adjective*
= complete

das **Kompliment**, *plural* Komplimente
= compliment

kompliziert *adjective*
= complicated

der **Komponist**, *plural* Komponisten
= composer

das **Kompott**, *plural* Kompotte
= stewed fruit

die **Konditorei**, *plural* Konditoreien
= patisserie, = cake shop

das **Kondom**, *plural* Kondome
= condom

das **Konfekt**
= confectionery

die **Konferenz**, *plural* Konferenzen
= conference

der **Konflikt**, *plural* Konflikte
= conflict

der **König**, *plural* Könige
= king

die **Königin**, *plural* Königinnen
= queen

das **Königreich**, *plural* Königreiche
= kingdom

die **Konkurrenz**, *plural* Konkurrenzen
= competition

konkurrenzfähig *adjective*
= competitive

können *irregular verb*
= to be able to
das kann ich nicht = I can't do that
können Sie Deutsch? = can you speak German?
das kann gut sein = that may well be

der **Könner**, *plural* Könner
= expert

könnt ▶ können

konnte, konnten, konntest, konntet ▶ können

das **Konsulat**, *plural* Konsulate
= consulate

der **Konsum**
= consumption

der **Kontakt**, *plural* Kontakte
= contact

die **Kontaktlinse**, *plural* Kontaktlinsen
= contact lens

der **Kontinent**, *plural* Kontinente
= continent

das **Konto**, *plural* Konten
= account

der **Kontoauszug**, *plural* Kontoauszüge
= bank statement

die **Kontrolle**, *plural* Kontrollen
• = check, = inspection
• = control

der **Kontrolleur**, *plural* Kontrolleure
= inspector

kontrollieren *verb*
• = to check, = to inspect
• = to control

konzentrieren *verb*
• = to concentrate
• sich auf etwas konzentrieren = to concentrate on something

das **Konzert**, *plural* Konzerte
= concert

der **Kopf**, *plural* Köpfe
• = head
sich den Kopf zerbrechen = to rack one's brains
seinen Kopf durchsetzen = to get one's own way
• ein Kopf Kohl/Salat = a cabbage/a lettuce

köpfen *verb*
• = to behead
• (*in soccer*) = to head

der **Kopfhörer**, *plural* Kopfhörer
= headphones

das **Kopfkissen**, *plural* Kopfkissen
= pillow

Kopfschmerzen (*plural*)
= headache

die **Kopie**, *plural* Kopien
= copy

der **Korb**, *plural* Körbe
jemandem einen Korb geben = to turn someone down
= basket

der **Kork**, *plural* Korke
= cork

der **Korken**, *plural* Korken
= cork

der **Korkenzieher**, *plural* Korkenzieher
= corkscrew

das **Korn**, *plural* Körner
= grain
= corn

der **Körper**, *plural* Körper
= body

der **Körperbau**
= build, = physique

K

körperlich *adjective*
= physical

der **Korridor**, *plural* Korridore
= corridor

korrigieren *verb*
= to correct

korrupt *adjective*
= corrupt

die **Kosmetik**
= beauty care

die **Kost**
= food

kostbar *adjective*
= valuable, = precious

kosten *verb*
* = to cost
* = to taste

Kosten (*plural*)
* = cost
* = expenses

kostenlos *adjective*
= free (of charge)

der **Kostenvoranschlag**, *plural*
Kostenvoranschläge
= estimate

köstlich *adjective*
* = delicious
* = funny

das **Kostüm**, *plural* Kostüme
* = suit
* (*fancy dress*) = costume

das **Kotelett**, *plural* Koteletts
= chop, = cutlet

die **Krabbe**, *plural* Krabben
* = crab
* = shrimp

der **Krach**, *plural* Kräche
= row

krachen *verb*
* = to crash
* = to crack

krächzen *verb*
= to croak

die **Kraft**, *plural* Kräfte
* = strength
= force
= power
* = worker

kräftig *adjective*
* = strong, = powerful
* = nourishing

der **Kraftstoff**, *plural* Kraftstoffe
= fuel

der **Kraftwagen**, *plural* Kraftwagen
= motor car

das **Kraftwerk**, *plural* Kraftwerke
= power station

der **Kragen**, *plural* Kragen
= collar

die **Krähe**, *plural* Krähen
= crow

die **Kralle**, *plural* Krallen
= claw

der **Kram**
* = stuff
* = affair

kramen *verb*
= to rummage about

der **Krampf**, *plural* Krämpfe
= cramp

der **Kran**, *plural* Kräne
= crane

der **Kranich**, *plural* Kraniche
= crane

krank *adjective*
= sick, = ill
krank werden = to fall ill

der/die **Kranke**, *plural* Kranken
= sick man/woman
(*in hospital*) = patient

kränken *verb*
= to hurt

das **Krankenhaus**, *plural* Krankenhäuser
= hospital

die **Krankenkasse**, *plural* Krankenkassen
= health insurance

die **Krankenschwester**, *plural*
Krankenschwestern
= nurse

der **Krankenwagen**, *plural*
Krankenwagen
= ambulance

die **Krankheit**, *plural* Krankheiten
= illness, = disease

kratzen *verb*
= to scratch

der **Kratzer**, *plural* Kratzer
= scratch

kraulen *verb*
* = to do the crawl
* = to tickle

das **Kraut**, *plural* Kräuter
* = herb
* = cabbage

---

der **Krawall**, plural Krawalle
- = riot
- = row

die **Krawatte**, plural Krawatten
= tie

der **Krebs**, plural Krebse
- = crab
- (illness) = cancer
- = Cancer

der **Kredit**, plural Kredite
- = credit
- = loan

die **Kreide**, plural Kreiden
= chalk

kreieren verb
= to create

der **Kreis**, plural Kreise
- = circle
- = district

der **Kreislauf**
- = cycle
- = circulation

das **Kreuz**, plural Kreuze
- = cross
- (of a motorway) = intersection
- = small of the back
- (playing cards) = clubs

kreuzen verb
- = to cross
- sich kreuzen = to cross

die **Kreuzfahrt**, plural Kreuzfahrten
= cruise

die **Kreuzung**, plural Kreuzungen
- = crossroads
- (plant, animal) = cross

das **Kreuzworträtsel**, plural Kreuzworträtsel
= crossword (puzzle)

kriechen irregular verb (! sein)
= to crawl

der **Krieg**, plural Kriege
= war

kriegen* verb
= to get

der **Krimi**, plural Krimis
= crime story
= thriller

kriminell adjective
= criminal

die **Krippe**, plural Krippen
- = manger
- = crib
- = crèche

die **Krise**, plural Krisen
= crisis

die **Kritik**, plural Kritiken
- = criticism
- = review

kritisch adjective
= critical

kritisieren verb
- = to criticize
- = to review

das **Krokodil**, plural Krokodile
= crocodile

die **Krone**, plural Kronen
= crown

krönen verb
= to crown

die **Krücke**, plural Krücken
= crutch

der **Krug**, plural Krüge
- = jug
- = mug

der **Krümel**, plural Krümel
= crumb

krümelig adjective
= crumbly

krumm adjective
= bent
= crooked

krümmen verb
- = to bend
- sich krümmen = to bend, (with laughter) = to double up

der **Krüppel**, plural Krüppel
= cripple

die **Kruste**, plural Krusten
= crust

die **Küche**, plural Küchen
- = kitchen
- = cooking
  kalte Küche = cold food
  warme Küche = hot food

der **Kuchen**, plural Kuchen
= cake

die **Küchenschabe**, plural Küchenschaben
= cockroach

der **Kuckuck**, plural Kuckucke
= cuckoo

die **Kugel**, plural Kugeln
- = ball
- = sphere
- = bullet

der **Kugelschreiber**, plural Kugelschreiber
= ballpoint (pen)

die **Kuh**, plural Kühe
= cow

K

kühl *adjective*
= cool

kühlen *verb*
* = to cool, = to chill
* = to refrigerate

der **Kühler**, *plural* Kühler
= radiator

die **Kühlerhaube**, *plural* Kühlerhauben
= bonnet, = hood

der **Kühlschrank**, *plural* Kühlschränke
= refrigerator, = fridge

die **Kultur**, *plural* Kulturen
= culture

der **Kulturbeutel**, *plural* Kulturbeutel
= toilet bag

kulturell *adjective*
= cultural

der **Kummer**
* = sorrow, = grief
* = worry
* = trouble

kümmern *verb*
= to concern
sich um jemanden kümmern = to take care of someone
kümmere dich um deine eigenen Angelegenheiten = mind your own business

der **Kunde**, *plural* Kunden
= customer
= client

der **Kundendienst**
= customer service

kündigen *verb*
* = to cancel
* = to give notice

die **Kundin**, *plural* Kundinnen
= customer
= client

die **Kundschaft**
= customers, = clientele

die **Kunst**, *plural* Künste
* = art
* = skill

der **Künstler**, *plural* Künstler
= artist

die **Künstlerin**, *plural* Künstlerinnen
= artist

künstlerisch *adjective*
= artistic

künstlich *adjective*
= artificial

der **Kunststoff**, *plural* Kunststoffe
= plastic

das **Kunststück**, *plural* Kunststücke
* = trick
* = feat

das **Kunstwerk**, *plural* Kunstwerke
= work of art

das **Kupfer**
= copper

die **Kupplung**, *plural* Kupplungen
* (*of a car*) = clutch
* = coupling

der **Kurs**, *plural* Kurse
* = course
* = price
= exchange rate

die **Kurve**, *plural* Kurven
* = curve
* = bend, = corner

kurz
1 *adjective*
= short
= brief
vor kurzem = a short time ago
2 *adverb* = shortly, = briefly
kurz gesagt = in a word

kurzärmelig *adjective*
= short-sleeved

kürzen *verb*
= to shorten

kurzfristig
1 *adjective* = short-term
2 *adverb*
* = at short notice
* = for a short time

kürzlich *adverb*
= recently

der **Kurzschluss** (**Kurzschluß**ⓞⓛⓓ), *plural* Kurzschlüsse
= short circuit

kurzsichtig *adjective*
= short-sighted

Kurzwaren (*plural*)
= haberdashery, = notions

die **Kusine**, *plural* Kusinen
= cousin

der **Kuss** (**Kuß**ⓞⓛⓓ), *plural* Küsse
= kiss

küssen *verb*
= to kiss

die **Küste**, *plural* Küsten
= coast

die **Kutsche**, *plural* Kutschen
= coach, = carriage

das **Kuvert**, *plural* Kuverts
= envelope

das **Labor**, *plural* Labors
= laboratory

die **Lache**, *plural* Lachen
= pool

lächeln *verb*
= to smile

lachen *verb*
= to laugh

lächerlich *adjective*
= ridiculous

der **Lachs**, *plural* Lachse
= salmon

der **Lack**, *plural* Lacke
* = varnish
* (*on a car*) = paint

lackieren *verb*
* = to varnish
* (*with paint*) = to spray

der **Laden**, *plural* Läden
* = shop, = store
* = shutter

die **Ladung**, *plural* Ladungen
* = cargo
* (*electrical*) = charge
* = summons

lag ▶liegen

die **Lage**, *plural* Lagen
= situation

das **Lager**, *plural* Lager
* = camp
* = warehouse
* = stock
* (*in a machine*) = bearing

lagern *verb*
= to store

die **Lähmung**, *plural* Lähmungen
= paralysis

das **Laken**, *plural* Laken
= sheet

das **Lamm**, *plural* Lämmer
= lamb

die **Lampe**, *plural* Lampen
= lamp

das **Land**, *plural* Länder
* = country
* = land
* (*in Germany*) = state

die **Landebahn**, *plural* Landebahnen
= runway

landen *verb* (**!** *sein*)
* = to land
* im Krankenhaus landen✖ = to end up in hospital

die **Landkarte**, *plural* Landkarten
= map

ländlich *adjective*
= rural, = country

die **Landschaft**, *plural* Landschaften
* = countryside
* = landscape

der **Landtag**
= state parliament

die **Landwirtschaft**
= agriculture, = farming

lang
1 *adjective*
* = long
* = tall
2 *adverb*
eine Stunde lang = for an hour

langärmelig *adjective*
= long-sleeved

lange *adverb*
* = a long time
* hier ist es lange nicht so schön = it's not nearly as nice here

die **Länge**, *plural* Längen
* = length
* = longitude

die **Langeweile**
= boredom

langsam *adjective*
= slow

längst *adverb*
* = a long time ago
* = for a long time
* hier ist es längst nicht so schön = it's not nearly as nice here

langweilen *verb*
* = to bore
* sich langweilen = to be bored

langweilig *adjective*
= boring

der **Lärm**
= noise

las ▶lesen

der **Laser**, *plural* Laser
= laser

lassen *irregular verb*
* = to let
  etwas machen lassen = to have something done *or* made
  jemanden warten lassen = to keep someone waiting

- to leave
  lass das! = stop it!
- **die Tür lässt sich leicht öffnen** = the door opens easily

lässig adjective
= casual

die **Last**, plural Lasten
- = load
- = burden

lästig adjective
= troublesome

der **Lastwagen**, plural Lastwagen
= lorry, = truck

das **Latein**
= Latin

das **Laub**
= leaves

der **Lauf**, plural Läufe
- = run
- = course
  im Laufe des Abends = during the course of the evening
- = race
- (of a gun) = barrel

die **Laufbahn**, plural Laufbahnen
= career

laufen irregular verb (**!** sein)
- = to run
- = to walk
- (of a machine) = to be running, = to be on

laufend
1 adjective
- = running
- = current
  auf dem Laufenden sein = to be up to date
- = regular
2 adverb = constantly
= continually

der **Läufer**, plural Läufer
- = runner
- = rug

die **Laufmasche**, plural Laufmaschen
= ladder (in tights)

die **Laune**, plural Launen
= mood

launisch adjective
= moody

die **Laus**, plural Läuse
= louse

lauschen verb
= to listen

---

laut adjective
= loud, = noisy
lauter stellen = to turn up

läuten verb
= to ring

lauter adjective
= nothing but

der **Lautsprecher**, plural Lautsprecher
= loudspeaker

die **Lautstärke**
= volume

lauwarm adjective
= lukewarm

die **Lawine**, plural Lawinen
= avalanche

leben verb
= to live
= to be alive
leb wohl! = farewell!

das **Leben**, plural Leben
= life

lebendig adjective
- = living
- = lively

die **Lebensgefahr**
= mortal danger
der Patient war in Lebensgefahr = the patient was critically ill

lebensgefährlich
1 adjective
- = extremely dangerous
- (of an injury) = critical
2 adverb = critically

Lebenshaltungskosten (plural)
= cost of living

lebenslänglich
1 adjective = life
2 adverb = for life

der **Lebenslauf**, plural Lebensläufe
= CV, = résumé

Lebensmittel (plural)
= food, = groceries

das **Lebensmittelgeschäft**, plural Lebensmittelgeschäfte
= grocer's (shop), = food shop

der **Lebensmittelhändler**, plural Lebensmittelhändler
= grocer

der **Lebensunterhalt**
= livelihood, = living

die **Lebensversicherung**, plural Lebensversicherungen
= life insurance

die **Leber**, plural Lebern
= liver

das **Lebewesen**, *plural* Lebewesen
= living being, = living thing

lebhaft *adjective*
* = lively
* = vivid

leblos *adjective*
= lifeless

das **Leck**, *plural* Lecks
= leak

lecken *verb*
* = to lick
* = to leak

lecker *adjective*
= delicious

ledig *adjective*
= single

lediglich *adverb*
= merely

leer *adjective*
= empty

leeren *verb*
* = to empty
* sich leeren = to empty

der **Leerlauf**
= neutral

die **Leerung**, *plural* Leerungen
= collection

legen *verb*
* = to lay, = to put
* sich legen = to lie down, (*of a storm*) = to die down

die **Legende**, *plural* Legenden
= legend

leger *adjective*
= casual

der **Lehm**
= clay

die **Lehne**, *plural* Lehnen
* = back
* = arm

lehnen *verb*
* = to lean
* sich an etwas lehnen = to lean against something

das **Lehrbuch**, *plural* Lehrbücher
= textbook

der **Lehrer**, *plural* Lehrer
= teacher
= instructor

die **Lehrerin**, *plural* Lehrerinnen
= teacher
= instructor

der **Lehrling**, *plural* Lehrlinge
= apprentice
= trainee

der **Leibwächter**, *plural* Leibwächter
= bodyguard

die **Leiche**, *plural* Leichen
= (dead) body, = corpse

leicht *adjective*
* = light
* ein leichter Akzent = a slight accent
* = easy
  jemandem leicht fallen = to be easy for somebody
  es ist ihnen nicht leicht gefallen = it wasn't easy for them

die **Leichtathletik**
= athletics, = track and field

leichtfallen⊙ᴸᴰ ▶ leicht

leichtsinnig *adjective*
= careless
= reckless

leid *adjective*
jemanden leid sein = to be fed up with somebody
etwas leid werden = to get fed up with something

das **Leid**
* = sorrow, = grief
* = harm
* es tut mir Leid = I'm sorry
  er tut mir Leid = I feel sorry for him

leiden *irregular verb*
= to suffer
jemanden gut leiden können = to like someone

die **Leidenschaft**, *plural* Leidenschaften
= passion

leidenschaftlich *adjective*
= passionate

leider *adverb*
= unfortunately
leider ja = I'm afraid so

leihen *irregular verb*
* = to lend
* sich etwas leihen = to borrow something

die **Leihgebür**, *plural* Leihgebühren
* = rental
* = borrowing fee

der **Leihwagen**, *plural* Leihwagen
= hire car

leihweise *adverb*
= on loan

der **Leim**, *plural* Leime
= glue

die **Leine**, *plural* Leinen
* = rope
* (*for washing*) = line
* (*for a dog*) = lead

L

das **Leinen**
= linen

die **Leinwand**, *plural* Leinwände
- = screen
- = canvas

leise
1 *adjective* = quiet
2 *adverb* = quietly
die Musik leiser stellen = to turn the
music down

leisten *verb*
- = to achieve
jemandem Hilfe leisten = to help
someone
- sich etwas leisten = to treat oneself to
something
sich etwas nicht leisten können = to not
be able to afford something

die **Leistung**, *plural* Leistungen
- = achievement
- = performance
- = payment

leiten *verb*
- = to lead
- (*if it's a business*) = to manage
- = to conduct
- (*if it's traffic*) = to direct

die **Leiter**¹ *plural* Leitern
= ladder

der **Leiter**² *plural* Leiter
- = leader
- = manager
- = director
- (*of a school*) = headmaster

die **Leiterin**, *plural* Leiterinnen
- = leader
- = manageress
- = director
- (*of a school*) = headmistress

die **Leitplanke**, *plural* Leitplanken
= crash barrier

die **Leitung**, *plural* Leitungen
- = direction
- = management
- (*phone*) = line
- = pipe
(*electric*) = lead, = cable
- unter der Leitung von (*of an orchestra*) =
conducted by

das **Leitungswasser**
= tap water

lenken *verb*
- = to steer
- = to guide

das **Lenkrad**, *plural* Lenkräder
= steering wheel

die **Lenkstange**, *plural* Lenkstangen
= handlebars

die **Lenkung**
= steering

lernen *verb*
- = to learn
- = to study

lesen *irregular verb*
= to read

das **Lesezeichen**, *plural* Lesezeichen
= bookmark

(das) **Lettland**
= Latvia

letzte ▶letzter

der/die/das **Letzte**, *plural* Letzten
der/die Letzte = the last (one)
das Letzte =the last (thing)
sie kam als Letzte = she arrived last

letztens *adverb*
- = lastly
- = recently

letzter/letzte/letztes *adjective*
- = last
zum letzten Mal = for the last time.
in letzter Zeit = recently
- = latest

leuchten *verb*
= to shine

der **Leuchter**, *plural* Leuchter
= candlestick

der **Leuchtturm**, *plural* Leuchttürme
= lighthouse

leugnen *verb*
= to deny

Leute (*plural*)
= people

das **Lexikon**, *plural* Lexika
- = encyclopaedia
- = dictionary

das **Licht**, *plural* Lichter
= light

das **Lichtbild**, *plural* Lichtbilder
= photograph

die **Lichtung**, *plural* Lichtungen
= clearing

das **Lid**, *plural* Lider
= (eye)lid

der **Lidschatten**, *plural* Lidschatten
= eye shadow

lieb *adjective*
- = dear
sein liebstes Spielzeug = his favourite
toy
es wäre mir lieber = I should prefer it
- = nice, = good

- jemanden lieb haben = to be fond of somebody

die **Liebe**, *plural* Lieben
   = love

lieben *verb*
   = to love

lieber *adverb*
- = rather
- = better

liebevoll *adjective*
   = loving

der **Liebling**, *plural* Lieblinge
- = darling
- = favourite, = favorite

Lieblings- *prefix*
   = favourite, = favorite

liebste ▶ liebster

liebsten *adverb*
   am liebsten = best (of all)

liebster/liebste/liebstes *adjective*
- = dearest
- = favourite, = favorite

das **Lied**, *plural* Lieder
   = song

lief ▶ laufen

liefern *verb*
- = to deliver
- = to supply

die **Lieferung**, *plural* Lieferungen
   = delivery

der **Lieferwagen**, *plural* Lieferwagen
   = (delivery) van

liegen *irregular verb*
- = to lie
- = to be situated, = to be
- liegen bleiben = to stay, = to be left
  (*forgotten*) = to be left behind
  die Arbeit ist liegen geblieben =the job
  was left undone
- liegen lassen = to leave
  alles stehen und liegen lassen = to drop
  everything
- es liegt mir nicht = it doesn't suit me
- an etwas liegen = to be due to something
  das liegt an ihm = it's up to him

der **Liegestuhl**, *plural* Liegestühle
   = deckchair

ließ ▶ lassen

liest ▶ lesen

der **Lift**, *plural* Lifte *or* Lifts
   = lift, = elevator

lila *adjective*
   = mauve
   (*darker*) = purple

die **Limo**, *plural* Limos *or* Limo
   ▶ Limonade

die **Limonade**, *plural* Limonaden
- = lemonade
- = fizzy drink

lindern *verb*
   = to relieve
   = to calm

das **Lineal**, *plural* Lineale
   = ruler

die **Linie**, *plural* Linien
- = line
- (*of a bus*) = route
  Linie 7 = number 7

linker/linke/linkes *adjective*
- = left
- = left-wing

links *adverb*
- = on the left
  nach links = left
- = inside out

die **Linse**, *plural* Linsen
- = lens
- = lentil

die **Lippe**, *plural* Lippen
   = lip

der **Lippenstift**, *plural* Lippenstifte
   = lipstick

die **List**, *plural* Listen
- = cunning
- = trick

die **Liste**, *plural* Listen
   = list

listig *adjective*
   = cunning

(das) **Litauen**
   = Lithuania

der **Liter**, *plural* Liter
   = litre, = liter

die **Literatur**, *plural* Literaturen
   = literature

der **Lkw**, *plural* Lkws
   (*Lastkraftwagen*) = lorry, = truck

das **Lob**
   = praise

loben *verb*
   = to praise

das **Loch**, *plural* Löcher
   = hole

die **Locke**, *plural* Locken
   = curl

locken *verb*
- = to tempt
- = to curl

L

locker *adjective*
* = loose
* (*of a rope*) = slack

lockig *adjective*
= curly

der **Löffel**, *plural* Löffel
* = spoon
* = spoonful

logisch *adjective*
= logical

der **Lohn**, *plural* Löhne
* = wages, = pay
* = reward

lohnen: sich lohnen *verb*
= to be worth it

das **Lokal**, *plural* Lokale
= bar
= restaurant

die **Lokomotive**, *plural* Lokomotiven
= locomotive, = engine

los
1 *adjective*
* es ist viel los = there is a lot going on
  was ist mit ihm los? = what's up with
  him?
* etwas los sein = to be rid of something
2 *adverb*
  los! = go on!
  Achtung, fertig, los! = ready, steady, go!

das **Los**, *plural* Lose
* = lot
* (*in a lottery*) = ticket
  das große Los ziehen = to hit the jackpot

löschen *verb*
* = to put out, = to extinguish
* seinen Durst löschen = to quench one's
  thirst
* = to cancel, = to delete

lose *adjective*
= loose

lösen *verb*
* = to undo
* = to solve
* eine Fahrkarte lösen = to buy a ticket
* sich lösen = to come undone, (*of a puzzle
  or mystery*) = to be solved

los|fahren *irregular verb* (**!** *sein*)
* = to set off
* = to drive off

los|gehen *irregular verb* (**!** *sein*)
* = to set off, = to start
* (*of a button*) = to come off
* (*of a bomb*) = to go off

los|lassen *irregular verb*
* = to let go of, = to release

* = to let go

die **Lösung**, *plural* Lösungen
= solution

los|werden *irregular verb* (**!** *sein*)
= to get rid of

die **Lotterie**, *plural* Lotterien
= lottery

das **Lotto**, *plural* Lottos
= (national) lottery

der **Löwe**, *plural* Löwen
* = lion
* = Leo

die **Löwin**, *plural* Löwinnen
= lioness

die **Lücke**, *plural* Lücken
= gap

die **Luft**, *plural* Lüfte
= air
in die Luft gehen✖ = to blow one's top

der **Luftballon**, *plural* Luftballons
= balloon

luftdicht *adjective*
= airtight

lüften *verb*
* = to air
* ein Geheimnis lüften = to reveal a secret

die **Luftmatratze**, *plural* Luftmatratzen
= air-bed

die **Luftpost**
= airmail

die **Lüftung**
= ventilation

die **Luftwaffe**
= air force

die **Lüge**, *plural* Lügen
= lie

lügen *irregular verb*
= to lie

der **Lügner**, *plural* Lügner
= liar

die **Lügnerin**, *plural* Lügnerinnen
= liar

die **Lunge**, *plural* Lungen
= lungs

die **Lungenentzündung**
= pneumonia

die **Lupe**, *plural* Lupen
= magnifying glass

die **Lust**
* = pleasure
* = desire
  Lust haben, etwas zu tun = to feel like
  doing something

lustig adjective
* = jolly
* = funny
* sich über jemanden lustig machen = to make fun of someone

lutschen verb
= to suck

der **Lutscher**, plural Lutscher
= lollipop

der **Luxus**
= luxury

machen verb
* = to make
* = to do
  was macht die Arbeit? = how is work?
  das macht nichts = it doesn't matter
* sich an die Arbeit machen = to get down to work

die **Macht**, plural Mächte
= power

das **Mädchen**, plural Mädchen
* = girl
* = maid

der **Mädchenname**, plural Mädchennamen
= maiden name

die **Made**, plural Maden
= maggot

mag ▶mögen

das **Magazin**, plural Magazine
= magazine

der **Magen**, plural Mägen
= stomach

mager adjective
* = thin
* = lean
* = low-fat

die **Magie**
= magic

magst ▶mögen

mähen verb
= to mow

mahlen irregular verb
= to grind

die **Mahlzeit**, plural Mahlzeiten
= meal
Mahlzeit! = enjoy your meal!

die **Mahnung**, plural Mahnungen
* = reminder
* = admonition

der **Mai**
= May

der **Mais**
= maize, = corn

der **Major**, plural Majore
= major

der **Makler**, plural Makler
= estate agent

mal adverb
* (in maths) = times
* (with measurements) = by
* (in the future) = sometime
* schon mal = once before
* nicht mal = not even
* hört mal! = listen!

das **Mal**, plural Male
* = time
  nächstes Mal = next time
* = mark
* = mole

malen verb
= to paint

der **Maler**, plural Maler
= painter

die **Malerei**
= painting

die **Malerin**, plural Malerinnen
= painter

man pronoun
* = one, = you
* = they, = people
  man hat mir gesagt = I was told

mancher/manche/manches
1 adjective = many a, (plural) = some
2 pronoun = many a person, (plural) = some (people)

manchmal adverb
= sometimes

die **Mandel**, plural Mandeln
* = almond
* = tonsil

der **Mangel**, plural Mängel
* = lack, = shortage
* = defect

mangelhaft adjective
* = faulty, = defective
* (school mark) = unsatisfactory

Manieren (plural)
= manners

der **Mann**, plural Männer
* = man
* = husband

M

das **Männchen**, *plural* Männchen
= male

das **Mannequin**, *plural* Mannequins
= model

männlich *adjective*
* = male
* = manly
* (*in grammar*) = masculine

die **Mannschaft**, *plural* Mannschaften
* = team
* = crew

die **Manschette**, *plural* Manschetten
= cuff

der **Mantel**, *plural* Mäntel
= coat

die **Mappe**, *plural* Mappen
* = folder
* = briefcase
* (*satchel*) = bag

das **Märchen**, *plural* Märchen
= fairy tale

der **Marienkäfer**, *plural* Marienkäfer
= ladybird

die **Marine**, *plural* Marinen
= navy

die **Mark**, *plural* Mark
= mark

die **Marke**, *plural* Marken
* = make, = brand
* = tag
* = stamp
* = coupon

das **Markenzeichen**, *plural*
Markenzeichen
= trade mark

markieren *verb*
* = to mark
* = to fake

der **Markt**, *plural* Märkte
= market

die **Marmelade**, *plural* Marmeladen
= jam

der **Marmor**
= marble

der **Marsch**, *plural* Märsche
= march

der **März**
= March

die **Masche**, *plural* Maschen
= stitch

die **Maschine**, *plural* Maschinen
* = machine

* = plane

Masern (*plural*)
= measles

die **Maske**, *plural* Masken
= mask

das **Maß**, *plural* Maße
* = measure
* = degree

die **Masse**, *plural* Massen
* = mass
  (*of people*) = crowd
* (*in cooking*) = mixture

massenhaft *adverb*
= in huge quantities

massieren *verb*
= to massage

mäßig *adjective*
= moderate

die **Maßnahme**, *plural* Maßnahmen
= measure

der **Maßstab**, *plural* Maßstäbe
* = standard
* = scale

der **Mast**, *plural* Masten
* = mast
* = pole
  = pylon

das **Material**, *plural* Materialien
= material
= materials

die **Mathe✱**
= maths, = math

die **Mathematik**
= mathematics

die **Matratze**, *plural* Matratzen
= mattress

der **Matrose**, *plural* Matrosen
= sailor

matt *adjective*
* = weak
* = matt
* (*in chess*) matt! = checkmate!

die **Matte**, *plural* Matten
= mat

die **Mauer**, *plural* Mauern
= wall

das **Maul**, *plural* Mäuler
= mouth

der **Maulkorb**, *plural* Maulkörbe
= muzzle

das **Maultier**, *plural* Maultiere
= mule

der **Maulwurf**, *plural* Maulwürfe
= mole

✱ in informal situations

der **Maurer**, *plural* Maurer
= bricklayer

die **Maus**, *plural* Mäuse
= mouse

mechanisch *adjective*
= mechanical

meckern *verb*
* = to bleat
* = to grumble

die **Medaille**, *plural* Medaillen
= medal

Medien (*plural*)
= media

das **Medikament**, *plural* Medikamente
= medicine

die **Medizin**, *plural* Medizinen
= medicine

medizinisch *adjective*
* = medical
* = medicinal

das **Meer**, *plural* Meere
= sea

Meeresfrüchte (*plural*)
= seafood

das **Mehl**
= flour

mehr *adverb*
= more
nie mehr = never again

mehrere *pronoun*
= several

mehrfach
1 *adjective*
* = multiple
* = repeated
2 *adverb* = several times

die **Mehrheit**, *plural* Mehrheiten
= majority

mehrmals *adverb*
= several times

die **Mehrwertsteuer**
= value added tax

die **Mehrzahl**, *plural* Mehrzahlen
* = majority
* = plural

meiden *irregular verb*
= to avoid

die **Meile**, *plural* Meilen
= mile

mein *adjective*
= my

meine ▶meiner

meinen *verb*
* = to think
* = to mean
* = to say

meiner/meine/meins *pronoun*
= mine

meinetwegen *adverb*
* = for my sake
* = because of me
* = as far as I'm concerned

meins ▶meiner

die **Meinung**, *plural* Meinungen
= opinion

meist *adverb*
= mostly

der/die/das **meiste**
= most

meistens *adverb*
= mostly

der **Meister**, *plural* Meister
* = master
* = champion

die **Meisterin**, *plural* Meisterinnen
= champion

die **Meisterschaft**, *plural* Meisterschaften
* = championship
* = mastery

melden *verb*
* = to report
* = to register
* = to announce
* sich melden = to report, (*on the phone*) = to answer
sich bei jemandem melden = to get in touch with someone

die **Melodie**, *plural* Melodien
= melody, = tune

die **Melone**, *plural* Melonen
* = melon
* (*hat*) = bowler

die **Menge**, *plural* Mengen
* = quantity, = amount
* = crowd
* (*in maths*) = set

der **Mensch**, *plural* Menschen
= human being
= person
kein Mensch = nobody
die Menschen = people

menschenleer *adjective*
= deserted

die **Menschheit**
= mankind

menschlich *adjective*
* = human
* = humane

die **Mentalität**, *plural* Mentalitäten
= mentality

M

das **Menü**, *plural* Menüs
- = menu
- = set meal

merken *verb*
- = to notice
- sich etwas merken = to remember something

das **Merkmal**, *plural* Merkmale
= feature

merkwürdig *adjective*
= strange, = odd

die **Messe**, *plural* Messen
- = mass
- = trade fair

messen *irregular verb*
- = to measure
  Fieber messen = to take someone's temperature
- sich mit jemandem messen können = to be as good as someone

das **Messer**, *plural* Messer
= knife

das **Messing**
= brass

das **Metall**, *plural* Metalle
= metal

der **Meter**, *plural* Meter
= metre, = meter

das **Metermaß**, *plural* Metermaße
= tape measure
= metre rule, = meter rule

die **Methode**, *plural* Methoden
= method

der **Metzger**, *plural* Metzger
= butcher

die **Metzgerei**, *plural* Metzgereien
= butcher's (shop)

meutern *verb*
- = to mutiny
- = to grumble

miauen *verb*
= to miaow, = to mew

mich *pronoun*
- = me
- (*reflexive*) = myself

mies✱ *adjective*
= lousy

die **Miete**, *plural* Mieten
- = rent
  zur Miete wohnen = to live in rented accommodation
- = hire charge

mieten *verb*
- = to rent
- = to hire

der **Mietwagen**, *plural* Mietwagen
= hire car

das **Mikrofon**, *plural* Mikrofone
= microphone

das **Mikroskop**, *plural* Mikroskope
= microscope

der **Mikrowellenherd**, *plural* Mikrowellenherde
= microwave oven

die **Milch**
= milk

mild *adjective*
= mild

das **Militär**
= army

die **Milliarde**, *plural* Milliarden
(*thousand million*) = billion

die **Million**, *plural* Millionen
= million

der **Millionär**, *plural* Millionäre
= millionaire

die **Minderheit**, *plural* Minderheiten
= minority

minderjährig *adjective*
= under age

mindestens *adverb*
= at least

mindester/mindeste/mindestes *adjective*
= least

die **Mine**, *plural* Minen
- = mine
- (*in a pencil*) = lead
  (*for a ballpoint*) = refill

der **Minister**, *plural* Minister
= minister

die **Ministerin**, *plural* Ministerinnen
= minister

das **Ministerium**, *plural* Ministerien
= ministry, = department

die **Minute**, *plural* Minuten
= minute

mir *pronoun*
- = (to) me
- (*reflexive*) = myself

mischen *verb*
- = to mix
- (*when playing cards*) = to shuffle
- sich mischen = to mix

✱ in informal situations   ⓄⓁⒹ = old spelling

die **Mischung**, *plural* Mischungen
    = mixture
    = blend

miserabel✶ *adjective*
    = hopeless, = dreadful

missbrauchen
    (**mißbrauchen**ⓞⓛⓓ) *verb*
    = to abuse

der **Misserfolg** (**Mißerfolg**ⓞⓛⓓ), *plural*
    Misserfolge
    = failure

missglücken (**mißglücken**ⓞⓛⓓ)
    verb (! *sein*)
    = to fail

misshandeln (**mißhandeln**ⓞⓛⓓ)
    verb
    = to ill-treat

misslingen (**mißlingen**ⓞⓛⓓ)
    irregular verb (! *sein*)
    = to fail
    es misslang ihm = he failed

misstrauen (**mißtrauen**ⓞⓛⓓ) *verb*
    = to mistrust, = to distrust

das **Missverständnis**
    (**Mißverständnis**ⓞⓛⓓ), *plural*
    Missverständnisse
    = misunderstanding

der **Mist**
    * = manure, = dung
    * so ein Mist!✶ = rubbish!

mit
    1 *preposition* (+ *dative*) = with
    mit fünf Jahren = at the age of five
    mit der Bahn fahren = to go by train
    mit lauter Stimme = in a loud voice
    2 *adverb* = too, = as well
    er war nicht mit dabei = he wasn't there

der **Mitarbeiter**, *plural* Mitarbeiter
    * = colleague
    * = employee

die **Mitarbeiterin**, *plural* Mitarbeiterinnen
    * = colleague
    * = employee

mit|bringen *irregular verb*
    = to bring (along)

miteinander *adverb*
    = with each other, = with one another

mit|fahren *irregular verb* (! *sein*)
    = to go along
    mit jemandem mitfahren = to go with
        someone, = to get a lift with someone

mit|gehen *irregular verb* (! *sein*)
    mit jemandem mitgehen = to go with
        someone

das **Mitglied**, *plural* Mitglieder
    = member

mit|halten *irregular verb*
    = to keep up

mit|kommen *irregular verb* (! *sein*)
    * = to come too
    * = to keep up

das **Mitleid**
    = pity

mit|machen *verb*
    * = to join in
    * = to take part in
    (*experience*) = to go through

mit|nehmen *irregular verb*
    = to take (along)
    zum Mitnehmen = to take away, = to go

der **Mitschüler**, *plural* Mitschüler
    = fellow pupil

die **Mitschülerin**, *plural* Mitschülerinnen
    = fellow pupil

der **Mittag**, *plural* Mittage
    * = midday
    * = lunch(-break)

das **Mittagessen**, *plural* Mittagessen
    = lunch

mittags *adverb*
    = at midday

die **Mitte**, *plural* Mitten
    = middle
    = centre

die **Mitteilung**, *plural* Mitteilungen
    = announcement

das **Mittel**, *plural* Mittel
    * = means
    * ein Mittel gegen Husten = a cough
        remedy

das **Mittelalter**
    = Middle Ages

mittelmäßig *adjective*
    = mediocre

das **Mittelmeer**
    = Mediterranean (Sea)

der **Mittelpunkt**, *plural* Mittelpunkte
    = centre, = center
    im Mittelpunkt stehen = to be the centre
        of attention

der **Mittelstand**
    = middle class

mitten *adverb*
    = in the middle of
    mitten durch = right through

die **Mitternacht**
    = midnight

mittlerer/mittlere/mittleres
    adjective
    * = middle

M

- *(in quality, size)* = medium
- = average

mittlerweile *adverb*
- = meanwhile
- = by now

der **Mittwoch**
= Wednesday

mittwochs *adverb*
= on Wednesdays

Möbel *(plural)*
= furniture

der **Möbelwagen**, *plural* Möbelwagen
= removal van

das **Mobiltelefon**, *plural* Mobiltelefone
= mobile phone

möbliert *adjective*
= furnished

mochte, mochten, mochtest, mochtet ▶mögen

möchte ▶mögen

die **Mode**, *plural* Moden
= fashion

der **Moderator**, *plural* Moderatoren
(TV) = presenter

modisch *adjective*
= fashionable

mogeln *verb*
= to cheat

mögen *irregular verb*
- = to like
  ich möchte lieber Tee = I would prefer tea
  ich möchte gern wissen = I would like to know
  möchtest du nach Hause? = do you want to go home?
  ich mag nicht mehr = I've had enough
- das mag sein = maybe
  wer mag das sein? = whoever can it be?

möglich *adjective*
= possible
alles Mögliche = all sorts of things

die **Möglichkeit**, *plural* Möglichkeiten
= possibility

möglichst *adverb*
= if possible
möglichst früh = as early as possible

die **Möhre**, *plural* Möhren
= carrot

der **Monat**, *plural* Monate
= month

monatlich
1 *adjective* = monthly

2 *adverb* = monthly, = every month

der **Mond**, *plural* Monde
= moon

der **Montag**
= Monday

montags *adverb*
= on Mondays

das **Moos**, *plural* Moose
= moss

die **Moral**
- = moral
- = morals

moralisch *adjective*
= moral

der **Mord**, *plural* Morde
= murder

der **Mörder**, *plural* Mörder
= murderer

die **Mörderin**, *plural* Mörderinnen
= murderess

morgen *adverb*
= tomorrow
morgen in einer Woche = a week tomorrow
bis morgen! = see you tomorrow!

der **Morgen**, *plural* Morgen
= morning
heute Morgen = this morning

morgens *adverb*
= in the morning

die **Mosel**
= Moselle

der **Moslem**, *plural* Moslems
= Muslim

moslemisch *adjective*
= Muslim

die **Moslime**, *plural* Moslimen
= Muslim

das **Motiv**, *plural* Motive
- = motive
- = motif

der **Motor**, *plural* Motoren
= engine, = motor

das **Motorrad**, *plural* Motorräder
= motorcycle, = motorbike

die **Motte**, *plural* Motten
= moth

die **Möwe**, *plural* Möwen
= seagull

die **Mücke**, *plural* Mücken
- = gnat, = midge
- = mosquito

müde *adjective*
= tired

die **Müdigkeit**
= tiredness

die **Mühe**, *plural* Mühen
= effort
= trouble

die **Mühle**, *plural* Mühlen
= mill
(*for coffee*) = grinder

mühsam *adjective*
= laborious

der **Müll**
= rubbish, = garbage

die **Mülltonne**, *plural* Mülltonnen
= dustbin, = garbage can

die **Mumie**, *plural* Mumien
= mummy

(das) **München**
= Munich

der **Mund**, *plural* Münder
= mouth
halt den Mund!✗ = shut up!

die **Mundharmonika**, *plural*
Mundharmonikas
= mouth organ

mündlich *adjective*
= oral

die **Mündung**, *plural* Mündungen
= mouth

die **Münze**, *plural* Münzen
= coin

murmeln *verb*
* = to mumble
* = to murmur

murren *verb*
= to grumble

mürrisch *adjective*
= grumpy

die **Muschel**, *plural* Muscheln
* = mussel
* = (sea) shell

das **Museum**, *plural* Museen
= museum

die **Musik**
= music

der **Musiker**, *plural* Musiker
= musician

die **Musikerin**, *plural* Musikerinnen
= musician

der **Muskel**, *plural* Muskeln
= muscle

muss (mußⓞⓛⓓ**)** ▶müssen

müssen *irregular verb*
= to have to
er muss es tun = he has (got) to do it,
= he must do it
muss das sein? = is that necessary?
sie muss gleich hier sein = she will be
here at any moment

das **Muster**, *plural* Muster
* = pattern
* = sample
* = model

der **Mut**
= courage
jemandem Mut machen = to encourage
someone

mutig *adjective*
= courageous, = brave

die **Mutter**[1] *plural* Mütter
= mother

die **Mutter**[2] *plural* Muttern
= nut

die **Muttersprache**, *plural*
Muttersprachen
= mother tongue, = native language

der **Muttertag**, *plural* Muttertage
= Mother's Day

die **Mutti**, *plural* Muttis
= mum, = mom

die **Mütze**, *plural* Mützen
= cap

der **Mythos**, *plural* Mythen
= myth

N

Nn

na *interjection*
= well
na und? = so what?

der **Nabel**, *plural* Nabel
= navel

nach
1 *preposition* (+ *dative*)
* = to
nach Hause gehen = to go home
nach oben = upwards, (*indoors*) =
upstairs
nach rechts abbiegen = to turn right
* = after
zehn nach zwei = ten past two
* = according to
meiner Meinung nach = in my opinion

2 *adverb*
nach und nach = bit by bit, = gradually

nach|ahmen *verb*
= to imitate, = to copy

der **Nachbar**, *plural* Nachbarn
= neighbour, = neighbor

die **Nachbarin**, *plural* Nachbarinnen
= neighbour, = neighbor

nachdem *conjunction*
= after
je nachdem = it depends, = depending on

nach|denken *irregular verb*
= to think

nachdenklich *adjective*
= thoughtful

nacheinander *adverb*
= one after the other

die **Nachfrage**, *plural* Nachfragen
= demand

nach|geben *irregular verb*
= to give in

nach|gehen *irregular verb* (**!** *sein*)
• = to follow
einer Sache nachgehen = to look into a
matter
• (*lose time*) = to be slow

nachher *adverb*
= afterwards, = later
bis nachher! = see you later!

nach|kommen *irregular verb* (**!** *sein*)
• = to follow, = to come later
• einem Versprechen nachkommen = to
carry out a promise

nach|lassen *irregular verb*
• = to let up, = to ease
• (*of health*) = to deteriorate
• etwas vom Preis nachlassen = to take
something off the price

nachlässig *adjective*
= careless

nach|machen *verb*
= to copy, = to imitate

der **Nachmittag**, *plural* Nachmittage
= afternoon

nachmittags *adverb*
= in the afternoon

die **Nachnahme**
per Nachnahme = cash on delivery

der **Nachname**, *plural* Nachnamen
= surname

nach|prüfen *verb*
= to check

die **Nachricht**, *plural* Nachrichten
= news
eine Nachricht hinterlassen = to leave a
message

der **Nachrichtensprecher**, *plural*
Nachrichtensprecher
= newsreader

nach|schlagen *irregular verb*
= to look up

nach|sehen *irregular verb*
• = to check
• = to look up

nach|sitzen *irregular verb*
= to be in detention
nachsitzen müssen = to have detention

nächste ▶nächster

der/die/das **Nächste**, *plural* Nächsten
= the next one
der Nächste, bitte! = next please
als Nächstes = next

nächstens *adverb*
= shortly

nächster/nächste/nächstes
adjective
• = next
• = nearest
in nächster Nähe = close by

die **Nacht**, *plural* Nächte
= night

der **Nachteil**, *plural* Nachteile
= disadvantage

der **Nachtfalter**, *plural* Nachtfalter
= moth

das **Nachthemd**, *plural* Nachthemden
= nightdress
= nightshirt

die **Nachtigall**, *plural* Nachtigallen
= nightingale

der **Nachtisch**, *plural* Nachtische
= dessert, = sweet

nachträglich
1 *adjective*
• = subsequent
• = belated
2 *adverb*
• = later, = afterwards
• = belatedly

nachts *adverb*
= at night
um drei Uhr nachts = at 3 o'clock in the
morning

der **Nacken**, *plural* Nacken
= neck

nackt *adjective*
= naked
= bare

✖ in informal situations   ⓄⓁⒹ = old spelling

die **Nadel**, *plural* Nadeln
* = needle
* = pin

der **Nagel**, *plural* Nägel
= nail

nageln *verb*
= to nail

nah✶ ▶nahe

nahe
1 *adjective*
* = near, = nearby
* = close
der Nahe Osten = the Middle East
2 *adverb* = closely
nahe bei = close to
nahe gelegen = close by
3 *preposition* (+ *dative*)
= near, = close to

die **Nähe**
= closeness, = proximity
in der Nähe = nearby

nähen *verb*
* = to sew
* (*when closing a wound*) = to stitch

näher
1 *adjective*
* = closer
* (*in distance*) = shorter
* nähere Einzelheiten = further details
2 *adverb*
= closer, = more closely

nähern: sich nähern *verb*
= to approach

das **Nähgarn**
= cotton

nahm ▶nehmen

die **Nahrung**
= food

die **Naht**, *plural* Nähte
= seam

der **Name**, *plural* Namen
= name

nämlich *adverb*
* = namely
* = because

nannte ▶nennen

die **Narbe**, *plural* Narben
= scar

die **Nase**, *plural* Nasen
= nose
die Nase voll haben✶ = to have had
enough

das **Nasenloch**, *plural* Nasenlöcher
= nostril

das **Nashorn**, *plural* Nashörner
= rhinoceros

nass (naß⑩) *adjective*
= wet

die **Nation**, *plural* Nationen
= nation

die **Nationalhymne**, *plural*
Nationalhymnen
= national anthem

die **Nationalität**, *plural* Nationalitäten
= nationality

die **Natur**, *plural* Naturen
= nature

natürlich
1 *adjective* = natural
2 *adverb* = naturally, = of course

das **Naturschutzgebiet**, *plural*
Naturschutzgebiete
= nature reserve

die **Naturwissenschaft**, *plural*
Naturwissenschaften
= natural science

der **Nebel**, *plural* Nebel
= fog, = mist

neben *preposition* (+ *dative* or
accusative)
* = next to, = beside
* = apart from

nebenan *adverb*
= next door

nebenbei *adverb*
* = in addition
* = by the way, = in passing

nebensächlich
= trivial, = unimportant

neblig *adjective*
= foggy, = misty

necken *verb*
= to tease

der **Neffe**, *plural* Neffen
= nephew

negativ *adjective*
= negative

nehmen *irregular verb*
* = to take
* sich etwas nehmen = to take something,
(*take food*) = to help oneself to
something

der **Neid**
= envy, = jealousy

neidisch *adjective*
= envious, = jealous

nein *adverb*
= no

die **Nelke**, *plural* Nelken
= carnation

N

nennen *irregular verb*
* = to call
* sein Name wurde nicht genannt = his name was not mentioned
* sich nennen = to be called, = to call oneself

der **Nerv**, *plural* Nerven
= nerve
er geht mir auf die Nerven = he gets on my nerves

nervös *adjective*
= nervous

die **Nessel**, *plural* Nesseln
= nettle

das **Nest**, *plural* Nester
* = nest
* (*village*) = little place

nett *adjective*
= nice

netto *adverb*
= net

das **Netz**, *plural* Netze
* = net
* = network
* (*of a spider*) = web

neu
1 *adjective* = new
die neueste Mode = the latest fashion
das ist mir neu = that's news to me
2 *adverb* = newly
es ist neu eingetroffen = it has just come in
etwas neu schreiben = to rewrite something

neuerdings *adverb*
= recently

die **Neugier**
= curiosity

neugierig *adjective*
= curious, = inquisitive

die **Neuigkeit**, *plural* Neuigkeiten
= piece of news
Neuigkeiten = news

das **Neujahr**
= New Year, = New Year's Day

neulich *adverb*
= recently, = the other day

neun *adjective*
= nine

neunter/neunte/neuntes *adjective*
= ninth

neunzehn *adjective*
= nineteen

neunzig *adjective*
= ninety

(das) **Neuseeland**
= New Zealand

nicht *adverb*
= not
nicht wahr? = isn't he/she/it?
du magst das, nicht (wahr)? = you like that, don't you?
gar nicht = not at all
nicht mehr = no more
bitte nicht = please don't

die **Nichte**, *plural* Nichten
= niece

nichts *pronoun*
= nothing

nicken *verb*
= to nod

nie *adverb*
= never

nieder
1 *adjective* = low
2 *adverb* = down

die **Niederlage**, *plural* Niederlagen
= defeat

die **Niederlande** (*plural*)
= the Netherlands

niedlich *adjective*
= sweet, = cute

niedrig *adjective*
= low

niemals *adverb*
= never

niemand *pronoun*
= no one, = nobody

die **Niere**, *plural* Nieren
= kidney

niesen *verb*
= to sneeze

das **Nilpferd**, *plural* Nilpferde
= hippopotamus

nimmt ▶nehmen

nirgends *adverb*
= nowhere

noch
1 *adverb*
* = still
noch nicht = not yet
* = just
gerade noch = only just
* = else
wer war noch da? = who else was there?
* = even
noch größer = even bigger

• (*other uses*)
noch einmal = again
noch ein Bier = another beer
2 *conjunction* = nor
weder . . . noch = neither . . . nor

nochmals *adverb*
= again

die **Nonne**, *plural* Nonnen
= nun

der **Norden**
= north

nördlich *adjective*
• = northern
• = northerly

nörgeln *verb*
= to grumble

normalerweise *adverb*
= normally

(das) **Norwegen**
= Norway

norwegisch *adjective*
= Norwegian

die **Not**, *plural* Nöte
• = need
zur Not = if need be
• = distress, = hardship

der **Notausgang**, *plural* Notausgänge
= emergency exit

der **Notdienst**
Notdienst haben = to be on call

die **Note**, *plural* Noten
• = note
Noten lesen = to read music
• = mark, = grade

der **Notfall**, *plural* Notfälle
= emergency

notfalls *adverb*
= if need be

die **Notfallstation**, *plural* Notfallstationen
= accident and emergency department

notieren *verb*
• = to note down
• sich etwas notieren = to make a note of
something

nötig
1 *adjective* = necessary
2 *adverb* = urgently

die **Notiz**, *plural* Notizen
• = note
keine Notiz von etwas nehmen = to take
no notice of something
• (*in a newspaper*) = report, = item

die **Notlage**, *plural* Notlagen
= crisis

der **Notruf**, *plural* Notrufe

• = emergency call
• = emergency number

notwendig *adjective*
= necessary

die **Notwendigkeit**, *plural*
Notwendigkeiten
= necessity

der **November**
= November

nüchtern *adjective*
• = sober
• auf nüchternen Magen = on an empty
stomach

Nudeln (*plural*)
• = noodles
• = pasta

null *adjective*
• = nought, = zero
• (*in sport*) = nil
(*in tennis*) = love

die **Null**, *plural* Nullen
• = nought, = zero
• (*person*) = failure

die **Nummer**, *plural* Nummern
• = number
• (*periodical*) = issue
• (*in a circus*) = act
• (*of clothing*) = size

nummerieren *verb*
= to number

das **Nummernschild**, *plural*
Nummernschilder
= number plate, = license plate

nun *adverb*
= now

nur *adverb*
= only
er soll es nur versuchen! = just let him
try!

(das) **Nürnberg**
= Nuremberg

die **Nuss** (**Nuß**ⓄⓁⒹ), *plural* Nüsse
= nut

nutzen *verb*
• = to use
• = to be useful

der **Nutzen**
• = benefit
• = profit

nützen *verb*
• = to be useful
nichts nützen = to be no use
• = to use

nützlich *adjective*
= useful

nutzlos *adjective*
= useless

Oo

---

ob *conjunction*
= whether
ob sie wohl krank ist? = I wonder if she is
ill
und ob! = you bet!

der/die **Obdachlose**, *plural* Obdachlosen
= homeless person

oben *adverb*
* = up
nach oben = up
von oben = from above, (*indoors*) = from
upstairs
* = on top
oben auf = on top of
* = at the top
* = upstairs
* (*in text*) = above
oben genannt = above-mentioned

der **Ober**, *plural* Ober
= waiter

oberer/obere/oberes *adjective*
= upper, = top

die **Oberfläche**, *plural* Oberflächen
= surface

oberflächlich *adjective*
= superficial

das **Oberhaupt**, *plural* Oberhäupter
= head

das **Oberhemd**, *plural* Oberhemden
= shirt

der **Oberschenkel**, *plural* Oberschenkel
= thigh

die **Oberschule**, *plural* Oberschulen
= secondary school

das **Objektiv**, *plural* Objektive
= lens

das **Obst**
= fruit

obszön *adjective*
= obscene

obwohl *conjunction*
= although, = though

der **Ochse**, *plural* Ochsen
= ox

öde *adjective*
* = desolate
* = dreary

oder *conjunction*
= or
sie ist doch hier, oder? = she is here, isn't
she?

der **Ofen**, *plural* Öfen
* = oven
* = stove
* = heater

offen
1 *adjective*
* = open
ein Tag der offenen Tür = an open day
offen haben = to be open
offen bleiben = to stay open, = to be left
open
* = vacant
* = frank
* (*of a bill*) = outstanding
2 *adverb*
* = openly
* = frankly
offen gesagt = frankly

offenbar *adjective*
= obvious

offenbleiben⊙ʟᴅ ▶ offen

offensichtlich *adjective*
= obvious

öffentlich *adjective*
= public
der öffentliche Dienst = the civil
service

die **Öffentlichkeit**
= public
in aller Öffentlichkeit = in public

offiziell *adjective*
= official

der **Offizier**, *plural* Offiziere
= officer

öffnen *verb*
* = to open
* sich öffnen = to open

die **Öffnung**, *plural* Öffnungen
= opening

oft *adverb*
= often

öfter *adverb*
= quite often

öfters* *adverb*
= quite often

---

ohne
1 *preposition* (+ *accusative*) = without
ohne weiteres = easily, = readily
ohne mich! = count me out!
2 *conjunction* = without

die **Ohnmacht**, *plural* Ohnmachten
• = faint
in Ohnmacht fallen = to faint
• = powerlessness

ohnmächtig *adjective*
• = unconscious
ohnmächtig werden = to faint
• = powerless

das **Ohr**, *plural* Ohren
= ear

der **Ohrring**, *plural* Ohrringe
= earring

oje *interjection*
= oh dear!

der **Ökoladen**, *plural* Ökoläden
= health-food shop, = health-food store

die **Ökologie**
= ecology

der **Oktober**
= October

das **Öl**, *plural* Öle
= oil

die **Olympiade**, *plural* Olympiaden
= Olympic Games, = Olympics

die **Oma**, *plural* Omas
= granny

der **Omnibus**, *plural* Omnibusse
= bus, = coach

der **Onkel**, *plural* Onkel
= uncle

der **Opa**, *plural* Opas
= grandad

die **Oper**, *plural* Opern
= opera

die **Operation**, *plural* Operationen
= operation

operieren *verb*
• = to operate
• = to operate on

das **Opfer**, *plural* Opfer
• = sacrifice
• = victim

der **Optiker**, *plural* Optiker
= optician

die **Orange**, *plural* Orangen
= orange

das **Orchester**, *plural* Orchester
= orchestra

ordentlich *adjective*
• = tidy
• = respectable
(*of a meal, job*) = proper

ordinär *adjective*
= vulgar, = crude

ordnen *verb*
• = to arrange
• = to put in order

die **Ordnung**
= order
er ist in Ordnung✶ = he's all right

das **Organ**, *plural* Organe
• = organ
• = voice

organisieren *verb*
• = to organize
• organisieren✶ = to get (hold of)

die **Orgel**, *plural* Orgeln
= organ

orientieren: sich orientieren
verb
= to get one's bearings
sich über etwas orientieren = to inform
oneself about something

die **Orientierung**
• = orientation
• die Orientierung verlieren = to lose one's
bearings
• zu Ihrer Orientierung = for your
information

der **Orientierungssinn**
= sense of direction

originell *adjective*
= original

der **Orkan**, *plural* Orkane
= hurricane

der **Ort**, *plural* Orte
• = place
an Ort und Stelle = in the right place,
(*immediately*) = on the spot
• = (small) town

örtlich *adjective*
= local

die **Ortschaft**, *plural* Ortschaften
= village

die **Öse**, *plural* Ösen
= eye

der **Ossi✶**, *plural* Ossis
= East German

der **Osten**
= east

die **Osterglocke**, *plural* Osterglocken
= daffodil

das **Ostern**, *plural* Ostern
= Easter

O

(das) **Österreich**
= Austria

der **Österreicher**, *plural* Österreicher
= Austrian

die **Österreicherin**, *plural*
Österreicherinnen
= Austrian

österreichisch *adjective*
= Austrian

östlich *adjective*
* = eastern
* = easterly

die **Ostsee**
= Baltic (Sea)

der **Ozean**, *plural* Ozeane
= ocean

der *or das* **Ozon**
= ozone

Pp

paar *pronoun*
ein paar = a few

das **Paar**, *plural* Paare
* = pair
* = couple

das **Päckchen**, *plural* Päckchen
= package, small packet

die **Packung**, *plural* Packungen
= packet, pack

der **Pädagoge**, *plural* Pädagogen
* = educationalist
* = teacher

paddeln *verb* (**!** *sein*)
= to paddle

das **Paket**, *plural* Pakete
* = parcel, = package
* = packet

der **Palast**, *plural* Paläste
= palace

die **Palme**, *plural* Palmen
= palm (tree)

die **Pampelmuse**, *plural* Pampelmusen
= grapefruit

die **Panik**, *plural* Paniken
= panic
in Panik geraten = to panic

die **Panne**, *plural* Pannen
* = breakdown
* = mishap

der **Papagei**, *plural* Papageien
= parrot

das **Papier**, *plural* Papiere
= paper

der **Papierkorb**, *plural* Papierkörbe
= waste-paper basket

die **Pappe**, *plural* Pappen
= cardboard

der **Pappkarton**, *plural* Pappkartons
= cardboard box

der **Papst**, *plural* Päpste
= pope

die **Parabolantenne**, *plural*
Parabolantennen
= satellite dish

der **Paragraph**, *plural* Paragraphen
* = section
* = clause

das **Parfüm**, *plural* Parfüms
= perfume

der **Park**, *plural* Parks
= park

parken *verb*
= to park

das **Parkhaus**, *plural* Parkhäuser
= multi-storey car park

der **Parkplatz**, *plural* Parkplätze
* = car park, = parking lot
* = parking space

die **Parkuhr**, *plural* Parkuhren
= parking meter

das **Parkverbot**
'Parkverbot' = 'no parking'

das **Parlament**, *plural* Parlamente
= parliament

die **Partei**, *plural* Parteien
= party
für jemanden Partei ergreifen = to side
with someone

das **Parterre**, *plural* Parterres
= ground floor, (*US*) = first floor

die **Partie**, *plural* Partien
* = part
* = game

der **Partner**, *plural* Partner
= partner

die **Partnerin**, *plural* Partnerinnen
= partner

die **Party**, *plural* Partys
= party

der **Pass** (**Paß**(OLD)), *plural* Pässe
* = passport
* = pass

der **Passagier**, *plural* Passagiere
= passenger

passen *verb*
* = to fit
* = to be suitable
  jemandem passen = to suit someone
  zu etwas passen = to go well with
    something
* (*in sport*) = to pass

passend *adjective*
* = suitable
* = matching

passieren *verb* (**!** *sein*)
= to happen

der **Pate**, *plural* Paten
= godfather

das **Patenkind**, *plural* Patenkinder
= godchild

patent *adjective*
= capable, = clever

der **Patient**, *plural* Patienten
= patient

die **Patientin**, *plural* Patientinnen
= patient

die **Patin**, *plural* Patinnen
= godmother

die **Pause**, *plural* Pausen
* = break
* = pause
* = interval, = intermission

pausenlos *adjective*
= continuous, = nonstop

der **Pazifik**
= the Pacific

das **Pech**
* = bad luck
* = pitch

das **Pedal**, *plural* Pedale
= pedal

peinlich *adjective*
* = embarrassing
* = meticulous

die **Peitsche**, *plural* Peitschen
= whip

peitschen *verb*
* = to whip
* = to lash

der **Pelz**, *plural* Pelze
= fur

der **Pendler**, *plural* Pendler
= commuter

die **Pension**, *plural* Pensionen
* = pension
  in Pension gehen = to retire
* = guesthouse
  bei voller Pension = with full board

das **Pensum**
= quota

per *preposition* (+ *accusative*)
* = by
* = per

perfekt *adjective*
= perfect

die **Perle**, *plural* Perlen
* = pearl
* = bead

die **Person**, *plural* Personen
* = person
* = character

das **Personal**
= personnel, = staff

der **Personalausweis**, *plural*
Personalausweise
= identity card

persönlich *adjective*
= personal

die **Perücke**, *plural* Perücken
= wig

pessimistisch *adjective*
= pessimistic

die **Pest**
= plague

der **Pfad**, *plural* Pfade
= path

der **Pfadfinder**, *plural* Pfadfinder
= (Boy) Scout

die **Pfadfinderin**, *plural* Pfadfinderinnen
= (Girl) Guide

das **Pfand**, *plural* Pfänder
* = pledge
* = forfeit
* (*on a bottle*) = deposit

die **Pfanne**, *plural* Pfannen
= (frying) pan

der **Pfannkuchen**, *plural* Pfannkuchen
= pancake

der **Pfarrer**, *plural* Pfarrer
* = vicar
* = priest

der **Pfau**, *plural* Pfauen
= peacock

der **Pfeffer**, *plural* Pfeffer
= pepper

der **Pfefferkuchen**
= gingerbread

P

die **Pfeife**, *plural* Pfeifen
- = whistle
- = pipe

pfeifen *irregular verb*
= to whistle

der **Pfeil**, *plural* Pfeile
= arrow

der **Pfeiler**, *plural* Pfeiler
- = pillar
- = pier

der **Pfennig**, *plural* Pfennige
= pfennig

das **Pferd**, *plural* Pferde
- = horse
- (*in chess*) = knight

der **Pferdeschwanz**, *plural*
Pferdeschwänze
= ponytail

pfiff ▶pfeifen

das **Pfingsten**, *plural* Pfingsten
= Whitsun

der **Pfirsich**, *plural* Pfirsiche
= peach

die **Pflanze**, *plural* Pflanzen
= plant

pflanzen *verb*
= to plant

das **Pflaster**, *plural* Pflaster
- = pavement, = surface
- = plaster

die **Pflaume**, *plural* Pflaumen
= plum

die **Pflege**
= care
(*in hospital*) = nursing

Pflegeeltern (*plural*)
= foster parents

das **Pflegeheim**, *plural* Pflegeheime
= nursing home

pflegeleicht *adjective*
= easy-care

pflegen *verb*
= to care for, = to look after
(*in hospital*) = to nurse

der **Pfleger**, *plural* Pfleger
= nurse

die **Pflicht**, *plural* Pflichten
= duty
Pflicht sein = to be compulsory

pflichtbewusst
(**pflichtbewußt**ⓞⓛⓓ) *adjective*
= conscientious

× in informal situations   ⓞⓛⓓ = old spelling

pflücken *verb*
= to pick

pflügen *verb*
= to plough, = to plow

der **Pförtner**, *plural* Pförtner
= porter

die **Pfote**, *plural* Pfoten
= paw

pfui *interjection*
= ugh!

das **Pfund**, *plural* Pfunde
= pound

die **Pfütze**, *plural* Pfützen
= puddle

die **Phantasie**, *plural* Phantasien
= imagination
Phantasien = fantasies

phantastisch *adjective*
= fantastic

der **Philosoph**, *plural* Philosophen
= philosopher

die **Philosophie**, *plural* Philosophien
= philosophy

die **Physik**
= physics

der **Pickel**, *plural* Pickel
= spot, = pimple

das **Picknick**, *plural* Picknicks
= picnic

das **Pik**
(*playing cards*) = spades

die **Pille**, *plural* Pillen
= pill

der **Pilz**, *plural* Pilze
- = mushroom
- = fungus

der **Pinguin**, *plural* Pinguine
= penguin

der **Pinsel**, *plural* Pinsel
= brush

die **Pistole**, *plural* Pistolen
= pistol

der **Pkw**, *plural* Pkws
(*Personenkraftwagen*) = car

die **Plage**, *plural* Plagen
= nuisance

plagen *verb*
- = to torment
- = to pester

das **Plakat**, *plural* Plakate
= poster

der **Plan**, *plural* Pläne
- = plan
- = map

planen *verb*
= to plan

das **Plastik**[1]
= plastic

die **Plastik**[2] *plural* Plastiken
= sculpture

die **Platte**, *plural* Platten
- (*wooden*) = board
  (*of a table*) = top
- (*stone*) = slab
- (*metal, glass*) = sheet
- = hotplate
- = plate
  (*for serving*) = dish
  kalte Platte = cold meats and cheeses
- = record, = disc

der **Plattenspieler**, *plural* Plattenspieler
= record player

der **Platz**, *plural* Plätze
- = square
- (*for sport*) = ground, = pitch
  (*for tennis*) = court
  (*for golf*) = course
- = place
  viel Platz haben = to have a lot of room
- = seat
  Platz nehmen = to take a seat, = to sit down

platzen *verb* (**!** sein)
- = to burst
- der Plan ist geplatzt✶ = the plan fell through

plaudern *verb*
= to chat

pleite✶ *adjective*
= broke

plötzlich
1 *adjective* = sudden
2 *adverb* = suddenly

plump *adjective*
- = plump
- = clumsy

der **Po✶**, *plural* Pos
= bottom

die **Poesie**
= poetry

der **Pokal**, *plural* Pokale
- = goblet
- = cup

der **Pole**, *plural* Polen
= Pole

(das) **Polen**
= Poland

die **Police**, *plural* Policen
= policy

polieren *verb*
= to polish

die **Polin**, *plural* Polinnen
= Pole

die **Politik**
- = politics
- = policy

der **Politiker**, *plural* Politiker
= politician

die **Politikerin**, *plural* Politikerinnen
= politician

politisch *adjective*
= political

die **Polizei**
= police

polizeilich
1 *adjective* = police
2 *adverb* = by the police

die **Polizeiwache**, *plural* Polizeiwachen
= police station

der **Polizist**, *plural* Polizisten
= policeman

die **Polizistin**, *plural* Polizistinnen
= policewoman

polnisch *adjective*
= Polish

das **Polster**, *plural* Polster
- = upholstery
- = pad

Pommes frites (*plural*)
= chips, = French fries

das **Pony**[1] *plural* Ponys
= pony

der **Pony**[2] *plural* Ponys
= fringe

das **Portemonnaie**, *plural* Portemonnaies
= purse

der **Portier**, *plural* Portiers
= porter

das **Portmonee**, *plural* Portmonees
= purse

das **Porto**
= postage

das **Porzellan**
= porcelain, = china

die **Post**
- = post, = mail
- = post office

das **Postamt**, *plural* Postämter
= post office

P

der **Postbote**, *plural* Postboten
= postman, = mailman

das **Postfach**, *plural* Postfächer
= PO box

die **Postkarte**, *plural* Postkarten
= postcard

die **Postleitzahl**, *plural* Postleitzahlen
= postcode, = Zip code

prächtig *adjective*
= splendid

prahlen *verb*
= to boast

praktisch
1 *adjective* = practical
ein praktischer Arzt = a general
practitioner
2 *adverb*
• = practically
• = in practice

die **Praline**, *plural* Pralinen
= chocolate

das **Präservativ**, *plural* Präservative
= condom

der **Präsident**, *plural* Präsidenten
= president

die **Präsidentin**, *plural* Präsidentinnen
= president

die **Praxis**, *plural* Praxen
• = practice
• (*doctor's*) = surgery

predigen *verb*
= to preach

der **Preis**, *plural* Preise
• = price
• = prize, = award

das **Preisausschreiben**, *plural*
Preisausschreiben
= competition

preiswert *adjective*
= reasonable, = cheap

die **Prellung**, *plural* Prellungen
= bruise

der **Premierminister**, *plural*
Premierminister
= prime minister

prima✗ *adjective*
= brilliant

der **Prinz**, *plural* Prinzen
= prince

die **Prinzessin**, *plural* Prinzessinnen
= princess

privat *adjective*
= private

pro *preposition* (+ *accusative*)
= per

die **Probe**, *plural* Proben
• = test
• = sample
• = rehearsal

probeweise *adverb*
= on a trial basis

probieren *verb*
= to try, = to taste

der **Profi**, *plural* Profis
= professional

das **Programm**, *plural* Programme
• = programme, = program
• (*on TV*) = channel

programmieren *verb*
= to program

der **Programmierer**, *plural*
Programmierer
= programmer

das **Promille**
= alcohol level
zu viel Promille haben = to be over the
limit

die **Prosa**
= prose

der **Prospekt**, *plural* Prospekte
= brochure

prost *interjection*
= cheers!

das **Protokoll**, *plural* Protokolle
• = protocol
• = minutes

protzen *verb*
= to show off

der **Proviant**
= provisions

das **Prozent**, *plural* Prozente
= per cent
auf etwas Prozente bekommen = to get a
discount on something

der **Prozentsatz**, *plural* Prozentsätze
= percentage

der **Prozess** (**Prozeß**ⓄⓁⒹ), *plural*
Prozesse
• = court case, = trial
• = process

prüfen *verb*
• = to test, = to check
• = to examine

die **Prüfung**, *plural* Prüfungen
• = examination, = exam
• = test

✗ in informal situations   ⓄⓁⒹ = old spelling

die **Prügelei**, *plural* Prügeleien
= fight

prügeln *verb*
• = to beat
• sich prügeln = to fight

der **Psychiater**, *plural* Psychiater
= psychiatrist

die **Psychiaterin**, *plural* Psychiaterinnen
= psychiatrist

psychisch *adjective*
= psychological

die **Psychologie**
= psychology

das **Publikum**
• = public
• = audience, = spectators

der **Pudding**, *plural* Puddings
= blancmange
= pudding

der **Puder**, *plural* Puder
= powder

der **Pulli✕**, *plural* Pullis
= sweater, = jumper

der **Pullover**, *plural* Pullover
= sweater, = jumper

der **Puls**, *plural* Pulse
= pulse

das **Pult**, *plural* Pulte
= desk

das **Pulver**, *plural* Pulver
= powder

der **Pulverkaffee**
= instant coffee

die **Pumpe**, *plural* Pumpen
= pump

pumpen *verb*
• = to pump
• jemandem Geld pumpen✕ = to lend
someone money
• sich etwas pumpen✕ = to borrow
something

der **Punker**, *plural* Punker
= punk

die **Punkerin**, *plural* Punkerinnen
= punk

der **Punkt**, *plural* Punkte
• = dot, = spot
Punkt vier Uhr = at 4 o'clock on the dot
• = full stop, = period
• = point

pünktlich *adjective*
= punctual

die **Puppe**, *plural* Puppen
• = doll
• = puppet

der **Purzelbaum**, *plural* Purzelbäume
= somersault

pusten✕ *verb*
= to blow

die **Pute**, *plural* Puten
= turkey

der **Putz**
= plaster

putzen *verb*
• = to clean
• sich (+ *dative*) die Nase putzen = to
blow one's nose

putzig✕ *adjective*
= cute

das **Puzzle**, *plural* Puzzles
= jigsaw (puzzle)

die **Pyramide**, *plural* Pyramiden
= pyramid

das **Quadrat**, *plural* Quadrate
= square

der **Quadratmeter**, *plural* Quadratmeter
= square metre, = square meter

quaken *verb*
• (*of a duck*) = to quack
• (*of a frog*) = to croak

die **Qual**, *plural* Qualen
• = torment
• = agony

quälen *verb*
• = to torment
• = to torture
• = to pester
• sich quälen = to suffer, = to struggle

der **Quälgeist✕**, *plural* Quälgeister
= pest

die **Qualität**, *plural* Qualitäten
= quality

die **Qualle**, *plural* Quallen
= jellyfish

das **Quartett**, *plural* Quartette
= quartet

das **Quartier**, *plural* Quartiere
• = accommodation
• = quarters

der **Quatsch*x**
= rubbish, = nonsense

quatschen*x *verb*
= to chat

die **Quelle**, *plural* Quellen
* = source
* = spring

quellen *irregular verb* (**!** *sein*)
* = to pour
* = to swell

quer *adverb*
* = across
  = crosswise
  = diagonally
* quer durch = straight through

die **Querstraße**, *plural* Querstraßen
= side street, = side road

quetschen *verb*
= to crush, = to squash

quietschen *verb*
= to squeak

quitt*x *adjective*
= quits

die **Quittung**, *plural* Quittungen
= receipt

Rr

der **Rabatt**, *plural* Rabatte
= discount

die **Rache**
= revenge

rächen *verb*
* = to avenge
* sich an jemandem rächen = to take
  revenge on someone

das **Rad**, *plural* Räder
* = wheel
* = bike
* Rad fahren = to cycle, = to ride a bike
  er fährt gern Rad = he likes cycling

der **Radfahrer**, *plural* Radfahrer
= cyclist

die **Radfahrerin**, *plural* Radfahrerinnen
= cyclist

der **Radfahrweg**, *plural* Radfahrwege
= cycle lane

der **Radiergummi**, *plural* Radiergummis
= rubber, = eraser

das **Radieschen**, *plural* Radieschen
= radish

das **Radio**, *plural* Radios
= radio

der **Radler**, *plural* Radler
= cyclist

die **Radlerin**, *plural* Radlerinnen
= cyclist

raffiniert *adjective*
= crafty, = cunning

der **Rahmen**, *plural* Rahmen
* = frame
* = framework

die **Rakete**, *plural* Raketen
= rocket

ran*x ▶heran

der **Rand**, *plural* Ränder
= edge
= rim
(*of a page*) = margin
etwas am Rande erwähnen = to mention
something in passing
mit etwas nicht zu Rande kommen = not
be able to cope with something

der **Randstreifen**, *plural* Randstreifen
= hard shoulder

der **Rang**, *plural* Ränge
* = rank
* (*in a theatre*) = circle

rangieren *verb*
* = to rank
* = to shunt, = to switch

rannte ▶rennen

rasch *adjective*
= quick

rascheln *verb*
= to rustle

rasen *verb* (**!** *sein*)
= to tear along

der **Rasen**, *plural* Rasen
= lawn, = grass

der **Rasierapparat**, *plural* Rasierapparate
= razor
= shaver

rasieren *verb*
* = to shave
* sich rasieren = to shave

das **Rasierwasser**
= aftershave

die **Rasse**, *plural* Rassen
= race

---

rassisch *adjective*
= racial

rassistisch *adjective*
= racist

rasten *verb*
= to rest

der **Rastplatz**, *plural* Rastplätze
= picnic area (*on a motorway*)

die **Raststätte**, *plural* Raststätten
= services (*on a motorway*)

der **Rat**, *plural* Räte
• = (piece of) advice
• = council

raten *irregular verb*
• = to advise
• = to guess

das **Rathaus**, *plural* Rathäuser
= town hall

rationell *adjective*
= efficient

ratlos *adjective*
= helpless

ratsam *adjective*
= advisable

der **Ratschlag**, *plural* Ratschläge
= (piece of) advice

das **Rätsel**, *plural* Rätsel
= puzzle
= mystery

rätselhaft *adjective*
= mysterious

die **Ratte**, *plural* Ratten
= rat

rau *adjective*
• = rough
• = harsh
• einen rauen Hals haben = to have a sore throat

der **Raub**
• = robbery
• = loot

rauben *verb*
= to steal, = to rob

das **Raubtier**, *plural* Raubtiere
= predator

der **Rauch**
= smoke

rauchen *verb*
= to smoke

der **Raucher**, *plural* Raucher
= smoker

die **Raucherin**, *plural* Raucherinnen
= smoker

rauf* ▶herauf, hinauf

rauh⃝ᴸᴰ ▶rau

der **Raum**, *plural* Räume
• = room
• = space
• = area

räumen *verb*
• = to clear
• = to vacate

die **Raumfahrt**
= space travel

der **Raumschiff**, *plural* Raumschiffe
= space ship

Raupe, die, *plural* Raupen
= caterpillar

raus* ▶heraus, hinaus

das **Rauschgift**, *plural* Rauschgifte
= drug
Rauschgift nehmen = to take drugs

rauschgiftsüchtig *adjective*
= addicted (to drugs)

der/die **Rauschgiftsüchtige**, *plural* Rauschgiftsüchtigen
= drug addict

raus|kriegen* *verb*
= to get out
ein Geheimnis rauskriegen = to find out a secret
er hat die Aufgabe nicht rausgekriegt = he couldn't do the exercise

räuspern: sich räuspern *verb*
= to clear one's throat

die **Razzia**, *plural* Razzien
= raid

reagieren *verb*
= to react

rebellieren *verb*
= to rebel

rechnen *verb*
• = to count, = to calculate
gut rechnen können = to be good at figures
• = to reckon
mit etwas rechnen = to expect something, (*rely on*) = to count on something
• = to work out

das **Rechnen**
= arithmetic

der **Rechner**, *plural* Rechner
• = calculator
• = computer

die **Rechnung**, *plural* Rechnungen
• = bill, = check
= invoice
• = calculation

R

recht
1 *adjective*
* = right
  jemandem recht sein = to be all right
  with someone
* = real
  ich habe keine rechte Lust = I don't really
  feel like it
2 *adverb*
* = correctly
* = very
* = quite
  recht vielen Dank = many thanks

das **Recht**, *plural* Rechte
* = law
* = right
  mit Recht = rightly
  Recht haben = to be right
* jemandem Recht geben = to agree with
  someone

rechte ▶rechter

das **Rechteck**, *plural* Rechtecke
= rectangle

rechteckig *adjective*
= rectangular

rechter, rechte, rechtes *adjective*
* = right
* = right-wing

rechtfertigen *verb*
= to justify

rechtlich *adjective*
= legal

rechts *adverb*
= on the right
von rechts = from the right
rechts sein = to be right-wing

der **Rechtsanwalt**, *plural* Rechtsanwälte
= lawyer, = solicitor
= barrister

die **Rechtsanwältin**, *plural*
Rechtsanwältinnen
= lawyer, = solicitor
= barrister

die **Rechtschreibung**
= spelling

rechtzeitig
1 *adjective* = timely
2 *adverb* = in time

der **Redakteur**, *plural* Redakteure
= editor

die **Redakteurin**, *plural* Redakteurinnen
= editor

die **Rede**, *plural* Reden
= speech
nicht der Rede wert = not worth
mentioning

reden *verb*
= to speak, = to talk

reduzieren *verb*
* = to reduce
* sich reduzieren = to decrease

das **Reformhaus**, *plural* Reformhäuser
= health-food shop, = health-food store

das **Regal**, *plural* Regale
= shelf
= shelves

die **Regel**, *plural* Regeln
* = rule
  in der Regel = as a rule
* (*menstruation*) = period

regelmäßig *adjective*
= regular

regeln *verb*
* = to regulate
  den Verkehr regeln = to direct the traffic
* (*sort out*) = to settle

die **Regelung**, *plural* Regelungen
* = regulation
* = settlement

der **Regen**
= rain

der **Regenbogen**, *plural* Regenbogen
= rainbow

der **Regenschirm**, *plural* Regenschirme
= umbrella

der **Regenwurm**, *plural* Regenwürmer
= earthworm

die **Regie**
= direction
Regie führen = to direct

regieren *verb*
* = to govern
* = to rule

die **Regierung**, *plural* Regierungen
* = government
* (*of a monarch*) = reign

der **Regisseur**, *plural* Regisseure
= director

die **Regisseurin**, *plural* Regisseurinnen
= director

regnen *verb*
= to rain

reiben *irregular verb*
* = to rub
* = to grate

reibungslos *adjective*
= smooth

reich *adjective*
= rich

das **Reich**, *plural* Reiche
= empire

✱ in informal situations   ⓄⓁⒹ = old spelling

reichen *verb*
- = to hand, = to pass
- = to be enough
  mit dem Geld reichen = to have enough money
  mir reichts!✖ = I've had enough!
- bis zu etwas reichen = to reach (up to) something

reichlich
1 *adjective* = ample, = large
2 *adverb* = plenty of

der **Reichtum**, *plural* Reichtümer
= wealth

reif *adjective*
- = ripe
- = mature

der **Reifen**, *plural* Reifen
- = tyre, = tire
- = hoop

die **Reifenpanne**, *plural* Reifenpannen
= puncture

die **Reihe**, *plural* Reihen
- = row
- = series
  du bist an der Reihe = it's your turn

die **Reihenfolge**, *plural* Reihenfolgen
= order

das **Reihenhaus**, *plural* Reihenhäuser
= terraced house

reimen *verb*
- = to rhyme
- sich reimen = to rhyme

rein1 *adjective*
= pure
= clean
etwas ins Reine schreiben = to make a fair copy of something
etwas ins Reine bringen = to clear something up

rein2 *adverb*
rein✖ ▶herein, hinein

reinigen *verb*
= to clean

die **Reinigung**, *plural* Reinigungen
- = cleaning
- = cleaner's

der **Reis**
= rice

die **Reise**, *plural* Reisen
= journey, = trip
(*by boat*) = voyage

das **Reisebüro**, *plural* Reisebüros
= travel agency

der **Reisebus**, *plural* Reisebusse
= coach

der **Reiseführer**, *plural* Reiseführer
- = guidebook
- = courier

reisen *verb* (**!** *sein*)
= to travel

der/die **Reisende**, *plural* Reisenden
= traveller, = traveler

der **Reisepass** (**Reisepaß**OLD), *plural* Reisepässe
= passport

der **Reisescheck**, *plural* Reiseschecks
= traveller's cheque, = traveler's check

reißen *irregular verb*
- = to tear
- = to pull
- sich um etwas reißen = to fight for something
- (**!** *sein*) = to tear, = to break

der **Reißverschluss** (**Reißverschluß**OLD), *plural* Reißverschlüsse
= zip, = zipper

die **Reißzwecke**, *plural* Reißzwecken
= drawing pin, = thumbtack

reiten *irregular verb* (**!** *sein*)
= to ride

der **Reiter**, *plural* Reiter
= rider

die **Reiterin**, *plural* Reiterinnen
= rider

der **Reitweg**, *plural* Reitwege
= bridle path

der **Reiz**, *plural* Reize
- = stimulus
- = attraction

reizen *verb*
- = to provoke
- = to attract, = to tempt
- (*when playing cards*) = to bid

reizend *adjective*
= charming, = delightful

reizvoll *adjective*
= attractive

die **Reklame**, *plural* Reklamen
= advertisement
(*on TV*) = commercial
für etwas Reklame machen = to advertise something

der **Rektor**, *plural* Rektoren
- (*of a school*) = head, = principal
- (*of a university*) = vice-chancellor

die **Religion**, *plural* Religionen
= religion

rennen *irregular verb* (**!** *sein*)
= to run

das **Rennen**, *plural* Rennen
= race

renovieren *verb*
= to renovate, = to redecorate

die **Renovierung**, *plural* Renovierungen
= renovation, = redecoration

die **Rente**, *plural* Renten
= pension
in Rente gehen = to retire

der **Rentner**, *plural* Rentner
= pensioner

die **Rentnerin**, *plural* Rentnerinnen
= pensioner

die **Reparatur**, *plural* Reparaturen
= repair

reparieren *verb*
= to repair

reservieren *verb*
= to reserve

respektieren *verb*
= to respect

der **Rest**, *plural* Reste
= rest, = remainder
die Reste = the remains, (*of food*) = the
leftovers

das **Restaurant**, *plural* Restaurants
= restaurant

restlich *adjective*
= remaining

restlos *adjective*
= complete

das **Resultat**, *plural* Resultate
= result

retten *verb*
* = to save, = to rescue
* sich retten = to escape

die **Rettung**
= rescue

der **Rettungsring**, *plural* Rettungsringe
= lifebelt

der **Rettungswagen**, *plural*
Rettungswagen
= ambulance

das **Rezept**, *plural* Rezepte
* = prescription
* = recipe

das **R-Gespräch**, *plural* R-Gespräche
= reverse-charge call, = collect call

der **Rhein**
= Rhine

das **Rheuma**
= rheumatism

der **Rhythmus**, *plural* Rhythmen
= rhythm

richten *verb*
* = to direct
* = to aim
* eine Frage an jemanden richten = to put
a question to someone
* = to judge
* sich richten = to be directed
sich nach jemandes Wünschen richten =
to fit in with someone's wishes

der **Richter**, *plural* Richter
= judge

richtig *adjective*
* = right, = correct
* = real

die **Richtlinie**, *plural* Richtlinien
= guideline

die **Richtung**, *plural* Richtungen
* = direction
* = trend

riechen *irregular verb*
= to smell

rief ▶rufen

der **Riegel**, *plural* Riegel
= bolt
ein Riegel Schokolade = a bar of
chocolate

der **Riemen**, *plural* Riemen
* = strap
* = oar

der **Riese**, *plural* Riesen
= giant

riesig *adjective*
= huge, = enormous

das **Riff**, *plural* Riffe
= reef

die **Rille**, *plural* Rillen
= groove

das **Rindfleisch**
= beef

der **Ring**, *plural* Ringe
= ring

das **Ringen**
= wrestling

ringsherum *adverb*
= all around

der **Rinnstein**, *plural* Rinnsteine
= gutter

die **Rippe**, *plural* Rippen
= rib

das **Risiko**, *plural* Risiken
= risk

riskant *adjective*
= risky

✖ in informal situations   ⓞⓛⓓ = old spelling

riskieren *verb*
= to risk

riss (**riß**ᴼᴸᴰ) ▶reißen

der **Riss** (**Riß**ᴼᴸᴰ), *plural* Risse
• = tear
• = crack

ritt ▶reiten

der **Ritter**, *plural* Ritter
= knight

der **Roboter**, *plural* Roboter
= robot

der **Rock**, *plural* Röcke
= skirt

der **Roggen**
= rye

roh *adjective*
• = raw
• = rough
• = brutal

das **Rohr**, *plural* Rohre
• = pipe
• = reed

die **Röhre**, *plural* Röhren
• = tube
• = valve, = tube

die **Rolle**, *plural* Rollen
• = roll
• = reel
• = role, = part
es spielt keine Rolle = it doesn't matter

rollen *verb*
= to roll

der **Roller**, *plural* Roller
= scooter

das **Rollo**, *plural* Rollos
= roller blind

der **Rollschuh**, *plural* Rollschuhe
= roller-skate

das **Rollschuhlaufen**
= roller-skating

der **Rollstuhl**, *plural* Rollstühle
= wheelchair

die **Rolltreppe**, *plural* Rolltreppen
= escalator

(das) **Rom**
= Rome

der **Roman**, *plural* Romane
= novel

romantisch *adjective*
= romantic

röntgen *verb*
= to X-ray

rosa *adjective*
= pink

der **Rosenkohl**
= (Brussels) sprouts

der **Rost**, *plural* Roste
• = grate, = grill
• = rust

rösten *verb*
• = to roast
• = to toast

rostig *adjective*
= rusty

rot *adjective*
= red

das **Rotkehlchen**, *plural* Rotkehlchen
= robin

rüber* ▶herüber, hinüber

der **Rücken**, *plural* Rücken
• = back
• (*of a book*) = spine

die **Rückenlehne**, *plural* Rückenlehnen
= back (of a chair)

die **Rückfahrkarte**, *plural* Rückfahrkarten
= return ticket

die **Rückgabe**, *plural* Rückgaben
= return

rückgängig *adjective*
etwas rückgängig machen = to cancel something

die **Rückhand**
= backhand

das **Rücklicht**, *plural* Rücklichter
= rear light

die **Rückseite**, *plural* Rückseiten
= back, = reverse

die **Rücksicht**
= consideration

rücksichtslos *adjective*
• = inconsiderate
• = ruthless

rücksichtsvoll *adjective*
= considerate

der **Rückstand**
= residue
im Rückstand sein = to be behind

rückwärts *adverb*
= backwards

der **Rückweg**, *plural* Rückwege
= way back, = return journey

die **Rückzahlung**, *plural* Rückzahlungen
= repayment

das **Ruder**, *plural* Ruder
• = oar
• = rudder

R

das **Ruderboot**, plural Ruderboote
= rowing boat, = rowboat

rudern verb (! sein)
= to row

der **Ruf**, plural Rufe
- = call
- = telephone number
- = reputation

rufen irregular verb
= to call

die **Rufnummer**, plural Rufnummern
= telephone number

die **Ruhe**
- = silence, = quiet
- = peace
- = rest

ruhen verb
= to rest

der **Ruhetag**, plural Ruhetage
= closing day
'Montag Ruhetag' = 'closed on Mondays'

ruhig adjective
- = quiet
- = peaceful
- = calm

der **Ruhm**
= fame

das **Rührei**
= scrambled eggs

rühren verb
- = to move
- = to stir
- sich rühren = to move

die **Ruine**, plural Ruinen
= ruin

ruinieren verb
= to ruin

rülpsen verb
= to belch, = to burp

(das) **Rumänien**
= Romania

der **Rumpf**, plural Rümpfe
- = trunk
- (of a ship) = hull
  (of a plane) = fuselage

rund adjective
= round

die **Runde**, plural Runden
- = round
- = lap
- = circle

die **Rundfahrt**, plural Rundfahrten
= tour

die **Rundfrage**, plural Rundfragen
= poll

der **Rundfunk**
= radio

rundherum adverb
= all around

das **Rundschreiben**, plural
Rundschreiben
= circular

runter✶ ▶herunter, hinunter

runzlig adjective
= wrinkled

die **Rüsche**, plural Rüschen
= frill

der **Ruß**
= soot

der **Russe**, plural Russen
= Russian

der **Rüssel**, plural Rüssel
= trunk

die **Russin**, plural Russinnen
= Russian

russisch adjective
= Russian

(das) **Russland** (**Rußland** ⓞⓛⓓ)
= Russia

die **Rüstung**, plural Rüstungen
- = arms
- = armour

die **Rutschbahn**, plural Rutschbahnen
= slide

rutschen verb (! sein)
= to slide, = to slip

rutschig adjective
= slippery

rütteln verb
= to shake

Ss

der **Saal**, plural Säle
= hall

die **Sache**, plural Sachen
- = matter, = business
  zur Sache kommen = to get to the point
- = thing
  meine Sachen (clothing) = my things

das **Sachgebiet**, plural Sachgebiete
= field, = area

sachlich adjective
• = objective
• = factual

sächlich adjective
= neuter

(das) **Sachsen**
= Saxony

der **Sack**, plural Säcke
• = sack
• = bag

die **Sackgasse**, plural Sackgassen
= cul-de-sac

der **Saft**, plural Säfte
• = juice
• = sap

saftig adjective
= juicy

die **Sage**, plural Sagen
= legend, = saga

die **Säge**, plural Sägen
= saw

sagen verb
• = to say
was ich noch sagen wollte = by the way
• = to tell
jemandem etwas sagen = to tell
someone something
sag mal = tell me
• = to mean
das hat nichts zu sagen = that doesn't
mean anything

sägen verb
= to saw

sah ▶sehen

die **Sahne**
= cream

die **Saison**, plural Saisons
= season

die **Saite**, plural Saiten
= string

das **Sakko**, plural Sakkos
= jacket

der **Salat**, plural Salate
• = lettuce
• = salad

die **Salbe**, plural Salben
= ointment

salopp adjective
= casual, = informal

das **Salz**, plural Salze
= salt

salzig adjective
= salty

der **Samen**, plural Samen
• = seed
• = semen, = sperm

sammeln verb
• = to collect, = to gather
• sich sammeln = to gather

die **Sammlung**, plural Sammlungen
= collection

der **Samstag**
= Saturday

samstags adverb
= on Saturdays

samt preposition (+ dative)
= together with

der **Samt**, plural Samte
= velvet

sämtlicher/sämtliche/
sämtliches pronoun
= all (the)
meine sämtlichen Bücher = all my books

die **Sandale**, plural Sandalen
= sandal

sandig adjective
= sandy

sanft adjective
= gentle
= soft

sang ▶singen

der **Sänger**, plural Sänger
= singer

die **Sängerin**, plural Sängerinnen
= singer

der **Sanitäter**, plural Sanitäter
= paramedic

der **Sarg**, plural Särge
= coffin

saß ▶sitzen

der **Satellit**, plural Satelliten
= satellite

das **Satellitenfernsehen**
= satellite television

satt adjective
• = full (up)
• jemanden satt haben✕ = to be fed up
with someone

der **Sattel**, plural Sättel
= saddle

der **Satz**, plural Sätze
• = sentence
• = leap
• (in tennis) = set
• (in music) = movement
• (of tax, interest) = rate

sauber adjective
* = clean
* = neat
* sauber machen = to clean (up)

sauer adjective
* = sour
  = pickled
  saurer Regen = acid rain
* er ist sauer✘ = he's annoyed

der **Sauerstoff**
  = oxygen

saufen✘ irregular verb
  = to drink, = to booze

saugen verb
* = to suck
* = to vacuum, = to hoover

das **Säugetier**, plural Säugetiere
  = mammal

der **Säugling**, plural Säuglinge
  = baby

die **Säule**, plural Säulen
  = column

der **Saum**, plural Säume
  = hem

die **Säure**, plural Säuren
  = acid

die **S-Bahn**, plural S-Bahnen
  = city and suburban railway

das **Schach**, plural Schachs
  = chess
  Schach! = check!

die **Schachtel**, plural Schachteln
  = box

schade adjective
  schade sein = to be a pity
  schade! = pity!, = (what a) shame!
  zu schade für jemanden sein = to be too
    good for someone

schaden verb
  = to damage, = to harm

der **Schaden**, plural Schäden
* = damage
* = disadvantage

schädlich adjective
  = harmful

das **Schaf**, plural Schafe
  = sheep

der **Schäfer**, plural Schäfer
  = shepherd

der **Schäferhund**, plural Schäferhunde
  = sheepdog

schaffen verb
* = to manage
  eine Prüfung schaffen = to pass an exam
* jemandem zu schaffen machen = to
    trouble someone
  geschafft sein✘ = to be worn out
* (irregular) = to create

der **Schaffner**, plural Schaffner
  = conductor

die **Schaffnerin**, plural Schaffnerinnen
  = conductress

der **Schal**, plural Schals
  = scarf

die **Schale**, plural Schalen
* = skin, = peel
* = shell
* = dish, = bowl

schälen verb
* = to peel
* sich schälen = to peel

die **Schallplatte**, plural Schallplatten
  = record

schalten verb
* = to switch, = to turn
* = to change gear
* schnell schalten✘ = to catch on quickly

der **Schalter**, plural Schalter
* = switch
* = counter

die **Schaltung**, plural Schaltungen
* = gear change
* = circuit

schämen: sich schämen verb
  = to be ashamed

die **Schande**
  = disgrace
  = shame

scharf adjective
* = sharp
  scharf sein (in photography) = to be in
    focus
* (of food) = hot
  scharf auf etwas sein✘ = to be really keen
    on something
* = hard
* = fierce

der **Schatten**, plural Schatten
* = shadow
* = shade

schattig adjective
  = shady

der **Schatz**, plural Schätze
* = treasure
* mein Schatz✘ = my darling

schätzen verb
* = to estimate

✘ in informal situations   ◆ considered offensive

* = to reckon
* = to value

die **Schau**, plural Schauen
= show

schauen verb
= to look

der **Schauer**, plural Schauer
= shower

die **Schauergeschichte**, plural
Schauergeschichten
= horror story

die **Schaufel**, plural Schaufeln
* = shovel
* = dustpan

das **Schaufenster**, plural Schaufenster
= shop window

die **Schaukel**, plural Schaukeln
= swing

der **Schaukelstuhl**, plural Schaukelstühle
= rocking chair

der **Schaum**
= foam, = froth
= lather

schäumen verb
= to foam, = to froth
= to lather

das **Schauspiel**, plural Schauspiele
* = play
* = spectacle

der **Schauspieler**, plural Schauspieler
= actor

die **Schauspielerin**, plural
Schauspielerinnen
= actress

der **Scheck**, plural Schecks
= cheque, = check

das **Scheckbuch**, plural Scheckbücher
= chequebook, = checkbook

die **Scheibe**, plural Scheiben
* = disc
* = pane
* = slice

der **Scheibenwischer**, plural
Scheibenwischer
= windscreen wiper

scheiden irregular verb
* = to separate
* sich scheiden = to differ
* sich scheiden lassen = to get divorced

die **Scheidung**, plural Scheidungen
= divorce

der **Schein**, plural Scheine
* = light

* = appearance, = pretence
  etwas nur zum Schein machen = to only
    pretend to do something
* = certificate
* (money) = note

scheinbar adjective
= apparent

scheinen irregular verb
* = to shine
* = to seem

der **Scheinwerfer**, plural Scheinwerfer
= headlamp, = headlight

die **Scheiße** = shit

scheitern verb (! sein)
= to fail

der **Schelm**, plural Schelme
= rogue

der **Schenkel**, plural Schenkel
= thigh

schenken verb
= to give

die **Schere**, plural Scheren
* = (pair of) scissors
* (of a crab) = claw

der **Scherz**, plural Scherze
= joke

scheu adjective
= shy

scheuern verb
* = to scrub
* = to rub

die **Scheune**, plural Scheunen
= barn

der **Schi**, plural Schier
▶Ski

die **Schicht**, plural Schichten
* = layer
* = class
* = shift

schick adjective
* = chic, = stylish
* ein schickes Auto✖ = a great car

schicken verb
= to send

das **Schicksal**, plural Schicksale
= fate

das **Schiebedach**, plural Schiebedächer
= sun-roof

schieben irregular verb
* = to push
  etwas auf jemanden schieben = to blame
    somebody for something
* schieben✖ = to deal in

der **Schiedsrichter**, plural Schiedsrichter
= referee, = umpire

S

schief
1 *adjective*
= crooked
2 *adverb*
das Bild hängt schief = the picture is not
   straight

schielen *verb*
= to squint

schien ▶ scheinen

das **Schienbein**, *plural* Schienbeine
= shin

die **Schiene**, *plural* Schienen
• = rail
  = runner
• = splint

schießen *irregular verb*
• = to shoot
• ein Tor schießen = to score a goal
• schießen✶ (! *sein*) (*rush*) = to shoot

das **Schiff**, *plural* Schiffe
• = ship
• (*in a church*) = nave

schikanieren *verb*
= to bully

das **Schild**, *plural* Schilder
• = sign
• = badge
• = label

die **Schildkröte**, *plural* Schildkröten
= tortoise
= turtle

der **Schimmel**, *plural* Schimmel
• = mould, = mold
• = white horse

der **Schimpanse**, *plural* Schimpansen
= chimpanzee

schimpfen *verb*
• = to grumble
• = to tell off

der **Schinken**, *plural* Schinken
= ham

der **Schirm**, *plural* Schirme
= umbrella
= shade
= sunshade

der **Schlaf**
= sleep

der **Schlafanzug**, *plural* Schlafanzüge
= pyjamas, = pajamas

schlafen *irregular verb*
= to sleep
= to be asleep
schlafen gehen = to go to bed

der **Schlafsaal**, *plural* Schlafsäle
= dormitory

der **Schlafsack**, *plural* Schlafsäcke
= sleeping bag

das **Schlafzimmer**, *plural* Schlafzimmer
= bedroom

der **Schlag**, *plural* Schläge
• = blow
  Schläge kriegen = to get a beating
  Schlag auf Schlag = all at once
• (*in sport*) = shot, = stroke
• (*of the heart*) = beat
• (*electric*) = shock

schlagen *irregular verb*
• = to hit
• = to beat
• = to bang
• (*of a clock*) = to strike
• sich schlagen = to fight

der **Schlager**, *plural* Schlager
= hit

der **Schläger**, *plural* Schläger
(*in tennis*) = racket
(*in baseball*) = bat
(*in golf*) = club
(*in hockey*) = stick

die **Schlagsahne**
= whipping cream
= whipped cream

die **Schlagzeile**, *plural* Schlagzeilen
= headline

der **Schlamm**
= mud

schlampig *adjective*
= sloppy

die **Schlange**, *plural* Schlangen
• = snake
• = queue, = line
  Schlange stehen = to queue, = to stand
  in line

schlank *adjective*
= slim

schlau *adjective*
• = crafty
• = clever

der **Schlauch**, *plural* Schläuche
= hose, = tube

schlecht *adjective*
• = bad
• mir ist schlecht = I feel sick
• es geht ihr schlecht = she's not well

schleichen *irregular verb* (! *sein*)
• = to creep
  = to crawl
• sich schleichen = to creep

---

die **Schleife**, *plural* Schleifen
  • = bow
  • = loop

schleifen¹ *verb*
  = to drag

schleifen² *irregular verb*
  = to sharpen

schleimig *adjective*
  = slimy

schleppen *verb*
  = to drag
  = to tow

der **Schlepplift**, *plural* Schlepplifte
  = T-bar lift

schleudern *verb*
  • = to hurl
  • (*of a washing machine*) = to spin
  • (! *sein*) = to skid

schlicht *adjective*
  = plain, = simple

schlief ▶schlafen

schließen *irregular verb*
  • = to close (down)
  • = to lock
  • = to conclude
    einen Vertrag schließen = to enter into a contract
  • sich schließen = to close

das **Schließfach**, *plural* Schließfächer
  = locker

schließlich *adverb*
  • = finally
  • = after all

schlimm *adjective*
  = bad

der **Schlips**, *plural* Schlipse
  = tie

der **Schlitten**, *plural* Schlitten
  = sledge, = toboggan

der **Schlittschuh**, *plural* Schlittschuhe
  = [ice-]skate
  Schlittschuh laufen = to [ice-]skate

das **Schlittschuhlaufen**
  = ice-skating

der **Schlitz**, *plural* Schlitze
  • = slit, = slot
  • (*in trousers*) = flies

schloss (**schloß**ⓄⓁⒹ) ▶schließen

das **Schloss** (**Schloß**ⓄⓁⒹ), *plural* Schlösser
  • = lock
  • = castle

der **Schluck**, *plural* Schlucke
  • = mouthful
  • = gulp

der **Schluckauf**
  = hiccups

schlucken *verb*
  = to swallow

schlug ▶schlagen

der **Schlüpfer**, *plural* Schlüpfer
  = knickers

der **Schluss** (**Schluß**ⓄⓁⒹ), *plural* Schlüsse
  • = end, = ending
  • = conclusion

der **Schlüssel**, *plural* Schlüssel
  • = key
  • = spanner

schmal *adjective*
  • = narrow
  • = thin

schmecken *verb*
  = to taste

schmeicheln *verb*
  = to flatter

schmeißen* *irregular verb*
  = to chuck
  mit etwas schmeißen = to chuck something

schmelzen *irregular verb*
  = to melt

der **Schmerz**, *plural* Schmerzen
  • = pain
  • = grief

schmerzen *verb*
  = to hurt

schmerzhaft *adjective*
  = painful

das **Schmerzmittel**, *plural* Schmerzmittel
  = painkiller

der **Schmetterling**, *plural* Schmetterlinge
  = butterfly

schmieren *verb*
  • = to lubricate
  • (*with butter*) = to spread
  • = to scrawl
  • = to smudge

die **Schminke**, *plural* Schminken
  = make-up

schmiss (**schmiß**ⓄⓁⒹ) ▶schmeißen

der **Schmuck**
  • = jewellery, = jewelry
  • = decoration

schmücken *verb*
  = to decorate

schmuggeln *verb*
  = to smuggle

schmusen *verb*
  = to cuddle

S

der **Schmutz**
= dirt

schmutzig *adjective*
= dirty

der **Schnabel**, *plural* Schnäbel
= beak

die **Schnalle**, *plural* Schnallen
= buckle

schnarchen *verb*
= to snore

die **Schnauze**, *plural* Schnauzen
- = snout, = muzzle
- die Schnauze halten✱ = to keep one's mouth shut

die **Schnecke**, *plural* Schnecken
= snail

der **Schnee**
= snow

schneiden *irregular verb*
= to cut
= to slice
Gesichter schneiden = to pull faces

der **Schneider**, *plural* Schneider
= tailor

die **Schneiderin**, *plural* Schneiderinnen
= dressmaker

schneien *verb*
= to snow

schnell *adjective*
= quick, = fast

der **Schnellzug**, *plural* Schnellzüge
= express (train)

schnitt ▶schneiden

das **Schnitzel**, *plural* Schnitzel
- = escalope
- = scrap

schnitzen *verb*
= to carve

der **Schnorchel**, *plural* Schnorchel
= snorkel

der **Schnuller**, *plural* Schnuller
= dummy, = pacifier

der **Schnupfen**, *plural* Schnupfen
= cold

die **Schnur**, *plural* Schnüre
- = (piece of) string
- = cord
- = flex

der **Schnurrbart**, *plural* Schnurrbärte
= moustache, = mustache

der **Schnürsenkel**, *plural* Schnürsenkel
= (shoe)lace

die **Schokolade**, *plural* Schokoladen
= chocolate

schon *adverb*
- = already
  komm schon! = come on!
- = even
  das ist schon möglich = that's quite possible
- = just
  schon deshalb = for that reason alone

schön *adjective*
- = beautiful
- = nice
- = good
  na schön = all right then

schonen *verb*
- = to look after
- sich schonen = to take things easy

die **Schönheit**, *plural* Schönheiten
= beauty

der **Schornstein**, *plural* Schornsteine
= chimney, = funnel

schoss (**schoß**OLD) ▶schießen

der **Schoß**, *plural* Schöße
= lap

der **Schotte**, *plural* Schotten
= Scot, = Scotsman

die **Schottin**, *plural* Schottinnen
= Scot, = Scotswoman

schottisch *adjective*
= Scottish

(das) **Schottland**
= Scotland

schräg *adjective*
= diagonal
= sloping

der **Schrank**, *plural* Schränke
= cupboard, = wardrobe

die **Schraube**, *plural* Schrauben
= screw

schrauben *verb*
= to screw

der **Schraubenzieher**, *plural* Schraubenzieher
= screwdriver

der **Schreck**, *plural* Schrecke
= fright

schrecklich *adjective*
= terrible

der **Schrei**, *plural* Schreie
= cry, = shout
der letzte Schrei✱ = the latest thing

✱ in informal situations   OLD = old spelling

schreiben *irregular verb*
- = to write
  wie schreibt man das? = how is it spelt?
- = to type

die **Schreibkraft**, *plural* Schreibkräfte
= typist

die **Schreibmaschine**, *plural*
Schreibmaschinen
= typewriter

der **Schreibtisch**, *plural* Schreibtische
= desk

Schreibwaren (*plural*)
= stationery

schreien *irregular verb*
= to cry, = to shout

schrieb ▶ schreiben

die **Schrift**, *plural* Schriften
- = writing
- = script
- = type

schriftlich
1 *adjective* = written
2 *adverb* = in writing

der **Schriftsteller**, *plural* Schriftsteller
= writer

die **Schriftstellerin**, *plural*
Schriftstellerinnen
= writer

der **Schritt**, *plural* Schritte
= step

der **Schrott**
= scrap (metal)

die **Schublade**, *plural* Schubladen
= drawer

schubsen *verb*
= to shove

schüchtern *adjective*
= shy

der **Schuh**, *plural* Schuhe
= shoe

das **Schuhwerk**
= shoes

die **Schuld**, *plural* Schulden
- = blame
  es ist nicht seine Schuld = it is not his
  fault
- = guilt
- = debt
  Schulden haben = to be in debt

schulden *verb*
= to owe

schuldig *adjective*
- = guilty
- **jemandem etwas schuldig sein** = to owe
  someone something

die **Schule**, *plural* Schulen
= school

schulen *verb*
= to train

der **Schüler**, *plural* Schüler
- = pupil
- = student
- = schoolboy

die **Schülerin**, *plural* Schülerinnen
- = pupil
- = student
- = schoolgirl

schulfrei *adjective*
ein schulfreier Tag = a day off school

der **Schulhof**, *plural* Schulhöfe
= playground

die **Schulter**, *plural* Schultern
= shoulder

schummeln✗ *verb*
= to cheat

die **Schuppe**, *plural* Schuppen
= scale
Schuppen = dandruff

die **Schürze**, *plural* Schürzen
= apron

der **Schuss** (**Schuß**ⓞⓛⓓ), *plural* Schüsse
- = shot
- (*small amount*) = dash
- (*in skiing*) = schuss

die **Schüssel**, *plural* Schüsseln
= bowl, = dish

der **Schuster**, *plural* Schuster
= shoemaker

schütteln *verb*
= to shake

schütten *verb*
- = to pour
- = to tip
- **es schüttet** = it is pouring (with rain)

der **Schutz**
= protection
= shelter

der **Schütze**, *plural* Schützen
- = marksman
- = Sagittarius

schützen *verb*
= to protect

schwach *adjective*
- = weak
- = poor

die **Schwäche**, *plural* Schwächen
= weakness

der **Schwager**, *plural* Schwäger
= brother-in-law

S

die **Schwägerin**, *plural* Schwägerinnen
= sister-in-law

die **Schwalbe**, *plural* Schwalben
= swallow

der **Schwamm**, *plural* Schwämme
= sponge

der **Schwan**, *plural* Schwäne
= swan

schwanger *adjective*
= pregnant

die **Schwangerschaft**, *plural*
Schwangerschaften
= pregnancy

schwanken *verb*
* = to sway
* = to fluctuate
* = to waver
* (**!** *sein*) = to stagger

der **Schwanz**, *plural* Schwänze
= tail

schwänzen✶ *verb*
= to skip
die Schule schwänzen = to play truant *or*
hookey

der **Schwarm**, *plural* Schwärme
= swarm

schwarz
1 *adjective*
= black
ins Schwarze treffen = to hit the nail on
the head
2 *adverb* = illegally

schweben *verb*
* in Gefahr schweben = to be in danger
* (**!** *sein*) = to float

(das) **Schweden**
= Sweden

schwedisch *adjective*
= Swedish

schweigen *irregular verb*
= to be silent, = to say nothing

das **Schwein**, *plural* Schweine
* = pig
* (*meat*) = pork
* du Schwein!✶ = you swine!
* Schwein haben✶ = to be lucky

das **Schweinefleisch**
= pork

der **Schweiß**
= sweat

die **Schweiz**
= Switzerland

der **Schweizer**, *plural* Schweizer
= Swiss

die **Schweizerin**, *plural* Schweizerinnen
= Swiss

schweizerisch *adjective*
= Swiss

schwer *adjective*
* = heavy
zwei Kilo schwer sein = to weigh 2 kilos
* = difficult
* (*of an injury*) = serious
* schwer arbeiten = to work hard
* jemandem schwer fallen = to be hard for
someone

schwerhörig *adjective*
= hard of hearing

das **Schwert**, *plural* Schwerter
= sword

die **Schwester**, *plural* Schwestern
* = sister
* = nurse

Schwiegereltern (*plural*)
= parents-in-law

die **Schwiegermutter**, *plural*
Schwiegermütter
= mother-in-law

der **Schwiegervater**, *plural*
Schwiegerväter
= father-in-law

schwierig *adjective*
= difficult

die **Schwierigkeit**, *plural* Schwierigkeiten
= difficulty

das **Schwimmbad**, *plural* Schwimmbäder
= swimming baths

das **Schwimmbecken**, *plural*
Schwimmbecken
= swimming pool

schwimmen *irregular verb* (**!** *sein*)
* = to swim
* = to float

die **Schwimmweste**, *plural*
Schwimmwesten
= life-jacket

schwindlig *adjective*
= dizzy

schwitzen *verb*
= to sweat

schwören *irregular verb*
= to swear

schwul✶ *adjective*
(*homosexual*) = gay

schwül *adjective*
= close

✶ in informal situations

der **Schwung**, *plural* Schwünge
* = swing
* (*of a person*) = drive

sechs *adjective*
= six

sechseckig *adjective*
= hexagonal

sechster/sechste/sechstes *adjective*
= sixth

sechzehn *adjective*
= sixteen

sechzig *adjective*
= sixty

der **See**[1] *plural* Seen
= lake

die **See**[2]
= sea

die **Seele**, *plural* Seelen
= soul

der **Seemann**, *plural* Seeleute
= seaman, = sailor

das **Segel**, *plural* Segel
= sail

das **Segelboot**, *plural* Segelboote
= sailing boat, = sailboat

segeln *verb* (! *sein*)
= to sail

segnen *verb*
= to bless

sehen *irregular verb*
= to see
= to look
nach jemandem sehen = to look after someone

die **Sehenswürdigkeit**, *plural* Sehenswürdigkeiten
= sight

die **Sehnsucht**
= longing

sehr *adverb*
= very
danke sehr = thank you very much

seid ▶sein

die **Seide**, *plural* Seiden
= silk

die **Seife**, *plural* Seifen
= soap

das **Seil**, *plural* Seile
= rope
= cable

die **Seilbahn**, *plural* Seilbahnen
= cable railway

sein[1] *irregular verb* (! *sein*)
* = to be
wie dem auch sei = be that as it may
aus Wolle sein = to be made of wool
mir ist schlecht = I feel sick
* sein lassen = to stop
lass das sein! = stop it!
* (*forming the perfect tense*)
sie ist angekommen = she (has) arrived
wir sind gerettet worden = we were saved

sein[2] *adjective*
= his
(*of a thing*) = its
(*referring to the German pronoun 'man'*)
= one's

seiner/seine/seins *pronoun*
= his
(*referring to the German pronoun 'man'*)
= one's own

seinlassen ▶sein[1]

seins ▶seiner

seit
1 *preposition* (+ *dative*) = since
ich bin seit zwei Wochen hier = I've been here for two weeks
2 *conjunction* = since

seitdem
1 *conjunction* = since
2 *adverb* = since then

die **Seite**, *plural* Seiten
* = side
auf der einen Seite = on the one hand
* = page

seither *adverb*
= since then

die **Sekretärin**, *plural* Sekretärinnen
= secretary

die **Sekunde**, *plural* Sekunden
= second

selbst
1 *pronoun*
ich/du/er/sie/es selbst = I myself/you yourself/he himself/she herself/it itself
wir/ihr/sie selbst = we ourselves/you yourselves/they themselves
Sie selbst = you yourself/you yourselves
von selbst = automatically, = by itself
2 *adverb* = even

selbständig *adjective*
* = independent
* = self-employed
sich selbständig machen = to set up on one's own

die **Selbstbedienung**
= self-service

selbstbewusst
(**selbstbewußt** ⓞⓛⓓ) *adjective*
= self-confident

der **Selbstmord**, *plural* Selbstmorde
= suicide

selbstständig *adjective* ▶ selbständig

selbstverständlich
1 *adjective* = natural
2 *adverb* = naturally, = of course

das **Selbstvertrauen**
= self-confidence

selten
1 *adjective* = rare
2 *adverb* = rarely

seltsam *adjective*
= strange, = odd

das **Semester**, *plural* Semester
= semester, = term

die **Semmel**, *plural* Semmeln
= roll

senden *verb*
• = to send
• = to broadcast, = to transmit

die **Sendung**, *plural* Sendungen
• = programme
• = consignment

der **Senf**, *plural* Senfe
= mustard

der **Senior**, *plural* Senioren
• = senior
• = senior citizen

senken *verb*
• = to lower
• sich senken = to come down

senkrecht *adjective*
= vertical

der **September**
= September

die **Serie**, *plural* Serien
= series
= serial

servieren *verb*
= to serve

die **Serviette**, *plural* Servietten
= napkin, = serviette

der **Sessel**, *plural* Sessel
= armchair

der **Sessellift**, *plural* Sessellifte
= chair-lift

setzen *verb*
• = to put
= to set down

• (*in games*) = to move
• = to bet
• sich setzen = to sit (down)

seufzen *verb*
= to sigh

sexuell *adjective*
= sexual

sich *pronoun*
• (*as part of a reflexive verb*)
(*with er/sie/es*) = himself/herself/itself
(*with plural sie*) = themselves
(*with Sie*) = yourself, (*plural*) = yourselves
(*referring to one*) = oneself
sich freuen = to be pleased
sich die Haare kämmen = to comb one's
hair
• = each other, = one another

sicher
1 *adjective*
• = safe
• = certain, = sure
2 *adverb*
• = safely
• = certainly, = surely
sicher! = certainly!

die **Sicherheit**
• = safety
• = security
• = certainty

der **Sicherheitsgurt**, *plural*
Sicherheitsgurte
= seatbelt

die **Sicherheitsnadel**, *plural*
Sicherheitsnadeln
= safety-pin

sicherlich *adverb*
= certainly

die **Sicherung**, *plural* Sicherungen
• = safeguard
• = safety catch
• = fuse

die **Sicht**
• = view
auf lange Sicht = in the long term
• = visibility

sichtbar *adjective*
= visible

sie *pronoun*
(*singular*) = she, (*accusative*) = her
(*thing*) = it
(*plural*) = they, (*accusative*) = them

Sie *pronoun*
= you
warten Sie! = wait!

das **Sieb**, *plural* Siebe
= sieve, = strainer

sieben *adjective*
= seven

siebter/siebte/siebtes *adjective*
= seventh

siebzehn *adjective*
= seventeen

siebzig *adjective*
= seventy

die **Siedlung**, *plural* Siedlungen
* = (housing) estate
* = settlement

der **Sieg**, *plural* Siege
= victory, = win

das **Siegel**, *plural* Siegel
= seal

der **Sieger**, *plural* Sieger
= winner

die **Siegerin**, *plural* Siegerinnen
= winner

sieht ▶sehen

die **Silbe**, *plural* Silben
= syllable

das **Silber**
= silver

silbern *adjective*
= silver

das **Silvester**
= New Year's Eve

sind ▶sein

singen *irregular verb*
= to sing

sinken *irregular verb* (! sein)
* = to sink
* = to go down

der **Sinn**, *plural* Sinne
* = sense
* = meaning
* = point
  es hat keinen Sinn = there's no point

sinnlos *adjective*
= pointless

sinnvoll *adjective*
* = sensible
* = meaningful

die **Sitte**, *plural* Sitten
* = custom
* Sitten = manners

die **Situation**, *plural* Situationen
= situation

der **Sitz**, *plural* Sitze
* = seat
* (*of clothes*) = fit

sitzen *irregular verb*
* = to sit
* = to fit

der **Sitzplatz**, *plural* Sitzplätze
= seat

die **Sitzung**, *plural* Sitzungen
* = meeting
* = session

das **Skelett**, *plural* Skelette
= skeleton

der **Ski**, *plural* Skier *or* Ski
= ski
Ski fahren *or* laufen = to ski

das **Skifahren**, das **Skilaufen**
= skiing

der **Skiläufer**, *plural* Skiläufer
= skier

die **Skiläuferin**, *plural* Skiläuferinnen
= skier

die **Skizze**, *plural* Skizzen
= sketch

der **Skorpion**, *plural* Skorpione
* = scorpion
* = Scorpio

der **Slip**, *plural* Slips
= briefs

die **Slowakei**
= Slovakia

der **Smaragd**, *plural* Smaragde
= emerald

der **Smoking**, *plural* Smokings
= dinner jacket, = tuxedo

so
1 *adverb*
* = so
* = like this, = like that
  gut so = that's fine
* = as
  so gut ich konnte = as best I could
* so = such
  so ein Zufall! = what a coincidence!
2 *conjunction*
so dass = so that

sobald *conjunction*
= as soon as

die **Socke**, *plural* Socken
= sock

sodass *conjunction*
= so that

sofort *adverb*
* = immediately
* = in a moment

die **Sohle**, *plural* Sohlen
= sole

der **Sohn**, *plural* Söhne
= son

solange *conjunction*
= as long as

S

solch *pronoun*
= such

solcher/solche/solches
1 *adjective* = such
eine solche Frau = a woman like that
2 *pronoun*
solche wie die = people like that

der **Soldat**, *plural* Soldaten
= soldier

sollen *irregular verb*
• = should
• = be supposed to
was soll das heißen? = what is that
supposed to mean?
• (*other uses*)
er soll warten = let him wait
sagen Sie ihm, er soll hereinkommen =
tell him to come in

sollte, sollten, solltest, solltet
▶ sollen

der **Sommer**, *plural* Sommer
= summer

sommerlich *adjective*
= summery, = summer

die **Sommersprosse**, *plural*
Sommersprossen
= freckle

das **Sonderangebot**, *plural*
Sonderangebote
= special offer

sonderbar *adjective*
= odd, = strange

sondern *conjunction*
= but

der **Sonnabend**
= Saturday

sonnabends *adverb*
= on Saturdays

die **Sonne**, *plural* Sonnen
= sun

der **Sonnenaufgang**
= sunrise

der **Sonnenbrand**
= sunburn

die **Sonnenbrille**, *plural* Sonnenbrillen
= sunglasses

der **Sonnenschein**
= sunshine

der **Sonnenschirm**, *plural* Sonnenschirme
= sunshade

der **Sonnenstich**
= sunstroke

der **Sonnenuntergang**
= sunset

sonnig *adjective*
= sunny

der **Sonntag**
= Sunday

sonntags *adverb*
= on Sundays

sonst *adverb*
• = usually
• = else
sonst noch was? = anything else?
sonst niemand = no one else
• = otherwise

sooft *conjunction*
= whenever

die **Sorge**, *plural* Sorgen
= worry
sich Sorgen machen = to worry

sorgen *verb*
• für etwas sorgen = to take care of
something
dafür sorgen, dass = to make sure that
• sich sorgen = to worry

sorgfältig *adjective*
= careful

die **Sorte**, *plural* Sorten
= sort, = kind

die **Soße**, *plural* Soßen
= sauce, = gravy
= dressing

soviel
1 *conjunction* = as far as
2 *adverb* ⓄⓁⒹ ▶ viel

sowenig ⓄⓁⒹ ▶ wenig

sowie *conjunction*
• = as well as
• = as soon as

sowieso *adverb*
= anyway

sowohl *adverb*
sowohl er wie auch sie = both he and she

der **Sozialarbeiter**, *plural* Sozialarbeiter
= social worker

sozialistisch *adjective*
= socialist

die **Sozialwohnung**, *plural*
Sozialwohnungen
= council flat

die **Soziologie**
= sociology

die **Spalte**, *plural* Spalten
• = crack
• (*in text*) = column

(das) Spanien
= Spain

spanisch *adjective*
= Spanish

spannend *adjective*
= exciting

die **Spannung**, *plural* Spannungen
• = tension
• = voltage

sparen *verb*
= to save
auf etwas sparen = to save up for something

sparsam *adjective*
• = economical
• = thrifty

der **Spaß**, *plural* Späße
• = fun
es macht mir Spaß = I enjoy it
viel Spaß! = have a good time!
• = joke

spät *adjective*
= late
wie spät ist es? = what time is it?

der **Spaten**, *plural* Spaten
= spade

später *adjective*
= later

spätestens *adverb*
= at the latest

der **Spatz**, *plural* Spatzen
= sparrow

spazieren *verb* (! *sein*)
• to stroll
• spazieren gehen = to go for a walk

der **Spaziergang**, *plural* Spaziergänge
= walk

der **Speck**
= bacon

der **Speicher**, *plural* Speicher
• = loft, = attic
• (*of a computer*) = memory

speichern *verb*
• = to store
• (*computing*) = to save

die **Speise**, *plural* Speisen
• = food
• = dish

die **Speisekarte**, *plural* Speisekarten
= menu

die **Spende**, *plural* Spenden
= donation

spenden *verb*
= to donate
= to give, = to contribute

sperren
= to close
= to block
den Strom sperren = to cut off the electricity
einen Scheck sperren = to stop a cheque

Spesen (*plural*)
= expenses

der **Spiegel**, *plural* Spiegel
= mirror

das **Spiegelbild**, *plural* Spiegelbilder
= reflection

spiegeln *verb*
• = to reflect
• sich spiegeln = to be reflected

das **Spiel**, *plural* Spiele
= game
auf dem Spiel stehen = to be at stake
ein Spiel Karten = a pack of cards

spielen *verb*
• = to play
• = to gamble
• = to act
der Film spielt in Berlin = the film is set in Berlin

die **Spielhalle**, *plural* Spielhallen
= amusement arcade

der **Spielplatz**, *plural* Spielplätze
= playground

das **Spielzeug**
• = toy
• = toys

der **Spinat**
= spinach

die **Spinne**, *plural* Spinnen
= spider

spinnen *irregular verb*
• = to spin
• sie spinnt✘ = she's crazy

das **Spinnennetz**, *plural* Spinnennetze
= spider's web, = cobweb

der **Spion**, *plural* Spione
= spy

spitz *adjective*
= pointed

die **Spitze**, *plural* Spitzen
• = point, = tip
• = top, = peak
Spitze sein✘ = to be great
• = front
an der Spitze liegen = to be in the lead
• = lace

der **Spitzname**, *plural* Spitznamen
= nickname

der **Splitter**, *plural* Splitter
= splinter

S

der **Sportler**, plural Sportler
= sportsman

die **Sportlerin**, plural Sportlerinnen
= sportswoman

sportlich adjective
= sporting
= sporty

der **Sportwagen**, plural Sportwagen
* = sports car
* = pushchair, = stroller

spotten verb
= to mock

sprach ▶sprechen

die **Sprache**, plural Sprachen
* = language
* = speech
etwas zur Sprache bringen = to bring
something up

sprang ▶springen

sprechen irregular verb
= to speak, = to talk

die **Sprechstunde**, plural Sprechstunden
= surgery

der **Sprengstoff**, plural Sprengstoffe
= explosive

spricht ▶sprechen

das **Sprichwort**, plural Sprichwörter
= proverb

springen irregular verb (**!** sein)
* = to jump, = to bounce
* = to dive

die **Spritze**, plural Spritzen
* = syringe
* = injection
* = hose

spritzen verb
* = to inject
* = to spray
= to splash
(of fat) = to spit

der **Spruch**, plural Sprüche
= saying

der **Sprudel**, plural Sprudel
= sparkling mineral water

sprühen verb
* = to spray
* (of eyes) = to sparkle
* (of sparks) = to fly

der **Sprung**, plural Sprünge
* = jump, = leap
* = dive
* (in china) = crack

das **Sprungbrett**, plural Sprungbretter
= diving board

spucken verb
= to spit

das **Spülbecken**, plural Spülbecken
= sink

spülen verb
* = to rinse
* = to wash up
* = to flush

die **Spur**, plural Spuren
* = track
* = lane
* = trail

spüren verb
= to sense, = to feel

der **Staat**, plural Staaten
= state

staatlich
1 adjective = state
2 adverb = by the state

die **Staatsangehörigkeit**
= nationality

stabil adjective
= stable
= sturdy

der **Stachel**, plural Stacheln
* = spine
* = spike
* = sting

die **Stachelbeere**, plural Stachelbeeren
= gooseberry

das **Stadion**, plural Stadien
= stadium

das **Stadium**, plural Stadien
= stage

die **Stadt**, plural Städte
= town, = city

städtisch adjective
= urban, = municipal

die **Stadtmitte**
= town centre, = downtown area

der **Stadtplan**, plural Stadtpläne
= street map

stahl ▶stehlen

der **Stahl**
= steel

der **Stall**, plural Ställe
= stable
(for cows) = shed
(for pigs) = sty
(for sheep) = pen
(for hens) = coop
(for rabbits) = hutch

✱ in informal situations   ⌐OLD⌐ = old spelling

der **Stamm**, *plural* Stämme
* = trunk
* = tribe

stand ▶ stehen

ständig *adjective*
= constant

die **Stange**, *plural* Stangen
= bar
= pole

starb ▶ sterben

stark *adjective*
* = strong
* = severe, = heavy
* das ist stark■ = that's great

die **Stärke**, *plural* Stärken
* = strength, = power
* = starch

starrsinnig *adjective*
= obstinate

der **Start**, *plural* Starts
* = start
* = take-off

die **Startbahn**, *plural* Startbahnen
= runway

die **Station**, *plural* Stationen
* = station
* = stop
  Station machen = to stop over
* (*in a hospital*) = ward

statt
1 *preposition* (+ *genitive*) = instead of
2 *conjunction*
statt zu arbeiten = instead of working

stattdessen *adverb*
= instead

statt|finden *irregular verb*
= to take place

der **Stau**, *plural* Staus
* = congestion
* = traffic jam, = tailback

der **Staub**
= dust

der **Staubsauger**, *plural* Staubsauger
= vacuum cleaner, = Hoover®

staunen *verb*
= to be amazed

stechen *irregular verb*
* = to prick
* = to stab
* (*of an insect*) = to sting, = to bite

die **Steckdose**, *plural* Steckdosen
= socket

stecken *verb*
= to put

der **Stecker**, *plural* Stecker
= plug

die **Stecknadel**, *plural* Stecknadeln
= pin

stehen *irregular verb*
* = to stand
* = to be
  es steht schlecht um ihn = he is in a bad way
* (**!** *sein*) stehen bleiben = to stop
  das Spiel steht eins zu eins = the score is one all
  in der Zeitung steht = it says in the paper
* die Uhr steht = the clock has stopped
* jemandem (gut) stehen = to suit someone
* zu jemandem stehen = to stand by someone

stehen bleiben ⓞⓛⓓ ▶ stehen

stehlen *irregular verb*
= to steal

steif *adjective*
= stiff

steigen *irregular verb* (**!** *sein*)
= to climb
in den Bus steigen = to get on the bus

steigern *verb*
* = to raise, = to boost
* sich steigern = to increase

steil *adjective*
= steep

der **Stein**, *plural* Steine
= stone

der **Steinbock**, *plural* Steinböcke
* = ibex
* = Capricorn

die **Stelle**, *plural* Stellen
* = place
  an Stelle = instead of
  auf der Stelle = immediately
* = job, = post

stellen *verb*
* = to put, = to place
  etwas zur Verfügung stellen = to provide something
* eine Uhr stellen = to set a clock
  die Heizung höher stellen = to turn the heating up
* sich krank stellen = to pretend to be ill

die **Stellenanzeige**, *plural* Stellenanzeigen
= job advertisement

die **Stellung**, *plural* Stellungen
= position

der **Stellvertreter**, *plural* Stellvertreter
= deputy

der **Stempel**, *plural* Stempel
* = stamp
* = postmark
* = hallmark

S

stempeln *verb*
* = to stamp
* = to postmark

die **Steppdecke**, *plural* Steppdecken
= quilt

sterben *irregular verb* (**!** *sein*)
= to die

die **Stereoanlage**, *plural* Stereoanlagen
= stereo (system)

der **Stern**, *plural* Sterne
= star

die **Sternwarte**, *plural* Sternwarten
= observatory

das **Steuer**¹ *plural* Steuer
* = steering wheel
* = helm

die **Steuer**² *plural* Steuern
= tax

die **Steuererklärung**, *plural*
Steuererklärungen
= tax return

steuerfrei *adjective*
= tax-free

steuern *verb*
* = to steer
* (*in an aircraft*) = to fly

steuerpflichtig *adjective*
= taxable

die **Steuerung**, *plural* Steuerungen
* = steering
* = controls

die **Stewardess** (**Stewardeß** ⓞⓛⓓ),
plural Stewardessen
= stewardess, = air hostess

der **Stich**, *plural* Stiche
* (*with a needle*) = prick
* (*with a knife*) = stab
* (*of an insect*) = sting, = bite
* (*when sewing*) = stitch
* (*when playing cards*) = trick
* jemanden im Stich lassen = to leave
someone in the lurch

sticken *verb*
= to embroider

der **Stiefbruder**, *plural* Stiefbrüder
= stepbrother

der **Stiefel**, *plural* Stiefel
= boot

das **Stiefkind**, *plural* Stiefkinder
= stepchild

die **Stiefmutter**, *plural* Stiefmütter
= stepmother

das **Stiefmütterchen**, *plural*
Stiefmütterchen
= pansy

die **Stiefschwester**, *plural*
Stiefschwestern
= stepsister

der **Stiefvater**, *plural* Stiefväter
= stepfather

stiehlt ▶ stehlen

der **Stiel**, *plural* Stiele
* = handle
* = stem

der **Stier**, *plural* Stiere
* = bull
* = Taurus

der **Stift**, *plural* Stifte
* (*nail*) = tack
* = pencil

der **Stil**, *plural* Stile
= style

still *adjective*
= quiet
= still

stillen *verb*
* = to satisfy
= to quench
* = to breast-feed

die **Stimme**, *plural* Stimmen
* = voice
* = vote

stimmen *verb*
* = to be right
stimmt das? = is that right?
* = to vote
* = to tune

die **Stimmung**, *plural* Stimmungen
= mood
= atmosphere

stinken *irregular verb*
= to smell, = to stink

stirbt ▶ sterben

die **Stirn**, *plural* Stirnen
= forehead

der **Stock**¹ *plural* Stöcke
= stick

der **Stock**² *plural* Stock
= floor, = storey

das **Stockwerk**, *plural* Stockwerke
= floor, = storey

der **Stoff**, *plural* Stoffe
* = material
* = substance

stöhnen *verb*
= to groan, = to moan

✖ in informal situations ⓞⓛⓓ = old spelling

stolpern *verb*
= to stumble, = to trip

stolz *adjective*
= proud

stopfen *verb*
• = to stuff
• = to darn

stoppen *verb*
= to stop

die **Stoppuhr**, *plural* Stoppuhren
= stopwatch

der **Stöpsel**, *plural* Stöpsel
• = plug
• = stopper

der **Storch**, *plural* Störche
= stork

stören *verb*
= to disturb, = to bother

die **Störung**, *plural* Störungen
= disturbance
eine technische Störung = a technical fault
entschuldigen Sie die Störung = I'm sorry to bother you

der **Stoß**, *plural* Stöße
• = push, = knock
• = pile, = stack

stoßen *irregular verb*
• = to push, = to knock
(*with one's foot*) = to kick
• (**!** *sein*) gegen etwas stoßen = to bump into something
auf etwas stoßen = to come across something
• sich stoßen = to knock oneself
sich an etwas stoßen = to object to something

die **Stoßstange**, *plural* Stoßstangen
= bumper

die **Stoßzeit**, *plural* Stoßzeiten
= rush hour

stottern *verb*
= to stutter, = to stammer

die **Strafe**, *plural* Strafen
= punishment
= penalty, = fine
= sentence

der **Strahl**, *plural* Strahlen
• = ray, = beam
• (*of water*) = jet

strahlen *verb*
= to shine
= to beam

der **Strand**, *plural* Strände
= beach

die **Straße**, *plural* Straßen
= street, = road

die **Straßenbahn**, *plural* Straßenbahnen
= tram, = streetcar

der **Strauch**, *plural* Sträucher
= bush

der **Strauß**[1] *plural* Sträuße
= bunch of flowers, = bouquet

der **Strauß**[2] *plural* Strauße
= ostrich

die **Strecke**, *plural* Strecken
• = distance
• = route, = line

strecken *verb*
• = to stretch (out)
• sich strecken = to stretch

streicheln *verb*
= to stroke

streichen *irregular verb*
• = to paint
'frisch gestrichen' = 'wet paint'
• (*with butter*) = to spread
• = to delete, = to cross off
• jemandem über den Kopf streichen = to stroke someone's head

das **Streichholz**, *plural* Streichhölzer
= match

die **Streife**, *plural* Streifen
= patrol

der **Streifen**, *plural* Streifen
• = stripe
• = strip

die **Streifenkarte**, *plural* Streifenkarten
= multiple ticket (*for economy travel*)

der **Streifenwagen**, *plural* Streifenwagen
= patrol car

der **Streik**, *plural* Streiks
= strike

streiken *verb*
= to strike

der **Streit**, *plural* Streite
= quarrel, = argument

streiten *irregular verb*
• = to quarrel, = to argue
• sich streiten = to quarrel, = to argue

Streitkräfte (*plural*)
= armed forces

streng *adjective*
= strict

der **Stress** (**Streß**(OLD))
= stress

stressig× *adjective*
= stressful

S

streuen verb
= to spread
= to sprinkle

stricken verb
= to knit

die **Strickjacke**, plural Strickjacken
= cardigan

das **Stroh**
= straw

der **Strohhalm**, plural Strohhalme
= straw

der **Strom**, plural Ströme
• = river
• = stream
  es regnet in Strömen = it's pouring with rain
• = electricity

strömen verb (**!** sein)
= to stream

die **Strömung**, plural Strömungen
= current

der **Strumpf**, plural Strümpfe
• = stocking
• = sock

die **Strumpfhose**, plural Strumpfhosen
= tights, = pantyhose

die **Stube**, plural Stuben
= room

das **Stück**, plural Stücke
• = piece, = bit
• = item
  fünfzig Pfennig das Stück = 50 pfennigs each
• = play

der **Student**, plural Studenten
= student

die **Studentin**, plural Studentinnen
= student

studieren verb
= to study

das **Studium**, plural Studien
= study
= studies

die **Stufe**, plural Stufen
= step

der **Stuhl**, plural Stühle
= chair

stumm adjective
• = dumb
• = silent

stumpf adjective
• = blunt
• = dull

die **Stunde**, plural Stunden
• = hour
• = lesson

stundenlang adverb
= for hours

der **Stundenplan**, plural Stundenpläne
= timetable

stündlich adjective
= hourly

stur✱ adjective
= stubborn

der **Sturm**, plural Stürme
= storm

der **Stürmer**, plural Stürmer
= forward

stürmisch adjective
• = stormy
• = tumultuous

der **Sturz**, plural Stürze
= fall

stürzen verb
• (**!** sein) = to fall
• (**!** sein) = to rush
• = to overthrow
• **sich in etwas stürzen** = to throw oneself into something
  sich auf jemanden stürzen = to pounce on someone

der **Sturzhelm**, plural Sturzhelme
= crash helmet

stützen verb
= to support
  sich auf jemanden stützen = to lean on someone

suchen verb
• = to search
• = to look for
  'Zimmer gesucht' = 'room wanted'

süchtig adjective
= addicted

(das) **Südafrika**
= South Africa

der **Süden**
= south

südlich adjective
• = southern
• = southerly

der **Südosten**
= southeast

der **Südwesten**
= southwest

die **Summe**, plural Summen
= sum

summen verb
= to hum
= to buzz

✱ in informal situations

super *adjective*
= great

der **Supermarkt**, *plural* Supermärkte
= supermarket

die **Suppe**, *plural* Suppen
= soup

surfen *verb*
= to surf

süß *adjective*
= sweet

die **Süßigkeit**, *plural* Süßigkeiten
= sweet, = candy

Süßwaren (*plural*)
= confectionery
= sweets, = candy

sympathisch *adjective*
= likeable

die **Szene**, *plural* Szenen
= scene

der **Tabak**, *plural* Tabake
= tobacco

die **Tabelle**, *plural* Tabellen
= table

das **Tablett**, *plural* Tabletts
= tray

die **Tablette**, *plural* Tabletten
= tablet

die **Tafel**, *plural* Tafeln
• = board, = blackboard
• eine Tafel Schokolade = a bar of
    chocolate

der **Tag**, *plural* Tage
= day
guten Tag = good morning/afternoon

das **Tagebuch**, *plural* Tagebücher
= diary

tagelang *adverb*
= for days

die **Tageskarte**, *plural* Tageskarten
• = today's menu
• = day ticket

die **Tagesmutter**, *plural* Tagesmütter
= childminder

die **Tagesschau**
= news

täglich
1 *adjective* = daily
2 *adverb*
zweimal täglich = twice a day

tagsüber *adverb*
= during the day

die **Taille**, *plural* Taillen
= waist

der **Takt**, *plural* Takte
• = tact
• = time, = rhythm

taktlos *adjective*
= tactless

taktvoll *adjective*
= tactful

das **Tal**, *plural* Täler
= valley

tanken *verb*
= to fill up (*with petrol*)

die **Tankstelle**, *plural* Tankstellen
= petrol station, = gas station

die **Tanne**, *plural* Tannen
= fir

der **Tannenbaum**, *plural* Tannenbäume
= fir tree

die **Tante**, *plural* Tanten
= aunt

der **Tanz**, *plural* Tänze
= dance

tanzen *verb*
= to dance

der **Tänzer**, *plural* Tänzer
= dancer

die **Tänzerin**, *plural* Tänzerinnen
= dancer

die **Tapete**, *plural* Tapeten
= wallpaper

tapfer *adjective*
= brave

die **Tasche**, *plural* Taschen
• = bag
• = pocket

das **Taschenbuch**, *plural* Taschenbücher
= paperback

das **Taschengeld**
= pocket money

die **Taschenlampe**, *plural*
Taschenlampen
= torch, = flashlight

das **Taschenmesser**, *plural*
Taschenmesser
= penknife

T

das **Taschentuch**, *plural* Taschentücher
= handkerchief

die **Tasse**, *plural* Tassen
= cup

die **Taste**, *plural* Tasten
* = key
* (*on a phone*) = button

tasten *verb*
* = to feel
* sich tasten = to feel one's way

das **Tastentelefon**, *plural* Tastentelefone
= push-button phone

tat ▶ tun

die **Tat**, *plural* Taten
* = action
  in der Tat = indeed
* crime

der **Täter**, *plural* Täter
= culprit
= offender

die **Tätigkeit**, *plural* Tätigkeiten
= activity
= job

die **Tatsache**, *plural* Tatsachen
= fact

tatsächlich
1 *adjective* = actual
2 *adverb* = actually

der **Tau**¹
= dew

das **Tau**² *plural* Taue
= rope

taub *adjective*
= deaf

die **Taube**, *plural* Tauben
= dove, = pigeon

tauchen *verb*
* = to dive
* = to dip

der **Taucher**, *plural* Taucher
= diver

die **Taucherin**, *plural* Taucherinnen
= diver

tauen *verb*
= to melt, = to thaw

die **Taufe**, *plural* Taufen
= christening
= baptism

taufen *verb*
= to christen
= to baptize

✴ in informal situations

tauschen *verb*
= to exchange, = to swap

täuschen *verb*
* = to deceive
* sich täuschen = to be mistaken

tausend *adjective*
= a thousand, = one thousand

das **Taxi**, *plural* Taxis
= taxi

der **Taxistand**, *plural* Taxistände
= taxi rank, = taxi stand

die **Technik**, *plural* Techniken
* = technology
* = technique

der **Techniker**, *plural* Techniker
= technician

technisch *adjective*
= technical
= technological

der **Tee**, *plural* Tees
= tea

der **Teich**, *plural* Teiche
= pond

der **Teig**, *plural* Teige
= dough
= pastry
(*for baking*) = mixture

der **Teil**¹ *plural* Teile
* = part
  zum Teil = partly
* = share

das **Teil**² *plural* Teile
* = part
  = spare part
* = share

teilen *verb*
* = to divide
* = to share
* sich etwas mit jemandem teilen = to
  share something with someone

teil|nehmen *irregular verb*
an etwas teilnehmen = to take part in
something

der **Teilnehmer**, *plural* Teilnehmer
* = participant
* = competitor

die **Teilnehmerin**, *plural* Teilnehmerinnen
* = participant
* = competitor

teils *adverb*
= partly

die **Teilung**, *plural* Teilungen
= division

die **Teilzeitarbeit**
= part-time work

das **Telefax**, *plural* Telefax *or* Telefaxe
= fax

das **Telefon**, *plural* Telefone
= telephone

das **Telefonbuch**, *plural* Telefonbücher
= telephone directory, = phone book

telefonieren *verb*
= to telephone, = to make a phone call

telefonisch
1 *adjective* = telephone
2 *adverb* = by telephone

die **Telefonkarte**, *plural* Telefonkarten
= phone card

die **Telefonzelle**, *plural* Telefonzellen
= telephone box, = telephone booth

telegrafieren *verb*
= to send a telegram

der **Teller**, *plural* Teller
= plate

der **Tempel**, *plural* Tempel
= temple

die **Temperatur**, *plural* Temperaturen
= temperature

das **Tempo**, *plural* Tempos
= speed

das **Tennis**
= tennis

der **Tennisschläger**, *plural*
Tennisschläger
= tennis racket

der **Teppich**, *plural* Teppiche
= carpet
= rug

der **Termin**, *plural* Termine
= date
= appointment

der **Tesafilm**®
= Sellotape®

teuer *adjective*
= expensive

der **Teufel**, *plural* Teufel
= devil

der **Text**, *plural* Texte
= text

die **Textverarbeitung**
= word processing

das **Textverarbeitungssystem**,
plural Textverarbeitungssysteme
= word processor

das **Theater**, *plural* Theater
• = theatre
• so ein Theater!✴ = such a fuss!

das **Theaterstück**, *plural* Theaterstücke
= play

das **Thema**, *plural* Themen
= theme, = subject

die **Themse**
= Thames

der **Thron**, *plural* Throne
= throne

der **Thunfisch**, *plural* Thunfische
= tuna

tief *adjective*
= deep
= low

die **Tiefe**, *plural* Tiefen
= depth

die **Tiefgarage**, *plural* Tiefgaragen
= underground car park

das **Tiefkühlfach**, *plural* Tiefkühlfächer
= freezer compartment

die **Tiefkühlkost**
= frozen food

das **Tier**, *plural* Tiere
= animal

der **Tierarzt**, *plural* Tierärzte
= vet, = veterinarian

der **Tierkreis**
= zodiac

der **Tierpark**, *plural* Tierparks
= zoo

die **Tinte**, *plural* Tinten
= ink

der **Tintenfisch**, *plural* Tintenfische
= octopus
= squid

tippen *verb*
• = to type
• = to tap
• auf etwas tippen = to bet on something
im Lotto tippen = to do the lottery

der **Tisch**, *plural* Tische
= table

der **Tischler**, *plural* Tischler
= joiner, = carpenter

das **Tischtuch**, *plural* Tischtücher
= tablecloth

toben *verb*
• = to rage
(*play boisterously*) = to go wild
• (**!** *sein*) = to rush

die **Tochter**, *plural* Töchter
= daughter

der **Tod**, *plural* Tode
= death

T

tödlich *adjective*
- = fatal
- = deadly

die **Toilette**, *plural* Toiletten
= toilet

toll✶ *adjective*
= brilliant, = fantastic

die **Tollwut**
= rabies

die **Tomate**, *plural* Tomaten
= tomato

der **Ton¹** *plural* Töne
- = tone, = note
- = sound
- (*of colour*) = shade

der **Ton²**
= clay

das **Tonband**, *plural* Tonbänder
= tape

das **Tonbandgerät**, *plural* Tonbandgeräte
= tape recorder

die **Tonne**, *plural* Tonnen
- = barrel
- (*for rubbish*) = bin
- = tonne

der **Topf**, *plural* Töpfe
- = pot, = jar
- = pan

die **Töpferei**, *plural* Töpfereien
= pottery

das **Tor**, *plural* Tore
- = gate
- = goal

die **Torte**, *plural* Torten
= gateau, = cake

der **Torwart**, *plural* Torwarte
= goalkeeper

tot *adjective*
= dead

der/die **Tote**, *plural* Toten
= dead man/woman, = fatality
die Toten = the dead

die **Tour**, *plural* Touren
- = tour, = trip
- auf diese Tour✶ = in this way

der **Tourismus**
= tourism

der **Tourist**, *plural* Touristen
= tourist

die **Touristin**, *plural* Touristinnen
= tourist

die **Tournee**, *plural* Tournees
= tour

die **Tracht**, *plural* Trachten
- = (national) costume
- eine Tracht Prügel = a good hiding

traditionell *adjective*
= traditional

traf ▶treffen

tragen *irregular verb*
- = to carry
- = to wear
- = to support
- = to bear

der **Träger**, *plural* Träger
- = porter
- (*holder*) = bearer
- (*on a dress*) = strap
- = girder

der **Trainer**, *plural* Trainer
= trainer, = coach
(*of a soccer team*) = manager

trainieren *verb*
= to train, = to coach

der **Trainingsanzug**, *plural*
Trainingsanzüge
= tracksuit

der **Traktor**, *plural* Traktoren
= tractor

die **Träne**, *plural* Tränen
= tear

trank ▶trinken

der **Transport**, *plural* Transporte
- = transport
- = consignment

transportieren *verb*
= to transport

trat ▶treten

die **Traube**, *plural* Trauben
= grape

trauen *verb*
- = to trust
- = to marry
- sich trauen = to dare

die **Trauer**
- = grief
- = mourning

der **Traum**, *plural* Träume
= dream

träumen *verb*
= to dream

traurig *adjective*
= sad

die **Trauung**, *plural* Trauungen
= wedding

---

treffen *irregular verb*
- = to hit, = to strike
- = to meet
- (*if it's an arrangement, a choice, a decision*) = to make
- **sich treffen** = to meet
  sich gut treffen = to be convenient

das **Treffen**, *plural* Treffen
  = meeting

der **Treffpunkt**, *plural* Treffpunkte
  = meeting place

treiben *irregular verb*
- = to drive
- = to do
  Handel treiben = to trade
- (**!** *sein*) = to drift

der **Treibhauseffekt**
  = greenhouse effect

der **Treibstoff**
  = fuel

trennen *verb*
- = to separate
- = to divide, = to split
- **sich trennen** = to separate, = to split up
  sich von etwas trennen = to part with something

die **Trennung**, *plural* Trennungen
- = separation
- = division

die **Treppe**, *plural* Treppen
  = stairs, = steps
  eine Treppe = a flight of stairs

treten *irregular verb*
- (**!** *sein*) = to step
- = to tread
- = to kick

treu *adjective*
  = faithful, = loyal

der **Trickfilm**, *plural* Trickfilme
  = cartoon

trifft ▶ treffen

trinken *irregular verb*
  = to drink

das **Trinkgeld**, *plural* Trinkgelder
  = tip

das **Trinkwasser**
  = drinking water

tritt ▶ treten

der **Tritt**, *plural* Tritte
- = step
- = kick

triumphieren *verb*
- = to rejoice
- = to be triumphant

trocken *adjective*
  = dry

trocknen *verb*
  = to dry

der **Trockner**, *plural* Trockner
  = drier

die **Trommel**, *plural* Trommeln
  = drum

trommeln *verb*
- = to drum
- = to play the drums

die **Trompete**, *plural* Trompeten
  = trumpet

Tropen (*plural*)
  = tropics

tropfen *verb*
  = to drip

der **Tropfen**, *plural* Tropfen
  = drop

trösten *verb*
  = to comfort, = to console

trotz *preposition* (+ *genitive*)
  = despite, = in spite of

trotzdem *adverb*
  = nevertheless
  trotzdem danke = thanks anyway

trüb(**e**) *adjective*
  = dull

trug ▶ tragen

die **Truhe**, *plural* Truhen
  = chest, = trunk

Trümmer (*plural*)
  = ruins

der **Trumpf**, *plural* Trümpfe
  = trump (card)
  = trumps

die **Trunkenheit**
  = drunkenness
  Trunkenheit am Steuer = drink-driving

tschechisch *adjective*
  = Czech

tschüs ▶ tschüss

tschüss *interjection*
  = bye!

das **Tuch**, *plural* Tücher
- = cloth
- = scarf

tüchtig *adjective*
- = competent
- = big

die **Tulpe**, *plural* Tulpen
  = tulip

tun *irregular verb*
- = to do
  das tut man nicht = it isn't done

T

- = to put
- **das Radio tuts noch✗** = the radio is still working
- **er tut nur so** = he's just pretending **freundlich tun** = to act friendly
- **es hat sich einiges getan** = quite a lot has happened

der **Tunnel**, *plural* Tunnel
  = tunnel

tupfen *verb*
- = to dab
- = to touch

die **Tür**, *plural* Türen
  = door

die **Türkei**
  = Turkey

der **Turm**, *plural* Türme
- = tower
- (*in chess*) = rook, = castle

das **Turnen**
  = gymnastics
  = physical education, = PE

die **Turnhalle**, *plural* Turnhallen
  = gymnasium

das **Turnier**, *plural* Tourniere
  = tournament

tuscheln *verb*
  = to whisper

die **Tüte**, *plural* Tüten
  = bag

der **Typ**, *plural* Typen
- = type
- **ein netter Typ✗** = a nice bloke

typisch *adjective*
  = typical

U u

die **U-Bahn**, *plural* U-Bahnen
  = underground, = subway

übel *adjective*
  = bad
  mir ist übel = I feel sick

die **Übelkeit**
  = nausea

üben *verb*
  = to practise

✗ in informal situations

über
1 *preposition*
- (*+ dative*)
  (*indicating position*) = over, = above
  (*more than*) = above
  über jemandem wohnen = to live above someone
- (*+ accusative*)
  (*indicating direction*) = over
  (*concerning*) = about, = on
  (*indicating an amount*) = for
  (*more than, during*) = over
  über die Straße gehen = to go across the street
  über München fahren = to go via Munich
  heute über eine Woche = a week today
2 *adverb*
  über und über = all over

überall *adverb*
  = everywhere

der **Überblick**, *plural* Überblicke
- = overall view
- = summary

überblicken *verb*
- = to overlook
- = to assess

übereinander *adverb*
  = one on top of the other
  übereinander sprechen = to talk about each other

überein|stimmen *verb*
  = to agree

überfahren *irregular verb*
  = to run over

die **Überfahrt**, *plural* Überfahrten
  = crossing

der **Überfall**, *plural* Überfälle
  = attack
  (*on a bank*) = raid

überfallen *irregular verb*
  = to attack, = to mug
  = to raid

überflüssig *adjective*
  = superfluous

die **Überführung**, *plural* Überführungen
- = transfer
- (*road*) = flyover
  (*for pedestrians*) = footbridge

überfüllt *adjective*
  = crowded

der **Übergang**, *plural* Übergänge
- = crossing
- = transition

übergeben *irregular verb*
- = to hand over
- **sich übergeben** = to be sick, = to vomit

überhaupt *adverb*
* = altogether
  überhaupt nicht = not at all
  überhaupt nichts = nothing at all
* = anyway

überholen *verb*
= to overtake

überlassen *irregular verb*
jemandem etwas überlassen = to leave
  someone something, = to give someone
  something

über|laufen *irregular verb* (**!** *sein*)
= to overflow

überleben *verb*
= to survive

überlegen *verb*
* = to think
* sich etwas überlegen = to think
  something over
  es sich anders überlegen = to change
  one's mind

übermorgen *adverb*
= the day after tomorrow

**übernächster/übernächste/
übernächstes** *adjective*
= next but one
übernächstes Jahr = the year after next

übernachten *verb*
= to stay the night

übernehmen *irregular verb*
* = to take over
* = to take on

überraschen *verb*
= to surprise

die **Überraschung**, *plural*
Überraschungen
= surprise

übers = über das

die **Überschrift**, *plural* Überschriften
= heading

die **Überschwemmung**, *plural*
Überschwemmungen
= flood

übersehen *irregular verb*
= to overlook

übersetzen *verb*
= to translate

der **Übersetzer**, *plural* Übersetzer
= translator

die **Übersetzerin**, *plural* Übersetzerinnen
= translator

die **Übersetzung**, *plural* Übersetzungen
= translation

die **Überstunde**, *plural* Überstunden
Überstunden machen = to work overtime

übertragen *irregular verb*
* = to transfer
* = to communicate
* (*on TV*) = to broadcast

die **Übertragung**, *plural* Übertragungen
* (*on TV*) = broadcast
* (*of an illness*) = communication

übertreiben *irregular verb*
* = to exaggerate
* = to overdo

die **Übertreibung**, *plural* Übertreibungen
= exaggeration

überweisen *irregular verb*
* = to transfer
* = to refer

überzeugen *verb*
* = to convince, = to persuade
* sich überzeugen = to satisfy oneself

die **Überzeugung**, *plural* Überzeugungen
= conviction

überziehen[1] *irregular verb*
* = to cover
* = to overdraw

über|ziehen[2] *irregular verb*
(*if it's clothes*) = to put on

üblich *adjective*
= usual

übrig *adjective*
= remaining, = spare
übrig sein = to be left over

übrigens *adverb*
= by the way

die **Übung**, *plural* Übungen
= exercise
außer Übung sein = to be out of practice

das **Ufer**, *plural* Ufer
(*of a river*) = bank
(*of the sea*) = shore

die **Uhr**, *plural* Uhren
= clock
= watch
es ist zwei Uhr = it is 2 o'clock
wie viel Uhr ist es? = what time is it?

die **Uhrzeit**, *plural* Uhrzeiten
= time

die **UKW**
(*Ultrakurzwelle*) = VHF

ulkig *adjective*
= funny

um
1 *preposition* (+ *accusative*)
* = around
* (*indicating time*) = at
  (*approximately*) = around, = about
  um zwei Uhr = at 2 o'clock

U

• = for
um etwas bitten = to ask for something
sich um etwas streiten = to quarrel over something
sich um jemanden sorgen = to worry about someone
• (*indicating difference*) = by
2 *adverb* = around, = about
3 *conjunction*
um zu = (in order) to

umarmen *verb*
= to hug

der **Umbau**, *plural* Umbauten
= renovation
= conversion

um|binden *irregular verb*
= to put on

um|blättern *verb*
= to turn over

um|bringen *irregular verb*
= to kill

um|drehen *verb*
• to turn
• sich umdrehen = to turn round, (*when lying down*) = to turn over

um|fallen *irregular verb* (**!** *sein*)
= to fall down

die **Umfrage**, *plural* Umfragen
= survey

die **Umgangssprache**
= slang

umgeben *irregular verb*
= to surround

die **Umgebung**, *plural* Umgebungen
= surroundings
= neighbourhood

umgekehrt *adjective*
= opposite
es war umgekehrt = it was the other way round

der **Umhang**, *plural* Umhänge
= cloak

um|kehren *verb* (**!** *sein*)
= to turn back

der **Umkleideraum**, *plural* Umkleideräume
= changing room

der **Umlaut**, *plural* Umlaute
= umlaut

die **Umleitung**, *plural* Umleitungen
= diversion

um|rechnen *verb*
= to convert

× in informal situations

um|rühren *verb*
= to stir

ums = um das

der **Umsatz**, *plural* Umsätze
= turnover

um|schalten *verb*
= to turn over
auf Rot umschalten = to change to red

der **Umschlag**, *plural* Umschläge
• = envelope
• = cover

um|sehen: sich umsehen *irregular verb*
= to look round

umso *conjunction*
umso besser = all the better
umso mehr = all the more

umsonst *adverb*
• = in vain
• = free, = for nothing

umständlich *adjective*
= laborious

um|steigen *irregular verb* (**!** *sein*)
= to change

der **Umtausch**
= exchange

um|tauschen *verb*
= to change, = to exchange

die **Umwelt**
= environment

umweltfreundlich *adjective*
= environmentally friendly

die **Umweltverschmutzung**
= pollution

um|ziehen *irregular verb*
• (**!** *sein*) = to move
• = to change
• sich umziehen = to get changed

der **Umzug**, *plural* Umzüge
= move

unabhängig *adjective*
= independent

die **Unabhängigkeit**
= independence

unangenehm *adjective*
• = unpleasant
• = embarrassing

unanständig *adjective*
= indecent, = vulgar

unartig *adjective*
= naughty

unbehaglich *adjective*
= uncomfortable, = uneasy

unbekannt *adjective*
= unknown

unbequem *adjective*
= uncomfortable

und *conjunction*
= and

undankbar *adjective*
= ungrateful

undeutlich *adjective*
= unclear

undicht *adjective*
= leaking, = leaky
eine undichte Stelle = a leak

unentbehrlich *adjective*
= indispensable

unentschieden *adjective*
= undecided
unentschieden spielen = to draw

unerträglich *adjective*
= unbearable

unerwartet *adjective*
= unexpected

unfähig *adjective*
= incompetent

der **Unfall**, *plural* Unfälle
= accident

unfreundlich *adjective*
= unfriendly

der **Unfug**
= nonsense

(das) **Ungarn**
= Hungary

ungeduldig *adjective*
= impatient

ungefähr
1 *adjective* = approximate
2 *adverb* = approximately, = about

ungefährlich *adjective*
= safe

das **Ungeheuer**, *plural* Ungeheuer
= monster

ungemütlich *adjective*
= uncomfortable

ungenügend *adjective*
• = insufficient
• (*mark at school*) = unsatisfactory

ungerade *adjective*
eine ungerade Zahl = an odd number

ungerecht *adjective*
= unjust

ungern *adverb*
= reluctantly

ungesund *adjective*
= unhealthy

ungewöhnlich *adjective*
= unusual

das **Ungeziefer**
= vermin

unglaublich *adjective*
= incredible, = unbelievable

das **Unglück**, *plural* Unglücke
• = accident
• = misfortune
• = bad luck

unglücklich *adjective*
• = unhappy
• = unfortunate

unheimlich *adjective*
• = eerie
• unheimlich viel✖ = a terrific amount

unhöflich *adjective*
= impolite

die **Universität**, *plural* Universitäten
= university

Unkosten (*plural*)
= expenses

das **Unkraut**
= weed

unmodern *adjective*
= old-fashioned

unmöglich *adjective*
= impossible

unnötig *adjective*
= unnecessary

unordentlich *adjective*
= untidy

die **Unordnung**
= disorder
= mess

unpraktisch *adjective*
= impractical

unpünktlich *adjective*
= unpunctual
unpünktlich sein = to be late

das **Unrecht**
= wrong
zu Unrecht = wrongly

unregelmäßig *adjective*
= irregular

die **Unruhe**, *plural* Unruhen
= restlessness
= agitation
Unruhen = unrest

uns *pronoun*
• = us

U

- *(reflexive)* = ourselves
  wir waschen uns die Hände = we are washing our hands

unschuldig *adjective*
= innocent

unser *adjective*
= our

unserer/unsere/unsers *pronoun*
= ours

der **Unsinn**
= nonsense

unten *adverb*
= at the bottom
(indoors) = downstairs
nach unten = down

unter
1 *preposition* (+ *dative or accusative*)
- = under
  (lower than) = below
- = among
  unter anderem = among other things
  unter sich = by themselves
  2 *adjective* = lower
  die untere Etage = the bottom floor

das **Unterbewusstsein**
(**Unterbewußtsein** OLD)
= subconscious

unterbrechen *irregular verb*
= to interrupt

die **Unterbrechung**, *plural* Unterbrechungen
= interruption

unter|bringen *irregular verb*
- = to put
- *(as a guest)* = to put up

die **Unterdrückung**
= suppression

untere ▶unterer

untereinander *adverb*
- among ourselves/yourselves/themselves
- one below the other

unterer/untere/unteres *adjective*
= lower

die **Unterführung**, *plural* Unterführungen
= subway, = underpass

unter|gehen *irregular verb* (**!** *sein*)
- *(of the sun)* = to set
- *(of a ship)* = to sink
- *(of the world)* = to come to an end

die **Untergrundbahn**, *plural* Untergrundbahnen
= underground, = subway

unterhalten *irregular verb*
- = to entertain

- *(feed)* = to support
- **sich unterhalten** = to talk, *(have fun)* = to enjoy oneself

die **Unterhaltung**, *plural* Unterhaltungen
- = conversation
- = entertainment

das **Unterhemd**, *plural* Unterhemden
= vest

die **Unterhose**, *plural* Unterhosen
= underpants

unterirdisch *adjective*
= underground

die **Unterkunft**, *plural* Unterkünfte
= accommodation, = accommodations

Unterlagen (*plural*)
= documents, = papers

unternehmen *irregular verb*
= to undertake
etwas unternehmen = to do something

der **Unterricht**
= lessons
jemandem Unterricht geben = to teach someone

unterrichten *verb*
- = to teach
- = to inform
- **sich unterrichten** = to inform oneself

der **Unterrock**, *plural* Unterröcke
= slip

untersagt *adjective*
= prohibited

unterscheiden *irregular verb*
- = to distinguish
- = to tell apart
- **sich unterscheiden** = to differ, = to be different

der **Unterschied**, *plural* Unterschiede
= difference

unterschreiben *irregular verb*
= to sign

die **Unterschrift**, *plural* Unterschriften
= signature

unterstreichen *irregular verb*
= to underline

unterstützen *verb*
= to support

untersuchen *verb*
- = to examine
- = to investigate

die **Untersuchung**, *plural* Untersuchungen
- = examination, = check-up
- = investigation

die **Untertasse**, *plural* Untertassen
= saucer

---

die **Unterwäsche**
= underwear

unterwegs
1 adverb = on the way
2 adjective
unterwegs sein = to be on the way
den ganzen Tag unterwegs sein = to be out all day

untreu adjective
= disloyal
(in marriage) = unfaithful

ununterbrochen adjective
= uninterrupted

unvergleichlich adjective
= incomparable

unverheiratet adjective
= unmarried

unverkäuflich adjective
= not for sale
ein unverkäufliches Muster = a free sample

unverschämt adjective
= impertinent

unverständlich adjective
= incomprehensible

unwahrscheinlich adjective
• = unlikely, = improbable
• das ist unwahrscheinlich!✖ = that's incredible!

das **Unwetter**, plural Unwetter
= storm

unwichtig adjective
= unimportant

unzerbrechlich adjective
= unbreakable

unzufrieden adjective
= dissatisfied

üppig adjective
= lavish

uralt adjective
= ancient

der **Urenkel**, plural Urenkel
= great-grandson
die Urenkel = the great-grandchildren

die **Urenkelin**, plural Urenkelinnen
= great-granddaughter

Urgroßeltern (plural)
= great-grandparents

die **Urkunde**, plural Urkunden
= certificate

der **Urlaub**, plural Urlaube
= holiday, = vacation
Urlaub haben = to be on holiday or vacation

der **Urlauber**, plural Urlauber
= holidaymaker, = vacationer

die **Ursache**, plural Ursachen
= cause
keine Ursache! = don't mention it!

der **Ursprung**, plural Ursprünge
= origin

ursprünglich adjective
= original

das **Urteil**, plural Urteile
• = judgement
• = verdict
• = opinion

der **Urwald**, plural Urwälder
= jungle

usw. abbreviation
(und so weiter) = etc.

Vv

die **Vanille**
= vanilla

der **Vater**, plural Väter
= father

der **Vati**, plural Vatis
= dad

der **Vegetarier**, plural Vegetarier
= vegetarian

die **Vegetarierin**, plural Vegetarierinnen
= vegetarian

vegetarisch adjective
= vegetarian

das **Veilchen**, plural Veilchen
= violet

die **Vene**, plural Venen
= vein

das **Ventil**, plural Ventile
= valve

verabreden verb
• to arrange
• sich mit jemandem verabreden = to arrange to meet someone

die **Verabredung**, plural Verabredungen
• = appointment
• = date
• = arrangement

verabschieden verb
• = to say goodbye to
• sich verabschieden = to say goodbye

die **Verachtung**
= contempt

verändern verb
* to change
* sich verändern = to change

die **Veränderung**, plural Veränderungen
= change

veranstalten verb
= to organize

die **Veranstaltung**, plural
Veranstaltungen
= event
Veranstaltungen = activities

verantwortlich adjective
= responsible

die **Verantwortung**
= responsibility

verarbeiten verb
= to process

der **Verband**, plural Verbände
* = association
* = bandage

verbessern verb
* = to improve
* = to correct

die **Verbesserung**, plural Verbesserungen
* = improvement
* = correction

verbeugen: sich verbeugen verb
= to bow

verbieten irregular verb
= to forbid
= to ban

verbilligt adjective
= reduced

verbinden irregular verb
* = to connect
* = to join
* = to combine
* (with a dressing) = to bandage
* (on the phone) = to put through
falsch verbunden sein = to have got the
wrong number

die **Verbindung**, plural Verbindungen
* = connection
sich in Verbindung setzen = to get in
touch
* = combination
* (in chemistry) = compound

verblühen verb (! sein)
= to fade

verbot ▶verbieten

das **Verbot**, plural Verbote
= ban

──────────

verboten adjective
= forbidden

der **Verbrauch**
= consumption

verbrauchen verb
= to consume, = to use

der **Verbraucher**, plural Verbraucher
= consumer

das **Verbrechen**, plural Verbrechen
= crime

der **Verbrecher**, plural Verbrecher
= criminal

verbreitet adjective
= widespread

verbrennen irregular verb
* (! sein) = to burn
* sich verbrennen = to burn oneself
sich den Finger verbrennen = to burn
one's finger

verbringen irregular verb
= to spend

der **Verdacht**
= suspicion

verdächtig adjective
= suspicious

der/die **Verdächtige**, plural Verdächtigen
= suspect

die **Verdauung**
= digestion

verderben irregular verb
* = to spoil
ich habe mir den Magen verdorben =
I have an upset stomach
* (! sein) = to go off

verdienen verb
= to earn

der **Verdienst**, plural Verdienste
* = salary
* = achievement

verdoppeln verb
* to double
* sich verdoppeln = to double

verdünnen verb
= to dilute

verdursten verb (! sein)
= to die of thirst

verehren verb
= to worship

der **Verehrer**, plural Verehrer
= admirer

die **Verehrerin**, plural Verehrerinnen
= admirer

der **Verein**, *plural* Vereine
= society
= organization
(*sports*) = club

vereinbaren *verb*
= to arrange

die **Vereinbarung**, *plural* Vereinbarungen
= agreement
= arrangement

Vereinigte Staaten (*plural*)
= United States

die **Vereinigung**, *plural* Vereinigungen
= organization

verfahren *irregular verb*
• (! *sein*) = to proceed
• sich verfahren = to lose one's way

verfallen *irregular verb* (! *sein*)
• = to decay
• (*run out*) = to expire

die **Verfassung**, *plural* Verfassungen
• = constitution
• (*of a person*) = state

verfaulen *verb* (! *sein*)
= to rot

verfolgen *verb*
• = to follow
• = to persecute

verführen *verb*
• = to tempt
• = to seduce

die **Verführung**, *plural* Verführungen
• = temptation
• = seduction

vergangen *adjective*
= last

die **Vergangenheit**
• = past
• (*in grammar*) = past tense

der **Vergaser**, *plural* Vergaser
= carburettor

vergaß ▶ vergessen

vergeben *irregular verb*
• = to forgive
• = to award

vergeblich
1 *adjective* = futile
2 *adverb* = in vain

vergessen *irregular verb*
= to forget

vergesslich (**vergeßlich**ⓄⓁⒹ)
adjective
= forgetful

die **Vergewaltigung**, *plural*
Vergewaltigungen
= rape

vergiften *verb*
= to poison

vergisst (**vergißt**ⓄⓁⒹ) ▶ vergessen

der **Vergleich**, *plural* Vergleiche
= comparison

vergleichen *irregular verb*
= to compare

das **Vergnügen**, *plural* Vergnügen
= pleasure
viel Vergnügen! = have fun!

vergnügt *adjective*
= cheerful

vergrößern *verb*
• = to enlarge
• = to increase
• = to magnify
• = to extend
• sich vergrößern = to expand, (*in amount*)
= to increase

die **Vergrößerung**, *plural* Vergrößerungen
• = expansion
• (*in photography*) = enlargement

verhaften *verb*
= to arrest

verhalten: sich verhalten
irregular verb
= to behave

das **Verhältnis**, *plural* Verhältnisse
• = relationship
• (*in maths*) = ratio

verhältnismäßig *adverb*
= relatively

verhandeln *verb*
= to negotiate
über etwas verhandeln = to negotiate
something

die **Verhandlung**, *plural* Verhandlungen
• = negotiation
• = hearing

verheimlichen *verb*
= to keep secret

verheiratet *adjective*
= married

verhindern *verb*
= to prevent

verhungern *verb* (! *sein*)
= to starve

verirren: sich verirren *verb*
= to get lost

der **Verkauf**, *plural* Verkäufe
= sale
zum Verkauf = for sale

verkaufen *verb*
= to sell
zu verkaufen = for sale

der **Verkäufer**, *plural* Verkäufer
- = seller
- = sales assistant

die **Verkäuferin**, *plural* Verkäuferinnen
- = seller
- = sales assistant

der **Verkehr**
= traffic

die **Verkehrsampel**, *plural* Verkehrsampeln
= traffic lights

verkehrt *adjective*
= wrong
verkehrt herum = inside out, = upside down

verklagen *verb*
= to sue

die **Verkleidung**, *plural* Verkleidungen
= disguise
(*at a party*) = fancy dress

verkommen *irregular verb* (**!** *sein*)
- (*of food*) = to go off
- (*of a house*) = to become dilapidated

verkratzt *adjective*
= scratched

der **Verlag**, *plural* Verlage
= publishing house, = publisher's

verlangen *verb*
= to demand
= to require
du wirst am Telefon verlangt = you're wanted on the phone

verlängern *verb*
= to extend
= to lengthen
einen Pass verlängern = to renew a passport

die **Verlängerung**, *plural* Verlängerungen
- = extension
- = renewal
- (*in sport*) = extra time

verlassen *irregular verb*
- = to leave
- sich auf etwas verlassen = to rely on something

verlaufen *irregular verb*
- (**!** *sein*) = to go
- sich verlaufen = to lose one's way

verlegen[1] *verb*
- = to mislay
- = to postpone
- = to publish
- (*if it's a cable, pipe, carpet*) = to lay

verlegen[2] *adjective*
= embarrassed

die **Verlegenheit**
= embarrassment

der **Verleih**, *plural* Verleihe
- = renting out, = hiring out
- = rental firm, = hire shop

verleihen *irregular verb*
- = to hire out, = to rent out
- = to lend
- = to award

verlernen *verb*
= to forget

verletzen *verb*
- = to injure
- = to hurt
- sich verletzen = to hurt oneself

der/die **Verletzte**, *plural* Verletzten
= injured person
= casualty

die **Verletzung**, *plural* Verletzungen
= injury

verlieben: sich verlieben *verb*
= to fall in love

verlieren *irregular verb*
= to lose

verloben: sich verloben *verb*
= to get engaged

die **Verlobung**, *plural* Verlobungen
= engagement

verlor ▶verlieren

die **Verlosung**, *plural* Verlosungen
= prize draw

der **Verlust**, *plural* Verluste
= loss

vermeiden *irregular verb*
= to avoid

vermieten *verb*
= to rent out, = to hire out
ein Zimmer vermieten = to let a room

der **Vermieter**, *plural* Vermieter
= landlord

die **Vermieterin**, *plural* Vermieterinnen
= landlady

vermissen *verb*
= to miss

die **Vermittlung**, *plural* Vermittlungen
- = arrangement
- (*office*) = agency
- = switchboard
- = telephone exchange
- = mediation

das **Vermögen**, *plural* Vermögen
= fortune

vermuten *verb*
= to suspect

vermutlich *adverb*
= probably

vernichten *verb*
= to destroy

die **Vernunft**
= reason

vernünftig *adjective*
= sensible

verpacken *verb*
= to pack
= to wrap up

die **Verpackung**, *plural* Verpackungen
= packaging

verpassen *verb*
= to miss

die **Verpflegung**
= food
Unterkunft und Verpflegung = board and
lodging

verpflichten: sich verpflichten
verb
• = to promise
• = to sign a contract

die **Verpflichtung**, *plural* Verpflichtungen
= obligation
= commitment

verprügeln *verb*
= to beat up

der **Verrat**
= betrayal

verraten *irregular verb*
• = to betray
• = to give away
• = to tell
• sich verraten = to give oneself away

verrechnen: sich verrechnen
verb
= to make a mistake
= to miscalculate

verreisen *verb* (! *sein*)
= to go away

verrosten *verb* (! *sein*)
= to rust

verrostet *adjective*
= rusty

verrückt *adjective*
= mad, = crazy

versagen *verb*
= to fail

versammeln *verb*
• = to assemble
• sich versammeln = to assemble

die **Versammlung**, *plural* Versammlungen
= meeting

verschenken *verb*
= to give away

verschieben *irregular verb*
• = to postpone
• = to move

verschieden *adjective*
= different
= various

verschlafen *irregular verb*
= to oversleep

der **Verschluss** (**Verschluß**⊙ᴸᴰ), *plural*
Verschlüsse
= fastener
(*on a bottle*) = top

die **Verschmutzung**, *plural*
Verschmutzungen
= pollution

verschreiben *irregular verb*
• = to prescribe
• sich verschreiben = to make a mistake

verschwenden *verb*
= to waste

verschwinden *irregular verb* (! *sein*)
= to disappear

das **Versehen**, *plural* Versehen
= oversight
aus Versehen = by mistake

versichern *verb*
• = to insure
• = to assert
jemandem versichern = to assure
someone

die **Versicherung**, *plural* Versicherungen
• = insurance
• = assurance

versöhnen: sich versöhnen *verb*
= to become reconciled
sich mit jemandem versöhnen = to make
it up with someone

versorgen *verb*
• = to supply
• = to provide for
• = to look after

verspäten: sich verspäten *verb*
= to be late

die **Verspätung**, *plural* Verspätungen
= lateness
mit Verspätung = late
zehn Minuten Verspätung haben = to be
ten minutes late

versprechen *irregular verb*
• = to promise
• sich versprechen = to make a slip of the
tongue

das **Versprechen**, *plural* Versprechen
= promise

V

verstaatlichen *verb*
= to nationalize

verstand ▶ verstehen

der **Verstand**
= mind
= reason

verständigen *verb*
• = to notify
• sich verständigen = to communicate, = to make oneself understood

die **Verständigung**, *plural* Verständigungen
• = communication
• = notification

verständlich *adjective*
• = comprehensible
jemandem etwas verständlich machen = to make something clear to someone
• = understandable

das **Verständnis**
= understanding

der **Verstärker**, *plural* Verstärker
= amplifier

verstauchen: sich verstauchen *verb*
sich den Fuß verstauchen = to sprain one's ankle

das **Versteck**, *plural* Verstecke
= hiding place

verstecken *verb*
• = to hide
• sich verstecken = to hide

verstehen *irregular verb*
• = to understand
etwas falsch verstehen = to misunderstand something
• sich verstehen = to get on

verstellen *verb*
• = to adjust
• = to block
• = to disguise
• sich verstellen = to pretend

der **Versuch**, *plural* Versuche
• = attempt
• = experiment

versuchen *verb*
= to try, = to attempt

verteidigen *verb*
= to defend

die **Verteidigung**, *plural* Verteidigungen
= defence

verteilen *verb*
= to distribute

der **Vertrag**, *plural* Verträge
= contract

vertragen *irregular verb*
• = to stand, = to take
• sich vertragen = to get on

vertrauen *verb*
= to trust

das **Vertrauen**
= trust, = confidence

vertraulich *adjective*
= confidential

vertreten *irregular verb*
• = to stand in for
• = to represent

der **Vertreter**, *plural* Vertreter
• = representative
• = deputy

die **Vertreterin**, *plural* Vertreterinnen
• = representative
• = deputy

die **Vertretung**, *plural* Vertretungen
• = representative
• = deputy
• = supply teacher

verunglücken *verb* (**!** sein)
= to have an accident

verursachen *verb*
= to cause

verurteilen *verb*
• = to sentence
• = to condemn

die **Verwaltung**, *plural* Verwaltungen
= administration

verwandeln *verb*
= to change

verwandt *adjective*
= related

der/die **Verwandte**, *plural* Verwandten
= relative

die **Verwandtschaft**, *plural* Verwandtschaften
• (*family*) = relatives
• = relationship

verwechseln *verb*
= to mix up
jemanden mit jemandem verwechseln = to mistake someone for someone

verwenden *verb*
= to use

die **Verwendung**
= use

verwirrt *adjective*
= confused

verwöhnen *verb*
= to spoil

der/die **Verwundete**, *plural* Verwundeten
= casualty
die Verwundeten = the wounded

verzählen: sich verzählen *verb*
= to miscount

verzeihen *irregular verb*
= to forgive
verzeihen Sie! = excuse me!

die **Verzeihung**
= forgiveness
jemanden um Verzeihung bitten = to
apologize to someone
Verzeihung! = sorry!

verzichten *verb*
= to do without

verzögern *verb*
• = to delay
• sich verzögern = to be delayed

die **Verzögerung**, *plural* Verzögerungen
= delay

verzweifelt *adjective*
= desperate

die **Verzweiflung**
= despair

der **Vetter**, *plural* Vettern
= cousin

das **Video**, *plural* Videos
= video

die **Videokamera**, *plural* Videokameras
= video camera

der **Videorekorder**, *plural* Videorekorder
= video recorder

die **Videothek**, *plural* Videotheken
= video shop, = video store

das **Vieh**
= cattle

viel
1 *pronoun*
• = a great deal of, = a lot of
(*plural*) = many, = a lot of
• = much, = a lot, (*plural*) = too many
zu viel = too much
vielen Dank = thank you very much
viel Spaß! = have fun!
2 *adverb* = much, = a lot
viel weniger = much less
das dauert viel zu lange = it will take far
too long
so viel wie möglich = as much as possible

vielleicht *adverb*
= perhaps

vier *adjective*
= four

viereckig *adjective*
= rectangular

vierte ▶vierter

das **Viertel**, *plural* Viertel
= quarter

die **Viertelstunde**, *plural* Viertelstunden
= quarter of an hour

vierter/vierte/viertes *adjective*
= fourth

vierzehn *adjective*
= fourteen

vierzig *adjective*
= forty

die **Villa**, *plural* Villen
= villa

der **Virus**, *plural* Viren
= virus

der **Vogel**, *plural* Vögel
= bird

das **Volk**, *plural* Völker
= people

das **Volkslied**, *plural* Volkslieder
= folk song

voll
1 *adjective* = full
die volle Wahrheit = the whole truth
2 *adverb*
= fully, = completely

völlig
1 *adjective* = complete
2 *adverb* = completely

vollkommen
1 *adjective*
• = perfect
• = complete
2 *adverb*
• = perfectly
• = completely

die **Vollpension**
= full board

vollständig *adjective*
= complete

vom = von dem

von *preposition* (+ *dative*)
• = from
von jetzt an = from now on
• (*instead of the genitive*) = of
ein Vetter von mir = a cousin of mine
• = by
er ist Lehrer von Beruf = he is a teacher
by profession
• = about
von etwas sprechen = to talk about
something

voneinander *adverb*
= from each other, = from one another

vor *preposition*
• (+ *dative or accusative*) = in front of

V

* (+ *dative*) (*indicating time, succession*)
  = before
  sie kamen vor uns an = they arrived
  before us
  vor drei Tagen = three days ago
  vor kurzem = recently
  zehn vor eins = ten to one
* (+ *dative*) (*because of*) = with
  vor Kälte zittern = to tremble with cold
  vor jemandem Angst haben = to be
  frightened of someone

voraus *adverb*
jemandem voraus sein = to be ahead of
someone
im Voraus = in advance

voraus|gehen *irregular verb* (**!** *sein*)
= to go on ahead

voraus|setzen *verb*
= to take for granted
vorausgesetzt, dass = provided that

die **Voraussetzung**, *plural*
Voraussetzungen
* = condition
* = assumption

vorbei *adverb*
* = past
* (*finished*) = over

vorbei|fahren *irregular verb* (**!** *sein*)
= to drive past, = to pass

vorbei|gehen *irregular verb* (**!** *sein*)
* = to pass
* (*visit*) = to drop in

vorbei|kommen *irregular verb* (**!** *sein*)
* = to pass
* = to get past
* (*visit*) = to drop in

vor|bereiten *verb*
* = to prepare
* sich vorbereiten = to prepare

die **Vorbereitung**, *plural* Vorbereitungen
= preparation

vor|beugen *verb*
* = to prevent
* sich vorbeugen = to lean forward

das **Vorbild**, *plural* Vorbilder
= example

vorderer/vordere/vorderes
adjective
= front

der **Vordergrund**
= foreground

vor|drängen: sich vordrängen
verb
= to push forward

die **Vorfahrt**
= right of way
'Vorfahrt beachten' = 'give way'

die **Vorfahrtsstraße**, *plural*
Vorfahrtsstraßen
= major road

der **Vorfall**, *plural* Vorfälle
= incident

die **Vorführung**, *plural* Vorführungen
* = performance
* (*of a machine*) = demonstration

der **Vorgänger**, *plural* Vorgänger
= predecessor

die **Vorgängerin**, *plural* Vorgängerinnen
= predecessor

vor|gehen *irregular verb* (**!** *sein*)
* = to go on ahead
* = to go forward
* = to proceed
* (*of a clock*) = to be fast
* = to happen, = to go on

vorgestern *adverb*
= the day before yesterday

vor|haben *irregular verb*
= to intend
etwas vorhaben = to have something
planned

die **Vorhand**
= forehand

der **Vorhang**, *plural* Vorhänge
= curtain, = drape

vorher *adverb*
= beforehand, = before

die **Vorhersage**, *plural* Vorhersagen
* = forecast
* = prediction

vorhin *adverb*
= just now

voriger/vorige/voriges *adjective*
= last

vor|kommen *irregular verb* (**!** *sein*)
* = to occur, = to happen
* = to exist
* = to seem
  jemandem verdächtig vorkommen = to
  seem suspicious to someone
* = to come forward

vor|lassen *irregular verb*
jemanden vorlassen = to let someone go
first

vorläufig
1 *adjective* = provisional
2 *adverb* = provisionally

vor|lesen *irregular verb*
= to read (out)
= to read aloud

die **Vorlesung**, *plural* Vorlesungen
= lecture

vorletzter/vorletzte/vorletztes
adjective
= last ... but one
vorletztes Jahr = the year before last

der **Vormittag**, *plural* Vormittage
= morning

vormittags *adverb*
= in the morning

vorn *adverb*
= at the front
nach vorn = to the front
von vorn = from the beginning
da vorn = over there

der **Vorname**, *plural* Vornamen
= first name

vorne ▶ vorn

vornehm *adjective*
= elegant

vor|nehmen *irregular verb*
* = to carry out
* sich vornehmen, etwas zu tun = to plan
to do something

der **Vorort**, *plural* Vororte
= suburb

der **Vorrat**, *plural* Vorräte
= supply, = stock

die **Vorschau**, *plural* Vorschauen
= preview
(*of a film*) = trailer

der **Vorschlag**, *plural* Vorschläge
= suggestion

vor|schlagen *irregular verb*
= to suggest

die **Vorschrift**, *plural* Vorschriften
= regulation

die **Vorschule**, *plural* Vorschulen
= infant school

der **Vorschuss** (**Vorschuß**ⓞⓛⓓ), *plural*
Vorschüsse
= advance

vor|sehen: sich vorsehen *verb*
= to be careful

die **Vorsicht**
= care
Vorsicht! = careful!, (*on a sign*) = caution!

vorsichtig *adjective*
= careful

die **Vorsichtsmaßnahme**, *plural*
Vorsichtsmaßnahmen
= precaution

die **Vorspeise**, *plural* Vorspeisen
= starter

der **Vorsprung**, *plural* Vorsprünge
(*advantage*) = lead

vor|stellen *verb*
* = to introduce
* (*turn on*) = to put forward
* sich vorstellen = to introduce oneself,
(*when applying for a job*) = to go for an
interview
* sich etwas vorstellen = to imagine
something
stell dir vor! = can you imagine?

die **Vorstellung**, *plural* Vorstellungen
* = performance
* = introduction
(*for a job*) = interview
* = idea
* = imagination

der **Vorteil**, *plural* Vorteile
= advantage

der **Vortrag**, *plural* Vorträge
= talk

vorübergehend
1 *adjective* = temporary
2 *adverb* = temporarily

das **Vorurteil**, *plural* Vorurteile
= prejudice

die **Vorwahl**, *plural* Vorwahlen
= dialling code, = area code

vorwärts *adverb*
= forward(s)
vorwärts kommen = to make progress

vorwiegend *adverb*
= predominantly

der **Vorwurf**, *plural* Vorwürfe
= reproach
jemandem Vorwürfe machen = to
reproach someone

vor|zeigen *verb*
= to show

vor|ziehen *irregular verb*
* = to prefer
* = to pull up
den Vorhang vorziehen = to draw the
curtain

vorzüglich *adjective*
= excellent

vulgär *adjective*
= vulgar

der **Vulkan** *plural* Vulkane
= volcano

V

die **Waage**, *plural* Waagen
* scales
* Libra

waagerecht *adjective*
= horizontal

wach *adjective*
= awake
wach werden = to wake up

die **Wache**, *plural* Wachen
* = guard
* = (police) station

der **Wachhund**, *plural* Wachhunde
= guard dog

das **Wachs**, *plural* Wachse
= wax

wachsen[1] *irregular verb* (**!** *sein*)
= to grow

wachsen[2] *verb*
= to wax

das **Wachstum**
= growth

der **Wächter**, *plural* Wächter
= guard

wackelig *adjective*
= wobbly

wackeln *verb*
= to wobble

die **Wade**, *plural* Waden
= calf

die **Waffe**, *plural* Waffen
= weapon

wagen *verb*
= to risk
es wagen, etwas zu tun = to dare to do something

der **Wagen**, *plural* Wagen
* = car
* (*of a train*) = carriage
* = cart

der **Wagenheber**, *plural* Wagenheber
= jack

die **Wahl**, *plural* Wahlen
* = choice
* = election

wählen *verb*
* = to choose
* = to elect
* = to vote
* (*when phoning*) = to dial

das **Wahlfach**, *plural* Wahlfächer
= optional subject

der **Wahnsinn**
= madness

wahnsinnig *adjective*
* = mad
* wahnsinnigen Durst haben✱ = to be terribly thirsty

wahr *adjective*
= true

während
1 *conjunction* = while
2 *preposition* (+ *genitive*) = during

die **Wahrheit**, *plural* Wahrheiten
= truth

die **Wahrsagerin**, *plural* Wahrsagerinnen
= fortune-teller

wahrscheinlich
1 *adjective* = probable
2 *adverb* = probably

die **Währung**, *plural* Währungen
= currency

die **Waise**, *plural* Waisen
= orphan

der **Wal**, *plural* Wale
= whale

der **Wald**, *plural* Wälder
= wood, = forest

der **Waliser**, *plural* Waliser
= Welshman

die **Waliserin**, *plural* Waliserinnen
= Welshwoman

walisisch *adjective*
= Welsh

die **Wallfahrt**, *plural* Wallfahrten
= pilgrimage

die **Walnuss** (**Walnuß**⃝ᴼᴸᴰ), *plural* Walnüsse
= walnut

die **Wand**, *plural* Wände
= wall

wandern *verb* (**!** *sein*)
= to hike, = to ramble
= to go walking

die **Wanderung**, *plural* Wanderungen
= hike, = ramble

wann *adverb*
= when
seit wann wohnst du hier? = how long have you been living here?

die **Wanne**, *plural* Wannen
= tub
= bath

das **Wappen**, *plural* Wappen
  = coat of arms

war ▶ sein

die **Ware**, *plural* Waren
  • = article
  = product
  • Waren = goods

waren ▶ sein

das **Warenhaus**, *plural* Warenhäuser
  = department store

das **Warenzeichen**, *plural* Warenzeichen
  = trademark

warf ▶ werfen

warm *adjective*
  = warm
  eine warme Mahlzeit = a hot meal

die **Wärme**
  = warmth
  wir haben zwanzig Grad Wärme = the
  temperature is 20 degrees

wärmen *verb*
  = to warm

warnen *verb*
  = to warn

die **Warnung**, *plural* Warnungen
  = warning

warst, wart ▶ sein

warten *verb*
  = to wait

der **Wärter**, *plural* Wärter
  = keeper
  = attendant
  = warder, = guard

die **Wärterin**, *plural* Wärterinnen
  = keeper
  = attendant
  = warder, = guard

das **Wartezimmer**, *plural* Wartezimmer
  = waiting room

die **Wartung**, *plural* Wartungen
  = service

warum *adverb*
  = why

die **Warze**, *plural* Warzen
  = wart

was *pronoun*
  • what
  was kostet das? = how much is it?
  was für? = what kind of?
  was für ein Glück! = what luck!
  • = that
  vieles, was er sagt = a lot that he says
  • (*short for* etwas) = something

(*in questions and negatives*) = anything
hier ist was zu essen = here's something
  to eat
hast du was zu lesen? = have you got
  anything to read?

das **Waschbecken**, *plural* Waschbecken
  = washbasin

die **Wäsche**
  • = washing
  • = underwear

waschen *irregular verb*
  • to wash
  • sich waschen = to have a wash
  sich die Hände waschen = to wash one's
  hands

die **Wäscherei**, *plural* Wäschereien
  = laundry

der **Waschlappen**, *plural* Waschlappen
  = flannel

die **Waschmaschine**, *plural*
  Waschmaschinen
  = washing machine

der **Waschsalon**, *plural* Waschsalons
  = launderette

die **Waschstraße**, *plural* Waschstraßen
  = car wash

das **Wasser**
  = water

der **Wasserball**, *plural* Wasserbälle
  • = beach ball
  • = water polo

wasserdicht *adjective*
  = waterproof
  = watertight

der **Wasserfall**, *plural* Wasserfälle
  = waterfall

der **Wasserhahn**, *plural* Wasserhähne
  = tap, = faucet

der **Wassermann**
  = Aquarius

das **Wasserskilaufen**
  = water-skiing

wässrig (**wäßrig**ᴼᴸᴰ) *adjective*
  = watery

die **Watte**
  = cotton wool

wattiert *adjective*
  = padded

weben *verb*
  = to weave

der **Wechsel**, *plural* Wechsel
  • = change
  • (*of foreign currency*) = exchange

das **Wechselgeld**
  = change

der **Wechselkurs**, *plural* Wechselkurse
= exchange rate

wechseln *verb*
= to change

wecken *verb*
= to wake (up)

der **Wecker**, *plural* Wecker
= alarm clock

weder *conjunction*
weder . . . noch = neither . . . nor

weg *adverb*
= away
sie ist schon weg = she's already gone
Hände weg! = hands off!

der **Weg**, *plural* Wege
= way
= path
sich auf den Weg machen = to set off

wegen *preposition* (+ *genitive*)
= because of

weg|fahren *irregular verb* (**!** *sein*)
= to leave

weg|gehen *irregular verb* (**!** *sein*)
• = to go away
= to leave
• (*for entertainment*) = to go out
• (*of a stain*) = to come out

weg|lassen *irregular verb*
• = to let go
• = to leave out

weg|laufen *irregular verb* (**!** *sein*)
= to run away

weg|legen *verb*
= to put down
= to put away

weg|räumen *verb*
= to clear away

weg|schicken *verb*
= to send off
= to send away

weg|tun *irregular verb*
= to put away

der **Wegweiser**, *plural* Wegweiser
= signpost

weg|werfen *irregular verb*
= to throw away

weh *adjective*
= sore
weh tun⊙ᴸᴰ ▶wehtun
o weh! = oh dear!

wehen *verb*
= to blow

der **Wehrdienst**
= military service

wehren: sich wehren *verb*
= to defend oneself

wehrlos *adjective*
= defenceless

wehtun *irregular verb* = to hurt

das **Weibchen**, *plural* Weibchen
= female

weiblich *adjective*
• = female
• (*in grammar*) = feminine

weich *adjective*
= soft

die **Weiche**, *plural* Weichen
= points

die **Weide**, *plural* Weiden
• = willow
• = pasture

weigern: sich weigern *verb*
= to refuse

das **Weihnachten**, *plural* Weihnachten
= Christmas

der **Weihnachtsmann**, *plural*
Weihnachtsmänner
= Father Christmas

weil *conjunction*
= because

der **Wein**, *plural* Weine
• = vine
• = wine

der **Weinberg**, *plural* Weinberge
= vineyard

weinen *verb*
= to cry

die **Weintraube**, *plural* Weintrauben
= grape

weise *adjective*
= wise

die **Weisheit**, *plural* Weisheiten
= wisdom

weiß¹ *adjective*
= white

weiß² ▶wissen

weit
1 *adjective*
• = wide
• = long
eine weite Reise = a long journey
2 *adverb*
• = wide, = widely
• = far
von weitem = from a distance
bei weitem = by far
ich bin so weit = I'm ready

weiten: sich weiten *verb*
= to widen
= to stretch

weiter adverb
- = further
  etwas weiter tun = to go on doing something
  und so weiter = and so on
- = in addition
  ich brauche nichts weiter = I don't need anything else
  weiter niemand = no one else

weiterer/weitere/weiteres adjective
= further
ohne weiteres = just like that
bis auf weiteres = for the time being

weiter|fahren irregular verb (! sein)
= to go on

weiter|gehen irregular verb (! sein)
= to go on

weiterhin adverb
- = still
  etwas weiterhin tun = to go on doing something
- = in future

weiter|machen verb
= to carry on

der **Weitsprung**
= long jump

der **Weizen**
= wheat

welcher/welche/welches
1 adjective = which
um welche Zeit? = at what time?
2 pronoun
- = which one
  welcher von euch? = which (one) of you?
- = some
  (in questions) = any
  ich möchte welches = I'd like some
  hast du welche? = have you got any?

die **Welle**, plural Wellen
= wave

der **Wellensittich**, plural Wellensittiche
= budgerigar

wellig adjective
= wavy

die **Welt**, plural Welten
= world
zur Welt kommen = to be born

das **Weltall**
= universe

der **Weltmeister**, plural Weltmeister
= world champion

die **Weltmeisterin**, plural
Weltmeisterinnen
= world champion

die **Weltmeisterschaft**, plural
Weltmeisterschaften
= world championship

der **Weltraum**
= space

wem pronoun
= to whom

wen pronoun
= whom, = who

die **Wende**
- = change
- = reunification (of Germany)

wenden: sich wenden irregular verb
= to turn
sich an jemanden wenden = to consult someone

wenig
1 pronoun = little
(plural) **wenige** = few
in wenigen Tagen = in a few days
2 adverb = little
wenig bekannt = little known
so wenig wie möglich = as little as possible
zu wenig = too little, (plural) = too few

weniger
1 pronoun = less
(plural) = fewer
immer weniger = less and less, = fewer and fewer
2 conjunction = less
fünf weniger zwei = five minus two
3 adverb = less

wenigste ▶ wenigster

wenigstens adverb
= at least

wenigster/wenigste/wenigstes pronoun
= least
am wenigsten = least

wenn conjunction
- = when
  immer wenn = whenever
- (conditional) = if
  außer wenn = unless

wer pronoun
- = who
- (informal for jemand) = someone
  (in questions) = anyone

werben irregular verb
- = to advertise
- = to recruit

der **Werbespot**, plural Werbespots
= advert, = commercial

die **Werbung**
= advertising

werden irregular verb (! sein)
- = to become
  müde werden = to get tired
  wach werden = to wake up
  mir wurde schlecht = I felt sick

W

- *(forming the future tense)* = shall, = will
  er wird es kaufen = he'll buy it
- *(forming the passive tense)*
  unsere Wohnung wird gestrichen = our
  flat is being painted
- *(in the conditional)*
  wir würden kommen = we would come

werfen *irregular verb*
= to throw

das **Werk**, *plural* Werke
- = work
- *(factory)* = works

die **Werkstatt**, *plural* Werkstätten
= workshop

der **Werktag**, *plural* Werktage
= working day

das **Werkzeug**, *plural* Werkzeuge
= tool

wert *adjective*
wert sein = to be worth
nichts wert sein = to be worthless

der **Wert**, *plural* Werte
= value
im Wert von . . . = worth . . .

wertlos *adjective*
= worthless

wertvoll *adjective*
= valuable

das **Wesen**, *plural* Wesen
- *(character)* = nature
- = creature

wesentlich
1 *adjective* = essential
im Wesentlichen = essentially
2 *adverb* = considerably

weshalb *adverb*
= why

die **Wespe**, *plural* Wespen
= wasp

wessen *pronoun*
= whose

der **Wessi✶**, *plural* Wessis
= West German

die **Weste**, *plural* Westen
= waistcoat, = vest

der **Westen**
= west

westlich *adjective*
- = western
- = westerly

weswegen *adverb*
= why

der **Wettbewerb**, *plural* Wettbewerbe
= competition, = contest

die **Wette**, *plural* Wetten
= bet
um die Wette laufen = to race

wetten *verb*
= to bet
mit jemandem um etwas wetten = to bet
someone something

das **Wetter**
= weather

der **Wettkampf**, *plural* Wettkämpfe
= contest

das **Wettrennen**, *plural* Wettrennen
= race

wichtig *adjective*
= important

wickeln *verb*
= to wind
ein Kind wickeln = to change a baby

der **Widder**, *plural* Widder
- = ram
- = Aries

widerlich *adjective*
= disgusting

widersprechen *irregular verb*
= to contradict

der **Widerspruch**, *plural* Widersprüche
= contradiction

der **Widerstand**
- = resistance
- = opposition

widerstandsfähig *adjective*
= resistant

widerstehen *irregular verb*
= to resist

die **Widmung**, *plural* Widmungen
= dedication

wie
1 *adverb*
- = how
  wie ist das Wetter? = what is the weather
  like?
  wie bitte? = sorry?
  wie spät ist es? = what is the time?
- wie viel = how much, *(plural)* = how
  many
  um wie viel Uhr? = at what time?
2 *conjunction*
- = as
  so schnell wie möglich = as quickly as
  possible
  nichts wie = nothing but
- = like
  genau wie du = just like you

---

wieder *adverb*
= again
etwas wieder finden = to find something (again)

wieder|bekommen *irregular verb*
= to get back

wiederfinden ⊙ᴸᴰ ▶wieder

wieder|geben *irregular verb*
* = to give back
* = to portray

wiederholen *verb*
* = to repeat
* (*learn*) = to revise
* **sich wiederholen** (*happen again*) = to recur, (*say again*) = to repeat oneself

die **Wiederholung**, *plural* Wiederholungen
* = repetition
* (*at school*) = revision

das **Wiederhören**
(*on the phone*) **auf Wiederhören!** = goodbye!

wieder|kommen *irregular verb*
(**!** *sein*)
= to come back
= to come again

das **Wiedersehen**, *plural* Wiedersehen
= reunion
auf Wiedersehen! = goodbye!

die **Wiedervereinigung**, *plural* Wiedervereinigungen
= reunification

die **Wiege**, *plural* Wiegen
= cradle

wiegen *irregular verb*
= to weigh

wiehern *verb*
= to neigh

(das) **Wien**
= Vienna

die **Wiese**, *plural* Wiesen
= meadow

wieso *adverb*
= why

wieviel ⊙ᴸᴰ ▶wie

wievielter/wievielte/wievieltes *adjective*
= which
zum wievielten Mal? = how many times?

das **Wildleder**
= suede

will ▶wollen

der **Wille**
= will
seinen Willen durchsetzen = to get one's way

willkommen *adjective*
= welcome

willst ▶wollen

die **Wimper**, *plural* Wimpern
= eyelash

die **Wimperntusche**, *plural* Wimperntuschen
= mascara

der **Wind**, *plural* Winde
= wind

die **Windel**, *plural* Windeln
= nappy, = diaper

der **Windhund**, *plural* Windhunde
= greyhound

windig *adjective*
= windy

die **Windmühle**, *plural* Windmühlen
= windmill

Windpocken (*plural*)
= chickenpox

die **Windschutzscheibe**, *plural* Windschutzscheiben
= windscreen, = windshield

der **Winkel**, *plural* Winkel
* = angle
* = corner

winken *verb*
= to wave

der **Winter**, *plural* Winter
= winter

der **Winterschlaf**
= hibernation

winzig *adjective*
= tiny

wir *pronoun*
= we
wir sind es = it's us

die **Wirbelsäule**, *plural* Wirbelsäulen
= spine

wird ▶werden

wirft ▶werfen

wirken *verb*
* = to have an effect
gegen etwas wirken = to be effective against something
* (*appear*) = to seem

wirklich
1 *adjective* = real
2 *adverb* = really

die **Wirklichkeit**
= reality

wirksam *adjective*
= effective

W

die **Wirkung**, plural Wirkungen
= effect

wirst ▶ werden

der **Wirt**, plural Wirte
= landlord

die **Wirtin**, plural Wirtinnen
= landlady

die **Wirtschaft**, plural Wirtschaften
* = economy
* = pub

wirtschaftlich adjective
= economic

das **Wirtshaus**, plural Wirtshäuser
= pub

wischen
= to wipe
Staub wischen = to dust

wissen irregular verb
= to know

das **Wissen**
= knowledge

die **Wissenschaft**, plural Wissenschaften
= science

der **Wissenschaftler**, plural
Wissenschaftler
= scientist

die **Wissenschaftlerin**, plural
Wissenschaftlerinnen
= scientist

die **Witwe**, plural Witwen
= widow

der **Witwer**, plural Witwer
= widower

der **Witz**, plural Witze
= joke

witzig adjective
= funny

wo
1 adverb = where
2 conjunction
* (because) = seeing that
* = although
= when

woanders adverb
= elsewhere, = somewhere else

die **Woche**, plural Wochen
= week

das **Wochenende**, plural Wochenenden
= weekend

wochenlang adverb
= for weeks

der **Wochentag**, plural Wochentage
= weekday

wochentags adverb
= on weekdays

wöchentlich adjective
= weekly

wofür adverb
= for what
wofür brauchst du das Geld? = what do
you need the money for?

woher adverb
= where … from
woher weißt du das? = how do you know
that?

wohin adverb
= where (… to)

wohl adverb
* = well
sich wohl fühlen = to feel well, (be
comfortable) = to feel happy
* = probably
du bist wohl verrückt = you must be mad

das **Wohl**
= welfare
= well-being
zum Wohl! = cheers!

der **Wohlstand**
= prosperity

wohltätig adjective
= charitable

wohnen verb
= to live
(for a short time) = to stay

wohnhaft adjective
= resident

das **Wohnheim**, plural Wohnheime
= hostel
(for old people) = home

der **Wohnort**, plural Wohnorte
= place of residence

der **Wohnsitz**, plural Wohnsitze
= place of residence

die **Wohnung**, plural Wohnungen
= flat, = apartment

der **Wohnwagen**, plural Wohnwagen
= caravan

das **Wohnzimmer**, plural Wohnzimmer
= living room

der **Wolf**, plural Wölfe
= wolf

die **Wolke**, plural Wolken
= cloud

der **Wolkenkratzer**, plural Wolkenkratzer
= skyscraper

wolkig adjective
= cloudy

die **Wolldecke**, *plural* Wolldecken
= blanket

die **Wolle**
= wool

wollen *irregular verb*
= to want
er wollte gerade gehen = he was just
about to go

womit *adverb*
• (*in questions*) = what ... with
womit schreibt er? = what is he writing
with?
• = with which
womit er schreibt = with which he is
writing

wonach *adverb*
• (*in questions*) = after what
wonach suchst du? = what are you
looking for?
• = after which

woran *adverb*
• (*in questions*) = what ... of
= on what
woran hast du ihn erkannt? = how did
you recognize him?
• = of which

woraus *adverb*
• (*in questions*) = what ... from
woraus ist das? = what is it made of?
• = from which

worin *adverb*
• (*in questions*) = in what, = what ... in
• in which

das **Wort**, *plural* Worte *or* Wörter
= word

das **Wörterbuch**, *plural* Wörterbücher
= dictionary

wörtlich *adjective*
= word for word

der **Wortschatz**
= vocabulary

worüber *adverb*
• (*in questions*) = what ... over
= about what
worüber lachst du? = what are you
laughing about?
• = over which
= about which

worum *adverb*
• (*in questions*) = about what
worum geht es? = what's it about?
• = for which

wovon *adverb*
• (*in questions*) = what ... from
= about what
• = from which
= about which

wovor *adverb*
• (*in questions*) = what ... of
wovor hast du Angst? = what are you
afraid of?
• = of which

wozu *adverb*
= why, = what for

das **Wrack**, *plural* Wracks
= wreck

wuchs ▶ wachsen

der **Wuchs**
= growth

wund *adjective*
= sore

die **Wunde**, *plural* Wunden
= wound

das **Wunder**, *plural* Wunder
• = miracle
• = wonder

wunderbar *adjective*
= wonderful

wundern: sich wundern *verb*
= to be surprised

der **Wunsch**, *plural* Wünsche
= wish
auf Wunsch = on request

wünschen *verb*
• = to wish
was wünschen Sie? = can I help you?
• sich etwas wünschen = to want
something

wurde ▶ werden
er wurde gerufen = he was called

würde ▶ werden
er würde kommen = he would come

wurden, würden ▶ werden

wurdest, würdest ▶ werden

wurdet, würdet ▶ werden

der **Wurf**, *plural* Würfe
= throw

der **Würfel**, *plural* Würfel
= cube
(*in games*) = dice

würfeln *verb*
= to throw the dice

der **Wurm**, *plural* Würmer
= worm

die **Wurst**, *plural* Würste
= sausage

die **Wurzel**, *plural* Wurzeln
= root

würzen *verb*
= to season

würzig *adjective*
= spicy

wusch ▶ waschen

wusste (**wußte**⊙ᴸᴰ) ▶ wissen

die **Wüste**, *plural* Wüsten
= desert

die **Wut**
= rage

wütend *adjective*
= furious

Xx

x-beliebig✶ *adjective*
= any

x-mal✶ *adverb*
= umpteen times

Yy

die **Yacht**, *plural* Yachten
= yacht

das **Yoga**
= yoga

das **Ypsilon**, *plural* Ypsilons
= Y

Zz

zäh *adjective*
= tough

die **Zahl**, *plural* Zahlen
= number
= figure

zahlen *verb*
= to pay
= to pay for
bitte zahlen! = the bill please!

zählen *verb*
= to count
zählen zu = to be among

der **Zähler**, *plural* Zähler
= meter

zahlreich *adjective*
= numerous

die **Zahlung**, *plural* Zahlungen
= payment

die **Zählung**, *plural* Zählungen
* = count
* = census

zahm *adjective*
= tame

zähmen *verb*
= to tame

der **Zahn**, *plural* Zähne
= tooth

der **Zahnarzt**, *plural* Zahnärzte
= dentist

die **Zahnärztin**, *plural* Zahnärztinnen
= dentist

das **Zahnfleisch**
= gum
= gums

die **Zahnpasta**, *plural* Zahnpasten
= toothpaste

Zahnschmerzen (*plural*)
= toothache

die **Zange**, *plural* Zangen
= pliers

zanken: sich zanken *verb*
= to squabble

zappeln *verb*
= to wriggle

zart *adjective*
= delicate
= tender

zärtlich *adjective*
= affectionate

der **Zauber**
= magic
= spell

der **Zauberer**, *plural* Zauberer
= magician, = conjurer

zauberhaft *adjective*
= enchanting

zaubern *verb*
= to do magic

der **Zaun**, *plural* Zäune
= fence

z.B. *abbreviation*
(*zum Beispiel*) = e.g.

✶ in informal situations   ⊙ᴸᴰ = old spelling

der **Zebrastreifen**, *plural* Zebrastreifen
= zebra-crossing, = crosswalk

der **Zeh**, *plural* Zehen
= toe

die **Zehe**, *plural* Zehen
• = toe
• (*of garlic*) = clove

zehn *adjective*
= ten

das **Zehntel**, *plural* Zehntel
= tenth

zehnter/zehnte/zehntes *adjective*
= tenth

das **Zeichen**, *plural* Zeichen
• = sign
• = signal

zeichnen *verb*
= to draw

die **Zeichnung**, *plural* Zeichnungen
= drawing

der **Zeigefinger**, *plural* Zeigefinger
= index finger

zeigen *verb*
• to show
• auf jemanden zeigen = to point at someone
• sich zeigen = to appear, (*emerge*) = to become clear

der **Zeiger**, *plural* Zeiger
= hand

die **Zeile**, *plural* Zeilen
= line

die **Zeit**, *plural* Zeiten
= time
sich Zeit lassen = to take one's time

das **Zeitalter**, *plural* Zeitalter
= age

zeitlich *adverb*
= chronologically
zeitlich begrenzt = for a limited time

die **Zeitlupe**
= slow motion

der **Zeitraum**, *plural* Zeiträume
= period

die **Zeitschrift**, *plural* Zeitschriften
= magazine

die **Zeitung**, *plural* Zeitungen
= newspaper

zeitweise *adverb*
= at times

die **Zelle**, *plural* Zellen
• = cell
• = booth

das **Zelt**, *plural* Zelte
= tent

der **Zement**
= cement

der **Zentimeter**, *plural* Zentimeter
= centimetre, = centimeter

das **Zentimetermaß**, *plural* Zentimetermaße
= tape measure

zentral *adjective*
= central

die **Zentrale**, *plural* Zentralen
• = central office
= headquarters
• = (telephone) exchange

die **Zentralheizung**, *plural* Zentralheizungen
= central heating

das **Zentrum**, *plural* Zentren
= centre

zerbrechen *irregular verb*
• = to break
• (**!** *sein*) = to break
die Tasse ist zerbrochen = the cup has broken

zerbrechlich *adjective*
= fragile

die **Zeremonie**, *plural* Zeremonien
= ceremony

zerreißen *irregular verb*
• = to tear
= to tear up
• (**!** *sein*) = to tear

zerschneiden *irregular verb*
= to cut (up)

zerstören *verb*
= to destroy

die **Zerstörung**
= destruction

zerstreut *adjective*
= absent-minded

der **Zettel**, *plural* Zettel
• = piece of paper
• **✗**= note

das **Zeug✗**
= stuff

der **Zeuge**, *plural* Zeugen
= witness

die **Zeugin**, *plural* Zeuginnen
= witness

das **Zeugnis**, *plural* Zeugnisse
• = certificate
• (*at school*) = report

die **Ziege**, *plural* Ziegen
= goat

Z

der **Ziegel**, plural Ziegel
* = tile
* = brick

ziehen irregular verb
* = to pull
  = to pull out
  (gently) = to draw
  einen Strich ziehen = to draw a line
* (in a lottery) = to draw
* sich ziehen (of a path, road) = to run
* (cultivate) = to grow
* es zieht = there is a draught
* (! sein) = to move
  wir ziehen nach London = we are moving
  to London

das **Ziel**, plural Ziele
* = destination
* = goal, aim
* (in sport) = finish

zielen verb
  = to aim

die **Zielscheibe**, plural Zielscheiben
  = target

ziemlich adverb
  = quite

zierlich adjective
  = dainty

die **Ziffer**, plural Ziffern
  = figure

das **Zifferblatt**, plural Zifferblätter
  = face, = dial

die **Zigarette**, plural Zigaretten
  = cigarette

die **Zigarre**, plural Zigarren
  = cigar

der **Zigeuner**, plural Zigeuner
  = gypsy

die **Zigeunerin**, plural Zigeunerinnen
  = gypsy

das **Zimmer**, plural Zimmer
  = room
  Zimmer mit Frühstück = bed and
  breakfast

das **Zinn**
  = zinc

Zinsen (plural)
  = interest

der **Zinssatz**, plural Zinssätze
  = interest rate

zirka adverb
  = about

der **Zirkel**, plural Zirkel
  = pair of compasses

---

* in informal situations

der **Zirkus**, plural Zirkusse
  = circus

zischen verb
  = to hiss

zitieren verb
  = to quote

die **Zitrone**, plural Zitronen
  = lemon

zittern verb
  = to tremble, = to shake
  (with cold) = to shiver

der **Zivildienst**
  = community service

die **Zivilisation**, plural Zivilisationen
  = civilization

zog ▶ ziehen

zögern verb
  = to hesitate

der **Zoll**, plural Zölle
* = customs
* = duty

zollfrei adjective
  = duty-free

der **Zopf**, plural Zöpfe
  = plait, = braid

der **Zorn**
  = anger

zornig adjective
  = angry

zu
1 preposition (+ dative)
* = to
  zu . . . hin = towards
  zu Hause = at home
* = with
  die Jacke passt nicht zu dem Rock = the
  jacket doesn't go with that skirt
* (with time, price) = at
  das Stück zu fünf Mark = at 5 marks each
* (showing purpose) = for
  zum Spaß = for fun
* (indicating change, a result) = into
  zu etwas werden = to turn into
  something
* (towards)
  nett zu jemandem sein = to be nice to
  someone
* zu Fuß = on foot
* (with numbers and quantities)
  wir waren zu zweit = there were two of us
  das Ergebnis war zwei zu eins = the
  result was 2–1
* (on the occasion of)
  was schenkst du ihm zum Geburtstag? =
  what are you giving him for his
  birthday?
  jemandem zu etwas gratulieren = to
  congratulate someone on something

2 *adverb*
- = too
  zu sehr = too much
- (*indicating direction*) = towards
- Tür zu!✖ = shut the door!
3 *conjunction* = to
  nichts zu trinken = nothing to drink
  zu verkaufen = for sale

das **Zubehör**
  = accessories

zu|bereiten *verb*
  = to prepare

zu|binden *irregular verb*
  = to tie (up)

züchten *verb*
  = to breed

zucken *verb*
  = to twitch

der **Zucker**
  = sugar

der **Zuckerguß**
  = icing

zuckern *verb*
  = to sweeten

zu|decken *verb*
  = to cover (up)

zueinander *adverb*
  = to one another
  sie passen gut zueinander = they go well
  together

zuerst *adverb*
- = first
- = at first

der **Zufall**, *plural* Zufälle
  = chance
  = coincidence

zufällig
1 *adjective* = chance
2 *adverb* = by chance

zufrieden *adjective*
  = content
  mit etwas zufrieden sein = to be satisfied
  with something

der **Zug**, *plural* Züge
- = train
- = procession
- = draught
- (*of a person*) = characteristic
- (*in board games*) = move
- (*when drinking*) = swig
- (*when smoking*) = drag

die **Zugabe**, *plural* Zugaben
- = free gift
- (*at a concert*) = encore

der **Zugang**, *plural* Zugänge
  = access

die **Zugbrücke**, *plural* Zugbrücken
  = drawbridge

zu|geben *irregular verb*
- = to add
- = to admit

der **Zügel**, *plural* Zügel
  = rein

zügig *adjective*
  = quick

zu|greifen *irregular verb*
- to grab it/them
- (*at table*) = to help oneself
- = to lend a hand

zugunsten *preposition* (+ *genitive*)
  = in favour of

zu|haben *irregular verb*
  = to be closed

das **Zuhause**
  = home

zu|hören *verb*
  = to listen

der **Zuhörer**, *plural* Zuhörer
  = listener
  die Zuhörer = the audience

die **Zuhörerin**, *plural* Zuhörerinnen
  = listener

zu|kleben *verb*
- = to seal
- = to glue

zu|knöpfen *verb*
  = to button up

die **Zukunft**
  = future

zukünftig *adjective*
  = future

zu|lassen *irregular verb*
- = to allow
  ein Auto zulassen = to register a car
- = to leave closed

die **Zulassung**, *plural* Zulassungen
- = registration
- = admission

zuletzt *adverb*
- = last
  nicht zuletzt = not least
- = in the end

zum = zu dem

zu|machen *verb*
  = to close
  = to fasten

zunächst *adverb*
- = first
- = at first

der **Zuname**, *plural* Zunamen
  = surname

Z

das **Zündholz**, *plural* Zündhölzer
= match

die **Zündung**, *plural* Zündungen
= ignition

zu|nehmen *irregular verb*
* = to increase
* = to put on weight

die **Zunge**, *plural* Zungen
= tongue

zur = zu der
zur Schule = to school

zurecht|kommen *irregular verb*
(**!** *sein*)
= to cope, = to manage

zurück *adverb*
= back
Berlin, hin und zurück = return to Berlin

zurück|bekommen *irregular verb*
= to get back

zurück|bringen *irregular verb*
* = to bring back
* = to take back

zurück|fahren *irregular verb*
* = to drive back
* (**!** *sein*) = to go back, (*by car*) = to drive back

zurück|führen *verb*
* = to lead back
* = to attribute

zurück|geben *irregular verb*
= to give back

zurück|gehen *irregular verb* (**!** *sein*)
* = to go back
* = to go down, = to decrease

zurück|halten *irregular verb*
* = to hold back
* sich zurückhalten = to restrain oneself

zurück|kommen *irregular verb*
(**!** *sein*)
= to come back
(*arrive*) = to get back

zurück|lassen *irregular verb*
= to leave behind

zurück|legen *verb*
* = to put back
* = to keep, = to put aside
* (*when walking*) = to cover
* sich zurücklegen = to lie back

**zurück|lehnen: sich
zurücklehnen** *verb*
= to lean back

zurück|nehmen *irregular verb*
= to take back

zurück|rufen *irregular verb*
= to call back

zurück|treten *irregular verb* (**!** *sein*)
* = to step back
* = to resign

zurück|zahlen *verb*
= to pay back

zurück|ziehen *irregular verb*
* = to draw back
* sich zurückziehen = to withdraw, = to retire

zurzeit *adverb*
= at the moment

die **Zusage**, *plural* Zusagen
= acceptance

zusammen *adverb*
* = together
* = altogether

die **Zusammenarbeit**
= co-operation

zusammen|arbeiten *verb*
= to co-operate

zusammen|bauen *verb*
= to assemble

zusammen|brechen *irregular verb*
(**!** *sein*)
= to collapse

zusammen|fassen *verb*
= to summarize

die **Zusammenfassung**, *plural*
Zusammenfassungen
= summary

zusammen|halten *irregular verb*
= to hold together
= to keep together
wir halten zusammen = we'll stick together

der **Zusammenhang**, *plural*
Zusammenhänge
* = context
* = connection

zusammen|kommen *irregular verb*
(**!** *sein*)
= to meet

zusammen|legen *irregular verb*
* = to put together
* = to fold up
* (*pool money*) = to club together

**zusammen|nehmen: sich
zusammennehmen** *irregular verb*
= to pull oneself together

zusammen|passen *verb*
= to match
(*of people*) = to be well matched
(*of parts*) = to fit together

OLD = old spelling

der **Zusammenstoß**, plural
Zusammenstöße
= collision, = crash

zusammen|stoßen irregular verb
(! sein)
= to collide, = to crash

zusammen|zählen verb
= to add up

zusätzlich
1 adjective = additional, = extra
2 adverb = in addition, = extra

zu|schauen verb
= to watch

der **Zuschauer**, plural Zuschauer
= spectator
(TV) = viewer
die Zuschauer = the audience

die **Zuschauerin**, plural Zuschauerinnen
= spectator
(TV) = viewer

der **Zuschlag**, plural Zuschläge
= surcharge
(on a train) = supplement

zu|schließen irregular verb
= to lock (up)

der **Zuschuss** (**Zuschuß**OLD), plural
Zuschüsse
= contribution
= grant

zu|sehen irregular verb
= to watch
zusehen, dass = to see to it that

der **Zustand**, plural Zustände
= condition
= state

zuständig adjective
= responsible

die **Zustellung**, plural Zustellungen
= delivery

zu|stimmen verb
= to agree

die **Zustimmung**, plural Zustimmungen
= agreement

zu|stoßen irregular verb (! sein)
= to happen

die **Zutat**, plural Zutaten
= ingredient

zu|trauen verb
jemandem etwas zutrauen = to
think someone capable of
something

zu|treffen irregular verb
auf etwas zutreffen = to apply to
something

der **Zutritt**
= entry
Zutritt haben = to have access

zuverlässig adjective
= reliable

zuviel OLD ▶ viel

zuwenig OLD ▶ wenig

zu|zahlen verb
= to pay extra

zu|ziehen irregular verb
• = to pull tight
die Vorhänge zuziehen = to draw the
curtains
• sich eine Verletzung zuziehen = to
sustain an injury

zuzüglich preposition (+ genitive)
= plus

der **Zwang**, plural Zwänge
• = force
• = obligation

zwängen verb
= to squeeze

zwanglos adjective
= casual, = informal

zwanzig adjective
= twenty

zwar adverb
= admittedly
und zwar = to be exact

der **Zweck**, plural Zwecke
= purpose
es hat keinen Zweck = there's no point

zwei adjective
= two

zweideutig adjective
= ambiguous

zweifach adjective
= twice

der **Zweifel**, plural Zweifel
= doubt

zweifellos adverb
= undoubtedly

zweifeln verb
= to doubt
an etwas zweifeln = to doubt something

der **Zweig**, plural Zweige
= branch

zweimal adverb
= twice

zweisprachig adjective
= bilingual

Z

zweit adverb
zu zweit = in twos
wir waren zu zweit = there were two of us

zweite ▶ zweiter

zweiteilig *adjective*
  = two-piece
  = two-part

zweitens *adverb*
  = secondly

zweiter/zweite/zweites *adjective*
  = second

der **Zwerg**, *plural* Zwerge
  = dwarf

die **Zwiebel**, *plural* Zwiebeln
  * = onion
  * = bulb

der **Zwilling**, *plural* Zwillinge
  * = twin
  * Zwillinge = Gemini

zwingen *irregular verb*
  * to force
  * sich zwingen = to force oneself

zwischen *preposition* (+ *dative or accusative*)
  = between
  (*in a crowd*) = among

zwischendurch *adverb*
  = in between
  = now and again

der **Zwischenfall**, *plural* Zwischenfälle
  = incident

der **Zwischenraum**, *plural* Zwischenräume
  = gap, = space

die **Zwischenzeit**
  in der Zwischenzeit = in the meantime

zwo✗ *adjective*
  = two

zwölf *adjective*
  = twelve

zwoter/zwote/zwotes✗ *adjective*
  = second

zynisch *adjective*
  = cynical

✗ in informal situations

Dictionary know-how

Dictionary know-how

This section contains a number of short exercises which will help you to use your dictionary more effectively. You will find answers to all of the exercises at the end of the section.

1 Which is which?

Here is an extract from a German holiday advertisement. Find fifteen nouns and underline them, and eight adjectives and circle them — or make two lists. If you are not sure of some words, look them up in the German–English part of the dictionary and see if the term 'noun' or 'adjective' is used to describe them.

URLAUB AUF DEM BAUERNHOF

Besonders geeignet für Familien mit kleinen Kindern, Hunde erlaubt. Gemütliche Zimmer mit Dusche und Balkon. Gute, österreichische Küche. Wir haben eigene Ponys und Fahrräder und einen großen Spielplatz. Kinder fünfzig Prozent Ermäßigung.

2 Der, die, or das?

Here are some English nouns which appear in the English–German part of the dictionary. Find out their German equivalents and make a list with three columns: *der* for masculine nouns, *die* for feminine nouns and *das* for neuter nouns. If there is more than one German equivalent, put each one in the right gender column.

bag	cake	door	child
penguin	library	raincoat	thunderstorm
shirt	underpants	house	sun
moon	glasses	book	snow
plane	tyre	ear	adventure

3 Jumbled-up buildings

Each of these German words is a building, but the letters have been jumbled up. Put them in the right order and look up the word on the German–English side of the dictionary to find the right article for each building.

TOPS	RICHEK	LEUSCH	HABFOHN
HUSTARA	HUFAUSAK	KUSEPRARMT	AHSU

4 **Nouns and pronouns**

The following example shows how pronouns can replace nouns:

Emma erklärt Peter die Regeln

sie erklärt Peter die Regeln

sie erklärt ihm die Regeln

sie erklärt sie ihm *(note the change of order)*

Underline the pronouns in the example sentences above, and change the next two sentences in the same way.

Gabi zeigt Fritz das Bild

der Mann gibt der Frau die Tasche

5 **Verbspotting**

Rearrange the following groups of words to form correct sentences. Then list the infinitive of the verb in each sentence—as it appears on the German–English side of the dictionary.

fährt nach Berlin er heute

Dienstag jeden ihr Fußball spielt?

Postkarte was nach kostet eine England?

zeigt uns er neue die Wohnung

wie Film der hieß?

6 **Where does the verb go?**

German verbs often consist of more than one word. This happens when they combine with another word or with an auxiliary verb to form the perfect or future tense. Place the two missing German words in the correct position in the following sentences. For example:

Er *(can tell)* gute Geschichten. **(kann erzählen)**
= Er kann gute Geschichten erzählen.

Der kleine Junge *(can walk)* noch nicht. **(kann laufen)**

Meine Schwester *(has bought)* ein neues Kleid für die Party. **(hat gekauft)**

Er *(will go)* mit dem Zug nach Frankfurt. **(wird fahren)**

Seine Mutter *(would like to visit)* uns in Italien. **(möchte besuchen)**

Ich *(must sign)* den Brief noch. **(muss unterschreiben)**

7 Separable or inseparable?

Here is a list of German verbs. Some have prefixes which are always separable, and others have prefixes which are never separable. Sort the separable from the inseparable verbs in two lists. If you are not sure of some of them, look them up on the German–English side of the dictionary. Separable verbs are marked in the dictionary with a vertical bar after the prefix.

verstehen	**ausgehen**	**zerstören**	**losfahren**
ankommen	**beginnen**	**einsteigen**	**verlaufen**
festhalten	**aufhören**	**mitmachen**	**erfinden**

8 Splitting verbs

Put the separable verbs in the right place in the following sentences. Be careful with the ending of the first part of each verb.

Die Kinder . . . nach Weihnachten . . . . **(wiederkommen)**

Heute . . . wir ein Picknick . . . . **(mitnehmen)**

Ich . . . morgens um sieben Uhr . . . . **(aufstehen)**

Er . . . erst nach Weihnachten . . . . **(zurückfahren)**

9 Subject or object?

Subjects and objects have been left out of sentences in this German newspaper report. Choose suitable words from the the list below to fill in the gaps. Look up the words on the German–English side of the dictionary and add the right article to the nouns.

FRANZ KATER VERHAFTET

Die .... verhaftete einen gefährlichen .... am Dienstag Abend. Franz Kater stahl letzte Woche ein wertvolles .... aus einer Galerie. Obwohl es dunkel war, erkannten zwei .... den Einbrecher sofort. Kater trug einen braunen .... und eine schwarze...................................... . Er zog eine .... aus der Tasche. "Hände hoch, oder .... schieße", schrie der .... Nach genauer Untersuchung stellte die .... fest, dass .... nur eine .... hatte.

Einbrecher	Spielzeugpistole	Polizei	Bild	Mantel	Polizei
Polizisten	ich		Mütze	er	Pistole	Einbrecher

10 **Finding separable verbs**

Find the separable verb(s) in each sentence and write them down in the infinitive — as they appear on the German–English side of the dictionary. Leave out the vertical bar, which is only there in the dictionary to show you that the verb is separable.

Um wie viel Uhr kommt ihr an?

Der Vater holt die Kinder von der Schule ab.

Wann findet das Konzert statt?

Die Kinder sehen viel fern.

11 **Word search**

Fourteen German words are hidden in this grid. They are listed below on the right. Most read across, but some read down. When you have found them, ring them, list them by part of speech (noun, adjective, etc.), and add the right article to nouns.

G	P	A	L	A	S	T	X	G	E
F	A	H	R	E	R	I	N	A	J
K	Q	M	J	U	N	G	I	S	L
Ä	Q	U	A	D	R	A	T	E	P
L	A	B	B	A	D	E	N	G	F
T	L	T	X	Y	F	A	C	H	A
E	T	D	E	R	Z	W	T	O	H
Z	E	I	C	H	N	U	N	G	R
U	L	C	H	O	R	W	A	Y	E
L	Ä	C	H	E	L	N	K	S	R

alt	**Gas**
baden	**jung**
Chor	**Kälte**
der	**lächeln**
Fach	**Palast**
Fahrer	**Quadrat**
Fahrerin	**Zeichnung**

12 **Find the plural**

Use your dictionary to find the plural of the following nouns.

der Mantel	**die** ....
ein Mädchen	**zwei** ....
ein Korb	**zehn** ....
eine Möglichkeit	**viele** ....
das Buch	**die** ....
ein Radio	**drei** ....
eine Verkäuferin	**zwei** ....
eine Kette	**viele** ....
das Auto	**die** ....
ein Tischtuch	**zwei** ....

13 **Building a sentence**

In a German main clause the subject usually comes before the verb. If there are two objects, the indirect object comes before the direct object. For example:

```
    ●        ■          ▶              ▲
Der Lehrer | gibt | dem Mädchen | das Buch
```

Make ten sentences using the following words. You don't always have to use both direct and indirect object in your sentences.

- ● **subjects:**   der Junge, das Mädchen
- ■ **verbs:**   kauft, schreibt, singt, spielt, gibt
- ▲ **direct objects:**   Klavier, eine CD, einen Brief, ein Lied
- ▶ **indirect objects:** dem Lehrer, seiner Mutter, ihr

14 **Time—manner—place**

A useful rule for word order when speaking or writing German is
TIME–MANNER–PLACE. For example:

Ich fahre morgen mit dem Zug nach Frankfurt
(*time* = morgen), (*manner* = mit dem Zug), (*place* = nach Frankfurt).

Practise the TIME–MANNER–PLACE sequence by inserting the words in the brackets in the right place in each of the following sentences.

Emma fährt jeden Morgen zur Universität. (mit dem Rad)

Wir sind mit dem Auto nach Italien gefahren. (letzten Sommer)

Wir fahren dieses Jahr zu Weihnachten. (nach München)

15 **Find the meaning**

Some words have more than one meaning, and it's important to check that you have chosen the right one. In this dictionary different meanings of a word are marked by a bullet point (•).

We have given you one meaning of the German words below. Use your dictionary to find another one.

die Dame	• lady	• ....
die Decke	• blanket	• ....
aufheben	• to pick up	• ....
dick	• thick	• ....
der Zug	• train	• ....
der Hahn	• tap	• ....
der Satz	• set	• ....

16 **Asking questions**

In German questions are often introduced by a pronoun such as *wer* or an adverb such as *wann*. In these cases the verb is the second element. For example:

statement   Emma wohnt in London

question   Wer wohnt in London?

Look up the bracketed words on the English-German side of the dictionary and use them to turn these statements into questions.

Das Buch liegt auf dem Tisch.   (*what*)

Peter wohnt in dieser Wohnung.   (*who*)

Wir fahren morgen nach Oxford.   (*when*)

Die Großeltern wohnen in Spanien.   (*where*)

17 **Umlauts**

The double dots of all the umlauts (ä, ö, ü) have been left out in this letter. Use your dictionary to help put the dots over the right vowels.

Liebe Gabi,

danke fur die Einladung zu deiner Party. Ich wurde gern kommen, aber mochte nicht alleine zuruckfahren. Ist es moglich, zwei Nachte bei dir zu bleiben? Mein Vater kann mich dann nach funf abholen. Ruf mich bald an, damit wir uns uber alles unterhalten konnen.

Herzliche Gruße
     deine Karin

18 **Find the word**

German nouns are often made up of two or more separate words. Ten such compound nouns have been split in two and put in separate lists. Choosing the first part of the word from list 1 and the second from list 2 , use your dictionary to help you find out what they are. Sometimes different word combinations make different nouns.

(list 1)

DAUER, AUTO, BAHN, OHR, SCHLAF, SEIL, FLUG, ZAHN, TELEFON, BRIEF

(list 2)

BUCH, BAHN, ZIMMER, MARKE, WELLE, RING, HAFEN, ZEIT, HOF, ARZT

19 **Which preposition?**

Look up the preposition 'to' and choose the right German word for the preposition gaps in the following sentences.

Nächste Woche fahren wir . . . Deutschland.

Ich muss . . . die Toilette gehen.

Peter schreibt einen Brief . . . seine Schwester.

Es ist jetzt zehn Minuten . . . fünf.

Wie komme ich . . . Bahnhof?

20 **Find the verb**

Some words in English can be both nouns and verbs, for example, **race**. For this exercise, look up the following English words on the English–German side of the dictionary and then give the German for the verb only.

insult   kiss   dance   measure   rain

Answers

1

Nouns: Urlaub, Bauernhof, Familien, Kindern, Hunde, Zimmer, Dusche, Balkon, Küche, Ponys, Fahrräder, Spielplatz, Kinder, Prozent, Ermäßigung.

Adjectives: geeignet, kleinen, gemütliche, gute, österreichische, eigene, großen, fünfzig

2

Masculine nouns: der Kuchen, der Pinguin, der Regenmantel, der Mond, der Schnee, der Reifen.

Feminine nouns: die Tasche/die Tüte, die Tür, die Bibliothek, die Unterhose, die Sonne, die Brille.

Neuter nouns: das Kind, das Gewitter, das Hemd, das Haus, das Buch, das Flugzeug, das Ohr, das Abenteuer.

3

die Post, die Kirche, die Schule, der Bahnhof, das Rathaus, das Kaufhaus, der Supermarkt, das Haus.

4

Emma erklärt Peter die Regeln, **sie** erklärt Peter die Regeln, **sie** erklärt **ihm** die Regeln, **sie** erklärt **sie ihm**;

Gabi zeigt Fritz das Bild, **sie** zeigt Fritz das Bild, **sie** zeigt **ihm** das Bild, **sie** zeigt **es ihm**;

der Mann gibt der Frau die Tasche, **er** gibt der Frau die Tasche, **er** gibt **ihr** die Tasche, **er** gibt **sie ihr.**

5

er fährt heute nach Berlin (fahren); spielt ihr jeden Dienstag Fußball? (spielen); was kostet eine Postkarte nach England? (kosten); er zeigt uns die neue Wohnung (zeigen); wie hieß der Film? (heißen).

6

Der kleine Junge kann noch nicht laufen.

Meine Schwester hat ein neues Kleid für die Party gekauft.

Er wird mit dem Zug nach Frankfurt fahren.

Seine Mutter möchte uns in Italien besuchen.

Ich muss den Brief noch unterschreiben.

7

Separable verbs: ausgehen, losfahren, ankommen, einsteigen, festhalten, aufhören, mitmachen.

Inseparable verbs: verstehen, zerstören, beginnen, verlaufen, erfinden.

8

Die Kinder kommen nach Weihnachten wieder.

Heute nehmen wir ein Picknick mit.

Ich stehe morgens um sieben Uhr auf.

Er fährt erst nach Weihnachten zurück.

9

Die **Polizei** verhaftete einen gefährlichen **Einbrecher** am Dienstag Abend. Franz Kater stahl letzte Woche ein wertvolles **Bild** aus einer Galerie. Obwohl es dunkel war, erkannten zwei **Polizisten** den Einbrecher sofort. Kater trug einen braunen **Mantel** und eine schwarze **Mütze**. Er zog eine **Pistole** aus der Tasche. "Hände hoch, oder **ich** schieße", schrie der **Einbrecher**. Nach genauer Untersuchung stellte die **Polizei** fest, dass **er** nur eine **Spielzeugpistole** hatte.

Subjects: die Polizei, die Polizisten, ich, der Einbrecher, die Polizei, er.

Objects: der Einbrecher, das Bild, der Mantel, die Mütze, die Pistole, die Spielzeugpistole.

10

ankommen; abholen; stattfinden; fernsehen.

11

Masculine nouns: der Palast, der Fahrer, der Chor; **feminine nouns:** die Fahrerin, die Kälte, die Zeichnung; **neuter nouns:** das Gas, das Quadrat, das Fach; **adjectives:** alt, jung; **verbs:** lächeln, baden; **article:** der.

12

der Mantel, die Mäntel; ein Mädchen, zwei Mädchen; ein Korb, zehn Körbe; eine Möglichkeit, viele Möglichkeiten; das Buch, die Bücher; ein Radio, drei Radios; eine Verkäuferin, zwei Verkäuferinnen; eine Kette, viele Ketten; das Auto, die Autos; ein Tischtuch, zwei Tischtücher.

13

der Junge kauft (dem Lehrer/seiner Mutter/ihr) eine CD

der Junge schreibt (dem Lehrer/seiner Mutter/ihr) einen Brief

der Junge singt (dem Lehrer/seiner Mutter/ihr) ein Lied

der Junge spielt Klavier/eine CD

der Junge gibt (dem Lehrer/seiner Mutter/ihr) eine CD

das Mädchen kauft (dem Lehrer/ihr) eine CD

das Mädchen schreibt (dem Lehrer/ihr) einen Brief

das Mädchen singt (dem Lehrer/ihr) ein Lied

das Mädchen spielt Klavier/eine CD

das Mädchen gibt (dem Lehrer/ihr) eine CD

14

Emma fährt jeden Morgen mit dem Rad zur Universität.

Wir sind letzten Sommer mit dem Auto nach Italien gefahren.

Wir fahren dieses Jahr zu Weihnachten nach München.

15

Possible answers:

die Dame	• queen
	• draughts, checkers
die Decke	• cloth
	• ceiling
aufheben	• to keep
dick	• fat
der Zug	• procession
	• draught
	• characteristic
	• move
	• swig
	• drag
der Hahn	• cock
der Satz	• sentence
	• leap
	• movement
	• rate

16

Was liegt auf dem Tisch?

Wer wohnt in dieser Wohnung?

Wann fahren wir nach Oxford?

Wo wohnen die Großeltern?

17

Liebe Gabi,

danke für die Einladung zu deiner Party. Ich würde gern kommen, aber möchte nicht alleine zurückfahren. Ist es möglich, zwei Nächte bei dir zu bleiben? Mein Vater kann mich dann nach fünf abholen. Ruf mich bald an, damit wir uns über alles unterhalten können.

Herzliche Grüße

deine Karin

18

Dauerwelle, Autobahn, Bahnhof, Ohrring, Schlafzimmer, Seilbahn, Flughafen, Zahnarzt, Telefonbuch, Briefmarke; **extra nouns:** Flugbahn, Flugzeit, Automarke.

19

Nächste Woche fahren wir **nach** Deutschland.

Ich muss **auf** die Toilette gehen.

Peter schreibt einen Brief **an** seine Schwester.

Es ist jetzt zehn Minuten **vor** fünf.

Wie komme ich **zum** Bahnhof?

20

beleidigen, küssen, tanzen, messen, regnen.

English–German

Aa

a *article*
= ein/eine/ein

> **!** *Note that the article changes according to the gender of the noun it goes with:* a table = ein Tisch *(masculine);* a flower = eine Blume *(feminine);* a house = ein Haus *(neuter).*

not a = kein/keine/kein

ability *noun*
(talent) = (die) Begabung

able *adjective*
(competent) = fähig
to be able to do something = etwas tun können

about
1 *preposition*
(on the subject of) = über (+ *accusative*)
a programme about life in Germany = eine Sendung über das Leben in Deutschland
2 *adverb*
(approximately) = ungefähr
in about three weeks = in ungefähr drei Wochen
she is about to [cry | sneeze | go ...] = sie [weint | niest | geht ...] gleich

above
1 *preposition* = über (+ *dative*)
their flat is above the shop = ihre Wohnung ist über dem Geschäft
the shelf above it = das Regal darüber
2 *adverb* = oben
above all = vor allem

abroad *adverb*
= im Ausland
to travel abroad = ins Ausland reisen

absent *adjective*
= abwesend
to be absent from school = in der Schule fehlen

accent *noun*
= (der) Akzent
to speak with a German accent = mit deutschem Akzent sprechen

accept *verb*
(receive) = annehmen

access *noun*
• = (der) Zugang
access to the internet = Zugang zum Internet
• *(road)* = (die) Zufahrt

accident *noun*
• *(causing injury or damage)* = (der) Unfall
the accident and emergency department = die Notfallstation

• *(chance)* = (der) Zufall
by accident = zufällig

accommodation *(British)*,
accommodations *(US) noun*
= (die) Unterkunft
accommodation is very expensive in London = Wohnungen *or* Zimmer sind in London sehr teuer

accompany *verb*
= begleiten

account *noun*
• *(in a bank)* = (das) Konto
there's money in my account = ich habe Geld auf meinem Konto
• **you have to take expenses into account** = man muß die Unkosten berücksichtigen

accountant *noun*
= (der) Buchhalter/(die) Buchhalterin

accurate *adjective*
• *(correct)* = richtig
• *(precise)* = genau
an accurate description = eine genaue Beschreibung

accuse *verb*
= beschuldigen
he accused them of stealing his bike = er beschuldigte sie, sein Rad gestohlen zu haben

across *preposition*
• = über (+ *accusative*)
to go across the street = über die Straße gehen (**!** *sein*)
• *(on the other side of)* = auf der anderen Seite (+ *genitive*)
across the river = auf der anderen Seite des Flusses
he lives across the street = er wohnt gegenüber

act *verb*
• *(take action)* = handeln
• *(perform as an actor)* = spielen

activity *noun*
= (die) Aktivität
activities = Veranstaltungen

actor *noun*
= (der) Schauspieler

actress *noun*
= (die) Schauspielerin

actually *adverb*
• *(in fact)* = eigentlich
I haven't actually seen the film yet = ich habe den Film eigentlich noch nicht gesehen

- (*really*) = wirklich
  did he actually say that? = hat er das wirklich gesagt?
- (*by the way*) = übrigens

adapt *verb*
  (*get used to*) = sich anpassen
  to adapt to = sich anpassen (+ *dative*)
  she quickly adapted to her new environment = sie hat sich schnell der neuen Umgebung angepasst

add *verb*
- = hinzufügen
  to add a spoonful of lemon juice = einen Löffel Zitronensaft dazugeben
- (*in maths*) = addieren

addicted *adjective*
  = süchtig
  to become addicted to drugs = drogensüchtig werden (**!** *sein*)

address *noun*
  = (die) Adresse, = (die) Anschrift
  what's his address? = wo wohnt er?

adhesive *noun*
  = (der) Klebstoff

adjust *verb*
- (*get used to*) = sich gewöhnen
  to adjust to something = sich an etwas (*accusative*) gewöhnen
- (*alter setting*) = einstellen

administration *noun*
  = (die) Verwaltung

admire *verb*
  = bewundern

admit *verb*
- (*own up*) = zugeben
  he won't admit to being jealous = er will nicht zugeben, dass er eifersüchtig ist
- (*allow in*) = hereinlassen
  he was admitted to hospital = er wurde im Krankenhaus aufgenommen

adolescent *noun*
  = (der/die) Jugendliche

adopt *verb*
  = adoptieren

adore *verb*
  = lieben
  she adores strawberries = sie mag Erdbeeren wahnsinnig gern

adult *noun*
  = (der/die) Erwachsene

advance *noun*
  in advance = im Voraus
  here's £30 in advance = hier sind dreißig Pfund als Vorschuss

advantage *noun*
- (*positive point*) = (der) Vorteil
  to have an advantage over someone = jemandem gegenüber im Vorteil sein

- **to take advantage of a situation** = eine Situation ausnutzen

adventure *noun*
  = (das) Abenteuer

advert, advertisement *noun*
- (*on TV*) = (der) Werbespot
- (*in a newspaper*) = (die) Anzeige
  to answer a job advertisement = sich auf eine Stellenanzeige melden

advertising *noun*
  = (die) Werbung

advice *noun*
  = (der) Rat
  to ask someone's advice = jemanden um Rat fragen
  a piece of advice = ein Ratschlag

advise *verb*
  = raten (+ *dative*)
  to advise someone to rest = jemandem raten, sich auszuruhen
  to advise against it = davon abraten

aerial *noun*
  = (die) Antenne

aerobics *noun*
  = (das) Aerobic
  to do aerobics = Aerobic machen

aeroplane *noun*
  = (das) Flugzeug

affect *verb*
- (*have an effect on*) = sich auswirken auf (+ *accusative*)
- (*distress*) = treffen
  they were badly affected by the loss = der Verlust traf sie hart

afford *verb*
  to be able to afford a car = sich (*dative*) ein Auto leisten können
  he can't afford to move = er kann es sich (*dative*) nicht leisten umzuziehen

afraid *adjective*
- (*scared*)
  to be afraid = Angst haben
  to be afraid of spiders = Angst vor Spinnen haben
- (*expressing regret*)
  I'm afraid not = leider nicht
  I'm afraid I can't come = ich kann leider nicht kommen

Africa *noun*
  = (das) Afrika ▶ **Countries p. 208**

African
  1 *noun* = (der) Afrikaner/(die) Afrikanerin
  2 *adjective* = afrikanisch ▶ **Countries p. 208**

after
  1 *preposition* = nach (+ *dative*)
  we'll leave after breakfast = wir fahren nach dem Frühstück ab
  the day after tomorrow = übermorgen
  after that = danach

2 *conjunction* = nachdem
  after brushing her teeth, she went to bed =
    nachdem sie sich die Zähne geputzt
    hatte, ging sie ins Bett
  after all = schließlich

afternoon *noun*
  = (der) Nachmittag
  in the afternoon = am Nachmittag
  this afternoon = heute Nachmittag
  on Monday afternoon =
    am Montagnachmittag

aftershave *noun*
  = (das) Rasierwasser

afterward (*US*), **afterwards** (*British*)
    adverb
• (*later*) = nachher
• (*after a particular event*) = danach
  he died soon afterwards = er starb kurz
    danach

again *adverb*
  = wieder
  are you going to Germany again this year?
    = fahrt ihr dieses Jahr wieder nach
    Deutschland?
  let's try again = versuchen wir es noch
    einmal
  again and again = immer wieder

against *preposition*
• (*close to*) = gegen (+ *accusative*)
  he leaned against the wall = er lehnte sich
    gegen die Wand
• (*not in favour of*) = gegen (+ *accusative*)
  to be against violence = gegen Gewalt sein

age
1 *noun* = (das) Alter
  under age = minderjährig
2 *verb* = altern
  he has aged = er ist alt geworden

aged *adjective*
  = im Alter von
  a boy aged 10 = ein zehnjähriger Junge

ago *adverb*
  = vor (+ *dative*)
  two weeks ago = vor zwei Wochen

agree *verb*
• (*have the same opinion*) = einer Meinung
    sein
  I don't agree with you = ich bin anderer
    Meinung
• (*give one's consent*) = einwilligen
  to agree to a plan = mit einem Plan
    einverstanden sein
• (*reach a decision*) = sich einigen
  to agree on a price = sich auf einen Preis
    einigen

agreement *noun*
• (*settlement*) = (die) Abmachung
• (*contract*) = (das) Abkommen
• (*when sharing an opinion*) = (die)
    Übereinstimmung

to be in agreement with someone = mit
  jemandem einer Meinung sein

agriculture *noun*
  = (die) Landwirtschaft

ahead *adverb*
• **we went on ahead** = wir sind vorgegangen
  I would like to send my baggage on ahead
    = ich möchte mein Gepäck
    vorausschicken
• **ahead of** = vor (+ *dative*)
  the people ahead of us = die Leute vor uns

Aids *noun*
  = (das) Aids

aim
1 *noun*
  = (das) Ziel
2 *verb*
• (*try*) = versuchen
• (*direct*)
  to be aimed at someone = auf jemanden
    abgezielt sein
  (*when using a weapon*)
  to aim a rifle at someone = ein Gewehr auf
    jemanden richten

air
1 *noun* = (die) Luft
2 *verb*
  to air a room = ein Zimmer lüften

air-conditioning *noun*
  = (die) Klimaanlage

aircraft *noun*
  = (das) Flugzeug

air hostess *noun*
  = (die) Stewardess

airline *noun*
  = (die) Fluggesellschaft

airmail *noun*
  = (die) Luftpost
  to send a letter by airmail = einen Brief mit
    or per Luftpost schicken

airplane (*US*) ▶ aeroplane

airport *noun*
  = (der) Flughafen

alarm clock *noun*
  = (der) Wecker

alcohol *noun*
  = (der) Alkohol

A levels *noun*
  ≈ (das) Abitur

alive *adjective*
  = lebendig
  to be alive = leben

all
1 *adjective*
• (*with a singular noun*) = ganz
  all the time = die ganze Zeit
• (*with a plural noun*) = alle
  all trains stop here = alle Züge halten hier

2 *pronoun*
- (*everybody*) = alle
  all of them = sie alle
- (*everything*) = alles
  that's all = das ist alles
  all of the town = die ganze Stadt

3 *adverb*
- = ganz
  to be all alone = ganz allein sein
  all at once = auf einmal
- (*score in sport*) **two all** = zwei zu zwei

allergy *noun*
= (die) Allergie

allow *verb*
to allow someone to leave = jemandem erlauben zu gehen
to be allowed to take a week off = eine Woche Urlaub nehmen dürfen
she's not allowed to hitchhike = sie darf nicht per Anhalter fahren
smoking is not allowed = Rauchen ist nicht gestattet

all right *adjective*
- (*when giving an opinion*) = ganz gut
  the film was all right = der Film war ganz gut
- (*when talking about health*)
  I'm all right = mir gehts ganz gut

> ! Note that **gehts**, *written as one word, is short for* **geht es**.

- (*when giving an opinion*) = in Ordnung, = okay✶

almond *noun*
= (die) Mandel

almost *adverb*
= fast
I almost forgot = ich hätte es fast vergessen

alone
1 *adjective* = allein
leave me alone! = lass mich in Ruhe!
2 *adverb* = allein
she doesn't like living alone = sie lebt nicht gern allein

along *preposition*
= entlang (+ *accusative*)

> ! Note that **entlang** *is usually put after the noun, which is in the accusative. When* **entlang** *is used with a verb, it forms a new, compound verb.*

along the street = die Straße entlang
to run along = entlanglaufen (! *sein*)

aloud *adverb*
= laut
to read aloud = vorlesen

already *adverb*
= schon
have you finished already? = bist du schon fertig?

also *adverb*
= auch

alternative *noun*
= (die) Alternative
you have no alternative = du hast keine andere Wahl

although *conjunction*
= obwohl
although it was cold, he didn't have a coat on = obwohl es kalt war, hatte er keinen Mantel an

altogether *adverb*
= insgesamt
how much is that altogether? = wie viel macht das insgesamt?

always *adverb*
= immer

amazing *adjective*
= erstaunlich

ambassador *noun*
= (der) Botschafter/ (die) Botschafterin

ambition *noun*
= (der) Ehrgeiz

ambitious *adjective*
= ehrgeizig

ambulance *noun*
= (der) Krankenwagen

America *noun*
= (das) Amerika ▶**Countries p. 208**

American
1 *noun* = (der) Amerikaner/ (die) Amerikanerin
2 *adjective* = amerikanisch ▶**Countries p. 208**

among, amongst *preposition*
- = unter (+ *dative*)
  among other things = unter anderem
- (*one of*)
  Japan is among the world's richest countries = Japan gehört zu den reichsten Ländern der Welt

amount *noun*
- (*quantity*) = (die) Menge
  I've got a huge amount of work = ich habe eine Menge Arbeit
- (*sum of money*) = (der) Betrag

amusement arcade *noun*
= (die) Spielhalle

amusing *adjective*
= amüsant

an ▶a

ancestor *noun*
= (der) Vorfahre

anchor *noun*
= (der) Anker

and *conjunction*
- = und

✶ in informal situations

and so on = und so weiter
try and come = versuche zu kommen
faster and faster = immer schneller
for weeks and weeks = wochenlang
it's nice and warm today = heute ist es
  schön warm
* (*in numbers*)
three hundred and fifty =
  dreihundertfünfzig ▶**Numbers p. 282**

anger *noun*
= (der) Zorn

angry *adjective*
= zornig
to be angry with someone = auf jemanden
  böse sein
you'll make her angry = du verärgerst sie
to get angry with someone = sich über
  jemanden ärgern

animal *noun*
= (das) Tier

ankle *noun*
= (der) Knöchel

anniversary *noun*
= (der) Jahrestag
my parents' wedding anniversary = der
  Hochzeitstag meiner Eltern

announcement *noun*
(*public statement*) = (die) Bekanntmachung

annoy *verb*
= ärgern
to be annoyed with someone = sich über
  jemanden ärgern
he's starting to annoy me = er regt mich
  langsam auf

annoyed *adjective*
= ärgerlich
she's annoyed with me = sie ist ärgerlich
  auf mich
he got very annoyed = er hat sich darüber
  sehr geärgert

annoying *adjective*
= ärgerlich
he is very annoying = er geht mir auf die
  Nerven

annual
1 *noun* = (das) Jahresalbum
2 *adjective* = jährlich
the annual meeting = die
  Jahresversammlung

another
1 *adjective*
* (*additional*) = noch ein
I'll buy another ticket = ich kaufe noch eine
  Karte
it will take another three weeks = es wird
  noch drei Wochen dauern
* (*different*) = ein anderer/eine andere/ein
  anderes
we can visit him another time = wir
  können ihn ein anderes Mal besuchen

2 *pronoun*
* (*one more*) = noch einer/noch eine/noch
  eins
* (*different one*) = ein anderer/eine
  andere/ein anderes
one after another = einer nach dem
  anderen/eine nach der anderen/eins nach
  dem anderen

answer
1 *noun*
* (*reply*) = (die) Antwort
to give the right answer = die richtige
  Antwort geben
there's no answer (*at the door*) = niemand
  macht die Tür auf, (*on the phone*) =
  niemand meldet sich
* (*solution*) = (die) Lösung
2 *verb* = antworten (+ *dative*)
he wouldn't answer me = er wollte mir
  nicht antworten
to answer a question = eine Frage
  beantworten
to answer the door = an die Tür gehen
to answer the phone (*on one occasion*) =
  ans Telefon gehen, (*speak*) = sich melden
to answer back = eine freche Antwort
  geben

answering machine *noun*
= (der) Anrufbeantworter

ant *noun*
= (die) Ameise

antibiotic *noun*
= (das) Antibiotikum
to be on antibiotics = Antibiotika nehmen

antique shop *noun*
= (das) Antiquitätengeschäft

anxious *adjective*
* (*worried*) = besorgt
she was anxious about the children = sie
  war um die Kinder besorgt
* (*keen*)
she was anxious to talk to him = sie wollte
  unbedingt mit ihm sprechen

any
1 *adjective*
* (*some*) = irgendein, (*plural*) =
  irgendwelche
  (*every*) = jeder/jede/jedes, (*plural*) = alle
if you have any difficulties = wenn du
  irgendwelche Schwierigkeiten hast
have you got any vegetables? = haben Sie
  Gemüse?
* (*with the negative*) = kein
he didn't have any friends = er hatte keine
  Freunde
* (*whatever*) = jeder beliebige/jede
  beliebige/jedes beliebige
choose any two numbers = nimm zwei
  beliebige Zahlen
2 *pronoun*
* (*in questions*) = welcher/welche/welches
I need some pins—have you got any? =
  ich brauche Stecknadeln—hast du
  welche?

- (*in negatives*) = keiner/keine/keins
  there aren't any = es gibt keine
- (*no matter which one*) = jeder/jede/jedes,
  (*plural*) = alle
3 *adverb* = noch
  would you like any more? = möchtest du
  noch etwas?

anyone *pronoun*
- (*in questions*) = irgendjemand
- (*in negatives*) = niemand
  there isn't anyone in = niemand ist zu
  Hause
- (*everyone*) = jeder
  anyone can do it = das kann jeder

anything *pronoun*
- (*in questions*) = irgendetwas
  do you have anything for the children? =
  habt ihr irgendetwas für die Kinder?
- (*in negatives*) = nichts
  she didn't say anything = sie hat nichts
  gesagt
- (*everything*) = alles
  I eat anything = ich esse alles

anyway *adverb*
- (*besides*) = sowieso
  I didn't want to go there anyway = ich
  wollte da sowieso nicht hingehen
- (*all the same*) = trotzdem
  thanks anyway = trotzdem danke
- (*in conversation*) = jedenfalls

anywhere *adverb*
- (*in questions*) = irgendwo
  can you see a phone booth anywhere? =
  kannst du irgendwo eine Telefonzelle
  sehen?
- (*in negatives*) = nirgends
  we couldn't find him anywhere = er war
  nirgends zu finden
- (*in any place*) = überall
  anywhere but London = überall, außer
  London
- (*to any place*)
  to go anywhere (*wherever*) = überallhin
  gehen, (*somewhere*) = irgendwohin
  gehen

apart *adverb*
  = auseinander
  to live apart = getrennt leben
  apart from = außer (+ *dative*)

apartment *noun*
  = (die) Wohnung

apologize *verb*
  = sich entschuldigen
  to apologize to someone = sich bei
  jemandem entschuldigen

apology *noun*
  = (die) Entschuldigung

appear *verb*
- (*seem*) = scheinen

  he appears to be happy = er scheint
  glücklich zu sein
- (*come into view*) = erscheinen (**!** *sein*)
- (*be on TV*) = auftreten (**!** *sein*)

appendix *noun*
- (*of a book*) = (der) Anhang
- (*in anatomy*) = (der) Blinddarm

appetite *noun*
  = (der) Appetit

applause *noun*
  = (der) Beifall

apple *noun*
  = (der) Apfel

application *noun*
- (*for a job*) = (die) Bewerbung
- (*for membership*) = (der) Antrag

apply *verb*
  = sich bewerben
  I've applied for the job = ich habe mich um
  die Stellung beworben
- (*make a formal request*) = beantragen
  to apply for a passport = einen Pass
  beantragen

appointment *noun*
  = (der) Termin

appreciate *verb*
- (*be grateful*) = dankbar sein für
  (+ *accusative*)
  I appreciate your help = ich bin dir für
  deine Hilfe dankbar
- (*enjoy*) = schätzen
  she appreciates good wine = sie schätzt
  guten Wein

approach *verb*
  = sich nähern (+ *dative*)
  to approach someone = sich jemandem
  nähern

approve *verb*
  to approve of someone = mit jemandem
  einverstanden sein

approximately *adverb*
  = ungefähr
  approximately 200 kilometres = ungefähr
  zweihundert Kilometer
  at approximately 8 o'clock = gegen acht Uhr

apricot *noun*
  = (die) Aprikose

April *noun*
  = (der) April ▶**Dates p. 213**
  April fool! = April, April!

apron *noun*
  = (die) Schürze

Aquarius *noun*
  = (der) Wassermann

arch noun
= (der) Bogen

architect noun
= (der) Architekt/(die) Architektin

area noun
• (region) = (die) Gegend
• (part of a building) = (der) Bereich
• a picnic area = ein Picknickplatz

argue verb
(quarrel) = sich streiten
to argue about something = sich über
etwas (accusative) streiten

argument noun
• (quarrel) = (der) Streit
to have an argument with someone = sich
mit jemandem streiten
• (reasons for or against) = (das) Argument

Aries noun
= (der) Widder

arithmetic noun
= (das) Rechnen

arm noun
= (der) Arm

armchair noun
= (der) Sessel

armed adjective
= bewaffnet

arms noun
= Waffen (plural)

army noun
• (force) = (das) Heer
• (profession) = (das) Militär
to join the army = zum Militär gehen

around
1 preposition = um (+ accusative) ... herum
the people around me = die Leute um mich
herum
all around = ringsherum
2 adverb
• = herum

! Note that around is often used with
verbs—look around, turn around, etc. You
will find translations for these under the
entries look, turn, etc.

• (approximately) = ungefähr
• (in the area)
he's not around = er ist nicht da
around here = hier in der Gegend

arrange verb
(organize) = arrangieren
to arrange an appointment = einen Termin
vereinbaren
to arrange to go to the cinema =
vereinbaren, ins Kino zu gehen

arrest verb
= verhaften
to be arrested by the police = von der
Polizei verhaftet werden (! sein)

arrival noun
= (die) Ankunft
on arrival = bei der Ankunft

arrive verb
= ankommen (! sein)
I arrive at midday = ich komme mittags an

arrow noun
= (der) Pfeil

arse noun (British)
= (der) Arsch

art noun
• = (die) Kunst
a work of art = ein Kunstwerk
• (school subject) = (die) Kunsterziehung

artificial adjective
= künstlich

artist noun
= (der) Künstler/(die) Künstlerin

artistic adjective
= künstlerisch
to be artistic = künstlerisch begabt sein

arts noun
the arts (fine arts) = die schönen Künste,
(humanities) = die Geisteswissenschaften

arts and crafts noun
• (at school) = (das) Werken
• (for sale) = (das) Kunstgewerbe

art school noun
= (die) Kunsthochschule

as
1 conjunction
• (when) = als
I used to live there as a child = als Kind
habe ich dort gewohnt
• (while) = während
the phone rang as I was opening the door
= während ich die Tür aufmachte,
klingelte das Telefon
• (introducing a statement) = wie
as you know, we moved to Berlin in June =
wie du weißt, sind wir im Juni nach
Berlin gezogen
• (since) = da
as you were out, I left a message = da du
nicht zu Hause warst, habe ich eine
Nachricht hinterlassen
• (when used with the same)
they have the same car as us = sie haben
das gleiche Auto wie wir
2 preposition = als
to work as a doctor = als Arzt tätig sein
3 adverb
• (in comparisons)
as [intelligent | rich | strong ...] as = so
[intelligent | reich | stark ...] wie
I have as much work as you = ich habe so
viel Arbeit wie du

- (*expressing degree*)
  as fast as you can = so schnell du kannst
  to pay as little as possible = so wenig wie
    möglich zahlen
  as far as I'm concerned = was mich betrifft
  as well = auch
  as for us = was uns betrifft
  as soon as = sobald
  as long as (*for the duration*) = solange,
    (*provided that*) = vorausgesetzt
  I'll go with you as long as it's free = ich
    komme mit, vorausgesetzt, dass es
    umsonst ist

ash *noun*
- (die) Asche
- (*tree*) = (die) Esche

ashamed *adjective*
  to be ashamed = sich schämen
  **you should be ashamed of yourself for
    telling lies** = du solltest dich schämen zu
    lügen

ashes *noun*
  = (die) Asche

ashtray *noun*
  = (der) Aschenbecher

Asia *noun*
  = (das) Asien ▶**Countries p. 208**

Asian
1 *noun* = (der) Asiat/(die) Asiatin
2 *adjective* = asiatisch ▶**Countries p. 208**

ask *verb*
- = fragen
  he asked her the way = er fragte sie nach
    dem Weg
  to ask someone's advice = jemanden um
    Rat fragen
  to ask someone to call = jemanden bitten
    anzurufen
  to ask someone a favour = jemanden um
    einen Gefallen bitten
  to ask a question = eine Frage stellen
- (*invite*) = einladen
  to ask some friends for dinner = Freunde
    zum Essen einladen
  he asked her out = er hat sie eingeladen
- (*make inquiries*) = sich erkundigen
  did you ask about the plane tickets? = hast
    du dich nach den Flugkarten erkundigt?
- **ask for** = verlangen
  to ask for money = Geld verlangen

asleep *adjective*
  to be asleep = schlafen
  to fall asleep = einschlafen

ass *noun* (*US: backside*) = (der) Arsch✊

✊ considered offensive

assassinate *verb*
  = ermorden

assemble *verb*
- (*come together*) = sich versammeln
- (*put together*) zusammenbauen

assignment *noun*
  (*for school*) = (die) Aufgabe

assistance *noun*
  = (die) Hilfe

assistant *noun*
- = (der) Helfer/(die) Helferin
- (*in school*) = (der) Assistent/(die) Assistentin

association *noun*
  = (der) Verband

assume *verb*
  = annehmen

assure *verb*
  = versichern
  he assured her it was not true = er
    versicherte ihr, dass es nicht stimmte

astronaut *noun*
  = (der) Astronaut/(die) Astronautin

at *preposition*

> **!** *The German preposition and the
> following article are often shortened to
> form one word:* an dem *becomes* am, in
> dem *becomes* im, bei dem *becomes*
> beim.

- (*when talking about a position*) = an
    (+ *dative*)
  at the station = am Bahnhof
  he's not at his desk = er ist nicht an
    seinem Schreibtisch
- (*when talking about a place*) = in
    (+ *dative*)
  at [**school** | **a hotel** | **the chemist's** ...] = in [der
    Schule | einem Hotel | der Drogerie ...]
  at home = zu Hause

> **!** *You will find translations for phrases like*
> **at the back of, at the front of,** *etc., under
> the entries* **back, front,** *etc.*

- (*at the house, shop of*) = bei (+ *dative*)
  let's meet at my mother's = treffen wir uns
    bei meiner Mutter
  at the supermarket = im Supermarkt
- (*when talking about time*) = um
    (+ *accusative*)
  the film starts at 9 o'clock = der Film fängt
    um neun Uhr an
  at [**Christmas** | **Easter** | **Whitsun** ...] = zu
    [Weihnachten | Ostern | Pfingsten ...]
- (*when talking about age*)
  at your age = in deinem Alter
  she could read at four = sie konnte schon
    mit vier lesen

athlete *noun*
  = (der) Athlet/(die) Athletin

athletics *noun*
(*British*) = (die) Leichtathletik
(*US*) = (der) Sport

Atlantic *noun*
the Atlantic, the Atlantic Ocean = der Atlantik

atlas *noun*
= (der) Atlas

atmosphere *noun*
= (die) Atmosphäre

attach *verb*
= befestigen
to be attached to the wall = an der Wand befestigt sein
to attach a letter to an application = einen Brief einer Bewerbung beiheften

attack
1 *verb* = angreifen
to attack a town = eine Stadt angreifen
to attack someone in the street = jemanden auf der Straße überfallen
2 *noun* = (der) Angriff

attempt
1 *verb* = versuchen
2 *noun* = (der) Versuch

attend *verb*
to attend a wedding = bei einer Hochzeit anwesend sein
to attend a meeting = an einer Besprechung teilnehmen
to attend a comprehensive school = eine Gesamtschule besuchen

attention *noun*
= (die) Aufmerksamkeit
to catch someone's attention = jemandes Aufmerksamkeit erregen
he drew her attention to a mistake = er machte sie auf einen Fehler aufmerksam
to pay attention = aufpassen
to pay attention to something = etwas beachten

attic *noun*
= (der) Dachboden

attitude *noun*
• (*way of acting*) = (die) Haltung
• (*way of thinking*) = (die) Einstellung
you'll have to change your attitude = du musst deine Einstellung ändern

attract *verb*
= anziehen
the exhibition has attracted more visitors than expected = die Ausstellung hat mehr Besucher als erwartet angezogen

attractive *adjective*
to be attractive = attraktiv sein
an attractive offer = ein reizvolles Angebot

audience *noun*
• (*in a theatre*) = (das) Publikum
• (*for TV*) = Zuschauer (*plural*)
• (*for radio*) = Zuhörer (*plural*)

August *noun*
= (der) August ▶ Dates p. 213

aunt *noun*
= (die) Tante

au pair *noun*
= (das) Au-pair-Mädchen

Australia *noun*
= (das) Australien ▶ Countries p. 208

Australian
1 *noun* = (der) Australier/(die) Australierin
2 *adjective* = australisch ▶ Countries p. 208

Austria *noun*
= (das) Österreich ▶ Countries p. 208

Austrian
1 *noun* = (der) Österreicher/(die) Österreicherin
2 *adjective* = österreichisch ▶ Countries p. 208

author *noun*
= (der) Autor/(die) Autorin

authority *noun*
• (*power*) = (die) Autorität
• (*organization*) = (die) Behörde
the school authorities = die Schulleitung

authorize *verb*
to authorize someone to [sell | pay | sign ...] = jemanden ermächtigen zu [verkaufen | zahlen | unterschreiben ...]

autograph *noun*
= (das) Autogramm

automatic *adjective*
= automatisch

autumn *noun*
= (der) Herbst
in the autumn = im Herbst

available *adjective*
• (*on sale*) = erhältlich
• (*free*)
to be available = zur Verfügung stehen, (*of a person*) = frei sein
are you available this afternoon? = sind Sie heute Nachmittag frei?

avalanche *noun*
= (die) Lawine

average
1 *noun* = (der) Durchschnitt
to be above average = über dem Durchschnitt liegen
2 *adjective* = durchschnittlich

avoid *verb*
• (*prevent*) = vermeiden
I had to brake hard to avoid an accident = ich musste scharf bremsen, um einen Unfall zu vermeiden
to avoid spending money = vermeiden, Geld auszugeben

A

* (*keep away from*) = meiden
  to avoid someone = jemanden meiden
* (*if it's a car, cyclist*) ausweichen (+ *dative*)
  to avoid a car = einem Auto ausweichen

awake *adjective*
  to be awake = wach sein
  I'm wide awake now = ich bin jetzt
    hellwach

award
1 *noun* = (der) Preis
2 *verb*
  to award a prize to someone = jemandem
    einen Preis verleihen

aware *adjective*
* (*conscious*)
  to be aware of [a problem | danger | the risk …]
    = sich (*dative*) [eines Problems | einer
    Gefahr | des Risikos …] bewusst sein
* (*up to date*) = informiert
  to be aware of what's happening =
    informiert sein, was vor sich geht

away *adverb*
* (*absent*)
  to be away = nicht da sein
  to be away on business = geschäftlich
    unterwegs sein
* (*when talking about distance*)
  to be far away = weit weg sein
  London is 40 kilometres away = London
    liegt vierzig Kilometer entfernt

awful *adjective*
  = furchtbar

awkward *adjective*
  it's an awkward situation = das ist eine
    schwierige Situation
  to ring at an awkward time = zu einem
    ungünstigen Zeitpunkt anrufen

ax (*US*), **axe** (*British*) *noun*
  = (die) Axt

baby *noun*
  = (das) Baby
  to have a baby = ein Kind bekommen

babysitter *noun*
  = (der) Babysitter

back
1 *noun*
* (*part of the body*) = (der) Rücken
* (*rear*) = (der) hintere Teil
  at the back of the room = hinten im
    Zimmer
  the back of a chair = die Rückenlehne

* (*reverse side*) = (die) Rückseite
2 *adverb*
* (*returning to original position*) = zurück
  I'll be back in five minutes = ich bin in fünf
    Minuten wieder zurück
  back to front = verkehrt herum
* (*before in time*) = zurück
  a month back = vor einem Monat

  ! *Note that* **back** *is often used with
    verbs—***come back**, **get back**, *etc. You will
    find translations for these under the
    entries* **come**, **get**, *etc.*

back down
  = klein beigeben
back up
* (*support*) = unterstützen
* (*confirm*) = bestätigen

back door *noun*
  = (die) Hintertür

background *noun*
* (*of a picture*) = (der) Hintergrund
* (*of a person*) = (die) Herkunft
  family background = Familienverhältnisse
    (*plural*)

backward (*US*), **backwards** (*British*)
    adverb
  = rückwärts
  to lean backwards = sich nach hinten
    lehnen

bacon *noun*
  = (der) Speck
  bacon and eggs = Eier mit Speck

bad *adjective*
* (*not good*) = schlecht
* (*serious*) = schlimm
  a bad mistake = ein schlimmer Fehler
  a bad accident = ein schwerer Unfall
* (*naughty*) = unartig
* (*weak*) = schwach
  to have a bad heart = ein schwaches Herz
    haben

badly *adverb*
* (*not well*) = schlecht
  he did badly in his exams = er hat in der
    Prüfung schlecht abgeschnitten
* (*seriously*) = schwer
  he was badly injured = er war schwer
    verletzt
* (*very much*) = dringend
  to want something badly = sich (*dative*)
    etwas sehr wünschen

badminton *noun*
  = (der) Federball, = (das) Badminton

bad-tempered *adjective*
  = schlecht gelaunt

bag *noun*
* (*handbag, luggage*) = (die) Tasche
  he packed his bags = er hat sein Gepäck
    gepackt
* (*made of paper, plastic*) (die) Tüte
  a bag of cement = ein Sack Zement

baggage *noun*
= (das) Gepäck

bake *verb*
= backen

baker *noun*
= (der) Bäcker ▶**Professions p. 298**

bakery *noun*
= (die) Bäckerei

balance
1 *noun*
• (*equilibrium*) = (das) Gleichgewicht
  to lose one's balance = das Gleichgewicht verlieren
• (*of a bank account*) = (der) Kontostand
• (*remainder*) = (der) Rest
2 *verb*
• (*keep steady*) = balancieren
• (*weigh up*) = abwägen

balcony *noun*
= (der) Balkon

bald *adjective*
= kahl
(*of a person*) = kahlköpfig
to go bald = eine Glatze bekommen

ball *noun*
• (*in football, tennis, golf*) = (der) Ball
• (*in billiards, croquet*) = (die) Kugel
• (*dance*) = (der) Ball
  I'm going to the ball = ich gehe auf den Ball

ballet *noun*
= (das) Ballett

balloon *noun*
= (der) Luftballon

ballpoint (**pen**) *noun*
= (der) Kugelschreiber

ban *verb*
= verbieten
to ban someone from doing something = jemandem verbieten, etwas zu tun
he was banned from driving = er erhielt Fahrverbot

banana *noun*
= (die) Banane

band *noun*
(*musical group*) = (die) Band

bandage *noun*
= (der) Verband

bang
1 *noun*
(*noise*) = (der) Knall
2 *verb*
• (*hit*)
  I banged my head on the ceiling = ich habe mir den Kopf an der Decke gestoßen
  he banged his fist on the table = er hat mit der Faust auf den Tisch geschlagen
• (*shut loudly*) = zuknallen

bank *noun*
= (die) Bank

bank account *noun*
= (das) Bankkonto

bank holiday *noun*
= (der) gesetzliche Feiertag

banknote *noun*
= (der) Geldschein

bankrupt *adjective*
= bankrott
to go bankrupt = Bankrott machen

bank statement *noun*
= (der) Kontoauszug

bar *noun*
• (*place*) = (die) Bar
• (*counter*) = (die) Theke
• (*piece of metal*) = (die) Stange
  behind bars = hinter Gittern
• (*block*)
  a bar of soap = ein Stück Seife
  a bar of chocolate = eine Tafel Schokolade

barbecue *noun*
• (*apparatus*) = (der) Grill
• (*party*) = (das) Grillfest

bare *adjective*
• (*uncovered*) = nackt
  to have bare feet = barfuß sein
• (*empty*) = leer
  bare walls = kahle Wände

barely *adverb*
= kaum

bargain *noun*
• (*cheap buy*) = (der) gute Kauf
• (*agreement*) = (das) Geschäft

bark *verb*
= bellen

barn *noun*
= (die) Scheune

barrel *noun*
= (das) Fass

barrier *noun*
• (*fence*) = (die) Absperrung
• (*problem*) = (die) Barriere

barrister *noun*
= (der) Rechtsanwalt/(die) Rechtsanwältin
  ▶**Professions p. 298**

base
1 *noun*
• (*bottom part*) = (der) Fuß
• (*place*) = (der) Sitz
  military base = (der) Stützpunkt
2 *verb*
  to be based in London = in London wohnen
  to be based on a true story = auf einer wahren Geschichte basieren

basement *noun*
= (das) Kellergeschoss

basic *adjective*
* grundlegend
  the basic problem = das Hauptproblem
* (*simple*) = einfach

basically *adverb*
= grundsätzlich

basin *noun*
= (das) Becken

basis *noun*
= (die) Grundlage
on a weekly basis = wöchentlich

basket *noun*
= (der) Korb

basketball
= (der) Basketball

bat *noun*
* (*animal*) = (die) Fledermaus
* (*in games*) = (der) Schläger

bath *noun*
* = (das) Bad
  to have a bath = baden
* (*tub*) = (die) Badewanne

bathroom *noun*
= (das) Badezimmer

battery *noun*
= (die) Batterie

battle *noun*
* (*in war*) = (die) Schlacht
* (*contest*) = (der) Kampf

bay *noun*
= (die) Bucht

be *verb*
* = sein (**!** *sein*)
  we are [rich | happy | lazy ...] = wir sind [reich | glücklich | faul ...]
  it is getting late = es wird spät
  she'll be 18 next week = sie wird nächste Woche achtzehn
* (*exist*) = sein (**!** *sein*)
  there is/are = da ist/da sind, = es gibt
* (*describing a job*) = sein (**!** *sein*)
  I am a doctor = ich bin Arzt ▶**Professions p. 298**
* (*describing health, the weather*) = sein (**!** *sein*)
  to be ill = krank sein
  how are you? = wie geht es dir?
  she is hot = ihr ist heiß
* (*describing a visit or travelling*) = sein (**!** *sein*)
  I've never been to Spain = ich bin noch nie in Spanien gewesen
* (*referring to cost*) = kosten
  how much is it? = wie viel kostet es?
* (*referring to time, measurements*) = sein (**!** *sein*)
  what time is it? = wie viel Uhr ist es?

* (*in the continuous tense*)
  I am going = ich gehe
  it's raining = es regnet
* (*at the end of sentences*)
  it's cold, isn't it? = es ist kalt, nicht wahr?
* (*when giving orders*)
  you are to do it at once = du musst es sofort machen
* (*expressing the future*)
  the president is to arrive at noon = der Präsident soll um zwölf Uhr eintreffen
* (*forming the passive*) = werden (**!** *sein*)
  to be attacked = überfallen werden

beach *noun*
= (der) Strand

bead *noun*
= (die) Perle

beak *noun*
= (der) Schnabel

beam *noun*
* (*made of wood*) = (der) Balken
* (*of light*) = (der) Strahl

bean *noun*
= (die) Bohne

bear
1 *noun* = (der) Bär
2 *verb*
* (*tolerate*) = ertragen
* (*carry*) = tragen

beard *noun*
= (der) Bart

beat *verb*
= schlagen
beat up
= verprügeln

beautiful *adjective*
= schön

beauty *noun*
= (die) Schönheit

because
1 *conjunction* = weil
  I'm shivering because I'm cold = ich zittere, weil mir kalt ist
2 *adverb*
  because of = wegen (+ *genitive*)
  because of the rain = wegen des Regens
  because of me = meinetwegen

become *verb*
= werden (**!** *sein*)
  to become king = König werden
  what became of him? = was ist aus ihm geworden?

bed *noun*
= (das) Bett
  to go to bed = ins *or* zu Bett gehen (**!** *sein*)

bedroom *noun*
= (das) Schlafzimmer

bee *noun*
= (die) Biene

beef *noun*
= (das) Rindfleisch

beer *noun*
= (das) Bier
two beers please = zwei Bier bitte

beetle *noun*
= (der) Käfer

before
1 *preposition*
• (*of time*) = vor (+ *dative*)
before the holidays = vor den Ferien
• (*in front of*) = vor (+ *dative*)
before my eyes = vor meinen Augen
2 *adverb*
• (*of time*) = vorher
long before = lange vorher
• (*already*) = schon einmal
I've seen that film before = ich habe den
Film schon einmal gesehen
3 *conjunction* = bevor
before the train leaves = bevor der Zug
abfährt

beg *verb*
• = betteln
to beg for money = um Geld betteln
• (*ask*) = bitten
to beg someone to do something =
jemanden bitten, etwas zu tun
I beg your pardon = entschuldigen Sie bitte

begin *verb*
= anfangen, = beginnen
it began to rain = es fing an zu regnen
to begin with = zunächst

beginner *noun*
= (der) Anfänger/ (die) Anfängerin

beginning *noun*
= (der) Anfang
in the beginning = am Anfang
at the beginning of May = Anfang Mai

behalf *noun*
on behalf of (*British*), **in behalf of** (*US*) = für
(+ *accusative*)

behave *verb*
• = sich verhalten
to behave well = sich gut benehmen
they behaved badly towards him = sie
haben ihn schlecht behandelt
• **to behave oneself** = sich benehmen

behavior (*US*), **behaviour** (*British*)
noun
• = (das) Verhalten
• (*manners*) **good/bad behaviour** =
gutes/schlechtes Benehmen

behind
1 *preposition* = hinter (+ *dative or*
accusative)

> **!** *Note that* **hinter** *is followed by a noun in*
> *the dative when position is described.*
> *The accusative follows when there is*
> *movement towards something.*

he stood behind the fence = er stand
hinter dem Zaun
she put it behind the sofa = sie hat es
hinter das Sofa gestellt
2 *adverb*
• = hinten
to look behind = nach hinten sehen
to stay behind = dableiben (**!** *sein*)
to leave something behind = etwas
zurücklassen
• (*late*) = im Rückstand

Belgian
1 *noun* = (der) Belgier/(die) Belgierin
2 *adjective* = belgisch ▶**Countries p. 208**

Belgium *noun*
= (das) Belgien ▶**Countries p. 208**

belief *noun*
= (der) Glaube

believe *verb*
= glauben
I don't believe you = das glaube ich dir
nicht
to believe in God = an Gott glauben

bell *noun*
• = (die) Glocke
• (*on a door or bike*) = (die) Klingel

belong *verb*
• (*be the property of*)
to belong to = gehören (+ *dative*)
it belongs to me = es gehört mir
• (*be a member of*)
to belong to = angehören (+ *dative*)
• (*be kept or stored*) = gehören
the cutlery belongs in this drawer = das
Besteck gehört in diese Schublade

belongings *noun*
= Sachen (*plural*)

below
1 *preposition*
• (*showing position*) = unter (+ *dative*)
the kitchen is below my bedroom = die
Küche ist unter meinem Schlafzimmer
• (*with movement to a different place*) =
unter (+ *accusative*)
he went below deck = er ging unter Deck
2 *adverb* = unten
the flat below = die Wohnung darunter

belt *noun*
= (der) Gürtel

bench *noun*
= (die) Bank

bend
1 *noun*
• (*in a road*) = (die) Kurve
• (*in a river, pipe*) = (die) Biegung

2 *verb*
- (*bow*) = beugen
  bend your knees = beuge die Knie
- (*make crooked*) = biegen
- (*make a bend*)
  the trees bend in the wind = die Bäume biegen sich im Wind
  the road bends = die Straße macht eine Kurve
- **to bend down** = sich bücken

beneath
1 *preposition* = unter (+ *dative or accusative*)

> ! Note that *unter* is followed by a noun in the dative when position is described. The accusative follows when there is movement towards something.

the dog lay beneath the table = der Hund lag unter dem Tisch
the baby crawled beneath the chair = das Baby kroch unter den Stuhl
2 *adverb* = unten

benefit
1 *noun*
  (*advantage*) = (der) Vorteil
  it will be to your benefit = das wird zu deinem Vorteil sein
2 *verb* = nützen (+ *dative*)

berry *noun*
= (die) Beere

beside *preposition*
= neben (+ *dative or accusative*)

> ! Note that *neben* is followed by a noun in the dative when position is described. The accusative follows when there is movement towards something.

he stood beside me = er stand neben mir
she sat down beside me = sie hat sich neben mich gesetzt

besides *adverb*
= außerdem
  besides, it's too late = außerdem ist es zu spät

best
1 *noun*
  the best = der/die/das Beste
  to do one's best = sein Bestes tun
  to make the best of it = das Beste daraus machen
  all the best! = alles Gute!
2 *adjective* = bester/beste/bestes
  the best hotel = das beste Hotel
3 *adverb* = am besten
  blue suits you best = Blau steht dir am besten
  I like oranges best = ich mag Orangen am liebsten
  (*on food*) **best before . . .** = mindestens haltbar bis . . .

bet
1 *noun* = (die) Wette

2 *verb* = wetten
  I bet you he'll win = ich wette mit dir, dass er gewinnt
  to bet on a horse = auf ein Pferd setzen

betray *verb*
= verraten

better
1 *adjective* = besser
  he was ill but now he is better = er war krank, aber jetzt geht es ihm besser
2 *adverb* = besser
  we'd better go now = wir gehen jetzt besser

between
1 *preposition* = zwischen (+ *dative or accusative*)

> ! Note that *zwischen* is followed by a noun in the dative when position is described. The accusative follows when there is movement towards something.

I stood between them = ich stand zwischen ihnen
he ran between them = er lief zwischen sie
between 8 and 11 o'clock = zwischen acht und elf Uhr
between now and next year = bis nächstes Jahr
2 *adverb*
  in between = dazwischen

beyond *preposition*
- (*at the other side of*) = jenseits (+ *genitive*)
- (*later than*) = nach (+ *dative*)
  beyond midnight = nach Mitternacht
- (*out of reach*) = außer (+ *dative*)
  it's beyond me = das ist mir unverständlich

bicycle *noun*
= (das) Fahrrad
  to ride a bicycle = Rad fahren (! *sein*)
  he rides a bicycle = er fährt Rad

big
1 *adjective* = groß
  a big book = ein großes Buch, (*thick*) = ein dickes Buch
2 *adverb*
  to talk big = angeben

bike *noun*
= (das) Rad

bikini *noun*
= (der) Bikini

bilingual *adjective*
= zweisprachig

bill *noun*
= (die) Rechnung
  may we have the bill? = die Rechnung bitte

billion *noun*
- (*thousand million*) = (die) Milliarde
- (*million million*) = (die) Billion

bin *noun*
= (der) Mülleimer

binoculars noun
= (das) Fernglas

biology noun
= (die) Biologie

bird noun
= (der) Vogel

biro ® noun (British)
= (der) Kugelschreiber

birth noun
= (die) Geburt
place of birth = (der) Geburtsort

birth certificate noun
= (die) Geburtsurkunde

birth control noun
= (die) Geburtenregelung

birthday noun
= (der) Geburtstag
happy birthday! = herzlichen Glückwunsch zum Geburtstag!

biscuit noun
= (der) Keks

bishop noun
= (der) Bischof

bit noun
a bit = ein bisschen
not a bit = überhaupt nicht

bite
1 noun = (der) Biss
(by an insect) = (der) Stich
2 verb = beißen
(of an insect) = stechen
he bites his nails = er kaut an den Nägeln

bitter adjective
= bitter

black adjective
= schwarz ▶ Colours p. 204

blackberry noun
= (die) Brombeere

blackboard noun
= (die) Tafel

blackcurrant noun
= (die) schwarze Johannisbeere

blackmail
1 noun = (die) Erpressung
2 verb
to blackmail someone = jemanden erpressen

bladder noun
= (die) Blase

blade noun
• (of a knife or sword) = (die) Klinge
• **a blade of grass** = ein Grashalm

blame
1 noun = (die) Schuld
to put the blame on someone = die Schuld auf jemanden schieben

2 verb
to blame someone for something = jemandem die Schuld an etwas (dative) geben
no one is to blame = keiner ist schuld daran

blank adjective
= leer
a blank tape = eine unbespielte Kassette

blanket noun
= (die) Decke

blast noun
= (die) Explosion

blaze
1 noun = (das) Feuer
2 verb = brennen

bleach
1 noun = (das) Bleichmittel
2 verb = bleichen

bleed verb
= bluten

bless verb
= segnen
(said after a sneeze) **bless you!** = Gesundheit!

blind
1 adjective = blind
to go blind = blind werden (! sein)
2 verb = blenden
the sun blinded them = die Sonne blendete sie
3 noun
(on a window) = (das) Rollo

blink verb
• (of a person) = blinzeln
• (of light) = blinken

blister noun
= (die) Blase

blizzard noun
= (der) Schneesturm

block
1 noun
• (large piece) = (der) Block
(wood) = (der) Klotz
a block of ice = ein Eisblock
• (building) = (der) Block
a block of flats = ein Wohnblock
2 verb
(obstruct) = blockieren
block off
to block off a road = eine Straße sperren
block out
to block out the light = das Licht wegnehmen
block up
to block up a hole = ein Loch zustopfen
the pipe is blocked up = das Rohr ist verstopft

B

blonde
1 *adjective* = blond
2 *noun* = (die) Blondine

blood *noun*
= (das) Blut

bloom
1 *noun* = (die) Blüte
  to be in full bloom = in voller Blüte stehen
2 *verb* = blühen

blossom *verb*
= blühen

blouse *noun*
= (die) Bluse

blow
1 *verb*
• = blasen
  to blow bubbles = Blasen machen
  blow your nose! = putz dir die Nase!
• (*of wind*) = wehen
  the flag is blowing in the wind = die Fahne
    weht im Wind
• (*of a referee*) = pfeifen
  he blew his whistle = er hat gepfiffen
• (*of a fuse or bulb*) = durchbrennen (**!** *sein*)
2 *noun* = (der) Schlag

blow down
= umwehen

blow off
= wegblasen

blow out
= ausblasen

blow up
• (*in an explosion*)
  the building blew up = das Gebäude ist
    explodiert
• (*inflate*) = aufblasen

blue *adjective*
= blau ▶**Colours p. 204**

blunt *adjective*
• = stumpf
• **a blunt question** = eine direkte Frage

blur *verb*
= verwischen

blush *verb*
= erröten (**!** *sein*)

board
1 *noun*
• (*piece of wood, game*) = (das) Brett
• (*committee*) = (der) Ausschuss
  the board of directors = der Vorstand
• (*accommodation*)
  board and lodging = Unterkunft und
    Verpflegung
  full board = Vollpension
2 *verb*
  to board a train = in einen Zug einsteigen
    (**!** *sein*)

boarding card *noun*
= (die) Bordkarte

× in informal situations

boarding school *noun*
= (das) Internat

boast *verb*
= prahlen
  he boasts about his car = er prahlt mit
    seinem Auto

boat *noun*
= (das) Boot

body *noun*
= (der) Körper
  a dead body = eine Leiche

bodyguard *noun*
= (der) Leibwächter

bog *noun*
= (der) Sumpf

boil *verb*
= kochen
  the kettle is boiling = das Wasser kocht
  to boil the kettle = Wasser aufsetzen
  you must boil the water = das Wasser muss
    abgekocht werden
  boiled potatoes = Salzkartoffeln

boil over
= überkochen (**!** *sein*)

bolt
1 *noun*
• (*lock*) = (der) Riegel
• (*screw*) = (der) Bolzen
2 *verb*
  (*lock*) = verriegeln

bomb
1 *noun* = (die) Bombe
2 *verb* = bombardieren

bond *noun*
= (die) Verbindung

bone *noun*
• = (der) Knochen
• (*of fish*) = (die) Gräte

bonnet *noun*
• (*hat*) = (die) Haube
• (*of a car*) = (die) Motorhaube

book
1 *noun* = (das) Buch
2 *verb* = buchen
  to book a flight = einen Flug buchen
  this performance is fully booked = diese
    Vorstellung ist ausverkauft

bookcase *noun*
= (das) Bücherregal

booking *noun*
= (die) Buchung

bookshop *noun*
= (die) Buchhandlung

boom
1 *noun*
  (*in the economy*) = (der) Boom
2 *verb* = dröhnen

boost *verb*
= steigern
to boost profits = den Gewinn steigern

boot *noun*
- (*footwear*) = (der) Stiefel
- (*of a car*) = (der) Kofferraum

border
1 *noun*
- (*frontier*) = (die) Grenze
- (*edge*) = (der) Rand
- (*in a garden*) = (die) Rabatte
- (*of a picture or dress*) = (die) Bordüre
2 *verb*
(*of countries*) = grenzen an (+ *accusative*)

bore *verb*
= langweilen

bored *adjective*
to be bored = sich langweilen

boredom *noun*
= (die) Langeweile

boring *adjective*
= langweilig

born *adjective*
to be born = geboren werden (**!** *sein*)
I was born in Italy = ich bin in Italien
geboren

borrow *verb*
= sich (*dative*) borgen, = sich (*dative*)
leihen
to borrow money from someone = sich
Geld von jemandem borgen

boss *noun*
= (der) Chef/(die) Chefin
boss about
= herumkommandieren

bossy *adjective*
= herrisch

both
1 *adjective* = beide
both my sons = meine beiden Söhne
2 *pronoun* = beide
they are both red = sie sind beide rot
3 *adverb*
both boys and girls = sowohl Jungen als
auch Mädchen
both of us = wir beide

bother *verb*
- (*inconvenience*) = stören
I'm sorry to bother you = es tut mir Leid,
dich zu stören
- (*take trouble*) = sich kümmern
to bother about something = sich um
etwas (*accusative*) kümmern
- (*trouble oneself*)
you needn't bother to wait = du brauchst
nicht zu warten
he didn't even bother to say goodbye = er
hat sich nicht einmal verabschiedet
I can't be bothered = ich habe keine Lust

bottle *noun*
= (die) Flasche

bottle bank *noun*
= (der) Altglascontainer

bottom
1 *noun*
- (*lowest part*) = (der) Boden
the bottom of the mountain = der Fuß des
Berges
at the bottom of the sea = auf dem
Meeresgrund
at the bottom of the page = unten auf der
Seite
at the bottom of the bag = unten in der
Tasche
- (*part of the body*) = (der) Hintern✖
2 *adjective*
- (*lowest*) = unterster/unterste/unterstes
in the bottom drawer = in der untersten
Schublade
- (*last, worst*) = schlechtester/schlechteste/
schlechtestes

bounce *verb*
- (*jump*) = springen (**!** *sein*)
- (*of a cheque*) = nicht gedeckt sein

bound *adjective*
- **to be bound to do something** = etwas ganz
bestimmt tun
she's bound to be late = sie kommt ganz
bestimmt zu spät
- (*heading in the direction of*)
to be bound for London = nach London
unterwegs sein

boundary *noun*
= (die) Grenze

bow[1] *noun*
- (*knot*) = (die) Schleife
- (*weapon*) = (der) Bogen

bow[2]
1 *noun* = (die) Verbeugung
2 *verb*
(*as a formal greeting*) = sich verbeugen

bowl *noun*
= (die) Schüssel
(*shallower*) = (die) Schale
(*for soup*) = (der) Teller

bowling *noun*
= (das) Kegeln

bow tie *noun*
= (die) Fliege

box *noun*
= (die) Schachtel
a box of chocolates = eine Schachtel
Pralinen
(*wooden*) = (die) Kiste
a cardboard box = ein Karton

boxer *noun*
(*person*) = (der) Boxer ▶**Professions p. 298**

boxing *noun*
= (das) Boxen

Boxing Day *noun*
= (der) zweite Weihnachtstag

boy *noun*
= (der) Junge

boyfriend *noun*
= (der) Freund

bra *noun*
= (der) BH

bracelet *noun*
= (das) Armband

brain *noun*
= (das) Gehirn

brake
1 *noun* = (die) Bremse
2 *verb* = bremsen

branch *noun*
• (*of a tree*) = (der) Ast
• (*of a shop*) = (die) Filiale

brand *noun*
(*name*) = (die) Marke

brand-new *adjective*
= nagelneu

brass *noun*
= (das) Messing

brave *adjective*
= tapfer

Brazil *noun*
= (das) Brasilien ▶ Countries p. 208

bread *noun*
= (das) Brot
a piece of bread and butter = ein
  Butterbrot

break
1 *noun*
• (*pause*) = (die) Pause
to take a break = Pause machen
• (*interruption*) = (die) Unterbrechung
the summer break = die Sommerferien
2 *verb*
• (*get damaged*) = zerbrechen (**!** *sein*), =
  kaputtgehen✱ (**!** *sein*)
the rope broke = das Seil ist zerrissen
• (*crack, smash*) = zerbrechen
• (*damage*) = kaputtmachen✱
• (*injure*)

> **!** *When you break a bone in your body,
> you don't use the possessive in German.
> See the following two examples.*

I broke my arm = ich habe mir den Arm
  gebrochen
she broke her leg = sie hat sich (*dative*) das
  Bein gebrochen

✱ in informal situations

• (*not keep*) = brechen
to break a promise = ein Versprechen
  brechen
• (*tell*) **to break the news that . . .** = melden,
  dass . . .

break down
(*of a car*) = eine Panne haben
(*of a machine*) = versagen

break in
= einbrechen (**!** *sein*)

break into
= einbrechen in (+ *accusative*) (**!** *sein*)
our house was broken into = bei uns
  wurde eingebrochen

break out
= ausbrechen (**!** *sein*)
the fire broke out in the cellar = das Feuer
  brach im Keller aus
he broke out of prison = er ist aus dem
  Gefängnis ausgebrochen

break up
• (*of a couple*) = sich trennen
• (*bring to an end*) = abbrechen

breakfast *noun*
= (das) Frühstück
to have breakfast = frühstücken

breast *noun*
= (die) Brust

breath *noun*
= (der) Atem
to be out of breath = außer Atem sein
to hold one's breath = den Atem anhalten

breathe *verb*
= atmen

breed
1 *noun* = (die) Rasse
2 *verb*
• (*rear animals*) = züchten
• (*reproduce*) = sich vermehren

breeze *noun*
= (die) Brise

brew *verb*
• **to brew beer** = Bier brauen
• **the tea is brewing** = der Tee zieht noch

bribe *verb*
= bestechen

brick *noun*
= (der) Ziegelstein
made of brick = aus Ziegel

bride *noun*
= (die) Braut

bridge *noun*
= (die) Brücke

brief *adjective*
= kurz

bright *adjective*
• (*vivid*) = leuchtend
bright blue = leuchtend blau
the light was too bright = das Licht war zu
  grell

* (*luminous, sunny*) = hell
a bright light = ein helles Licht
cloudy with bright spells = bewölkt mit Aufheiterungen
* (*shiny*) = glänzend

brilliant *adjective*
* (*very clever*) = genial
* (*wonderful*) = toll

bring *verb*
* (*take along*) = mitbringen
he brought me some flowers = er hat mir Blumen mitgebracht
* (*transport, result in*) = bringen
to bring someone home = jemanden nach Hause bringen
* (*lead*) = führen
the path brings you to the village = der Weg führt ins Dorf
bring back
* (*return*) = zurückbringen
* (*get shopping, gift*) = mitbringen
bring down
to bring prices down = die Preise senken
bring in
to bring in lots of money = viel Geld einbringen
bring up
(*educate*) = erziehen

bristle *noun*
* (*of a brush*) = (die) Borste
* (*on chin*) = (die) Bartstoppel

Britain *noun*
= (das) Großbritannien ▶**Countries p. 208**

British
1 *noun*
the British = die Briten
2 *adjective* = britisch ▶**Countries p. 208**

broad *adjective*
* (*wide*) = breit
* (*wide-ranging*) = weit
a broad range of programmes = ein umfassendes Programmangebot
* **in broad daylight** = am helllichten Tag

broadcast
1 *noun* = (die) Sendung
2 *verb* = senden

brochure *noun*
= (die) Broschüre

broke *adjective*
= pleite✗

broken *adjective*
= zerbrochen, = kaputt✗
to have a broken leg = ein gebrochenes Bein haben
in broken German = in gebrochenem Deutsch

bronze
1 *noun* = (die) Bronze
2 *adjective* = Bronze-
a bronze statue = eine Bronzestatue

broom *noun*
= (der) Besen

brother *noun*
= (der) Bruder

brother-in-law *noun*
= (der) Schwager

brown *adjective*
= braun ▶**Colours p. 204**

bruise
1 *noun*
* (*on a person*) = (der) blaue Fleck
* (*on fruit*) = (die) Druckstelle
2 *verb*
I bruised my knee = ich habe einen blauen Fleck am Knie bekommen

brush
1 *noun*
* (*for hair, teeth, shoes*) = (die) Bürste
* (*broom*) = (der) Besen
* (*for use with a dustpan*) = (der) Handfeger
* (*for painting*) = (der) Pinsel
2 *verb* = bürsten
he brushed the children's hair = er bürstete den Kindern die Haare
I brushed my teeth = ich putzte mir die Zähne

bubble *noun*
= (die) Blase

bucket *noun*
= (der) Eimer

bud *noun*
= (die) Knospe

budgerigar *noun*
= (der) Wellensittich

buggy *noun* (*British*)
= (der) Sportwagen

build *verb*
* = bauen
* (*establish*) = aufbauen

builder *noun*
* (*workman*) = (der) Bauarbeiter
* (*contractor*) = (der) Bauunternehmer
▶**Professions p. 298**

building *noun*
= (das) Gebäude

built-in *adjective*
= eingebaut
a built-in wardrobe = ein Einbauschrank

built-up *adjective*
(*of an area*) = bebaut

bulb *noun*
* (*light bulb*) = (die) Birne
* (*of a plant*) = (die) Zwiebel

Bulgaria *noun*
= (das) Bulgarien ▶**Countries p. 208**

B

bulge *verb*
- (*swell out*) = sich wölben
- (*be full*) = voll gestopft sein
  a bulging suitcase = ein prall gefüllter Koffer

bull *noun*
= (der) Bulle

bullet *noun*
= (die) Kugel

bulletin *noun*
- (*on TV, radio*) = (die) Kurzmeldung
- (*publication*) = (das) Bulletin

bully
1 *noun*
- (*in school*) = Schüler, der Schwächere schikaniert
- (*adult*) = (der) Tyrann
2 *verb* = schikanieren

bump
1 *noun*
- (*on a surface*) = (die) Unebenheit
- (*swelling on the body*) = (die) Beule
- (*sound*) = (der) Bums
- (*jolt*) = (der) Stoß
2 *verb* = stoßen
  he bumped his head = er hat sich (*dative*) den Kopf gestoßen
  to bump into someone (*meet*) = jemanden zufällig treffen

bumper *noun*
= (die) Stoßstange

bun *noun*
- (*bread roll*) = (das) Brötchen, = (die) Semmel
- (*hairstyle*) = (der) Knoten

bunch *noun*
- (*of flowers*) = (der) Strauß
- (*of keys*) = (das) Bund
  a bunch of grapes = eine ganze Weintraube

bundle *noun*
= (das) Bündel

bunk *noun*
= (die) Koje

bunk beds *noun*
= (das) Etagenbett

burden *noun*
= (die) Last

bureaucracy *noun*
= (die) Bürokratie

burger *noun*
= (der) Hamburger

burglar *noun*
= (der) Einbrecher

burglar alarm *noun*
= (die) Alarmanlage

burglary *noun*
= (der) Einbruch

burn
1 *noun*
- (*on the skin*) = (die) Verbrennung
- (*on material*) = (die) Brandstelle
2 *verb*
- = verbrennen
  the candle is burning = die Kerze brennt
- (*injure oneself*)
  to burn one's finger = sich (*dative*) den Finger verbrennen
- (*when cooking*) = anbrennen
- (*in the sun*)
  he burns easily = er bekommt leicht einen Sonnenbrand

burn down
= abbrennen (**!** *sein*)

burst *verb*
- = platzen (**!** *sein*)
  the tyre has burst = der Reifen ist geplatzt
- **you burst my balloon** = du hast meinen Luftballon platzen lassen

burst into
  to burst into the room = ins Zimmer stürzen (**!** *sein*)
  to burst into tears = in Tränen ausbrechen (**!** *sein*)

burst out
  to burst out laughing = in Lachen ausbrechen (**!** *sein*)

bury *verb*
- (*dead person*) = begraben
- (*hide underground*) = vergraben

bus *noun*
= (der) Bus

bush *noun*
= (der) Busch

business *noun*
- (*commercial activities*) = Geschäfte (*plural*)
  business is good at the moment = momentan gehen die Geschäfte gut
- (*company*) = (der) Betrieb
- (*trade, profession*) = (die) Branche
  he works in the hotel business = er ist in der Hotelbranche
- (*matters that concern a person*) = (die) Angelegenheit
  mind your own business = kümmere dich um deine eigenen Angelegenheiten
  it's none of your business = das geht dich nichts an

businessman/businesswoman *noun*
= (der) Geschäftsmann/(die) Geschäftsfrau

bus stop *noun*
= (die) Bushaltestelle

busy *adjective*
- (*occupied*) = beschäftigt
  she was busy packing = sie war mit Packen beschäftigt
  he is very busy = er hat sehr viel zu tun

- (*full of people*) = belebt
  it's always very busy before Christmas = vor Weihnachten ist es immer sehr voll
- (*full of traffic*) = verkehrsreich

but

1 *conjunction* = aber
  it was sunny but cold = es war sonnig aber kalt

> **!** *After a negative, especially when contradicting the previous statement,* sondern *is used.*

  he is not rich, but poor = er ist nicht reich, sondern arm
  not only . . . but also . . . = nicht nur . . ., sondern auch . . .

2 *preposition*
- (*except*) = außer (+ *dative*)
  we have nothing but water to drink = wir haben nichts außer Wasser zu trinken
  the last but one = der/die/das Vorletzte
- **but for** (*without*) = ohne (+ *accusative*)

butcher *noun*
= (der) Fleischer, = (der) Metzger
  ▶ **Professions p. 298**

butter *noun*
= (die) Butter

butterfly *noun*
= (der) Schmetterling

button *noun*
= (der) Knopf

buy *verb*
= kaufen
  to buy a present for someone = jemandem ein Geschenk kaufen

buyer *noun*
= (der) Käufer/(die) Käuferin

buzz *verb*
= summen

by

1 *preposition*
- (*close to*) = an (+ *dative*)
  by the sea = am Meer
- (*expressing cause*) = von (+ *dative*)
  he was bitten by a dog = er wurde von einem Hund gebissen
- (*by means of*) = durch (+ *accusative*)
  we escaped by the back door = wir flüchteten durch die Hintertür
- (*travelling by means of*) = mit (+ *dative*)
  by bus = mit dem Bus
- (*indicating the author, painter*) = von (+ *dative*)
- (*during*) = bei (+ *dative*)
  by day/night = bei Tag/Nacht
- (*not later than*) = bis (+ *accusative*)
  by next Thursday = bis nächsten Donnerstag
  by now = inzwischen
- (*indicating an amount*)
  to increase by 20% = um zwanzig Prozent erhöhen

- (*indicating a rate*) = pro (+ *accusative*)
  to be paid by the hour = pro Stunde bezahlt werden (**!** *sein*)
- (*in measurements*)
  2 metres by 4 = zwei mal vier Meter
  10 divided by 2 = zehn geteilt durch zwei
- (*in other phrases*)
  by mistake = versehentlich
  little by little = nach und nach
  one by one = einzeln

2 *adverb*
  (*past*) = vorbei
  to go by (*walk*) = vorbeigehen (**!** *sein*), (*drive*) = vorbeifahren (**!** *sein*)
  as time goes by = mit der Zeit

Cc

cab *noun*
= (das) Taxi

cabbage *noun*
= (der) Kohl

cabin *noun*
- (*on a ship or plane*) = (die) Kabine
- (*for a ship's crew*) = (die) Kajüte
- (*wooden house*) = (die) Hütte

cable car *noun*
= (die) Seilbahn

cable TV *noun*
= (das) Kabelfernsehen

café *noun*
= (das) Café

cage
1 *noun* = (der) Käfig
2 *verb* = einsperren

cake *noun*
= (der) Kuchen

calculator *noun*
= (der) Taschenrechner

calendar *noun*
= (der) Kalender

calf *noun*
- (*young cow*) = (das) Kalb
- (*part of the leg*) = (die) Wade

call

1 *verb*
- (*name, describe*) = nennen
  they called the baby Sam = sie haben das Baby Sam genannt
  she's called Emma = sie heißt Emma
  what is it called in German? = wie heißt das auf Deutsch?

* (*summon*) = rufen
  he is calling us = er ruft uns
  to call a taxi = ein Taxi rufen
  to call a flight = einen Flug aufrufen
* (*phone*) = anrufen
  who's calling? = wer spricht da, bitte?
* (*arrange*)
  to call a meeting = eine Versammlung
  einberufen
* (*wake*) = wecken
* (*pay a visit*) = vorbeikommen (**!** *sein*)
  they called yesterday = sie kamen gestern
  vorbei
* (*stop en route*)
  the train calls at Reading = der Zug hält in
  Reading
2 *noun*
* (*phone call*) = (der) Anruf
  to return someone's call = jemanden
  zurückrufen
* (*visit*) = (der) Besuch
* (*shout*) = (der) Ruf
  a call for help = ein Hilferuf
  to be on call = Bereitschaftsdienst haben
call back
* (*return*) = zurückkommen (**!** *sein*)
* (*phone back*) = zurückrufen
call off
= absagen
call on
* (*visit*) = besuchen
* (*urge*)
  to call on someone to do something =
  jemanden auffordern, etwas zu tun
call out
= rufen
they called out my name = mein Name
wurde aufgerufen
call up
(*phone*) = anrufen

call box *noun*
= (die) Telefonzelle

calm
1 *adjective* = ruhig
2 *noun* = (die) Ruhe
3 *verb*
* = beruhigen
* (*ease, relieve*) = lindern
calm down
= sich beruhigen

camcorder *noun*
= (der) Camcorder

camel *noun*
= (das) Kamel

camera *noun*
* (*for taking photos*) = (der) Fotoapparat
* (*film, video*) = (die) Kamera

camp
1 *noun* = (das) Lager
2 *verb* = zelten

camping *noun*
= (das) Camping

campsite *noun*
= (der) Campingplatz

can¹ *verb*
* = können
  I can't see it = ich kann es nicht sehen
  I can speak German = ich spreche Deutsch
* (*be allowed to*) = dürfen, = können

  > **!** Note that **dürfen** *is usually used to*
  > *translate* can *in the sense of* **may**.
  can I smoke? = darf ich rauchen?

can² *noun*
= (die) Dose

Canada *noun*
= (das) Kanada ▶ **Countries p. 208**

Canadian
1 *noun* = (der) Kanadier/(die) Kanadierin
2 *adjective* = kanadisch ▶ **Countries p. 208**

canal *noun*
= (der) Kanal

cancel *verb*
* (*call off*) = absagen
* (*change plan*) = rückgängig machen
  you must cancel the booking = du musst
  die Buchung rückgängig machen
  to cancel a newspaper = eine Zeitung
  abbestellen

cancer *noun*
* = (der) Krebs
* **Cancer** = (der) Krebs

candle *noun*
= (die) Kerze

candy *noun* (*US*)
* (*confectionery*) = Süßigkeiten (*plural*)
* (*sweet*) = (der) *or* (das) Bonbon

canoe *noun*
= (das) Kanu

can opener *noun*
= (der) Dosenöffner

canteen *noun*
= (die) Kantine

cap *noun*
= (die) Kappe

capable *adjective*
= fähig
to be capable of doing something = fähig
sein, etwas zu tun
to be capable of anything = zu allem fähig
sein

capital
1 *noun*
* (*money*) = (das) Kapital
* (*city*) = (die) Hauptstadt
* (*letter*) = (der) Großbuchstabe
2 *adjective* = groß
  a capital P = ein großes P

Capricorn *noun*
= (der) Steinbock

captain
1 *noun* = (der) Kapitän
2 *verb*
  to captain a team = Mannschaftskapitän
  sein

capture *verb*
  to capture an animal = ein Tier fangen
  to capture a city = eine Stadt einnehmen

car *noun*
  = (das) Auto, = (der) Wagen
  we went there by car = wir sind mit dem
  Auto hingefahren

caravan *noun*
  = (der) Wohnwagen

card *noun*
• = (die) Karte
• (*cardboard*) = (die) Pappe

care
1 *noun*
• (*caution*) = (die) Vorsicht
  to take care crossing the street =
  vorsichtig beim Überqueren der Straße
  sein
  to take care not to make mistakes =
  aufpassen, dass man keine Fehler macht
• (*attention*)
  medical care = ärztliche Betreuung
  to take care of the children = sich um die
  Kinder kümmern
2 *verb*
  to care about something = etwas wichtig
  finden
  to care about someone = jemanden mögen
  I don't care = das ist mir egal

career *noun*
• (*job*) = (der) Beruf
• (*progress in professional life*) =
  (die) Laufbahn

careful *adjective*
• (*cautious*) = vorsichtig
  be careful! = Vorsicht!
• (*thorough*) = sorgfältig

careless *adjective*
  = nachlässig

carnival *noun*
• (*British: festival*) = (der) Karneval
• (*US: funfair*) = (der) Jahrmarkt

carousel *noun*
• (*merry-go-round*) = (das) Karussell
• (*for baggage*) = (das) Gepäckförderband

car park *noun*
  = (der) Parkplatz
  (*multi-storey*) = (das) Parkhaus

carpenter *noun*
  = (der) Tischler

carpet *noun*
  = (der) Teppich

carriage *noun*
• (*British: of a train*) = (das) Abteil
• (*horse-drawn*) = (die) Kutsche

carry *verb*
  = tragen
  I can carry the case = ich kann den Koffer
  tragen
  to carry the baggage upstairs = das Gepäck
  herauftragen

! *When the sentence emphasizes the
destination of the carrying,* **bringen** *is
used.*

  he carried the case to her room = er hat
  den Koffer auf ihr Zimmer gebracht
carry on
  (*continue*) = weitermachen
  carry on with your work = mach deine
  Arbeit weiter

cartoon *noun*
• (*film*) = (der) Zeichentrickfilm
• (*drawing*) = (der) Cartoon

case¹ *noun*
  = (der) Fall
  in case = falls

case² *noun*
• (*suitcase*) = (der) Koffer
• (*for spectacles*) = (das) Etui
• (*crate*) = (die) Kiste

cash
1 *noun*
  = (das) Bargeld
  to pay cash = bar zahlen
2 *verb* = einlösen
  to cash a cheque = einen Scheck einlösen

cash card *noun*
  = (die) Bankkarte

cash desk *noun*
  = (die) Kasse

cash dispenser *noun*
  = (der) Geldautomat

cashier *noun*
  = (der) Kassierer/(die) Kassiererin

cassette *noun*
  = (die) Kassette

cassette recorder *noun*
  = (der) Kassettenrekorder

cast *noun*
  (*of a play*) = (die) Besetzung

castle *noun*
• = (das) Schloss
  (*fortified*) = (die) Burg
• (*in chess*) = (der) Turm

casual *adjective*
• (*relaxed*) = zwanglos
• (*offhand*) = lässig
• (*informal*) = leger

casualty *noun*
• (*injured person*) = (der/die) Verletzte
• (*hospital department*) = (die) Unfallstation

cat *noun*
= (die) Katze

catalog (*US*), **catalogue** (*British*) *noun*
• (der) Katalog

catch *verb*
• = fangen
  the cat caught a bird = die Katze hat einen Vogel gefangen
  to catch a thief = einen Dieb fassen
• (*trap, become hooked*)
  he caught his finger in the door = er hat sich (*dative*) den Finger in der Tür geklemmt
  to get caught on something = an etwas (*dative*) hängen bleiben (✘ *sein*)
• (*get or take*) = nehmen
  to catch a |bus | plane | train …| = |einen Bus | ein Flugzeug | einen Zug …| nehmen
• (*be in time*) = erreichen
  he ran to catch his train = er rannte, um seinen Zug zu erreichen
• (*take by surprise*) = erwischen
  to catch someone stealing = jemanden beim Stehlen erwischen
  to get caught = erwischt werden (✘ *sein*)
• (*hear*) = verstehen
• (*become ill with*) = bekommen
  to catch flu = die Grippe békommen
  to catch a cold = sich erkälten
catch up
• (*reach*) = einholen
  I'll catch up with you = ich hole euch ein
• = aufholen
  to have a lot to catch up on = viel aufzuholen haben

caterpillar *noun*
= (die) Raupe

cathedral *noun*
= (die) Kathedrale

cattle *noun*
= (das) Vieh

cauliflower *noun*
= (der) Blumenkohl

cause *verb*
= verursachen

cautious *adjective*
= vorsichtig

cave *noun*
= (die) Höhle

CD *noun*
= (die) CD

CD player *noun*
= (der) CD-Player

ceiling *noun*
= (die) Decke

celebrate *verb*
= feiern

---

celery *noun*
= (der) Sellerie

cell *noun*
(*in prison*) = (die) Zelle

cellar *noun*
= (der) Keller

cement *noun*
= (der) Zement

cemetery *noun*
= (der) Friedhof

center (*US*) ▶centre

centimeter (*US*), **centimetre** (*British*) *noun*
= (der) Zentimeter

central heating *noun*
= (die) Zentralheizung

centre *noun* (*British*)
= (das) Zentrum
(*middle*) = (die) Mitte

century *noun*
= (das) Jahrhundert

certain *adjective*
• (*sure*) = sicher
  I'm absolutely certain = ich bin mir ganz sicher
• (*particular*) = bestimmt
• (*not named*) = gewiss

certainly *adverb*
= bestimmt
(*of course*) = sicher

certificate *noun*
• (*for performance*) = (die) Bescheinigung
  a birth certificate = eine Geburtsurkunde
• (*at school*) = (das) Zeugnis

chain *noun*
= (die) Kette

chair *noun*
= (der) Stuhl

chair lift *noun*
= (der) Sessellift

chalk *noun*
= (die) Kreide

champagne *noun*
= (der) Champagner

champion *noun*
= (der) Meister/(die) Meisterin
  the world ice-skating champion = der Weltmeister/die Weltmeisterin im Eiskunstlauf

championship *noun*
= (die) Meisterschaft

chance noun
- (*likely event*) = (die) Aussicht

> **!** Note that **chance** in this sense is often translated by the plural, **Aussichten**.

  will she win?—she has a good chance = gewinnt sie?—sie hat gute Aussichten
- (*opportunity*) = (die) Gelegenheit
  to have the chance to [travel | work abroad …] = die Gelegenheit haben [zu reisen | , im Ausland zu arbeiten …]
- (*luck*) = (das) Glück
  by chance = zufällig
  on the off chance = auf gut Glück

change
1 noun
- = (die) Veränderung
  (*alteration*) = (die) Änderung
  I haven't got a change of clothes with me = ich habe nichts anderes zum Anziehen dabei
- (*different experience*) = (die) Abwechslung
  we could go to the cinema for a change = wir könnten zur Abwechslung mal ins Kino gehen
- (*money back*) = (das) Wechselgeld
  (*coins*) = (das) Kleingeld
2 verb
- (*become different*) = sich verändern
  the town has changed a lot = die Stadt hat sich sehr verändert
- (*make different*) = ändern
  to change one's address = seine Anschrift ändern
- (*replace*) = auswechseln
  to change a light bulb = eine Glühbirne auswechseln
- (*exchange in a shop*) = umtauschen
  to change a shirt for a smaller size = ein Hemd gegen eine kleinere Größe umtauschen
- (*switch*) = wechseln
  I'd like to change jobs = ich würde gerne meine Stellung wechseln
- (*exchange*) = tauschen
  to change places with someone = mit jemandem den Platz tauschen
- (*put on other clothes*) = sich umziehen
- (*when using transport*) = umsteigen (**!** *sein*)
- (*get foreign currency*) = wechseln

changing room noun
  = (der) Umkleideraum

channel noun
- (*TV station*) = (der) Kanal
  to change channels = auf einen anderen Kanal schalten
- = (der) Kanal
  the English Channel = der Ärmelkanal

Channel Islands noun
  the Channel Islands = die Kanalinseln

Channel Tunnel noun
  the Channel Tunnel = der Eurotunnel

chapter noun
  = (das) Kapitel

character noun
- = (der) Charakter
- (*in a play or film*) = (die) Rolle

charge
1 verb
- (*ask for payment*) = berechnen
  to charge someone for [delivery | the damage | packing …] = jemandem [die Lieferung | den Schaden | die Verpackung …] berechnen
- (*run*) = stürmen (**!** *sein*)
2 noun
- (*price*) = (die) Gebühr
  free of charge = kostenlos
- (*care*) = (die) Verantwortung
  to be in charge = die Verantwortung haben

charming adjective
  = reizend

charter flight noun (*British*)
  = (der) Charterflug

chase
1 verb = jagen
2 noun = (die) Verfolgungsjagd
chase away
  = wegjagen

chat
1 verb = plaudern
2 noun = (die) Plauderei
  to have a chat with someone = mit jemandem plaudern
chat up
  = anmachen✗

cheap adjective
  = billig

cheat
1 verb = betrügen
  they cheated him out of all his money = sie haben ihn um sein ganzes Geld betrogen
  (*in games*) = mogeln
  to cheat at cards = beim Kartenspielen mogeln
2 noun = (der) Betrüger/(die) Betrügerin
  (*in games*) = (der) Mogler/(die) Moglerin

check
1 verb
- (*examine accuracy*) = nachprüfen
- (*inspect*) = kontrollieren
  they checked our passports = sie haben unsere Pässe kontrolliert
- (*test*) = überprüfen
  to check on something = etwas überprüfen
  to check with someone = bei jemandem nachfragen
2 noun
- (*inspection for quality*) = (die) Kontrolle
- (*US: bill*) = (die) Rechnung
  to pick up the check = zahlen
- (*US: cheque*) = (der) Scheck
check in
  (*at an airport*) = einchecken
check out
  = abreisen (**!** *sein*)

checkbook noun (US)
= (das) Scheckbuch

checkers noun (US)
= (das) Damespiel

check-in noun
(at an airport) = (der) Abfertigungsschalter
(at a hotel) = (die) Rezeption

checkout noun
= (die) Kasse

check-up noun
= (die) Untersuchung

cheek noun
(part of the face) = (die) Backe

cheeky adjective
= frech

cheerful adjective
= fröhlich

cheers interjection
(when drinking) = prost!

cheese noun
= (der) Käse

chef noun
= (der) Koch

chemist noun
• (in a pharmacy) = (der) Apotheker/(die)
  Apothekerin ▶ **Professions p. 298**
• (in a laboratory) = (der) Chemiker/(die)
  Chemikerin
• (dispensing) = (die) Apotheke
  (shop) = (die) Drogerie

chemistry noun
= (die) Chemie

cheque noun (British)
= (der) Scheck
to pay by cheque = mit Scheck bezahlen

chequebook noun (British)
= (das) Scheckbuch

cherry noun
= (die) Kirsche

chess noun
= (das) Schach

chest noun
• (part of the body) = (die) Brust
• (piece of furniture) = (die) Truhe

chestnut
1 noun = (die) Kastanie
2 adjective = kastanienbraun ▶ **Colours p. 204**

chest of drawers noun
= (die) Kommode

chew verb
= kauen

chewing gum noun
= (der) Kaugummi

chicken noun
= (das) Huhn

child noun
= (das) Kind
when I was a child = als ich klein war

childminder noun (British)
= (die) Tagesmutter

chilly adjective
= kühl

chimney noun
= (der) Schornstein

chimpanzee noun
= (der) Schimpanse

chin noun
= (das) Kinn

China noun
= (das) China ▶ **Countries p. 208**

Chinese
1 noun
• (people) the Chinese = die Chinesen
• (language) = (das) Chinesisch
2 adjective = chinesisch ▶ **Countries p. 208**
  a Chinese restaurant = ein China-
  Restaurant

chips noun
• (British: fried potatoes) = Pommes frites
  (plural)
• (US: crisps) = Chips (plural)

chocolate noun
• = (die) Schokolade
• (sweet) = (die) Praline

choice noun
• = (die) Wahl
  we had no choice = wir hatten keine
  andere Wahl
• (variety) = (die) Auswahl
  you have a choice of three = du hast drei
  zur Auswahl

choir noun
= (der) Chor

choke
1 verb = sich verschlucken
  to choke to death = ersticken (**!** sein)
2 noun = (der) Choke

choose verb
• (select) = wählen
• (select from a group) = sich (dative)
  aussuchen
  choose something from the menu = suche
  dir etwas auf der Karte aus

christening noun
= (die) Taufe

Christian name noun
= (der) Vorname

✗ in informal situations

Christmas noun
= (das) Weihnachten
Happy Christmas! = Frohe Weihnachten!

Christmas Day noun
= (der) erste Weihnachtstag

Christmas Eve noun
= (der) Heiligabend

church noun
= (die) Kirche

cider noun
≈ (der) Apfelwein

cigar noun
= (die) Zigarre

cigarette noun
= (die) Zigarette

cinema noun
= (das) Kino

circle noun
• (shape) = (der) Kreis
• (in a theatre) = (der) Rang

circumstances noun
= Umstände (plural)
under no circumstances = unter gar
keinen Umständen

circus noun
= (der) Zirkus

citizen noun
= (der) Bürger/(die) Bürgerin

city noun
= (die) Großstadt
the City = die City

city center (US), **city centre** (British)
noun
= (das) Stadtzentrum

civilized adjective
= zivilisiert

civil servant noun
= (der) Beamte/(die) Beamtin

clap
1 verb = klatschen
2 noun
• (applause)
to give someone a clap = jemandem
Beifall klatschen
• **a clap of thunder** = ein Donnerschlag

clarinet noun
= (die) Klarinette

class noun
• = (die) Klasse
to travel first class = erster Klasse reisen
• (lesson) = (die) Stunde
we talked about it in class = wir haben es
im Unterricht besprochen
to take a history class (British: to give one)
= Geschichte unterrichten, (US: to attend
one) = Geschichte haben
• (style) = (der) Stil

classical adjective
= klassisch

classroom noun
= (das) Klassenzimmer

claw noun
• (of a cat) = (die) Kralle
• (of a crab) = (die) Schere

clay noun
= (der) Lehm
(in pottery) = (der) Ton

clean
1 adjective = sauber
are your hands clean? = hast du saubere
Hände?
2 verb = putzen
to clean the windows = die Fenster putzen
to have a jacket cleaned = eine Jacke ·
reinigen lassen
clean up
= sauber machen

clear
1 adjective
• = klar
the instructions are not very clear = die
Gebrauchsanweisung ist nicht ganz klar
is that clear? = ist das klar?✶
he has a clear advantage = er ist eindeutig
im Vorteil
on a clear day = bei klarem Wetter
your writing must be clear = du musst
deutlich schreiben
• (free from spots) = rein
to have clear skin = reine Haut haben
• (not blocked) = frei
2 verb
• (empty) = räumen
to clear the building = das Gebäude
räumen
to clear the table = den Tisch abräumen
• (disappear) = sich auflösen
the fog cleared after an hour = der Nebel
hat sich nach einer Stunde aufgelöst
• (go through)
to clear customs = vom Zoll abgefertigt
werden (**!** sein)
clear away
= wegräumen
clear up
• **to clear up the living room** = das
Wohnzimmer aufräumen
• **if the weather clears up, we'll go for a walk**
= wenn sich das Wetter aufklärt, gehen
wir spazieren

clever adjective
• (intelligent) = klug
to be clever at chess = gut im
Schachspielen sein
• (smart) = clever
• (skilful) = geschickt

client noun
= (der) Kunde/(die) Kundin

climate *noun*
 = (das) Klima

climb *verb*
• = hinaufsteigen (**!** *sein*)
 to climb over a wall = über eine Mauer
 klettern (**!** *sein*)
• (*rise higher*) = steigen (**!** *sein*)
 the aircraft is still climbing = das Flugzeug
 steigt noch immer

cloakroom *noun*
• (*for coats*) = (die) Garderobe
• (*British: toilets*) = (die) Toilette

clock *noun*
 = (die) Uhr

close¹
1 *adjective*
• (*near*) = nahe, = nah

 ! *In everyday speech,* nah *is used more
 often than* nahe.

 the station is quite close to the hotel = der
 Bahnhof ist ganz nah am Hotel
• (*of a friend*) = eng
• (*of a relative, an acquaintance*) = nahe
• (*other uses*)
 a close contest = ein harter Wettkampf
 it's very close today = heute ist es sehr
 schwül
 that was a close shave = das war knapp **✶**
2 *adverb* = nah(e)
 to come closer = näher kommen (**!** *sein*)
 to live close (by) = in der Nähe wohnen
close to
• (*when talking about location*) = nah(e) an
 (+ *dative or accusative*)

 ! *Note that* an *is followed by a noun in the
 dative when position is described. The
 accusative follows when there is
 movement towards something.*

• (*when talking about a situation*) = nah(e)
 to be close to tears = den Tränen nahe sein
 to come close to leaving = nahe daran sein
 wegzugehen

close² *verb*
• = zumachen, = schließen
 the shop closes at midday = das Geschäft
 macht mittags zu
 the door closed suddenly = die Tür schloss
 sich plötzlich
• **to close a road** = eine Straße sperren
close down
 = schließen
close off
 = sperren
close up
 = zumachen

closed *adjective*
 = geschlossen

cloth *noun*
• (*material*) = (der) Stoff
• (*for household use*) = (das) Tuch

clothes *noun*
 = Kleider (*plural*)
 to put on one's clothes = sich anziehen
 to take off one's clothes = sich ausziehen

cloud *noun*
 = (die) Wolke

cloudy *adjective*
 = bewölkt

club *noun*
• (*association, nightclub*) = (der) Klub
• (*for playing golf*) = (der) Schläger
• (*playing cards*) **clubs** = (das) Kreuz

clue *noun*
• (*in an investigation*) = (der) Anhaltspunkt
• (*in a crossword*) = (die) Frage

clumsy *adjective*
 = ungeschickt

coach
1 *noun*
• (*bus*) = (der) Bus
• (*trainer*) = (der) Trainer
• (*British: of a train*) = (der) Wagen
2 *verb* = trainieren

coal *noun*
 = (die) Kohle

coast *noun*
 = (die) Küste

coastguard *noun*
 = (die) Küstenwache

coat *noun*
• (*garment*) = (der) Mantel
• (*of an animal*) = (das) Fell

coat-hanger *noun*
 = (der) Kleiderbügel

cobweb *noun*
 = (das) Spinnennetz

cock *noun*
 (*British: rooster*) = (der) Hahn

cockroach *noun*
 = (die) Küchenschabe

cocoa *noun*
 = (der) Kakao

coconut *noun*
 = (die) Kokosnuss

cod *noun*
 = (der) Kabeljau

coffee *noun*
 = (der) Kaffee
 two white coffees = zwei Kaffee mit Milch

coffin *noun*
 = (der) Sarg

✶ in informal situations

coin noun
= (die) Münze

coincidence noun
= (der) Zufall

Coke® noun
= (die) or (das) Cola®

cold
1 adjective = kalt
I'm cold = mir ist kalt
2 noun
• (illness) = (die) Erkältung, = (der) Schnupfen
to catch a cold = sich erkälten
• (temperature) = (die) Kälte

collapse verb
• (of a building) = einstürzen (! sein)
• (of a person) = zusammenbrechen (! sein)
• (fail) = scheitern (! sein)

collar noun
• (on a shirt) = (der) Kragen
• (for a pet) = (das) Halsband

colleague noun
= (der) Kollege/(die) Kollegin

collect
1 verb
• = sammeln
to collect wood = Holz sammeln
to collect the exercise books = die Hefte
einsammeln
he collects stamps = er sammelt
Briefmarken
• (fetch) = abholen
to collect the children from school = die
Kinder von der Schule abholen
2 adverb (US)
to call someone collect = ein R-Gespräch
mit jemandem führen

collection noun
• (collected objects, money for charity) = (die)
Sammlung
• (in church) = (die) Kollekte
• (from a letterbox) = (die) Leerung
• (designer's new fashion) = (die) Kollektion

collision noun
= (der) Zusammenstoß

color (US), **colour** (British)
1 noun
• = (die) Farbe
• (of a person's skin) = (die) Hautfarbe
2 verb
• (paint) = malen
to colour the picture (in) = das Bild
ausmalen
• (dye) = färben

color film (US), **colour film** (British)
noun
= (der) Farbfilm

colorful (US), **colourful** (British)
adjective
= bunt

comb
1 noun = (der) Kamm
2 verb
to comb one's hair = sich (dative) die Haare
kämmen

come verb
• = kommen (! sein)
is the bus coming? = kommt der Bus?
he'll be coming around 10 o'clock = er
kommt gegen zehn Uhr
Christmas is coming = bald ist
Weihnachten
turn left when you come to the traffic lights
= wenn du an der Ampel bist, bieg
links ab
• (be a native or product of) = kommen
(! sein)
she comes from Italy = sie ist Italienerin
• (be available) = erhältlich sein
the dress comes in four colours = das
Kleid ist in vier Farben erhältlich
• (referring to position in a contest)
to come first = Erster/Erste werden (! sein)
come back
= zurückkommen (! sein)
when are you coming back from holiday?
= wann kommst du aus dem Urlaub
zurück?
come down
(be reduced) = fallen (! sein)
come in
• (enter) = hereinkommen (! sein)
• (arrive) = ankommen (! sein)
the train comes in at 5 o'clock = der Zug
kommt um fünf Uhr an
come off
• (become detached) = abgehen (! sein)
the button has come off = der Knopf ist
abgegangen
• (succeed) = klappen
come on
• (start to work) = angehen (! sein)
the light comes on when you open the
door = wenn man die Tür aufmacht, geht
das Licht an
• (encouraging someone)
come on! = komm!
come out
• (emerge) = herauskommen (! sein)
when he came out of the shop = als er aus
dem Laden herauskam
• (become available) = herauskommen
(! sein)
the magazine comes out every month =
die Zeitschrift kommt monatlich heraus
• (wash out) = herausgehen (! sein)
• (describing a photograph) =
herauskommen (! sein)
the photo didn't come out = das Foto ist
nichts geworden
• (be revealed) = herauskommen (! sein)
the truth will come out = die Wahrheit
kommt bestimmt heraus
the exam results are coming out today =
die Prüfungsergebnisse werden heute
bekannt gegeben

C

Colours

Adjectives

Most colours take adjectival endings:

a blue shirt	= ein blaues Hemd
the brown jacket	= die braune Jacke
the dress is red	= das Kleid ist rot

But some, such as **lila** (= purple), **orange** (= orange) and **rosa** (= pink), never change:

a purple dress	= ein lila Kleid
pink carnations	= rosa Nelken

When two adjectives are put together, they form a new adjective spelt as one word:

a light-blue suit	= ein hellblauer Anzug
the curtains are dark green	= die Vorhänge sind dunkelgrün
black and white stripes	= schwarzweiße Streifen
navy blue	= marineblau

For adjectives with the ending *-ish*, to show that something is approximately a certain colour, the German equivalent is **-lich**. Note that certain colours add an umlaut:

yellowish	= gelblich
greenish	= grünlich
bluish	= bläulich
reddish	= rötlich

Nouns

All colours are neuter nouns, written with a capital letter:

green	= das Grün
the blue of the sky	= das Blau des Himmels
my favourite colour is red	= meine Lieblingsfarbe ist Rot

Some colour phrases

to paint something green	= etwas grün anmalen
dressed in green	= in Grün, = grün gekleidet
blue suits her	= Blau steht ihr gut
the traffic lights are red	= die Ampel steht auf Rot

---

come round
- (*visit*) = vorbeikommen (**!** *sein*)
- (*regain consciousness*) = wieder zu sich (*dative*) kommen (**!** *sein*)

come to
(*amount to*) = sich belaufen auf (+ *accusative*)
that comes to £20 = das macht zwanzig Pfund

come up
- (*be discussed*) = erwähnt werden (**!** *sein*)
his name came up = sein Name wurde erwähnt
- (*occur*) = passieren (**!** *sein*)
- (*rise*) = aufgehen (**!** *sein*)

comfortable *adjective*
- = bequem
the sofa is very comfortable = das Sofa ist sehr bequem
- (*relaxed*)
to feel comfortable = sich wohl fühlen

comic strip *noun*
= (der) Comic

commercial
1 *adjective* = kommerziell
2 *noun* = (der) Werbespot

commit *verb*
- (*carry out*) = begehen
to commit suicide = Selbstmord begehen
- (*make a promise*)
to commit oneself to doing something = sich verpflichten, etwas zu tun

common *adjective*
- (*frequent*) = häufig
it's a common mistake = das ist ein häufiger Fehler
- (*usual*) = normal
- (*shared*) = gemeinsam
in common = gemeinsam

communicate *verb*
to communicate with someone = sich mit jemandem verständigen

community *noun*
= (die) Gemeinschaft

company noun
- (business) = (die) Gesellschaft, = (die) Firma
- (group of actors) = (die) Truppe
- (presence of other people) =
    (die) Gesellschaft
  to keep someone company = jemandem
    Gesellschaft leisten
  to expect company = Besuch erwarten

compare verb
  = vergleichen
  compared with or **to** = verglichen mit

compartment noun
- (of a train) = (das) Abteil
- (section) = (das) Fach

compass noun
  = (der) Kompass
  a pair of compasses = ein Zirkel

competent adjective
  = fähig

competition noun
- (rivalry or rivals) = (die) Konkurrenz
- (contest) = (der) Wettbewerb
  (in a newspaper) = (das) Preisausschreiben

competitive adjective
  = konkurrenzfähig

complain verb
  = sich beschweren
  to complain about the noise = sich über
    den Krach beschweren
  she complained to the headmistress = sie
    hat sich bei der Direktorin beschwert

complete
1 adjective
- (total) = völlig
  this is a complete waste of time = das ist
    völlige Zeitvergeudung
- (finished) = fertig
2 verb
- (finish) = beenden
- (fill in) = ausfüllen

completely adverb
  = völlig

complicated adjective
  = kompliziert

compliment noun
  = (das) Kompliment

comprehensive school noun (British)
  = (die) Gesamtschule

compulsory adjective
  = obligatorisch
  a compulsory subject = ein Pflichtfach
  to be compulsory = Pflicht sein

computer noun
  = (der) Computer

computer game noun
  = (das) Computerspiel

computer programmer noun
  = (der) Programmierer/(die)
    Programmiererin

computer studies noun
  = (die) Informatik

computing noun
  = (die) Computertechnik

concentrate verb
  = sich konzentrieren

concerned adjective
  to be concerned about someone = um
    jemanden besorgt sein

concert noun
  = (das) Konzert

concrete
1 noun = (der) Beton
2 adjective = Beton-
  a concrete floor = ein Betonboden

condemn verb
  (sentence) = verurteilen

condition noun
- (physical state) = (der) Zustand
- (proviso) = (die) Bedingung
  on condition that ... = unter der
    Bedingung, dass ...

condom noun
  = (das) Kondom

conductor noun
- (of an orchestra or choir) =
    (der) Dirigent/(die) Dirigentin
- (of a bus or tram) = (der) Schaffner/
    (die) Schaffnerin

cone noun
- = (der) Kegel
- (ice cream) = (die) Eistüte

confectionery noun
  = Süßigkeiten (plural)

conference noun
  = (die) Konferenz

confidence noun
- (trust) = (das) Vertrauen
  to have confidence in someone = zu
    jemandem Vertrauen haben
- (self-confidence) = (das) Selbstvertrauen
  to lack confidence = kein Selbstvertrauen
    haben

confident adjective
  (self-confident) = selbstbewusst
  I am confident that ... = ich bin mir sicher,
    dass ...

confidential adjective
  = vertraulich

confiscate verb
  = beschlagnahmen

confused adjective
  = verwirrt

confusing *adjective*
= verwirrend

congratulate *verb*
= gratulieren
they congratulated me on passing the exam = sie gratulierten mir zur bestandenen Prüfung

congratulations *noun*
congratulations! = herzlichen Glückwunsch!

conjurer *noun*
= (der) Zauberer/(die) Zauberin

connection *noun*
• (*link*) = (der) Zusammenhang
in connection with = in Zusammenhang mit
• (*train, phone connection*) = (der) Anschluss

conquer *verb*
= erobern

conscientious *adjective*
= gewissenhaft

conscious *adjective*
• (*aware*) = bewusst
he's very conscious of his height = er ist sich (*dative*) seiner Größe sehr bewusst
• (*after an operation*)
to be conscious = bei Bewusstsein sein

consent *noun*
= (die) Zustimmung

consequence *noun*
= (die) Folge

considerate *adjective*
= rücksichtsvoll

consideration *noun*
to take the [price | accommodation | time ...] into consideration = [den Preis | die Unterkunft | die Zeit ...] berücksichtigen

construct *verb*
= bauen

consulate *noun*
= (das) Konsulat

consult *verb*
= um Rat fragen

consumer *noun*
= (der) Verbraucher/(die) Verbraucherin

contact
1 *noun* = (der) Kontakt
to be in contact with someone = mit jemandem in Kontakt sein
to lose contact = den Kontakt verlieren
2 *verb* = sich in Verbindung setzen mit (+ *dative*)

contact lens *noun*
= (die) Kontaktlinse

contain *verb*
= enthalten

container *noun*
= (der) Behälter

content *adjective*
= zufrieden

contents *noun*
= (der) Inhalt

contest *noun*
= (der) Wettbewerb

continent *noun*
= (der) Kontinent

continental quilt *noun* (*British*)
= (die) Daunendecke

continue *verb*
• = fortsetzen
to continue doing something = etwas weiterhin tun
if the bad weather continues, we'll have to cancel the picnic = wenn das schlechte Wetter anhält, müssen wir das Picknick absagen
• (*walk*) = weitergehen (**!** *sein*)
(*in a car*) = weiterfahren (**!** *sein*)
• (*go on doing something*) = weitermachen
• (*go on speaking*) = fortfahren (**!** *sein*)

continuous *adjective*
= ununterbrochen

contraception *noun*
= (die) Empfängnisverhütung

contract *noun*
= (der) Vertrag

contradict *verb*
= widersprechen (+ *dative*)
don't contradict! = widersprich mir nicht!

contradiction *noun*
= (der) Widerspruch

contribute *verb*
• (*give money*) = beisteuern
(*donate*) = spenden
• (*participate*) = beitragen
to contribute to a discussion = zu einer Diskussion beitragen

control
1 *noun* = (die) Kontrolle
to be in control of a business = ein Geschäft leiten
to take control of the situation = die Situation unter sich (*dative*) haben
to get out of control = außer Kontrolle geraten (**!** *sein*)
she lost control = sie verlor die Beherrschung
2 *verb*
to control a firm = eine Firma leiten
to control the traffic = den Verkehr regeln
to control a dog = einen Hund unter Kontrolle halten

✻ in informal situations

convenient adjective
• (useful, practical) = praktisch
 it's more convenient to take the bus = es ist viel praktischer mit dem Bus zu fahren
• (suitable) = günstig
 to be convenient for someone = jemandem passen

conversation noun
 = (das) Gespräch
 to be in conversation with someone = sich mit jemandem unterhalten

convertible noun
 (car) = (das) Kabrio

convince verb
 = überzeugen

cook
1 verb = kochen
2 noun = (der) Koch/(die) Köchin

cookbook noun
 = (das) Kochbuch

cooker noun (British)
 = (der) Kochherd

cookery book noun (British)
 = (das) Kochbuch

cookie noun (US)
 = (der) Keks

cooking noun
• (food) = (die) Küche
• (preparing food) = (das) Kochen

cool
1 adjective
• (not hot) = kühl
• (calm) = ruhig, = gelassen
 stay cool! = bleib ruhig!
• (great) = cool, = geil **✶**
2 noun
 to lose one's cool = durchdrehen✶
 to keep one's cool = gelassen bleiben (**!** sein)
cool down
• (get colder) = sich abkühlen
• (calm down) = sich beruhigen

co-operate verb
 = zusammenarbeiten

cope verb
 = zurechtkommen (**!** sein)

copper noun
 = (das) Kupfer

copy
1 noun
• (imitation) = (die) Kopie
• (book, newspaper) = (das) Exemplar
2 verb
• = kopieren
• (in school) = abschreiben
• (imitate) = nachahmen

cork noun
• (material) = (der) Kork
• (for a bottle) = (der) Korken

corkscrew noun
 = (der) Korkenzieher

corn noun
• (British: wheat) = (das) Korn
• (US: maize) = (der) Mais
• (on the foot) = (das) Hühnerauge

corner noun
• (of a street, building) = (die) Ecke
 the post office is just round the corner = die Post ist gleich um die Ecke
• (bend in the road) = (die) Kurve
• (in football, hockey) = (der) Eckball

corpse noun
 = (die) Leiche

correct
1 adjective = richtig
 that is correct = das stimmt
2 verb = verbessern
 (in school, when typing) = korrigieren

cost verb
 = kosten

cost of living noun
 = Lebenshaltungskosten (plural)

costume noun
 = (das) Kostüm
 (national costume) = (die) Tracht

cosy adjective (British)
 = gemütlich

cot noun
 (British: for a baby) = (das) Kinderbett
 (US: camp bed) = (das) Feldbett

cottage cheese noun
 = (der) Hüttenkäse

cotton noun
• (material) = (die) Baumwolle
• (thread) = (das) Nähgarn

cotton wool noun
 = (die) Watte

couch noun
 = (die) Couch
 (in a doctor's surgery) = (die) Liege

cough
1 verb = husten
2 noun = (der) Husten
 to have a cough = Husten haben

could verb
• ▶ can

 ! The subjunctive of **können** is often used to translate **could**, expressing a speculation, wish, or suggestion.
• (as speculation)
 it could well be true = es könnte ja wahr sein

Countries and cities

In German, most countries and cities are neuter, but the **das** is not normally used:

Austria = Österreich
to come from Austria = aus Österreich kommen (**!** *sein*)
Munich = München
he lives in Munich = er wohnt in München

A few countries are feminine, and the **die** is normally used:

Switzerland = die Schweiz
we went to Switzerland = wir sind in die Schweiz gefahren
Turkey = die Türkei

A few countries are plural, and the **die** is normally used:

the United States = die Vereinigten Staaten
the Netherlands = die Niederlande
in the USA = in den USA

Nationality

In German, when you refer to a person's nationality, you use a noun but leave out the article:

he is German = er ist Deutscher
she is German = sie ist Deutsche
he is English = er ist Engländer
she is English = sie ist Engländerin

Adjectives

When referring to countries, adjectives are written with a small letter:

English = englisch
German = deutsch
French = französisch

To form adjectives, cities add an **-er**:

the Berlin shops = die Berliner Geschäfte
Munich beer = das Münchner Bier

---

* (*indicating uncertainty*)
  he could be right = er könnte Recht haben
* (*expressing a wish*)
  if only I could sing well = wenn ich nur gut singen könnte
* (*asking or suggesting*)
  could I speak to Anna? = könnte ich Anna sprechen?
  it would be nice if you could come = es wäre schön, wenn du kommen könntest

count *verb*
= zählen

count on
* (*rely on*) = sich verlassen auf
  (+ *accusative*)
* (*expect*) = rechnen mit (+ *dative*)

counter *noun*
* (*in a shop*) = (der) Ladentisch
  (*in a bank, post office*) = (der) Schalter
  (*in a bar*) = (die) Theke
* (*in board games*) = (die) Spielmarke

country
1 *noun*

* (*state*) = (das) Land
* (*scenery*) = (die) Landschaft
* (*not town*) = (das) Land
  to live in the country = auf dem Land wohnen
2 *adjective* = Land-
  country life = (das) Landleben

countryside *noun*
* (*scenery*) = (die) Landschaft
* (*not town*) = (das) Land

couple *noun*
* **a couple of days** (*two*) = zwei Tage, (*a few*) = ein paar Tage
* (*pair*) = (das) Paar

courage *noun*
= (der) Mut

courageous *adjective*
= mutig

course *noun*
* (*series of lessons*) = (der) Kurs
  a language course = ein Sprachkurs
* (*part of a meal*) = (der) Gang
* (*for golf*) = (der) Platz

✻ in informal situations

• (*other uses*)
of course = natürlich
in the course of = im Laufe (+ *genitive*)

court *noun*
• (*of law*) = (das) Gericht
to go to court = vor Gericht gehen (**!** *sein*)
• (*for playing sports*) = (der) Platz
• (*of a monarch*) = (der) Hof

courtyard *noun*
= (der) Hof

cousin *noun*
(*male*) = (der) Vetter, (*female*) = (die) Kusine

cover
1 *verb*
• (*for protection*) = bedecken
(*cover over*) = zudecken
(*with a loose cover*) = beziehen
• (*spread over*) **to cover a cake with
chocolate icing** = einen Kuchen mit
Schokoladenguss überziehen
• (*be found on*)
to be covered in dust = völlig verstaubt
sein
• (*insure*) = versichern
to be covered against theft = gegen
Diebstahl versichert sein
• (*report*) = berichten über (+ *accusative*)
• (*pay for*) decken
to cover expenses = die Kosten decken
2 *noun*
• (*lid*) = (der) Deckel
• (*for a cushion, duvet*) = (der) Bezug
• (*blanket*) = (die) Decke
• (*of a book*) = (der) Einband
• (*of a magazine*) = (der) Umschlag

cow *noun*
= (die) Kuh

coward *noun*
= (der) Feigling

cozy *adjective* (*US*)
= gemütlich

crab *noun*
= (die) Krabbe

crack
1 *verb*
• (*break or damage*)
(*if it's glass, china*) = anschlagen
(*if it's wood*) = anknacksen
(*if it's a nut, problem*) = knacken
to crack something open = etwas
aufbrechen
• (*get damaged*)
(*of glass, china*) = einen Sprung
bekommen
(*of wood*) = einen Riss bekommen
2 *noun*
• (*narrow gap*) = (der) Spalt
• (*in a cup, mirror*) = (der) Sprung
• (*in wood, a wall*) = (der) Riss
• (*loud noise*) = (der) Knall

cradle *noun*
= (die) Wiege

crafty *adjective*
= gerissen

cramp *noun*
= (der) Krampf

crane *noun*
• (*machine*) = (der) Kran
• (*bird*) = (der) Kranich

crash
1 *noun*
• (*collision*) = (der) Zusammenstoß
to have a crash = einen Unfall haben
a plane crash = ein Flugzeugunglück
• (*loud noise*) = (das) Krachen
2 *verb*
(*collide*) = einen Unfall haben
to crash into a lorry = mit einem Lastwagen
zusammenstoßen (**!** *sein*)
the plane crashed = das Flugzeug ist
abgestürzt

crate *noun*
= (die) Kiste

crawl *verb*
= kriechen (**!** *sein*)

crayon *noun*
(*wax*) = (der) Wachsstift
(*pencil*) = (der) Buntstift

crazy *adjective*
= verrückt
to be crazy about someone = verrückt
nach jemandem sein*****

cream
1 *noun*
• (*to eat*) = (die) Sahne
strawberries and cream = Erdbeeren mit
Sahne
• (*for face, burns*) = (die) Creme
2 *adjective* (*colour*) = cremefarben

create *verb*
= schaffen
to create difficulties = Schwierigkeiten
machen
to create a good impression = einen guten
Eindruck machen

creative *adjective*
= kreativ

crèche *noun*
= (die) Kinderkrippe

credit
1 *noun*
(*in banking*) = (der) Kredit
2 *verb* = gutschreiben

credit card *noun*
= (die) Kreditkarte

crime *noun*
= (das) Verbrechen

criminal
1 *noun* = (der/die) Kriminelle
2 *adjective* = kriminell

crisis *noun*
= (die) Krise

crisps *noun* (*British*)
= Chips (*plural*)

critical *adjective*
= kritisch

criticize *verb*
= kritisieren

crockery *noun*
= (das) Geschirr

crocodile *noun*
= (das) Krokodil

crooked *adjective*
• = schief
• (*bent*) = krumm

cross
1 *verb*
• (*go across*) = überqueren
  the train crossed the bridge = der Zug fuhr
  über die Brücke
• (*intersect*) = sich kreuzen
  our letters crossed = unsere Briefe haben
  sich gekreuzt
• (*other uses*)
  to cross one's legs = die Beine
  übereinander schlagen
  to cross a cheque = einen Scheck zur
  Verrechnung ausstellen
  it crossed my mind = es fiel mir ein
2 *noun* = (das) Kreuz
3 *adjective* = verärgert
  to get cross = ärgerlich werden (**!** *sein*)

cross off
= streichen

cross out
= ausstreichen

crossroads *noun*
= (die) Kreuzung

crossword *noun*
= (das) Kreuzworträtsel

crow *noun*
= (die) Krähe

crowd
1 *noun*
• (*large number of people*) =
  (die) Menschenmenge
  crowds of people = Menschenmassen
• (*spectators*) = Zuschauer (*plural*)
2 *verb* = sich drängen
  we crowded into a small room = wir
  drängten uns in ein kleines Zimmer

crowded *adjective*
= überfüllt

crown
1 *noun* = (die) Krone
2 *verb* = krönen

cruel *adjective*
= grausam

cruelty *noun*
= (die) Grausamkeit

cruise *noun*
= (die) Kreuzfahrt
to go on a cruise = eine Kreuzfahrt machen

crush *verb*
= quetschen

crust *noun*
= (die) Kruste

crutch *noun*
= (die) Krücke
to be on crutches = an Krücken gehen
  (**!** *sein*)

cry
1 *verb* = weinen
2 *noun*
  (*shout*) = (der) Schrei

cry out
= aufschreien

cuckoo *noun*
= (der) Kuckuck

cucumber *noun*
= (die) Gurke

cuddle *noun*
= (die) Liebkosung
to have a cuddle = schmusen

cuff *noun*
= (die) Manschette

cul-de-sac *noun*
= (die) Sackgasse

culprit *noun*
= (der) Täter/(die) Täterin

cultural *adjective*
= kulturell

culture *noun*
= (die) Kultur

cunning *adjective*
= listig

cup *noun*
• (*crockery*) = (die) Tasse
  a cup of coffee = eine Tasse Kaffee
• (*trophy*) = (der) Pokal
  the cup final = das Pokalendspiel
  the World Cup = die Weltmeisterschaft

cupboard *noun*
= (der) Schrank

curb *noun* (*US*) ▶kerb

cure
1 *verb* = heilen
2 *noun*
  (*thing that cures*) = (das) Heilmittel

curious *adjective*
= neugierig

curl
1 *noun* = (die) Locke
2 *verb*
   (*go curly*) = sich locken

curly *adjective*
= lockig

currant *noun*
= (die) Korinthe

currency *noun*
= (die) Währung
   foreign currency = Devisen (*plural*)

current *noun*
• (*water*) = (die) Strömung
• (*electricity*) = (der) Strom

curry *noun*
• (*powder*) = (das) *or* (der) Curry
• (*dish*) = (das) Currygericht

cursor *noun*
= (der) Cursor

curtain *noun*
= (der) Vorhang

cushion *noun*
= (das) Kissen

custard *noun* (*British*)
= (die) Vanillesoße

custom *noun*
• (*tradition*) = (der) Brauch
• (*habit*) = (die) Gewohnheit

customer *noun*
= (der) Kunde/(die) Kundin

customs *noun*
= (der) Zoll

customs officer *noun*
= (der) Zollbeamte/(die) Zollbeamtin

cut
1 *verb* = schneiden
   to cut an apple in half = einen Apfel
      halbieren
   to cut one's finger = sich in den Finger
      schneiden
   she cut herself = sie hat sich geschnitten
   to have one's hair cut = sich (*dative*) die
      Haare schneiden lassen
2 *noun*
• (*wound*) = (die) Schnittwunde
• (*hairstyle*) = (der) Schnitt
• (*reduction*) = (die) Kürzung
   (*in prices*) = (die) Senkung
cut out
• **to cut a photo out of a magazine** = ein Foto
      aus einer Zeitschrift ausschneiden
• **the engine cut out** = der Motor setzte aus
cut up
   = zerschneiden

cute *adjective*
• (*sweet, attractive*) = niedlich
• (*US: cunning*) = schlau

cutlery *noun*
= (das) Besteck

CV *noun* (*British*)
= (der) Lebenslauf

cycle *verb*
= Rad fahren (**!** *sein*)
   he cycles = er fährt Rad

cycle lane *noun*
= (die) Fahrradspur

cycling *noun*
= (das) Radfahren

cycling shorts *noun*
= (die) Radlerhose

cyclist *noun*
= (der) Radfahrer/(die) Radfahrerin

cynical *adjective*
= zynisch

Czech Republic *noun*
   the Czech Republic = die Tschechische
      Republik

Dd

dad *noun*
= (der) Vati

daddy *noun*
= (der) Papa

daffodil *noun*
= (die) Osterglocke

daisy *noun*
= (das) Gänseblümchen

damage
1 *noun* = (der) Schaden
2 *verb*
• (*physically*) = beschädigen
   the building was damaged by fire = das
      Gebäude wurde durch ein Feuer
      beschädigt
• (*harm*) = schädigen
   it damaged his reputation = das hat seinen
      Ruf geschädigt

damp
1 *noun* = (die) Feuchtigkeit
2 *adjective* = feucht

dance
1 *noun* = (der) Tanz
2 *verb* = tanzen

dancer *noun*
= (der) Tänzer/(die) Tänzerin

dancing *noun*
= (das) Tanzen

dandruff noun
• Schuppen (plural)

Dane noun
= (der) Däne/(die) Dänin

danger noun
= (die) Gefahr

dangerous adjective
= gefährlich

Danish
1 noun
(language) = (das) Dänisch
2 adjective = dänisch ▶ **Countries p. 208**

dark
1 noun = (die) Dunkelheit
in the dark = im Dunkeln
2 adjective
= dunkel

> ! Adjectives ending in -el drop the e when
> followed by a vowel, so dunkel becomes
> dunkler/dunkle/dunkles.

a dark night = eine dunkle Nacht
he's got dark hair = er ist dunkelhaarig

darkness noun
= (die) Dunkelheit

darling noun
= (der) Liebling

dart noun
= (der) Pfeil
(game) **darts** = (das) Darts

data noun
= Daten (plural)

database noun
• = (die) Datenbank

date
1 noun
• (das) Datum ▶ **Dates p. 213**
date of birth = (das) Geburtsdatum
• (meeting) = (die) Verabredung
2 verb = datieren
a letter dated 3rd August = ein vom dritten
August datierter Brief

daughter noun
= (die) Tochter

daughter-in-law noun
= (die) Schwiegertochter

dawn noun
= (die) Morgendämmerung
at dawn = bei Tagesanbruch

day noun
= (der) Tag ▶ **Dates p. 213**
during the day = tagsüber
these days = heutzutage
the day after tomorrow = übermorgen
the day before yesterday = vorgestern
the next day = am nächsten Tag

daylight noun
= (das) Tageslicht

dazzle verb
= blenden

dead
1 adjective = tot
2 noun
the dead = die Toten

deaf
1 adjective = taub
2 noun
the deaf = die Tauben

deal
1 noun
• (in business) = (das) Geschäft
• a great deal of = viel
2 verb
• (when playing cards) = geben
to deal the cards = geben
deal with
• (handle) = sich befassen mit (+ dative)
• (cope with) = fertig werden mit (+ dative)
(! sein)

dear
1 adjective
• (expensive) = teuer
• (precious) = lieb
• (in letter-writing) = Lieber/Liebe ▶ **Letter-
writing p. 262**
2 interjection
oh dear! = oje!

death noun
= (der) Tod

debt noun
= (die) Schuld
(money owed) = Schulden (plural)
to be in debt = Schulden haben

decade noun
= (das) Jahrzehnt

December noun
= (der) Dezember ▶ **Dates p. 213**

decide verb
• (make up one's mind) = sich entschließen
she can never decide what to do = sie
kann sich niemals entschließen, was sie
tun soll
• (come to a decision) = sich entscheiden
to decide on doing something = sich
entscheiden, etwas zu tun

decision noun
= (die) Entscheidung
to make a decision = eine Entscheidung
treffen

declare verb
= erklären
(at customs) anything to declare? = etwas
zu verzollen?

decorate verb
• (with ornaments) = schmücken
to decorate the Christmas tree = den
Weihnachtsbaum schmücken

Dates

Days

The days of the week are all masculine:

Sunday	= Sonntag
Monday	= Montag
Tuesday	= Dienstag
Wednesday	= Mittwoch
Thursday	= Donnerstag
Friday	= Freitag
Saturday	= Samstag, = Sonnabend

To translate *on* with days, use **am**, the shortened form of **an dem**:

on Sunday = am Sonntag

Months

The months of the year are all masculine:

January	= Januar
February	= Februar
March	= März
April	= April
May	= Mai
June	= Juni
July	= Juli
August	= August
September	= September
October	= Oktober
November	= November
December	= Dezember

To translate *in* with months, use **im**, the shortened form of **in dem**:

in January	= im Januar
what day is it today?	= welchen Tag haben wir heute?, = welcher Tag ist heute?
what is the date today?	= den Wievielten haben wir heute?, = der Wievielte ist heute?
the ninth of May, 9th May	= der neunte Mai, = 9. Mai
it's the first of June	= heute ist der erste Juni
on the nineteenth of January	= am neunzehnten Januar

At the top of a letter, the date is in the accusative:

5th March = den 5. März, = den fünften März

• **to decorate a room** (*with paint*) = ein Zimmer streichen, (*with wallpaper*) = ein Zimmer tapezieren

decoration *noun*
= (die) Verzierung
Christmas decorations = (der) Weihnachtsschmuck

deep *adjective*
= tief

deer *noun*
= (der) Hirsch

defeat
1 *noun* = (die) Niederlage
2 *verb* = schlagen

defence *noun* (*British*)
= (die) Verteidigung

defend *verb*
= verteidigen

defense (*US*) ▶ defence

definite *adjective*
• (*precise*) = klar
• (*obvious*) = eindeutig
• (*certain*) = sicher

definitely *adverb*
• (*certainly*) = bestimmt
I'm definitely coming = ich komme ganz bestimmt
• (*clearly*) = eindeutig

definition *noun*
= (die) Definition

degree *noun*
• (*from a university*) = (der) akademische Grad
• (*in measurements*) = (der) Grad
20 degrees = zwanzig Grad

deliberately *adverb*
= absichtlich

delicatessen noun
= (das) Feinkostgeschäft

delicious adjective
= köstlich

delighted adjective
= hocherfreut
she was delighted with her present = sie
hat sich sehr über ihr Geschenk gefreut

deliver verb
(supply) = liefern
(put through a letterbox) = austragen

delivery noun
(of goods) = (die) Lieferung
(of letters) = (die) Zustellung

demand
1 noun
• (request) = (die) Nachfrage
in demand = gefragt
• (claim) = (die) Forderung
2 verb = verlangen

democracy noun
= (die) Demokratie

democratic adjective
= demokratisch

demolish verb
= abreißen

demonstration noun
• (by protesters) = (die) Demonstration
• (presentation) = (die) Vorführung

Denmark noun
= (das) Dänemark ▶ **Countries p. 208**

dentist noun
= (der) Zahnarzt/(die) Zahnärztin
▶ **Professions p. 298**

deny verb
= bestreiten

department noun
• (part of a firm or shop) = (die) Abteilung
• (division of government) =
(das) Ministerium

department store noun
= (das) Kaufhaus

departure noun
= (die) Abfahrt
(of a plane) = (der) Abflug

depend verb
to depend on = abhängen von (+ dative)
it depends on him = das hängt von ihm ab
it depends = es kommt darauf an

deposit
1 noun
• (initial payment) = (die) Anzahlung
• (when renting a house) = (die) Kaution
• (in a bank account) = (das) Guthaben
2 verb
• **to deposit money in a bank** = Geld bei
einer Bank einzahlen
• (place down) = ablegen

depressed adjective
= deprimiert

depressing adjective
= deprimierend

deprive verb
= entziehen

depth noun
= (die) Tiefe
I'm out of my depth (when swimming) = ich
kann nicht mehr stehen

deputy
1 noun = (der) Stellvertreter/
(die) Stellvertreterin
2 adjective = stellvertretend

describe verb
= beschreiben

description noun
= (die) Beschreibung

desert
1 noun = (die) Wüste
2 verb = verlassen

deserve verb
= verdienen
he deserves to be punished = er verdient
Strafe

design
1 noun
• (pattern) = (das) Muster
• (plan) = (der) Entwurf
• (construction) = (die) Konstruktion
• (subject of study) = (das) Design
2 verb
• = entwerfen
• (intend, plan)
to be designed for = vorgesehen sein für
(+ accusative)

desire
1 noun = (der) Wunsch
2 verb = wünschen

desk noun
• (piece of furniture) = (der) Schreibtisch
• (in the classroom) = (das) Pult
• (at an airport, station) = (der) Schalter
• (in a hotel) = (der) Empfang

despair noun
= (die) Verzweiflung
in despair = verzweifelt

desperate adjective
= verzweifelt

dessert noun
= (der) Nachtisch

destroy verb
= zerstören

destruction noun
= (die) Zerstörung

detached adjective
• (torn off) = abgetrennt

- (*unemotional*) = distanziert
- (*separate*)
  a detached house = ein Einzelhaus

detail noun
= (die) Einzelheit
to go into details = auf Einzelheiten
eingehen (**!** *sein*)
in detail = ausführlich

detective noun
= (der) Kriminalbeamte/
(die) Kriminalbeamtin
private detective = (der) Detektiv/
(die) Detektivin

determined adjective
= entschlossen
to be determined to do something = fest
entschlossen sein, etwas zu tun

develop verb
- = entwickeln
- **to develop into a row** = sich zu einem Streit
  entwickeln

development noun
= (die) Entwicklung

devil noun
= (der) Teufel

dew noun
= (der) Tau

diagram noun
= (die) schematische Darstellung

dial
1 noun
- (*of a clock*) = (das) Zifferblatt
- (*of a telephone*) = (die) Wählscheibe
2 verb
to dial a number = eine Nummer wählen

diamond noun
- (*precious stone*) = (der) Diamant
  (*in jewellery*) = (der) Brillant
- (*playing cards*) **diamonds** = (das) Karo

diaper noun (*US*)
= (die) Windel

diarrhoea noun
= (der) Durchfall

diary noun
- (*for writing personal thoughts*) =
  (das) Tagebuch
- (*for appointments*) = (der) Terminkalender

dice noun
= (der) Würfel
to throw the dice = würfeln

dictionary noun
= (das) Wörterbuch

die verb
- (*of a person*) = sterben (**!** *sein*)
  to die of pneumonia = an
  Lungenentzündung sterben
- (*of a plant*) = eingehen (**!** *sein*)
  (*of a flower*) = verwelken (**!** *sein*)

diet noun
= (die) Diät
(*for slimming*) = (die) Schlankheitskur
to go on a diet = eine Schlankheitskur
machen

difference noun
= (der) Unterschied
it makes no difference = es ist egal

different adjective
= anderer/andere/anderes
a different book = ein anderes Buch
to be different = anders sein
he is different from his brother = er ist
anders als sein Bruder

difficult adjective
= schwierig

difficulty noun
= (die) Schwierigkeit

dig verb
= graben
dig up
= ausgraben

dilute verb
= verdünnen

dining room noun
= (das) Esszimmer

dinner noun
= (das) Abendessen
dinner's ready = das Essen ist fertig

dinosaur noun
= (der) Dinosaurier

direct
1 adjective = direkt
2 verb
- (*give directions*)
  he directed me to the station = er hat mir
  den Weg zum Bahnhof gesagt
- (*in film or theatre*) = Regie führen
  to direct a film = bei einem Film Regie
  führen

direction noun
- (*the way*) = (die) Richtung
  to ask for directions = nach dem Weg
  fragen
- (*instructions*)
  directions (**for use**) =
  (die) Gebrauchsanweisung

director noun
- (*of a film, play*) = (der) Regisseur/
  (die) Regisseurin
- (*of a company*) = (der) Direktor/
  (die) Direktorin

dirt noun
= (der) Schmutz

dirty
1 adjective = schmutzig
2 verb = schmutzig machen

D

disadvantage *noun*
= (der) Nachteil

disagree *verb*
= nicht übereinstimmen

disappear *verb*
= verschwinden (**!** *sein*)

disappoint *verb*
= enttäuschen

disappointment *noun*
= (die) Enttäuschung

disapprove *verb*
to disapprove of something = gegen etwas
(*accusative*) sein

disaster *noun*
= (die) Katastrophe

discipline
1 *noun* = (die) Disziplin
2 *verb*
(*punish*) = bestrafen

disco *noun*
= (die) Disko

discover *verb*
= entdecken

discovery *noun*
= (die) Entdeckung

discuss *verb*
(*talk about*) = besprechen
to discuss politics = über Politik
diskutieren

disease *noun*
= (die) Krankheit

disguise
1 *noun* = (die) Verkleidung
2 *verb* = verkleiden
she disguised herself as a witch = sie hat
sich als Hexe verkleidet

disgust
1 *noun* = (der) Ekel
2 *verb* = anekeln

disgusting *adjective*
= eklig

dish *noun*
• (*bowl*) = (die) Schüssel
(*shallow*) = (die) Schale
to do the dishes = abwaschen
• (*food*) = (das) Gericht

dishonest *adjective*
= unehrlich

dishwasher *noun*
= (die) Geschirrspülmaschine

disk *noun*
= (die) Diskette

dislike *verb*
= nicht mögen
I dislike him = ich mag ihn nicht

dismiss *verb*
• (*reject*) = ablehnen
• (*from a job*) = entlassen

disobey *verb*
= nicht gehorchen (+ *dative*)

display
1 *noun*
• (*of objects for sale*) = (die) Auslage
• (*exhibition*) = (die) Ausstellung
2 *verb*
• (*show*) = ausstellen
• (*show off*) = zur Schau stellen

dispute *noun*
= (der) Streit

disrupt *verb*
= unterbrechen

dissatisfied *adjective*
= unzufrieden

distance *noun*
= (die) Entfernung
from a distance = aus der Entfernung

distant *adjective*
= fern

distinguish *verb*
= unterscheiden
to distinguish between right and wrong =
das Richtige vom Falschen unterscheiden

distract *verb*
= ablenken

distribute *verb*
= verteilen

disturb *verb*
= stören
I hope I'm not disturbing you = hoffentlich
störe ich nicht

disturbing *adjective*
= beunruhigend

dive
1 *noun*
(*into water*) = (der) Kopfsprung
2 *verb*
• (*into water*) = einen Kopfsprung machen
• (*swim under water*) = tauchen

divide *verb*
= teilen
to divide something in two = etwas in zwei
Teile teilen
they divided the money between them =
sie teilten das Geld untereinander
six divided by two is three = sechs geteilt
durch zwei ist drei

diving board *noun*
= (das) Sprungbrett

✱ in informal situations

division noun
- (sharing) = (die) Teilung
- (separation) = (die) Trennung
- (in maths) = (die) Division

divorce
1 noun = (die) Scheidung
2 verb = sich scheiden lassen
  his parents are divorced = seine Eltern sind geschieden

DIY noun (British)
= (das) Heimwerken

dizzy adjective
= schwindlig
  I feel dizzy = mir ist schwindlig

do verb
- = tun, = machen
  he did his homework = er hat seine Hausaufgaben gemacht
  to do the [washing-up | cooking | cleaning ...] = [abwaschen | kochen | putzen ...]
  can you do me a favour? = kannst du mir einen Gefallen tun?
  to do one's hair = sich frisieren
- (used as an auxiliary verb)
  I don't like cats = ich mag Katzen nicht
  do you like strawberries?—yes, I do = magst du Erdbeeren?—ja, sehr gerne
  I love chocolate—so do I = ich esse Schokolade wahnsinnig gern—ich auch
  do you know her?—no, I don't = kennst du sie?—nein
  may I sit down?—yes, please do = darf ich mich setzen?—ja bitte
  he lives in London, doesn't he? = er wohnt in London, nicht wahr?
- (be enough) = reichen
  ten pounds will do = zehn Pfund reichen
- (perform)
  he did well = er hat gut abgeschnitten
  how is he doing? = wie geht es ihm?
- (have a job)
  what do you do? = was machen Sie beruflich?

do up
- (fasten) = zumachen
- (renovate, adorn)
  to do up a house = ein Haus renovieren
  to do oneself up = sich zurechtmachen

do without
  to do without something = ohne etwas (accusative) auskommen (**!** sein)

doctor noun
= (der) Arzt/(die) Ärztin ▶**Professions p. 298**
  to go to the doctor's = zum Arzt gehen (**!** sein)

document noun
= (das) Dokument

dog noun
= (der) Hund

doghouse (US) ▶kennel

doll noun
= (die) Puppe

dollar noun
= (der) Dollar ▶**Money p. 274**

dolphin noun
= (der) Delphin

dominate verb
= beherrschen

domino noun
= (der) Dominostein
  dominoes (game) = (das) Domino

donation noun
= (die) Spende

donkey noun
= (der) Esel

donut noun (US) ▶doughnut

door noun
= (die) Tür

dormitory noun
= (der) Schlafsaal

double
1 adjective
- (twice as much) = doppelt
  a room double the size = ein doppelt so großes Zimmer
  at double the cost = zum doppelten Preis
  to underline something with a double line = etwas doppelt unterstreichen
- (with numbers or letters)
  double eight = acht acht
- (for two) = Doppel-
  a double bed = ein Doppelbett
2 adverb
  (twice) = doppelt
3 noun
- (twice the amount) = (das) Doppelte
- (in tennis, badminton)
  to play a game of doubles = ein Doppel spielen
4 verb = verdoppeln
  his fortune has doubled = sein Vermögen hat sich verdoppelt

double-decker noun
(bus) = (der) Doppeldeckerbus

doubt
1 noun = (der) Zweifel
2 verb = bezweifeln
  I doubt (that) she will come = ich bezweifle, dass sie kommt

doughnut noun (British)
= (der) Berliner, = (der) Krapfen

down
1 adverb
- (in a static position) = unten
  it's down there = es ist da unten
- (moving downwards) = nach unten
  to jump down = hinunterspringen/ herunterspringen (**!** sein), = runterspringen✱ (**!** sein)

> **!** Note that hin and her show direction. In written German, **hinunter** is used for movement away and **herunter** for movement towards the speaker. In everyday spoken German, **runter** can cover both.

I'm coming down = ich komme runter**✶**
* (when writing)
  to write something down = etwas aufschreiben
2 preposition
  he ran down the hill = er lief den Hügel herunter
  to fall down the stairs = die Treppe runterfallen**✶** (**!** sein)

> **!** Note that **hinunter**, **herunter** and **runter** are usually put after the noun, which is in the accusative: When used with a verb, they form new, compound verbs.

downstairs
1 adverb = unten
  to go downstairs = nach unten gehen (**!** sein)
2 noun = (das) Erdgeschoss
3 adjective
  the downstairs bedroom = das Schlafzimmer im Erdgeschoss

dozen noun
= (das) Dutzend

draft noun (US) ▶draught

drag verb
= schleppen

drain
1 noun = (der) Abfluss
  the drains = die Kanalisation
2 verb
* (when cooking)
  to drain the vegetables = das Gemüse abgießen
* (drain away) = ablaufen (**!** sein)

drama noun
= (das) Drama

dramatic adjective
= dramatisch

drapes noun (US)
= Vorhänge (plural)

draught noun (British)
= (der) Luftzug
  there is a draught in here = hier zieht es

draughts noun (British)
= (das) Damespiel
  to play draughts = Dame spielen

draw
1 verb
* (with a pencil) = zeichnen
  to draw a line = einen Strich ziehen

* (pull) = ziehen
  to draw the curtains (open) = die Vorhänge aufziehen, (close) = die Vorhänge zuziehen
* (take out) = herausziehen
  he drew a knife from his pocket = er zog ein Messer aus der Tasche
  to draw money from one's account = Geld von seinem Konto abheben
* (attract) = anziehen
  the circus drew a large crowd = der Zirkus hat viele Zuschauer angezogen
* (in a lottery) = ziehen
  to draw a ticket = ein Los ziehen
* (in sports) = unentschieden spielen
* (of a date or an event)
  to draw near = heranrücken (**!** sein)
  to draw to an end = zu Ende gehen (**!** sein)
2 noun
* (in sport) = (das) Unentschieden
* (in a lottery) = (die) Ziehung
draw back
= zurückziehen
draw up
  to draw up a list = eine Liste aufstellen

drawer noun
= (die) Schublade

drawing noun
* (picture) = (die) Zeichnung
* (activity) = (das) Zeichnen

dream
1 noun = (der) Traum
2 verb = träumen

dress
1 noun
* (worn by women) = (das) Kleid
* (clothing) = (die) Kleidung
2 verb
* (clothe) = anziehen
  to dress a child = ein Kind anziehen
* (put one's clothes on) = sich anziehen
dress up
* (put smart clothes on) = sich schön anziehen
* (put on a disguise) = sich verkleiden

dressing gown noun
= (der) Morgenrock

drill
1 noun
  (tool) = (der) Bohrer
2 verb = bohren

drink noun
* = (das) Getränk
  (alcoholic) = (der) Drink
  to have a drink = etwas trinken
  a drink of water = ein Glas Wasser
* (alcohol) = (der) Alkohol
2 verb = trinken

drive
1 noun
* (in a car) = (die) Fahrt
  to go for a drive = eine Autofahrt machen
* (driveway) = (die) Einfahrt

---

2 *verb*
- (*in a vehicle*) = fahren (**!** *sein*)
- (*force*) **to drive someone to do something** = jemanden dazu bringen, etwas zu tun

drive away
= wegfahren (**!** *sein*)

drive back
= zurückfahren (**!** *sein*)

drive out
= hinauswerfen

driver *noun*
= (der) Fahrer/(die) Fahrerin

driver's license (*US*), **driving licence** (*British*) *noun*
= (der) Führerschein

driving test *noun*
= (die) **Fahrprüfung**
Jill has passed her driving test = Jill hat den Führerschein gemacht

drop
1 *noun*
- (*of liquid*) = (der) Tropfen
- (*decrease*) = (der) Rückgang
  a drop in temperature = ein Temperaturrückgang
2 *verb*
- (*fall*) = fallen (**!** *sein*)
- (*let fall*) = fallen lassen
  she dropped her bag = sie ließ ihre Tasche fallen
- (*lower*) = senken
  he dropped his price = er hat den Preis gesenkt
- (*fall lower*) = sinken (**!** *sein*)
  prices are dropping = die Preise sinken
- (*omit*) = auslassen

drop in
(*visit*) = vorbeikommen (**!** *sein*)

drop out
he dropped out of school = er hat die Schule aufgegeben
he dropped out of the race = er ist aus dem Rennen ausgeschieden

drought *noun*
= (die) Dürre

drown *verb*
- (*die*) = ertrinken (**!** *sein*)
- (*kill*) = ertränken

drug
1 *noun*
- (*addictive substance*) = (die) Droge, = (das) Rauschgift
  to be on drugs = Drogen nehmen
- (*medicine*) = (das) Medikament
2 *verb*
  to drug someone = jemanden betäuben

drug addict *noun*
= (der/die) Drogensüchtige

drum *noun*
= (die) Trommel

drunk *adjective*
= betrunken
to get drunk = sich betrinken

dry
1 *adjective* = trocken
2 *verb* = trocknen
  to dry the dishes = das Geschirr abtrocknen
  he dried his hands = er trocknete sich (*dative*) die Hände ab

dryer *noun*
- (*for washing*) = (der) Wäschetrockner
- (*for hair*) = (der) Föhn

duchess *noun*
= (die) Herzogin

duck
1 *noun* = (die) Ente
2 *verb*
  (*bend down*) = sich ducken

due *adjective*
- (*owing*) = zustehend
  I am due some holidays = mir stehen Ferien zu
- (*now payable*) = fällig
- (*expected*)
  to be due to do something = etwas tun sollen
  the train is due at 2 o'clock = der Zug soll um zwei Uhr ankommen
- **due to** = aufgrund (+ *genitive*)

duke *noun*
= (der) Herzog

dull *adjective*
- (*of a colour*) = fahl
- (*of a person or book*) = langweilig
- (*of the weather*) = trüb

dumb *adjective*
(*unable to speak*) = stumm

dump
1 *noun*
  (*for rubbish*) = (die) Müllkippe
2 *verb* = werfen

during *preposition*
= während (+ *genitive*)
  during the summer = während des Sommers

dusk *noun*
= (die) Abenddämmerung

dust
1 *noun* = (der) Staub
2 *verb* = abstauben

dustbin *noun*
= (die) Mülltonne

dustman *noun*
= (der) Müllmann

dustpan *noun*
= (die) Kehrschaufel

D

Dutch
1 *noun*
- (*people*) **the Dutch** = die Holländer
- (*language*) = (das) Holländisch
2 *adjective* = holländisch ▶**Countries p. 208**

duty *noun*
- (*moral obligation*) = (die) Pflicht
  it is your duty to return the money = du hast die Pflicht, das Geld zurückzugeben
- (*task*) = (die) Aufgabe
- (*of a soldier or nurse*)
  to be on duty = Dienst haben
- (*tax*) = (der) Zoll

duvet *noun*
= (das) Federbett

dye
1 *noun* = (die) Farbe
2 *verb* = färben
  to dye one's hair = sich (*dative*) die Haare färben

Ee

---

each
1 *adjective* = jeder/jede/jedes

> **!** Note that **jeder, jede** and **jedes** *change their endings in the same way as* **der/die/das.**

each morning = jeden Morgen
2 *pronoun*
- (*each one*) = jeder/jede/jedes

> **!** Note that **jeder** (*masculine*), **jede** (*feminine*) and **jedes** (*neuter*) *agree in gender with the noun they stand for.*

each of you = jeder/jede von euch
each other = einander
- (*per*) = je
  oranges are 30p each = Orangen kosten je dreißig Pence
  £10 each (*per person*) = zehn Pfund pro Person, (*per item*) = zehn Pfund pro Stück

eager *adjective*
  to be eager to do something = etwas unbedingt tun wollen

eagle *noun*
= (der) Adler

ear *noun*
= (das) Ohr

earl *noun*
= (der) Graf

early
1 *adverb* = früh
  to be early = früh dran sein
  early in the morning = früh am Morgen
  early next week = Anfang nächster Woche
2 *adjective* = früh
  to have an early night = früh zu Bett gehen (**!** *sein*)

earn *verb*
= verdienen

earring *noun*
= (der) Ohrring

earth *noun*
= (die) Erde

earthquake *noun*
= (das) Erdbeben

easily *adverb*
= leicht

east
1 *noun* = (der) Osten
  to the east of London = östlich von London
2 *adjective* = östlich, = Ost-
  the east coast = die Ostküste
3 *adverb* = nach Osten

Easter *noun*
= (das) Ostern
  at Easter = zu Ostern

easy *adjective*
= leicht

eat *verb*
- (*of people*) = essen
- (*of animals*) = fressen

economic *adjective*
= wirtschaftlich

economical *adjective*
= sparsam

economy *noun*
- (*of a country*) = (die) Wirtschaft
- (*saving*) = (die) Sparsamkeit

economy class *noun*
= (die) Touristenklasse

edge *noun*
- (*of a road, paper*) = (der) Rand
  on the edge of town = am Stadtrand
- (*of a table, bed*) = (die) Kante
- (*of a knife*) = (die) Schneide

educate *verb*
= erziehen

education *noun*
- (*process*) = (die) Erziehung
- (*studies, training*) = (die) Ausbildung
- (*knowledge, result of good education*)
  = (die) Bildung

effect *noun*
= (die) Wirkung
  to take effect (*of law*) = in Kraft treten (**!** *sein*)

effective *adjective*
= wirksam

effort *noun*
= (die) Anstrengung
to make an effort = sich (*dative*) Mühe geben

egg *noun*
= (das) Ei

eggcup *noun*
= (der) Eierbecher

Egypt *noun*
= (das) Ägypten ▶Countries p. 208

eight *adjective*
= acht ▶Numbers p. 282

eighteen *adjective*
= achtzehn ▶Numbers p. 282

eighth ▶Numbers p. 282, ▶Dates p. 213
1 *adjective* = achter/achte/achtes
2 *noun*
(*fraction*) = (das) Achtel

eighty *adjective*
= achtzig ▶Numbers p. 282

either
1 *pronoun*
• (*one or other*) = einer von beiden/eine von beiden/eins von beiden
I don't like either of them = ich mag keinen von beiden/keine von beiden/keins von beiden
• (*both*) = beide (*plural*)
I can't see either (of them) = ich kann beide nicht sehen
2 *adjective*
• (*one or other*) = einer von beiden/eine von beiden/eins von beiden
• (*each*) = beide (*plural*)
on either side of the road = auf beiden Seiten der Straße
either day is fine = beide Tage sind okay✗
3 *adverb*
I can't do it either = ich kann es auch nicht machen
4 *conjunction*
• **either ... or** = entweder ... oder
they are coming on either Monday or Tuesday = sie kommen entweder am Montag oder am Dienstag
• (*after a negative*)
I didn't see either Helen or Paul = ich habe weder Helen noch Paul gesehen

elbow *noun*
= (der) Ellbogen

elderly *adjective*
= älterer/ältere/älteres

eldest *adjective*
= ältester/älteste/ältestes

elect *verb*
= wählen

election *noun*
= (die) Wahl

electric *adjective*
= elektrisch

electrician *noun*
= (der) Elektriker/(die) Elektrikerin
▶Professions p. 298

electricity *noun*
• (*supply*) = (der) Strom
• (*in physics*) = (die) Elektrizität

elegant *adjective*
= elegant

elephant *noun*
= (der) Elefant

eleven *adjective*
= elf ▶Numbers p. 282

eliminate *verb*
= ausschalten

elm *noun*
= (die) Ulme

else *adverb*
= sonst
nothing else = sonst nichts
anything else? = sonst noch etwas?
what else did he say? = was hat er sonst noch gesagt?
everything else = alles andere
anyone else = jeder andere
or else = sonst

elsewhere *adverb*
= woanders

e-mail *noun*
= (die) E-mail

embark *verb*
= an Bord gehen (**!** *sein*)

embarrass *verb*
to embarrass someone = jemanden in Verlegenheit bringen
I feel embarrassed about it = das ist mir peinlich

embarrassing *adjective*
= peinlich

embarrassment *noun*
= (die) Verlegenheit

embassy *noun*
= (die) Botschaft

emerald *noun*
= (der) Smaragd

emerge *verb*
• = herauskommen (**!** *sein*)
he emerged from the building = er kam aus dem Gebäude heraus
• (*become apparent*) = sich herausstellen
the truth finally emerged = die Wahrheit hat sich endlich herausgestellt

emergency *noun*
= (der) Notfall
in an emergency = im Notfall

emergency exit *noun*
= (der) Notausgang

emotion *noun*
= (das) Gefühl

emotional *adjective*
• (*of a person*) = gefühlsbetont
• (*of a situation*) = emotionsgeladen

emperor *noun*
= (der) Kaiser

emphasize *verb*
= betonen

employ *verb*
• (*keep in service*) = beschäftigen
• (*appoint*) = einstellen

employee *noun*
= (der/die) Angestellte

employer *noun*
= (der) Arbeitgeber/(die) Arbeitgeberin

employment *noun*
= (die) Arbeit

empress *noun*
= (die) Kaiserin

empty
1 *adjective* = leer
2 *verb* = leeren

encourage *verb*
= ermutigen

encyclopaedia *noun*
= (das) Lexikon

end
1 *noun* = (das) Ende
at the end of the year = am Ende des Jahres
at the end of May = Ende Mai
she read to the end of the page = sie hat die Seite zu Ende gelesen
in the end = schließlich
2 *verb*
• (*bring to an end*) = beenden
• (*come to an end*) = enden

endure *verb*
= ertragen

enemy *noun*
= (der) Feind

energy *noun*
= (die) Energie

engaged *adjective*
• (*of a couple*) = verlobt
to get engaged = sich verloben
• (*of a phone, lavatory*) = besetzt

engagement *noun*
• (*before marriage*) = (die) Verlobung
• (*appointment*) = (die) Verabredung

engine *noun*
• (*of a car, plane*) = (der) Motor
• (*of a ship*) = (die) Maschine
• (*of a train*) = (die) Lokomotive

engineer *noun*
= (der) Ingenieur/(die) Ingenieurin
▶**Professions p. 298**

England *noun*
= (das) England ▶**Countries p. 208**

English
1 *noun*
• (*people*) **the English** = die Engländer
• (*language*) = (das) Englisch
2 *adjective* = englisch ▶**Countries p. 208**

Englishman *noun*
= (der) Engländer

Englishwoman *noun*
= (die) Engländerin

enjoy *verb*
• (*like*)
to enjoy |**reading** | **swimming** | **going to the cinema** …| = gerne |lesen | schwimmen | ins Kino gehen …|
I enjoyed the |**book** | **film** | **trip** …| = |das Buch | der Film | der Ausflug …| hat mir gut gefallen
he enjoyed the meal = das Essen hat ihm geschmeckt
• **to enjoy oneself** = sich amüsieren

enormous *adjective*
= riesig

enough
1 *pronoun* = genug
we have enough to eat = wir haben genug zu essen
that's enough = das reicht
2 *adverb* = genug
3 *adjective* = genug
we haven't got enough room = wir haben nicht genug Platz

enquire, enquiry ▶inquire, inquiry

enter *verb*
• (*go in*) = gehen in (+ *accusative*) (**!** *sein*)
he entered the room = er ging in das Zimmer
• (*come in*) = hereinkommen (**!** *sein*)
• (*participate*) = teilnehmen an (+ *dative*)
to enter a competition = an einem Preisausschreiben teilnehmen

entertain *verb*
= unterhalten

entertainment *noun*
• (*amusement*) = (die) Unterhaltung
• (*show*) = (die) Veranstaltung

enthusiasm *noun*
= (die) Begeisterung

entrance *noun*
= (der) Eintritt

entry *noun*
= (der) Eintritt
to force an entry into a building = sich
  (*dative*) Zutritt zu einem Gebäude
  verschaffen
no entry (*to pedestrians*) = Zutritt
  verboten, (*to cars*) = Einfahrt verboten

envelope *noun*
= (der) Briefumschlag

environment *noun*
= (die) Umwelt

envy
1 *noun* = (der) Neid
2 *verb* = beneiden

episode *noun*
• (*event*) = (die) Episode
• (*on TV or radio*) = (die) Folge

equal
1 *adjective* = gleich
in equal amounts = gleich viel
of equal [size | strength | height …] = gleich
  [groß | stark | hoch …]
2 *verb* = gleichen (+ *dative*)

equality *noun*
= (die) Gleichberechtigung

equator *noun*
the equator = der Äquator

equipment *noun*
• = (die) Ausstattung
• (*things needed for an activity*) = (die)
  Ausrüstung
skiing equipment = (die) Skiausrüstung

error *noun*
= (der) Fehler

escalator *noun*
= (die) Rolltreppe

escape
1 *noun* = (die) Flucht
2 *verb*
• = entkommen (**!** *sein*)
to escape from something = aus etwas
  (*dative*) entkommen
to escape from someone = jemandem
  entkommen
• (*from prison*) = ausbrechen (**!** *sein*)

especially *adverb*
= besonders

essay *noun*
= (der) Aufsatz

essential *adjective*
= wesentlich

establish *verb*
• (*set up*) = gründen
• (*prove*) = beweisen

estate agent *noun*
= (der) Immobilienmakler/(die)
  Immobilienmaklerin

estimate
1 *noun*
  (*quote*) = (der) Kostenvoranschlag
2 *verb* = schätzen

etc. *abbreviation*
= usw.

EU *noun*
= (die) EU

euro *noun*
= (der) Euro

eurocheque *noun*
= (der) Euroscheck

Europe *noun*
= (das) Europa ▶**Countries p. 208**

European
1 *noun* = (der) Europäer/(die) Europäerin
2 *adjective* = europäisch ▶**Countries p. 208**

even
1 *adjective*
• (*flat, smooth*) = eben
an even surface = eine ebene Fläche
• (*regular*) = gleichmäßig
• **an even number** = eine gerade Zahl
• (*equal*) = gleich
2 *adverb*
• = sogar
she works even on holiday = sie arbeitet
  sogar in den Ferien
• (*with a negative*)
not even = nicht einmal
he didn't even try = er hat es nicht einmal
  versucht
• (*with a comparison*) = sogar noch
it is even colder today = es ist sogar noch
  kälter heute

evening *noun*
= (der) Abend
in the evening = am Abend

event *noun*
= (das) Ereignis

eventually *adverb*
= schließlich

ever *adverb*
• (*at any time*) = je
have you ever been to Rome? = warst du
  je in Rom?
not ever = nie
nothing ever happens = es passiert nie
  etwas
• (*always*) = immer
for ever = für immer

every
  adjective = jeder/jede/jedes

  ! *Note that* **jeder**, **jede** *and* **jedes** *change
  their endings in the same way as*
  der/die/das.
every other day = jeden zweiten Tag
every one = jeder Einzelne/jede
  Einzelne/jedes Einzelne
every few days = alle paar Tage

E

everybody *pronoun*
  = alle (*plural*)
  everybody knows that = das wissen alle
  (*each one*) = jeder
  everybody has their own method = jeder
    macht es auf seine eigene Weise

everyday *adjective*
  = alltäglich

everyone ▶everybody

everything *pronoun*
  = alles

everywhere *adverb*
  = überall

evidence *noun*
  • (*proof*) = (der) Beweis
  • (*given in court*) = (die) Aussage
  to give evidence = aussagen

evil
  1 *noun* = (das) Böse
  2 *adjective* = böse

exact *adjective*
  = genau

exactly *adverb*
  = genau

exaggerate *verb*
  = übertreiben

exaggeration
  = (die) Übertreibung

exam *noun*
  = (die) Prüfung

examination *noun*
  • (*at school*) = (die) Prüfung
  • (*medical check-up*) = (die) Untersuchung

examine *verb*
  • (*at school*) = prüfen
  • (*medically*) = untersuchen

excellent *adjective*
  = ausgezeichnet

except *preposition*
  = außer (+ *dative*)
  **you couldn't hear anything except (for) the
    clock ticking** = man hörte nichts außer
    dem Ticken der Uhr

exception *noun*
  = (die) Ausnahme

exchange
  1 *noun*
  • (*of ideas, students*) = (der) Austausch
  • (*of money, bought items*) = (der) Umtausch
  2 *verb* = umtauschen
  she exchanged the bag for a scarf = sie
    tauschte die Tasche gegen einen Schal
    um

exchange rate *noun*
  = (der) Wechselkurs

excited *adjective*
  = aufgeregt

exciting *adjective*
  = aufregend

excuse
  1 *noun*
  • (*justifying something*) =
      (die) Entschuldigung
  • (*pretext*) = (die) Ausrede
  2 *verb* = entschuldigen
  excuse me! = Entschuldigung!

exercise
  1 *noun*
  • (*piece of work*) = (die) Übung
  • (*to keep fit*) = (die) Bewegung
  to do exercises = Gymnastik machen
  to take exercise = sich bewegen
  2 *verb*
  (*keep fit*) = trainieren

exhaust *noun*
  (*of a car*) = (der) Auspuff

exhausted *adjective*
  = erschöpft

exhibition *noun*
  = (die) Ausstellung

existence *noun*
  = (die) Existenz

exit *noun*
  • (*door*) = (der) Ausgang
  • (*from a motorway*) = (die) Ausfahrt

expect *verb*
  • = erwarten
  she is expecting a baby = sie erwartet ein
    Kind
  the results were worse than expected =
    die Ergebnisse waren schlechter als
    erwartet
  I expect so = wahrscheinlich
  to expect someone to do something = von
    jemandem erwarten, dass er/sie etwas tut
  they are expected to be there on time =
    man erwartet von ihnen, dass sie
    pünktlich da sind
  • (*suppose*) = glauben
  I expect so = ich glaube schon

expense *noun*
  = Kosten (*plural*)
  at my expense = auf meine Kosten

expenses *noun*
  • (*outgoings*) = Ausgaben (*plural*)
  • (*of a businessman*) = Spesen (*plural*)

expensive *adjective*
  = teuer

explain *verb*
  = erklären

explanation *noun*
  = (die) Erklärung

explode *verb*
- (*go off*) = explodieren (**!** *sein*)
- (*set off*) = zur Explosion bringen

exploit *verb*
= ausbeuten

explore *verb*
= erforschen

explosion *noun*
= (die) Explosion

export
1 *noun* = (der) Export
2 *verb* = exportieren

expose *verb*
- (*reveal*) = aufdecken
- (*expose to danger*) = aussetzen
- **to expose a film** = einen Film belichten

express
1 *adjective* = Eil-
  an express letter = ein Eilbrief
  an express train = ein Schnellzug
2 *adverb*
  to send a letter express = einen Brief per
    Eilboten schicken
3 *verb* = ausdrücken
  to express oneself = sich ausdrücken

expression *noun*
= (der) Ausdruck

extent *noun*
- (*of knowledge, power*) = (der) Umfang
- (*of damage*) = (das) Ausmaß
- (*degree*)
  to a certain extent = in gewissem Maße

external *adjective*
= äußerer/äußere/äußeres

extra
1 *noun*
- (*additional thing*) = (das) Extra
- (*actor*) = (der) Statist/(die) Statistin
2 *adjective* = zusätzlich
3 *adverb*
- (*additionally*) = extra
- (*especially*) = besonders
  you need to be extra careful = du musst
    besonders vorsichtig sein

extraordinary *adjective*
- (*wonderful*) = außerordentlich
- (*strange*) = seltsam

extreme
1 *noun* = (das) Extrem
2 *adjective*
- (*outermost*) = äußerster/äußerste/
    äußerstes
- (*radical*) = extrem

extremely *adverb*
= äußerst

extrovert *adjective*
= extravertiert

eye *noun*
= (das) Auge

eyebrow *noun*
= (die) Augenbraue

eyelash *noun*
= (die) Wimper

eyelid *noun*
= (das) Augenlid

eyeliner *noun*
= (der) Eyeliner

eye shadow *noun*
= (der) Lidschatten

eyesight *noun*
  to have good/bad eyesight =
    gute/schlechte Augen haben

Ff

fabric *noun*
= (der) Stoff

face
1 *noun*
- (*of a person*) = (das) Gesicht
  he has a scar on his face = er hat eine
    Narbe im Gesicht
  to make a face = ein Gesicht schneiden
- (*of a clock, watch*) = (das) Zifferblatt
2 *verb*
- (*be opposite*) = gegenüberstehen
  (+ *dative*)
  she was facing me = sie stand mir
    gegenüber
  the house facing the church = das Haus
    gegenüber der Kirche
- (*look towards*)
  my room faces the garden = mein Zimmer
    geht auf den Garten
- (*of a building*)
  to face south = nach Süden liegen
- (*confront*) = gegenüberstehen (+ *dative*)
  to be faced with difficulties =
    Schwierigkeiten gegenüberstehen
- (*bear*) = verkraften
  not to be able to face something = etwas
    nicht verkraften können

face up to
= ins Auge sehen (+ *dative*)
  to face up to the facts = den Tatsachen ins
    Auge sehen

fact *noun*
= (die) Tatsache
  in fact (*in reality*) = tatsächlich, (*actually*) =
    eigentlich

factory *noun*
= (die) Fabrik

F

fade *verb*
- (*of a fabric*) = verbleichen (**!** *sein*)
- (*of a colour, memory*) = verblassen (**!** *sein*)
- (*of a sound*) = abklingen (**!** *sein*)
- (*of a flower*) = verwelken (**!** *sein*)

fail *verb*
- (*not succeed*) = scheitern (**!** *sein*)
  to fail in something = mit etwas scheitern
  to fail to do something = etwas nicht tun
  (*in an exam*) = durchfallen (**!** *sein*)
- (*not succeed at*) = nicht bestehen
  I failed my driving test = ich habe meine
  Fahrprüfung nicht bestanden
- (*not allow to pass*)
  to fail a candidate = einen Prüfling
  durchfallen lassen
- (*not work*) = versagen
  the brakes failed = die Bremsen versagten

failure *noun*
- (*lack of success*) = (der) Misserfolg
- (*unsuccessful person*) = (der) Versager
- (*of electricity, an engine*) = (der) Ausfall
  a power failure = ein Stromausfall

faint
1 *verb* = ohnmächtig werden (**!** *sein*)
2 *adjective* = schwach

fair
1 *noun* = (der) Jahrmarkt
  (*trade fair*) = (die) Messe
2 *adjective*
- (*in colour*)
  to have fair hair = blonde Haare haben
  to have fair skin = helle Haut haben
- (*just, reasonable*) = fair, = gerecht
- (*of weather*) = gut

fair-haired *adjective*
  = blond

fairy *noun*
  = (die) Fee

fairy story, fairy tale *noun*
  = (das) Märchen

faith *noun*
- (*religious belief*) = (der) Glaube
- (*confidence*) = (das) Vertrauen
  to have faith in someone = Vertrauen zu
  jemandem haben

faithful *adjective*
  = treu
  to be faithful to someone = jemandem treu
  sein

fall
1 *noun*
- (*of an object*) = (der) Fall
- (*of a person, regime*) = (der) Sturz
- (*in prices, temperature*) = (das) Sinken
- (*US: autumn*)
  the fall = der Herbst

2 *verb*
- (*drop, decrease*) = fallen (**!** *sein*)
  to fall to the ground = auf den Boden fallen

> **!** *To indicate direction, a prefix is often
> added to the verb, forming a
> separable verb such as* **herunterfallen**.

  to fall downstairs = die Treppe
  herunterfallen (**!** *sein*)
- (*become*)
  to fall asleep = einschlafen (**!** *sein*)
  to fall in love with someone = sich in
  jemanden verlieben

fall down
- (*of a person*) = hinfallen (**!** *sein*)
- (*of a building*) = einstürzen (**!** *sein*)
- (*of a tent, toy*) = umfallen (**!** *sein*)

fall off
  = herunterfallen (**!** *sein*)

fall out
  = herausfallen (**!** *sein*)

fall over
- (*of a person*) = hinfallen (**!** *sein*)
- (*stumble*)
  he fell over the stool = er fiel über den
  Hocker

fall through
  (*of an agreement*) = ins Wasser fallen
  (**!** *sein*)

false *adjective*
  = falsch

false teeth *noun*
  = (das) Gebiss

familiar *adjective*
  = bekannt
  the name sounds familiar = der Name ist
  mir bekannt

family *noun*
  = (die) Familie

famine *noun*
  = (die) Hungersnot

famous *adjective*
  = berühmt

fan *noun*
- (*held in the hand*) = (der) Fächer
- (*electric, for cooling*) = (der) Ventilator
- (*supporter*) = (der) Fan

fancy *adjective*
  = extravagant

fancy dress *noun*
  = (die) Verkleidung
  in fancy dress = verkleidet

fantastic *adjective*
  (*wonderful*) = phantastisch

fantasy *noun*
  = (die) Phantasie

✘ in informal situations   **◆** considered offensive

far
1 *adverb*
- (*in distance, time*) = weit
  how far is it to London? = wie weit ist es
  bis London?
  it's very far away = es ist sehr weit weg
  far into the future = bis weit in die Zukunft
  as far back as 1950 = schon 1950
- (*very much*) = viel
  far better = viel besser
2 *adjective*
- (*remote*) = weit entfernt
- (*remote in time*) = fern
- (*other*)
  at the far end = am anderen Ende
- (*other uses*)
  by far = bei weitem
  so far = bisher
  as far as I know = soweit ich weiß

fare *noun*
- (*on a bus, train*) = (der) Fahrpreis
- (*on a plane*) = (der) Flugpreis

farm *noun*
  = (der) Bauernhof

farmer *noun*
  = (der) Bauer/(die) Bäuerin ▶**Professions
  p. 298**

fart *verb*
  = furzen☞

farther ▶further

fascination *noun*
  = (die) Faszination

fashion *noun*
  = (die) Mode
  to be in fashion = in Mode sein
  to go out of fashion = aus der Mode
  kommen (**!** *sein*)

fashionable *adjective*
  = modisch

fast
1 *adjective* = schnell
  to be fast (*of a clock*) = vorgehen (**!** *sein*)
  my watch is fast = meine Uhr geht vor
2 *adverb* = schnell
  to be fast asleep = fest schlafen

fasten *verb*
  to fasten a zip = einen Reißverschluss
  zumachen
  to fasten one's seatbelt = sich anschnallen

fat
1 *adjective*
- (*of a person, animal*) = dick, = fett☓
- (*of meat*) = fett
2 *noun* = (das) Fett

fatal *adjective*
  a fatal accident = ein tödlicher Unfall
  a fatal mistake = ein verhängnisvoller
  Fehler

fate *noun*
  = (das) Schicksal

father *noun*
  = (der) Vater

Father Christmas *noun*
  = (der) Weihnachtsmann

father-in-law *noun*
  = (der) Schwiegervater

fattening *adjective*
  to be fattening = dick machen

faucet *noun* (*US*)
  = (der) Wasserhahn

fault *noun*
- (*responsibility*) = (die) Schuld
  it's your fault = du hast Schuld
- (*flaw*) = (der) Fehler

favor (*US*) ▶favour

favorite (*US*) ▶favourite

favour (*British*)
1 *noun*
- (*kind act*) = (der) Gefallen
  to do someone a favour = jemandem einen
  Gefallen tun
- (*advantage*)
  that's in his favour = das ist zu seinen
  Gunsten
- (*support*)
  in favour of = zugunsten (+ *genitive*)
  to be in favour of something = für etwas
  (*accusative*) sein
  I am in favour = ich bin dafür
2 *verb*
- (*benefit*) = begünstigen
- (*prefer*) = bevorzugen

favourite (*British*)
1 *adjective* = Lieblings-
  my favourite film = mein Lieblingsfilm
2 *noun*
- (*in a race or contest*) = (der) Favorit/
  (die) Favoritin
- (*favoured person*) = (der) Liebling

fax
1 *noun* = (das) Fax
2 *verb* = faxen

fear
1 *noun* = (die) Angst
  fear of = Angst vor (+ *dative*)
2 *verb* = fürchten

feast *noun*
  = (das) Festessen

feather *noun*
  = (die) Feder

February *noun*
  = (der) Februar ▶**Dates p. 213**

fed up *adjective*
  I am fed up with him = ich habe die Nase
  voll von ihm☓

F

fee *noun* = (die) Gebühr
(*of a doctor, lawyer*) = (das) Honorar
school fees = (das) Schulgeld

feed *verb*
= füttern

feel *verb*
* (*emotionally, physically*)
  to feel [sad | happy | tired …] = [traurig |
  glücklich | müde …] sein
  to feel [young | old | ill …] = sich [jung | alt |
  krank …] fühlen
  she felt a pain = sie spürte einen Schmerz
  I feel hot = mir ist heiß
* (*to the touch*) = fühlen
  to feel [soft | hard | damp …] = sich [weich |
  hart | feucht …] anfühlen
* (*want*)
  to feel like something = Lust auf etwas
  (*accusative*) haben
  I don't feel like it = ich habe keine Lust
  dazu
feel up to
  to feel up to work = sich der Arbeit
  gewachsen fühlen

feeling *noun*
= (das) Gefühl
I have a feeling he's right = ich habe das
Gefühl, dass er Recht hat

female
1 *adjective* = weiblich
2 *noun*
* (*woman*) = (die) Frau
* (*animal*) = (das) Weibchen

feminine
1 *adjective* = weiblich, = feminin
2 *noun*
(*in grammar*) = (das) Femininum

feminist
1 *noun* = (die) Feministin/(der) Feminist
2 *adjective* = feministisch

fence *noun*
= (der) Zaun

fencing *noun*
(*sport*) = (das) Fechten

ferry *noun*
= (die) Fähre

fertile *adjective*
= fruchtbar

festival *noun*
* (*holiday*) = (der) Feiertag
* (*artistic event*) = Festspiele (*plural*)

fetch *verb*
* (*go and get*) = holen
  (*collect*) = abholen
* (*be sold for*) = einbringen
  to fetch a good price = einen guten Preis
  einbringen

✱ in informal situations

few
1 *adjective*
* (*not many*) = wenige
  few people = wenige Leute
* (*several*) **a few** = ein paar
  every few days = alle paar Tage
  the first few weeks = die ersten paar
  Wochen
2 *pronoun* = wenige
  there are so few of them = es gibt nur so
  wenige
  a few of us = ein paar von uns
  quite a few = eine ganze Menge

fiddle *verb*
to fiddle with something = an etwas
(*dative*) fummeln

field *noun*
= (das) Feld

fierce *adjective*
= wild

fifteen *adjective*
= fünfzehn ▶ **Numbers p. 282**

fifth ▶ **Numbers p. 282**, ▶ **Dates p. 213**
1 *adjective* = fünfter/fünfte/fünftes
2 *noun*
(*fraction*) = (das) Fünftel

fifty *adjective*
= fünfzig ▶ **Numbers p. 282**

fight
1 *noun*
* (*battle*) = (der) Kampf
* (*brawl*) = (die) Schlägerei
  (*between children*) = (die) Rauferei
* (*quarrel*) = (der) Streit
2 *verb*
* (*do battle*) = kämpfen
  to fight someone = mit jemandem
  kämpfen
* (*brawl*) = sich schlagen
  (*of children*) = sich raufen
* (*quarrel*) = sich streiten
* (*combat*) **to fight [disease | poverty | a fire …]** =
  [Krankheit | Armut | ein Feuer …] bekämpfen

figure *noun*
* (*number*) = (die) Zahl
* (*person*) = (die) Gestalt
* (*body shape*) = (die) Figur

file
1 *noun*
* (*for documents*) = (die) Akte
* (*in computing*) = (die) Datei
* (*for nails*) = (die) Feile
* (*line*) = (die) Reihe
  in single file = im Gänsemarsch
2 *verb*
* **to file documents** = Akten ablegen
* (*smooth*) = feilen
  to file one's nails = sich (*dative*) die Nägel
  feilen

filing cabinet *noun*
= (der) Aktenschrank

fill verb
- (make full) = füllen
- (become full) = sich füllen

fill in
= ausfüllen

film
1 noun = (der) Film
2 verb = filmen

filthy adjective
= dreckig

final
1 adjective
- (last) = letzter/letzte/letztes
  the final day = der letzte Tag
- (definitive) = endgültig
  her final decision = ihre endgültige
    Entscheidung
  the final result = das Endresultat
2 noun
  (in sport) = (das) Finale

finally adverb
= schließlich

finance
1 noun
- (funds) = Geldmittel (plural)
- (resources) = Finanzen (plural)
2 verb = finanzieren

financial adjective
= finanziell

find verb
= finden

find out
= herausfinden

fine
1 adjective
- (very good) = gut
  I'm fine = mir geht es gut
  to feel fine = sich wohl fühlen
  a fine day = ein schöner Tag
- (delicate) = fein
2 adverb = gut
  they get along fine = sie verstehen sich gut
3 noun = (die) Geldstrafe
4 verb
  to fine someone = jemanden zu einer
    Geldstrafe verurteilen
  he was fined £10 = er musste zehn Pfund
    Strafe bezahlen

finger noun
= (der) Finger

fingernail noun
= (der) Fingernagel

finish
1 verb
- (end) = beenden
- (eat up food, meal) = aufessen
  (drink up) = austrinken
  (use up) = aufbrauchen
- (complete)
  to finish doing something = etwas zu Ende
    tun
  she finished (reading) the book = sie las
    das Buch zu Ende
- **to be finished with something** = mit etwas
    fertig sein
  have you finished your work? = bist du mit
    der Arbeit fertig?
- (come to an end) = aufhören
  (of a performance, meeting) = zu Ende sein
2 noun
- = (der) Schluss
- (finishing line) = (das) Ziel

Finland noun
= (das) Finnland ▶Countries p. 208

fir noun
= (die) Tanne

fire
1 noun = (das) Feuer
  to be on fire = brennen
  to catch fire = Feuer fangen
  to light a fire = das Feuer anmachen
  to set fire to a house = ein Haus in Brand
    stecken
2 verb
- (shoot)
  to fire at someone = auf jemanden
    schießen
  to fire a gun = ein Gewehr abfeuern
- (dismiss) = feuern✗

fire brigade noun
= (die) Feuerwehr

fire engine noun
= (das) Feuerwehrauto

fire extinguisher noun
= (der) Feuerlöscher

fireman noun
= (der) Feuerwehrmann

fireplace noun
= (der) Kamin

fire station noun
= (die) Feuerwache

firework noun
= (der) Feuerwerkskörper

fireworks display noun
= (das) Feuerwerk

firm
1 noun = (die) Firma
2 adjective
- (hard) = fest
- (strict) = streng

first ▶Numbers p. 282, ▶Dates p. 213
1 adjective = erster/erste/erstes
  for the first time = zum ersten Mal
  at first sight = auf den ersten Blick
2 adverb
- (before others, to begin with) = zuerst
  who saw him first? = wer hat ihn zuerst
    gesehen?

• (*for the first time*) = zum ersten Mal
I first met him in Berlin = ich traf ihn zum ersten Mal in Berlin
at first = zuerst
3 *noun*
• **the first** = der/die/das Erste
she was the first to arrive = sie kam als Erste an
Elizabeth the First = Elisabeth die Erste
• (*in dates*)
it's the first today = heute ist der Erste

first aid *noun*
= (die) erste Hilfe

first class
1 *adjective* = erstklassig
a first-class ticket = eine Fahrkarte erster Klasse
a first-class stamp = eine Briefmarke für bevorzugt beförderte Post
2 *adverb*
he travels first class = er reist erster Klasse

first floor *noun*
• (*British*) = (der) erste Stock
• (*US*) = (das) Erdgeschoss

firstly *adverb*
= zuerst

first name *noun*
= (der) Vorname

fish
1 *noun* = (der) Fisch
2 *verb*
(*with a net*) = fischen
(*with a rod*) = angeln

fisherman *noun*
= (der) Fischer

fishing *noun*
= (die) Fischerei

fishing rod *noun*
= (die) Angel

fist *noun*
= (die) Faust

fit
1 *adjective*
• (*suitable*) = geeignet
fit to eat = essbar
the house is not fit to live in = das Haus ist nicht bewohnbar
• (*healthy*) = gesund, = fit✘
to keep fit = fit bleiben
2 *noun* = (der) Anfall
a coughing fit = ein Hustenanfall
3 *verb*
• (*be the right size*) = passen
these shoes don't fit me = diese Schuhe passen mir nicht
• (*install*) = einbauen
to fit a carpet = einen Teppich legen

• (*match*) = zutreffen auf (+ *accusative*)
fit in
• (*in a room or car*) = hineinpassen, = reinpassen✘
• (*adapt*) = sich einfügen
to fit in with a group = sich in eine Gruppe einfügen

fitted kitchen *noun*
= (die) Einbauküche

five *adjective*
= fünf ▶ **Numbers p. 282**

fix *verb*
• (*repair*) = reparieren
• (*establish*) = festlegen
to fix a [date | price ...] = [einen Termin | einen Preis ...] festlegen
• (*prepare*) = machen
to fix someone a meal = jemandem etwas zu essen machen

fizzy *adjective*
= kohlensäurehaltig

flag *noun*
= (die) Fahne

flame *noun*
= (die) Flamme

flannel *noun* (*British*)
= (der) Waschlappen

flash
1 *noun* = (der) Blitz
a flash of lightning = ein Blitz
2 *verb*
his eyes flashed = seine Augen blitzten
the light flashed all the time = das Licht blinkte die ganze Zeit
to flash a warning = zur Warnung blinken

flask *noun*
(*vacuum flask*) = (die) Thermosflasche®

flat
1 *adjective*
• (*not curved*) = flach
(*of a surface*) = eben
• (*of a tyre*) = platt
to have a flat tyre = eine Reifenpanne haben
2 *noun* (*British*) = (die) Wohnung

flatter *verb*
= schmeicheln (+ *dative*)

flavor (*US*), **flavour** (*British*)
1 *noun* = (der) Geschmack
2 *verb* = abschmecken

flaw *noun*
= (der) Fehler

flea *noun*
= (der) Floh

fleet *noun*
= (die) Flotte

✘ in informal situations

flesh *noun*
= (das) Fleisch

flexible *adjective*
- (*bendable*) = biegsam
- (*adaptable*) = flexibel

flicker *verb*
= flackern

flight *noun*
= (der) Flug

float *verb*
- (*on water*) = treiben (**!** *sein*)
  (*of a person*) = sich treiben lassen
- (*in the air*) = schweben (**!** *sein*)

flock *noun*
- (*of sheep*) = (die) Herde
- (*of birds*) = (der) Schwarm

flood
1 *noun*
= (die) Überschwemmung
2 *verb*
- (*overflow*) = über die Ufer treten (**!** *sein*)
  the river floods every spring = der Fluss
    tritt jeden Frühling über die Ufer
- (*fill with water*) = überschwemmen
  the houses were flooded = die Häuser
    wurden überschwemmt

floor *noun*
- (*ground*) = (der) Boden
- (*storey*) = (der) Stock

floorboard *noun*
= (die) Diele

floppy disk *noun*
= (die) Diskette

florist *noun*
= (der) Blumenhändler/(die)
  Blumenhändlerin ▶**Professions p. 298**

flour *noun*
= (das) Mehl

flow *verb*
= fließen (**!** *sein*)

flower
1 *noun* = (die) Blume
2 *verb* = blühen

flu *noun*
= (die) Grippe
to have flu = die Grippe haben

fluent *adjective*
= fließend
she speaks fluent German = sie spricht
  fließend Deutsch

fluff *noun*
= Fusseln (*plural*)

fluid
1 *noun* = (die) Flüssigkeit
2 *adjective* = flüssig

flush
1 *noun*
(*on the face*) = (das) Erröten
2 *verb*
(*wash away*) = spülen

flute *noun*
= (die) Flöte

fly
1 *verb*
- (*of a pilot*) = fliegen
  to fly a plane = ein Flugzeug fliegen
  to fly a kite = einen Drachen steigen lassen
- (*of a bird, plane*) = fliegen (**!** *sein*)
  I flew Lufthansa = ich bin mit Lufthansa
    geflogen
- (*of a flag*) = wehen
  to fly the German flag = die deutsche Fahne
    führen
2 *noun* = (die) Fliege

foam *noun*
- (*on sea, drink*) = (der) Schaum
- (*rubber or plastic material*) =
  (der) Schaumstoff

focus
1 *noun*
- (*in photography*)
  in focus = scharf
- (*centre*) = (der) Brennpunkt
  to be the focus of attention = im
    Brennpunkt des Interesses stehen
2 *verb*
- **to focus a camera on something** = eine
  Kamera scharf auf etwas (*accusative*)
  einstellen
- (*concentrate*) = sich konzentrieren

fog *noun*
= (der) Nebel

foggy *adjective*
= neblig

fold
1 *verb* = falten
he folded his arms = er verschränkte die
  Arme
2 *noun*
- (*in fabric, skin*) = (die) Falte
- (*in paper*) = (der) Kniff
fold up
= zusammenfalten
to fold up a chair = einen Stuhl
  zusammenklappen

follow *verb*
= folgen (+ *dative*) (**!** *sein*)
she followed him into the room = sie folgte
  ihm ins Zimmer
as follows = wie folgt

follower *noun*
= (der) Anhänger/(die) Anhängerin

following
1 *adjective* = folgend
2 *preposition* = nach (+ *dative*)
following the accident = nach dem Unfall**

F

fond adjective
  to be fond of someone = jemanden gern
    haben

food noun
• = (das) Essen
  to buy food = Lebensmittel einkaufen
• (for animals) = (das) Futter

fool
1 noun = (der) Dummkopf
2 verb
  to fool someone = jemanden täuschen
fool around
  = herumalbern

foot noun
  = (der) Fuß
  on foot = zu Fuß

football noun
• (soccer, ball) = (der) Fußball
• (American football) = (der) Football

footballer noun
  = (der) Fußballspieler/(die) Fußballspielerin

footpath noun
  = (der) Fußweg

footprint noun
  = (der) Fußabdruck

footstep noun
  = (der) Schritt

for preposition
• = für (+ accusative)
  to work for a firm = bei einer Firma
    arbeiten
  to go for a swim = schwimmen gehen
    (**!** sein)
  to go for a walk = spazieren gehen (**!** sein)
  something for [a cough | a cold | a headache] =
    etwas gegen [Husten | Schnupfen |
    Kopfschmerzen]
  he is for nuclear power = er ist für
    Kernenergie
  to ask for help = um Hilfe bitten
  for this reason = aus diesem Grund
• (in time expressions) = seit (+ dative)
  she has lived here for 8 years = sie wohnt
    seit acht Jahren hier
  I've been waiting for 3 hours = ich habe
    drei Stunden lang gewartet
  for hours = stundenlang
  he will be in Paris for a year = er bleibt ein
    Jahr in Paris
• (indicating distance)
  we drove for 80 kilometres = wir fuhren
    achtzig Kilometer
  for kilometres = kilometerweit
• (indicating cost or an amount)
  he bought it for £10 = er hat es für zehn
    Pfund gekauft
  a cheque for £20 = ein Scheck über
    zwanzig Pfund
  for nothing = umsonst

• (representing)
  T for Tom = T wie Tom
  what is the French for cat? = wie heißt
    Katze auf Französisch?
• (on the occasion of) = zu (+ dative)
  I got a book for my birthday = ich habe ein
    Buch zu meinem Geburtstag bekommen
  what's for lunch? = was gibts zum
    Mittagessen?
  what for? = wozu?

forbid verb
  = verbieten
  to forbid someone to do something =
    jemandem verbieten, etwas zu tun

force
1 noun
• (power) = (die) Kraft
• (violence) = (die) Gewalt
  the police force = die Polizei
  the (**armed**) **forces** = die Streitkräfte
• (of a law)
  to be in force = gültig sein
  to come into force = in Kraft treten (**!** sein)
2 verb = zwingen
force open
  = aufbrechen

forecast
1 noun = (die) Voraussage
  (weather report) = (die) Vorhersage
2 verb = voraussagen
  to forecast rain = Regen vorhersagen

forehead noun
  = (die) Stirn

foreign adjective
  = ausländisch
  foreign countries = fremde Länder
  a foreign language = eine Fremdsprache

foreigner noun
  = (der) Ausländer/(die) Ausländerin

Foreign Secretary noun (British)
  = (der) Außenminister/(die) Außenministerin

forest noun
  = (der) Wald

forever adverb
• (for all time) = ewig
• (continually) = ständig
  he is forever complaining = er beklagt sich
    ständig

forge verb
  = fälschen

forgery noun
  = (die) Fälschung

forget verb
  = vergessen
  to forget about something = etwas
    vergessen
  he forgot to do the shopping = er hat
    vergessen einzukaufen

forgive *verb*
= verzeihen (+ *dative*)
he forgave her for lying to him = er hat ihr verziehen, dass sie ihn angelogen hatte

fork *noun*
= (die) Gabel

form
1 *noun*
• (*type, shape, mood*) = (die) Form
  a form of life = eine Lebensform
  to be in good form = gut in Form sein
  off form = nicht in Form
• (*document*) = (das) Formular
  to fill in a form = ein Formular ausfüllen
• (*British: class in school*) = (die) Klasse
2 *verb*
• (*develop*) = bilden
  to form a circle = einen Kreis bilden
  to form an opinion = sich (*dative*) ein Urteil bilden
  to form an impression = einen Eindruck gewinnen
• (*be formed*) = sich bilden
  bubbles form on the surface = Blasen bilden sich auf der Oberfläche

formal *adjective*
• (*official*) = formell
• (*of manner, clothes, language*) = förmlich
• (*festive*) = feierlich

former *adjective*
• (*previous*) = ehemalig
  the former minister = der ehemalige Minister
  in former times = früher
• (*first of two*)
  the former = der/die/das Erstere

fortnight *noun*
= vierzehn Tage (*plural*)

fortnightly *adverb*
= alle vierzehn Tage

fortunate *adjective*
= glücklich
to be fortunate = Glück haben

fortunately *adverb*
= glücklicherweise

fortune *noun*
• (*wealth*) = (das) Vermögen
• (*luck*) = (das) Glück

fortune-teller *noun*
= (die) Wahrsagerin

forty *adjective*
= vierzig ▶ **Numbers p. 282**

forward
1 *adverb*
• (*in the direction faced*) = vorwärts
• (*to the front*) = nach vorn
2 *adjective*
• (*at the front*) = vorderer/vordere/vorderes
• (*cheeky*) = frech

3 *verb* = nachsenden
  to forward a letter = einen Brief nachsenden
4 *noun*
  (*in sport*) = (der) Stürmer

fossil *noun*
= (das) Fossil

foundation *noun*
• (*basis*) = (die) Grundlage
• (*cosmetics*) = (das) Make-up
• **foundations** (*of a building*) = (das) Fundament

fountain *noun*
= (der) Brunnen

four *adjective*
= vier ▶ **Numbers p. 282**

fourteen *adjective*
= vierzehn ▶ **Numbers p. 282**

fourth ▶ **Numbers p. 282**, ▶ **Dates p. 213**
1 *adjective* = vierter/vierte/viertes
2 *noun* (*fraction*) = (das) Viertel

fox *noun*
= (der) Fuchs

fraction *noun*
• (*in maths*) = (der) Bruch
• (*small amount*) = (der) Bruchteil

fracture
1 *noun* = (der) Bruch
2 *verb* = brechen

fragile *adjective*
= zerbrechlich

frame
1 *noun*
• (*of a picture, window*) = (der) Rahmen
• (*of spectacles*) = (das) Gestell
2 *verb* = einrahmen

France *noun*
= (das) Frankreich ▶ **Countries p. 208**

frank *adjective*
= offen

fraud *noun*
= (der) Betrug

freckle *noun*
= (die) Sommersprosse

free
1 *adjective*
• (*at liberty, available*) = frei
  to set a prisoner free = einen Gefangenen freilassen
  he is free to do what he wants = er kann tun, was er will
  is this seat free? = ist dieser Platz frei?
  are you free on Monday? = bist du am Montag frei?
• (*without charge*) = kostenlos
2 *adverb*
• (*without charge*) = umsonst

students get their meals free = Studenten bekommen das Essen umsonst
- (*without restriction*) = frei

freedom *noun*
= (die) Freiheit

freeze *verb*
- (*become covered with ice*) = zufrieren (**!** *sein*)
  the lake was frozen = der See war zugefroren
- (*of food, liquid*) = gefrieren (**!** *sein*)
- (*preserve food*) = einfrieren
- (*feel cold*) = sehr frieren
  I'm freezing = ich friere sehr
- (*fix at a certain level*) = einfrieren
  to freeze prices = Preise einfrieren

freezer *noun*
- (*deep freeze*) = (der) Gefrierschrank
- (*part of a fridge*) = (das) Gefrierfach

freezing *adjective*
= eiskalt

French
1 *noun*
- (*people*) the French = die Franzosen
- (*language*) = (das) Französisch
2 *adjective* = französisch ▶**Countries p. 208**

French fries *noun*
= Pommes frites (*plural*)

Frenchman *noun*
= (der) Franzose

Frenchwoman *noun*
= (die) Französin

frequently *adverb*
= häufig

fresh *adjective*
= frisch

Friday *noun*
= (der) Freitag ▶**Dates p. 213**

fridge *noun*
= (der) Kühlschrank

friend *noun*
= (der) Freund/(die) Freundin
  to be friends with someone = mit jemandem befreundet sein
  he made friends with her = er hat sich mit ihr befreundet

friendly *adjective*
= freundlich
  to be friendly with someone = mit jemandem befreundet sein

friendship *noun*
= (die) Freundschaft

fright *noun*
= (der) Schreck
  to give someone a fright = jemanden erschrecken

frighten *verb*
- (*scare*) = Angst machen (+ *dative*)
- (*startle*) = erschrecken

frightened *adjective*
  to be frightened = Angst haben
  she is frightened of dogs = sie hat Angst vor Hunden

frightening *adjective*
= beängstigend

fringe *noun*
(*hairstyle*) = (der) Pony

frog *noun*
= (der) Frosch

from *preposition*
- (*indicating a starting place*) = von (+ *dative*)
  the journey from London to Munich = die Reise von London nach München
  we live ten minutes from the city centre = wir wohnen zehn Minuten vom Stadtzentrum
  ! Note the contraction vom = von dem.
- (*indicating place of origin*) = aus (+ *dative*)
  he comes from Germany = er kommt aus Deutschland
  the train from Berlin = der Zug aus Berlin
  where is he from? = woher kommt er?
- (*referring to time*) = von (+ *dative*)
  the shop is open from 8 to 12 = das Geschäft hat von acht bis zwölf offen
  from Sunday on = ab Sonntag
  from then on = von da an
  from that day = seit dem Tag
- (*according to*) = nach (+ *dative*)
  from his description = nach seiner Beschreibung
  from what she said = nach dem, was sie sagte
- (*ranging*)
  there were from 20 to 30 people there = es waren zwischen zwanzig und dreißig Leute da
- different from = anders als

front
1 *noun*
- (*exterior*) = (die) Vorderseite
- (*of a house*) = (die) Vorderfront
- (*of a jacket, building*) = (das) Vorderteil
- (*of a train, queue*) = (das) vordere Ende
- at the front = vorne
  in *or* at the front of = vorne in (+ *dative*)
  to sit at the front = vorne sitzen
2 *adjective* = vorderer/vordere/vorderes
  the front wheel = das Vorderrad
  in front of = vor (+ *dative or accusative*)
  ! Note that vor is followed by a noun in the dative when position is described. The accusative follows when there is movement towards something.

front door *noun*
= (die) Haustür

frontier *noun*
= (die) Grenze

front page *noun*
= (die) Titelseite

front seat noun
= (der) Vordersitz

frost noun
= (der) Frost

frosty adjective
= frostig

frown verb
= die Stirn runzeln

frozen adjective
• (very cold) = gefroren
I'm frozen = mir ist eiskalt
• (of food) = tiefgekühlt
frozen food = (die) Tiefkühlkost

fruit noun
• (a single fruit or type) = (die) Frucht
• (collectively) = (das) Obst

frustrating adjective
= frustrierend

fry verb
= braten

frying pan (British), **frypan** (US) noun
= (die) Bratpfanne

fuel noun
• (for a car) = (der) Kraftstoff
• (for heating) = (der) Brennstoff

fulfil (British), **fulfill** (US) verb
= erfüllen
to fulfil an ambition = eine Ambition
verwirklichen

full adjective
= voll
at full speed = in voller Fahrt
full of = voller (+ genitive)
the streets were full of people = die
Straßen waren voller Menschen

full board noun
= (die) Vollpension

full moon noun
= (der) Vollmond

full stop noun
= (der) Punkt

fumes noun
= Dämpfe (plural)
(from cars) = Abgase (plural)

fun noun
= (der) Spaß
dancing is fun = Tanzen macht Spaß
for fun = aus Spaß
to have fun = sich amüsieren

function
1 noun
• (purpose) = (die) Funktion
• (reception) = (die) Veranstaltung
2 verb = funktionieren

funeral noun
= (die) Beerdigung

funny adjective
• (amusing) = lustig
• (odd) = komisch
it's funny that he hasn't phoned = es ist
komisch, dass er nicht angerufen hat

fur
1 noun
• (on an animal) = (das) Fell
• (on a coat) = (der) Pelz
2 adjective = Pelz-
a fur coat = ein Pelzmantel

furious adjective
= wütend

furnish verb
(with furniture) = einrichten
a furnished flat = eine möblierte Wohnung

furniture noun
= Möbel (plural)
a piece of furniture = ein Möbelstück

further
1 adverb = weiter
it was further than I thought = es war
weiter als ich dachte
further off = weiter entfernt
2 adjective
• (more distant) = weiter entfernt
at the further end of the street = am
anderen Ende der Straße
• (additional) = weiterer/weitere/weiteres
a further 50 people = weitere fünfzig Leute
3 verb = fördern
to further one's career = seine Karriere
fördern

fuss
1 noun = (das) Theater
to make a fuss about something = viel
Theater um etwas machen
2 verb
(worry) = sich aufregen
to fuss over someone = jemanden
bemuttern

future
1 noun = (die) Zukunft
in future = in Zukunft
2 adjective = zukünftig
his future wife = seine zukünftige Frau
at a future date = zu einem späteren
Zeitpunkt

Gg

gale noun
= (der) Sturm

gallery noun
= (die) Galerie

game *noun*
= (das) Spiel
to have a game of football = Fußball
  spielen
to play a game of chess with someone =
  eine Partie Schach mit jemandem spielen
games (*at school*) = (der) Sport

gang *noun*
• (*group of friends*) = (die) Clique
• (*group of criminals*) = (die) Bande

gap *noun*
• (*space*) = (die) Lücke
• (*period of time*) = (die) Pause
• (*difference*) = (der) Unterschied
  a big age gap = ein großer
  Altersunterschied

garage *noun*
• (*for keeping cars*) = (die) Garage
• (*for repairing cars*) = (die) Autowerkstatt
• (*petrol station*) = (die) Tankstelle

garbage *noun* (*US*)
= (der) Müll

garden *noun*
= (der) Garten

gardener *noun*
= (der) Gärtner/(die) Gärtnerin

gardening *noun*
= (die) Gartenarbeit

garlic *noun*
= (der) Knoblauch

garment *noun*
= (das) Kleidungsstück

gas *noun*
• (*fuel*) = (das) Gas
  to use gas for cooking = mit Gas kochen
• (*US: petrol*) = (das) Benzin

gasoline *noun* (*US*)
= (das) Benzin

gas station *noun* (*US*)
= (die) Tankstelle

gate *noun*
• (*entrance*) = (das) Tor
• (*in an airport*) = (der) Flugsteig

gather *verb*
• (*collect*) = sammeln
• (*come together*) = sich versammeln
  people gathered in the park = die Leute
  versammelten sich im Park

gay *adjective*
• (*happy*) = fröhlich
• (*homosexual*) = schwul✘

GCSE *noun* (*British*)
≈ (die) Abschlussprüfung

✘ in informal situations

gear *noun*
• (*in a car, on a bike*) = (der) Gang
  to change gear = schalten
  is the car in gear? = ist der Gang eingelegt?
• (*equipment*) = (die) Ausrüstung
• (*clothing*) = Sachen (*plural*), = (das) Zeug✘

Gemini *noun*
= Zwillinge (*plural*)

general
1 *noun* = (der) General
2 *adjective* = allgemein
  in general = im Allgemeinen

generation *noun*
= (die) Generation

generous *adjective*
= großzügig

genetics *noun*
= (die) Genetik

Geneva *noun*
= (das) Genf ▶Countries p. 208
Lake Geneva = der Genfer See

genius *noun*
= (das) Genie

gentle *adjective*
= sanft

gentleman *noun*
= (der) Herr

genuine *adjective*
= echt
  is that a genuine Picasso? = ist das ein
  echter Picasso?

geography *noun*
= (die) Geographie, = (die) Erdkunde

German
1 *noun*
• (*person*) = (der) Deutsche/(die) Deutsche
  the Germans = die Deutschen
• (*language*) = (das) Deutsch
  I am learning German = ich lerne Deutsch
  in German = auf Deutsch
2 *adjective* = deutsch ▶Countries p. 208

Germany *noun*
= (das) Deutschland ▶Countries p. 208

get *verb*

  ! Note that get is a very common word in
  English and does not have a multi-
  purpose German equivalent. This entry
  covers most frequent uses, but to find
  translations for other expressions, such
  as get well, get in shape, etc, look up well,
  shape, etc.

• (*become*) = werden (**!** sein)
  to get [old | wet | rich …] = [alt | nass | reich …]
  werden
• (*ask or persuade*)
  to get someone to do something =
  jemanden dazu bringen, etwas zu tun

- (*cause to be done or happen*)
 to get something done = etwas machen lassen
 to get one's hair cut = sich (*dative*) die Haare schneiden lassen
 to get dressed = sich anziehen
 to get to know someone = jemanden kennen lernen
- (*arrive*) = ankommen (**!** *sein*)
 I'll let you know when we get there = ich sage dir Bescheid, wenn wir ankommen
- (*obtain, receive*) = bekommen, = kriegen✱
 to get a present from someone = ein Geschenk von jemandem bekommen
 to get a shock = einen Schreck kriegen✱
 to get a good mark = eine gute Note kriegen✱
- (*procure*) = besorgen
 they can get you a car = sie können euch ein Auto besorgen
- (*buy*) = kaufen
- (*fetch*) = holen
 he's gone to get help = er holt Hilfe
 to get someone from the station = jemanden vom Bahnhof abholen
- (*prepare*) = machen
 to get breakfast = Frühstück machen
- (*have illness*) = haben
 I've got toothache = ich habe Zahnschmerzen
- (*use for transport*) = nehmen
 to get a taxi to the station = ein Taxi zum Bahnhof nehmen
- (*answer the door or phone*)
 I'll get it (*open the door*) = ich mache auf, (*answer the phone*) = ich gehe ans Telefon
 to get someone (*on the phone*) = jemanden erreichen
- (*start*)
 to get working = sich an die Arbeit machen
 to get talking = ins Gespräch kommen (**!** *sein*)
- (*understand*) = verstehen, = kapieren✱
 I don't get it = ich kapier es nicht✱

 ! For translations of **got to**, see the entry **got**.

get away
- (*leave*) = wegkommen (**!** *sein*)
- (*escape*) = entkommen (+ *dative*) (**!** *sein*)
- (*go unpunished*) = ungestraft davonkommen (**!** *sein*)

get back
- (*return*) = zurückkommen (**!** *sein*)
- (*regain*) = zurückbekommen

get down to
 to get down to something = sich an etwas (*accusative*) machen

get off
- (*leave a bus, train*) = aussteigen (**!** *sein*)
- (*remove*) = entfernen

get on
- (*enter a bus, train*) = einsteigen (**!** *sein*)
- (*have a good relationship*) = sich verstehen
 he gets on well with her = er versteht sich gut mit ihr

- (*progress*) = vorankommen (**!** *sein*)

get out
- (*leave*) = herauskommen (**!** *sein*)
- (*bring out*) = herausbringen
- (*leave a car, train*) = aussteigen (**!** *sein*)

get through
- (*contact by phone*) = durchkommen (**!** *sein*)
 I couldn't get through to her = ich konnte nicht zu ihr durchkommen

get up
 = aufstehen (**!** *sein*)

ghost *noun*
 = (der) Geist

giant *noun*
 = (der) Riese

G

gift *noun*
- (*present*) = (das) Geschenk
- (*talent*) = (die) Begabung
 he has a gift for languages = er ist sprachbegabt

girl *noun*
 = (das) Mädchen

girlfriend *noun*
 = (die) Freundin

give *verb*
- = geben
 to give someone something to eat = jemandem etwas zu essen geben
 to give a speech = einen Vortrag halten
 to give one's name = seinen Namen angeben
- (*donate*) = spenden
- (*give as a gift*) = schenken
 to give someone a present = jemandem etwas schenken
- (*pass on*)
 give him my regards = richten Sie ihm schöne Grüße von mir aus
 to give someone a message = jemandem eine Nachricht hinterlassen
 to give the latest news = das Neueste mitteilen

 ! For translations of phrases such as **to give someone a fright, a hand** or **a lift**, look up the entries **fright, hand** or **lift**.

give away
- (*get rid off*) = weggeben
 (*give as a present*) = verschenken
- (*reveal*) = verraten
 to give away a secret = ein Geheimnis verraten

give back
 = zurückgeben

give in
 = nachgeben
 to give in to someone = jemandem nachgeben

give out
 (*hand out*) = austeilen

give up
- (*stop*) = aufgeben

- (*surrender*) = sich stellen
  to give oneself up to the police = sich der Polizei stellen

give way
  (*British: when driving*) = die Vorfahrt beachten

glad *adjective*
  = froh
  we were glad to see him = wir haben uns gefreut, ihn zu sehen

glass *noun*
  = (das) Glas
  a glass of water = ein Glas Wasser

glasses *noun*
  = (die) Brille
  she wears glasses = sie trägt eine Brille

glitter *verb*
  = glitzern

global warming *noun*
  = (der) globale Temperaturanstieg

globe *noun*
  = (der) Globus

gloomy *adjective*
- (*dark*) = düster
- (*sad*) = pessimistisch

glove *noun*
  = (der) Handschuh

glow
1 *noun*
  = (der) Schein
2 *verb*
  (*of a candle*) = scheinen
  (*of a fire, cheeks*) = glühen

glue
1 *noun* = (der) Klebstoff
2 *verb* = kleben

> **!** *Note that* **kleben** *forms a separable verb with prepositions such as* **an**, **auf** *and* **zusammen**.

  he glued them together = er klebte sie zusammen

go
1 *verb*
- (*on foot*) = gehen (**!** *sein*)
  (*by vehicle, bicycle*) = fahren (**!** *sein*)
  (*by plane*) = fliegen (**!** *sein*)
  to go to [**town** | **the market** | **the beach** | **work** ...] = [in die Stadt | auf den Markt | zum Strand | zur Arbeit ...] gehen
  to go for a [**walk** | **jog** | **sleep** ...] = [spazieren | joggen | schlafen ...] gehen
  we are going to Austria this year = dieses Jahr fahren wir nach Österreich
  to go on holiday = in die Ferien fahren
  to go [**shopping** | **swimming** | **skiing** ...] = [einkaufen | schwimmen | Ski fahren ...] gehen
  where are you going? = wo gehst du hin?
- (*leave*) = weggehen (**!** *sein*)
  (*in a vehicle*) = wegfahren (**!** *sein*)
  (*on a journey*) = abfahren (**!** *sein*)
- (*when talking about time*) = vergehen (**!** *sein*)
  time goes very slowly = die Zeit vergeht sehr langsam
- (*disappear*) = verschwinden (**!** *sein*), = weg sein✖
  my bike's gone = mein Rad ist weg✖
- (*belong*) = gehören
  the chair goes in the corner = der Stuhl gehört in die Ecke
- (*function*) = laufen (**!** *sein*)
  (*of a watch, clock*) = gehen (**!** *sein*)
  to get something going = etwas in Gang bringen
- (*in polite inquiries*) = gehen (**!** *sein*)
  how's it going? = wie gehts?
- (*become*) = werden (**!** *sein*)
  to go red = rot werden
- (*expressing the future*)
  to be going to do something = etwas tun werden
  I am going to [**leave London** | **learn to drive** | **phone you** ...] = ich werde [London verlassen | fahren lernen | dich anrufen ...]
- (*make a sound or signal*) = losgehen (**!** *sein*)
- (*US: take away*) **to go** = zum Mitnehmen
  one pizza to go = eine Pizza zum Mitnehmen

2 *noun*
- (*turn*)
  whose go is it? = wer ist dran?✖
- (*try*) = (der) Versuch
  have another go! = versuch es nochmal!
  to have a go at doing something = versuchen, etwas zu tun

go ahead
  (*take place*) = stattfinden

go away
  = weggehen (**!** *sein*)
  (*on a journey*) = wegfahren (**!** *sein*)

go back
  = zurückgehen (**!** *sein*)
  go back to sleep = wieder einschlafen (**!** *sein*)
  (*drive back*) = zurückfahren (**!** *sein*)

go down
- (*drop*) = fallen (**!** *sein*)
  the prices have gone down = die Preise sind gefallen
- (*come down*) = hinuntergehen (**!** *sein*)
  (*drive down*) = hinunterfahren (**!** *sein*)
- (*sink*) = untergehen (**!** *sein*)

go in
  (*enter*) = hineingehen (**!** *sein*)
  (*drive in*) = hineinfahren (**!** *sein*)

go off
- (*British: lose interest in*) = nicht mehr mögen
- (*of a gun or alarm*) = losgehen (**!** *sein*)
- (*leave*) = weggehen (**!** *sein*)
  (*drive off*) = wegfahren (**!** *sein*)

✖ in informal situations

- (*go bad*) = schlecht werden (**!** *sein*)
- (*switch off*) = ausgehen (**!** *sein*)

go on
- (*continue*) = weitermachen
  to go on [talking | working | reading ...] = weiter [reden | arbeiten | lesen ...]
- (*happen*) = los sein
  what's going on? = was ist los?
- (*switch on*) = angehen (**!** *sein*)

go out
- (*leave*) = hinausgehen (**!** *sein*)
- (*have an evening out*) = ausgehen (**!** *sein*)
  to go out for a meal = essen gehen (**!** *sein*)
- (*switch off, stop burning*) = ausgehen (**!** *sein*)

go over
(*check*) = überprüfen

go through
- (*search*) = durchsuchen
- (*suffer*) = durchmachen
- (*check*) = durchgehen (**!** *sein*)
- **to go through a lot of money** = viel Geld ausgeben

go up
- (*by stairs*) = hinaufgehen (**!** *sein*)
  (*by lift*) = hochfahren (**!** *sein*)
- (*increase*) = steigen (**!** *sein*)

go with
(*match*) = passen zu (+ *dative*)
the jacket doesn't go with the skirt = die Jacke passt nicht zu dem Rock

go without
= verzichten auf (+ *accusative*)

goal *noun*
- (*in football, hockey*) = (das) Tor
  to score a goal = ein Tor schießen
- (*aim*) = (das) Ziel

goalkeeper *noun*
= (der) Torwart

goat *noun*
= (die) Ziege

god *noun*
= (der) Gott

goddaughter *noun*
= (die) Patentochter

goddess *noun*
= (die) Göttin

godfather *noun*
= (der) Pate

godmother *noun*
= (die) Patin

godson *noun*
= (der) Patensohn

gold
1 *noun* = (das) Gold
2 *adjective* = golden

golf *noun*
= (das) Golf

good
1 *adjective*

- = gut
  a good book = ein gutes Buch
  to have a good time = sich amüsieren
  to be good at chemistry = gut in Chemie sein
  to be good at doing something = etwas gut können
  that tastes good = das schmeckt gut
  good morning/night = guten Morgen/gute Nacht
  good afternoon = guten Tag
- (*healthy*) = gesund
  [fruit | fresh air | exercise ...] **is good for you** = [Obst | frische Luft | Bewegung ...] ist gesund
- (*well-behaved*) = artig, = brav
- (*kind*) = nett
  it was very good of you = es war sehr nett von Ihnen

2 *noun*
- (*use*) = (der) Nutzen
  it's no good [crying | complaining | shouting ...] = es nützt nichts [zu weinen | sich zu beschweren | zu schreien ...]
- **for good** = für immer

goodbye *interjection*
= auf Wiedersehen
(*on the phone*) = auf Wiederhören

Good Friday *noun*
= (der) Karfreitag

goods *noun*
= Waren (*plural*)

goose *noun*
= (die) Gans

gooseberry *noun*
= (die) Stachelbeere

gorilla *noun*
= (der) Gorilla

gossip
1 *noun* = (der) Klatsch
2 *verb* = klatschen

got *verb*
▶ get
- **to have got** = haben
  I've got a lot of work = ich habe viel Arbeit
- **to have got to** = müssen
  I have got to [go | work | get dressed ...] = ich muss [gehen | arbeiten | mich anziehen ...]

government *noun*
= (die) Regierung

graceful *adjective*
= graziös

grade *noun*
- (*quality*) = (die) Klasse
- (*mark*) = (die) Note
  to get good grades = gute Noten bekommen
- (*US: class*) = (die) Klasse

grade school *noun* (*US*)
= (die) Grundschule

G

gradually *adverb*
= allmählich

gram *noun*
= (das) Gramm ▶**Measures p. 270**
100 grams of butter = hundert Gramm
Butter

grammar *noun*
= (die) Grammatik

grandchild *noun*
= (das) Enkelkind

granddaughter *noun*
= (die) Enkelin

grandfather *noun*
= (der) Großvater

grandmother *noun*
= (die) Großmutter

grandparents *noun*
= Großeltern (*plural*)

grandson *noun*
= (der) Enkel

grape *noun*
= (die) Traube

grapefruit *noun*
= (die) Grapefruit, = (die) Pampelmuse

grass *noun*
* = (das) Gras
* (*lawn*) = (der) Rasen
  to cut the grass = den Rasen mähen

grasshopper *noun*
= (die) Heuschrecke

grateful *adjective*
= dankbar
to be grateful to someone = jemandem
dankbar sein
I'd be very grateful to you = ich wäre Ihnen
sehr dankbar

grave *noun* = (das) Grab

graveyard *noun*
= (der) Friedhof

gray (*US*) ▶grey

grease *noun*
* (*for a machine*) = (das) Schmierfett
* (*animal fat*) = (das) Fett

greasy *adjective*
= fettig

great *adjective*
* (*of size, importance*) = groß
  to have a great advantage = einen großen
  Vorteil haben
  to have a great deal of free time = viel
  Freizeit haben
* (*when showing enthusiasm*) = großartig, =
  prima✻

Great Britain *noun*
= (das) Großbritannien ▶**Countries p. 208**

great-grandfather *noun*
= (der) Urgroßvater

great-grandmother *noun*
= (die) Urgroßmutter

Greece *noun*
= (das) Griechenland ▶**Countries p. 208**

greedy *adjective*
= gierig

Greek
1 *noun*
* (*person*) = (der) Grieche/(die) Griechin
* (*language*) = (das) Griechisch
2 *adjective* = griechisch ▶**Countries p. 208**

green *adjective*
= grün ▶**Colours p. 204**

greenhouse *noun*
= (das) Gewächshaus

greenhouse effect *noun*
= (der) Treibhauseffekt

grey *adjective* (*British*)
= grau ▶**Colours p. 204**
to go grey = grau werden (**!** *sein*)

greyhound *noun*
= (der) Windhund

grill
1 *noun* = (der) Grill
2 *verb* = grillen

grin *verb*
= grinsen
to grin at someone = jemanden angrinsen

groan *verb*
* (*in pain*) = stöhnen
* (*when annoyed*) = sich beklagen

grocer *noun*
= (der) Lebensmittelhändler ▶**Professions
p. 298**

groceries *noun*
= Lebensmittel (*plural*)

ground *noun*
* (*soil, surface, terrain*) = (der) Boden
* (*special area*) = (das) Gelände
  sports ground = (der) Sportplatz
* (*position in a contest, debate*) = (der) Boden
  to gain ground = Boden gewinnen
* (*US: electricity*) = (die) Erde

ground floor *noun* (*British*)
= (das) Erdgeschoss

grounds *noun*
* (*part of property*) = Anlagen (*plural*)
* (*reason*) = (der) Grund
  to have grounds for something = einen
  Grund für etwas (*accusative*) haben
  to have no grounds for complaint = keinen
  Grund zur Klage haben
  to have grounds for divorce = einen
  Scheidungsgrund haben

✻ in informal situations

group *noun*
= (die) Gruppe

grow *verb*
• (*get bigger*) = wachsen (**!** *sein*)
  the population is still growing = die Bevölkerung wächst noch
  to grow a beard = sich (*dative*) einen Bart wachsen lassen
• (*cultivate*) = anbauen
  to grow vegetables = Gemüse anbauen
• (*become*) = werden (**!** *sein*)
  to grow old = alt werden
grow up
= erwachsen werden (**!** *sein*)
  he grew up in London = er ist in London aufgewachsen

grumble *verb*
= murren

grumpy *adjective*
= grantig

guarantee
1 *verb* = garantieren
  to guarantee a watch for a year = ein Jahr Garantie auf eine Uhr geben
2 *noun* = (die) Garantie

guard
1 *verb*
• (*watch over*) = bewachen
  the dog guards the house = der Hund bewacht das Haus
• (**protect**) = beschützen
2 *noun*
• (*in a prison*) = (der) Wärter/(die) Wärterin
• (*in a bank, building*) = (der) Wächter
• (*in the army*) = (die) Wache
  to be on guard = Wache stehen

guard dog *noun*
= (der) Wachhund

guess *verb*
• = raten
• (*guess correctly*) = erraten
  I guessed right = ich habe es richtig erraten
• (*suppose*) = glauben
  I guess so = ich glaube schon

guest *noun*
= (der) Gast

guesthouse *noun*
= (die) Pension

guide
1 *noun*
• (*person*) = (der) Führer/(die) Führerin
  (*for tourists*) = (der) Fremdenführer/(die) Fremdenführerin
• (*book*) = (der) Reiseführer
• (*indicator*) = (der) Anhaltspunkt
2 *verb* = führen

guidebook *noun*
= (der) Reiseführer

guide dog *noun*
= (der) Blindenhund

guidelines *noun*
= Richtlinien (*plural*)

guilt *noun*
= (die) Schuld

guilty *adjective*
• = schuldig
  to be guilty of murder = des Mordes schuldig sein
  to feel guilty about something = ein schlechtes Gewissen wegen etwas (*genitive*) haben
• (*prompted by guilt*) = schuldbewusst

guitar *noun*
= (die) Gitarre

gulf *noun*
= (der) Golf

gum *noun*
(*in the mouth*) = (das) Zahnfleisch

gun *noun*
• (*rifle*) = (das) Gewehr
• (*pistol*) = (die) Pistole

gutter *noun*
• (*beside a road*) = (der) Rinnstein
• (*on a roof*) = (die) Regenrinne

gym *noun*
• (*gymnasium*) = (die) Turnhalle
• (*school lesson*) = (das) Turnen

gymnasium *noun*
= (die) Turnhalle

gymnastics *noun*
= (die) Gymnastik, = (das) Turnen

gypsy *noun*
= (der) Zigeuner/(die) Zigeunerin

Hh

habit *noun*
= (die) Gewohnheit
(*bad habit*) = (die) Angewohnheit
  to do something out of habit = etwas aus Gewohnheit tun
  to be in the habit of doing something = die Gewohnheit *or* die Angewohnheit haben, etwas zu tun
  to get out of the habit of [watching TV | cooking | reading …] = sich (*dative*) abgewöhnen [fernzusehen | zu kochen | zu lesen …]

hail
1 *noun* = (der) Hagel
2 *verb* = hageln

hair *noun*
(*collectively*) = Haare (*plural*)
(*a single hair*) = (das) Haar

> **!** *A person's* **hair** *is normally translated by the plural* **Haare**.

to wash one's hair = sich (*dative*) die Haare waschen

hairbrush *noun*
= (die) Haarbürste

haircut *noun*
= (der) Haarschnitt
to have a haircut = sich (*dative*) die Haare schneiden lassen

hairdresser *noun*
• (*stylist*) = (der) Friseur/(die) Friseuse
  ▶**Professions p. 298**
• (*salon*) = Friseursalon
  to go to the hairdresser's = zum Friseur gehen (**!** *sein*)

hair-dryer *noun*
= (der) Föhn

hairstyle *noun*
= (die) Frisur

half ▶**Numbers p. 282**
1 *noun*
• (*fraction*) = (die) Hälfte
  half the money = die Hälfte des Geldes
• (*period in a game*) = (die) Spielhälfte
2 *adjective* = halb
  half a litre of milk = ein halber Liter Milch
  two and a half cups = zweieinhalb Tassen
  (at) half price = zum halben Preis
3 *pronoun*
• (*when talking about quantities, numbers*)
  half of his pocket money = die Hälfte von seinem Taschengeld
  you don't listen half the time = du hörst die halbe Zeit nicht zu
• (*when talking about time, age*)
  one and a half hours = anderthalb Stunden
  she is five and a half = sie ist fünfeinhalb

> **!** *When telling the time,* **half past** *is translated by* **halb**, *but in German the half-hour is 'half way to' the next hour.*

half past three = halb vier
4 *adverb* = halb
  half as much = halb so viel

hall *noun*
• (*in a house, flat*) = (der) Flur
• (*in an airport, hotel*) = (die) Halle
• (*for public events*) = (der) Saal

ham *noun*
= (der) Schinken

---

hamburger *noun*
• = (der) Hamburger
• (*US: ground beef*) = (das) Hackfleisch

hammer
1 *noun* = (der) Hammer
2 *verb* = hämmern

hamster *noun*
= (der) Hamster

hand
1 *noun*
• (*part of the body*) = (die) Hand
  to hold someone's hand = jemandem die Hand halten
• (*on a clock*) = (der) Zeiger
• (*other uses*)
  to give someone a hand = jemandem helfen
  on the one hand ..., on the other hand ... = einerseits ..., andererseits ...
  to get out of hand = außer Kontrolle geraten (**!** *sein*)
2 *verb* = reichen
  to hand someone a book = jemandem ein Buch reichen
hand in
  to hand in homework = die Hausaufgaben abgeben
  to hand in an application = einen Antrag einreichen
hand out
= austeilen
hand over
= übergeben

handbag *noun*
= (die) Handtasche

handbrake *noun*
= (die) Handbremse

handicapped *adjective*
= behindert

handkerchief *noun*
= (das) Taschentuch

handle
1 *noun*
• (*on a drawer, bag, cutlery*) = (der) Griff
• (*on a door*) = (die) Klinke
• (*of a cup*) = (der) Henkel
• (*of a broom, saucepan*) = (der) Stiel
2 *verb*
• (*deal with*) = fertig werden mit (+ *dative*) (**!** *sein*)
  to handle a situation = mit einer Situation fertig werden
• (*control*) = handhaben

handlebars *noun*
= (die) Lenkstange

hand luggage *noun*
= (das) Handgepäck

handsome *adjective*
= gut aussehend

handwriting *noun*
= (die) Handschrift

handy *adjective*
• (*of an object*) = praktisch
• (*of a person*) = geschickt
  to have something handy = etwas
    griffbereit haben
  to come in handy = nützlich sein

hang *verb*
• (*attach to a hook, line*) = aufhängen
  to hang a picture on the wall = ein Bild an
    der Wand aufhängen
• (*be attached*) = hängen
• (*kill*) = hängen
hang around
• (*wait*) = warten
  to keep someone hanging around =
    jemanden warten lassen
• (*waste time*) = rumhängen✖
hang on
• (*grasp*) = sich festhalten
  to hang on to something = sich an etwas
    (*dative*) festhalten
• (*wait*) = warten
hang up
• (*put the phone down*) = auflegen
• (*attach to a hook, line*) = aufhängen

hang-gliding *noun*
= (das) Drachenfliegen

hangover *noun*
= (der) Kater✖

happen *verb*
• (*occur*) = passieren (**!** *sein*), = geschehen
  (**!** *sein*)
  when did it happen? = wann ist es passiert?
  what's happening? = was ist los?
• (*by chance*)
  I happened to meet him = ich habe ihn
    zufällig getroffen
  as it happens = zufälligerweise

happy *adjective*
= glücklich
  to be happy with [the new job | her work | one's
    life …] = mit [der neuen Stelle | ihrer Arbeit |
    seinem Leben …] zufrieden sein
  to be happy to do something = gerne etwas
    tun

harbor (*US*), **harbour** (*British*) *noun*
= (der) Hafen

hard
1 *adjective*
• = hart
  to be hard on someone = hart zu
    jemandem sein
• (*difficult*) = schwer
2 *adverb*
  to listen hard = gut zuhören
  to pull hard = kräftig ziehen
  to try hard = sich sehr bemühen
  to rain hard = stark regnen
  it hit him hard = es hat ihn schwer getroffen
  to be hard up = knapp bei Kasse sein

hard-boiled egg *noun*
= (das) hart gekochte Ei

hard disk *noun*
= (die) Festplatte

hardly *adverb*
= kaum

hardware *noun*
• (*for computers*) = (die) Hardware
• (*for use in the home, garden*) =
  Haushaltsgeräte (*plural*)

hardware shop (*British*), **hardware
store** (*US*) *noun*
= (das) Haushaltswarengeschäft

hard-working *adjective*
= fleißig

hare *noun*
= (der) Hase

harm
1 *verb*
• (*injure a person*) = verletzen
  to harm someone = jemanden verletzen
• (*hurt reputation, environment, health*) =
  schaden (+ *dative*)
2 *noun* = (der) Schaden
  there's no harm in asking = es kann nichts
    schaden zu fragen
  no harm done = nichts ist passiert

harmful *adjective*
= schädlich

harmless *adjective*
= unschädlich

harp *noun*
= (die) Harfe

harvest
1 *noun* = (die) Ernte
2 *verb* = ernten

hat *noun*
= (der) Hut

hatch *verb*
• **to hatch eggs** = Eier ausbrüten
• **when will the eggs hatch?** = wann
  schlüpfen die Jungen aus?

hate
1 *verb* = hassen
  I hate having to get up early = ich hasse es,
    früh aufstehen zu müssen
  the two brothers hate each other = die
    beiden Brüder hassen sich
2 *noun* = (der) Hass

hatred *noun*
= (der) Hass

haunted *adjective*
  a haunted castle = ein Spukschloss
  this house is haunted = in diesem Haus
    spukt es

have
1 *verb*
• (*possess*) = haben
  have got = haben
  she has (got) a dog = sie hat einen Hund

H

- (*eat, do*)

> ! The general verb **have** *is usually translated by a more specific German verb.*

  to have a meal = etwas essen
  to have a game of football = Fußball spielen
- (*get*) = bekommen, = kriegen✱
  I had a letter from Bob yesterday = gestern bekam ich einen Brief von Bob
- (*experience, suffer*) = haben
  to have flu = die Grippe haben
  to have a good time = sich amüsieren
- (*get done*)
  to have something done = etwas machen lassen
- **to have to** = müssen
2 *auxiliary verb*
  = haben, (*with some verbs*) = sein

> ! The auxiliary verb *is used to form the perfect tense. Most German verbs form the perfect with* **haben**. *Some take* **sein**, *and these are mainly verbs expressing motion and involving a change of place.*

  I have lost my bag = ich habe meine Tasche verloren
  they have arrived = sie sind angekommen
  you've been there, haven't you? = du warst schon mal dort, nicht?

> ! Note that **nicht** *is only used in this way in spoken German; it is short for* **nicht wahr.**

  to have a [coat | sweater | skirt …] on = einen [Mantel | Pullover | Rock …] anhaben
  he had nothing on = er hatte nichts an

hay *noun*
  = (das) Heu

hazelnut *noun*
  = (die) Haselnuss

he *pronoun*
  = er

head
1 *noun*
- (*part of the body*) = (der) Kopf
  from head to foot = von Kopf bis Fuß
  to have a good head for figures = gut rechnen können
- (*person in charge*) = (der) Leiter/(die) Leiterin
  (*of a firm*) = (der) Chef/(die) Chefin
  the head of state = das Staatsoberhaupt
  the head of a family = das Familienoberhaupt
- (*British: principal*) = (der) Direktor/(die) Direktorin
- (*top part of a table, bed*) = (das) Kopfende
- (*when counting*) (*person*) = (der) Kopf
  £10 per head = zehn Pfund pro Kopf
  (*animal*) = (das) Stück

✱ in informal situations

2 *verb*
- (*be in charge of*) = leiten
- (*be bound*)
  to head for = zusteuern auf (+ *accusative*) (! *sein*)
  to head (off) home = nach Hause fahren (! *sein*)
- (*in football*) = köpfen

headache *noun*
  = Kopfschmerzen (*plural*)
  I've got a headache = ich habe Kopfschmerzen

headlamp, headlight *noun*
  = (der) Scheinwerfer

headline *noun*
  = (die) Schlagzeile

headphones *noun*
  = (der) Kopfhörer

heal *verb*
  = heilen

health *noun*
  = (die) Gesundheit
  to be in good health = guter Gesundheit sein
  to be in poor health = kränklich sein

health club *noun*
  = (das) Fitnesscenter

healthy *adjective*
  = gesund

hear *verb*
  = hören
  I've heard a lot about it = ich habe viel davon gehört
  to have heard of something = schon mal von etwas (*dative*) gehört haben

heart *noun*
- (*organ, or heart shape*) = (das) Herz
  to learn something by heart = etwas auswendig lernen
  she took his warning to heart = sie hat sich (*dative*) seine Warnung zu Herzen genommen
- (*courage*) = (der) Mut
  to lose heart = den Mut verlieren
- (*playing cards*) **hearts** = (das) Herz

heart attack *noun*
  = (der) Herzanfall

heat
1 *noun*
- (*temperature*) = (die) Hitze
  I can't stand the heat = ich kann die Hitze nicht aushalten
  to cook at a low heat = bei niedriger Temperatur kochen
- (*qualifying round*) = (der) Vorlauf
2 *verb*
  to heat food = Essen heiß machen
  to heat a room = einen Raum heizen

heat up
= aufwärmen

heater noun
= (das) Heizgerät

heating noun
= (die) Heizung

heaven noun
= (der) Himmel

heavily adverb
to sleep heavily = tief schlafen
to rain heavily = stark regnen

heavy adjective
• = schwer
heavy losses have been reported =
 schwere Verluste wurden gemeldet
a heavy coat = ein dicker Mantel
to wear heavy shoes = feste Schuhe tragen
• (in quantity, intensity) = stark
heavy traffic = starker Verkehr

hedge noun
= (die) Hecke

hedgehog noun
= (der) Igel

heel noun
• (part of the foot, sock) = (die) Ferse
• (part of a shoe) = (der) Absatz

height noun
• (of a person) = (die) Größe
what height are you? = wie groß bist du?
• (of a building, tree) = (die) Höhe
what height is it? = wie hoch ist es?

helicopter noun
= (der) Hubschrauber

hell noun
= (die) Hölle
to make someone's life hell = jemandem
 das Leben zur Hölle machen

helmet noun
= (der) Helm

help
1 verb
• (be of assistance) = helfen (+ dative)
to help someone (to) do something =
 jemandem helfen, etwas zu tun
to help someone [with the shopping | with their
 homework …] = jemandem [beim
 Einkaufen | bei den Hausaufgaben …] helfen
can I help you? = kann ich dir helfen?, (in a
 shop) = kann ich Ihnen behilflich sein?
• (serve)
to help oneself = sich (dative) etwas
 nehmen
I helped myself to more pototoes = ich
 habe mir mehr Kartoffeln genommen
help yourself! = greif zu!

• (avoid)
I couldn't help [laughing | thinking about it |
 crying …] = ich musste einfach [lachen |
 darüber nachdenken | weinen …]
I can't help it = ich kann nichts dafür
it can't be helped = es lässt sich nicht
 ändern
2 interjection = Hilfe!
3 noun
 (assistance) = (die) Hilfe
to ask someone for help = jemanden um
 Hilfe bitten
help out
= aushelfen

helpful adjective
• (willing to help) = hilfbereit
• (useful) = nützlich

helpless adjective
= hilflos

hem noun
= (der) Saum

hen noun
= (die) Henne

her
1 adjective = ihr

> ❗ Note that ihr changes its endings in the
> same way as ein.

I hate her dog = ich hasse ihren Hund
2 pronoun

> ❗ In German this pronoun changes
> according to its function in the sentence.
> As a direct object it is in the accusative,
> sie, and as an indirect object it is in the
> dative, ihr.

• (in the accusative) = sie
I know her = ich kenne sie
I've read a lot about her = ich habe viel
 über sie gelesen
• (in the dative) = ihr
you must help her = du musst ihr helfen
he gave her the money = er hat ihr das
 Geld gegeben
• (in the nominative, as a complement) = sie
it was her = sie war es
if I were her = wenn ich sie wäre

herb noun
= (das) Kraut

herd noun
= (die) Herde

here adverb
• = hier
is it far from here? = ist es weit von hier?
here's my telephone number = hier ist
 meine Telefonnummer
in here = hier drinnen
• (to this place) = hierher
when she came here = als sie hierher kam
to bring something here = etwas hierher
 bringen
come here! = komm her!

hers *pronoun*
= ihrer/ihre/ihrs

> ! *Note that the pronoun agrees in number
> and gender with the noun it stands for:*
> hers *(meaning the pencil)* is red = ihrer
> *(der Bleistift)* ist rot; hers *(meaning the
> shoes)* are new = ihre *(die Schuhe)* sind
> neu.

my shirt is white but hers is blue = mein
  Hemd ist weiß, aber ihrs ist blau
the gloves are hers = die Handschuhe
  gehören ihr
a friend of hers = ein Freund von ihr

herself *pronoun*
• *(when translated by a reflexive verb in
  German)* = sich
  she wants to enjoy herself = sie möchte
    sich amüsieren
• *(used for emphasis)* = selbst
  she said it herself = sie hat es selbst gesagt
• by herself = allein
  she did it all by herself = sie hat es ganz
    allein gemacht

hesitate *verb*
= zögern

heterosexual *noun*
= (der/die) Heterosexuelle

hi *interjection*
= hallo!

hiccup *noun*
= (der) Schluckauf
to have hiccups = einen Schluckauf haben

hide *verb*
• = verstecken
  to hide (oneself) = sich verstecken
• *(keep secret)* = verheimlichen
  to hide the facts = die Tatsachen
    verheimlichen

hi-fi *noun*
= (die) Hi-Fi-Anlage

high
1 *adjective* = hoch
  the wall is high = die Mauer ist hoch

> ! *The adjective* hoch *loses its c when it
> has an ending, becoming*
> hoher/hohe/hohes.

a high wall = eine hohe Mauer
a tower 200 metres high = ein zweihundert
  Meter hoher Turm
high tide = (die) Flut
to get high marks = sehr gute Noten
  bekommen
he was high (on drugs) = er war high
2 *adverb* = hoch

high heels *noun*
= hochhackige Schuhe (*plural*)

highlights *noun*
• *(on TV, radio)* = Highlights (*plural*)
• *(in hair)* = Strähnchen (*plural*)

high school *noun*
≈ (die) Oberschule

highway *noun*
• *(British: public road)* = (die) öffentliche
  Straße
• *(US: main road)* = (der) Highway

hijack *verb*
= entführen

hike
1 *noun* = (die) Wanderung
2 *verb* = wandern (! *sein*)

hill *noun*
= (der) Hügel
(*higher*) = (der) Berg

him *pronoun*

> ! *In German this pronoun changes
> according to its function in the sentence.
> As a direct object it is in the accusative,*
> ihn, *and as an indirect object it is in the
> dative,* ihm.

• *(in the accusative)* = ihn
  she loves him = sie liebt ihn
  I've got nothing against him = ich habe
    nichts gegen ihn
• *(in the dative)* = ihm
  you must help him = du musst ihm helfen
  give him the money = gib ihm das Geld
• *(in the nominative, as a complement)* = er
  it was him = er war es
  if I were him = wenn ich er wäre

himself *pronoun*
• *(when translated by a reflexive verb in
  German)* = sich
  he enjoyed himself = er hat sich amüsiert
• *(used for emphasis)* = selbst
  he said it himself = er hat es selbst gesagt
• by himself = allein
  he was all by himself = er war ganz allein

hip *noun*
= (die) Hüfte

hire
1 *verb*
• *(rent)* = mieten
  to hire a car = ein Auto mieten
• *(hire out)* = vermieten
  they hire boats (out) here = Boote werden
    hier vermietet
• *(employ)* = einstellen
  to hire staff = Personal einstellen
2 *noun*
  car hire = (die) Autovermietung
  for hire = zu vermieten

hire car *noun*
= (der) Mietwagen, = (der) Leihwagen

his
1 *adjective* = sein

> ! *Note that* sein *changes its endings in
> the same way as* ein.

I hate his dog = ich hasse seinen Hund

2 *pronoun* = seiner/seine/seins

> **!** *Note that the pronoun agrees in number and gender with the noun it stands for:* his (*meaning the pencil*) **is red** = seiner (*der Bleistift*) ist rot; his (*meaning the shoes*) **are new** = seine (*die Schuhe*) sind neu.

my shirt is white but his is blue = mein Hemd ist weiß, aber seins ist blau
these books are his = diese Bücher gehören ihm
a friend of his = ein Freund von ihm

history *noun*
= (die) Geschichte

hit
1 *verb*
• (*strike*) = schlagen
to hit someone = jemanden schlagen
• (*come into contact with*) = anstoßen
to hit one's head on the door = sich (*dative*) den Kopf an der Tür stoßen
• (*collide with*) = prallen gegen (+ *accusative*) (**!** *sein*)
to hit a wall = gegen eine Wand prallen
• (*strike with a missile, affect*) = treffen
to hit the target = das Ziel treffen
it hit him hard = es hat ihn schwer getroffen
2 *noun*
(*song*) = (der) Hit
(*film, book*) = (der) Erfolg

hitchhike *verb*
= per Anhalter fahren (**!** *sein*)

hitchhiker *noun*
= (der) Anhalter/(die) Anhalterin

hoarse *adjective*
= heiser

hobby *noun*
= (das) Hobby

hockey *noun*
= (das) Hockey

hold
1 *verb*
• = halten
to hold hands = sich an der Hand halten
• (*arrange*) = abhalten
to hold a meeting = eine Versammlung abhalten
• (*keep*) = festhalten
to hold someone for several days = jemanden mehrere Tage lang festhalten
to hold someone prisoner = jemanden gefangen halten
• (*have*) = haben
to hold a German passport = einen deutschen Pass haben
• (*contain*) = enthalten
• (*other uses*)
to hold someone responsible for something = jemanden für etwas (*accusative*) verantwortlich machen

(*on the phone*) **to hold** (**the line**) = warten
hold the line please = warten Sie bitte
2 *noun*
• (*grip*) = (der) Griff
to keep hold of something = etwas festhalten
• (*contact*)
to get hold of someone = jemanden erreichen
to get hold of something = etwas bekommen
hold back
= zurückhalten
hold on
• (*wait*) = warten
• (*so as not to fall*) = festhalten
to hold on to something = sich an etwas (*dative*) festhalten
hold up
• (*raise*) = hochhalten
• (*delay*) = aufhalten
to hold up the traffic = den Verkehr aufhalten
• (*rob*) = überfallen

hole *noun*
= (das) Loch
to be full of holes = voller Löcher sein

holiday *noun*
• (*British: vacation*) = (der) Urlaub, = Ferien (*plural*)

> **!** *People with paid jobs usually have* Urlaub; *schoolchildren and students have* Ferien.

to go on holiday = in Urlaub *or* in die Ferien fahren
the school holidays = die Schulferien
• (*national festival*) = (der) Feiertag
• (*British: day off*) = (der) freie Tag

Holland *noun*
= (das) Holland ▶ Countries p. 208

home
1 *noun*
• = (das) Zuhause
he has no home = er hat kein Zuhause
to go home = nach Hause gehen (**!** *sein*)
to live at home = im Elternhaus wohnen
• (*flat*) = (die) Wohnung, (*house*) = (das) Haus
• (*own country*) = (die) Heimat
to be far from home = fern der Heimat sein
• (*for elderly or ill people*) = (das) Heim
a retirement home = ein Altersheim
• (*in sports*)
a home win = ein Heimsieg
2 *adverb*
• (*to home*) = nach Hause
to go home = nach Hause gehen (**!** *sein*)
I met her on my way home = ich habe sie auf dem Weg nach Hause getroffen
• (*at home*) = zu Hause
I've got to stay (at) home = ich muss zu Hause bleiben

H

- **to feel at home** (*comfortable*) = sich wohl fühlen
  to make oneself at home = es sich (*dative*) bequem machen

homeless *noun*
  the homeless = die Obdachlosen (*plural*)

homesick *adjective*
  to be homesick = Heimweh haben

homework *noun*
  = Hausaufgaben (*plural*)

homosexual *noun*
  = (der/die) Homosexuelle

honest *adjective*
  = ehrlich
  to be honest with someone = ehrlich zu jemandem sein

honestly *adverb*
  = ehrlich

honey *noun*
  = (der) Honig

honeymoon *noun*
  = Flitterwochen (*plural*)

honor (*US*), **honour** (*British*)
1 *noun* = (die) Ehre
2 *verb*
- (*show respect for*) = ehren
- (*fulfil*) = sich halten an (+ *accusative*)
  to honour a cheque = einen Scheck honorieren

hood *noun*
- (*headwear*) = (die) Kapuze
- (*on a convertible car*) = (das) Verdeck
- (*US: car bonnet*) = (die) Motorhaube

hoof *noun*
  = (der) Huf

hook *noun*
  = (der) Haken
  the phone was off the hook = das Telefon war ausgehängt

hooligan *noun*
  = (der) Hooligan

hoover *verb* (*British*)
  = saugen

hop *verb*
  = hüpfen (**!** *sein*)

hope
1 *verb* = hoffen
  to hope for something = auf etwas (*accusative*) hoffen
  I hope to [meet her | speak fluent German | get the job ...] = ich hoffe, [sie zu treffen | fließend Deutsch zu sprechen | die Stelle zu bekommen ...]
  I hope so = hoffentlich

2 *noun*
  = (die) Hoffnung
  to give up hope = die Hoffnung aufgeben
  in the hope of something = in der Hoffnung auf etwas (*accusative*)

horizon *noun*
  = (der) Horizont

horn *noun*
- (*on a car*) = (die) Hupe
- (*of an animal, instrument*) = (das) Horn

horoscope *noun*
  = (das) Horoskop

horrible *adjective*
  = furchtbar

horror *noun*
  = (das) Entsetzen
  to have a horror of doing something = einen Horror davor haben, etwas zu tun

horse *noun*
  = (das) Pferd

horseriding *noun*
  = (das) Reiten

horseshoe *noun*
  = (das) Hufeisen

hose *noun*
  = (der) Schlauch

hospital *noun*
  = (das) Krankenhaus

hospitality *noun*
  = (die) Gastfreundschaft

host *noun*
- (*to guests*) = (der) Gastgeber
- (*on a TV programme*) = (der) Moderator

hostage *noun*
  = (die) Geisel
  to take someone hostage = jemanden als Geisel nehmen

hostel *noun*
  (*for refugees, workers*) = (das) Wohnheim

hostess *noun*
- (*to guests*) = (die) Gastgeberin
- (*on a TV programme*) = (die) Moderatorin
- (*air hostess*) = (die) Stewardess

hostile *adjective*
- (*opposing*) = feindlich
- (*unfriendly*) = feindselig
  to give someone a hostile look = jemanden feindselig ansehen

hot *adjective*
- (*very warm*) = heiß
  I'm very hot = mir ist sehr heiß
  a hot meal = ein warmes Essen
- (*spicy*) = scharf

hot dog *noun*
  = (der) *or* (das) Hotdog

hotel *noun*
= (das) Hotel

hour *noun*
= (die) Stunde ▶ **Time p. 331**
I earn £5 an hour = ich verdiene fünf Pfund pro Stunde

house
1 *noun* = (das) Haus
I went to my friend's house = ich bin zu meinem Freund nach Hause gegangen
at my house = bei mir (zu Hause)
2 *verb* = unterbringen

housework *noun*
= (die) Hausarbeit

housing estate *noun*
= (die) Wohnsiedlung

hovercraft *noun*
= (das) Luftkissenboot

how *adverb*
• = wie
how do you spell his name? = wie wird sein Name geschrieben?
how are you? = wie gehts dir?, *(formal)* wie geht es Ihnen?

! Note that **gehts**, *written as one word, is short for* **geht es.**

how do you do? = guten Tag
how about something to eat? = wie wäre es mit etwas zu essen?
• *(asking about amount)* = wie
how far? = wie weit?
how many? = wie viele?
how much? = wie viel?
how much is it? = wie viel kostet es?

however *adverb*
• = jedoch, = aber
• **however rich he is** = wie reich er auch sein mag
however long it takes = egal, wie lange es dauert

huge *adjective*
= riesig

humid *adjective*
= feucht

humor *(US)* ▶ humour

humorous *adjective*
= lustig

humour *noun (British)*
= (der) Humor
to have a sense of humour = Humor haben

hundred *adjective*
= hundert ▶ **Numbers p. 282**

Hungary *noun*
= (das) Ungarn ▶ **Countries p. 208**

hunger *noun*
= (der) Hunger

hungry *adjective*
= hungrig
I am hungry = ich habe Hunger

hunting *noun*
= (die) Jagd

hurdles *noun*
(race) = (der) Hürdenlauf

hurrah, hurray *interjection*
= hurra!

hurry
1 *verb*
• *(hurry up)* = sich beeilen
you'll have to hurry to catch the train = du musst dich beeilen, um den Zug zu erwischen
you must hurry home = du musst schnell nach Hause
• *(hurry along)*
to hurry someone = jemanden zur Eile antreiben
2 *noun* = (die) Eile
to be in a hurry = es eilig haben
there's no hurry = es eilt nicht

hurt *verb*
• *(injure)* = verletzen
to hurt oneself = sich verletzen
I hurt my arm playing tennis = ich habe mir den Arm beim Tennisspielen verletzt
• *(be painful)* = wehtun (+ *dative*)
my arm is hurting = der Arm tut mir weh
• *(cause emotional pain)* = kränken
to feel hurt = sich gekränkt fühlen

husband *noun*
= (der) Ehemann

hut *noun*
= (die) Hütte

hygienic *adjective*
= hygienisch

hypnotize *verb*
= hypnotisieren

hysterical *adjective*
= hysterisch

I

I i

I *pronoun*
= ich
I've got to go now = ich muss jetzt gehen

ice *noun*
= (das) Eis

ice cream *noun*
= (das) Eis
two ice creams, please = zwei Eis bitte

ice hockey noun
= (das) Eishockey

ice-skating noun
= (das) Schlittschuhlaufen

icing noun
= (der) Zuckerguss

idea noun
= (die) Idee
what a good idea = was für eine gute Idee
I haven't the slightest idea = ich habe
keine Ahnung

identity card noun
= (der) Personalausweis

idiot noun
= (der) Idiot

if conjunction
• = wenn
if you meet him, don't tell him = wenn du
ihn triffst, sage nichts
if you like = wenn du willst

! *The subjunctive is often used in clauses
following* if. *For information on the
subjunctive,* ▶ **p. 351**

if I were you = wenn ich du ware
• (*whether, usually following* to know *or to
wonder*) = ob
I don't know if he is coming = ich weiß
nicht, ob er kommt
as if = als ob

ignore verb
= ignorieren

ill adjective
= krank
to be ill with flu = die Grippe haben

illegal adjective
= illegal

illness noun
= (die) Krankheit

illustration noun
= (die) Illustration

imagination noun
• (*ability to imagine*) = (die) Phantasie
• (*fancy*) = (die) Einbildung
it's all in your imagination = das bildest du
dir nur ein

imagine verb
= sich (*dative*) vorstellen
I imagine it's easy = ich stelle mir das
leicht vor
can you imagine? = stell dir vor!

imitate verb
= nachahmen

immediately adverb
= sofort

---

immigrant
1 noun = (der) Einwanderer/(die) Einwanderin
2 adjective = Einwanderer-

! *Note that* **Einwanderer-** *forms the first
part of a compound noun.*

an immigrant child = ein Einwandererkind

impatient adjective
= ungeduldig

important adjective
= wichtig

impossible adjective
= unmöglich

impress verb
= beeindrucken
to be impressed by something = von etwas
(*dative*) beeindruckt sein

impression noun
= (der) Eindruck

improve verb
• (*make better*) = verbessern
to improve one's financial situation = seine
finanzielle Lage verbessern
• (*get better*) = besser werden (! *sein*)
your German is improving = dein Deutsch
wird besser
• (*of an ill or injured person*)
he has greatly improved = es geht ihm viel
besser

improvement noun
= (die) Verbesserung

in
1 preposition
• (*in a place or position*) = in (+ *dative or
accusative*)

! *Note that* in *is followed by a noun in the
dative when position is described. The
accusative follows when there is
movement towards something.*

to sit in the garden = im Garten sitzen

! *Note that* im *is the shortened form of* in
dem; in das *can also be shortened, to* ins.

to go in the garden = in den Garten gehen
(! *sein*)
in the street = auf der Straße
in the world = auf der Welt
in Japan = in Japan
• (*among*) = bei (+ *dative*)
it's normal in children of that age = das ist
normal bei Kindern in dem Alter
• (*wearing, with colours*) = in (+ *dative*)
she was dressed in black = sie war in
Schwarz
• (*the way something is done*)
they were sitting in a circle = sie saßen im
Kreis
in German = auf Deutsch
he spoke in a soft voice = er sprach mit
leiser Stimme
we'll pay in cash = wir zahlen bar

- (*during*) = in (+ *dative*)
  in 1995 = (im Jahre) 1995
  in October = im Oktober
  at 2 o'clock in the morning = um zwei Uhr morgens
- (*with an occupation*)
  he is in banking = er ist im Bankwesen
  he is in the army = er ist beim Militär
- (*other uses*)
  one in ten (**people**) = jeder Zehnte
  a rise in prices = ein Preisanstieg
2 *adverb*
- (*indoors*) = herein-/hinein-, = rein-✱

> ! *Note that* herein-, hinein- *and* rein- *form the prefixes to separable verbs;* herein- *has the sense of* towards *the speaker, and* hinein- *has the sense of* away from. *So* herein- *often goes with verbs like* kommen (to come in = hereinkommen), *and* hinein- *goes with verbs like* gehen (to go in = hineingehen). *The less formal* rein- *can be used for both movements, towards and away.*

  you can come in = du kannst hereinkommen
  can I go in? = kann ich reingehen?✱
- (*at home*) = zu Hause
  she's not in = sie ist nicht zu Hause
- (*indoors*) = drinnen
  in here = hier drinnen
  in there = da drinnen
- (*arrived*) = da
  he's not in yet = er ist noch nicht da
- (*other uses*)
  to keep in with someone = sich mit jemandem gut stellen
  to let oneself in for something = sich auf etwas (*accusative*) einlassen
3 *adjective*
  (*in fashion*) = in Mode, = in✱

inch *noun*
= (der) Inch ▶**Measures p. 270**

incident *noun*
= (der) Vorfall

include *verb*
= einschließen
service is included in the price = die Bedienung ist im Preis eingeschlossen

including *preposition*
= einschließlich (+ *genitive*)
they were all invited, including the children = sie waren alle eingeladen, einschließlich der Kinder

income *noun*
= (das) Einkommen

income tax *noun*
= (die) Einkommenssteuer

incompetent *adjective*
= unfähig

inconsiderate *adjective*
= rücksichtslos

inconvenient *adjective*
= ungünstig
at an inconvenient time = zu einem ungünstigen Zeitpunkt

incorrect *adjective*
= unrichtig
that is incorrect = das stimmt nicht

increase
1 *verb*
- (*raise*) = erhöhen
  they increased his salary = sie erhöhten sein Gehalt
- (*rise*) = steigen (! *sein*)
  to increase in value = im Wert steigen
- (*get bigger*) = größer werden (! *sein*)
2 *noun*
- (*becoming greater*) = (die) Zunahme
- (*amount*) = (die) Erhöhung
  a price increase = eine Preiserhöhung

incredible *adjective*
= unglaublich

India *noun*
= (das) Indien ▶**Countries p. 208**

Indian
1 *noun*
- (*a person from India*) = (der) Inder/(die) Inderin
- (*a Native American*) = (der) Indianer/(die) Indianerin
2 *adjective*
- (*of India*) = indisch
  (*Native American*) = indianisch ▶**Countries p. 208**

indicate *verb*
- (*point to*) = zeigen auf (+ *accusative*)
- (*of a car, driver*) = blinken

indigestion *noun*
= (die) Magenverstimmung
to have indigestion = eine Magenverstimmung haben

individual
1 *noun* = (der/die) Einzelne
2 *adjective*
- (*single*) = einzeln
- (*distinctive*) = individuell

indoor *adjective*
- (*of a pool, court*) = Hallen-
  an indoor swimming pool = ein Hallenbad
- (*taking place inside*) = im Haus

indoors *adverb*
= drinnen, = im Haus
to stay indoors = drinnen bleiben (! *sein*)
to go indoors = ins Haus gehen (! *sein*)

industry *noun*
= (die) Industrie

inevitable *adjective*
= unvermeidlich

infant *noun*
• (*baby*) = (der) Säugling
• (*small child*) = (das) kleine Kind

infant school *noun*
= (die) Vorschule

infection *noun*
= (die) Infektion

influence
1 *noun* = (der) Einfluss
  to have influence with someone = bei
    jemandem Einfluss haben
2 *verb* = beeinflussen

inform *verb*
• (*tell*) = informieren
  to inform someone of something =
    jemanden über etwas (*accusative*)
    informieren
  we are pleased to inform you that . . . = wir
    freuen uns, Ihnen mitteilen zu können,
    dass . . .
  to keep someone informed = jemanden
    auf dem Laufenden halten
• (*denounce*)
  to inform on someone = jemanden
    anzeigen

informal *adjective*
• (*of manner, discussion*) = zwanglos
• (*of language, tone*) = ungezwungen

information *noun*
= (die) Auskunft
  a piece of information = eine Auskunft
  to give someone information about
    something = jemandem Auskunft über
    etwas (*accusative*) geben

information desk *noun*
= (das) Auskunftsbüro, = (die) Information

information technology *noun*
= (die) Informatik

ingredient *noun*
= (die) Zutat

inhabitant *noun*
= (der) Einwohner/(die) Einwohnerin

injection *noun*
= (die) Spritze

injured *adjective*
= verletzt

injury *noun*
= (die) Verletzung

injury time *noun*
= (die) Nachspielzeit

ink *noun*
= (die) Tinte

inn *noun*
= (das) Gasthaus

✶ in informal situations

innocent *adjective*
= unschuldig

inquire *verb*
  to inquire about something = sich nach
    etwas (*dative*) erkundigen

inquiry *noun*
• (*question*) = (die) Erkundigung
  to make inquiries about something = sich
    nach etwas (*dative*) erkundigen
• (*asking*) = (die) Anfrage
• (*investigation*) = (die) Untersuchung

insect *noun*
= (das) Insekt

inside
1 *preposition*
= in (+ *dative or accusative*)

> **!** *Note that* in *is followed by a noun in the
> dative when position is described. The
> accusative follows when there is
> movement towards something.*

  to be inside the house = im Haus sein

> **!** *Note that* im *is the shortened form of* in
> dem; in das *can also be shortened, to* ins.

  to go inside the house = ins Haus gehen
    (**!** *sein*)
2 *adjective* = Innen-

> **!** *Note that* Innen- *forms the first part of a
> compound noun.*

  inside pocket = (die) Innentasche
3 *adverb*
• (*on or in the inside*) = innen
  inside out = links (herum)
• (*indoors*) = drinnen
  he's inside = er ist drinnen
• (*to the inside*) = nach innen hinein/herein,
    = nach innen rein✶

> **!** *Note that* herein *has the sense of*
> towards *the speaker, and* hinein *has the
> sense of* away from. *The less formal* rein
> *can be used for both movements,
> towards and away.*

  we brought the chairs inside = wir haben
    die Stühle reingebracht✶

inspect *verb*
• (*look at closely*) = inspizieren
• (*test*) = prüfen
• (*check tickets, passport*) = kontrollieren

inspector *noun*
• (*of passengers' tickets*) =
    (der) Kontrolleur/(die) Kontrolleurin
• (*in the police*) = (der) Kommissar/
    (die) Kommissarin

instead *adverb*
• = stattdessen
  I don't feel like going to the cinema, we
    could play tennis instead = ich habe
    keine Lust, ins Kino zu gehen, stattdessen
    könnten wir Tennis spielen

- **instead of** = (an)statt (+ *genitive*)
  he hired a bicycle instead of a car = er hat
  ein Fahrrad statt eines Autos gemietet
  instead of working he watched television =
  anstatt zu arbeiten, hat er ferngesehen
  his wife came instead of him = seine Frau
  kam an seiner Stelle

instruction *noun*
= (die) Anweisung
instructions for use =
(die) Gebrauchsanweisung

instrument *noun*
= (das) Instrument

insult
1 *noun* = (die) Beleidigung
2 *verb* = beleidigen

insurance *noun*
= (die) Versicherung
travel insurance = (die) Reiseversicherung

insure *verb*
= versichern
to insure against theft = sich gegen
Diebstahl versichern

intelligent *adjective*
= intelligent

intend *verb*
- = beabsichtigen
  to intend to do something = beabsichtigen,
  etwas zu tun
- **to be intended for something** = für etwas
  (*accusative*) gedacht sein
  this course is intended for adults = dieser
  Kurs ist für Erwachsene

intensive care *noun*
= (die) Intensivpflege
to be in intensive care = auf der
Intensivstation sein

interest
1 *noun*
- = (das) Interesse
  to show interest in something = Interesse
  an etwas (*dative*) zeigen
  he has lost interest in politics = er hat das
  Interesse an Politik verloren
- (*financial*) = Zinsen (*plural*)
  the rate of interest = der Zinssatz
2 *verb* = interessieren

interested *adjective*
= interessiert
to be interested in politics = sich für Politik
interessieren

interesting *adjective*
= interessant

interfere *verb*
- (*meddle*) = sich einmischen
- (*damage*)
  to interfere with something = etwas
  beeinträchtigen

interior decoration *noun*
= (die) Innenausstattung

international *adjective*
= international

Internet *noun*
= (das) Internet
on the Internet = im Internet

interpreter *noun*
= (der) Dolmetscher/(die) Dolmetscherin

interrupt *verb*
= unterbrechen
he interrupted me = er hat mich
unterbrochen

interval *noun*
- (*in time or space*) = (der) Abstand
  at regular intervals = in regelmäßigen
  Abständen
  at 30-minute intervals = in Abständen von
  dreißig Minuten
  at two-hourly intervals = alle zwei Stunden
- (*break during a performance*) = (die) Pause

interview
1 *noun*
- (*for a job*) = (das) Vorstellungsgespräch
  to go for an interview = sich vorstellen
- (*with a journalist*) = (das) Interview
2 *verb*
- (*for a job*)
  to interview someone = ein
  Vorstellungsgespräch mit jemandem
  führen
- (*of a journalist*) = interviewen
- (*of the police*) = vernehmen

into *preposition*
- (*when referring to a place or location*) = in
  (+ *accusative*)

  ! *Note that in the meaning of into,* in *is
  always followed by a noun in the
  accusative, because there is movement
  towards something.*

  to go into the garden = in den Garten
  gehen (! *sein*)
  to get into the car = ins Auto steigen
  (! *sein*)

  ! *Note that* ins *is a shortened form of* in
  das.

- (*against*) = gegen (+ *accusative*)
  he drove into the tree = er ist gegen den
  Baum gefahren
- (*indicating change*) = in (+ *accusative*)
  to translate a letter into German = einen
  Brief ins Deutsche übersetzen
- (*in division*) = durch (+ *accusative*)
  five into twenty goes four = zwanzig durch
  fünf ist vier

introduce *verb*
- (*when people meet*) = vorstellen
  he introduced me to Peter = er hat mich
  Peter vorgestellt
  to introduce oneself = sich vorstellen

- (*on radio or TV*)
  to introduce a programme = ein Programm
  ankündigen
- (*bring into operation*)
  to introduce a [law | reform | change …] = [ein
  Gesetz | eine Reform | eine Änderung …]
  einführen

introduction *noun*
- (*of one person to another*) =
  (die) Vorstellung
- (*in a book, speech*) = (die) Einleitung
- (*of a law, reform*) = (die) Einführung

invent *verb*
= erfinden

invention *noun*
= (die) Erfindung

investigate *verb*
= untersuchen

investigation *noun*
= (die) Untersuchung

invisible *adjective*
= unsichtbar

invitation *noun*
= (die) Einladung

invite *verb*
= einladen
  to invite someone round = jemanden zu
  sich (*dative*) einladen

involved *adjective*
= verwickelt
  he was involved in an accident = er war in
  einen Unfall verwickelt

Ireland *noun*
= (das) Irland ▶**Countries p. 208**

Irish
1 *noun*
- (*people*) **the Irish** = die Iren
- (*language*) = (das) Irisch
2 *adjective* = irisch ▶**Countries p. 208**

iron
1 *noun*
- (*metal*) = (das) Eisen
- (*for clothes*) = (das) Bügeleisen
2 *verb* = bügeln

island *noun*
= (die) Insel

it *pronoun*

> **!** Note that the German translation for *it*
> can be masculine, feminine or neuter,
> depending on the gender of the noun *it*
> represents.

- (*as the subject of a sentence, in the
  nominative*) = er/sie/es
  it's gone = er/sie/es ist weg
  where is the newspaper?—it's on the table
  = wo ist die Zeitung?—sie ist auf dem
  Tisch
- (*as the object of a sentence, in the
  accusative*) = ihn/sie/es
  have you found it? = hast du ihn/sie/es
  gefunden?
  that's my newspaper, give it to me = das ist
  meine Zeitung, gib sie mir
- (*used to represent something general*)
  it's [difficult | easy | awful …] = es ist [schwierig |
  einfach | furchtbar …]
  it's a nice house = das ist ein hübsches
  Haus
  it's me = ich bins
  we talked about it = wir haben darüber
  gesprochen
  of it/from it/about it = davon
  out of it = daraus
  who is it? = wer ist da?
  what is it? = was ist los?

IT *noun*
= (die) Informatik

Italian
1 *noun*
- (*person*) = (der) Italiener/(die) Italienerin
- (*language*) = (das) Italienisch
2 *adjective* = italienisch ▶**Countries p. 208**

Italy *noun*
= (das) Italien ▶**Countries p. 208**

itchy *adjective*
  my back is itchy = mein Rücken juckt

its *adjective*
  (*masculine*) = sein
  (*feminine*) = ihr
  (*neuter*) = sein

> **!** Note that **sein** and **ihr** change their
> endings in the same way as **ein**. Gender
> depends on the noun to which the
> adjective refers.

  the dog was black and its tail was white =
  der Hund war schwarz und sein Schwanz
  war weiß
  the cat is black and its eyes are green =
  die Katze ist schwarz und ihre Augen
  sind grün

itself *pronoun*
- (*when translated by a reflexive verb in
  German*) = sich
  the cat hurt itself = die Katze hat sich
  wehgetan
- (*used for emphasis*) = selbst
  the garden itself is quite large = der Garten
  selbst ist ziemlich groß
- **by itself** (*automatically*) = von selbst,
  (*alone*) = allein
  the heating comes on by itself = die
  Heizung geht von selbst an

Jj

jacket noun
- (clothing) = (die) Jacke
- (on a book) = (der) Umschlag

jail noun
= (das) Gefängnis
to be sent to jail = ins Gefängnis kommen (**!** sein)

jam noun
- (food) = (die) Marmelade
- (traffic) = (der) Stau

January noun
= (der) Januar ▶ **Dates p. 213**

Japan noun
= (das) Japan ▶ **Countries p. 208**

Japanese
1 noun
- (person) = (der) Japaner/(die) Japanerin
- (language) = (das) Japanisch
2 adjective = japanisch ▶ **Countries p. 208**

jar noun
- (for jam, sweets) = (das) Glas
- (larger, earthenware) = (der) Topf

jaw noun
= (der) Kiefer

jazz noun
= (der) Jazz

jealous adjective
= eifersüchtig
he is jealous of her = er ist eifersüchtig auf sie

jeans noun
= Jeans (plural)

jet noun
(plane) = (das) Düsenflugzeug, = (der) Jet✖

Jew noun
= (der) Jude/(die) Jüdin

jewel noun
= (der) Edelstein

jewellery (British), **jewelry** (US) noun
= (der) Schmuck
a piece of jewellery = ein Schmuckstück

Jewish adjective
= jüdisch

jigsaw noun
= (das) Puzzle

job noun
- (post) = (die) Stelle, = (der) Job✖
to look for a job = einen Job suchen✖

- (task) = (die) Arbeit
he made a good job of it = er hat es gut gemacht
- (duty) = (die) Aufgabe

jogging noun
= (das) Jogging
to go jogging = joggen gehen (**!** sein)

join verb
- (meet) = treffen
I'll join you in half an hour = ich treffe dich in einer halben Stunde
- (accompany) = mitkommen mit (+ dative) (**!** sein)
- (take part) = sich anschließen (+ dative)
to join a demonstration = sich einer Demonstration anschließen
- (become a member of a club, party) = beitreten (+ dative) (**!** sein)
- (become a member of a firm, the army) = eintreten (+ accusative) (**!** sein)
- (fasten together) = verbinden
join in
= mitmachen
to join in a game = bei einem Spiel mitmachen

joke
1 noun = (der) Witz
to play a joke on someone = jemandem einen Streich spielen
2 verb = Witze machen

journalist noun
= (der) Journalist/(die) Journalistin

journey noun
= (die) Reise
to go on a journey = verreisen (**!** sein)

joy noun
= (die) Freude

judge
1 noun
- (in court) = (der) Richter
- (at a sporting event) = (der) Schiedsrichter
- (in a competition) = (der) Preisrichter
2 verb
- (form an opinion about) = beurteilen
- (make a judgement) = urteilen
to judge by = urteilen nach (+ dative)

jug noun
= (der) Krug

juice noun
= (der) Saft

July noun
= (der) Juli ▶ **Dates p. 213**

jump
1 verb = springen (**!** sein)
he jumped across the stream = er sprang über den Bach
to jump the queue = sich vordrängen
2 noun = (der) Sprung

J

jump out
= herausspringen/hinausspringen (**!** *sein*),
= rausspringen� (**!** *sein*)

> **!** Note that **heraus-** *has the sense of* **towards** *the speaker, and* **hinaus-** *has the sense of* **away from.** *The less formal* **raus-** *can be used for both movements, towards and away.*

jumper *noun*
= (der) Pullover

June *noun*
= (der) Juni ▶**Dates p. 213**

junior *adjective*
• (*younger*) = jünger
• (*of lower rank*) = untergeordnet
• (*US: after name*) = junior

jury *noun*
• (*in court*)
the jury = die Geschworenen (*plural*)
• (*in a competition*) = (die) Jury

just¹
1 *adverb*
• (*very recently*) = gerade
I saw him just now = ich habe ihn gerade eben gesehen
• (*exactly*) = genau
it's just as good = das ist genauso gut
• (*immediately*)
it was just after 6 o'clock = es war kurz nach sechs Uhr
• (*only*) = nur
I've come just to say goodbye = ich bin nur gekommen, um auf Wiedersehen zu sagen
• (*barely*) = gerade noch
I got there just in time = ich kam gerade noch rechtzeitig an
• (*simply*) = einfach
just tell the truth = sag einfach die Wahrheit
• (*equally*)
he is just as tall as you = er ist genauso groß wie du
• (*at that very moment*)
to be just about to do something = dabei sein, etwas zu tun
I was just about to phone you = ich war gerade dabei, dich anzurufen
just a minute! = einen Moment!

just² *adjective*
= gerecht

justice *noun*
= (die) Gerechtigkeit

justify *verb*
= rechtfertigen

kangaroo *noun*
= (das) Känguru

karate *noun*
= (das) Karate

keen *adjective*
• (*eager*) = begeistert
to be keen on [tennis | swimming | sweets …] = [Tennis | Schwimmen | Bonbons …] mögen
to be keen to do something = etwas unbedingt tun wollen
he is very keen for you to come along = er will unbedingt, dass du mitkommst
• (*sharp*) = scharf

keep *verb*
• (*retain*) = behalten
you can keep the change = du kannst das Wechselgeld behalten
• (*maintain*) = halten
to keep something hot = etwas warm halten
• (*store*) = aufbewahren
to keep the wine in the cellar = den Wein im Keller aufbewaren
(*not throw away*) = aufheben
• (*detain*) = aufhalten
I won't keep you long = ich will dich nicht lange aufhalten
to keep someone waiting = jemanden warten lassen
to keep a seat = einen Platz freihalten
• (*not break*) = einhalten
to keep an appointment = eine Verabredung einhalten
• (*carry on, manage*) = führen
to keep the accounts = Buch führen
• (*continue*)
to keep walking = weitergehen (**!** *sein*)

> **!** Note that the prefix **weiter-** forms a separable verb.

keep going! = mach weiter!
• (*do repeatedly*)
to keep (on) interrupting = dauernd unterbrechen
• (*remain*) = bleiben (**!** *sein*)
to keep calm = ruhig bleiben (**!** *sein*)
• (*of food, stay in good condition*) = sich halten
• (*prevent*)
to keep someone from doing something = jemanden davon abhalten, etwas zu tun
to keep something from falling down = verhindern, dass etwas herunterfällt

keep away
= sich fernhalten, = wegbleiben✶ (**!** *sein*)

keep back
= zurückhalten
the police kept the crowd back = die
Polizei hielt die Menschenmenge zurück
keep down
to keep [prices | unemployment | wages …]
down = [Preise | Arbeitslosigkeit | Löhne …]
niedrig halten
keep your voice down = rede nicht so laut
keep off
to keep off the grass = den Rasen nicht
betreten
keep on
= weitermachen

! Note that the prefix **weiter-** forms a
separable verb when the action carries
on continuously. But **weiter** and the verb
are written as two separate words if the
action carries on over a long period of
time, with interruptions.

to keep on [talking | playing | reading …] =
[weiterreden | weiterspielen | weiterlesen …]
you must keep on practising = du musst
weiter üben
keep out
to keep out of a building = ein Gebäude
nicht betreten
to keep out of the sun = nicht in die Sonne
gehen (! sein)
**the curtain is supposed to keep the flies
out** = der Vorhang soll die Fliegen
abhalten

kennel noun
(British: doghouse) = (die) Hundehütte

kerb noun (British)
= (der) Randstein

kettle noun
= (der) Kessel

key
1 noun
• = (der) Schlüssel
• (on a computer, piano) = (die) Taste
2 verb = eintasten, = eingeben
to key (in) data = Daten eintasten

keyboard noun
= (die) Tastatur

keyhole noun
= (das) Schlüsselloch

kick
1 verb
to kick someone = jemandem einen Tritt
geben
to kick the ball = den Ball schießen
2 noun = (der) Tritt
kick off
= anstoßen
kick out
to kick someone out = jemanden
rausschmeißen✗

kid noun
• (young goat) = (das) Kitz
• (child) = (das) Kind

kidnap verb
= entführen, = kidnappen

kill verb
= töten
to kill an animal = ein Tier töten
to kill a man = einen Mann umbringen
he killed himself = er hat sich umgebracht

killer noun
= (der) Mörder/(die) Mörderin

kilometer (US), **kilometre** (British)
noun
= (der) Kilometer ▶**Measures p. 270**

kind
1 adjective
• (friendly) = nett
it is very kind of you to help me = es ist
sehr nett von Ihnen, mir zu helfen
• (affectionate) = lieb
a kind act = eine gute Tat
2 noun
• (type) = (die) Art
a kind of [novel | game | fish …] = so eine Art
[Roman | Spiel | Fisch …]
all kinds of [people | excuses | games …] = alle
möglichen [Leute | Ausreden | Spiele …]
• (brand) = (die) Sorte
a new kind of cheese = eine neue Käsesorte
what kind of car does he drive? = was für
ein Auto hat er?

kindness noun
= (die) Freundlichkeit

king noun
= (der) König

kingdom noun
= (das) Königreich

kiss
1 verb = küssen
they kissed (each other) = sie küssten sich
2 noun = (der) Kuss

kitchen noun
= (die) Küche

kite noun
= (der) Drachen

knee noun
= (das) Knie

kneel verb
= knien
(go down on one's knees) = niederknien
to kneel (down) to do something = sich
hinknien, um etwas zu tun

knife noun
= (das) Messer

knit verb
= stricken

knock
1 verb
• (strike lightly) = klopfen an (+ accusative)
he knocked on the door = er klopfte an die
Tür

K

- (*hit*) = stoßen
  he knocked his head = er hat sich (*dative*)
  den Kopf gestoßen
2 *noun*
- (*blow*) = (der) Schlag
- (*at the door*) = (das) Klopfen
  there is a knock at the door = es klopft an
  der Tür
knock down
- = herunterwerfen
  (*punch*) = niederschlagen
  (*in a car*) **he was knocked down by a car** =
  er ist von einem Auto angefahren worden
- (*demolish a building*) = abreißen
knock out
  = bewusstlos schlagen
  (*in boxing*) = k.o. schlagen
knock over
  = umstoßen

knot
1 *noun* = (der) Knoten
2 *verb* = knoten

know *verb*
- (*be acquainted with*) = kennen
  I don't know her = ich kenne sie nicht
  to get to know someone = jemanden
  kennen lernen
- (*have knowledge of*) = wissen
  how do you know that? = woher weißt du
  das?
  to let someone know something =
  jemandem über etwas (*accusative*)
  Bescheid sagen
- (*have an understanding of*) = können
  to know how to do something = etwas tun
  können
  do you know any German? = können Sie
  etwas Deutsch?

knowledge *noun*
- (*learning*) = Kenntnisse (*plural*)
  his scientific knowledge = seine
  wissenschaftlichen Kenntnisse
- (*awareness*) = (das) Wissen
  to my knowledge = meines Wissens
  not to my knowledge = meines Wissens
  nicht

Ll

laboratory *noun*
  = (das) Labor

lace *noun*
- (*material*) = (die) Spitze
- (*shoelace*) = (der) Schnürsenkel
  to tie one's laces = sich (*dative*) die
  Schnürsenkel binden

lack
1 *noun* = (der) Mangel
  lack of |money | interest | tact ...| = Mangel an
  [Geld | Interesse | Takt ...]
2 *verb* = fehlen an (+ *dative*)
  he lacks confidence = ihm fehlt es an
  Selbstvertrauen

ladder *noun*
  = (die) Leiter

lady *noun*
  = (die) Dame

lake *noun*
  = (der) See

lamb *noun*
  = (das) Lamm

lamp *noun*
  = (die) Lampe

lampshade *noun*
  = (der) Lampenschirm

land
1 *noun*
- = (das) Land
- (*property*) = (der) Grundbesitz
2 *verb*
  = landen (**!** *sein*)

landlady *noun*
- (*of a house, room*) = (die) Vermieterin
- (*of a pub*) = (die) Gastwirtin

landlord *noun*
- (*of a house, room*) = (der) Vermieter
- (*of a pub*) = (der) Gastwirt

landscape *noun*
  = (die) Landschaft

language *noun*
- = (die) Sprache
- (*way of speaking*) = (die) Ausdrucksweise
  bad language = Kraftausdrücke (*plural*)

language laboratory *noun*
  = (das) Sprachlabor

lap *noun*
- (*part of the body*) = (der) Schoß
- (*in a race*) = (die) Runde

large *adjective*
  = groß

last
1 *adjective* = letzter/letzte/letztes
  for the last time = zum letzten Mal
2 *pronoun*
  the last = der Letzte/die Letzte/das Letzte
  the night before last = vorgestern Nacht
3 *adverb*
- (*at the end*) = zuletzt
  I'll do the packing last = ich packe die
  Koffer zuletzt
- (*in final position*) = als Letzter/als Letzte
  they were last to arrive = sie kamen als
  Letzte an
  he spoke last = er hat als Letzter
  gesprochen

- (*most recently*) = das letzte Mal
  I last saw him in June = ich habe ihn das
    letzte Mal im Juni gesehen
  4 *verb* = dauern
  the film lasted 3 hours = der Film dauerte
    drei Stunden

late
1 *adjective*
- (*not on time*) = verspätet
  to be late = sich verspäten
  the train was 10 minutes late = der Zug
    hatte zehn Minuten Verspätung
  to make someone late = jemanden
    aufhalten
- (*far into the day or night*) = spät
  at this late hour = zu dieser späten Stunde
- (*towards the end of*)
  in late September = Ende September
- (*most recent*)
  the latest fashion = die neueste Mode
2 *adverb*
- (*not on time*) = zu spät
  they arrived an hour late = sie kamen eine
    Stunde zu spät an
- (*far into the day or night*) = spät
  to stay up late = bis spät aufbleiben (**!** *sein*)

later *adverb*
  = später
  later on = später
  see you later = bis später

Latin *noun*
  = (das) Latein

Latin America *noun*
  = (das) Lateinamerika ▶Countries p. 208

Latvia *noun*
  = (das) Lettland ▶Countries p. 208

laugh
1 *verb* = lachen
  to laugh at something = über etwas
    (*accusative*) lachen
  (*mock*) **to laugh at someone** = jemanden
    auslachen
2 *noun* = (das) Lachen
  with a laugh = lachend

laughter *noun*
  = (das) Gelächter

launderette *noun*
  = (der) Waschsalon

laundry *noun*
- (*place*) = (die) Wäscherei
- (*washing*) = (die) Wäsche
  to do the laundry = Wäsche waschen

law *noun*
- (*regulation*) = (das) Gesetz
  to break the law = gegen das Gesetz
    verstoßen
- (*set of rules in a country*) = (das) Recht
  according to German law = nach
    deutschem Recht
  it's against the law = das ist verboten

- (*as a university subject*) = Jura (*plural*)
  to study law = Jura studieren

lawn *noun*
  = (der) Rasen

lawnmower *noun*
  = (der) Rasenmäher

lawyer *noun*
  = (der) Rechtsanwalt/(die) Rechtsanwältin
    ▶Professions p. 298

lay *verb*
- (*put, fit*) = legen
  she laid her hand on his shoulder = sie
    legte ihre Hand auf seine Schulter
  to lay a carpet = einen Teppich legen
  (*of a bird*) **to lay an egg** = ein Ei legen
- (*set*) = decken
  to lay the table = den Tisch decken
lay down
- (*put down*) = hinlegen
  to lay something down on the table =
    etwas auf den Tisch legen
- (*impose*) = festlegen
  to lay down rules = Regeln festlegen
lay off
  to lay off workers = Arbeiter
    vorübergehend entlassen

lazy *adjective*
  = faul

lead¹
1 *verb*
- (*guide, have or conduct*) = führen
  he led me into the garden = er führte mich
    in den Garten
  to lead someone into difficulties =
    jemanden in Schwierigkeiten bringen
  to lead the way = vorangehen (**!** *sein*)
- (*be at the head of*) = anführen
  to lead a [team | demonstration | parade …] =
    [eine Mannschaft | eine Demonstration | einen
    Umzug …] anführen
- (*be ahead*) = führen
  to lead by 5 points = mit fünf Punkten
    führen
- (*cause*)
  to lead someone to do something =
    jemanden dazu bringen, etwas zu tun
  to be easily led = sich leicht beeinflussen
    lassen
- (*result in*)
  to lead to = führen zu (+ *dative*)
  to lead to an accident = zu einem Unfall
    führen
- (*in cards*) = ausspielen
2 *noun*
- (*in a match, contest*) = (die) Führung
  to take the lead = in Führung gehen
    (**!** *sein*)
- (*leading role*) = (die) Hauptrolle
- (*wire*) = (die) Schnur
- (*British: for a dog*) = (die) Leine

lead² *noun*
- (*metal*) = (das) Blei
- (*in a pencil*) = (die) Mine

leader *noun*
- (*of an army, movement*) = (der) Führer/ (die) Führerin
- (*of a political party*) = (der/die) Vorsitzende
- (*of an expedition, group*) = (der) Leiter/ (die) Leiterin
- (*of a gang*) = (der) Anführer/(die) Anführerin

leaf *noun*
= (das) Blatt

leak
1 *verb*
- (*of a roof, container*) = undicht sein
- (*of a boat*) = leck sein
2 *noun*
- (*in a roof, container*) = (die) undichte Stelle
- (*in a boat*) = (das) Leck
- (*of gas*) = (der) Gasausfluss

lean
1 *verb*
- = lehnen
  to lean against/on something = an etwas (+ *accusative*) lehnen
- (*of a person*) = sich lehnen
  he leant out of the window = er lehnte sich aus dem Fenster
2 *adjective*
= mager

lean on
= sich stützen auf (+ *accusative*)
  he leaned on his stick = er stützte sich auf seinen Stock

leap
1 *verb* = springen (**!** *sein*)
2 *noun* = (der) Sprung

learn *verb*
= lernen

leash *noun*
= (die) Leine

least
1 *adjective* = wenigster/wenigste/wenigstes
  they have the least money = sie haben das wenigste Geld
  to have least time = am wenigsten Zeit haben
2 *pronoun* = das wenigste
  that is the least you can do = das ist das wenigste, was man tun kann
3 *adverb* = am wenigsten
  I like that colour (the) least = die Farbe gefällt mir am wenigsten

> **!** Note that least *is often translated into German by forming the superlative of the opposite adjective:* the least expensive (*the cheapest*) = der/die/das billigste.

the least expensive shop = der billigste Laden
the least difficult question = die einfachste Frage

at least
- (*at the minimum*) = mindestens
  he's at least 30 = er ist mindestens dreißig
- (*if nothing more, anyway*) = wenigstens
  they could at least have phoned = sie hätten wenigstens anrufen können
  he's gone out, at least I think he has = er ist rausgegangen, glaube ich wenigstens

leave *verb*
- = verlassen
  she left her husband = sie hat ihren Mann verlassen
  the train leaves London at 11 o'clock = der Zug fährt um elf Uhr von London ab
- (*depart*) = (weg)gehen (**!** *sein*), (*by car*) = (weg)fahren (**!** *sein*), (*by plane*) = abfliegen (**!** *sein*)
  we are leaving now = wir gehen jetzt
  she leaves home at 8 o'clock = sie geht um acht Uhr von zu Hause weg
- (*let remain, deposit, in will*) = hinterlassen
  he didn't leave a message = er hat keine Nachricht hinterlassen
- (*forget*) = vergessen
  I left my gloves = ich habe meine Handschuhe vergessen
- (*postpone*) = lassen
  leave it until tomorrow = lass es bis morgen
- (*allow to remain*) = lassen
  to leave the light on = das Licht anlassen
  to leave the door open = die Tür offen lassen
- (*remain*) = übrig bleiben (**!** *sein*)
  was there any food left? = ist von dem Essen etwas übrig geblieben?
- (*entrust*) = überlassen
  leave it to me = überlassen Sie es mir

leave behind
- (*not take with one*) = zurücklassen
- (*by mistake*) = vergessen

leave out
- (*not show or mention*) = auslassen
- (*exclude a person*) = ausschließen
- (*allow to remain outdoors*) = draußen lassen
  they leave the cat out all night = sie lassen die Katze die ganze Nacht draußen

Lebanon *noun*
(the) Lebanon = der Libanon ▶ **Countries p. 208**

lecture *noun*
- (*British: at university*) = (die) Vorlesung
  to give a lecture = eine Vorlesung halten
- (*public talk*) = (der) Vortrag

left
1 *noun* = (die) linke Seite
  the first street on your left = die erste Straße links
2 *adjective* = linker/linke/linkes
  his left hand = seine linke Hand
3 *adverb* = links
  to turn left = nach links abbiegen (**!** *sein*)

leg *noun*
= (das) Bein
a leg of lamb = eine Hammelkeule

legal *adjective*
* (*concerning the law*) = rechtlich
* (*lawful*) = gesetzlich

leisure *noun*
= (die) Freizeit

lemon *noun*
= (die) Zitrone

lemonade *noun*
= (die) Limonade

lend *verb*
= leihen
to lend someone money = jemandem Geld leihen

length *noun*
* = (die) Länge
to be 30 metres in length = dreißig Meter lang sein ▶**Measures p. 270**
* (*of an event*) = (die) Dauer

lens *noun*
* (*of a camera*) = (das) Objektiv
* (*of spectacles*) = (das) Brillenglas
* (*contact lens*) = (die) Linse

Leo *noun*
= (der) Löwe

leopard *noun*
= (der) Leopard

less
1 *adjective* = weniger

> **!** Note that **weniger** never changes.

less [money | time | love …] = weniger [Geld | Zeit | Liebe …]
2 *pronoun* = weniger
he reads less than she does = er liest weniger als sie
3 *adverb* = weniger
we travel less in winter = wir reisen weniger im Winter
less and less = immer weniger
less 10 per cent discount = weniger zehn Prozent Rabatt

lesson *noun*
= (die) Stunde
a driving lesson = eine Fahrstunde

let¹ *verb*
* (*used in a suggestion*)
let's eat = essen wir
let's go home = gehen wir nach Hause
* (*allow*) = lassen
she lets her do what she likes = sie lässt sie tun, was sie will
to let someone in = jemanden hereinlassen

> **!** Note the use of the separable verb formed with the prefix **herein-**.

* **let alone** = geschweige denn
he can't read, let alone write = er kann nicht lesen, geschweige denn schreiben
let down
* (*disappoint*) = enttäuschen
* (*lengthen*) = länger machen
let go
* (*stop holding*) = loslassen
let go of my arm! = lass meinen Arm los!
* (*release from captivity*) = freilassen
let in
* (*into a room or house*) = hereinlassen
let me in! = lass mich herein!
* (*unintentionally*) = durchlassen
to let in water = Wasser durchlassen
let off
* (*not punish*) = frei ausgehen lassen
* (*allow to explode*)
to let off a bomb = eine Bombe hochgehen lassen
let out
* (*allow out*) = hinauslassen, = rauslassen✶
* (*utter*) = ausstoßen
* (*make wider*) = auslassen
* (*release*)
to let a prisoner out = einen Gefangenen entlassen

let² *verb*
= vermieten
to let a room to someone = jemandem ein Zimmer vermieten
'to let' = 'zu vermieten'

letter *noun*
* (*written message*) = (der) Brief
* (*of the alphabet*) = (der) Buchstabe

letterbox *noun*
= (der) Briefkasten

lettuce *noun*
= (der) Salat
a lettuce = ein Kopf Salat

level
1 *noun* = (die) Höhe
at sea level = auf Meereshöhe
2 *adjective*
* (*flat*) = eben
a level surface = eine ebene Oberfläche
a level teaspoon of sugar = ein gestrichener Teelöffel Zucker
* (*at the same height*) = auf gleicher Höhe

liar *noun*
= (der) Lügner/(die) Lügnerin

Libra *noun*
= (die) Waage

library *noun*
= (die) Bibliothek

licence (*British*), **license** (*US*) *noun*
= (die) Genehmigung

lick *verb*
= lecken

L

Letter-writing

Addressing the envelope

The addressed person's title appears on a separate line, in the accusative:

Mr = Herrn
Mrs = Frau
Miss = Fräulein
Ms = Frau

On the next line comes the person's name, and on the next the name of the street, followed by the house number. Then comes the postcode (= **die Postleitzahl**), followed by the town. The German postcode refers to a town or to part of a larger town or city.

Frau
Elisabeth Becker
Oderstraße 28
82577 München
Germany

Beginnings

To someone you know well:

Dear Hans, = Lieber Hans!
Dear Gabi, = Liebe Gabi!

The letter itself starts on the next line with a capital. Or you can use a comma instead of the exclamation mark, as in English, and this is followed by a small letter:

Dear Natalie and Peter, = Liebe Natalie, lieber Peter,

To someone you do not know:

Dear Mr Braun = Lieber Herr Braun
Dear Ms Fischer = Liebe Frau Fischer

In a formal business letter:

Dear Mr Schneider = Sehr geehrter Herr Schneider
Dear Sir or Madam = Sehr geehrte Damen und Herren

Endings

To someone you know well:

Yours = Herzliche Grüße

To someone you do not know:

Yours sincerely = Mit freundlichen Grüßen

In a formal business letter:

Yours faithfully = Mit freundlichen Empfehlungen, = Hochachtungsvoll

---

lid *noun*
= (der) Deckel

lie
1 *verb*
• = liegen
he is lying on the carpet = er liegt auf dem Teppich
to lie down on the sofa = sich auf das Sofa legen
• (*be situated*) = liegen (**!** sein)
the village lies in the valley = das Dorf liegt im Tal
• (*not tell the truth*) = lügen
to lie to someone = jemanden belügen
2 *noun* = (die) Lüge
to tell a lie = lügen
lie down
= sich hinlegen

life *noun*
= (das) Leben
throughout his life = sein ganzes Leben lang

lift
1 *verb* = heben
2 *noun*
• (*British: elevator*) = (der) Aufzug
• **to give someone a lift** (*in a car*) = jemanden mitnehmen
lift up
= hochheben

light
1 *noun*
• = (das) Licht
turn the light on = mach das Licht an
• (*lamp*) = (die) Lampe

- (*in the street*) = (die) Straßenlampe
- (**traffic**) **lights** = (die) Ampel
  the lights are green = die Ampel ist grün
- **have you got a light?** (*for a cigarette*) = haben Sie Feuer?

2 *adjective*
- (*not dark*) = hell
  light blue = hellblau ▶**Colours p. 204**
  it's still light outside = es ist immer noch hell draußen
- (*not heavy*) = leicht

3 *verb*
- (*with a match*) = anzünden
- (*illuminate*) = beleuchten

lighter *noun*
= (das) Feuerzeug

light bulb *noun*
= (die) Glühbirne

lightning *noun*
= (der) Blitz

like¹ *preposition*
- = wie (+ *nominative*)
  what's it like? = wie ist es?
  he cried like a child = er hat wie ein Kind geweint
  like this/that = so
- (*similar to*) = ähnlich (+ *dative*)
  she looks like her mother = sie sieht ihrer Mutter ähnlich

like² *verb*
- = mögen
  I like Paul but I don't like Peter = ich mag Paul, aber Peter mag ich nicht
  I like [reading | dancing | working …] = ich [lese | tanze | arbeite …] gerne
  do you like the dress? = gefällt dir das Kleid?
  I like chocolate/tea = ich esse gerne Schokolade/ich trinke gerne Tee
- (*want*)
  would you like some cake? = möchten Sie ein Stück Kuchen?
  I'd like a drink = ich würde gerne etwas trinken
  if you like = wenn du willst

likely *adjective*
= wahrscheinlich
it is likely that he will come = wahrscheinlich kommt er

❗ Note that the future is often translated by the German present tense.

limit
1 *noun* = (die) Grenze
2 *verb* = begrenzen

limited *adjective*
= begrenzt
a limited company = eine Gesellschaft mit beschränkter Haftung

line
1 *noun*

- = Linie
  a straight line = eine gerade Linie
- (*in writing*) = (die) Zeile
- (*US: queue*) = (die) Schlange
  to stand in line = Schlange stehen
- (*row*) = (die) Reihe
- (*wrinkle*) = (die) Falte
- (*for fishing*) = (die) Leine
- (*phone line*) = (die) Leitung
  it's a bad line = die Verbindung ist schlecht
- (*railway track*) = (das) Gleis
- (*line of business*) = (die) Branche

2 *verb*
= füttern
to line a coat = einen Mantel füttern

line up
- = aufstellen
- **the children lined up** = die Kinder stellten sich auf

linen *noun*
- (*fabric*) = (das) Leinen
- (*for household use*) = (die) Wäsche

link
1 *noun*
- (*connection*) = (die) Verbindung
- (*in a chain*) = (das) Glied
2 *verb* = verbinden

lion *noun*
= (der) Löwe

lioness *noun*
= (die) Löwin

lip *noun*
= (die) Lippe

lipstick *noun*
= (der) Lippenstift

Lisbon *noun*
= (das) Lissabon ▶**Countries p. 208**

list
1 *noun* = (die) Liste
2 *verb* = auflisten

listen *verb*
= zuhören (+ *dative*)
to listen to the teacher = dem Lehrer zuhören
to listen to the radio = Radio hören

liter (*US*) ▶litre

literature *noun*
= (die) Literatur

Lithuania *noun*
= (das) Litauen ▶**Countries p. 208**

litre *noun* (*British*)
= (der) Liter ▶**Measures p. 270**

litter *noun*
- (*rubbish*) = (der) Abfall
- (*baby animals*) = (der) Wurf

little
1 *adjective*
- (*small*) = klein
- (*not much*) = wenig

L

2 *pronoun*
  a little = ein wenig

> **!** Note that **ein wenig** *never changes.*

  I have a little left = ich habe ein wenig
    übrig
3 *adverb* = wenig
  he writes little now = er schreibt nur noch
    wenig
  a little (bit) slow = ein bisschen langsam

live¹ *verb*
- (*exist*) = leben
  you can't live on that = davon kann man
    nicht leben
- (*reside*) = wohnen
  he lives in a small village = er wohnt in
    einem kleinen Dorf
  he lives in Rome = er lebt in Rom

live²
1 *adjective*
- (*alive*) = lebendig
- (*of a performance*) = Live-
  a live broadcast = eine Livesendung
- (*of a wire*) = Strom führend
2 *adverb*
  to broadcast a concert live = ein Konzert
    live senden

lively *adjective*
  = lebhaft

living room *noun*
  = (das) Wohnzimmer

load
1 *noun*
- (*cargo*) = (die) Ladung
- **loads of** |money | work | toys ...| = jede Menge
  or ein Haufen✶ [Geld | Arbeit | Spielzeug ...]
2 *verb*
  to load a truck with wood = einen
    Lastwagen mit Holz beladen
  to load a camera = einen Film einlegen

loaf *noun*
  = (das) Brot
  a loaf of bread = ein Brot

loan
1 *noun*
- = (die) Leihgabe
- (*money*) = (das) Darlehen
2 *verb* = leihen

lobster *noun*
  = (der) Hummer

local *adjective*
  = lokal
  the local newspaper = die Lokalzeitung
  the local people = die Einheimischen
  our local shops = die Geschäfte bei uns in
    der Nähe
  a local call = ein Ortsgespräch

location *noun*
  = (die) Lage

✶ in informal situations

lock
1 *verb* = abschliessen
2 *noun* = (das) Schloss
lock in
  = einschließen
lock up
- = abschließen
- (*imprison*) = einsperren

locker *noun*
  = (das) Schließfach

log *noun*
  = (der) Baumstamm
  (*for a fire*) = (das) Holzscheit

logical *adjective*
  = logisch

lonely *adjective*
  = einsam

long
1 *adjective* = lang
  10 metres long = zehn Meter lang
  a long journey = eine weite Reise
  it's quite a long way = es ist ziemlich weit
  a long time = lange
  the film is two hours long = der Film dauert
    zwei Stunden
2 *adverb* = lange
  it won't take long = es dauert nicht lange
  I won't be long = ich bin gleich fertig
  all day long = den ganzen Tag
  as long as = solange

long-sighted *adjective*
  = weitsichtig

look
1 *verb*
- = sehen, = schauen
  he looked out of the window = er sah aus
    dem Fenster
  to look at someone = jemanden ansehen
- (*appear*) = aussehen
  what does he look like? = wie sieht er aus?
2 *noun*
- (*appearance*) = (das) Aussehen
  to have a look at something = sich (*dative*)
    etwas ansehen
- (*expression*) = (der) Blick
  a look of sadness = ein trauriger Blick
look after
- (*attend to*) = sich kümmern um
  (+ *accusative*)
- (*keep in good condition*) = pflegen
look around
  = sich umsehen
look back
- (*glance back*) = sich umsehen
- (*recall*)
  to look back on something = auf etwas
    (*accusative*) zurückblicken
look for
  = suchen
  he is looking for a job = er sucht eine Stelle

look forward to
= sich freuen auf (+ *accusative*)
to look forward to doing something = sich
darauf freuen, etwas zu tun

look on to
= gehen auf (+ *accusative*) (**!** *sein*)
my bedroom looks on to the garden =
mein Schlafzimmer geht auf den Garten

look out for
= aufpassen auf (+ *accusative*)
look out! = Vorsicht!

look up
• (*in a book*) = nachschlagen
to look up a word = ein Wort nachschlagen
• (*raise one's eyes*) = aufsehen
• **to look up to someone** = zu jemandem
aufsehen

loose *adjective*
• (*of a knot, screw, tooth*) = locker
• (*of a page*) = lose
• (*of clothes*) = weit

lord *noun*
= (der) Lord

lorry *noun* (*British*)
= (der) Lastwagen

lose *verb*
= verlieren
to lose weight = abnehmen
the clock loses (**time**) = die Uhr geht nach

loss *noun*
= (der) Verlust

lost *adjective*
= verloren
(*of a person*) = vermisst
to get lost = sich verlaufen

lot *pronoun*
a lot = viel
he drinks a lot = er trinkt viel
a lot of = viel, (*many*) = viele
to have a lot of [energy | time | money ...] =
viel [Energie | Zeit | Geld ...] haben
a lot of [children | dresses | books ...] = viele
[Kinder | Kleider | Bücher ...]

lottery *noun*
= (die) Lotterie, = (das) Lotto

loud *adjective*
• (*of sounds*) = laut
• (*of colours*) = grell

loudspeaker *noun*
= (der) Lautsprecher

lounge *noun*
• (*in a house*) = (das) Wohnzimmer
• (*in a hotel, airport*) = (die) Halle
the departure lounge = die Abflughalle
• (*US: bar*) = (die) Bar

love
1 *verb*
• = lieben
they love each other = sie lieben sich

• (*enjoy*)
to love doing something = etwas sehr
gerne tun
I love chocolate = ich mag Schokolade sehr
gerne
I'd love to come = ich würde sehr gerne
kommen
2 *noun* = (die) Liebe
to be in love with someone = in jemanden
verliebt sein

lovely *adjective*
• (*beautiful*) = schön
• (*pleasant*) = nett

low
1 *adjective*
• = niedrig
a low ceiling = eine niedrige Decke
low tide = (die) Ebbe
• (*of a sound, cloud, note*) = tief
2 *adverb*
• (*in a low position*) = niedrig
lower down the page = weiter unten auf
der Seite
• (*not loud*) = leise
(*at a low pitch*) = tief

loyal *adjective*
= treu

luck *noun*
= (das) Glück
to bring someone (**good**) **luck** = jemandem
Glück bringen
good luck! = viel Glück!
bad luck = (das) Pech

lucky *adjective*
= glücklich
my lucky number = meine Glückszahl
to be lucky = Glück haben

luggage *noun*
= (das) Gepäck

lump *noun*
• (*on the body*) = (die) Beule
• (*of sugar, coal*) = (das) Stück
• (*shapeless mass*) = (der) Klumpen

lunch *noun*
= (das) Mittagessen
to have lunch = zu Mittag essen

lung *noun*
= (der) Lungenflügel
lungs = (die) Lunge

Luxembourg *noun*
= (das) Luxemburg ▶**Countries p. 208**

luxury
1 *noun* = (der) Luxus
2 *adjective* = Luxus-
a luxury hotel = ein Luxushotel

L

Mm

machine *noun*
• = (die) Maschine
• (*slot-machine*) = (der) Automat

mad *adjective*
• (*crazy*) = verrückt
  are you mad? = bist du verrückt
  geworden?
• (*angry*) = wütend
  to be mad at someone = auf jemanden
  wütend sein
• (*keen*)
  to be mad about something = ganz wild
  auf etwas (*accusative*) sein✗

magazine *noun*
= (die) Zeitschrift
(*containing mostly photos*) = (das) Magazin

magic
1 *adjective*
• (*supernatural*) = magisch
• (*in tricks*) = Zauber-
  magic wand = (der) Zauberstab
2 *noun*
• (*witchcraft*) = (die) Magie
• (*tricks*) = (die) Zauberei

magnet *noun*
= (der) Magnet

magnificent *adjective*
= herrlich

magnifying glass *noun*
= (die) Lupe

maiden name *noun*
= (der) Mädchenname

mail
1 *noun*
  (*post*) = (die) Post
2 *verb*
• = mit der Post schicken
• (*send off*) = abschicken
  (*put in a postbox*) = einwerfen

mailbox *noun* (*US*)
= (der) Briefkasten

mailman *noun* (*US*)
= (der) Briefträger

main *adjective*
= Haupt-
  the main problem = das Hauptproblem

main course *noun*
= (das) Hauptgericht

main road *noun*
= (die) Hauptstraße

✗ in informal situations

maintain *verb*
• (*preserve*) = aufrechterhalten
• (*take care of*) = instand halten

maize *noun*
= (der) Mais

major
1 *adjective*
• (*important*) = groß
  of major importance = von großer
  Bedeutung
• (*serious*) = schwer
2 *noun* = (der) Major
3 *verb* (*US*)
  to major in English = Englisch als
  Hauptfach studieren

majority *noun*
= (die) Mehrheit

make
1 *verb*
• (*do, cause to be*) = machen
  to make [the bed | a noise | breakfast ...] = [das
  Bett | Lärm | Frühstück ...] machen
  it makes you [thirsty | tired | sad ...] = das
  macht einen [durstig | müde | traurig ...]
  to make someone laugh = jemanden zum
  Lachen bringen

  ! Note that the general verb **make** is often
  translated by a German verb relating
  more specifically to the action.

  to make a cake = einen Kuchen backen
  to make a speech = eine Rede halten
  to make a dress = ein Kleid nähen
  to make a film = einen Film drehen
  to make a phone call = telefonieren
  to make friends with someone = sich mit
  jemandem anfreunden
  to make room = Platz schaffen
• (*manufacture*) = herstellen
  to make wine from grapes = aus Trauben
  Wein machen
  made in Germany = in Deutschland
  hergestellt
  made of [gold | cotton | plastic ...] = aus [Gold |
  Baumwolle | Plastik ...]
• (*cause to do*)
  to make someone do something =
  jemanden dazu bringen, etwas zu tun
  to make someone wait = jemanden warten
  lassen
• (*force*) = zwingen
  they made me give them the money = sie
  haben mich gezwungen, ihnen das Geld
  zu geben
• (*earn*) = verdienen
  to make a lot of money = viel Geld
  verdienen
2 *noun* = (die) Marke
make do
= zurechtkommen (**!** *sein*)
make out
• (*understand*) = verstehen
  I can't make him out = ich kann ihn nicht
  verstehen

- (*write out*) = ausstellen
  to make a cheque out to someone = jemandem einen Scheck ausstellen

make up
- (*be friends again*) = sich versöhnen
- (*invent*) = erfinden
- (*compile*) = zusammenstellen
- **to make up one's mind** = sich entschließen

make-up *noun*
= (das) Make-up
to put on make-up = sich schminken

male
1 *adjective* = männlich
2 *noun*
- (*man*) = (der) Mann
- (*animal*) = (das) Männchen

man *noun*
- = (der) Mann
- (*human race*) = (der) Mensch

manage *verb*
- (*run*) = leiten
  he manages the hotel = er leitet das Hotel
- (*be able to*)
  to manage to |finish one's homework | find a job | be on time …| = es schaffen, [seine Hausaufgaben fertig zu machen | eine Stelle zu finden | pünktlich zu sein …]
- (*cope*) = zurechtkommen (**!** *sein*)
  can you manage? = kommst du zurecht?

manager *noun*
- (*of a company, bank*) = (der) Direktor
- (*of a shop*) = (der) Geschäftsführer
- (*of a soccer team*) = (der) Trainer

manageress *noun*
- (*of a company, bank*) = (die) Direktorin
- (*of a shop*) = (die) Geschäftsführerin
- (*of a soccer team*) = (die) Trainerin

manner *noun*
= (die) Art

manners *noun*
= Manieren (*plural*)
to have good manners = gute Manieren haben
it's bad manners to grin = es gehört sich nicht zu grinsen

manual *noun*
= (das) Handbuch

manufacture *verb*
= herstellen

many
1 *adjective* = viele
how many people were there? = wie viele Leute waren da?
so many = so viele
2 *pronoun* = viele
many find work abroad = viele finden Arbeit im Ausland
how many? = wie viele?

map *noun*
= (die) Karte
(*of a town*) = (der) Stadtplan

marble *noun*
= (der) Marmor

march *noun*
1 *verb* = marschieren (**!** *sein*)
2 *noun* = (der) Marsch

March *noun*
= (der) März ▶**Dates p. 213**

margarine *noun*
= (die) Margarine

mark
1 *noun*
- (*stain*) = (der) Fleck
  (*scratch*) = (der) Kratzer
- (*on the body*) = (das) Mal
- (*grade*) = (die) Note
  to get good marks = gute Noten bekommen
- (*German money*) = (die) Mark
- (*in races*)
  on your marks! = auf die Plätze!
2 *verb*
- (*stain*) = Flecken machen auf (+ *dative*)
  (*damage*) = beschädigen
- (*correct*) = korrigieren
- (*indicate*) = markieren
- (*in sports*) = decken

market
1 *noun* = (der) Markt
the job market = der Arbeitsmarkt
2 *verb*
(*sell*) = vertreiben

marketing *noun*
= (das) Marketing

marmalade *noun*
= (die) Orangenmarmelade

marriage *noun*
- = (die) Ehe
- (*wedding*) = (die) Hochzeit

married *adjective*
= verheiratet
to be married to someone = mit jemandem verheiratet sein

marry *verb*
= heiraten
to get married to someone = jemanden heiraten

marvellous (*British*), **marvelous** (*US*)
   adjective
= wunderbar

marzipan *noun*
= (das) Marzipan

mascara *noun*
= (die) Wimperntusche

masculine
1 *adjective* = männlich
2 *noun*
(*in grammar*) = (das) Maskulinum

M

mash verb
= stampfen

mashed potatoes noun
= (der) Kartoffelbrei

mask noun
= (die) Maske

mass noun
• (large number) = (die) Masse
 a mass of people = eine große
 Menschenmenge
• (in church) = (die) Messe

massive adjective
= riesig

mast noun
= (der) Mast

master
1 noun
• = (der) Herr
 (dog owner) = (das) Herrchen
• (artist) = (der) Meister
• (British: teacher) = (der) Lehrer
2 verb = beherrschen

mat noun
= (die) Matte

match
1 noun
• (game) = (das) Spiel
• (matchstick) = (das) Streichholz
2 verb = passen zu (+ dative)
 the shoes match the skirt = die Schuhe
 passen zu dem Rock

matchbox noun
= (die) Streichholzschachtel

mate
1 noun
• = (der) Gehilfe
• (British: friend) = (der) Freund,
 = (der) Kumpel✘
2 verb = sich paaren

material noun
• (substance) = (das) Material
• (cloth, information for a novel) = (der) Stoff

math noun (US)
= (die) Mathe✘

mathematics noun
= (die) Mathematik

maths noun (British)
= (die) Mathe✘

matter
1 noun
• (affair) = (die) Angelegenheit, = (die) Sache
 money matters = Geldangelegenheiten
 it's a private matter = das ist eine
 Privatsache

• (question) = (die) Frage
 a matter of = eine Frage (+ genitive)
 it's only a matter of time = es ist nur noch
 eine Frage der Zeit
• (problem)
 what's the matter with her? = was ist mit
 ihr los?
2 verb = etwas ausmachen
 it doesn't matter = das macht nichts
 does it really matter? = ist das wirklich so
 wichtig?

mattress noun
= (die) Matratze

mature adjective
= reif

maximum adjective
= maximal
 a maximum temperature of 40° = eine
 Höchsttemperatur von vierzig Grad

may verb
• (stating possibility) = können
 they may be able to come after all = sie
 können vielleicht doch kommen
• (when asking for or giving permission) =
 dürfen
 may I come in? = darf ich reinkommen✘?

May noun
= (der) Mai ▶ **Dates p. 213**

maybe adverb
= vielleicht

mayor noun
= (der) Bürgermeister/(die) Bürgermeisterin

maze noun
= (der) Irrgarten

me pronoun

> **!** In German this pronoun changes
> according to its function in the sentence.
> As a direct object it is in the accusative,
> **mich**, and as an indirect object it is in the
> dative, **mir**.

• (in the accusative) = mich
 she loves me = sie liebt mich
 did you do it for me? = hast du das für
 mich getan?
• (in the dative) = mir
 give me the money = gib mir das Geld
 he never talks to me = er redet nie mit mir
• (in the nominative, as a complement) = ich
 it's me = ich bins

> **!** Note that **bins**, written as one word, is
> short for **bin es**.

meadow noun
= (die) Wiese

meal noun
• = (die) Mahlzeit
• (food) = (das) Essen
 to cook a meal = Essen kochen
 to go out for a meal = essen gehen

✘ in informal situations

mean
1 *verb*
* = bedeuten
  what does that mean? = was bedeutet das?
* (*intend*) = beabsichtigen
  I meant to [invite them for dinner | order a pizza | go to the cinema ...] = ich wollte [sie zum Essen einladen | eine Pizza bestellen | ins Kino gehen ...]
  she meant well = sie meinte es gut
* (*be supposed to*)
  to be meant for something = für etwas (*accusative*) bestimmt sein
  she is meant to be doing her homework = sie soll ihre Hausaufgaben machen
* (*intend to say*) = meinen
  do you see what I mean? = verstehst du, was ich meine?
2 *adjective*
* (*not generous*) = geizig
* (*nasty*) = gemein

meaning *noun*
= (die) Bedeutung

means *noun*
* (*way*) = (das) Mittel, = (die) Möglichkeit
  means of transport = (das) Verkehrsmittel
  a means of earning money = eine Möglichkeit, Geld zu verdienen
  by means of = mit Hilfe (+ *genitive*)
* (*money*) = Mittel (*plural*)

meanwhile *adverb*
= inzwischen

measles *noun*
= Masern (*plural*)

measure
1 *verb* = messen
  to measure a room = ein Zimmer ausmessen
2 *noun*
  (*step*) = (die) Maßnahme
  to take measures = Maßnahmen ergreifen

measurement *noun*
= (das) Maß
to take someone's measurements = bei jemandem Maß nehmen

meat *noun*
= (das) Fleisch

mechanical *adjective*
= mechanisch

medal *noun*
= (der) Orden
(*in sport*) = (die) Medaille

media *noun*
the media = die Medien (*plural*)

medical *adjective*
= medizinisch
(*of treatment*) = ärztlich
to have medical treatment = in ärztlicher Behandlung sein

medicine *noun*
* (*subject, profession*) = (die) Medizin
* (*drug*) = (das) Medikament

Mediterranean
1 *noun*
  the Mediterranean (Sea) = das Mittelmeer
2 *adjective* = Mittelmeer-
  a Mediterranean climate = ein Mittelmeerklima

medium *adjective*
= mittlerer/mittlere/mittleres
it's a medium size = das ist eine mittlere Größe

meet *verb*
* (*by chance*) = treffen
  she met him in the shopping centre = sie hat ihn im Einkaufszentrum getroffen
  they met in the street = sie trafen sich auf der Straße
* (*by arrangement*) = sich treffen mit (+ *dative*)
  I meet her every Tuesday = ich treffe mich jeden Dienstag mit ihr
  to meet again = sich wieder treffen
* (*get to know*) = kennen lernen
  she met him on holiday = sie hat ihn auf Urlaub kennen gelernt
  I've never met her = ich kenne sie nicht
* (*collect*) = abholen
  she's meeting me at the airport = sie holt mich vom Flughafen ab
* (*fulfil*) = erfüllen
  to meet a condition = eine Bedingung erfüllen
meet up
= sich treffen

meeting *noun*
* = (das) Treffen
* (*discussion*) = (die) Besprechung

melon *noun*
= (die) Melone

melt *verb*
= schmelzen (**!** *sein*)

member *noun*
= (das) Mitglied
family member = (der/die) Angehörige

memory *noun*
* (*ability to remember*) = (das) Gedächtnis
* (*thing remembered*) = (die) Erinnerung
* (*of a computer*) = (der) Speicher

mend *verb*
(*fix*) = reparieren
(*by sewing*) = ausbessern

mental *adjective*
= geistig
mental illness = (die) Geisteskrankheit

mention *verb*
= erwähnen
thank you very much—don't mention it = herzlichen Dank—bitte

M

Measures

The metric system of measures is used in German.

Length

millimetre = (der) Millimeter (mm)   *metre* = (der) Meter (m)
centimetre = (der) Zentimeter (cm)   *kilometre* = (der) Kilometer (km)

Note that German uses a comma instead of a decimal point:

1 inch = 2,54 cm   *1 yard* = 91,44 cm
1 foot = 30,48 cm   *1 mile* = 1,61 km

how long is the rope? = wie lang ist das Seil?
it's 3 metres too long = es ist um drei Meter zu lang

Height

When talking about people:

how tall is he? = wie groß ist er?
he's six feet (1.83 metres) tall = er ist 1,83 groß, = er ist ein Meter dreiundachtzig groß
he's taller than me = er ist größer als ich
at a height of 2 metres = in zwei Meter Höhe

Distance

how far is it from Frankfurt to Munich? = wie weit is es von Frankfurt bis München?
it's about 300 kilometres = es sind ungefähr dreihundert Kilometer
the distance between the houses is 12 metres = die Entfernung zwischen den Häusern beträgt zwölf Meter
at a distance of 5 kilometres = in einer Entfernung von fünf Kilometern

Speed

kilometres per hour = Stundenkilometer (km/h)
he was doing 120 k.p.h. = er fuhr hundertzwanzig Stundenkilometer

Width/depth

how wide is it? = wie breit is es?
how deep is it? = wie tief ist es?
at a depth of 10 metres = in zehn Meter Tiefe

Weight

gram = (das) Gramm (g)   *1 oz* = 28,35 g
kilogram = (das) Kilogramm (kg)   *1 lb* = 453,6 g
kilo = (das) Kilo
tonne = (die) Tonne (t)

Note that a *pound* is translated by **ein Pfund**, but in German this is the equivalent of 500 grams (half a kilo).

When you are expressing a quantity of something in German, masculine and neuter nouns stay in the singular:

250 grams of cheese = zweihundertfünfzig Gramm Käse
3 pieces of cake = drei Stück Torte

But feminine nouns are in the plural:

2 bottles of coke = zwei Flaschen Cola

how much does it weigh? = wie viel wiegt es?
it weighs 3 pounds = es wiegt drei Pfund
to get 4 apples to the pound = vier Äpfel je Pfund bekommen

Capacity

litre = (der) Liter (l)
1 pint (British) = 0,568 Liter, *(US)* = 0,473 Liter
half a litre of mineral water = ein halber Liter Mineralwasser

Note that both **Liter** and **Meter** can be neuter as well as masculine.

Temperature

20 degrees Celsius or centigrade = zwanzig Grad Celsius

menu *noun*
- (*in a restaurant*) = (die) Speisekarte
- (*in computing*) = (das) Menü

mercy *noun*
= (die) Gnade
to be at someone's mercy = jemandem ausgeliefert sein

mess *noun*
- (*untidiness*) = (das) Durcheinander
your room is in a mess = dein Zimmer ist unordentlich
to make a mess on something = etwas schmutzig machen
- (*difficult situation*) = Schwierigkeiten (*plural*)
mess around
(*be silly*) = herumalbern
mess up
- (*botch*) = verpfuschen
- (*make dirty*) = schmutzig machen
(*untidy*) = in Unordnung bringen

message *noun*
= (die) Nachricht

messenger *noun*
= (der) Bote/(die) Botin

metal *noun*
= (das) Metall

meter *noun*
- (*for gas, electricity*) = (der) Zähler
- (*for parking*) = (die) Parkuhr
- (*US*) ▶metre

method *noun*
= (die) Methode

metre *noun* (*British*)
= (der) Meter ▶**Measures p. 270**

Mexico *noun*
= (das) Mexiko ▶**Countries p. 208**

microphone *noun*
= (das) Mikrofon

microscope *noun*
= (das) Mikroskop

microwave *noun*
(*oven*) = (der) Mikrowellenherd

midday *noun*
= (der) Mittag
at midday = mittags

middle *noun*
= (die) Mitte
in the middle of the night = mitten in der Nacht
in the middle of August = Mitte August
to be in the middle of [writing a letter | cooking ...] = gerade dabei sein [, einen Brief zu schreiben | zu kochen ...]

Middle Ages *noun*
the Middle Ages = das Mittelalter

middle class
1 *noun*
= (der) Mittelstand
2 *adjective* = bürgerlich

midnight *noun*
= (die) Mitternacht

midwife *noun*
= (die) Hebamme

might *verb*

> ! The subjunctive of **können** *is usually used to translate* **might**, *expressing a possibility or suggestion.*

- (*talking about a possibility*)
she might be right = sie könnte Recht haben
will you come?—I might = kommst du? —vielleicht
- (*referring to something that did not happen*)
she might have warned us = sie hätte uns warnen können
- (*making a polite suggestion*)
you might try leaving a message = Sie könnten versuchen, eine Nachricht zu hinterlassen

mild *adjective*
- (*gentle*) = mild
- (*not serious*) = leicht
a mild infection = eine leichte Infektion

mile *noun*
= (die) Meile ▶**Measures p. 270**
it's miles too big = es ist viel zu groß

military *adjective*
= militärisch

milk
1 *noun* = (die) Milch
2 *verb* = melken

mill *noun*
= (die) Mühle

millennium *noun*
= (das) Jahrtausend

million *noun*
= (die) Million ▶**Numbers p. 282**
a million marks = eine Million Mark

millionaire *noun*
= (der) Millionär/(die) Millionärin

mince
1 *noun* (*British*) = (das) Hackfleisch
2 *verb* = durchdrehen

mind
1 *noun*
- (*a person's thoughts*) = (der) Verstand
to have a logical mind = logisch denken
to take someone's mind off things = jemanden auf andere Gedanken bringen
to bear something in mind = etwas nicht vergessen

M

* (*a person's opinions or attitudes*)
  to make up one's mind to [live in Germany | change jobs | move ...] = sich entschließen [, in Deutschland zu leben | , die Stelle zu wechseln | umzuziehen ...]
  I've made up my mind = ich habe mich entschieden
  I've changed my mind = ich habe es mir anders überlegt
  she knows her own mind = sie weiß, was sie will
2 *verb*
* (*when expressing an opinion*)
  where would you like to sit?—I don't mind = wo willst du sitzen?—das ist mir egal
  I don't mind where I sit = mir ist egal, wo ich sitze
  she doesn't mind the heat = die Hitze macht ihr nichts aus
* (*in polite questions or requests*)
  would you mind [closing the window | turning the radio down | waiting ...]? = würden Sie bitte [das Fenster zumachen | warten | das Radio leiser stellen ...]?
* (*be careful*) = aufpassen
  mind the step! = Achtung Stufe!
  mind you don't fall = pass auf, dass du nicht stolperst
* (*take care of*) = sich kümmern um (+ *accusative*)
* (*worry*)
  never mind! = macht nichts!

mine¹ *pronoun*
= meiner/meine/meins

> **!** *Note that the pronoun agrees in number and gender with the noun it represents:* mine (*meaning the pencil*) is red = meiner (*der Bleistift*) ist rot; mine (*meaning the shoes*) are new = meine (*die Schuhe*) sind neu.

his shirt is white but mine is blue = sein Hemd ist weiß, aber meins ist blau
his sister is the same age as mine = seine Schwester ist genauso alt wie meine
a friend of mine = ein Freund von mir

mine²
1 *noun*
* (*for coal, metals*) = (das) Bergwerk
  to work down the mines = unter Tage arbeiten
* (*explosive*) = (die) Mine
2 *verb* = abbauen
  to mine for coal = Kohle abbauen

miner *noun*
= (der) Bergarbeiter

mineral water *noun*
= (das) Mineralwasser

minimum *adjective*
= Mindest-
  to pay the minimum price = den Mindestpreis zahlen

minister *noun*
* (*in government*) = (der) Minister/ (die) Ministerin
* (*of religion*) = (der/die) Geistliche

minor
1 *adjective* = kleinerer/kleinere/kleineres
  a minor injury = eine kleinere Verletzung
  a minor role = eine Nebenrolle
2 *noun* = (der/die) Minderjährige

minority *noun*
= (die) Minderheit

mint *noun*
* (*herb*) = (die) Minze
* (*sweet*) = (der) *or* (das) Pfefferminzbonbon

minus *preposition*
= minus (+ *genitive*)
  six minus two is four = sechs minus zwei ist vier
  it's minus four degrees = es ist minus vier Grad

minute *noun* ▶
* = (die) Minute ▶**Time p. 331**
* (*moment*) = (der) Moment
  in a minute = gleich
  wait a minute! = einen Moment bitte!

minutes *noun*
= (das) Protokoll
  to take the minutes = das Protokoll führen

miracle *noun*
= (das) Wunder

mirror *noun*
= (der) Spiegel

miserable *adjective*
* (*unhappy*) = unglücklich
  to look miserable = unglücklich aussehen
  to feel miserable = sich elend fühlen
* (*awful*)
  the weather is miserable = das Wetter ist fürchterlich

miss *verb*
* (*fail to hit*) = nicht treffen
  the stone missed his head = der Stein hat seinen Kopf nicht getroffen
  to miss the target = das Ziel verfehlen
* (*fail to see*) = übersehen
* (*fail to take, catch*) = verpassen
  to miss the train = den Zug verpassen
* (*fail to understand*) = nicht mitbekommen
* (*feel sad not to see*) = vermissen
  I miss you = ich vermisse dich
* (*fail to go to*) = versäumen
  to miss school = in der Schule fehlen

Miss *noun*
* = Fräulein, = Frau

> **!** *It is now usual to address adult women as* **Frau**, *whether or not they are married.*

  good morning, Miss Jones (*to a girl*) = guten Morgen, Fräulein Jones, (*to a woman*) = guten Morgen, Frau Jones

- (*in a letter*)
  Dear Miss Jones (*to a girl*) = Sehr geehrtes Fräulein Jones, (*to a woman*) = Sehr geehrte Frau Jones ▶**Letter-writing p. 262**

missing *adjective*
- = fehlend
  to be missing = fehlen
- (*lost*) = verschwunden
  he went missing yesterday = er wird seit gestern vermisst

mist *noun*
= (der) Nebel

mistake *noun*
= (der) Fehler
spelling mistake = (der) Rechtschreibfehler
by mistake = aus Versehen

misunderstand *verb*
= missverstehen

misunderstanding *noun*
= (das) Missverständnis

mix
1 *verb*
- (*put together*) = mischen
  to mix wine and water = Wein und Wasser mischen
  to mix cream into the sauce = Sahne in die Soße rühren
- (*go together*) = sich mischen
  oil doesn't mix with water = Öl mischt sich nicht mit Wasser
- (*be sociable*) = Kontakt mit anderen Menschen haben
2 *noun* = (die) Mischung
mix up
- (*get confused*) = durcheinander bringen
- (*mistake for*) = verwechseln
  I'm always mixing him up with his brother = ich verwechsele ihn immer mit seinem Bruder

mixture *noun*
= (die) Mischung

moan *verb*
- (*groan*) = stöhnen
- (*complain*) = jammern

mobile phone *noun*
= (das) Mobiltelefon, = (das) Handy

model *noun*
- (*of a train, building*) = (das) Modell
- (*fashion model*) = (das) Mannequin

modem *noun*
= (der) Modem

modern *adjective*
= modern

mole *noun*
- (*animal*) = (der) Maulwurf
- (*spot on the skin*) = (der) Leberfleck

moment *noun*
= (der) Moment
it will be ready in a moment = es ist gleich fertig
there's no one there at the moment = im Moment ist niemand da

Monday *noun*
= (der) Montag ▶**Dates p. 213**

money *noun*
= (das) Geld

monkey *noun*
= (der) Affe

monster *noun*
= (das) Ungeheuer

month *noun*
= (der) Monat

monument *noun*
= (das) Denkmal

mood *noun*
= (die) Laune
to be in a good mood = gute Laune haben
to not be in the mood for working = keine Lust zum Arbeiten haben

moody *adjective*
= launisch

moon *noun*
= (der) Mond

moor
1 *noun* = (das) Moor
2 *verb* = festmachen

moped *noun*
= (das) Moped

moral *adjective*
= moralisch

morals *noun*
= (die) Moral

more
1 *adjective*
- = mehr

  ! Note that mehr never changes.

  more [friends | time | work ...] = mehr [Freunde | Zeit | Arbeit ...]
  there's no more bread = es ist kein Brot mehr da
- (*in addition*) = noch
  he's buying two more tickets = er kauft noch zwei Karten
  more coffee? = noch etwas Kaffee?
2 *pronoun* = mehr
  to cost more = mehr kosten
3 *adverb*
- (*when comparing*)

  ! The comparative of adjectives, such as more difficult, is formed in German by adding the ending -er (schwieriger).

  it is more interesting than I thought = es ist interessanter als ich dachte

M

Money

The German unit of currency is the mark, sometimes called *Deutschmark* in English. There are 100 pfennigs in a mark.

Note that when you are expressing an amount of money, the noun stays in the singular:

2 marks = zwei Mark (2,— DM)
a hundred marks = hundert Mark (100 DM)
one Deutschmark = eine Deutsche Mark (1,— DM)
50 pfennigs = fünfzig Pfennig (0,50 DM)
one mark ninety pfennigs = eine Mark und neunzig Pfennig (1,90 DM)
one mark ninety = eine Mark neunzig (1,90 DM)
one ninety = eins neunzig (1,90 DM)

a 50-pfennig piece = ein Fünfzigpfennigstück, = ein 50-Pfennig-Stück
a 20-mark note = ein Zwanzigmarkschein, = ein 20-Mark-Schein

pound = (das) Pfund
£5 = fünf Pfund, = fünf englische Pfund
dollar = (der) Dollar
dollar bill = (der) Dollarschein

In Austria the unit of currency is the **Schilling** (der), and in Switzerland it is the **Franken** (der). The single European currency is the **Euro** (der).

Talking about money

how much is it? = wie viel kostet das?
the dress is 100 marks = das Kleid kostet hundert Mark
to pay cash = bar zahlen
3 marks to the pound = drei Mark für ein Pfund
do you cash traveller's cheques? = lösen Sie Reiseschecks ein?
a £50 cheque = ein Scheck über fünfzig Pfund
two 50-pfennig stamps = zwei Briefmarken zu fünfzig Pfennig

---

* (*when talking about time*) = mehr
he doesn't live here any more = er wohnt hier nicht mehr
* (*more often*) = öfter
I'd like to go to the theatre more = ich würde gerne öfter ins Theater gehen
* (*other uses*)
more and more = immer mehr
more or less = mehr oder weniger

morning *noun*
= (der) Morgen
in the morning = am Morgen
3 o'clock in the morning = drei Uhr morgens
good morning! = guten Morgen!
this morning = heute Morgen
on Friday morning = am Freitagmorgen
tomorrow morning = morgen früh

mosquito *noun*
= (die) Mücke
(*tropical*) = (der) Moskito

most
1 *adjective*
* (*majority of*) = die meisten
most shops are closed = die meisten Geschäfte haben zu

* (*largest amount of*) = der meiste/ die meiste/das meiste
who has the most money? = wer hat das meiste Geld?
2 *pronoun*
* (*majority*) = die meisten
most of the time = die meiste Zeit
* (*largest amount*) = das meiste
he earns the most money = er verdient das meiste Geld
3 *adverb*
* (*when comparing*)

> **!** *The superlative of adjectives, such as* **most difficult**, *is formed in German by adding the ending* -(e)st (der/die/das schwierigste).

the most [expensive shop | difficult problem | interesting programme …] = das teuerste Geschäft | das schwierigste Problem | die interessanteste Sendung …]
* (*to the greatest degree*) = am meisten
I drank most = ich habe am meisten getrunken
* (*very*) = äußerst
a most enjoyable evening = ein äußerst angenehmer Abend
* (*other uses*)
at most = höchstens
most of all = am allermeisten

mostly adverb
= hauptsächlich

moth noun
= (der) Nachtfalter
(in clothes) = (die) Motte

mother noun
= (die) Mutter

mother-in-law noun
= (die) Schwiegermutter

motor noun
= (der) Motor

motorbike, motorcycle noun
= (das) Motorrad

motorcyclist noun
= (der) Motorradfahrer/
(die) Motorradfahrerin

motorist noun
= (der) Autofahrer/(die) Autofahrerin

motor racing noun
= (das) Autorennen

motorway noun (British)
= (die) Autobahn

mountain noun
= (der) Berg

mountain bike noun
= (das) Mountainbike

mountaineering noun
= (das) Bergsteigen

mourning noun
= (die) Trauer
to be in mourning = in Trauer sein

mouse noun
= (die) Maus

moustache (British) noun
= (der) Schnurrbart

mouth noun
• (of a person) = (der) Mund
  to have a big mouth = einen großen Mund
  haben✶
• (of an animal) = (das) Maul
• (of a river) = (die) Mündung

mouth organ noun
= (die) Mundharmonika

move
1 verb
• (of a person) = sich bewegen
  he can't move = er kann sich nicht
  bewegen
  don't move! = still halten!
• (of a vehicle) = fahren (❗ sein)
• (put elsewhere)
  to move the furniture = die Möbel rücken
  to move something somewhere else =
  etwas woandershin tun

• (make a move) = bewegen
  I can't move my leg = ich kann mein Bein
  nicht bewegen
  can you move your head to the side? =
  kannst du deinen Kopf zur Seite tun?
• (touch emotionally) = rühren
  he was deeply moved = er war sehr
  gerührt
• (act) = handeln
  to move fast = schnell handeln
• (change location) = umziehen (❗ sein)
  to move to London = nach London
  umziehen
  to move house = umziehen (❗ sein)
2 noun
• (movement) = (die) Bewegung
  to make a move = aufbrechen (❗ sein)
• (step, decision) = (der) Schritt
  to make the first move = den ersten Schritt
  tun
• (change of location) = (der) Umzug
• (in a game) = (der) Zug
  it's your move = du bist am Zug
move around
• (travel around) = unterwegs sein
• (put elsewhere) = herumräumen
  to move the furniture around = umräumen
move away
• (live elsewhere) = wegziehen (❗ sein)
• (make a movement away) = wegrücken
  (❗ sein)
  to move away from the window = vom
  Fenster wegrücken
move back
= zurückrücken (❗ sein)
(of a vehicle) = zurückfahren (❗ sein)
move forward
= vorrücken (❗ sein)
(of a vehicle) = vorwärts fahren (❗ sein)
move in
= einziehen (❗ sein)
  to move in with friends = bei Freunden
  einziehen
move off
= sich in Bewegung setzen
(of a vehicle) = losfahren (❗ sein)
move out
= ausziehen (❗ sein)
move over
= zur Seite rücken (❗ sein)

movement noun
= (die) Bewegung
a movement of the hand = eine
  Handbewegung
the women's movement = die
  Frauenbewegung

movie noun (US)
= (der) Film
at the movies = im Kino

mow verb
= mähen

MP noun (British)
= (der/die) Abgeordnete

M

Mr noun
• = (der) Herr
  good morning, Mr Jones = guten Morgen,
  Herr Jones
  we are waiting for Mr Brown's call = wir
  warten auf Herrn Browns Anruf
• (in a letter)
  Dear Mr Jones = Sehr geehrter Herr Jones
    ▶**Letter-writing p. 262**

Mrs noun
• = (die) Frau
  good morning, Mrs White = guten Morgen,
  Frau White, (very formal) = guten
  Morgen, gnädige Frau
• (in a letter)
  Dear Mrs Black = Sehr geehrte Frau Black
    ▶**Letter-writing p. 262**

Ms noun
  = (die) Frau
  Dear Ms Jones = Sehr geehrte Frau Jones
    ▶**Letter-writing p. 262**

much
1 adverb
• (a lot) = viel
  he doesn't read much = er liest nicht viel
  I'd much rather stay here = ich bleibe viel
  lieber hier
  she earns twice as much as me = sie
  verdient doppelt so viel wie ich
• (often) = oft
  they don't go to the cinema much = sie
  gehen nicht oft ins Kino
• (when used with very, too, so) = sehr
  he misses her very much = er vermisst sie
  sehr
  I don't like driving very much = ich fahre
  nicht sehr gerne Auto
2 pronoun = viel

  ! Note that viel never changes.

  I don't need much = ich brauche nicht viel
  as much as you like = so viel du willst
  how much is it? = wie viel kostet es?
  not too much = nicht zu viel
3 adjective = viel
  I haven't got much time = ich habe nicht
  viel Zeit
  we have too much work = wir haben zu
  viel Arbeit

mud noun
  = (der) Schlamm

mudguard noun
  (on a bike) = (das) Schutzblech

mug
1 noun = (der) Becher
2 verb = überfallen
  to be mugged = überfallen und beraubt
  werden (! sein)

mule noun
  = (das) Maultier

multiply verb
  (in maths) = multiplizieren
  2 multiplied by 3 is 6 = drei mal zwei ist
  sechs

mum noun
  = (die) Mutti

mumble verb
  = murmeln

mummy noun
• (mother) = (die) Mama
• (body) = (die) Mumie

murder
1 noun = (der) Mord
  to be accused of murder = des Mordes
  beschuldigt werden
2 verb = ermorden
3 adjective = Mord-
  murder suspect = (der/die) Mordverdächtige

murderer noun
  = (der) Mörder/(die) Mörderin

muscle noun
  = (der) Muskel

museum noun
  = (das) Museum

mushroom noun
  = (der) Pilz

music noun
• = (die) Musik
• (score) = Noten (plural)

musical
1 adjective = musikalisch
2 noun = (das) Musical

musical instrument noun
  = (das) Musikinstrument

musician noun
  = (der) Musiker/(die) Musikerin

Muslim
1 noun = (der) Moslem/(die) Moslime
2 adjective = moslemisch

mussel noun
  = (die) Muschel

must verb
• = müssen, (with a negative) = dürfen
  we must go = wir müssen gehen
  we mustn't be late = wir dürfen nicht zu
  spät kommen
• (when assuming something is true) =
  müssen
  you must be Peter's sister = du musst
  Peters Schwester sein

mustache (US) ▶moustache

mustard noun
  = (der) Senf

mutton noun
  = (das) Hammelfleisch

my *adjective*
= mein

> **!** Note that mein *changes its endings in the same way as* ein.

they don't like my dog = sie mögen meinen Hund nicht

myself *pronoun*
• (*when translated by a reflexive verb in German*) = mich
I've cut myself = ich habe mich geschnitten
• (*reflexive dative pronoun*) = mir
I hurt myself = ich habe mir wehgetan
I thought to myself = ich habe mir gedacht
• (*used for emphasis*) = selbst
I told them myself = ich habe es ihnen selbst gesagt
all by myself = ganz allein

mysterious *adjective*
= rätselhaft

mystery *noun*
• (*puzzle*) = (das) Rätsel
• (*secret*) = (das) Geheimnis

Nn

nail
1 *noun*
= (der) Nagel
2 *verb* = nageln
to nail a picture to the wall = ein Bild an die Wand nageln

nail varnish *noun*
= (der) Nagellack

naked *adjective*
= nackt

name
1 *noun*
• (*of a person*) = (der) Name
what's your name? = wie heißt du?, (*polite*) = wie heißen Sie?
my name is Sam = ich heiße Sam
• (*of a book, film*) = (der) Titel
2 *verb* = nennen

napkin *noun*
= (die) Serviette

nappy *noun* (*British*)
= (die) Windel

narrow
1 *adjective*
• = schmal
a narrow road = eine schmale Straße

• (*restricted*) = eng
the shoe is too narrow = der Schuh ist zu eng
2 *verb*
• (*become less wide*) = sich verengen
• (*reduce*) = verkleinern
to narrow the gap = den Abstand verkleinern

narrow-minded *adjective*
= engstirning

nasty *adjective*
• (*spiteful*) = gemein
to be nasty to someone = gemein zu jemandem sein
• (*unpleasant*) = scheußlich
a nasty smell = ein scheußlicher Geruch
• (*serious*) = schlimm
a nasty accident = ein schlimmer Unfall

nation *noun*
• (*state*) = (die) Nation
• (*people*) = (das) Volk

national
1 *adjective* = national
a national newspaper = eine überregionale Zeitung
a national strike = ein landesweiter Streik
2 *noun*
(*citizen*) = (der) Staatsbürger/(die) Staatsbürgerin

national anthem *noun*
= (die) Nationalhymne

nationality *noun*
= (die) Nationalität

native
1 *adjective*
my native land = mein Heimatland
his native language = seine Muttersprache
she is a native German speaker = Deutsch ist ihre Muttersprache
2 *noun*
(*person born in a place*) = (der/die) Eingeborene
(*local inhabitant*) = (der/die) Einheimische

natural *adjective*
= natürlich

naturally *adverb*
= natürlich
naturally, we're delighted = natürlich freuen wir uns

nature *noun*
• = (die) Natur
to protect nature = die Natur schützen
to be suspicious by nature = von Natur aus misstrauisch sein
• (*sort, character*) = (die) Art

naughty *adjective*
= unartig

navel *noun*
= (der) Nabel

navy *noun*
= (die) Marine

navy blue *adjective*
= marineblau ▶**Colours p. 204**

near
1 *preposition* = nahe an (+ *dative*)
   the cinema is near the station = das Kino
   ist nahe am Bahnhof
   ! *Note that* am *is the shortened form of* an
   dem.

2 *adverb* = nahe, = nah✳

   ! *Note that in spoken German* nahe *is*
   often shortened to nah.

   they live quite near = sie wohnen ganz
   nah✳
   near by = nicht weit weg
3 *adjective* = nahe, = nah✳

   ! *The superlative of* nah(e) *is* der/die/das
   nächste.

   the nearest supermarket is just round the
   corner = der nächste Supermarkt ist
   gleich um die Ecke
   in the near future = demnächst

nearby *adverb*
= in der Nähe
is there a chemist nearby? = gibt es eine
Drogerie hier in der Nähe?

nearly *adverb*
= fast
we're nearly there = wir sind fast da
I nearly screamed = ich hätte fast
geschrien

neat *adjective*
• (*tidy*) = ordentlich
   her room is always very neat = ihr Zimmer
   ist immer sehr ordentlich
   neat handwriting = eine saubere
   Handschrift
• (*describing a person's looks*) = adrett
• (*clever*) = geschickt
   to find a neat solution = eine geschickte
   Lösung finden

necessary *adjective*
= nötig, = notwendig
to do no more than is necessary = nicht
mehr tun, als nötig ist

neck *noun*
• (*of a person*) = (der) Hals
   back of the neck = (der) Nacken
• (*of a garment*) = (der) Kragen

necklace *noun*
= (die) Halskette

need
1 *verb*

• (*have to*) = müssen, (*with a negative*) =
   brauchen
   to need to do something = etwas tun
   müssen
   I need to know = ich muss es wissen
   you don't need to ask for permission = du
   brauchst nicht um Erlaubnis zu fragen
• (*want*) = brauchen
   to need |money | friends | time ...| = [Geld |
   Freunde | Zeit ...] brauchen
2 *noun*
   there's no need = das ist nicht nötig
   there's no need to worry = du brauchst dir
   keine Sorgen zu machen

needle *noun*
= (die) Nadel

negative
1 *adjective* = negativ
   to have a negative influence on someone
   = jemanden negativ beeinflussen
2 *noun*
   (*of a photo*) = (das) Negativ

neglect *verb*
= vernachlässigen

negotiations *noun*
= Verhandlungen (*plural*)

neighbor (*US*), **neighbour** (*British*)
   noun
= (der) Nachbar/(die) Nachbarin

neither
1 *conjunction*
• **neither ... nor** = weder ... noch
   she speaks neither German nor English =
   sie spricht weder Deutsch noch Englisch
• (*nor*) = auch nicht
   I can't sleep—neither can I = ich kann
   nicht schlafen—ich auch nicht
   you don't like her and neither do I = du
   magst sie nicht, und ich mag sie auch
   nicht
2 *adjective* = keiner der beiden/keine der
   beiden/keins der beiden
   neither book is interesting = keins der
   beiden Bücher ist interessant
3 *pronoun* = keiner von beiden/keine von
   beiden/keins von beiden
   neither of them is coming = keiner von
   beiden kommt
   neither of us = keiner von uns beiden

nephew *noun*
= (der) Neffe

nerve *noun*
• = (der) Nerv
• (*courage*) = (der) Mut

nervous *adjective*
• (*anxious*) = ängstlich
   to be nervous of *or* **about something** =
   Angst vor etwas (*dative*) haben
   to be nervous about making a mistake =
   Angst davor haben, einen Fehler zu
   machen
• (*as a personality*) = nervös

✳ in informal situations

nest *noun*
= (das) Nest

net
1 *noun*
= (das) Netz
2 *adjective* = netto, = Netto-
net income = (das) Nettoeinkommen

Netherlands *noun*
the Netherlands = die Niederlande (*plural*)
▶**Countries p. 208**

nettle *noun*
= (die) Nessel

network *noun*
= (das) Netz

neutral
1 *adjective* = neutral
2 *noun*
(*when driving*) **to be in neutral** = im
Leerlauf sein

never *adverb*
• (*not ever*) = nie
never again = nie wieder
• (*used for emphasis*) = noch nie
I never knew that = das habe ich noch nie
gewusst
• **never mind** = macht nichts

nevertheless *adverb*
= trotzdem

new *adjective*
= neu

news *noun*
• (*new information*) = (die) Nachricht
piece of news = (die) Neuigkeit
what's the latest news? = was gibt es
Neues?
**we haven't had any news from her for
weeks** = wir haben schon wochenlang
nichts mehr von ihr gehört
• (*on TV, radio*) = Nachrichten (*plural*)
I saw it on the news = ich habe es in den
Nachrichten gesehen

newsagent *noun*
= (der) Zeitungshändler

newsflash *noun*
= (die) Kurzmeldung

newspaper *noun*
= (die) Zeitung
the Sunday newspaper = die
Sonntagszeitung

newsreader *noun*
= (der) Nachrichtensprecher/
(die) Nachrichtensprecherin

New Year *noun*
= (das) Neujahr
Happy New Year! = ein gutes neues Jahr!

New Year's (*US*), **New Year's Day**
(*British*) *noun*
= (das) Neujahr

New Year's Eve *noun*
= (das) Silvester

New Zealand *noun*
= (das) Neuseeland ▶**Countries p. 208**

next
1 *adjective*
• = nächster/nächste/nächstes
she's leaving next Friday = sie fährt
nächsten Freitag ab
• (*in a sequence*)
who's next? = wer ist der Nächste?
I'm next = ich bin an der Reihe, = ich bin
dran✱
next! = der Nächste!/die Nächste!
2 *adverb*
• (*in the past*) = danach
what happened next? = was geschah
danach?
• (*now*) = als nächstes
what shall we do next? = was machen wir
als Nächstes?
• (*in the future*) = das nächste Mal
when you next go to Paris, give Gary a call
= wenn du nächstes Mal nach Paris
fährst, ruf Gary an
• **next to** = neben (+ *dative or accusative*)

! Note that *neben* is followed by a noun in
the dative when position is described.
The accusative follows when there is
movement towards something.

we live next to the school = wir wohnen
neben der Schule
she sat down next to him = sie hat sich
neben ihn gesetzt
3 *pronoun*
she was (the) next to be examined = sie
wurde als Nächste geprüft
the week after next = übernächste Woche

next door *adverb*
= nebenan

nice *adjective*
• (*enjoyable*) = schön
it's nice to be able to relax = es ist schön,
wenn man sich entspannen kann
have a nice day! = viel Spaß!
• (*kind*) = nett
to be nice to someone = zu jemandem nett
sein
• (*attractive*) = hübsch
to look very nice (*of a woman*) = sehr
hübsch sein, (*of a man*) = gut aussehen
• (*tasty*) = gut

nickname *noun*
= (der) Spitzname

niece *noun*
= (die) Nichte

night *noun*
• (*as opposed to day*) = (die) Nacht
he's staying the night with friends = er
bleibt über Nacht bei Freunden
I couldn't sleep last night = ich konnte
heute Nacht nicht schlafen
to work at night = nachts arbeiten

N

• (*evening*) = (der) Abend
  he arrived last night = er kam gestern
  Abend an

nightdress *noun*
  = (das) Nachthemd

nightmare *noun*
  = (der) Alptraum

nil *noun*
  (*in sport*) = null
  to win one nil = eins zu null gewinnen

nine *adjective*
  = neun ▶**Numbers p. 282**

nineteen *adjective*
  = neunzehn ▶**Numbers p. 282**

ninety *adjective*
  = neunzig ▶**Numbers p. 282**

ninth *adjective*
  = neunter/neunte/neuntes
    ▶**Numbers p. 282**, ▶**Dates p. 213**

no
1 *adjective*
• (*not any*) = kein

  ! Note that **kein** *changes its endings in
  the same way as* **ein**.

  we have no money = wir haben kein Geld
  it's no use = das hat keinen Zweck
  I've no idea = ich habe keine Ahnung
• (*forbidden*)
  no [parking | smoking | dogs] = [Parken |
  Rauchen | Hunde] verboten
2 *adverb*
• = nein
  to say no = nein sagen
• (*not*) = nicht
  he no longer works here = er arbeitet nicht
  mehr hier

nobody ▶no one

nod *verb*
  = nicken
  to nod one's head = mit dem Kopf nicken

noise *noun*
• (*loud*) = (der) Lärm
  don't make too much noise = sei nicht zu
  laut
• (*any sound*) = (das) Geräusch

noisy *adjective*
  = laut

non-alcoholic *adjective*
  = alkoholfrei

none *pronoun*
  = keiner/keine/keins
  **none of [us | you | them ...] can speak
  Russian** = keiner von [uns | euch |
  ihnen ...] spricht Russisch
  have you got any money?—none at all =
  hast du Geld?—überhaupt keins
  none of it is true = nichts davon ist wahr
  there's none left = es ist nichts mehr übrig

nonsense *noun*
  = (der) Unsinn

non-smoker *noun*
  = (der) Nichtraucher/(die) Nichtraucherin

noon *noun*
  = (der) Mittag
  at noon = um zwölf (Uhr mittags)

no one *pronoun*
  = niemand
  no one saw him = niemand hat ihn
  gesehen

nor *conjunction*
• **neither ... nor** = weder ... noch
  she speaks neither German nor English =
  sie spricht weder Deutsch noch Englisch
• = auch nicht
  nor do we = wir auch nicht

normal
1 *adjective* = normal
  at the normal time = zur normalen Zeit
2 *noun*
  to get back to normal = sich normalisieren

normally *adverb*
• (*usually*) = normalerweise
• (*properly*) = normal

north
1 *noun* = (der) Norden
  to the north of London = nördlich von
  London
2 *adjective* = nördlich, = Nord-
  a north wind = ein Nordwind
3 *adverb* = nach Norden

North America *noun*
  = (das) Nordamerika ▶**Countries p. 208**

Northern Ireland *noun*
  = (das) Nordirland ▶**Countries p. 208**

Norway *noun*
  = (das) Norwegen ▶**Countries p. 208**

Norwegian
1 *noun*
• (*person*) = (der) Norweger/(die) Norwegerin
• (*language*) = (das) Norwegisch
2 *adjective* = norwegisch ▶**Countries p. 208**

nose *noun*
  = (die) Nase
  to nose around = herumschnüffeln

nostril *noun*
• (*of a person*) = (das) Nasenloch
• (*of a horse*) = (die) Nüster

not *adverb*
  = nicht
  hasn't he phoned you? = hat er dich nicht
  angerufen?
  we won't need a car = wir brauchen kein
  Auto
  not a chance = keine Möglichkeit
  not at all = überhaupt nicht, = gar nicht
  thanks a lot—not at all = vielen Dank—gern
  geschehen

note
1 *noun*
* (*written comment*) = (die) Notiz
  to take notes = sich (*dative*) Notizen machen
  to make a note of an address = sich (*dative*) eine Adresse notieren
* (*short letter*) = (der) kurze Brief, = (der) Zettel✶
  I left you a note = ich hab dir einen Zettel dagelassen✶
  to write a quick note = ein paar Zeilen schreiben
* (*British: banknote*) = (der) Schein
  a £10 note = ein Zehnpfundschein
* (*in music*) = (die) Note
2 *verb*
* (*notice*) = bemerken
* (*pay attention to*) = beachten
* (*write down*) = notieren
note down
= sich (*dative*) notieren

notebook *noun*
= (das) Notizbuch

nothing
1 *pronoun* = nichts
  to have nothing to do with something = nichts mit etwas (*dative*) zu tun haben
  there's nothing left = es ist nichts mehr übrig
2 *adverb*
  it's nothing like as difficult as Russian = es ist längst nicht so schwer wie Russisch
3 (*other uses*)
  it's caused me nothing but trouble = es hat mir nur Ärger gemacht
  for nothing = umsonst

notice
1 *verb* = bemerken
  I noticed he wasn't wearing glasses = ich bemerkte, dass er keine Brille trug
2 *noun*
* (*written sign*) = (der) Anschlag
* (*public announcement*) = (die) Bekanntmachung
* (*advance warning*) = (die) Ankündigung
  without any notice = ohne irgendwelche Ankündigung
  to be cancelled at short notice = kurzfristig abgesagt werden
  to hand in one's notice = kündigen
  to give someone notice = jemandem kündigen
* (*announcement of birth, marriage, death*) = (die) Anzeige
* (*attention*) = (die) Beachtung
  to take notice of something = etwas beachten
  to take no notice of someone = keine Notiz von jemandem nehmen

noticeable *adjective*
= bemerkenswert

novel
1 *noun* = (der) Roman
2 *adjective* = neu

November *noun*
= (der) November ▶ **Dates p. 213**

now *adverb*
= jetzt
  do it right now = mach es sofort
  it hasn't been a problem until now = bis jetzt war es kein Problem
  I should have told you before now = ich hätte es dir vorher sagen sollen
  he left just now = er ist gerade gegangen
  between now and next Monday = bis nächsten Montag
  now and again = hin und wieder
  it's now or never = jetzt oder nie

nowhere *adverb*
= nirgends
  there is nowhere to [shop | change | eat …] = man kann [nirgends einkaufen | sich nirgends umziehen | nirgends essen …]

nuclear *adjective*
= Kern-
  nuclear energy = (die) Kernenergie
  nuclear deterrent = (das) nukleare Abschreckungsmittel

nude
1 *adjective* = nackt
2 *noun* = (der/die) Nackte
  in the nude = nackt

nuisance *noun*
* (*annoying person*) = (der) Quälgeist✶
  stop making a nuisance of yourself = hör auf, alle verrückt zu machen
* (*annoying thing*) = (die) Plage
  the flies are a real nuisance = die Fliegen sind eine richtige Plage
  what a nuisance = wie ärgerlich

number
1 *noun*
* (*figure*) = (die) Zahl
  (*of a house, bus, telephone*) = (die) Nummer
  to dial the wrong number = sich verwählen
* (*quantity*) = (die) Anzahl
  we have received a number of applications = wir haben eine Anzahl Bewerbungen erhalten
  a number of [people | things | books …] = einige [Leute | Dinge | Bücher …]
  for a number of reasons = aus mehreren Gründen
  any number of = beliebig viele
* (*performance*) = (die) Nummer
2 *verb* = nummerieren
  the seats are numbered = die Plätze sind nummeriert

numberplate *noun* (*British*)
= (das) Nummernschild

N

Numbers

1	eins	1st	erster / erste / erstes
2	zwei	2nd	zweiter / zweite / zweites
3	drei	3rd	dritter / dritte / drittes
4	vier	4th	vierter / vierte / viertes
5	fünf	5th	fünfter / fünfte / fünftes
6	sechs	6th	sechster / sechste / sechstes
7	sieben	7th	siebter / siebte / siebtes
8	acht	8th	achter / achte / achtes
9	neun	9th	neunter / neunte / neuntes
10	zehn	10th	zehnter / zehnte / zehntes
11	elf	11th	elfter / elfte / elftes
12	zwölf	12th	zwölfter / zwölfte / zwölftes
13	dreizehn	13th	dreizehnter / dreizehnte / dreizehntes
14	vierzehn	14th	vierzehnter / vierzehnte / vierzehntes
15	fünfzehn	15th	fünfzehnter / fünfzehnte / fünfzehntes
16	sechzehn	16th	sechzehnter / sechzehnte / sechzehntes
17	siebzehn	17th	siebzehnter / siebzehnte / siebzehntes
18	achtzehn	18th	achtzehnter / achtzehnte / achtzehntes
19	neunzehn	19th	neunzehnter / neunzehnte / neunzehntes
20	zwanzig	20th	zwanzigster / zwanzigste / zwanzigstes
21	einundzwanzig	21st	einundzwanzigster / einundzwanzigste / einundzwanzigstes
30	dreißig	30th	dreißigster / dreißigste / dreißigstes
40	vierzig	40th	vierzigster / vierzigste / vierzigstes
50	fünfzig	50th	fünfzigster / fünfzigste / fünfzigstes
60	sechzig	60th	sechzigster / sechzigste / sechzigstes
70	siebzig	70th	siebzigster / siebzigste / siebzigstes
80	achtzig	80th	achtzigster / achtzigste / achtzigstes
90	neunzig	90th	neunzigster / neunzigste / neunzigstes
100	hundert	100th	hundertster / hundertste / hundertstes

In German, the endings of the ordinal numbers (*erster / erste / erstes*, etc.) change according to the gender and case of the noun which they describe:

the fourth goal = das vierte Tor   *in the third week* = in der dritten Woche

With large numbers, full stops or spaces are used instead of the English commas:

1,000,000 = 1.000.000 *or* 1 000 000

Ordinal numbers are usually written as figures followed by a full stop:

3rd = 3.

Fractions

When used as nouns, fractions have a capital letter:

half = (die) Hälfte   *fifth* = (das) Fünftel
third = (das) Drittel   *eighth* = (das) Achtel
quarter = (das) Viertel   *two thirds* = zwei Drittel

I've paid a third of the amount = ich habe ein Drittel des Betrages gezahlt

They are written with a small letter when used as an adjective:

$\frac{1}{2}$ = ein halb $\frac{5}{8}$ = fünf achtel
$1\frac{1}{2}$ = eineinhalb $\frac{2}{3}$ = zwei drittel

half a litre of milk = ein halber Liter Milch

Decimals

Note that German uses a comma instead of a decimal point:

0.1 (nought point one) = 0,1 (null Komma eins)
1.43 (one point four three) = 1,43 (eins Komma vier drei)

Calculations in German

$4 + 5 = 9$ (vier und fünf ist neun) $10 \times 3 = 30$ (zehn mal drei ist dreißig)
$10 - 3 = 7$ (zehn weniger drei ist sieben) $30 : 3 = 10$ (dreißig geteilt durch drei ist zehn)

Note that the German division sign is a colon.

nurse
1 *noun* = (die) Krankenschwester
(*male*) = (der) Pfleger
2 *verb*
• (*look after*) = pflegen
• (*breast-feed*) = stillen

nursery *noun*
• (*children's room*) = (das) Kinderzimmer
• (*day nursery*) = (die) Kindertagesstätte
• (*for plants*) = (die) Gärtnerei

nursery school *noun*
= (der) Kindergarten

nursing home *noun*
= (das) Pflegeheim

nut *noun*
• (*for eating*) = (die) Nuss
• (*for use with a bolt*) = (die) Mutter

oak *noun*
= (die) Eiche

oar *noun*
= (das) Ruder

obedient *adjective*
= gehorsam

obey *verb*
= gehorchen (+ *dative*)
to obey someone = jemandem gehorchen
to obey the law = sich an das Gesetz halten

object
1 *noun*
• (*thing*) = (der) Gegenstand
• (*aim*) = (der) Zweck
2 *verb* = Einwände erheben
to object to something = Einwände gegen
etwas (*accusative*) erheben
no one objected = keiner war dagegen

objection *noun*
= (der) Einwand

oblige *verb*
• (*have to*)
to be obliged to give up work = gezwungen
sein, die Arbeit aufzugeben
• (*be helpful*)
to oblige someone = jemandem einen
Gefallen tun
• (*be grateful*)
to be obliged to someone for something =
jemandem für etwas (*accusative*) sehr
verbunden sein

obscene *adjective*
= obszön

obsessed *adjective*
= besessen

obsession *noun*
• = (die) Besessenheit
• (*persistent idea*) = (die) fixe Idee

obstacle *noun*
= (das) Hindernis

obstinate *adjective*
= starrsinnig

obstruct *verb*
• (*impede*) = behindern
to obstruct a player = einen Spieler
behindern
• (*block*) = versperren
to obstruct someone's view = jemandem
die Sicht versperren

obtain *verb*
= erhalten

obvious *adjective*
= eindeutig

obviously
1 *adverb* = offensichtlich
he obviously needs help = er braucht
offensichtlich Hilfe
2 *interjection* = natürlich!

occasion *noun*
= (die) Gelegenheit
on special occasions = zu besonderen
Gelegenheiten
on a number of occasions = mehrmals

occasionally *adverb*
= gelegentlich

occupy *verb*
• (*live in*) = bewohnen
• (*take*) = besetzen
the seats are occupied = die Plätze sind
besetzt
• (*keep busy*) = beschäftigen
to keep oneself occupied = sich
beschäftigen
• (*conquer*) = einnehmen

occur *verb*
• (*take place*) = sich ergeben
• (*cross someone's mind*)
to occur to someone = jemandem
einfallen (! *sein*)

ocean *noun*
= (der) Ozean

o'clock *adverb*
at five o'clock = um fünf Uhr ▶ Time p. 331

October *noun*
= (der) Oktober ▶ Dates p. 213

octopus *noun*
= (der) Tintenfisch

odd *adjective*
• (*strange*) = seltsam

* (*not matching*) = einzeln
  odd socks/gloves = nicht zusammengehörende Socken/Handschuhe
  the odd one out = die Ausnahme
* **an odd number** = eine ungerade Zahl

odor (*US*), **odour** (*British*) *noun*
= (der) Geruch

of *preposition*
* von (+ *dative*)

> **!** Note that instead of translating **of** with **von**, *the genitive case can be used.*

  the father of the child = der Vater des Kindes *or* der Vater von dem Kind
  the names of the pupils = die Namen der Schüler
* (*with quantities*)
  a kilo of potatoes = ein Kilo Kartoffeln
  a child of ten = ein zehnjähriges Kind

> **!** Note that **davon** *can be used to translate* **of it** *or* **of them** *when talking about things, but not when referring to people.*

  half of it = die Hälfte davon
  I didn't have any of it = ich habe nichts davon bekommen
  how many of them? (*of things*) = wie viele davon?, (*of people*) = wie viele von ihnen?
  there are six of us = wir sind zu sechst
  some of us = einige von uns
  the whole of the town = die ganze Stadt
* (*made from*) = aus (+ *dative*)
  it's made of plastic = es ist aus Plastik

off
1 *adverb*
* (*leaving*)
  to be off = gehen (**!** *sein*), (*in a vehicle*) = fahren (**!** *sein*)
  I'm off now = ich gehe jetzt
  they are off to Italy tomorrow = sie fahren morgen nach Italien
* (*away*)
  the coast is a long way off = die Küste ist weit entfernt
  summer isn't far off now = bis zum Sommer ist es jetzt nicht mehr lange hin
* (*free*)
  to take a day off = sich (*dative*) einen Tag frei nehmen
  to have a day off = einen freien Tag haben
* (*on an appliance*)
  on/off = ein/aus
* (*turned off*)
  the lights are off = das Licht ist aus
  the water is off = das Wasser ist abgestellt
* (*cancelled*) = abgesagt
  the match is off = das Spiel ist abgesagt worden

2 *adjective*
  the milk is off = die Milch ist sauer
  the meat is off = das Fleisch ist schlecht
3 *preposition*
* (*near*)
  there's a florist just off the station = ganz in der Nähe vom Bahnhof ist ein Blumengeschäft
  the kitchen is just off the dining room = die Küche ist direkt neben dem Esszimmer
* (*not interested in*)
  to be off something = etwas (*accusative*) leid sein
  he's off his food = er hat keinen Appetit

> **!** Note that **off** *is often used with verbs—* **fall off**, **get off**, **turn off**, *etc. You will find translations for these under the entries* **fall**, **get**, **turn**, *etc.*

offence *noun* (*British*)
* (*crime*) = (die) Straftat
* (*insult*) = (die) Beleidigung
  to take offence = beleidigt sein

offend *verb*
= beleidigen

offense (*US*) ▶**offence**

offer
1 *verb* = anbieten
  to offer someone a job = jemandem eine Stelle anbieten
  to offer to [water the flowers | mind the children | feed the cat ...] = anbieten, [die Blumen zu gießen | auf die Kinder aufzupassen | die Katze zu füttern ...]
2 *noun* = (das) Angebot
  on special offer = im Sonderangebot

office *noun*
= (das) Büro

office hours *noun*
= Dienststunden (*plural*)

officer *noun*
* (*in the army*) = (der) Offizier
* (*in the police*) = (der) Beamte/(die) Beamtin

office worker *noun*
= (der/die) Büroangestellte

official
1 *adjective* = offiziell
2 *noun* = (der) Repräsentant/(die) Repräsentantin

often *adverb*
= oft

oil
1 *noun* = (das) Öl
2 *verb* = ölen

oil rig *noun*
= (die) Bohrinsel

okay, OK
1 *adjective*
* = in Ordnung, = okay✱

that's OK by me = mir ist es recht
is it OK if I come a little later? = ist es okay, wenn ich etwas später komme?✱
• (*when talking about health*)
he's OK at the moment = es geht ihm im Moment ganz gut
how are you?—OK = wie gehts?—ganz gut
2 *interjection* = gut!, = okay!✱

old *adjective*
• = alt
old people = alte Leute
how old are you? = wie alt bist du?
he's 40 years old = er ist vierzig Jahre alt
to get old = alt werden (**!** *sein*)
• (*previous*)
that's my old address = das ist meine alte Adresse
in the old days = früher

old-fashioned *adjective*
= altmodisch

old people's home *noun*
= (das) Altersheim

olive *noun*
= (die) Olive

olive oil *noun*
= (das) Olivenöl

Olympics *noun*
the Olympics = die Olympischen Spiele

on
1 *preposition*
• (*showing location*) = auf (+ *dative or accusative*)
(*on a vertical surface*) = an (+ *dative or accusative*)

! *Note that* auf *and* an *are followed by a noun in the dative when position is described. The accusative follows when there is movement towards something.*

put the cups on the table = stelle die Tassen auf den Tisch
I like the picture on the wall = mir gefällt das Bild an der Wand
on the right/left = rechts/links
• (*when talking about transport*)
to travel on the coach = mit dem Bus fahren (**!** *sein*)
the baggage is already on the plane = das Gepäck ist schon im Flugzeug
• (*about*) = über (+ *accusative*)
a book on drugs = ein Buch über Drogen
• (*when talking about time*) = an (+ *dative*)
on the 6th of December = am sechsten Dezember

! *Note that* am *is a shortened form of* an dem.

• **on television** = im Fernsehen
on tape = auf Band
• (*using*)
to be on antibiotics = Antibiotika nehmen

• (*earning*)
to be on a low income = wenig verdienen
I couldn't live on it = davon könnte ich nicht leben
2 *adverb*
• (*when talking about clothes*)
to have a [coat | sweater | bra …] **on** = einen [Mantel | Pullover | BH …] anhaben
to have a hat on = einen Hut aufhaben
• (*on an appliance*)
on/off = ein/aus
• (*turned on*)
why are the lights on? = warum ist das Licht an?
• (*showing*)
is there anything good on? (*TV*) = gibt es irgendwas Gutes im Fernsehen?
what's on at the cinema? = was läuft im Kino?
• (*when talking about time*)
from Tuesday on = ab Dienstag
from then on = von da an
a little later on = etwas später
• (*when talking about distance*)
a little further on = etwas weiter weg
• (*other uses*)
I've nothing on tonight = ich habe heute Abend nichts vor
it's on me = das spendiere ich

! *Note that* on *is often used with verbs—*count on, keep on, turn on, *etc. You will find translations for these under the entries* count, keep, turn, *etc.*

once
1 *adverb*
• (*one time*) = einmal
once a day = einmal täglich
once and for all = ein für alle Mal
at once (*immediately*) = sofort, (*at the same time*) = gleichzeitig
• (*in the old days*) = früher
(*in fairy tales*) **once upon a time there was** = es war einmal
2 *conjunction* = sobald
it will be easier once we have found a house = es wird einfacher sein, sobald wir ein Haus gefunden haben

one
1 *noun*
(*number*) = (die) Eins ▶ **Numbers p. 282**
2 *adjective*
• (*when counting*) = eins, (*with a noun*) = ein
one child = ein Kind
one day = eines Tages
one of my colleagues = einer meiner Kollegen
• (*only*) = einzig
it's the one thing that annoys me = das ist das Einzige, das mich ärgert
• (*same*) = ein
to keep all the keys in one drawer = alle Schlüssel in einer Schublade aufbewahren

O

3 *pronoun*
- (*person or thing*) = einer/eine/eins
  not one = keiner/keine/keins
  the biscuits are delicious, I'll have another one = die Kekse sind köstlich, ich nehme mir noch einen
  not one of them came = keiner von ihnen kam

> **!** *The pronoun is often translated by an adjective describing the specific person or thing.*

I like the new house but she prefers the old one = mir gefällt das neue Haus, aber sie mag das alte lieber
I'm going to wear the black one (*dress = das Kleid*) = ich ziehe das schwarze an
which one? = welcher/welche/welches?
this one = dieser/diese/dieses
I like that one = ich mag den da/die da/das da

> **!** *Note that in German the gender always depends on the noun referred to.*

- (*you*) = man
  one never knows = man kann nie wissen

one another *pronoun*
= einander

> **!** *Note that* **one another** *is usually translated by using a reflexive pronoun like* sich.

to love one another = sich lieben

oneself *pronoun*
- (*when used as a reflexive pronoun*) = sich
  to enjoy oneself = sich amüsieren
- (*used for emphasis*) = selbst
- **by oneself** = allein

one-way street *noun*
= (die) Einbahnstraße

onion *noun*
= (die) Zwiebel

only
1 *adverb* = nur
  you only have to ask = du brauchst nur zu fragen
2 *adjective* = einziger/einzige/einziges
  they are our only neighbours = sie sind unsere einzigen Nachbarn
  an only child = ein Einzelkind
3 *conjunction* = nur
  they need a car, only they can't afford it = sie brauchen ein Auto, nur können sie es sich nicht leisten

only just
- (*very recently*) = gerade erst
- (*by a narrow margin*) = gerade noch
  we only just caught the train = wir haben gerade noch den Zug erwischt

open
1 *verb*
- = öffnen, = aufmachen

---

to open [the door | a letter | the garage ...] = [die Tür | einen Brief | die Garage ...] öffnen *or* aufmachen
  the shop opens at 8 = das Geschäft öffnet um acht, = das Geschäft macht um acht auf
- (*open up*) = sich öffnen
- (*set up, start*) = eröffnen
  to open an account = ein Konto eröffnen
- (*be started*) = eröffnet werden (**!** *sein*)
2 *adjective*
- = offen
  the door is open = die Tür ist offen
  are the shops open today? = haben die Geschäfte heute auf?
- (*public*) = öffentlich
- (*frank*) = offen
- (*other uses*)
  to keep an open mind = alles offen lassen
  to leave the date open = das Datum offen lassen
3 *noun*
  in the open = im Freien
  to come into the open = herauskommen (**!** *sein*), = an den Tag kommen**✕** (**!** *sein*)

open up
- (*for business*) = öffnen
- (*talk*) = gesprächig werden (**!** *sein*)

opener *noun*
= (der) Öffner

opening hours *noun*
= Öffnungszeiten (*plural*)

open-minded *adjective*
= aufgeschlossen

opera *noun*
= (die) Oper

operate *verb*
- (*run*) = verkehren (**!** *sein*)
  the bus service does not operate after 8 pm = Busse verkehren nicht nach zwanzig Uhr
- (*make a machine work*) = bedienen
- (*of a surgeon*) = operieren
  to operate on someone = jemanden operieren

operation *noun*
= (die) Operation
  to have an operation = sich operieren lassen

operator *noun*
(*on the phone*) = (die) Vermittlung

opinion *noun*
= (die) Meinung
  in my opinion = meiner Meinung nach

opponent *noun*
= (der) Gegner

opportunity *noun*
= (die) Gelegenheit

✕ in informal situations

oppose *verb*
  to oppose a plan = gegen einen Plan sein
  to be opposed to nuclear weapons = gegen Kernwaffen sein

opposite
1 *preposition* = gegenüber (+ *dative*)
  she was sitting opposite me = sie saß mir gegenüber
2 *adjective*
• (*totally different*) = entgegengesetzt
  he was walking in the opposite direction = er ging in die entgegengesetzte Richtung
  the opposite sex = das andere Geschlecht
• (*other side*) = gegenüberliegend
  on the opposite side of the room = auf der gegenüberliegenden Zimmerseite
3 *adverb* = gegenüber
  who lives opposite? = wer wohnt gegenüber?
4 *noun* = (das) Gegenteil

opposition *noun*
  = (der) Widerstand
  (*in sport*) = (der) Gegner

optician *noun*
  = (der) Optiker/(die) Optikerin

optimistic *adjective*
  = optimistisch

option *noun*
  = (die) Wahl
  I don't have any option = ich habe keine andere Wahl
  to have the option of [going abroad | buying a house …] = die Möglichkeit haben, [ins Ausland zu gehen | ein Haus zu kaufen …]

or *conjunction*
• = oder
• (*in negative sentences*) = noch
  I can't come today or tomorrow = ich kann weder heute noch morgen kommen
• (*otherwise*) = sonst
  be careful or it will break = sei vorsichtig, sonst geht es kaputt✱

oral *adjective*
  = mündlich

orange
1 *noun*
  (*fruit*) = (die) Orange
2 *adjective* = orange ▶ **Colours p. 204**

orange juice *noun*
  = (der) Orangensaft

orchard *noun*
  = (der) Obstgarten

orchestra *noun*
  = (das) Orchester

order
1 *verb*
• (*tell*) = befehlen (+ *dative*)
  they ordered him to leave the country = sie befahlen ihm, das Land zu verlassen

• (*call for*) = anordnen
  to order the evacuation of a building = die Räumung eines Gebäudes anordnen
• (*ask for, book*) = bestellen
  I've ordered = ich habe schon bestellt
2 *noun*
• (*instruction*) = (der) Befehl
• (*in a shop, restaurant*) = (die) Bestellung
  to place an order = eine Bestellung aufgeben
  the books are on order = die Bücher sind bestellt
• (*arrangement*) = (die) Reihenfolge
  in alphabetical order = in alphabetischer Reihenfolge
• (*control*) = (die) Ordnung
  out of order = außer Betrieb
  in order to = um zu
  I phoned in order to book tickets = ich habe angerufen, um Karten zu buchen

ordinary *adjective*
• (*not unusual*) = normal
• (*not exceptional*) = gewöhnlich

organ *noun*
• (*musical instrument*) = (die) Orgel
• (*part of the body*) = (das) Organ

organization *noun*
  = (die) Organisation

original *adjective*
• (*first*) = ursprünglich
• (*not an imitation*) = original
  an original (**painting**) = ein Original
• (*new*) = originell
  an original idea = eine originelle Idee

orphan *noun*
  = (die) Waise

ostrich *noun*
  = (der) Strauß

other
1 *adjective* = anderer/andere/anderes
  the other pupils = die anderen Schüler
  we met them the other day = wir haben sie neulich getroffen
  the other evening = neulich abends
  every other day = jeden zweiten Tag
  any other questions? = sonst noch Fragen?
2 *pronoun* = anderer/andere/anderes
  the others = die anderen
  not any other = kein anderer/keine andere/kein anderes
  they came in one after the other = sie kamen hintereinander herein
  someone or other told me = irgendjemand hat es mir gesagt
  other than = außer (+ *dative*)

otherwise *adverb*
  = sonst

ought *verb*
• = sollen
  I ought to do my homework, but I'm too lazy = ich soll meine Hausaufgaben machen, aber ich bin zu faul

O

! *The subjunctive of* **sollen** *is usually used to translate* **ought,** *when making polite suggestions or when something is likely to happen.*

he ought to arrive tomorrow = er sollte morgen ankommen
- (*when implying that something was not right*)
he ought to have been more polite = er hätte höflicher sein sollen
you ought not to have done it = du hättest es nicht machen sollen

our *adjective*
= unser

! *Note that* **unser** *changes its endings in the same way as* **ein.**

he ran over our dog = er hat unseren Hund überfahren

ours *pronoun*
= unserer/unsere/unsers

! *Note that* **unserer** *and other forms sometimes drop an e in informal use, to become* **unsrer,** *etc. The pronoun agrees in number and gender with the noun it stands for.*

their garden is bigger than ours = ihr Garten ist größer als unserer
the grey car is ours = das graue Auto gehört uns
he's a friend of ours = er ist ein Freund von uns

ourselves *pronoun*
- (*when translated by a reflexive verb in German*) = uns
we want to enjoy ourselves = wir wollen uns amüsieren
- (*used for emphasis*) = selbst
we organized everything ourselves = wir haben alles selbst organisiert
- **by ourselves** = allein

out
1 *adverb*
- (*outside*) = draußen
it's quite cold out = es ist ziemlich kalt draußen
- (*absent*) = weg
he is out = er ist nicht da
he's been out all night = er war die ganze Nacht weg
- (*seen or heard*) = heraus, = raus✖
the book will be out in November = das Buch kommt im November heraus
the sun is out = die Sonne scheint
the ball was out (*out of play*) = der Ball war aus
out with it! = raus damit!✖
- (*not on*) = aus
the fire is out = das Feuer ist aus
- (*unconscious*) = bewusstlos

✖ in informal situations

2 *preposition*
out of = aus (*+ dative*)
to walk out of the building = aus dem Gebäude gehen (**!** *sein*)
to stay out of the sun = aus der Sonne bleiben (**!** *sein*)

! *Note that* **out** *is often used with verbs—blow out, find out, go out, etc. You will find translations for these under the entries* **blow, find, go,** *etc.*

outdoor *adjective*
outdoor games = Spiele im Freien
outdoor swimming pool = (das) Freibad
to lead an outdoor life = viel im Freien sein

outdoors *adverb*
= draußen

outlook *noun*
- (*attitude*) = (die) Einstellung
- (*for the future*) = Aussichten (*plural*)

outside
1 *noun* = (die) Außenseite
2 *preposition*
- (*in front of*) = vor (*+ dative*)
to wait outside the school = vor der Schule warten
- (*beyond*) = außerhalb (*+ genitive*)
outside the city = außerhalb der Stadt
3 *adverb*
- (*on the outside*) = draußen
they are sitting outside = sie sitzen draußen
- (*to the outside*) = nach draußen
to go outside = nach draußen gehen (**!** *sein*)
4 *adjective* = Außen-
outside wall = (die) Außenwand

oven *noun*
= (der) Ofen

over
1 *preposition*
- (*across, above*) = über (*+ dative or accusative*)

! *Note that* **über** *is followed by a noun in the dative when position is described. The accusative follows when there is movement towards something.*

to wear a sweater over a shirt = einen Pullover über dem Hemd anhaben
to climb over a fence = über einen Zaun klettern (**!** *sein*)
over there = da drüben
- (*during*) = über (*+ accusative*)
over the weekend = übers Wochenende

! *Note that* **übers** *is a shortened form of* **über das.**

- **all over** (*everywhere*) = überall, (*finished*) = zu Ende
2 *adverb*
- (*finished*) = zu Ende
when the film is over = wenn der Film zu Ende ist

- (*to one's home*)
  to invite someone over = jemanden zu sich
    (*dative*) einladen
  come over tomorrow evening = komm
    morgen Abend zu uns herüber
- (*remaining*) = übrig
  to be left over = übrig bleiben (**!** *sein*)
- (*repeated*)
  over again = noch einmal

  ! *Note that* over *is often used with
  verbs—*hand over, move over, *etc. You
  will find translations for these under the
  entries* hand, move, *etc.*

overdraft *noun*
= (die) Kontoüberziehung
  to have an overdraft = sein Konto
    überzogen haben

overtake *verb*
= überholen

overthrow *verb*
= stürzen

overweight *adjective*
  to be overweight = Übergewicht haben

owe *verb*
= schulden
  to owe someone money = jemandem Geld
    schulden

owl *noun*
= (die) Eule

own
1 *adjective* = eigen
  he would like his own car = er hätte gerne
    ein eigenes Auto
2 *pronoun* = eigen
  I don't need his pencil, I've got my own =
    ich brauche seinen Bleistift nicht, ich
    habe meinen eigenen
  on one's own = allein
3 *verb* = besitzen, = haben
  she owns two cars = sie hat zwei Autos
own up
  to own up to something = etwas
    (*accusative*) zugeben

owner *noun*
= (der) Eigentümer/(die) Eigentümerin

oxygen *noun*
= (der) Sauerstoff

ozone layer *noun*
= (die) Ozonschicht

Pacific *noun*
  the Pacific, the Pacific Ocean = der Pazifik

pack
1 *verb*
  (*fill*) = packen
  (*put into a container*) = einpacken
2 *noun* = (die) Packung
  pack of cards = (das) Kartenspiel
pack up
= packen
  to pack up one's belongings = seine
    Sachen packen

package *noun*
= (das) Paket

packet *noun*
= (das) Päckchen

paddle *noun*
= (das) Paddel

page *noun*
= (die) Seite

pain *noun*
= (der) Schmerz
  to be in pain = Schmerzen haben

painful *adjective*
= schmerzhaft

paint
1 *noun* = (die) Farbe
2 *verb*
- (*in art*) = malen
- (*decorate*) = streichen

paintbrush *noun*
= (der) Pinsel

painter *noun*
= (der) Maler/(die) Malerin

painting *noun*
- (*picture*) = (das) Gemälde
- (*activity*) = (die) Malerei
- (*by a decorator*) = Malerarbeiten (*plural*)

pair *noun*
= (das) Paar

pajamas (*US*) ▶pyjamas

Pakistan *noun*
= (das) Pakistan ▶**Countries p. 208**

palace *noun*
= (der) Palast

pale *adjective*
= blass
  to go *or* **turn pale** = blass werden (**!** *sein*)

pan noun
  (for frying) = (die) Pfanne
  (saucepan) = (der) Topf

pancake noun
  = (der) Pfannkuchen

panic verb
  = in Panik geraten (**!** sein)

pants noun
• (British: underwear) = (die) Unterhose,
   (woman's) = (der) Schlüpfer
• (US: trousers) = (die) Hose

paper noun
• = (das) Papier
  a piece of paper = ein Blatt Papier
• (newspaper) = (die) Zeitung

paperback noun
  = (das) Taschenbuch

parachute noun
  = (der) Fallschirm

parade noun
  = (der) Umzug

paralysed (British), **paralyzed** (US)
  adjective
  = gelähmt

parcel noun
  = (das) Paket

parents noun
  = Eltern (plural)

park
1 noun = (der) Park
2 verb = parken

parking meter noun
  = (die) Parkuhr

parking ticket noun
  = (der) Strafzettel

parliament noun
  = (das) Parlament

parrot noun
  = (der) Papagei

part noun
• (der) Teil
  part of the [book | work | story …] = ein Teil
  [des Buches | der Arbeit | der Geschichte …]
• (piece for a machine, car) = (das) Teil
  the different parts of an engine = die
  einzelnen Teile eines Motors
• (area) = (die) Gegend
• (role) = (die) Rolle
• **to take part in a demonstration** = an einer
  Demonstration teilnehmen

participate verb
  = teilnehmen
  to participate in something = an etwas
  (dative) teilnehmen

particular adjective
  = besonderer/besondere/besonderes
  nothing in particular = nichts Besonderes
  in particular = besonders

partner noun
  = (der) Partner/(die) Partnerin

part-time
1 adjective = Teilzeit-
  part-time work = (die) Teilzeitarbeit
2 adverb
  to work part-time = Teilzeit arbeiten

party noun
• (social event) = (die) Party, = (das) Fest
• (political organization) = (die) Partei

pass verb
• (go past) = vorbeigehen an (+ dative)
  (**!** sein)
  (drive past) = vorbeifahren an (+ dative)
  (**!** sein)
  to let someone pass = jemanden
  vorbeilassen
• (overtake) = überholen

> **!** Note that **überholen** is an inseparable
> verb.

  the car passed the lorry = das Auto
  überholte den Lastwagen
• (hand over) = reichen
• (spend) = verbringen
  to pass the time [reading | listening to the
  radio | playing the piano …] = sich (dative)
  die Zeit mit [Lesen | Radiohören |
  Klavierspielen …] vertreiben
• (succeed in an exam) = bestehen
• (of time) = vergehen (**!** sein)
  time passes quickly on holiday = auf
  Ferien vergeht die Zeit schnell
pass on
  = weitergeben
  to pass a message on to someone = eine
  Nachricht an jemanden weitergeben
pass out
  = ohnmächtig werden (**!** sein)

passage noun
• (corridor) = (der) Gang
• (voyage) = (die) Überfahrt

passenger noun
  = (der) Passagier/(die) Passagierin

passport noun
  = (der) Reisepass

password noun
  (in computing) = (das) Passwort

past
1 noun = (die) Vergangenheit
2 adjective
  (last) = letzter/letzte/letztes
  in the past few days = in den letzten paar
  Tagen
3 preposition
• (when talking about time) = nach (+ dative)
  ▶ **Time p. 331**

- (by)
  past something = an etwas (dative) vorbei
  to go past someone = an jemandem
  vorbeigehen (**!** sein)
- (after) = nach (+ dative)
  it's just past the traffic lights = es ist kurz
  nach der Ampel
  4 adverb = vorbei
  to go past = vorbeigehen (**!** sein)

pasta noun
  = Nudeln (plural)

pastry noun
- (for baking) = (der) Teig
- (cake) = (das) Gebäck

patch noun
- (on a garment) = (der) Flicken
- (spot) = (der) Fleck
- (area) = (die) Stelle
  patches of ice = stellenweise Eis

path noun
  = (der) Weg
  (narrower) = (der) Pfad

patience noun
  = (die) Geduld

patient
  1 noun = (der) Patient/(die) Patientin
  2 adjective = geduldig

patrol car noun
  = (der) Streifenwagen

pattern noun
- (design) = (das) Muster
- (for making garments) = (der) Schnitt

pavement noun (British)
  = (der) Bürgersteig

paw noun
  = (die) Pfote

pay
  1 verb
- = bezahlen, = zahlen

  > **!** Note that **bezahlen** is used when you
  > pay a person, a fine or a bill, and **zahlen**
  > when the object of the verb is money or
  > there is no object.

  he paid for the meal = er hat das Essen
  bezahlt
  the work doesn't pay very well = die Arbeit
  wird schlecht bezahlt
  to pay by credit card = mit Kreditkarte
  zahlen
  they pay £5 an hour = sie zahlen fünf
  Pfund pro Stunde
- (give)
  to pay someone a visit = jemanden
  besuchen
  to pay someone a compliment =
  jemandem ein Kompliment machen
  2 noun = (das) Gehalt
  pay back
  = zurückzahlen

PE noun
  = (der) Sport

pea noun
  = (die) Erbse

peace noun
  = (der) Frieden
  for my own peace of mind = zu meiner
  eigenen Beruhigung

peach noun
  = (der) Pfirsich

peacock noun
  = (der) Pfau

peanut noun
  = (die) Erdnuss

pear noun
  = (die) Birne

pearl noun
  = (die) Perle

pebble noun
  = (der) Kieselstein

pedestrian noun
  = (der) Fußgänger/(die) Fußgängerin

pedestrian crossing noun
  = (der) Fußgängerüberweg

peel verb
  = schälen
  I'm peeling = ich schäle mich

pen noun
  (ballpoint) = (der) Kugelschreiber
  (fountain) = (der) Füller

penalty noun
- (fine) = (die) Geldstrafe
- (in soccer) = (der) Elfmeter

pencil noun
  = (der) Bleistift

pencil case noun
  = (das) Federmäppchen

pencil sharpener noun
  = (der) Bleistiftspitzer

pen friend noun
  = (der) Brieffreund/(die) Brieffreundin

penguin noun
  = (der) Pinguin

penknife noun
  = (das) Taschenmesser

pensioner noun
  = (der) Rentner/(die) Rentnerin

people noun
  = Leute (plural)
  most people = die meisten Leute
  for three people = für drei Personen

pepper noun
- (spice) = (der) Pfeffer
- (vegetable) = (der) Paprika

P

per *preposition*
= pro (+ *accusative*)
per person = pro Person

per cent *noun*
= (das) Prozent

perfect *adjective*
= perfekt

perform *verb*
• (*do*)
to perform a task = eine Arbeit ausführen
• (*act*) = spielen
to perform a play = ein Theaterstück
aufführen

perfume *noun*
= (das) Parfüm

perhaps *adverb*
= vielleicht

period *noun*
• (*in time*) = (die) Zeit
trial period = (die) Probezeit
• (*school lesson*) = (die) Stunde
• (*in history, woman's cycle*) = (die) Periode
• (*full stop*) = (der) Punkt

permanent *adjective*
= ständig
a permanent job = eine feste Stelle

permission *noun*
= (die) Erlaubnis

person *noun*
= (der) Mensch, = (die) Person
an old person = ein alter Mensch

> **!** Note that **Person** is mainly used when
> counting people or as a grammatical
> term. When referring to a **person**, the
> word might seem rude and so is not
> translated.

he's not a very patient person = er ist nicht
sehr geduldig
a sick person = ein Kranker/eine Kranke

personal *adjective*
= persönlich

personality *noun*
= (die) Persönlichkeit

persuade *verb*
= überreden
(*convince*) = überzeugen
to persuade someone to [come | buy a car |
help …] = jemanden überreden [zu
kommen | , ein Auto zu kaufen | zu helfen …]

pessimistic *adjective*
= pessimistisch

pet *noun*
= (das) Haustier

petrol *noun* (*British*)
= (das) Benzin

petrol station *noun* (*British*)
= (die) Tankstelle

pet shop *noun*
= (die) Tierhandlung

pharmacy *noun*
= (die) Apotheke

pheasant *noun*
= (der) Fasan

phone
1 *noun* = (das) Telefon
he's on the phone = er telefoniert
to pick up the phone = den Hörer
abnehmen
2 *verb* = anrufen

phone book *noun*
= (das) Telefonbuch

phone booth *noun*
= (die) Telefonzelle

phone call *noun*
= (der) Telefonanruf

phone card *noun*
= (die) Telefonkarte

photo *noun*
= (das) Foto
to take a photo of someone = ein Foto von
jemandem machen

photocopier *noun*
= (das) Fotokopiergerät

photocopy *noun*
= (die) Fotokopie

photograph
1 *noun* = (die) Fotografie
2 *verb* = fotografieren

photographer *noun*
= (der) Fotograf/(die) Fotografin

physical *adjective*
= körperlich

physics *noun*
= (die) Physik

piano *noun*
= (das) Klavier

pick *verb*
• (*choose*) = aussuchen, (*for oneself*) = sich
(*dative*) aussuchen
• (*collect*) = pflücken
• (*take*)
to pick a book off the shelf = ein Buch aus
dem Regal nehmen
pick up
• (*lift*)
to pick the toys up off the floor = die
Spielsachen vom Boden aufheben
to pick a baby up = ein Baby hochnehmen
to pick up the phone = den Hörer
abnehmen

- (*collect*) = abholen
  he's picking me up from the station = er
  holt mich vom Bahnhof ab
- (*buy*) = kaufen
- (*learn*) = lernen
  to pick up a little French = ein bisschen
  Französisch lernen

picnic *noun*
= (das) Picknick

picture *noun*
- = (das) Bild
- (*film*) = (der) Film

piece *noun*
- (*bit*) = (das) Stück
  a piece of cheese = ein Stück Käse
- (*part of a machine or set*) = (das) Teil
  to take something to pieces = etwas in
  Einzelteile zerlegen, = etwas auseinander
  nehmen
  to fall to pieces = zerbrechen (**!** *sein*), =
  kaputtgehen✱ (**!** *sein*)
- (*coin*) = (das) Stück
  a 50-pence piece = ein Fünfzig-Pence-Stück

pierce *verb*
= durchstechen

pig *noun*
= (das) Schwein

pigeon *noun*
= (die) Taube

pile *noun*
- = (der) Haufen
  (*neat stack*) = (der) Stapel
- (*lots*) = (die) Menge
  piles of [CDs | books | magazines ...] = eine
  Menge | CDs | Bücher | Zeitschriften ...]

pill *noun*
= (die) Pille

pillow *noun*
= (das) Kopfkissen

pilot *noun*
= (der) Pilot/(die) Pilotin

pin
1 *noun* = (die) Stecknadel
2 *verb* = stecken

pinball *noun*
= (das) Flippern

pinch *verb*
- = kneifen
- (*hurt by being too tight*) = drücken

pineapple *noun*
= (die) Ananas

pine tree *noun*
= (die) Kiefer

pink *adjective*
= rosa ▶**Colours p. 204**

pint *noun*
= (das) Pint
let's go for a pint = gehen wir auf ein Bier

pipe *noun*
- = (das) Rohr
- (*for smoking*) = (die) Pfeife

pirate *noun*
= (der) Pirat

Pisces *noun*
= Fische (*plural*)

pitch *noun* (*British*)
= (das) Feld
football pitch = (der) Fußballplatz

pity
1 *noun*
- = (das) Mitleid
- (*when showing regret*)
  it's a pity you [can't come | have to go | didn't
  tell me ...] = schade, dass du [nicht kommen
  kannst | gehen musst | mir das nicht gesagt
  hast ...]
  what a pity! = wie schade!
2 *verb* = bemitleiden

pizza *noun*
= (die) Pizza

place *noun*
- (*location, town*) = (der) Ort
  Oxford is a nice place = Oxford ist ein
  netter Ort
  they come from all over the place = sie
  kommen von überall her
  this place is very dirty = es ist sehr
  schmutzig hier
- (*spot*) = (die) Stelle
- (*house*) = (das) Haus, (*flat*) = (die) Wohnung
  I've got my own place = ich habe meine
  eigene Wohnung
  at Alison's place = bei Alison
- (*in a queue*) = (der) Platz
  to find a place to park = einen Platz zum
  Parken finden
  out of place = fehl am Platz
- (*in a contest, team*) = (der) Platz
  to gain third place = den dritten Platz
  belegen
  a university place = ein Studienplatz

plain
1 *adjective*
- (*simple*) = einfach
- (*without pattern*) = einfarbig
- (*not good-looking*) = nicht hübsch
2 *noun* = (die) Ebene

plait *noun*
= (der) Zopf

plan
1 *noun* = (der) Plan
I don't have any plans for tonight = ich
habe heute Abend nichts vor

P

2 *verb*
- (*prepare*) = planen
  to plan a |trip | meeting | party ...| = |einen
  Ausflug | ein Treffen | eine Party ...| planen
- (*intend*) = vorhaben
  I'm planning to |visit Scotland | go to
  university ...| = ich habe vor, |nach
  Schottland zu fahren | auf die Universität zu
  gehen ...|

plane *noun*
= (das) Flugzeug

planet *noun*
= (der) Planet

plant
1 *noun* = (die) Pflanze
2 *verb* = pflanzen

plaster *noun*
- (*material*) = (der) Gips
  his leg is in plaster = er hat das Bein in
  Gips
- (*for walls*) = (der) Verputz
- (*sticking plaster*) = (das) Pflaster

plastic
1 *noun* = (das) Plastik
2 *adjective* = Plastik-
  plastic bag = (die) Plastiktüte

plate *noun*
= (der) Teller

platform *noun*
= (der) Bahnsteig
  on platform 4 = auf Gleis 4

play
1 *verb*
= spielen
  to play |football | cards | a game ...| = |Fußball |
  Karten | ein Spiel ...| spielen
  Germany are playing Ireland =
  Deutschland spielt gegen Irland

  ! *Note that in German the article is not
  translated when playing musical
  instruments.*

  to play the |piano | flute | guitar ...| = |Klavier |
  Flöte | Gitarre ...| spielen
  the film is playing at the Odeon = der Film
  läuft im Odeon
  to play a trick on someone = jemandem
  einen Streich spielen
2 *noun*
= (das) Theaterstück
play around
= Blödsinn machen
play back
= abspielen

player *noun*
= (der) Spieler/(die) Spielerin

playground *noun*
= (der) Spielplatz
  school playground = (der) Schulhof

please *adverb*
= bitte
  please come in = kommen Sie bitte herein

pleased *adjective*
- (*happy*) = erfreut
  to be pleased about something = sich über
  etwas (*accusative*) freuen
  I'm pleased to hear that you are well = ich
  freue mich zu hören, dass es euch gut
  geht
- (*satisfied*) = zufrieden

plenty *pronoun*
  to have plenty of |time | friends | money ...| =
  |viel Zeit | viele Freunde | viel Geld ...| haben

plot *noun*
- (*story*) = (die) Handlung
- (*plan*) = (das) Komplott
- **a plot of land** = ein Grundstück

plug *noun*
- (*electric*) = (der) Stecker
- (*in a sink, bath*) = (der) Stöpsel
plug in
= einstecken

plum *noun*
= (die) Pflaume

plumber *noun*
= (der) Installateur

plus *preposition*
= plus (+ *dative*)

pneumonia *noun*
= (die) Lungenentzündung

pocket *noun*
= (die) Tasche

pocketbook *noun* (*US*)
= (die) Handtasche

poem *noun*
= (das) Gedicht

point
1 *noun*
- = (der) Punkt
  a point of view = ein Standpunkt
- (*in a contest, game*) = (der) Punkt
- (*most important thing, meaning*) = (der) Sinn
  that's not the point = darum geht es nicht
  what's the point? = wozu?
  there's no point in |shouting | protesting ...| =
  es hat keinen Sinn zu |schreien |
  protestieren ...|
- (*talking about time*)
  to be on the point of |moving | selling the
  house | changing jobs ...| = im Begriff sein
  |umzuziehen | , das Haus zu verkaufen | , die
  Stelle zu wechseln ...|
- (*sharp end*) = (die) Spitze
- (*in numbers*)
  one point five = eins Komma fünf

2 *verb*
* (*indicate*)
  to point one's finger at someone = mit dem Finger auf jemanden zeigen
  to point at a [house | street …] = auf [ein Haus | eine Straße …] zeigen
  to point the way to the station = den Weg zum Bahnhof zeigen
* (*aim*) = richten
  to point a gun at someone = ein Gewehr auf jemanden richten
point out
  = zeigen auf (+ *accusative*)
  to point something out to someone = jemanden auf etwas (*accusative*) hinweisen

poison
1 *noun* = (das) Gift
2 *verb* = vergiften

Poland *noun*
  = (das) Polen ▶ **Countries p. 208**

Pole *noun*
  (der) Pole/(die) Polin

pole *noun*
  = (die) Stange

police *noun*
  = (die) Polizei

policeman *noun*
  = (der) Polizist

police station *noun*
  = (die) Polizeiwache

policewoman *noun*
  = (die) Polizistin

polish *verb*
  = polieren
  to polish the floor = den Fußboden bohnern

polite *adjective*
  = höflich

political *adjective*
  = politisch

politician *noun*
  = (der) Politiker/(die) Politikerin

politics *noun*
  = (die) Politik

pollute *verb*
  = verschmutzen

pollution *noun*
  = (die) Verschmutzung

pond *noun*
  = (der) Teich

pony *noun*
  = (das) Pony

ponytail *noun*
  = (der) Pferdeschwanz

pool *noun*
* (*swimming pool*) = (das) Schwimmbecken

* (*on the ground, floor*) = (die) Lache
* (*game*) = (das) Poolbillard

poor *adjective*
* = arm
* (*not satisfactory*) = schlecht

population *noun*
  = (die) Bevölkerung

pork *noun*
  = (das) Schweinefleisch

port *noun*
  = (der) Hafen

porter *noun*
  (*in a station, airport*) = (der) Gepäckträger
  (*in a hotel*) = (der) Portier

Portugal *noun*
  = (das) Portugal ▶ **Countries p. 208**

positive *adjective*
* (*definite*) = eindeutig
* (*convinced*) = sicher
* (*of a result, attitude*) = positiv

possibility *noun*
  = (die) Möglichkeit

possible *adjective*
  = möglich
  as quickly as possible = so schnell wie möglich

post (*British*)
1 *noun* = (die) Post
  by post = per Post, = mit der Post
2 *verb*
  to post a letter = einen Brief abschicken

postbox *noun* (*British*)
  = (der) Briefkasten

postcode *noun* (*British*)
  = die Postleitzahl

poster *noun*
  = (das) Plakat
  (*used as a picture*) = (das) *or* (der) Poster

postman *noun* (*British*)
  = (der) Briefträger

post office *noun*
  = (die) Post

postpone *verb*
  = verschieben
  to postpone the party until next week = die Party auf nächste Woche verschieben

pot *noun*
  = (der) Topf
  (*for tea, coffee*) = (die) Kanne
  a pot of tea = eine Kanne Tee

potato *noun*
  = (die) Kartoffel

pottery *noun*
* (*craft*) = (die) Töpferei
* (*objects*) = Töpferwaren (*plural*)

P

pound noun
= (das) Pfund ▶Measures p. 270, ▶Money
p. 274

pour verb
• (from a container) = gießen
• (serve a drink) = eingießen
  to pour someone a cup of tea = jemandem
  eine Tasse Tee eingießen
• (flow) = fließen (**!** sein)
• (enter or leave in large numbers) = strömen
  (**!** sein)
  refugees were pouring out of the city = die
  Flüchtlinge strömten aus der Stadt
• (rain)
  it's pouring = es gießt

powder noun
= (das) Pulver
  (cosmetics) = (der) Puder

power noun
• (control) = (die) Macht
  to be in power = an der Macht sein
• (influence)
  to have great power = großen Einfluss
  haben
• (strength) = (die) Kraft
• (electricity) = (der) Strom

power cut noun
= (die) Stromsperre

practical adjective
= praktisch

practice
1 noun (British)
• = (die) Übung
• (of a doctor, lawyer) = (die) Praxis
2 verb (US) ▶practise

practise
1 verb (British)
• = üben
• (rehearse) = proben
2 noun (US) ▶practice

praise verb
= loben

pram noun (British)
= (der) Kinderwagen

prawn noun
= (die) Garnele

prayer noun
= (das) Gebet

precaution noun
= (die) Vorsichtsmaßnahme

precious adjective
= kostbar

precise adjective
= genau

prefer verb
= vorziehen
  I prefer him to his brother = ich ziehe ihn
  seinem Bruder vor
  I prefer to phone = ich rufe lieber an

pregnant adjective
= schwanger

prejudice noun
• = (das) Vorurteil
• (bias) = (die) Voreingenommenheit

prepare verb
• (get ready) = vorbereiten
  to prepare pupils for an exam = Schüler
  auf eine Prüfung vorbereiten
• (get oneself ready) = sich vorbereiten
  to prepare for an exam = sich auf eine
  Prüfung vorbereiten

prepared adjective
• (willing)
  to be prepared to wait = bereit sein zu
  warten
• (ready) = vorbereitet
  to be prepared for an exam = auf eine
  Prüfung vorbereitet sein

prescription noun
= (das) Rezept

present
1 noun
• (gift) = (das) Geschenk
  to give someone a present = jemandem
  ein Geschenk machen
• (now)
  the present = die Gegenwart
  at present = zur Zeit
2 verb
• (give) = überreichen
  to present a prize to someone = jemandem
  einen Preis überreichen
• (on TV, radio) = moderieren

president noun
= (der) Präsident/(die) Präsidentin

press
1 verb
• = drücken
• (on something) = drücken auf
  (+ accusative)
  to press the bell = auf die Klingel drücken
2 noun
  the press = die Presse

pressure noun
= (der) Druck
  to put pressure on someone = jemanden
  unter Druck setzen

pretend verb
= vorgeben
  he's pretending to be annoyed = er gibt
  vor, böse zu sein
  to pretend that . . . = so tun, als ob . . .

pretty
1 adjective = hübsch
2 adverb
  (quite) = ziemlich

prevent *verb*
to prevent an accident = einen Unfall verhindern
to prevent someone from working = jemanden daran hindern zu arbeiten

previous *adjective*
• (*earlier*) = früher
in previous years = in früheren Jahren
• (*preceding*) = vorig
the previous owner = der vorige Besitzer

price *noun*
= (der) Preis

pride *noun*
= (der) Stolz

priest *noun*
= (der) Priester

primary school *noun*
= (die) Grundschule

prime minister *noun*
= (der) Premierminister/
(die) Premierministerin

prince *noun*
= (der) Prinz

princess *noun*
= (die) Prinzessin

principal *noun*
(*of a senior school*) = (der) Direktor/
(die) Direktorin
(*of a junior school*) = (der) Rektor/
(die) Rektorin

print
1 *verb*
= drucken
(*in computing*) = ausdrucken
2 *noun*
• (*photo*) = (der) Abzug
• (*in a book*) = (der) Druck
• (*of a finger, foot*) = (der) Abdruck

printer *noun*
(*for a computer*) = (der) Drucker

printout *noun*
= (der) Ausdruck

prison *noun*
= (das) Gefängnis

prisoner *noun*
= (der/die) Gefangene

private *adjective*
= privat, Privat-
my private life = mein Privatleben
in private = privat

prize *noun*
= (der) Preis

probably *adverb*
= wahrscheinlich

problem *noun*
= (das) Problem
no problem! = kein Problem!

process *noun*
= (der) Prozess
to be in the process of writing a letter = dabei sein, einen Brief zu schreiben

produce
1 *verb*
• (*make*) = herstellen
the company produces soft drinks = die Firma stellt alkoholfreie Getränke her
• (*create*)
to produce a film = einen Film produzieren
to produce a play = ein Theaterstück inszenieren
2 *noun* = Erzeugnisse (*plural*)

product *noun*
= (das) Produkt

production *noun*
= (die) Produktion

profession *noun*
= (der) Beruf

professional *adjective*
• (*relating to work*) = beruflich
• (*expert*) = fachmännisch
• (*not amateur*) = Berufs-
(*in sport*) = professionell
a professional musician = ein Berufsmusiker

profit *noun*
= (der) Gewinn
to sell something at a profit = etwas mit Gewinn verkaufen

program
1 *noun*
• (*for a computer*) = (das) Programm
• (*US*) ▶programme
2 *verb* = programmieren

programme *noun* (*British*)
• (*on TV, radio*) = (die) Sendung
• (*booklet, schedule*) = (das) Programm

progress *noun*
= (der) Fortschritt
to make progress = Fortschritte machen

project *noun*
(*at school*) = (die) Arbeit

promise
1 *verb* = versprechen
to promise to [write a letter | say nothing | come back soon …] = versprechen, [einen Brief zu schreiben | nichts zu sagen | bald wiederzukommen …]
to promise someone a letter = jemandem einen Brief versprechen
2 *noun* = (das) Versprechen

pronounce *verb*
= aussprechen

proof *noun*
= (der) Beweis
I have proof that they lied = ich kann beweisen, dass sie gelogen haben

P

Professions

Shops

In English you can say *at the baker's* or *at the baker's shop*. In German, you can also use the name of the trader or the shop.

> *he is at the baker's* = er ist beim Bäcker, = er ist in der Bäckerei
> *to go to the chemist's* = zum Apotheker *or* Drogisten gehen, = in die Apotheke *or* Drogerie gehen (**!** *sein*)

Note that in German you go to the **Apotheke** for medicines and to the **Drogerie** for toiletries.

> *to work at the hairdresser's* = beim Friseur arbeiten, = im Friseursalon arbeiten
> *to go to the hairdresser's* = zum Friseur gehen (**!** *sein*)

People

In sentences describing a person's profession, the article (*a* / *an*) is not translated in German:

> *my father is a doctor* = mein Vater ist Arzt
> *my mother is a teacher* = meine Mutter ist Lehrerin

But if an adjective describes the profession, the article is used with the adjective:

> *she is a good dentist* = sie ist eine gute Zahnärztin

Bei and **zu** are also used with professions:

> *at the lawyer's* = beim Anwalt / bei der Anwältin
> *to go to the doctor's* = zum Arzt / zur Ärztin gehen (**!** *sein*)

Useful shopping expressions

> *can I help you?* = kann ich Ihnen helfen?
> *what would you like?* = was wünschen Sie, bitte?
> *anything else?* = sonst noch etwas?
> *I'd like ...* = ich möchte ...
> *have you got ...?* = haben Sie ...?

---

properly *adverb*
= richtig

property *noun*
• (*possessions*) = (das) Eigentum
• (*land*) = (der) Besitz
(*house*) = (das) Haus

protect *verb*
= schützen
to protect someone from something =
jemanden vor etwas (*dative*) schützen

protest *verb*
= protestieren
to protest about something = gegen etwas
(*accusative*) protestieren

protester *noun*
(*at a demonstration*) = (der)
Demonstrant/(die) Demonstrantin

proud *adjective*
= stolz
she is proud of her work = sie ist auf ihre
Arbeit stolz

prove *verb*
= beweisen
to prove to be wrong = sich als falsch
erweisen

provide *verb*
to provide [work | food | entertainment ...] = für
[Arbeit | Essen | Unterhaltung ...] sorgen
to provide a car = ein Auto zur Verfügung
stellen

provided *conjunction*
provided (**that**) = vorausgesetzt, (dass)

psychiatrist *noun*
= (der) Psychiater/(die) Psychiaterin

pub *noun* (*British*)
= (die) Kneipe✱

public
1 *noun*
the public = die Öffentlichkeit
in public = öffentlich
2 *adjective*
= öffentlich
public holiday = (der) gesetzliche Feiertag

public transport *noun*
= öffentliche Verkehrsmittel (*plural*)

pudding *noun* (*British*)
= (der) Nachtisch

puddle *noun*
= (die) Pfütze

pull *verb*
• = ziehen

✱ in informal situations

(*pull on*) = ziehen an (+ *dative*)
to pull a rope = an einem Seil ziehen
to pull someone's sleeve = jemanden am
  Ärmel ziehen
he pulled a handkerchief out of his pocket
  = er zog ein Taschentuch aus der Tasche
to pull a face = eine Grimasse schneiden
• (*injure*)
to pull a muscle = sich (*dative*) einen
  Muskel zerren

pull down
• (*demolish*) = abreißen
• (*lower*) = herunterziehen

pull out
• **to pull out a tooth** = einen Zahn ziehen
• **the train is pulling out** = der Zug fährt ab

pull up
• (*raise*) = hochziehen
• (*stop*) = anhalten
• (*remove*) = herausziehen, = rausziehen✱

pullover noun
= (der) Pullover

pump noun
= (die) Pumpe
pump up
= aufpumpen

pumpkin noun
= (der) Kürbis

punch verb
= boxen

punctual adjective
= pünktlich

puncture noun
• (*hole*) = (das) Loch
• (*flat tyre*) = (die) Reifenpanne

punish verb
= bestrafen

pupil noun
= (der) Schüler/(die) Schülerin

puppet noun
= (die) Puppe

puppy noun
= (der) junge Hund

pure adjective
= rein

purple adjective
= lila ▶**Colours p. 204**
the purple dress = das lila Kleid

purpose noun
= (der) Zweck
on purpose = absichtlich

purse noun
• (*for money*) = (das) Portemonnaie
• (*US: handbag*) = (die) Handtasche

push verb
• (*move by pushing*) = schieben
to push a car = ein Auto schieben, (*to get it
  started*) = ein Auto anschieben

• (*roughly*) = schubsen
she pushed him down the stairs = sie
  schubste ihn die Treppe herunter
• (*press*) = drücken
to push a button = auf einen Knopf
  drücken
• (*sell*) = pushen✱
to push drugs = Rauschgift pushen

pushchair noun (*British*)
= (der) Sportwagen

put verb
• (*place*) = tun
to put sugar in one's coffee = sich (*dative*)
  Zucker in den Kaffee tun
• (*lay flat*) = legen
she put the pencil on the table = sie legte
  den Bleistift auf den Tisch
• (*place upright*) = stellen
I put the vase on the shelf = ich habe die
  Vase auf das Regal gestellt
• (*push in*) = stecken
she put her hands in her pockets = sie
  steckte die Hände in die Taschen

put away
= wegräumen

put back
• (*return to its place*) = zurücktun
• (*turn back*) = zurückstellen
to put the clocks back = die Uhren
  zurückstellen

put down
• (*vertically*) = hinstellen, (*horizontally*) =
  hinlegen
to put the phone down = den Hörer
  auflegen
• (*kill an animal painlessly*) = einschläfern

put forward
= vorstellen
to put the clocks forward = die Uhren
  vorstellen

put off
• (*postpone*) = verschieben
we'll have to put the party off till next week
  = wir müssen die Party auf nächste
  Woche verschieben
• (*switch off*) = ausmachen

put on
• (*when dressing*) = anziehen
to put jeans on = Jeans anziehen
to put a hat on = einen Hut aufsetzen
• (*switch on*)
to put the light on = das Licht anmachen
to put the kettle on = Wasser aufsetzen
to put a CD on = eine CD auflegen
• **to put on weight** = zunehmen
• **to put on a play** = ein Theaterstück
  aufführen

put out
(*extinguish*) = ausmachen
to put out the fire = das Feuer löschen
• (*take outside*) = hinaustun, = raustun✱

put up
• (*lift*) = heben
to put one's hand up = die Hand heben
• (*attach*) = anbringen

P

- (*pitch*)
  to put up a tent = ein Zelt aufschlagen
- (*raise*) = erhöhen
  to put the rent up = die Miete erhöhen
- (*give a place to stay*) = unterbringen
- **to put up with someone** = jemanden dulden

puzzle *noun*
= (das) Rätsel

pyjamas *noun* (*British*)
= (der) Schlafanzug

Qq

qualified *adjective*
= ausgebildet

quality *noun*
= (die) Qualität

quantity *noun*
= (die) Menge

quarrel
1 *noun* = (der) Streit
2 *verb* = sich streiten

quarter *noun*
= (das) Viertel ▶ **Time p. 331**
a quarter of an hour = eine Viertelstunde
an hour and a quarter = eineinviertel Stunden

quay *noun*
= (der) Kai

queen *noun*
= (die) Königin
(*in chess, cards*) = (die) Dame

question
1 *noun*
= (die) Frage
to ask someone a question = jemandem eine Frage stellen
2 *verb*
- (*ask questions*) = befragen
- (*doubt*) = bezweifeln

questionnaire *noun*
(der) Fragebogen

queue (*British*)
1 *noun*
= (die) Schlange
to join the queue = sich anstellen
2 *verb* = Schlange stehen

quick *adjective*
= schnell
to have a quick meal = schnell etwas essen
be quick! = mach schnell!

quickly *adverb*
= schnell

quiet
1 *adjective*
- (*silent, not talkative*) = still
  to keep quiet = still sein
  be quiet! = sei still!
  to have a quiet voice = eine leise Stimme haben
- (*calm*) = ruhig
2 *noun* = (die) Ruhe

quietly *adverb*
to speak quietly = leise reden

quit *verb*
- (*resign*) = kündigen
- (*US: give up*)
  to quit smoking = aufhören zu rauchen

quite *adverb*
- (*rather*) = ziemlich
- (*completely*) = ganz
  I'm not quite ready yet = ich bin noch nicht ganz fertig
- (*exactly*)
  I don't quite know what he does = ich weiß nicht genau, was er macht
  quite! = genau!

quiz *noun*
= (das) Quiz

Rr

rabbit *noun*
= (das) Kaninchen

rabies *noun*
= (die) Tollwut

race
1 *noun*
- (*contest*) = (das) Rennen
  to have a race (*running*) = um die Wette laufen (**!** *sein*), (*swimming*) = um die Wette schwimmen (**!** *sein*)
  the races = das Pferderennen
- (*ethnic group*) = (die) Rasse
2 *verb*
- (*compete with*)
  to race someone = mit jemandem um die Wette laufen (**!** *sein*)
- (*take part in a contest*)

  ! *Note that the translation can change according to the type of race.*

  (*running*) = laufen, (*swimming*) = schwimmen, (*sailing*) = segeln (**!** *all sein*)

racetrack *noun*
= (die) Rennbahn

racket, racquet *noun*
= (der) Schläger

radiator *noun*
• (*heater*) = (der) Heizkörper
• (*in a car*) = (der) Kühler

radio *noun*
= (das) Radio
I heard it on the radio = ich habe es im
Radio gehört

radish *noun*
= (das) Radieschen

rage *noun*
= (die) Wut
to fly into a rage = in Wut geraten (**!** *sein*)

raid
1 *verb*
to raid a bank = eine Bank überfallen
the police raided the house = die Polizei
hat in dem Haus eine Razzia gemacht
2 *noun*
(*by thieves*) = (der) Überfall
(*by the police*) = (die) Razzia

rail *noun*
• (*for holding on to*) = (das) Geländer
• (*for trains*) = (die) Schiene
to go by rail = mit der Bahn fahren (**!** *sein*)

railroad (*US*), **railway** (*British*) *noun*
• (*track*) = (die) Bahnstrecke
• (*system*) = (die) Eisenbahn, = (die) Bahn

railway station *noun*
= (der) Bahnhof

rain
1 *noun* = (der) Regen
2 *verb* = regnen
it's raining = es regnet

rainbow *noun*
= (der) Regenbogen

raincoat *noun*
= (der) Regenmantel

raise *verb*
• (*lift*) = heben
to raise one's hand = die Hand heben
• (*increase*) = erhöhen
to raise prices = die Preise erhöhen
• (*talk about*) = aufwerfen
to raise a question = eine Frage aufwerfen
• (*bring up*) = aufziehen
to raise children = Kinder aufziehen

range *noun*
• (*selection*) = (die) Auswahl
to have a range of something = eine
Auswahl an etwas (*dative*) haben
to have a range of options = verschiedene
Möglichkeiten haben
a range of subjects = verschiedene Fächer
in this price range = in dieser Preislage
• (*of mountains*) = (die) Kette

rarely *adverb*
= selten

rasher *noun*
(*of bacon*) = (die) Speckscheibe

raspberry *noun*
= (die) Himbeere

rat *noun*
= (die) Ratte

rather *adverb*
• (*when saying what one would prefer*)
= lieber
I'd rather [stay here | read the paper | wait ...] =
ich würde lieber [hier bleiben | die Zeitung
lesen | warten ...]
I'd rather you came with me = es wäre mir
lieber, wenn du mitkämst
• (*quite*) = ziemlich
she's rather young = sie ist ziemlich jung

raw *adjective*
= roh

razor *noun*
= (der) Rasierapparat

reach *verb*
• (*arrive at*) = ankommen in (+ *dative*)
(**!** *sein*)
they reached the town at 8 o'clock = sie
kamen um acht Uhr in der Stadt an
• (*be delivered to, contact by phone*)
= erreichen
the letter never reached her = der Brief hat
sie nie erreicht
• (*by stretching*) = reichen an (+ *accusative*)
to be able to reach the shelf = an das Regal
reichen können
can you reach? = kommst du daran?
• (*come to*) = kommen zu (+ *dative*) (**!** *sein*)
to reach a decision = zu einer
Entscheidung kommen
reach for
= greifen nach (+ *dative*)
reach out
= die Hand ausstrecken

react *verb*
= reagieren

read *verb*
= lesen
his writing is difficult to read = seine Schrift
ist schwer zu lesen
to read a story to someone = jemandem
eine Geschichte vorlesen
read out
= laut vorlesen
read through
= durchlesen

ready *adjective*
• (*prepared*) = fertig
to get ready = sich fertig machen
• (*willing*) = bereit
I'm ready to help them = ich bin bereit,
ihnen zu helfen

real *adjective*
• (*not imagined*) = wirklich

- (*not artificial*) = echt
  are they real diamonds? = sind das echte
    Brillanten?
- (*great*) = wirklich
  it's a real shame = das ist wirklich schade

reality *noun*
= (die) Wirklichkeit

realize *verb*
(*know*) = wissen

really *adverb*
= wirklich
it's really easy = es ist wirklich einfach
I don't really know him = ich kenne ihn
  eigentlich nicht

rear
1 *noun* = (der) hintere Teil
2 *adjective* = hinterer/hintere/hinteres
rear wheel = (das) Hinterrad
3 *verb* = aufziehen

reason *noun*
= (der) Grund
there's no reason to get annoyed = es
  besteht kein Grund, ärgerlich zu werden

receipt *noun*
= (die) Quittung

receive *verb*
= erhalten

recent *adjective*
(*not long past*) = jüngst
in recent years = in den letzten Jahren
recent research = die neueste Forschung

recently *adverb*
= kürzlich

reception *noun*
- (*in a hotel, company*) = (der) Empfang,
    = (die) Rezeption
- (*in a hospital*) = (die) Aufnahme
- (*formal event*) = (der) Empfang

receptionist *noun*
= (die) Empfangsdame
(*at the doctor's*) = (die) Sprechstundenhilfe

recipe *noun*
= (das) Rezept

recognize *verb*
= erkennen

recommend *verb*
= empfehlen

record
1 *noun*
- (*of events*) = (die) Aufzeichnung
- (*information*)
  records = Unterlagen (*plural*)
- (*musical disc*) = (die) Platte
- (*in sport*) = (der) Rekord
2 *verb*
- (*keep account of*) = aufzeichnen
- (*on tape*) = aufnehmen

recorder *noun*
= (die) Blockflöte

record player *noun*
= (der) Plattenspieler

recover *verb*
= sich erholen
to recover from an illness = sich von einer
  Krankheit erholen

recycle *verb*
= recyceln

red *adjective*
= rot ▶ **Colours p. 204**
to go red, to turn red = rot werden (**!** *sein*)

red-haired *adjective*
= rothaarig

reduce *verb*
to reduce the size of something = etwas
  verkleinern
to reduce speed = die Geschwindigkeit
  verringern
to reduce prices = die Preise herabsetzen

reduction *noun*
- (*in size*) = (die) Verkleinerung
- (*in number*) = (die) Verringerung
- (*in price*) = (die) Ermäßigung

redundant *adjective* (*British*)
to be made redundant = entlassen werden
  (**!** *sein*)

referee *noun*
= (der) Schiedsrichter/(die) Schiedsrichterin

reflect *verb*
= spiegeln
the lights were reflected in the water = die
  Lichter spiegelten sich im Wasser

reflection *noun*
= (das) Spiegelbild

refreshing *adjective*
= erfrischend

refrigerator *noun*
= (der) Kühlschrank

refugee *noun*
= (der) Flüchtling

refuse[1] *verb*
(*not allow*) = verweigern
to refuse someone admission = jemandem
  den Zutritt verweigern
to refuse to [stop | pay | go …] = sich weigern
  [aufzuhören | zu zahlen | zu gehen …]

refuse[2] *noun* (*British*)
= (der) Abfall, = (der) Müll

regards *noun*
= Grüße (*plural*)
give her my regards = grüße sie von mir

region *noun*
= (das) Gebiet

register noun
(at school) = (das) Klassenbuch
to take the register = die Anwesenheit der Schüler überprüfen

registration number noun (British)
= (die) Autonummer

regret
1 verb = bedauern
I regret not seeing him again = ich bedauere es, dass ich ihn nicht mehr gesehen habe
2 noun = (das) Bedauern
to have regrets = es bereuen

regular adjective
• = regelmäßig
• (usual) = üblich

regularly adverb
= regelmäßig

rehearsal noun
= (die) Probe

rehearse verb
= proben

reject verb
= ablehnen

relationship noun
= (die) Beziehung
to have a good relationship with one's parents = eine gute Beziehung zu seinen Eltern haben

relative noun
= (der/die) Verwandte

relax verb
= sich entspannen

relaxed adjective
= entspannt

relay race noun
= (die) Staffel

release verb
(free) = freilassen

reliable adjective
= zuverlässig

relieved adjective
I was relieved to get a letter from him = ich war erleichtert, als ich seinen Brief erhielt

religion noun
= (die) Religion

religious adjective
= religiös

religious education noun
= (der) Religionsunterricht

rely verb
to rely on (be dependent on) = angewiesen sein auf (+ accusative), (count on) = sich verlassen auf (+ accusative)
can we rely on you? = können wir uns auf euch verlassen?

remain verb
= bleiben (**!** sein)
(be left over) = übrig bleiben (**!** sein)

remark noun
= (die) Bemerkung

remarkable adjective
= bemerkenswert

remember verb
= sich erinnern an (+ accusative)
do you remember her? = kannst du dich an sie erinnern?
to remember to [post the letters | switch off the lights | lock the door …] = daran denken, [die Briefe abzuschicken | das Licht auszumachen | abzuschließen …]

remind verb
= erinnern
she reminds me of my sister = sie erinnert mich an meine Schwester
to remind someone to buy milk = jemanden daran erinnern, Milch zu kaufen

remote control noun
• (of a car or plane) = (die) Fernlenkung
• (of a TV or video) = (die) Fernbedienung

remove verb
= entfernen

rent
1 verb = mieten
2 noun = (die) Miete
rent out
= vermieten

repair verb
= reparieren
to have a bicycle repaired = ein Fahrrad reparieren lassen

repeat verb
= wiederholen

replace verb
• (substitute) = ersetzen
• (put back) = zurücktun

reply
1 verb = antworten
to reply to someone = jemandem antworten
to reply to a letter = auf einen Brief antworten
2 noun = (die) Antwort

report
1 verb
• (notify) = melden
to report someone to the police = jemanden anzeigen
• (in the news) = berichten
to report on an event = über ein Ereignis berichten
2 noun
• = (der) Bericht
• (British: at school) = (das) Zeugnis

R

report card noun (US)
= (das) Zeugnis

reporter noun
= (der) Reporter/(die) Reporterin

represent verb
- (act for) = vertreten
- (symbolize) = darstellen

republic noun
= (die) Republik

request noun
= (die) Bitte

rescue verb
= retten

resemble verb
= ähneln (+ dative)
to resemble each other = sich (dative) ähneln

resent verb
= übel nehmen
she resented his remark = sie hat ihm seine Äußerung übel genommen
he resents her for winning = er nimmt es ihr übel, dass sie gewonnen hat

reserve verb
- (keep) = reservieren
- (book) = reservieren lassen

resign verb
(from one's job) = kündigen
(from public office) = zurücktreten (! sein)

resist verb
= widerstehen (+ dative)

respect
1 verb = respektieren
2 noun = (der) Respekt
to have respect for someone = Respekt vor jemandem haben

responsibility noun
= (die) Verantwortung

responsible adjective
- (the cause of) = verantwortlich
- (in charge) = verantwortlich
- (sensible) = verantwortungsbewusst

rest
1 noun
- (what is left) = (der) Rest
- (break) = (die) Pause
to have a rest = eine Pause machen
2 verb = sich ausruhen

restaurant noun
= (das) Restaurant

result noun
- (outcome) = (das) Ergebnis
the exam results = die Prüfungsergebnisse
- (consequence) = (die) Folge
as the result of an accident = als Folge eines Unfalls
as a result of this = infolgedessen

retire verb
= in den Ruhestand treten (! sein)

return verb
- (go back) = zurückgehen (! sein), (drive) = zurückfahren (! sein)
- (come back) = zurückkommen (! sein)
- (give back) = zurückgeben
- (send back) = zurückschicken
- (put back) = zurückstellen, = zurücklegen

! Note that **zurückstellen** is used if something is put down in a vertical position and **zurücklegen** if it is put down in a horizontal position.

- (start again)
to return to school = wieder in die Schule gehen (! sein)

return ticket noun
= (die) Rückfahrkarte
(by air) = (der) Rückflugschein

reunification noun
= (die) Wiedervereinigung

reveal verb
to reveal a secret = ein Geheimnis enthüllen

revenge noun
= (die) Rache
to get one's revenge = sich rächen

revolution noun
= (die) Revolution

reward
1 noun = (die) Belohnung
2 verb = belohnen

rhinoceros noun
= (das) Nashorn

rhythm noun
= (der) Rhythmus

rib noun
= (die) Rippe

ribbon noun
= (das) Band

rice noun
= (der) Reis

rich adjective
= reich

rid verb
to get rid of = loswerden (! sein)

ride
1 verb
to ride a horse = reiten (! sein)
to ride a bike = Rad fahren (! sein)
he's riding his bike = er fährt Rad
2 noun
to go for a ride (in a car) = eine Fahrt machen, (on a horse) = ausreiten (! sein), (on a bike) = Rad fahren (! sein)

ridiculous adjective
= lächerlich

riding *noun*
= (das) Reiten

rifle *noun*
= (das) Gewehr

right
1 *adjective*
* (*not left*) = rechter/rechte/rechtes
 his right hand = seine rechte Hand
* (*correct*) = richtig
 the right answer = die richtige Antwort
 you're right = du hast Recht
 that's right = das stimmt
2 *noun*
* (*not left*) = (die) rechte Seite
 the first street on the right = die erste
 Straße rechts
* (*entitlement*) = (das) Recht
 to have a right to something = ein Recht
 auf etwas (*accusative*) haben
3 *adverb*
= rechts
to turn right = rechts abbiegen (**!** *sein*)

ring
1 *verb*
* (*British: phone*) = anrufen
* (*make a sound*) = klingeln
 I rang the bell = ich habe geklingelt
 the bell rang = es hat geklingelt
2 *noun*
* (*piece of jewellery*) = (der) Ring
 wedding ring = (der) Ehering
* (*circle*) = (der) Kreis
 to stand in a ring = im Kreis stehen
* (*in a circus*) = (die) Manege
ring back (*British*)
= zurückrufen
ring up (*British*)
= anrufen

rinse *verb*
= spülen

ripe *adjective*
= reif

rise *verb*
* = steigen (**!** *sein*)
* (*of the sun or moon*) = aufgehen (**!** *sein*)

risk
1 *noun* = (das) Risiko
 I took a risk = ich bin ein Risiko
 eingegangen
2 *verb* = riskieren
 to risk losing one's job = es riskieren, seine
 Stelle zu verlieren

rival *noun*
* (*person*) = (der) Rivale/(die) Rivalin
* (*company*) = (die) Konkurrenz

river *noun*
= (der) Fluss

road *noun*
= (die) Straße

road sign *noun*
= (das) Straßenschild

roadworks *noun*
= Straßenarbeiten (*plural*)

roar *verb*
(*of a lion or person*) = brüllen
(*of traffic*) = donnern
(*of an engine*) = dröhnen

roast
1 *verb* = braten
2 *adjective* = gebraten
 roast beef = (der) Rinderbraten
 roast potatoes = Bratkartoffeln (*plural*)
3 *noun* = (der) Braten

rob *verb*
 to rob a bank = eine Bank ausrauben
 to rob someone = jemanden berauben

robbery *noun*
= (der) Raub

robin *noun*
= (das) Rotkehlchen

robot *noun*
= (der) Roboter

rock *noun*
* (*substance*) = (der) Fels
* (*large stone*) = (der) Felsen
* (*music*) = (der) Rock

rocket *noun*
= (die) Rakete

rocking chair *noun*
= (der) Schaukelstuhl

role *noun*
= (die) Rolle

roll
1 *verb* = rollen (**!** *sein*)
2 *noun*
* (*of paper, cloth, plastic*) = (die) Rolle
 a roll of film = eine Rolle Film
* (*bread*) = (das) Brötchen, = (die) Semmel
roll about, roll around
 (*of an object*) = herumrollen (**!** *sein*)
 (*of a person*) = sich wälzen
roll over
= sich umdrehen
roll up
* **to roll up a carpet** = einen Teppich
 aufrollen
 to roll up a newspaper = eine Zeitung
 zusammenrollen
* **to roll up one's sleeves** = sich (*dative*) die
 Ärmel hochkrempeln

roller coaster *noun*
= (die) Achterbahn

roller-skate *noun*
= (der) Rollschuh

roller-skating *noun*
= (das) Rollschuhlaufen

R

Romania *noun*
= (das) Rumänien ▶**Countries p. 208**

romantic *adjective*
= romantisch

roof *noun*
= (das) Dach

room *noun*
* = (das) Zimmer
* (*space*) = (der) Platz
  to make room = Platz machen

root *noun*
= (die) Wurzel

rope *noun*
= (das) Seil

rose *noun*
= (die) Rose

rosy *adjective*
= rosig

rot *verb*
= verfaulen (**!** *sein*)

rotten *adjective*
= verfault

rough *adjective*
* (*not smooth*) = rau
  (*of a road, ground*) = uneben
* (*not gentle, not exact*) = grob
  a rough estimate = eine grobe Schätzung
* (*difficult*) = schwer
  to have a rough time = es schwer haben
* (*stormy*)
  a rough sea = eine stürmische See

round
1 *preposition* = um (+ *accusative*)
  to go round the corner = um die Ecke
    gehen (**!** *sein*)
  to go round a museum = ein Museum
    besuchen
2 *adverb*
  to go round and round = sich im Kreis
    drehen
  to invite someone round = jemanden zu
    sich (*dative*) einladen
  to go round to John's = zu John gehen
    (**!** *sein*)
  to look round = sich umsehen

> **!** *Note that* round *is often used with
> verbs—*come round, show round, *etc. You
> will find translations for these under the
> entries* come, show, *etc.*

3 *adjective* = rund
4 *noun* = (die) Runde

roundabout *noun* (*British*)
* (*at a fair*) = (das) Karussell
* (*for traffic*) = (der) Kreisverkehr

routine *noun*
= (die) Routine

row¹
1 *noun*
* = (die) Reihe
* (*sequence*)
  in a row = hintereinander
  to be absent for five days in a row = fünf
    Tage hintereinander fehlen
2 *verb* = rudern (**!** *sein*)

row² *noun*
= (der) Streit, = (der) Krach✖
  to have a row with someone = sich mit
    jemandem streiten

rowboat (*US*) ▶rowing boat

rowing *noun*
= (das) Rudern

rowing boat *noun* (*British*)
= (das) Ruderboot

royal *adjective*
= königlich

rub *verb*
= reiben
  to rub one's eyes = sich (*dative*) die Augen
    reiben
rub off
= abreiben
rub out
= ausradieren

rubber *noun*
* (*material*) = (der) *or* (das) Gummi
* (*British: eraser*) = (der) Radiergummi

rubber band *noun*
= (das) Gummiband

rubbish *noun* (*British*)
* (*refuse*) = (der) Abfall, = (der) Müll
* (*poor goods*) = (der) Schund✖
* (*nonsense*) = (der) Quatsch✖

rucksack *noun*
= (der) Rucksack

rude *adjective*
* (*impolite*) = unhöflich
* (*vulgar*) = unanständig

rug *noun*
* (*carpet*) = (der) Teppich
* (*blanket*) = (die) Decke

rugby *noun*
= (das) Rugby

ruin
1 *verb* = ruinieren
2 *noun* = (die) Ruine

rule
1 *noun* = (die) Regel
  the rules of the game = die Spielregeln
  as a rule = in der Regel
2 *verb* = regieren

ruler *noun*
* (*for measuring*) = (das) Lineal
* (*person*) (der) Herrscher/(die) Herrscherin

✖ in informal situations

rumor (US), **rumour** (British) noun
= (das) Gerücht

run
1 verb
* = laufen (**!** sein), (run fast) = rennen (**!** sein)
  to run a race = ein Rennen laufen
* (flee from danger) = weglaufen (**!** sein),
  = wegrennen (**!** sein)
* (manage) = führen
  to run a shop = ein Geschäft führen
* (work, operate) = laufen (**!** sein)
  to leave the engine running = den Motor
  laufen lassen
  the car runs on unleaded petrol = das Auto
  fährt mit bleifreiem Benzin
* (organize) = leiten
* (when talking about transport) = fahren
  (**!** sein)
  the train runs every hour = der Zug fährt
  jede Stunde
  the train is running 20 minutes late = der
  Zug hat zwanzig Minuten Verspätung
* (flow) = laufen (**!** sein)
* (of a river) = fließen (**!** sein)
  his nose is running = ihm läuft die Nase
* **to run a bath** = sich (dative) ein Bad
  einlaufen lassen
* (of colours)
  (in the wash) = auslaufen (**!** sein)
  (on a painting) = ineinander laufen (**!** sein)
* (remain valid, showing) = laufen (**!** sein)
  the contract runs until June = der Vertrag
  läuft bis Juni
* (drive) = fahren
  I ran her home = ich habe sie nach Hause
  gefahren
* (in an election) = kandidieren
  to run for president = für das Amt des
  Präsidenten kandidieren
2 noun (on foot) = (der) Lauf
  (in a car) = (die) Fahrt
  (of a play, show) = (die) Laufzeit
run away
= weglaufen (**!** sein), = wegrennen (**!** sein)
run off
= weglaufen (**!** sein)
run out
= ausgehen (**!** sein)
  we've run out of petrol = wir haben kein
  Benzin mehr
run over
(injure) = überfahren
runner noun
(person) = (der) Läufer/(die) Läuferin
rush
1 verb
* (run) = rasen (**!** sein)
  she rushed out of the house = sie raste aus
  dem Haus
* (hurry) = sich beeilen
  he rushed to finish his homework = er
  beeilte sich, seine Hausaufgaben fertig zu
  machen
  to rush something = etwas zu schnell
  machen

to be rushed into hospital = schnellstens
  ins Krankenhaus gebracht werden
  (**!** sein)
* (pressurize) = hetzen
2 noun = (die) Eile
  to be in a rush = in Eile sein

rush hour noun
= (die) Stoßzeit

Russia noun
= (das) Russland ▶ **Countries p. 208**

Russian
1 noun
* (person) = (der) Russe/(die) Russin
* (language) = (das) Russisch
2 adjective = russisch ▶ **Countries p. 208**

rusty adjective
= rostig
  to go rusty = rosten

Ss

sad adjective
= traurig

saddle noun
= (der) Sattel

safe
1 adjective
* (not dangerous) = sicher
  to feel safe from something = sich vor
  etwas (dative) sicher fühlen
  is the water safe to drink? = kann man das
  Wasser ohne Risiko trinken?
  have a safe journey! = gute Reise!
* (out of harm) = in Sicherheit
  he's safe = er ist in Sicherheit
2 noun = (der) Safe

safety noun
= (die) Sicherheit

safety pin noun
= (die) Sicherheitsnadel

Sagittarius noun
= (der) Schütze

sail
1 noun = (das) Segel
  to set sail = Segel setzen
2 verb
  (travel on water) = fahren (**!** sein)
  (in a sailing boat) = segeln (**!** sein)

sailboat (US) ▶ sailing boat

sailing noun
= (das) Segeln

sailing boat noun (British)
= (das) Segelboot

sailor noun
= (der) Seemann
(in the navy) = (der) Matrose

saint noun
= (der/die) Heilige

salad noun
= (der) Salat

salary noun
= (das) Gehalt

sale noun
• = (der) Verkauf
  for sale = zu verkaufen
  to put a house up for sale = ein Haus zum
  Verkauf anbieten
  on sale at your bookshop = in Ihrer
  Buchhandlung erhältlich
• (at reduced prices) = (der) Ausverkauf

sales assistant noun (British)
= (der) Verkäufer/(die) Verkäuferin

salmon noun
= (der) Lachs

salt noun
= (das) Salz

same
1 adjective
• **the same** = der gleiche/die gleiche/das
  gleiche
  I've got the same picture = ich habe das
  gleiche Bild
• (one and the same) =
  derselbe/dieselbe/dasselbe
  they go to the same school = sie gehen in
  dieselbe Schule
2 adverb
  the same = gleich
  the houses all look the same = die Häuser
  sehen alle gleich aus
3 pronoun
• **the same** = der Gleiche/
  die Gleiche/das Gleiche
  I'll have the same = ich nehme das Gleiche
  Happy New Year—the same to you = ein
  gutes neues Jahr–danke gleichfalls
• (one and the same) =
  derselbe/dieselbe/dasselbe
  to do the same as the others = dasselbe
  wie die anderen machen

sand noun
= (der) Sand

sandal noun
= (die) Sandale

Santa Claus noun
= (der) Weihnachtsmann

sardine noun
= (die) Sardine

satellite dish noun
= (die) Parabolantenne, =
  (die) Satellitenschüssel

satellite TV noun
= (das) Satellitenfernsehen

satisfactory adjective
= befriedigend

satisfied adjective
= zufrieden

Saturday noun
= (der) Samstag, = (der) Sonnabend ▶ **Dates
p. 213**

sauce noun
= (die) Soße

saucepan noun
= (der) Kochtopf

saucer noun
= (die) Untertasse

sausage noun
= (die) Wurst

save verb
• (rescue) = retten
  to save someone from something =
  jemanden vor etwas (dative) retten
  they saved his life = sie haben ihm das
  Leben gerettet
• (avoid spending, wasting) = sparen
  to save |time | money | energy ...] = [Zeit |
  Geld | Energie ...] sparen
  to save up for something = auf etwas
  (accusative) sparen
• (keep) = aufheben
  to save a piece of cake for someone =
  jemandem ein Stück Kuchen aufheben
• (spare) = ersparen
  to save someone a lot of work =
  jemandem viel Arbeit ersparen
• (stop) = abwehren
  to save a penalty = einen Elfmeter
  abwehren
• (in computing) = speichern

savings noun
= Ersparnisse (plural)

saw noun
= (die) Säge

say verb
= sagen
  he didn't say that = er hat das nicht gesagt
  what does the paper say? = was steht in
  der Zeitung?
  that is to say = das heißt
  that goes without saying = das versteht
  sich von selbst

scandal noun
= (der) Skandal

scare verb
(startle) = erschrecken
(frighten) = Angst machen (+ dative)

scare away
= verscheuchen

scared *adjective*
to be scared of someone = vor jemandem Angst haben

scarf *noun*
(*long*) = (der) Schal
(*square*) = (das) Tuch

scenery *noun*
= (die) Landschaft

school
1 *noun* = (die) Schule
to be at school = in der Schule sein
to go to school = zur Schule gehen (**!** *sein*)
2 *adjective* = Schul-
school uniform = (die) Schuluniform

schoolboy *noun*
= (der) Schüler

schoolgirl *noun*
= (die) Schülerin

schoolwork *noun*
= Schularbeiten (*plural*)

science *noun*
= (die) Wissenschaft
to study science = Naturwissenschaften studieren

scientist *noun*
= (der) Wissenschaftler/
(die) Wissenschaftlerin

scissors *noun*
= (die) Schere
a pair of scissors = eine Schere

score *verb*
to score a goal = ein Tor schießen

Scorpio *noun*
= (der) Skorpion

Scotland *noun*
= (das) Schottland ▶**Countries p. 208**

Scottish *adjective*
= schottisch ▶**Countries p. 208**

scratch *verb*
• (*when itchy*) = sich kratzen
to scratch one's arm = sich am Arm kratzen
• (*hurt*) = kratzen
• (*mark, damage*) = zerkratzen

scream *verb*
= schreien

screen *noun*
• (*of a TV, computer*) = (der) Bildschirm
(*in the cinema*) = (die) Leinwand
• (*partition*) = (die) Trennwand

screw *noun*
= (die) Schraube

sea *noun*
= (das) Meer, = (die) See

seafood *noun*
= Meeresfrüchte (*plural*)

seagull *noun*
= (die) Möwe

seal *noun*
• (*animal*) = (der) Seehund
• (*official mark, stamp*) = (das) Siegel

search *verb*
• = suchen
to search for someone = jemanden suchen
• (*examine*) = durchsuchen
to search a building for something = ein Gebäude nach etwas (*dative*) durchsuchen

seashell *noun*
= (die) Muschel

seasick *adjective*
= seekrank

season *noun*
= (die) Jahreszeit
(*holiday season, sporting*) = (die) Saison
strawberries are in season = es ist die Zeit für Erdbeeren

season ticket *noun*
(die) Dauerkarte

seat *noun*
• (*chair, bench*) = (der) Sitzplatz
have a seat = setz dich, (*formal*) = setzen Sie sich
• (*on a bus, in the theatre*) = (der) Platz

seatbelt *noun*
= (der) Sicherheitsgurt

second
1 *adjective* = zweiter/zweite/zweites
it's the second time I've called her = ich habe sie schon zum zweiten Mal gerufen
every second Monday = jeden zweiten Montag
to be second = Zweiter/Zweite sein
2 *noun*
• (*in a sequence*)
the second = der/die/das Zweite
the second of May = der zweite Mai ▶**Dates p. 213**
• (*part of a minute*) = (die) Sekunde

secondary school *noun*
= (die) höhere Schule

second-hand *adjective*
= gebraucht
a second-hand car = ein Gebrauchtwagen

secret
1 *adjective* = geheim
2 *noun* = (das) Geheimnis
to tell someone a secret = jemandem ein Geheimnis verraten
in secret = heimlich

secretary *noun*
= (der) Sekretär/(die) Sekretärin

S

see *verb*
* = sehen
  do they see each other often? = sehen sie sich oft?
  he saw it happen = er hat gesehen, wie es passiert ist
  see you soon = bis bald
  see you! = tschüss!
* (*check*) = nachsehen
  I'll go and see = ich sehe nach
* (*visit*) = besuchen
  (*see a doctor, solicitor*) = gehen zu (+ *dative*) (**!** *sein*)
* (*speak to*) = sprechen
  I want to see him about the flat = ich möchte ihn wegen der Wohnung sprechen
* (*make sure*)
  to see that the work is finished = zusehen, dass die Arbeit fertig wird
* (*accompany*) = begleiten
  I'll see you home = ich begleite dich nach Hause
* (*understand*) = verstehen
see off
  (*say goodbye to*) = verabschieden
see through
  to see through someone = jemanden durchschauen
see to
  = sich kümmern um (+ *accusative*)

seem *verb*
  = scheinen
  she seems [happy | tired | depressed …] = sie scheint [glücklich | müde | deprimiert …] zu sein
  it seems there are a lot of problems = anscheinend gibt es viele Probleme

seldom *adverb*
  = selten

self-confident *adjective*
  = selbstbewusst

selfish *adjective*
  = egoistisch

sell *verb*
  = verkaufen
  it sells well = es verkauft sich gut

send *verb*
  = schicken
  to send a parcel to someone = jemandem ein Paket schicken
  to send someone to do the shopping = jemanden einkaufen schicken
send away
  = wegschicken
send back
  = zurückschicken
send for
  to send for the doctor = den Arzt rufen
  to send for a catalogue = einen Katalog anfordern

send off
* **to send a player off** = einen Spieler vom Platz stellen
* **to send off for something** = sich (*dative*) etwas schicken lassen
send on
  = nachsenden

senior *adjective*
* (*in age*) = älter
* (*in rank*) = höher

senior high school *noun* (*US*)
  = (die) höhere Schule

sense *noun*
* (*common sense*) = (der) Verstand
* (*one of the five senses, meaning*) = (der) Sinn
  sense of taste = (der) Geschmackssinn
  it doesn't make sense = es ergibt keinen Sinn

sensible *adjective*
* (*reasonable*) = vernünftig
* (*practical*) = praktisch

sensitive *adjective*
  = empfindlich

sentence
1 *noun*
* (*in grammar*) = (der) Satz
* (*punishment*) = (die) Strafe
  a prison sentence = eine Gefängnisstrafe
2 *verb* = verurteilen
  to sentence someone to a year in prison = jemanden zu einem Jahr Gefängnis verurteilen

separate
1 *adjective*
* (*apart*)
  separate bedrooms = getrennte Schlafzimmer
  a separate toilet = eine separate Toilette
  all the children have separate rooms = die Kinder haben alle ihr eigenes Zimmer
* (*different*) = verschieden
  there are two separate problems = es gibt zwei verschiedene Probleme
2 *verb*
* = trennen
* (*of a couple*) = sich trennen

separated *adverb*
  = getrennt
  the couple are separated = das Paar lebt getrennt

separately *adverb*
* (*individually*) = einzeln
* (*alone*) = getrennt

September *noun*
  = (der) September ▶ **Dates p. 213**

serial *noun*
  = (die) Fortsetzungsgeschichte
  (*on TV, radio*) = (die) Serie

series *noun*
= (die) Serie

serious *adjective*
• = ernst
  to be serious about sport = Sport ernst
  nehmen
  to be serious about [going to university |
  getting married | finding a job …] = ernsthaft
  [auf die Universität gehen | heiraten | einen Job
  finden …] wollen
• (*of an illness, accident*) = schwer

serve *verb*
• (*in a shop*) = bedienen
  are you being served? = werden Sie schon
  bedient?
• (*at table*) = servieren
• (*in tennis*) = aufschlagen

service *noun*
• (*work, helping others*) = (der) Dienst
• (*in a shop, restaurant*) = (die) Bedienung
• (*religious ceremony*) = (der) Gottesdienst
• (*car maintenance*) = (die) Wartung
• (*system of transport*) = (die) Verbindung

service station *noun*
= (die) Tankstelle

set
1 *noun*
• (*collection, in tennis*) = (der) Satz
  a chess set = ein Schachspiel
• (*TV*) = (das) Gerät
2 *verb*
• (*decide on*) = festlegen
  to set a [date | price …] = [einen Termin | einen
  Preis …] festlegen
• (*adjust controls*) = einstellen
  to set an alarm clock = einen Wecker
  stellen
• (*at school*)
  to set homework = Hausaufgaben aufgeben
• (*be responsible for*)
  to set a record = einen Rekord aufstellen
  to set an example to someone =
  jemandem ein Beispiel geben
• (*locate*)
  the film is set in Paris = der Film spielt in
  Paris
• (*of the sun*) = untergehen (**!** *sein*)
• **to set the table** = den Tisch decken
set off
• (*leave*) = aufbrechen (**!** *sein*)
• (*cause to go off*)
  to set off an alarm = eine Alarmanlage
  auslösen
  to set off a bomb = eine Bombe explodieren
  lassen
set up
= aufbauen

settle *verb*
• (*end*)
  to settle an argument = einen Streit
  beilegen
• (*pay*) = bezahlen
  to settle a bill = eine Rechnung bezahlen
• (*decide on*) = entscheiden
• (*make one's home*) = sich niederlassen
settle down
• (*sit comfortably*) = sich gemütlich
  hinsetzen
• (*become established in a place*)
  = sich einleben
• (*calm down*) = sich beruhigen
  to settle down to work = mit der Arbeit
  anfangen
• (*marry*) = häuslich werden (**!** *sein*)

seven *adjective*
= sieben ▶**Numbers p. 282**

seventeen *adjective*
= siebzehn ▶**Numbers p. 282**

seventh *adjective*
= siebter/siebte/siebtes ▶**Numbers p. 282**,
  ▶**Dates p. 213**

seventy *adjective*
= siebzig ▶**Numbers p. 282**

several *adjective, pronoun*
= mehrere

severe *adjective*
• (*of an illness, conditions*) = schwer
• (*of a person, criticism*) = hart

sew *verb*
= nähen

sewing machine *noun*
= (die) Nähmaschine

sex *noun*
• (*gender*) = (das) Geschlecht
• (*sexuality*) = (der) Sex

shade *noun*
• (*out of the sun*) = (der) Schatten
  to sit in the shade = im Schatten sitzen
• (*of colour*) = (der) Ton
• (*for a lamp*) = (der) Schirm

shadow *noun*
= (der) Schatten

shake *verb*
• schütteln
  to shake one's head = den Kopf schütteln
  to shake hands with someone =
  jemandem die Hand geben
• (*cause to tremble, shock*) = erschüttern
• (*with cold, shock*) = zittern
  he was shaking with fear = er zitterte vor
  Angst
• (*from an explosion, earthquake*) = beben

shall *verb*

! *Note that* **shall** *is normally translated by*
werden, *since in German the future tense
is formed by* **werden** *and the infinitive of
the main verb. However, the present
tense and verbs implying the future, such
as* **können** (= *can*), **sollen** (= *should*) *and*
müssen (= *must*), *are often used to
express the future tense.*

S

* I shall **certainly come** = ich werde ganz
  bestimmt kommen *or* ich komme ganz
  bestimmt

  ! *Note that* **werden** *is always used when
  some doubt is expressed about the
  future.*

  I shall probably spend Christmas at home
  = ich werde wahrscheinlich Weihnachten
  zu Hause verbringen
* (*in questions*) = sollen
  shall I set the table? = soll ich den Tisch
  decken?

shame *noun*
* (*disgrace*) = (die) Schande
* **what a shame** = wie schade
  it's a shame he can't come = schade, dass
  er nicht kommen kann

shampoo *noun*
= (das) Shampoo

shape *noun*
= (die) Form
  to be in good shape = gut in Form sein
  to get in shape = in Form kommen (**!** *sein*)

share
1 *verb* = teilen
2 *noun* = (der) Teil
  to pay one's share = seinen Teil zahlen
share out
= aufteilen

shark *noun*
= (der) Hai

sharp *adjective*
* (*used for cutting*) = scharf
* (*with a point*) = spitz
* (*sudden*) = steil
  a sharp rise = ein steiler Anstieg
  a sharp bend = eine scharfe Kurve
* (*clever*) = clever
* (*severe, painful*) = heftig
* (*unscrupulous*) = gerissen
* (*in taste*) = sauer

shave *verb*
= sich rasieren

she *pronoun*
= sie

sheep *noun*
= (das) Schaf

sheet *noun*
* (*for a bed*) = (das) Laken
* (*of paper*) = (das) Blatt
* (*of glass*) = (die) Platte

shelf *noun*
* (*single board*) = (das) Brett
  (*set of shelves*) = (das) Regal
  the book is on the shelf = das Buch steht
  im Regal
* (*in an oven*) = (die) Schiene

! in informal situations   **!** considered offensive

shell *noun*
* (*of an egg, nut*) = (die) Schale
  (*of a snail*) = (das) Haus
  (*of a tortoise*) = (der) Panzer
  (*on a beach*) = (die) Muschel
* (*bomb*) = (die) Granate

shelter
1 *noun*
* (*from rain, danger*) = (der) Schutz
* (*for homeless people*) = (die) Unterkunft
2 *verb*
  (*take shelter*) = Schutz suchen
  (*from the rain*) = sich unterstellen
  to shelter someone from something =
  jemanden vor etwas (*dative*) schützen

shin *noun*
= (das) Schienbein

shine *verb*
* (*to give out light*) = leuchten
  (*of the sun, moon, a lamp*) = scheinen
  the sun shone in his eyes = die Sonne
  schien ihm in die Augen
* (*point*) = leuchten
  to shine a torch at something = etwas
  anleuchten

  ! *Note that it is not necessary to translate*
  torch.

* (*reflect light*) = glänzen

ship *noun*
= (das) Schiff

shirt *noun*
= (das) Hemd

shit *noun* = (die) Scheiße**!**

shiver *verb*
= zittern

shock
1 *noun*
* = (der) Schock
  to get a shock = einen Schock bekommen
  to give someone a shock = jemandem
  einen Schock versetzen
  to be in shock = unter Schock stehen
* (*from electricity*) = (der) Schlag
  to get a shock = einen Schlag bekommen
2 *verb*
* (*upset*) = erschüttern
* (*cause scandal*) = schockieren

shoe *noun*
= (der) Schuh

shoelace *noun*
= (der) Schnürsenkel

shoot *verb*
* (*using a weapon*) = schießen
  (*kill*) = erschießen
* (*move very fast*) = schießen**!** (**!** *sein*)
  to shoot past = vorbeischießen**!** (**!** *sein*)
* **to shoot a film** = einen Film drehen
shoot up
  (*grow*) = in die Höhe schießen (**!** *sein*)

shop
1 *noun* = (das) Geschäft, = (der) Laden
2 *verb* = einkaufen
  to go shopping = einkaufen gehen
    (**!** sein)

shop assistant *noun* (British)
= (der) Verkäufer/(die) Verkäuferin

shopkeeper *noun*
= (der) Geschäftsinhaber/
  (die) Geschäftsinhaberin, = (der)
  Ladenbesitzer/(die) Ladenbesitzerin

shopping *noun*
• (*activity*) = (das) Einkaufen
  to do the shopping = einkaufen
• (*things bought*) = Einkäufe (*plural*)

shopping cart *noun* (US)
  (der) Einkaufswagen

shopping centre (*British*), **shopping mall** (*US*) *noun*
= (das) Einkaufszentrum

shopping trolley *noun* (British)
= (der) Einkaufswagen

shop window *noun*
= (das) Schaufenster

shore *noun*
• (*coast*) = (die) Küste
  (*beach*) = (der) Strand
  to be on shore = an Land sein
• (*of a lake, river*) = (das) Ufer

short *adjective*
• (*not long*) = kurz
  to have short hair = kurze Haare haben
• (*not tall*) = klein
• (*lacking*)
  to be short of [money | time | paper ...] = zu
    wenig [Geld | Zeit | Papier ...] haben
  to be short of breath = außer Atem sein
  in short = kurz

short cut *noun*
= (die) Abkürzung

shortly *adverb*
• (*soon*) = in Kürze
• (*not long*) = gleich
  shortly before = kurz bevor
  shortly after = kurz danach

shorts *noun*
= Shorts (*plural*)

short-sighted *adjective*
= kurzsichtig

shot *noun*
• (*from a gun, in football*) = (der) Schuss
  to fire a shot at someone = einen Schuss
    auf jemanden abfeuern
• (*photo*) = (die) Aufnahme

should *verb*

> **!** Note that **should** *is usually translated by
> the imperfect subjunctive of* sollen. *For
> more about the subjunctive* ▶ **p .351.**

• (*ought*)
  one should always tell the truth = man
    sollte immer die Wahrheit sagen
  shouldn't he be at school? = sollte er nicht
    in der Schule sein?
• (*when something is likely to happen*)
  they should be home soon = sie müssten
    bald zu Hause sein
  that should be enough = das müsste
    reichen
• (*implying that something didn't happen*)
  the letter should have arrived yesterday =
    der Brief hätte gestern ankommen
    müssen
• (*when asking for advice*)
  should I call the doctor? = soll ich den Arzt
    rufen?
• (*expressing a wish*)
  I should like to know = ich möchte gerne
    wissen

shoulder *noun*
= (die) Schulter

shout
1 *verb* = schreien

> **!** Note that **schreien** *forms a separable
> verb with prepositions such as* an.

  to shout at someone = jemanden
    anschreien
2 *noun* = (der) Schrei

shovel *noun*
= (die) Schaufel

show
1 *verb*
• (*let someone see, indicate*) = zeigen
  to show someone a photo = jemandem ein
    Foto zeigen
  to show one's passport = den Pass
    vorzeigen
• (*go with*) = begleiten
  I'll show you to your room = ich begleite
    Sie auf Ihr Zimmer
  she showed him to his seat = sie führte
    ihn an seinen Platz
• (*be on*) = laufen (**!** sein)
  the film is showing at the Odeon = der
    Film läuft im Odeon
  to be shown on TV = im Fernsehen
    kommen (**!** sein)
2 *noun*
• (*on stage, TV*) = (die) Schau, = (die) Show
• (*exhibition*) = (die) Ausstellung
  to be on show = ausgestellt sein
show off
= angeben
show round
  to show someone round the town =
    jemandem die Stadt zeigen

shower *noun*
• (*for washing*) = (die) Dusche
  to have a shower = sich duschen
• (*rain*) = (der) Schauer

S

shrimp noun
= (die) Krabbe

shrink verb
(get smaller) = schrumpfen (**!** sein)
(of clothes) = einlaufen (**!** sein)

shut
1 adjective = zu
to stay shut = zubleiben (**!** sein)
2 verb
(close) = zumachen
(of a door, mouth, eyes) = schließen
the door won't shut = die Tür schließt nicht
the door shut after her = die Tür schloss
sich hinter ihr

shut up
• (be quiet) = den Mund halten✱
shut up! = halt den Mund!✱
• (lock in) = einsperren

shy adjective
= schüchtern

sick adjective
• (ill) = krank
to be sick (vomit) = sich übergeben
I feel sick = mir ist schlecht
• (fed up)
to be sick of |work | the neighbours | the
noise ...| = |die Arbeit | die Nachbarn | den
Lärm ...| satt haben
to be sick of doing something = es satt
haben, etwas zu tun

sickness noun
= (die) Krankheit
(vomiting) = (das) Erbrechen

side noun
• = (die) Seite
on the wrong side of the road = auf der
falschen Straßenseite
at or by the side of = neben (+ dative)
to take sides against someone = gegen
jemanden Partei ergreifen
to stand side by side = nebeneinander
stehen
• (team) = (die) Mannschaft

side with
= Partei ergreifen für (+ accusative)

sidewalk noun (US)
= (der) Bürgersteig

sigh verb
= seufzen

sight noun
to have good sight = gute Augen haben
to catch sight of someone = jemanden
sehen
to lose sight of someone = jemanden aus
dem Auge verlieren
to be out of sight = außer Sicht sein
at first sight = auf den ersten Blick

sights noun
= Sehenswürdigkeiten (plural)

sightseeing noun
to go sightseeing = die
Sehenswürdigkeiten besichtigen

sign
1 noun
• = (das) Zeichen
the dollar sign = das Dollarzeichen
to give someone a sign = jemandem ein
Zeichen geben
• (notice) = (das) Schild
2 verb = unterschreiben

sign on
(when unemployed) = sich arbeitslos
melden

signal
1 noun = (das) Signal
2 verb
• (make signs) = signalisieren
to signal to someone = jemandem ein
Signal geben
• (when driving) = die Fahrtrichtung
anzeigen

signature noun
= (die) Unterschrift

silence noun
(quiet) = (die) Stille
(saying nothing) = (das) Schweigen

silent adjective
(quiet) = still
(saying nothing) = schweigend

silk noun
= (die) Seide

silly adjective
= dumm

silver
1 noun
= (das) Silber
2 adjective = silbern
silver paper = (das) Silberpapier

similar adjective
= ähnlich

simple adjective
= einfach

since
1 preposition = seit (+ dative)

> **!** For an action starting in the past and
> going on to the present, the present tense
> is used after seit. But with a negative, the
> perfect tense is used.

she has been living in Germany since
1990 = sie lebt schon seit 1990 in
Deutschland
I haven't seen him since yesterday = ich
habe ihn seit gestern nicht gesehen
2 conjunction
• = seit
since she's known him = seit sie ihn kennt
• (because) = da
since she was ill, she couldn't come = da
sie krank war, konnte sie nicht kommen

3 *adverb* = seitdem
I haven't seen him since = ich habe ihn seitdem nicht mehr gesehen
ever since = seither

sincere *adjective*
= aufrichtig

sincerely *adverb*
= aufrichtig
Yours sincerely (*British*), **Sincerely yours** (*US*) = Mit freundlichen Grüßen ▶**Letterwriting p. 262**

sing *verb*
= singen

singer *noun*
= (der) Sänger/(die) Sängerin

single *adjective*
• (*just one*) = einzig
we visited three museums in a single day = wir haben drei Museen an einem einzigen Tag besucht
not a single word = kein einziges Wort
• (*individual*) = einzeln
every single one = jeder/jede/jedes Einzelne
• (*unmarried*) = ledig, = allein stehend

single bed *noun*
= (das) Einzelbett

single parent *noun*
= (der/die) Alleinerziehende

single room *noun*
= (das) Einzelzimmer

single ticket *noun* (*British*)
= (die) einfache Fahrkarte

sink
1 *noun* = (das) Spülbecken
2 *verb* = sinken

sister *noun*
= (die) Schwester

sister-in-law *noun*
= (die) Schwägerin

sit *verb*
• (*take a seat*) = sich setzen
sit over there = setzt euch da drüben hin
• (*be seated*) = sitzen
to sit on the floor = auf dem Boden sitzen
• **to sit an exam** = eine Prüfung machen
sit down
= sich hinsetzen
to be sitting down = sitzen
sit up
• (*after lying down*) = sich aufsetzen
to sit up straight = gerade sitzen
• (*stay up late*) = aufbleiben (**!** *sein*)

sitting room *noun*
= (das) Wohnzimmer

situated *adjective*
to be situated in the town centre = in der Stadtmitte liegen

situation *noun*
• = (die) Lage
• (*job*) = (die) Stelle

six *adjective*
= sechs ▶**Numbers p. 282**

sixteen *adjective*
= sechzehn ▶**Numbers p. 282**

sixth *adjective*
= sechster/sechste/sechstes ▶**Numbers p. 282**, ▶**Dates p. 213**

sixty *adjective*
= sechzig ▶**Numbers p. 282**

size *noun*
= (die) Größe
what size do you take? = welche Größe haben Sie?
she's about your size = sie ist ungefähr so groß wie du

skateboard *noun*
= (das) Skateboard

skating *noun*
(*ice-skating*) = (das) Schlittschuhlaufen, = (das) Eislaufen
(*roller-skating*) = (das) Rollschuhlaufen
to go skating = Schlittschuh laufen/Rollschuh laufen (**!** *sein*)

skating rink *noun*
(*for ice-skating*) = (die) Eisbahn
(*for roller-skating*) = (die) Rollschuhbahn

skeleton *noun*
= (das) Skelett

sketch *noun*
• (*drawing*) = (die) Skizze
• (*funny scene*) = (der) Sketch

ski
1 *noun* = (der) Ski
2 *verb* = Ski fahren, = Ski laufen (**!** *sein*)

skiing *noun*
= (das) Skifahren, = (das) Skilaufen

skilful *adjective* (*British*)
= geschickt

skill *noun*
= (das) Geschick
(*ability*) = (die) Fähigkeit

skilled *adjective*
(*trained*) = ausgebildet

skillful (*US*) ▶ skilful

skin *noun*
• = (die) Haut
• (*on fruit*) = (die) Schale

skinny *adjective*
= dünn

skip *verb*
• (*hop*) = hüpfen (**!** *sein*)
• (*with a rope*) = seilspringen (**!** *sein*)
• **to skip lunch** = das Mittagessen auslassen

S

skirt *noun*
= (der) Rock

sky *noun*
= (der) Himmel

skydiving *noun*
= (das) Fallschirmspringen

skyscraper *noun*
= (der) Wolkenkratzer

slap *verb*
to slap someone = jemanden schlagen,
  (*across the face*) = jemanden ohrfeigen

sled (*US*), **sledge** (*British*)
1 *noun* = (der) Schlitten
2 *verb* = Schlitten fahren (**!** *sein*)

sleep
1 *noun* = (der) Schlaf
to go to sleep = einschlafen (**!** *sein*)
to go back to sleep = wieder einschlafen
2 *verb* = schlafen

sleeping bag *noun*
= (der) Schlafsack

sleet *noun*
= (der) Schneeregen

sleeve *noun*
= (der) Ärmel

slice
1 *noun*
(*of bread, meat*) = (die) Scheibe
(*of cake, cheese*) = (das) Stück
2 *verb*
(*cut bread, meat*) = in Scheiben schneiden
(*cut cake, vegetable*) = in Stücke
  schneiden

slide
1 *verb* = rutschen (**!** *sein*)
2 *noun*
• (*transparency*) = (das) Dia
• (*in a playground*) = (die) Rutschbahn

slim
1 *adjective* = schlank
2 *verb* (*British*)
= abnehmen

slip *verb*
• (*slide*) = rutschen (**!** *sein*)
  the glass slipped out of my hand = das
    Glas ist mir aus der Hand gerutscht
• (*fall*) = ausrutschen (**!** *sein*)
  she slipped and broke her leg = sie
    rutschte aus und brach sich (*dative*) das
    Bein
• to slip out of the room = aus dem Zimmer
    schlüpfen (**!** *sein*)
  to slip a letter to someone = jemandem
    einen Brief zustecken
  it slipped my mind = es ist mir entfallen

slipper *noun*
= (der) Hausschuh

slippery *adjective*
(*of a road, surface*) = glatt
(*of an object*) = schlüpfrig

Slovakia *noun*
= (die) Slowakei ▶Countries p. 208

slow *adjective*
• = langsam
  to make slow progress = langsam vorwärts
    kommen (**!** *sein*)
• to be slow (*of a clock*) = nachgehen (**!** *sein*)
  my watch is slow = meine Uhr geht nach
slow down
= langsamer werden (**!** *sein*)

slowly *adverb*
= langsam

sly *adjective*
= schlau

small *adjective*
= klein

small ads *noun* (*British*)
= Kleinanzeigen (*plural*)

smart *adjective*
• (*British: elegant*) = elegant
• (*clever*) = clever

smash *verb*
• (*break*) = zerschlagen
• (*get broken*) = zerbrechen (**!** *sein*)
smash up
= zertrümmern

smell
1 *noun*
• (*odour*) = (der) Geruch
• (*sense*) = (der) Geruchssinn
2 *verb* = riechen
(*sniff at*) = riechen an (+ *dative*)
to smell of soap = nach Seife riechen

smelly *adjective*
= stinkend
to be smelly = stinken

smile
1 *verb* = lächeln
to smile at someone = jemanden
  anlächeln
2 *noun* = (das) Lächeln

smoke
1 *noun* = (der) Rauch
2 *verb* = rauchen

smooth *adjective*
= glatt
a smooth crossing = eine ruhige Überfahrt

snack *noun*
= (der) Imbiss

snail *noun*
= (die) Schnecke

snake *noun*
= (die) Schlange

snapshot *noun*
= (der) Schnappschuss

sneeze *verb*
= niesen

snore *verb*
= schnarchen

snorkel
1 *noun* = (der) Schnorchel
2 *verb* = schnorcheln (**!** *sein*)

snow
1 *noun* = (der) Schnee
2 *verb* = schneien
 it's snowing = es schneit

snowboarding *noun*
= (das) Snowboarding

snowflake *noun*
= (die) Schneeflocke

snowman *noun*
= (der) Schneemann

so
1 *adverb*
• so
 I have so much to do = ich habe so viel zu
  tun
• (*also*) = auch
 I'm 15 and so is he = ich bin fünfzehn und
  er auch
• (*other uses*)
 I think so = ich glaube schon
 I'm afraid so = leider ja
 so what? = na und?
 who says so? = wer hat das gesagt?
 so long! = tschüss!
2 *conjunction*
• (*therefore*) = also
 **he's on holiday so he won't be able to
  come** = er ist auf Urlaub, also kann er
  nicht kommen
• (*for a purpose*)
 be quiet so that I can work = sei still, damit
  ich arbeiten kann
 we left early so as not to miss the train =
  wir sind früh weggegangen, um den Zug
  nicht zu verpassen

soap *noun*
= (die) Seife

soap opera *noun*
= (die) Seifenoper

soccer *noun*
= (der) Fußball

social *adjective*
• = sozial
• (*sociable*) = gesellig

social studies *noun*
= (die) Gemeinschaftskunde

social worker *noun*
= (der) Sozialarbeiter/(die) Sozialarbeiterin

sock *noun*
= (die) Socke
 (*knee-length*) = (der) Kniestrumpf

sofa *noun*
= (das) Sofa

soft *adjective*
• (*not hard or tough*) = weich
• (*not harsh or severe*) = sanft
• (*not strict*) = nachsichtig

soft drink *noun*
= (das) alkoholfreie Getränk

software *noun*
= (die) Software

soil *noun*
= (die) Erde

solar energy *noun*
= (die) Sonnenenergie

soldier *noun*
= (der) Soldat

sole *noun*
 (*of the foot*) = (die) Fußsohle
 (*of a shoe*) = (die) Sohle

solicitor *noun* (*British*)
= (der) Rechtsanwalt/(die) Rechtsanwältin

solution *noun*
= (die) Lösung

solve *verb*
= lösen

some
1 *adjective*
• (*an amount*) = etwas
 can you lend me some money? = kannst
  du mir etwas Geld leihen?

 ! *Note that* some *is often not translated,
 unless it is emphasized.*

 we bought some beer = wir haben Bier
  gekauft
• (*a certain number of*) = einige
 some of his books are very old = einige
  von seinen Büchern sind sehr alt
• (*a few*) = ein paar
• (*certain*) = manche
 some people don't like flying = manche
  Leute fliegen nicht gerne
2 *pronoun*
• (*an amount*) = etwas
 have some more = nimm dir noch etwas
 some of it is quite good = manches ist
  nicht schlecht
• (*a number of them*) = einige
 some left very late = einige gingen sehr
  spät
 I know where you can find some = ich
  weiß, wo du welche finden kannst
• (*certain people or things*) = manche
 some think differently = manche sind
  anderer Meinung

S

somebody, someone *pronoun*
= jemand
someone or other = irgendjemand

something *pronoun*
= etwas
there's something wrong = irgendetwas
stimmt nicht

sometimes *adverb*
= manchmal

somewhere *adverb*
= irgendwo
(*go, travel*) = irgendwohin

son *noun*
= (der) Sohn

song *noun*
= (das) Lied

son-in-law *noun*
= (der) Schwiegersohn

soon *adverb*
• (*in a short time*) = bald
see you soon! = bis bald!
• (*quickly*) = schnell
you must come as soon as possible = du
musst so schnell wie möglich kommen
• (*early*) = früh
sooner or later = früher oder später

sore *adjective*
(*painful*) = schmerzhaft
(*inflamed*) = wund
to have a sore throat = Halsschmerzen
haben

sorry
1 *interjection*
• (*when apologizing*) = Entschuldigung!
• (*when asking someone to repeat*) = wie
bitte?
2 *adjective*
• (*sad, upset*) = traurig
• (*when apologizing*)
to say sorry = sich entschuldigen
sorry I'm late = es tut mir Leid, dass ich zu
spät komme
• (*feeling pity*)
she feels sorry for him = er tut ihr Leid

sort
1 *noun* = (die) Art
it's a sort of [game | bird | toy ...] = es ist so
eine Art [|Spiel | Vogel | Spielzeug ...]
all sorts of things = alles Mögliche
he's a funny sort of person = er ist ein
komischer Typ
2 *verb* = sortieren
sort out
• (*solve, deal with*) = klären
• (*organize*) = sortieren
• (*pick out*) = aussortieren

sound
1 *noun*

• (*noise*) = (das) Geräusch
they left without a sound = sie sind lautlos
gegangen
• (*of a bell, voice*) = (der) Klang
• (*of TV, radio*) = (der) Ton
2 *verb*
it sounds |funny | interesting | exciting ...| = es
hört sich [komisch | interessant |
aufregend ...] an

soup *noun*
= (die) Suppe

sour *adjective*
= sauer

south
1 *noun* = (der) Süden
to the south of London = südlich von
London
2 *adjective* = südlich, = Süd-
the south coast = die Südküste
3 *adverb* = nach Süden

South Africa *noun*
= (das) Südafrika ▶**Countries p. 208**

souvenir *noun*
= (das) Andenken, = (das) Souvenir

space *noun*
• (*room*) = (der) Platz
• (*outer space*) = (der) Weltraum
• (*gap*) = (der) Zwischenraum
(*for parking*) = (die) Lücke

spacecraft *noun*
= (das) Raumschiff

spade *noun*
• = (der) Spaten
• (*playing cards*) **spades** = (das) Pik

Spain *noun*
= (das) Spanien ▶**Countries p. 208**

Spanish
1 *noun*
• (*people*) **the Spanish** = die Spanier
• (*language*) = (das) Spanisch
2 *adjective* = spanisch ▶**Countries p. 208**

spare
1 *adjective*
• (*extra*) = Extra-
to have a spare key = einen Extraschlüssel
haben
• (*not in use*) = übrig
there is one spare ticket = eine Karte ist
noch übrig
2 *verb*
• **to have money to spare** = Geld übrig
haben
to have time to spare = Zeit haben

spare part *noun*
= (das) Ersatzteil

spare room *noun*
= (das) Gästezimmer

spare time *noun*
= (die) Freizeit

speak verb
= sprechen
to speak to someone about something =
mit jemandem über etwas (accusative)
sprechen
who's speaking? (on the phone) = wer ist
am Apparat?
speak up
= lauter sprechen

special adjective
= besonderer/besondere/besonderes
= speziell

! Note that **speziell** is mainly used when
talking about a particular interest,
question or subject.

my special interests = meine speziellen
Interessen
special offer = (das) Sonderangebot

speciality noun (British)
= (die) Spezialität

specially adverb
= speziell
(especially) = besonders

specialty (US) ▶speciality

spectator noun
= (der) Zuschauer/(die) Zuschauerin

speech noun
• (manner of speaking) = (die) Sprache
• (talk) = (die) Rede

speed
1 noun = (die) Geschwindigkeit
2 verb
• (travel fast) = schnell fahren (! sein), =
rasen (! sein)
• (drive too fast) = zu schnell fahren (! sein)
speed up
= beschleunigen

speed limit noun
= (die) Geschwindigkeitsbeschränkung

spell verb
(when speaking) = buchstabieren
(when writing) = schreiben
how do you spell that? = wie schreibt man
das?

spelling noun
= (die) Rechtschreibung

spend verb
• (pay money) = ausgeben
• (pass time) = verbringen

spider noun
= (die) Spinne

spill verb
• = verschütten
• (of a liquid) = überlaufen (! sein)

spinach noun
= (der) Spinat

spine noun
= (die) Wirbelsäule

spit verb
= spucken

spite noun
in spite of = trotz (+ genitive)

spiteful adjective
= boshaft

spoil verb
• (ruin) = verderben
he spoiled our evening = er hat uns
(dative) den Abend verdorben
• (pamper) = verwöhnen

sponge noun
= (der) Schwamm

spoon noun
= (der) Löffel

sport noun
= (der) Sport

sportsman noun
= (der) Sportler

sportswoman noun
= (die) Sportlerin

spot
1 noun
• (stain) = (der) Fleck
• (pimple) = (der) Pickel
• (drop) = (der) Tropfen
• (place) = (die) Stelle
on the spot = auf der Stelle
2 verb = entdecken

sprain verb
= verstauchen
to sprain one's wrist = sich (dative) das
Handgelenk verstauchen

spring noun
= (der) Frühling
in spring = im Frühling

spy
1 noun = (der) Spion/(die) Spionin
2 verb
to spy on someone = jemandem
nachspionieren

square
1 noun
• (shape) = (das) Quadrat
• (in a town) = (der) Platz
2 adjective = quadratisch
square metre = (der) Quadratmeter

squash
1 noun
• (game) = (das) Squash
• (drink) = (das) Fruchtsaftgetränk
2 verb = zerquetschen

squeak verb
= quietschen

S

squeeze verb
to squeeze a lemon = eine Zitrone
  auspressen
to squeeze someone's hand = jemandem
  die Hand drücken

squirrel noun
= (das) Eichhörnchen

stable noun
= (der) Stall

stadium noun
= (das) Stadion

staff noun
(of a company) = (das) Personal
(of a school, college) = Lehrkräfte
  (plural)

staff room noun
= (das) Lehrerzimmer

stage noun
= (die) Bühne

stain
1 noun = (der) Fleck
2 verb = beflecken

stairs noun
= (die) Treppe

stamp noun
• (for postage) = (die) Briefmarke
• (on a document) = (der) Stempel

stand verb
• = stehen
  to remain standing = stehen bleiben
    (! sein)
• (put) = stellen
  to stand a vase on the table = eine Vase auf
    den Tisch stellen
• (bear) = ausstehen
  I can't stand German = ich kann Deutsch
    nicht ausstehen
  I can't stand the noise any more = ich
    kann den Krach nicht mehr aushalten
• (other uses)
  to stand someone a coke = jemandem
    eine Cola spendieren
  to stand one's ground = nicht nachgeben
stand back
  = zurücktreten (! sein)
stand for
• (represent) = vertreten
• (mean) = bedeuten
stand out
• (be conspicuous) = auffallen (! sein)
• (be outstanding) = hervorstechen
stand up = aufstehen (! sein)
  to stand someone up = jemanden
    versetzen

star noun
• (in space) = (der) Stern
• (famous person) = (der) Star

✗ in informal situations

stare verb
to stare at someone = jemanden anstarren

start
1 verb
• = anfangen
  to start crying = anfangen zu weinen
  to start with = zuerst
• (set up) = gründen
  to start a shop = einen Laden aufmachen
• (cause) = auslösen
• to start a car = ein Auto starten
  the car won't start = das Auto springt nicht
    an
2 noun
• = (der) Anfang
  from the start = von Anfang an
• (in sport) = (der) Start
start off
• (begin) = anfangen
• (set off) = aufbrechen (! sein)
start over (US)
  = noch einmal von vorn anfangen

state noun
• (territory) = (der) Staat
• (condition) = (der) Zustand
  don't get in a state! = reg dich nicht auf!✗

statement noun
= (die) Erklärung

station noun
• (railway) = (der) Bahnhof
• (TV) = (der) Sender

stationer noun
stationer('s) = (das) Schreibwarengeschäft

stationery noun
= Schreibwaren (plural)

statue noun
= (die) Statue

stay
1 verb
• (remain) = bleiben (! sein)
  we stayed for a week = wir sind eine
    Woche geblieben
• (have accommodation) = wohnen
  (for a night) = übernachten
  to stay the night with friends = bei
    Freunden übernachten
2 noun = (der) Aufenthalt
stay away
  = wegbleiben (! sein)
  to stay away from school = nicht zur
    Schule gehen (! sein)
stay in
  = zu Hause bleiben (! sein)
stay up
  = aufbleiben (! sein)

steady adjective
• (constant) = stetig
• (stable) = stabil

steak noun
= (das) Steak

steal verb
= stehlen
to steal money from someone = jemandem Geld stehlen

steam noun
= (der) Dampf
steam up
= beschlagen (**!** sein)

steel noun
= (der) Stahl

steep adjective
= steil

steering wheel noun
= (das) Lenkrad

step
1 noun
• = (der) Schritt
  to take a step = einen Schritt machen
  to take steps to do something = Schritte unternehmen, um etwas zu tun
• (stair) = (die) Stufe
2 verb = treten (**!** sein)
step aside
= zur Seite treten (**!** sein)

stepbrother noun
= (der) Stiefbruder

stepfather noun
= (der) Stiefvater

stepmother noun
= (die) Stiefmutter

stepsister noun
= (die) Stiefschwester

stereo noun
• (sound) = (das) Stereo
• (equipment) = (die) Stereoanlage

stewardess noun
= (die) Stewardess

stick
1 verb
• (glue, tape) = kleben
• (become attached) = kleben
  to stick to something = an etwas (dative) kleben
• (jam) = klemmen
  the door is stuck = die Tür klemmt
  I'm stuck = ich kann nicht weiter
• (pin, insert) = stecken
2 noun = (der) Stock
stick out
• **his ears stick out** = seine Ohren stehen ab
• **to stick one's tongue out** = die Zunge herausstrecken

sticker noun
= (der) Aufkleber

sticky tape noun (British)
= (der) Tesafilm®, = (der) Klebestreifen

stiff adjective
= steif
to be stiff (after sport) = Muskelkater haben
to be bored stiff = sich zu Tode langweilen

still[1] adverb
• = noch
  does she still play the piano? = spielt sie noch Klavier?
• (even now) = immer noch

still[2]
1 adverb
  to sit still = stillsitzen
  to keep still = stillhalten
2 adjective = ruhig

stir verb
= rühren
he didn't stir = er hat sich nicht gerührt

stomach noun
= (der) Magen

stomach ache noun
= Magenschmerzen (plural)

stone noun
= (der) Stein

stop
1 verb
• (put an end to) = aufhören
  to stop [laughing | crying | working ...] = aufhören zu [lachen | weinen | arbeiten ...]
  stop it! = hör auf damit!
• (prevent) = verhindern
  to stop something happening = verhindern, dass etwas geschieht
  to stop someone from phoning = jemanden daran hindern anzurufen
• (not move) = halten
  (of a person, watch) = stehen bleiben (**!** sein)
  the bus didn't stop = der Bus hat nicht gehalten
• (make stop) = anhalten
  the policeman stopped the car = der Polizist hielt den Wagen an
• (of a machine, noise) = aufhören
2 noun
  (for a bus) = (die) Haltestelle

store noun
  (shop) = (der) Laden
  (department store) = (das) Kaufhaus

storm noun
= (der) Sturm

story noun
• = (die) Geschichte
• (in a newspaper) = (der) Bericht

straight
1 adjective
• = gerade
  a straight line = eine gerade Linie
  the picture isn't straight = das Bild hängt nicht gerade
• (not curly) = glatt

S

- (*honest*) = ehrlich
  to be straight with someone = zu
    jemandem offen sein
- (*clear, logical*) = klar
2 *adverb*
- = gerade
  to go straight ahead = immer geradeaus
    gehen (**!** sein)
- (*directly*) = direkt
- (*without delay*) = sofort
  to go straight home = sofort nach Hause
    gehen (**!** sein)

straight away *adverb*
  = sofort

strange *adjective*
- (*odd*) = seltsam
- (*unfamiliar*) = fremd

stranger *noun*
  = (der/die) Fremde

straw *noun*
- (*for drinking*) = (der) Strohhalm
- (*grain*) = (das) Stroh

strawberry *noun*
  = (die) Erdbeere

stream *noun*
  = (der) Bach

street *noun*
  = (die) Straße

streetlamp *noun*
  = (die) Straßenlampe

strength *noun*
- (*power of a person or an animal*) =
    (die) Kraft
- (*force, intensity*) = (die) Stärke

stress *noun*
  = (der) Stress

stressful *adjective*
  = stressig✶

stretch *verb*
  to stretch one's arms = die Arme strecken
  the jeans have stretched = die Jeans haben
    sich gedehnt

strict *adjective*
  = streng

strike
1 *noun* = (der) Streik
2 *verb*
- (*hit*) = schlagen
- (*go on strike*) = streiken

string *noun*
  = (die) Schnur
  a piece of string = eine Schnur

striped *adjective*
  = gestreift

---

stroke *verb*
  = streicheln

stroller *noun* (*US*)
  = (der) Sportwagen

strong *adjective*
- = stark
  a strong French accent = ein starker
    französischer Akzent
  a strong child = ein kräftiges Kind
- (*not easily damaged*) = stabil
- **a strong argument** = ein gutes Argument

stubborn *adjective*
  = starrsinning, = stur✶

student *noun*
  (*at school*) = (der) Schüler/(die) Schülerin
  (*at university*) = (der) Student/(die) Studentin

study
1 *verb* = lernen
  (*at university*) = studieren
2 *noun*
- = (das) Studium
- (*room*) = (das) Arbeitszimmer

stuff
1 *noun* = (das) Zeug
2 *verb*
- = stopfen
  she stuffed the socks in a drawer = sie hat
    die Socken in eine Schublade gestopft
- (*fill*) = vollstopfen✶
  to stuff oneself = sich vollstopfen✶

stuffing *noun*
  = (die) Füllung

stupid *adjective*
  = dumm

style *noun*
- = (der) Stil
- (*fashion*) = (die) Mode

stylish *adjective*
  = elegant

subject *noun*
- = (das) Thema
  to change the subject = das Thema
    wechseln
- (*at school*) = (das) Fach

subscription *noun*
  = (das) Abonnement

subtitles *noun*
  = Untertitel (*plural*)

suburb *noun*
  = (der) Vorort
  to live in the suburbs = am Stadtrand
    wohnen

subway *noun*
- (*British: passage*) = (die) Unterführung
- (*US: underground railway*) = (die) U-Bahn

✶ in informal situations

succeed *verb*
= gelingen (**!** *sein*)
I succeeded in persuading him = es ist mir
gelungen, ihn zu überzeugen

success *noun*
= (der) Erfolg

successful *adjective*
= erfolgreich

such
1 *adjective* = solcher/solche/solches

> **!** *Note that* solcher, solche *and* solches
> *change their endings in the same way as*
> der/die/das.

such a thing should not have happened =
so etwas hätte nicht passieren dürfen
2 *adverb*
they have such a lot of money = sie haben
so viel Geld

suddenly *adverb*
= plötzlich

suede *noun*
= (das) Wildleder

suffer *verb*
= leiden

sugar *noun*
= (der) Zucker

suggestion *noun*
= (der) Vorschlag

suit
1 *noun*
(*man's*) = (der) Anzug
(*woman's*) = (das) Kostüm
2 *verb*
• (*be convenient*) = passen (+ *dative*)
does Friday suit you? = passt Ihnen
Freitag?
• (*look good on*)
the hat suits you = der Hut steht Ihnen gut

suitable *adjective*
= geeignet
to be suitable for children = für Kinder
geeignet sein

suitcase *noun*
= (der) Koffer

sum *noun*
• (*amount*) = (die) Summe
• (*in maths*) = (die) Rechenaufgabe
to be good at sums = gut im Rechnen sein
sum up
= zusammenfassen

summer *noun*
= (der) Sommer
in summer = im Sommer

sun *noun*
= (die) Sonne

sunbathe *verb*
= sich sonnen

sunburn *noun*
= (der) Sonnenbrand

sunburnt *adjective*
to get sunburnt = einen Sonnenbrand
bekommen

Sunday *noun*
= (der) Sonntag ▶**Dates p. 213**

sunglasses *noun*
= (die) Sonnenbrille

sunny *adjective*
= sonnig

sunrise *noun*
= (der) Sonnenaufgang

sunset *noun*
= (der) Sonnenuntergang

sunshade *noun*
= (der) Sonnenschirm

sunshine *noun*
= (der) Sonnenschein

suntan *noun*
= (die) Bräune
to get a suntan = braun werden (**!** *sein*)

superintendent *noun*
(*in the police*) = (der) Kommissar/
(die) Kommissarin

supermarket *noun*
= (der) Supermarkt

superstitious *adjective*
= abergläubisch

supper *noun*
= (das) Abendessen

support *verb*
• (*help, give money to*) = unterstützen
• (*hold, help physically*) = stützen

supporter *noun*
(*of a team*) = (der) Fan
(*of a party*) = (der) Anhänger/
(die) Anhängerin

suppose *verb*
• (*imagine*) = annehmen
I suppose so = ich nehme es an,
(*doubtfully*) = ja, vermutlich
• (*be meant to*)
to be supposed to do something = etwas
tun sollen

sure *adjective*
• (*certain*) = sicher
are you sure? = bist du dir sicher?
to make sure the door is shut =
nachprüfen, dass die Tür zu ist
• (*bound*)
he's sure to [win | forget it | meet him ...] = er
[gewinnt | vergisst es | trifft ihn ...] bestimmt
• **sure of oneself** = selbstsicher

surf *verb*
= surfen (**!** *sein*)

S

surface
1 *noun* = (die) Oberfläche
2 *verb* = auftauchen (**!** *sein*)

surfboard *noun*
= (das) Surfbrett

surgeon *noun*
= (der) Chirurg/(die) Chirurgin

surgery *noun*
• (*British: place*) = (die) Praxis
• to have surgery = operiert werden

surname *noun*
= (der) Nachname

surprise
1 *noun* = (die) Überraschung
it came as a surprise to us = es hat uns
überrascht
2 *verb* = überraschen

surprised *adjective*
= überrascht
I'm not surprised = das wundert mich gar
nicht

surround *verb*
= umgeben

surroundings *noun*
= (die) Umgebung

survey *noun*
(*poll*) = (die) Umfrage
(*investigation*) = (die) Untersuchung

survive *verb*
= überleben

suspect
1 *verb*
• = verdächtigen
she is suspected of stealing the money =
man verdächtigt sie, das Geld gestohlen
zu haben
• (*assume*) = vermuten
2 *noun* = (der/die) Verdächtige

suspicious *adjective*
• (*feeling suspicion*) = misstrauisch
to be suspicious of someone = jemandem
misstrauen
• (*causing suspicion*) = verdächtig

swan *noun*
= (der) Schwan

swap *verb*
= tauschen
to swap something for something = etwas
gegen etwas (*accusative*) eintauschen

sweat
1 *noun* = (der) Schweiß
2 *verb* = schwitzen

sweater *noun*
= (der) Pullover

Sweden *noun*
= (das) Schweden ▶**Countries p. 208**

Swedish
1 *noun*
(*language*) = (das) Schwedisch
2 *adjective* = schwedisch ▶**Countries p. 208**

sweep *verb*
= kehren, = fegen

sweet
1 *adjective*
• = süß
to have a sweet tooth = gern Süßes mögen
• (*kind, gentle*) = lieb
2 *noun* = (der) *or* (das) Bonbon

swim *verb*
= schwimmen (**!** *sein*)

swimming *noun*
= (das) Schwimmen

swimming pool *noun*
= (das) Schwimmbecken

swimsuit *noun*
= (der) Badeanzug

swing
1 *verb*
• (*move back and forth*) = schwingen
• (*on a swing*) = schaukeln
• (*dangle*) = baumeln
to swing from a branch = an einem Ast
baumeln
2 *noun* = (die) Schaukel

Swiss
1 *noun*
(*person*) = (der) Schweizer/(die) Schweizerin
2 *adjective* = schweizerisch ▶**Countries p. 208**

switch
1 *noun* = (der) Schalter
2 *verb* = wechseln
to switch to another programme = auf ein
anderes Programm umschalten
switch off
= ausschalten
switch on
= einschalten

Switzerland *noun*
= die Schweiz ▶**Countries p. 208**

syllabus *noun*
= (der) Lehrplan

sympathetic *adjective*
(*showing understanding*) = verständnisvoll
(*showing pity*) = mitfühlend

syringe *noun*
= (die) Spritze

system *noun*
= (das) System

table *noun*
= (der) Tisch

tablet *noun*
= (die) Tablette

table tennis *noun*
= (das) Tischtennis

tackle *verb*
  (*in soccer, hockey*) = angreifen
  (*in American football, rugby*) = fassen
  to tackle a problem = ein Problem in
    Angriff nehmen

tactful *adjective*
= taktvoll

tail *noun*
= (der) Schwanz

take *verb*
• (*take hold of*) = nehmen
  to take someone by the hand = jemanden
    bei der Hand nehmen
• (*carry with one*) = mitnehmen
  I took my umbrella = ich habe meinen
    Regenschirm mitgenommen
• (*take to a place*) = bringen
  to take someone home = jemanden nach
    Hause bringen
  to take the children for a walk = mit den
    Kindern spazieren gehen (**!** *sein*)
• (*steal*) = stehlen
• (*cope with*) = aushalten
  I can't take the pain = ich kann die
    Schmerzen nicht aushalten
• (*need*) = brauchen
  it won't take long = es wird nicht lange
    dauern
• (*accept*) = annehmen
  we don't take cheques = wir nehmen
    keine Schecks an
• (*react to*) = aufnehmen
  to take something calmly = etwas gelassen
    aufnehmen
• (*use when travelling*) = nehmen
  to take a taxi = ein Taxi nehmen
• (*do, have*)
  to take driving lessons = Fahrstunden
    nehmen
  to take an exam = eine Prüfung machen
  to take a holiday = Ferien machen
  to take a photo = eine Aufnahme machen
• (*wear*) = haben
  to take size 10 = Größe zehn haben
take apart
= auseinander nehmen
take away
  (*remove*) = wegnehmen
  (*of food*) **'to take away'** = 'zum
    Mitnehmen'

take back
= zurückbringen
take down
• (*from a shelf*) = herunternehmen
• (*write down*) = aufschreiben
take off
• (*from an airport*) = abfliegen (**!** *sein*)
• (*remove*) = ausziehen
  to take one's clothes off = sich ausziehen
• **to take time off** = sich (*dative*) freinehmen
take out
• (*from a container, pocket*) = herausnehmen
• (*from a bank account*) = abheben
• **to take someone out** = mit jemandem
    ausgehen (**!** *sein*)
• **to take it out on someone** = seinen Ärger
    an jemandem auslassen
take part = teilnehmen
  to take part in a game = an einem Spiel
    teilnehmen
take place
= stattfinden
take up
• **to take up German** = anfangen, Deutsch zu
    lernen
• **to take up time** = Zeit in Anspruch nehmen

talented *adjective*
= talentiert

talk
1 *verb*
• = reden, = sprechen
  to talk to someone = mit jemandem
    sprechen *or* reden
  to talk in German = Deutsch sprechen
• (*gossip*) = reden
  they were talking about him = sie haben
    über ihn geredet
2 *noun*
• (*conversation*) = (das) Gespräch
• (*speech*) = (der) Vortrag

talkative *adjective*
= gesprächig

tall *adjective*
  (*of a person*) = groß
  (*of a building, tree*) = hoch

tame *adjective*
= zahm

tampon *noun*
(der) Tampon

tan *noun*
= (die) Bräune
  to get a tan = braun werden (**!** *sein*)

tank *noun*
• (*in a car*) = (der) Tank
  (*for water*) = (der) Wasserspeicher
• (*in war*) = (der) Panzer

tap
1 *noun* (*British*) = (der) Wasserhahn
2 *verb* = klopfen
  to tap on the door = an die Tür klopfen

T

tape
1 *noun*
- (*cassette*) = (die) Kassette
  to record something on tape = etwas auf Band aufnehmen
- (*for sticking*) = (der) Klebestreifen
  (*strip of material*) = (das) Band
2 *verb*
- (*record*) = aufnehmen
- (*stick*) = kleben

tape measure *noun*
= (das) Metermaß

tape recorder *noun*
= (das) Tonbandgerät

target
1 *noun* = (das) Ziel
  (*board*) = (die) Zielscheibe
2 *verb* = zielen auf (+ *accusative*)

tart *noun* (*British*)
= (das) Törtchen
an apple tart = ein Apfelkuchen

task *noun*
= (die) Aufgabe

taste
1 *noun* = (der) Geschmack
2 *verb*
- (*describing flavour*) = schmecken
  it tastes good = es schmeckt gut
- (*sample when eating or drinking*) = probieren

Taurus *noun*
= (der) Stier

tax *noun*
= (die) Steuer

taxi *noun*
= (das) Taxi

taxi rank (*British*), **taxi stand** (*US*) *noun*
= (der) Taxistand

tea *noun*
- = (der) Tee
- (*meal*) = (das) Abendessen

teach *verb*
- **to teach someone to [read | drive | swim ...]** = jemandem [Lesen | Autofahren | Schwimmen ...] beibringen
- (*work as a teacher*) = unterrichten
  to teach German = Deutsch unterrichten

teacher *noun*
= (der) Lehrer/(die) Lehrerin

team *noun*
  (*group*) = (das) Team
  (*in sport*) = (die) Mannschaft

teapot *noun*
= (die) Teekanne

tear¹ *verb*
- (*rip*) = zerreißen
  to tear a page out of a book = eine Seite aus einem Buch reißen
- (*get damaged*) = zerreißen (**!** *sein*)
  the string has torn = die Schnur ist zerrissen

> **!** A verb like **zerreißen** *that normally takes* **sein** *in the perfect tense takes* **haben** *when it has a direct object.*

  I have torn the string = ich habe die Schnur zerrissen
  I tore my dress = ich habe mir mein Kleid zerrissen
tear off
= abreißen
tear up
= zerreißen

tear² *noun*
  (*when crying*) = (die) Träne

tease *verb*
= necken

teaspoon *noun*
= (der) Teelöffel

technical *adjective*
= technisch

teenager *noun*
= (der) Teenager

telegram *noun*
= (das) Telegramm

telephone *noun*
= (das) Telefon

telephone directory *noun*
= (das) Telefonbuch

television *noun*
= (das) Fernsehen
  (*set*) = (der) Fernseher
  I saw it on television = ich habe es im Fernsehen gesehen
  to watch television = fernsehen

tell *verb*
- (*say to, inform*) = sagen
  to tell someone something = jemandem etwas sagen
  could you tell me how to get to the station? = könnten Sie mir sagen, wie ich zum Bahnhof komme?
  to tell someone how to do something = jemandem sagen, wie man etwas tut
- (*relate*) = erzählen
  to tell someone a story = jemandem eine Geschichte erzählen
- (*work out, know*) = wissen
  I can tell she doesn't like me = ich weiß, dass sie mich nicht mag
- (*make a distinction*) = erkennen
  to tell the difference = den Unterschied erkennen
  its difficult to tell the twins apart = die Zwillinge sind schwer zu unterscheiden

tell off
= ausschimpfen

temper noun
to lose one's temper = wütend werden
(**!** sein)

temperature noun
= (die) Temperatur
to have a temperature = Fieber haben

temporary adjective
= vorübergehend
temporary worker = (die) Aushilfe

ten adjective
= zehn ▶Numbers p. 282

tennis noun
= (das) Tennis

tennis court noun
= (der) Tennisplatz

tense adjective
= gespannt

tent noun
= (das) Zelt

tenth
1 adjective = zehnter/zehnte/zehntes
▶Numbers p. 282, ▶Dates p. 213
2 noun
(fraction) = (das) Zehntel

term noun
(at school) = (das) Halbjahr
(at university) = (das) Semester

terrible adjective
= schrecklich

terrified adjective
= verängstigt

terror noun
• (fear) = (die) panische Angst
• (thing or person causing fear) =
(der) Schrecken

terrorist noun
= (der) Terrorist/(die) Terroristin

test
1 verb
• (try out) = testen
• (at school) = prüfen
2 noun
• (of a person's ability) = (der) Test
(at school) = (die) Klassenarbeit
driving test = (die) Fahrprüfung
• (medical)
eye test = (der) Sehtest
to have a blood test = eine Blutprobe
machen

textbook noun
= (das) Lehrbuch

than conjunction
= als
he is older than me = er ist älter als ich

thank verb
= danken (+ dative)
thank you = danke schön
thank you for coming = danke, dass du
gekommen bist

thanks
1 interjection = danke!
2 noun = (der) Dank
many thanks = vielen Dank

that
1 adjective
= der/die/das, (stressed) =
dieser/diese/dieses

> **!** Note that dieser, diese and dieses
> change their endings in the same way as
> der/die/das.

I prefer that shirt = mir gefällt das Hemd
besser
that one = der da/die da/das da
I'll take that one = ich nehme das da
that poor child = dieses arme Kind
2 pronoun
• = das
what's that? = was ist das?
who's that? = wer ist das?, (on the phone) =
wer ist am Apparat?
is that John? = ist das John?
that's not true = das stimmt nicht
• (of the kind or in the way mentioned) = so
just like that = einfach so
that's right! = gut so!
a man like that = so ein Mann
• (introducing a relative clause) = der/die/das

> **!** Note that der, die and das agree in
> gender with the noun they stand for.

a shop that sells jewellery = ein Geschäft,
das Schmuck verkauft
is he the man that you saw in the cinema?
= ist das der Mann, den du im Kino
gesehen hast?
3 adverb = so
it wasn't that hot = es war nicht so heiß
4 conjunction = dass
I know that it's not easy = ich weiß, dass es
nicht leicht ist
he drove so slowly that he caused a traffic
jam = er fuhr so langsam, dass er einen
Stau verursachte

> **!** Note that there is always a comma
> before the conjunction dass.

the
1 article = der/die/das, (plural) = die

> **!** Note that the article changes according
> to the gender of the noun it goes with: the
> table = der Tisch (masculine); the flower =
> die Blume (feminine); the house = das
> Haus (neuter); the children = die Kinder
> (plural).

the fifth of March = der fünfte März
2 adverb
the more the better = je mehr, desto besser
all the better = umso besser

T

theater (*US*), **theatre** (*British*) *noun*
= (das) Theater

their *adjective*
= ihr

> **!** *Note that* ihr *changes its endings in the same way as* ein.

they are selling their car = sie verkaufen ihr Auto

theirs *pronoun*
= ihrer/ihre/ihrs

> **!** *Note that the pronoun agrees in number and gender with the noun it stands for:* theirs (*meaning the garden*) is small = ihrer (*der Garten*) ist klein; theirs (*meaning the shoes*) are new = ihre (*die Schuhe*) sind neu.

the new house is theirs = das neue Haus gehört ihnen
a friend of theirs = ein Freund von ihnen

them *pronoun*

> **!** *In German this pronoun changes according to its function in the sentence. As a direct object it is in the accusative,* sie, *and as an indirect object it is in the dative,* ihnen.

* (*in the accusative*) = sie
  I know them = ich kenne sie
* (*in the dative*) = ihnen
  he gave them the money = er hat ihnen das Geld gegeben
* (*in the nominative, for emphasis*)
  it's them who stole it = sie haben es gestohlen

themselves *pronoun*
* (*when translated by a reflexive verb in German*) = sich
  they want to enjoy themselves = sie möchten sich amüsieren
* (*used for emphasis*) = selbst
  they did it themselves = sie haben es selbst gemacht
* **by themselves** = allein

then *adverb*
* (*at that time*) = damals
  we met a lot then = wir trafen uns damals oft
  from then on = von da an
  since then = seitdem
* (*after, next*) = dann

there
1 *pronoun*
  there is = da ist, = es gibt
  there is no room = da ist kein Platz
  there will be a lot of people = es werden viele Leute da sein
2 *adverb*
* (*when talking about location*) = da

(*with movement to a place*) = dahin
who's there? = wer ist da?
put the books there = leg die Bücher dahin
they don't go there often = sie fahren nicht oft dahin
* (*when drawing attention*)
  there they are! = da sind sie ja!
  there you are (*when giving something*) = bitte schön
  there, there = nun, nun

therefore *adverb*
= deshalb

thermometer *noun*
= (das) Thermometer

these
1 *adjective* = diese

> **!** *Note that* diese *changes its endings in the same way as the plural article* die.

these books aren't mine = diese Bücher gehören mir nicht
these ones = diese (da)
2 *pronoun*
* = die
  I prefer these = die gefallen mir besser
  these are your things = das sind deine Sachen
* (*referring to near things or people*) = diese

they *pronoun*
* = sie
  they want to come too = sie wollen auch kommen
* (*indefinite use*) = man
  they say = man sagt

thick *adjective*
* (*not thin*) = dick
* (*stupid*) = dumm

thief *noun*
= (der) Dieb/(die) Diebin

thigh *noun*
= (der) Oberschenkel

thin *adjective*
= dünn

thing *noun*
* (*object*) = (das) Ding
* (*action, subject*) = (die) Sache
  the thing is, he wants money for it = die Sache ist, dass er Geld dafür haben will
  the best thing would be to call him = am besten wäre es, ihn anzurufen
  how are things? = wie gehts?

> **!** *Note that* gehts, *written as one word, is short for* geht es.

* **things** (*belongings*) = Sachen (*plural*)

think *verb*
* = denken
  to think of something = an etwas (*accusative*) denken
  we didn't think of closing the window = wir haben nicht daran gedacht, das Fenster zuzumachen

- (*believe*) = meinen
  what do you think? = was meinen Sie?
  I think so = ich glaube schon
  I don't think so = ich glaube nicht
- (*consider*) = nachdenken
  to think about something = über etwas
  (*accusative*) nachdenken
  what do you think of his proposal? = was
  halten Sie von seinem Vorschlag?
- (*regard as*) = halten für (+ *accusative*)
- (*remember*)
  I can't think of his name = ich kann mich
  nicht an seinen Namen erinnern
think over
  = sich (*dative*) überlegen
  I have to think it over first = ich muss es
  mir erst überlegen
think up
  = sich (*dative*) ausdenken

third
1 *adjective* = dritter/dritte/drittes ▶**Numbers**
  p. 282, ▶**Dates p. 213**
2 *noun*
  (*fraction*) = (das) Drittel

thirsty *adjective*
  = durstig
  I am thirsty = ich habe Durst

thirteen *adjective*
  = dreizehn ▶**Numbers p. 282**

thirty *adjective*
  = dreißig ▶**Numbers p. 282**

this
1 *adjective* = dieser/diese/dieses

> ! *Note that* dieser, diese *and* dieses
> *change their endings in the same way as*
> der/die/das.

  he wants to come this week = er will diese
  Woche kommen
  I'll take this one = ich nehme
  diesen/diese/dieses
  this morning = heute Morgen
2 *pronoun*
- = das
  what's this? = was ist das?
  who's this? = wer ist das?
  how much is this? = wie viel kostet das?
  like this = so
- (*referring to a near thing or person*) =
  dieser/diese/dieses
  this is the best = dieser ist der beste

thorn *noun*
  = (der) Dorn

those
1 *adjective* = diese, = die

> ! *Note that* diese *changes its endings in*
> *the same way as the plural article* die.

  those books are yours = diese Bücher
  gehören dir

2 *pronoun* = die (da)
  can I have those? = kann ich die da haben?
  those are my letters = das sind meine
  Briefe
  one of those = einer von denen

though *conjunction*
  = obwohl

thought *noun*
  = (der) Gedanke

thousand *adjective*
  = tausend
  one thousand, a thousand = eintausend
  ▶**Numbers p. 282**

thread *noun*
  = (der) Faden

threat *noun*
- = (die) Drohung
- (*danger*) = (die) Gefahr

threaten *verb*
  = drohen (+ *dative*)
  (*with a weapon*) = bedrohen

three *adjective*
  = drei ▶**Numbers p. 282**

throat *noun*
  = (der) Hals

through *preposition*
- durch (+ *accusative*)
  to drive through the desert = durch die
  Wüste fahren (**!** *sein*)
- (*when talking about time*)
  right through the day = den ganzen Tag
  hindurch
  open April through September (*US*) = von
  April bis September geöffnet

> ! *Note that* through *is often used with*
> *verbs*—get through, go through, see
> through, *etc. You will find translations for*
> *these under the entries* get, go, see, *etc.*

throw *verb*
- = werfen
  to throw a book on the floor = ein Buch auf
  den Boden werfen
  to throw stones at someone = mit Steinen
  nach jemandem werfen
  throw me the ball = wirf mir den Ball zu
  to throw oneself to the ground = sich auf
  den Boden werfen
- (*other uses*)
  to throw a party = eine Party schmeißen✗
throw away, throw out
  = wegwerfen

thumb *noun*
  = (der) Daumen

thunder *noun*
  = (der) Donner

thunderstorm *noun*
  = (das) Gewitter

T

Thursday *noun*
= (der) Donnerstag ▶ Dates p. 213

ticket *noun*
  (*for the theatre, an exhibition*) = (die) Karte
  (*for a bus, train*) = (die) Fahrkarte
  (*for a plane*) = (der) Flugschein
  (*for a locker, parking*) = (der) Schein

tickle *verb*
= kitzeln

tide *noun*
= Gezeiten (*plural*)
the tide is in/out = es is Flut/es ist Ebbe

tidy *adjective*
= ordentlich
tidy up
= aufräumen

tie
1 *verb* = binden
  to tie the horse to the fence = das Pferd an
    den Zaun binden
  to tie a knot = einen Knoten machen
2 *noun*
• (*necktie*) = (die) Krawatte, = (der) Schlips
• (*draw*) = (das) Unentschieden
tie up
  to tie someone up = jemanden fesseln
  to tie a boat up = ein Boot festbinden

tiger *noun*
= (der) Tiger

tight *adjective*
• (*firm*) = fest
• (*close-fitting*) = eng

tights *noun*
= (die) Strumpfhose
a pair of tights = eine Strumpfhose

tile *noun*
  (*on the wall*) = (die) Kachel
  (*on the floor*) = (die) Fliese
  (*on the roof*) = (der) Ziegel

till[1] ▶ until

till[2] *noun*
= (die) Kasse

timber *noun*
= (das) Holz

time *noun*
• = (die) Zeit
  I don't have time to visit them = ich habe
    keine Zeit, um sie zu besuchen
  to spend time reading = Zeit mit Lesen
    verbringen
  I've been waiting for some time = ich warte
    schon seit einiger Zeit
  a long time ago = vor langer Zeit

• (*when talking about a specific hour or
    period*)
  the time is 2 o'clock = es ist zwei Uhr
  what's the time? = wie spät ist es?
  what time does the film start? = um wie
    viel Uhr fängt der Film an?
  to arrive on time = pünktlich ankommen
    (**!** sein)
  just in time = gerade rechtzeitig
  in [five days' | a year's | two months' …] **time** =
    in [fünf Tagen | einem Jahr | zwei Monaten …]
  this time last year = heute vor einem Jahr
• (*moment, experience*)
  at times = manchmal
  at the right time = im richtigen Moment
  at any time = jederzeit
  for the time being = vorläufig
  in no time = im Handumdrehen
  to have a good time = sich amüsieren
• (*occasion*) = (das) Mal
  this time = diesmal
  three times a day = dreimal täglich
  the first time I saw him = das erste Mal, als
    ich ihn sah
  from time to time = von Zeit zu Zeit
• (*when comparing*)
  ten times quicker = zehnmal schneller

timetable *noun*
• (*for trains, buses*) = (der) Fahrplan
• (*at school*) = (der) Stundenplan
• (*at work, for events*) = (das) Programm

tin *noun*
• (*metal*) = (das) Blech
• (*British: can*) = (die) Dose

tin-opener *noun* (*British*)
= (der) Dosenöffner

tiny *adjective*
= winzig

tip *noun*
• (*point, end*) = (die) Spitze
• (*money*) = (das) Trinkgeld
• (*advice*) = (der) Rat, = (der) Tip✖

tire (*US*) ▶ tyre

tired *adjective*
= müde

tiring *adjective*
= ermüdend

tissue *noun*
= (das) Papiertaschentuch

to *preposition*
• (*in the direction of*) = zu (+ *dative*)
  to come to someone = zu jemandem
    kommen (**!** sein)
  he gave the parcel to me = er hat mir das
    Paket gegeben
  (*to a country, town*) = nach (+ *dative*)
  we went to Munich = wir sind nach
    München gefahren

✖ in informal situations

Time of day

For days of the week, months and dates, ▶ **Dates p. 213.**

what time is it? = wie spät ist es?, = wie viel Uhr ist es?
could you tell me the time? = können Sie mir sagen, wie spät es ist?
it's 3 o'clock = es ist drei Uhr

In German timetables and official situations, the 24-hour clock is used, so *4 pm* is **sechzehn Uhr**.

00.45 = null Uhr fünfundvierzig

8 o'clock = acht Uhr
8 o'clock in the morning = acht Uhr morgens *or* früh
4 o'clock in the afternoon = vier Uhr nachmittags, = sechzehn Uhr
8 o'clock in the evening = acht Uhr abends, = zwanzig Uhr

1.00 = ein Uhr, *(p.m.)* = dreizehn Uhr
1.05 = ein Uhr fünf, = fünf (Minuten) nach eins
1.15 = ein Uhr fünfzehn, = Viertel nach eins
1.25 = ein Uhr fünfundzwanzig, = fünf (Minuten) vor halb zwei
1.30 = ein Uhr dreißig, = halb zwei
1.35 = ein Uhr fünfunddreißig, = fünf (Minuten) nach halb zwei
1.45 = ein Uhr fünfundvierzig, = Viertel vor zwei
1.55 = ein Uhr fünfundfünfzig, = fünf (Minuten) vor zwei

Note that in German, *1.30 (half past one)* is translated by **halb zwei**; the half-hour is 'half way to' the next hour.

at 9 o'clock tomorrow = morgen um neun Uhr
at about eight = gegen acht Uhr
from ten o'clock onwards = ab zehn Uhr

(to the cinema, theatre, school, office) = in (+ *accusative*)
we went to the cinema = wir sind ins Kino gegangen

! *Note that* ins *is a shortened form of* in das.

(to a wedding, party, university) = auf (+ *accusative*)
to go to the toilet = auf die Toilette gehen (**!** *sein*)
• *(as far as, until)* = bis (+ *accusative*)
she counted up to 3 = sie hat bis drei gezählt
• *(indicating position)*
with my back to the wall = mit dem Rücken zur Wand
to the left/right = nach links/rechts
• *(send, address, fasten to)* = an (+ *accusative*)
I'm sending the letter to my mother = ich schicke den Brief an meine Mutter
• *(indicating a reaction, showing an attitude)*
to his surprise = zu seiner Überraschung
to the best of my knowledge = nach meinem besten Wissen
there's nothing to it = es ist nichts dabei
• *(in expressions of time)* = vor (+ *dative*)
5 minutes to 8 = fünf Minuten vor acht
• *(in verbal expressions with the infinitive)* = zu
the question is difficult to answer = die Frage ist schwer zu beantworten

! *Note that with separable verbs* zu *is put between the prefix and the verb.*
she tried to ring = sie versuchte anzurufen

! *Note that* zu *is not needed before the infinitive after the verbs* dürfen, können, mögen, müssen, sollen *or* wollen.
he had to go = er musste gehen
(showing purpose, and after too) = um ... zu
she went home to visit her mother = sie fuhr nach Hause, um ihre Mutter zu besuchen
too young to marry = zu jung, um zu heiraten
(following another verb)
to want to do something = etwas tun wollen
I forgot to tell you = ich habe vergessen, es dir zu sagen
(following an adjective) = zu
to be polite to someone = höflich zu jemandem sein

! *Note that* to *is often used with adjectives* (be grateful to someone, be nice to someone, *etc.) and with verbs* (to apologize to someone, to write to someone, *etc.). You will find translations for these under the entries* apologize, grateful, nice, write, *etc.*

toast *noun*
= (der) Toast

toaster *noun*
= (der) Toaster

today *adverb*
= heute

toe *noun*
= (der) Zeh

T

together *adverb*
= zusammen
(*at the same time*) = gleichzeitig

toilet *noun*
= (die) Toilette

toilet paper *noun*
= (das) Toilettenpapier

tomato *noun*
= (die) Tomate

tomorrow *adverb*
= morgen

tongue *noun*
= (die) Zunge

tonight *adverb*
(*this evening*) = heute Abend
(*during the night*) = heute Nacht

too *adverb*
* (*also*) = auch
* (*more than necessary*) = zu
  it's too big = es ist zu groß
  I ate too much = ich habe zu viel gegessen
* (*very*)
  he's not too happy = er ist nicht besonders
    glücklich

tool *noun*
= (das) Werkzeug

tooth *noun*
= (der) Zahn

toothache *noun*
= Zahnschmerzen (*plural*)
! *The translation for an* **ache** *is the plural*
Schmerzen.

toothbrush *noun*
= (die) Zahnbürste

toothpaste *noun*
= (die) Zahnpasta

top
1 *noun*
* (*highest part*) = (die) Spitze
  at the top of = oben auf (+ *dative*)
  at the top of the stairs = oben auf der
    Treppe
* (*cover, lid*)
  (*on a bottle, jar*) = (der) Deckel
  (*on a pen, tube*) = (die) Kappe
  (*of a table*) = (die) Platte
* (*highest level*)
  to be top of the class = der Erste/die Erste
    der Klasse sein
  to get to the top = Erfolg haben
2 *adjective*
* (*highest*) = oberster/oberste/oberstes
* (*best*) = bester/beste/bestes

torch *noun*
= (die) Taschenlampe

✗ in informal situations

tortoise *noun*
= (die) Schildkröte

total
1 *noun*
(*number*) = (die) Gesamtzahl
(*sum*) = (die) Gesamtsumme
2 *adjective*
(*comprising the whole*) = gesamt
(*complete*) = völlig
to have total freedom = völlige Freiheit
  haben

touch
1 *verb*
(*with one's hand*) = berühren
(*get hold of*) = anfassen
don't touch that! = fass das nicht an!
2 *noun*
to keep in touch with someone = mit
  jemandem in Verbindung bleiben (**!** *sein*)
to get in touch with someone = sich mit
  jemandem in Verbindung setzen

tough *adjective*
* (*not soft or sensitive*) = hart
* (*difficult*) = schwierig
* (*rough*) = rau
* (*resistant*) = widerstandsfähig

tour
1 *noun*
* (*journey*) = (die) Tour
* (*by a band, team*) = (die) Tournee
* (*inspection of a building, city*) =
    (die) Besichtigung
  to go on a tour of the castle = das Schloss
    besichtigen
2 *verb*
to go touring = herumreisen (**!** *sein*)

tourism *noun*
= (der) Tourismus

tourist *noun*
= (der) Tourist/(die) Touristin

tourist office *noun*
= (das) Fremdenverkehrsbüro

toward, towards *preposition*
* (*in the direction of*) = zu (+ *dative*)
  (*facing*) = nach (+ *dative*)
  towards the east = nach Osten
* (*with time*) = gegen (+ *accusative*)
  towards evening = gegen Abend
* (*when talking about attitudes*) = gegenüber
    (+ *dative*)
  ! *Note that* **gegenüber** *always follows a*
  pronoun or noun.
  towards you = dir gegenüber
  I'm fair towards him = ich bin ihm
    gegenüber fair

towel *noun*
= (das) Handtuch

tower *noun*
= (der) Turm

tower block noun (British)
= (das) Hochhaus

town noun
= (die) Stadt
to go to town = in die Stadt gehen (**!** sein)

town hall
= (das) Rathaus

toy noun
= (das) Spielzeug

track noun
* (path) = (der) Weg
* (for sports) = (die) Bahn
* (rails) = (das) Gleis
* (left by a person, animal or vehicle)
tracks = Spuren (plural)

tracksuit noun
= (der) Trainingsanzug

trade noun
* (business) = (der) Handel
* (craft) = (das) Handwerk

traffic noun
= (der) Verkehr

traffic jam noun
= (der) Stau

traffic lights noun
= (die) Ampel

train
1 noun = (der) Zug
by train = mit dem Zug
2 verb
* (teach) = ausbilden
to train someone as a teacher = jemanden zum Lehrer ausbilden
* (in sport) = trainieren

trainer noun (British)
* = (der) Trainer
* **trainers** (shoes) = Trainingsschuhe (plural)

translate verb
= übersetzen

translation noun
= (die) Übersetzung

translator noun
= (der) Übersetzer/(die) Übersetzerin

transport (British), **transportation** (US) noun
= (der) Transport

trap noun
= (die) Falle
to set a trap for someone = jemandem eine Falle stellen

trash noun (US)
= (der) Müll, = (der) Abfall

trash can noun (US)
= (der) Mülleimer

travel verb
= reisen (**!** sein)

travel agency noun
= (das) Reisebüro

traveler (US), **traveller** (British) noun
= (der/die) Reisende

traveler's check (US), **traveller's cheque** (British) noun
= (der) Reisescheck

tray noun
= (das) Tablett

treat verb
* (deal with) = behandeln
* (pay for)
to treat someone to an ice cream = jemandem ein Eis spendieren

treatment noun
= (die) Behandlung

tree noun
= (der) Baum

tremble verb
= zittern

trendy adjective
= modern

trial noun
= (der) Prozess
to be on trial for theft = wegen Diebstahls angeklagt sein

triangle noun
= (das) Dreieck

trick
1 noun
* (joke) = (der) Streich
* (to deceive, entertain) = (der) Trick
2 verb = täuschen, = hereinlegen✖

trip
1 noun
(journey) = (die) Reise
(day out) = (der) Ausflug
to make a trip to London = nach London fahren (**!** sein)
2 verb
* = stolpern (**!** sein)
* **to trip someone up** = jemandem ein Bein stellen

trouble noun
* (difficulties) = Schwierigkeiten (plural)
to get someone into trouble = jemanden in Schwierigkeiten bringen
* (effort) = (die) Mühe
to take the trouble = sich (dative) die Mühe machen
to go to a lot of trouble = sich (dative) viel Mühe geben

trousers noun
= (die) Hose

trout noun
= (die) Forelle

T

truck *noun*
= (der) Lastwagen

true *adjective*
= wahr
to come true = in Erfüllung gehen (**!** *sein*)

trunk *noun*
• (*of a tree*) = (der) Stamm
• (*large case*) = (der) Koffer
• (*for storage*) = (die) Truhe
• (*of an elephant*) = (der) Rüssel
• (*US: in a car*) = (der) Kofferraum

trust *verb*
• (*believe*) = trauen (+ *dative*)
• (*rely on*)
you can't trust him = man kann sich nicht auf ihn verlassen

truth *noun*
= (die) Wahrheit

try
1 *verb*
• = versuchen
to try to [come | ring | relax …] = versuchen [zu kommen | anzurufen | zu entspannen …]
try again = versuche es noch einmal
• (*test*)
to try a recipe = ein Rezept ausprobieren
to try on a pair of jeans = Jeans anprobieren
• (*taste*) = probieren
• (*in court*) = vor Gericht stellen
2 *noun* = (der) Versuch

T-shirt *noun*
= (das) T-Shirt

tube *noun*
• (*container*) = (die) Tube
• (*pipe*) = (das) Rohr
inner tube = (der) Schlauch
• (*British: underground*) = (die) U-Bahn

Tuesday *noun*
= (der) Dienstag ▶ **Dates p. 213**

tuna *noun*
= (der) Thunfisch

tunnel *noun*
= (der) Tunnel

turkey *noun*
= (die) Pute

Turkey *noun*
= die Türkei ▶ **Countries p. 208**

turn
1 *verb*
• (*twist*) = drehen
to turn the handle to the right = den Griff nach rechts drehen
• (*turn around*) = sich umdrehen
she turned and waved = sie drehte sich um und winkte

• (*change direction*)
to turn right = nach rechts abbiegen (**!** *sein*)
to turn the corner = um die Ecke biegen (**!** *sein*)
• (*become*) = werden (**!** *sein*)
to turn red = rot werden
2 *noun*
• (*bend*) = (die) Kurve
• (*in games*)
whose turn is it? = wer ist an der Reihe?
in turn = der Reihe nach
• (*rotation*) = (die) Drehung
• **at the turn of the century** = um die Jahrhundertwende

turn around
• (*face the other way*) = sich umdrehen
• (*rotate*) = sich drehen

turn away
= sich abwenden

turn back
= umkehren (**!** *sein*)

turn down
• **to turn the radio down** = das Radio leiser stellen
• (*reject*) = ablehnen

turn off
= ausschalten
to turn the lights off = das Licht ausschalten
to turn the tap off = den Hahn zudrehen
to turn off the oven = den Backofen ausmachen

turn on
= einschalten
to turn the lights on = das Licht einschalten
to turn the tap on = den Hahn aufdrehen
to turn on the oven = den Backofen anschalten

turn over
• (*roll over*) = sich umdrehen
• **to turn over the page** = umblättern

turn up
• **to turn up the heating** = die Heizung aufdrehen
to turn the music up = die Musik lauter machen
• (*show up*) = auftauchen (**!** *sein*)

turtle *noun*
= (die) Schildkröte

twelve *adjective*
= zwölf ▶ **Numbers p. 282**

twenty *adjective*
= zwanzig ▶ **Numbers p. 282**

twice *adverb*
= zweimal
twice a year = zweimal im Jahr

twin
1 *noun* = (der) Zwilling
2 *adjective*
his twin brother = sein Zwillingsbruder

twist *verb*
• (*bend out of shape*) = verbiegen
• **to twist one's ankle** = sich (*dative*) den Knöchel verrenken

- (*of a road, river*) = sich winden

two *adjective*
= zwei ▶**Numbers p. 282**

type
1 *noun*
(*kind*) = (die) Art
(*person*) = (der) Typ
2 *verb*
= mit der Maschine schreiben, = tippen✖

typewriter *noun*
= (die) Schreibmaschine

typical *adjective*
= typisch

typist *noun*
= (die) Schreibkraft

tyre *noun* (*British*)
= (der) Reifen

Uu

ugly *adjective*
= hässlich

umbrella *noun*
= (der) Regenschirm

unbearable *adjective*
= unerträglich

unbelievable *adjective*
= unglaublich

uncle *noun*
= (der) Onkel

uncomfortable *adjective*
= unbequem
I feel uncomfortable = mir ist unbehaglich zumute

unconscious *adjective*
- (*after an accident*) = bewusstlos
- (*unaware*) = unbewusst

under *preposition*
- = unter (+ *dative or accusative*)

> **!** Note that **unter** is followed by a noun in the dative when position is described. The accusative follows when there is movement towards something.

to hide under the bed = sich unter dem Bett verstecken
to push the chair under the table = den Stuhl unter den Tisch schieben
- (*less than*) = unter (+ *dative*)
(*in price*) = weniger als
children under 5 = Kinder unter fünf Jahren

- (*other uses*)
under German law = nach deutschem Recht
under construction = im Bau

underground
1 *adjective* = unterirdisch
2 *noun* (*British*) = (die) U-Bahn

underline *verb*
= unterstreichen

underneath
1 *adverb* = darunter
2 *preposition* = unter (+ *dative or accusative*)

> **!** Note that **unter** is followed by a noun in the dative when position is described. The accusative follows when there is movement towards something.

the dog lay underneath the table = der Hund lag unter dem Tisch
the baby crawled underneath the chair = das Baby kroch unter den Stuhl
underneath it = darunter

underpants *noun*
= (die) Unterhose

understand *verb*
= verstehen
I can understand her doing it = ich kann verstehen, warum sie es tut
to make onself understood = sich verständlich machen

understanding *adjective*
= verständnisvoll

underwear *noun*
= (die) Unterwäsche

undo *verb*
= aufmachen

undress *verb*
= sich ausziehen

uneasy *adjective*
= unbehaglich

unemployed *adjective*
= arbeitslos

unfair *adjective*
= unfair, = ungerecht

unfortunately *adverb*
= leider

unfriendly *adjective*
= unfreundlich

ungrateful *adjective*
= undankbar

unhappy *adjective*
- (*sad*) = unglücklich
- (*not satisfied*) = unzufrieden

unhealthy *adjective*
= ungesund

U

uniform *noun*
= (die) Uniform

union *noun*
- = (die) Union
- (*trade union*) = (die) Gewerkschaft

United Kingdom *noun*
= das Vereinigte Königreich

United States of America *noun*
= die Vereinigten Staaten von Amerika

universe *noun*
= (das) Weltall

university *noun*
= (die) Universität

unkind *adjective*
(*of a person*) = unfreundlich
(*of a remark*) = hässlich

unknown *adjective*
= unbekannt

unless *conjunction*
= es sei denn

unlock *verb*
= aufschließen

unlucky *adjective*
- **to be unlucky** = Pech haben
- (*bringing bad luck*) = Unglücks-
an unlucky number = eine Unglückszahl
it's unlucky to walk under a ladder = es
bringt Unglück, wenn man unter einer
Leiter durchgeht

unpack *verb*
= auspacken

unsuccessful *adjective*
= erfolglos

unsuitable *adjective*
= unpassend

untidy *adjective*
(*of a person, room*) = unordentlich
(*of a person's looks*) = ungepflegt

until
1 *preposition* = bis (+ *accusative*)
I'm staying until Thursday = ich bleibe bis
Donnerstag

! *Note that* until *followed by a noun is
usually translated as* bis zu, *which takes
the dative.*

until the evening = bis zum Abend

! *Note that* not until *is translated by* erst.

not until next week = erst nächste Woche
2 *conjunction* = bis
I'll wait until you get back home = ich
warte, bis du wieder nach Hause kommst
not until = erst wenn

unusual *adjective*
= ungewöhnlich

up

! *Note that* up *is often used with
verbs*—blow up, give up, own up, *etc. You
will find translations for these under the
entries* blow, give, own, *etc.*

1 *preposition*
to be up on something = oben auf etwas
(*dative*) sein
to go up the stairs = die Treppe
hinaufgehen (! *sein*)
to go up the street = die Straße
entlanggehen (! *sein*)
2 *adverb*
- = oben
it's up on the wardrobe = es liegt oben auf
dem Schrank
up there = da oben
- (*with movement*) = nach oben
to go up = nach oben gehen (! *sein*)
3 *adjective*
- (*out of bed*) = auf
to be up all night = die ganze Nacht auf
sein
- (*higher in amount*) = gestiegen
to be up by 10% = um zehn Prozent
gestiegen sein
prices are up = die Preise sind gestiegen
- (*wrong*)
what's up? = was ist los?✹
up to
- (*well enough*)
I'm not up to it = ich fühle mich nicht wohl
genug dazu
- (*when talking about who is responsible*)
it's up to [me | you | them ...] to help = [ich
sollte | ihr solltet | sie sollten ...] helfen
the decision isn't up to me = die
Entscheidung hängt nicht von mir ab
- (*until*) = bis
up to now = bis jetzt
- (*as many as*) = bis zu (+ *dative*)
to work up to 8 hours a day = bis zu acht
Stunden täglich arbeiten

upset
1 *adjective*
- **to be upset** (*annoyed*) = ärgerlich sein,
(*distressed*) = bestürzt sein
to get upset about something = sich über
etwas (*accusative*) aufregen
2 *verb*
- (*make unhappy*) = erschüttern
- (*mess up plans*) = ducheinander bringen
- (*annoy*) = ärgern
- (*knock over*) = umstoßen, (*spill*) =
verschütten

upstairs *adverb*
= oben

! *If movement is involved,* upstairs *is
translated by* nach oben.

to go upstairs = nach oben gehen (! *sein*)

urgent *adjective*
= dringend

us *pronoun*
= uns
they know us = sie kennen uns
it's us = wir sinds

! *Note that* sinds, *written as one word, is short for* sind es.

they are older than us = sie sind älter als wir

USA *noun*
= die USA (*plural*) ▶Countries p. 208

use
1 *verb*
* (*make use of*) = benutzen
he uses this room as an office = er benutzt dieses Zimmer als Büro
what is it used for? = wofür wird das benutzt?
to use a different word = ein anderes Wort gebrauchen
* (*take advantage of*) = ausnutzen
to use someone = jemanden ausnutzen
to use the opportunity to speak German = die Gelegenheit ausnutzen, Deutsch zu sprechen
* (*use up*) = verbrauchen
(*on food*) **use before ...** = mindestens haltbar bis ...
2 *noun*
* = (der) Gebrauch
to be in use = in Gebrauch sein
to make use of a room = von einem Zimmer Gebrauch machen
* (*using*) = (die) Benutzung
to have the use of a car = ein Auto benutzen können
* (*purpose*) = (die) Verwendung
* **to be of use to someone** = jemandem nützlich sein
that's no use = das nützt nichts
it's no use complaining = es hat keinen Zweck, sich zu beschweren
use up
to use up all the money = das ganze Geld verbrauchen
to use up the milk = die Milch aufbrauchen

used
1 *verb*
I used to read a lot = ich habe früher viel gelesen
2 *adjective*
to be used to [animals | noise | the cold ...] = an [Tiere | Lärm | die Kälte ...] gewöhnt sein
to get used to a new job = sich an eine neue Stelle gewöhnen

useful *adjective*
= nützlich

useless *adjective*
* (*not usable*) = unbrauchbar
* (*having no point*) = zwecklos
* (*having no purpose*) = nutzlos

* (*lacking ability*)
to be useless at chemistry = Chemie überhaupt nicht können
he's useless = er ist zu nichts zu gebrauchen

usually *adverb*
= normalerweise

vacant *adjective*
= frei

vacation (*US*) ▶ holiday

vacuum *verb*
= saugen

vacuum cleaner *noun*
= (der) Staubsauger

vain *adjective*
= eitel

valid *adjective*
= gültig

valley *noun*
= (das) Tal

valuable *adjective*
= wertvoll

value *noun*
* (*financial worth*) = (der) Wert
* (*usefulness*) = (der) Nutzen

van *noun*
= (der) Lieferwagen

vanilla *noun*
= (die) Vanille

various *adjective*
= verschieden
there are various ways of saying it = man kann es auf verschiedene Weise sagen

vary *verb*
* (*become different*) = sich ändern
* (*be different*) = verschieden sein

vase *noun*
= (die) Vase

veal *noun*
= (das) Kalbfleisch

vegetable *noun*
= (das) Gemüse
fresh vegetables = frisches Gemüse

vegetarian *noun*
= (der) Vegetarier/(die) Vegetarierin

V

vein *noun*
= (die) Vene

velvet *noun*
= (der) Samt

versus *preposition*
= gegen (+ *accusative*)

very
1 *adverb* = sehr
  to eat very little = sehr wenig essen
2 *adjective*
  on the very day = genau am selben Tag
  the very thing = genau das Richtige
  at the very beginning = ganz am Anfang
  the very first person = der Allererste/die
    Allererste

vest *noun*
• (*British: underwear*) = (das) Unterhemd
• (*US: waistcoat*) = (die) Weste

vet *noun*
= (der) Tierarzt/(die) Tierärztin

via *preposition*
= über (+ *accusative*)

vicious *adjective*
• (*violent*) = brutal
• (*nasty*) = boshaft

victory *noun*
= (der) Sieg

video
1 *noun*
• (*recording*) = (das) Video
• ▶video cassette, video recorder
2 *verb*
• (*record*) = aufzeichnen
• (*film*) = filmen

video camera *noun*
= (die) Videokamera

video cassette *noun*
= (die) Videokassette

video recorder *noun*
= (der) Videorekorder

video shop *noun*
= (die) Videothek

view *noun*
• (*line of sight*) = (die) Sicht
  it came into view = es kam in Sicht
• (*scene*) = (die) Aussicht
• (*opinion*) = (die) Ansicht
  in my view = meiner Ansicht nach

village *noun*
= (das) Dorf

vineyard *noun*
= (der) Weinberg

violent *adjective*
• (*fierce*) = heftig
• (*of behaviour*) = gewalttätig

violin *noun*
= (die) Geige

Virgo *noun*
= (die) Jungfrau

visit
1 *verb* = besuchen
  to visit someone = jemanden besuchen
  I'm only visiting = ich bin nur auf Besuch
    da
  to visit with someone (*US*) = bei jemandem
    zu Besuch sein
2 *noun* = (der) Besuch

visitor *noun*
= (der) Besucher/(die) Besucherin
  to have visitors = Besuch haben

vocabulary *noun*
= (der) Wortschatz

voice *noun*
= (die) Stimme
  to speak in a low voice = leise sprechen

volleyball *noun*
= (der) Volleyball

vomit *verb*
= sich übergeben

vote
1 *noun* = (die) Stimme
2 *verb*
  to vote for someone = jemanden wählen

wage *noun*
= (der) Lohn

waist *noun*
= (die) Taille

waistcoat *noun* (*British*)
= (die) Weste

wait *verb*
• = warten
  to wait for someone = auf jemanden
    warten
  to wait for something = auf etwas
    (*accusative*) warten
  to wait for someone to ring = darauf
    warten, dass jemand anruft
  to wait one's turn = warten, bis man an der
    Reihe ist
  I can't wait to see them = ich kann es kaum
    erwarten, sie zu sehen
• (*in a restaurant*)
  to wait at table (*British*), **to wait on table**
    (*US*) = servieren

wait up
= aufbleiben (**!** *sein*)

waiter *noun*
= (der) Kellner

waiting room *noun*
= (der) Warteraum
(*doctor's*) = (das) Wartezimmer

waitress *noun*
= (die) Serviererin, = (die) Bedienung

wake *verb*
to wake someone = jemanden wecken
wake up
* to wake someone up = jemanden
aufwecken
* to wake up at 10 o'clock = um zehn Uhr
aufwachen (**!** *sein*)

Wales *noun*
= (das) Wales ▶**Countries p. 208**

walk
1 *verb*
(*rather than run*) = gehen (**!** *sein*)
(*rather than drive or ride*) = laufen (**!** *sein*),
= zu Fuß gehen (**!** *sein*)
(*for pleasure*) = spazieren gehen (**!** *sein*)
to walk down the street = die Straße
entlanggehen (**!** *sein*)
the child can't walk yet = das Kind kann
noch nicht laufen
to walk the dog = mit dem Hund spazieren
gehen (**!** *sein*)
to walk someone home = jemanden nach
Hause bringen
2 *noun* = (der) Spaziergang
to go for a walk = spazieren gehen (**!** *sein*)
it's 5 minutes' walk = es ist fünf Minuten
zu Fuß
walk around
= herumlaufen (**!** *sein*)
walk away
= weggehen (**!** *sein*)
walk back
= zurücklaufen (**!** *sein*)
walk by
= vorbeigehen (**!** *sein*)
walk in
= hereinkommen (**!** *sein*)
walk out
* (*leave*) = gehen (**!** *sein*)
to walk out of the room = aus dem Zimmer
gehen
to walk out on someone = jemanden
verlassen
* (*go on strike*) = in den Streik treten (**!** *sein*)
walk up
to walk up to someone = auf jemanden
zugehen (**!** *sein*)

Walkman® *noun*
= (der) Walkman®

wall *noun*
(*inside a building*) = (die) Wand
(*outside*) = (die) Mauer

wallet *noun*
= (die) Brieftasche

wallpaper *noun*
= (die) Tapete

walnut *noun*
= (die) Walnuss

wander *verb*
to wander around town = durch die Stadt
bummeln (**!** *sein*)

want *verb*
* = wollen
he wants to [go home | play | sleep ...] = er
will [nach Hause gehen | spielen | schlafen ...]
do you want me to come? = willst du, dass
ich mitkomme?
* (*need*) = brauchen
do you want anything in town? = brauchst
du etwas aus der Stadt?
to be wanted by the police = polizeilich
gesucht werden (**!** *sein*)

war *noun*
= (der) Krieg

wardrobe *noun*
= (der) Kleiderschrank

warm
1 *adjective*
* (*not cold*) = warm
I'm very warm = mir ist sehr warm
it's nice and warm in this room = es ist
schön warm in diesem Zimmer
* (*enthusiastic*) = herzlich
a warm welcome = ein herzlicher Empfang
2 *verb*
to warm the plates = die Teller wärmen
to warm one's hands = sich (*dative*) die
Hände wärmen
warm up
* (*get warm*) = warm werden (**!** *sein*)
(*for sport*) = sich aufwärmen
* (*make warm*) = aufwärmen

warn *verb*
= warnen
to warn someone about the risks =
jemanden vor den Gefahren warnen
I warned him not to go by car = ich habe
ihn davor gewarnt, mit dem Auto zu
fahren

wash *verb*
* (*clean*) = waschen
to wash one's hands = sich (*dative*) die
Hände waschen
to wash the clothes = Wäsche waschen
to wash the dishes = abwaschen
* (*get clean*) = sich waschen
wash up
* (*British: do the dishes*) = abwaschen
* (*US: get clean*) = sich waschen

washbasin *noun*
= (das) Waschbecken

W

washing noun
= (die) Wäsche
to do the washing = die Wäsche waschen

washing machine noun
= (die) Waschmaschine

washing-up noun (British)
= (der) Abwasch
to do the washing-up = abwaschen

wasp noun
= (die) Wespe

waste
1 verb = verschwenden
to waste one's time = seine Zeit
verschwenden
2 noun = (die) Verschwendung
a waste of money = eine
Geldverschwendung
a waste of time = eine Zeitverschwendung

watch
1 verb
• (look at) = sich (dative) ansehen
to watch a film = sich (dative) einen Film
ansehen
to watch television = fernsehen
• (observe) = beobachten
we are being watched = wir werden
beobachtet
• (be careful with) = aufpassen auf
(+ accusative)
watch the children = pass auf die Kinder
auf
watch you don't fall = pass auf, dass du
nicht hinfällst
2 noun = (die) Uhr, = (die) Armbanduhr
watch for
= achten auf (+ accusative)
watch out
• (be careful) = aufpassen
• **to watch out for someone** (look for) = nach
jemandem Ausschau halten

water
1 noun = (das) Wasser
2 verb = gießen

waterfall noun
= (der) Wasserfall

water-skiing noun
= (das) Wasserskilaufen

wave
1 verb
• = winken
to wave to someone = jemandem
winken
to wave goodbye = zum Abschied
winken
to wave one's handkerchief = mit dem
Taschentuch winken
to wave flags = Fahnen schwenken

✱ in informal situations

• (direct)
to wave someone on = jemanden
weiterwinken
2 noun = (die) Welle

way noun
• (manner) = (die) Art
(method) = (die) Art und Weise
that's not the way to learn French = auf
diese Art und Weise kann man nicht
Französisch lernen
he does it the wrong way = er macht es
falsch
I like the way they live = mir gefällt ihre
Art zu leben
you can do it this way or that way = man
kann es so oder so machen
in a way = in gewisser Weise
• (route, road) = (der) Weg
I met him on the way to the station = ich
habe ihn auf dem Weg zum Bahnhof
getroffen
which is the way to the station? = wie
kommt man zum Bahnhof?
we can eat it on the way = wir können es
unterwegs essen
on the way back = auf dem Rückweg
to lose one's way = sich verlaufen, (in a
car) = sich verfahren
• **way in** = (der) Eingang
way out = (der) Ausgang
• (direction) = (die) Richtung
that's the wrong way = das ist die falsche
Richtung
this way = hier entlang, = in diese
Richtung
• **to be in someone's way** = jemandem im
Weg sein
to get out of the way = aus dem Weg gehen
(! sein)
• (distance) = (das) Stück
you still have a little way to go = du musst
noch ein kleines Stück gehen
it's a long way from here = es ist weit weg
von hier
• (what one wants)
if I had my own way, I'd stay = wenn es
nach mir ginge, bliebe ich hier
to get one's way = seinen Kopf durchsetzen
• **by the way** = übrigens

we pronoun
= wir

weak adjective
• = schwach
• (watery) = dünn

wealthy adjective
= reich

wear verb
• (be dressed in) = tragen
to wear jeans = Jeans tragen or anhaben✱
to wear black = Schwarz tragen
• (put on) = anziehen
I've got nothing to wear = ich habe nichts
anzuziehen

wear out
= abnutzen
he wears his shoes out quickly = er trägt
die Schuhe schnell ab
to wear oneself out = sich kaputtmachen✱

weather *noun*
= (das) Wetter
what's the weather like? = wie ist das
Wetter?
in [cold | bad | nice …] **weather** = bei [kaltem |
schlechtem | schönem …] Wetter
in wet weather = wenn es regnet

weather forecast *noun*
= (die) Wettervorhersage

wedding *noun*
= (die) Hochzeit

Wednesday *noun*
= (der) Mittwoch ▶ **Dates p. 213**

week *noun*
= (die) Woche
in two weeks' time = in zwei Wochen

weekend *noun*
= (das) Wochenende

weigh *verb*
= wiegen
what do you weigh? = wie viel wiegst du?
to weigh oneself = sich wiegen

weight *noun*
= (das) Gewicht
to lose weight = abnehmen

weird *adjective*
= bizarr

welcome
1 *verb* = begrüßen
to welcome someone = jemanden
begrüßen
2 *adjective*
• = willkommen
to be welcome = wilkommen sein
welcome to Germany = willkommen in
Deutschland
• (*acknowledging thanks*)
you're welcome = bitte, = gern geschehen
3 *noun* = (das) Willkommen

well
1 *adverb*
• = gut
the work is well paid = die Arbeit wird gut
bezahlt
she is well able to look after herself = sie
kann sich gut selbst versorgen
• (*other uses*)
you might as well go = du kannst ruhig
gehen
I can't very well say no = ich kann kaum
nein sagen
2 *adjective*
• = gesund
she is not well = es geht ihr nicht gut
get well soon! = gute Besserung!

• **as well** = auch
she can sing as well as dance = sie kann
singen und auch tanzen

well-known *adjective*
= bekannt

Welsh
1 *noun*
• (*people*) **the Welsh** = die Waliser
• (*language*) = (das) Walisisch
2 *adjective* = walisisch ▶ **Countries p. 208**

west
1 *noun* = (der) Westen
to the west of London = westlich von
London
2 *adjective* = westlich, = West-
the west coast = die Westküste
3 *adverb* = nach Westen

West Indies *noun*
= die Westindischen Inseln (*plural*)

wet
1 *adjective*
• (*damp*) = nass
to get wet = nass werden (**!** *sein*)
• (*when talking about the weather*) =
regnerisch
a wet day = ein regnerischer Tag
2 *verb* = nass machen

what
1 *pronoun*
(*in questions*) = was
what's in that box? = was ist in der
Schachtel?
what is your address? = wie ist Ihre
Adresse?
what's your name? = wie heißt du?
what is the weather like? = wie ist das
Wetter?
what for? = wozu?
• (*that which*) = was
you can do what you want = du kannst
machen, was du willst
what we need is a timetable = was wir
brauchen, ist ein Fahrplan
2 *adjective*
• = welcher/welche/welches
what book did you choose? = welches
Buch hast du dir ausgesucht?
• (*asking for an amount*) = wie viel, (*with
plural*) = wie viele
what weight is it? = wie viel wiegt es?
at what time? = um wie viel Uhr?
• (*in exclamations*) = was für
what a lovely day = was für ein schöner Tag
• (*other uses*)
what if? = was ist, wenn?
what about tennis? = wie wärs mit Tennis?

> **!** Note that **wärs** is a shortened form of
> **wäre es**, used in conversational German.

W

whatever pronoun
= was ... auch
whatever they do, they'll still lose = was sie
auch machen, sie verlieren trotzdem
whatever happens = was auch geschieht
take whatever you want = nimm, was du
willst

wheat noun
= (der) Weizen

wheel noun
= (das) Rad

wheelchair noun
= (der) Rollstuhl

when
1 conjunction
(with the present or future) = wenn, (with
the past) = als
when he comes we'll go for a walk = wenn
er kommt, gehen wir spazieren
I was still asleep when the bell rang = ich
schlief noch, als es klingelte
2 adverb = wann
I don't know when the film starts = ich
weiß nicht, wann der Film anfängt
3 pronoun
by when/till when? = bis wann?
from when? = ab wann?
since when? = seit wann?

where
1 adverb = wo
where are you going? = wo gehst du hin?
do you know where he comes from? =
weißt du, woher er kommt?
2 conjunction = wo
I'll leave the key where you can see it = ich
lasse den Schlüssel, wo du ihn sehen
kannst

whether conjunction
= ob
can you check whether it's correct? =
können Sie nachprüfen, ob es richtig ist?

which
1 adjective = welcher/welche/welches

! Note that welcher, welche and welches
change their endings in the same way as
der/die/das.

which book do you want? = welches Buch
willst du?
2 pronoun
• = welcher/welche/welches

! Note that welcher (masculine), welche
(feminine) and welches (neuter) agree in
gender with the noun they stand for.

which (one) do you want? =
welchen/welche/welches willst du?

• (as a relative pronoun) = der/die/das
the film which is on at the moment = der
Film, der gerade läuft
**the blue book, the title of which I've
forgotten** = das blaue Buch, dessen Titel
ich vergessen habe
(when referring back) = was
he's always late, which I can't stand = er
kommt immer zu spät, was ich nicht
leiden kann

while
1 conjunction = während
while I was writing a letter he watched TV
= während ich einen Brief schrieb, sah er
fern
she fell asleep while watching TV = sie
schlief beim Fernsehen ein
2 noun
a while = eine Weile
a while ago = vor kurzem

whisper verb
= flüstern

whistle
1 verb = pfeifen
2 noun = (die) Pfeife

white adjective
= weiß ▶**Colours p. 204**

who pronoun
• (in questions) = wer
who told you? = wer hat dir das erzählt?
(in the accusative) = wen
who did you invite? = wen hast du
eingeladen?
(in the dative) = wem
who did you go to the cinema with? = mit
wem bist du ins Kino gegangen?
• (as a relative pronoun) = der/die/das

! A relative pronoun must agree in gender
and number with the noun to which it
refers.

my friend who lives in London = meine
Freundin, die in London wohnt

whole
1 noun
the whole = das Ganze
the whole of [the country | London | August ...]
= [das ganze Land | ganz London | den ganzen
August ...]
on the whole = im Großen und Ganzen
2 adjective = ganz
three whole weeks = drei ganze Wochen

whose pronoun
• (in questions) = wessen
whose dog is that? = wessen Hund ist das?
whose is this? = wem gehört das?
• (as a relative pronoun) = dessen/deren/
dessen

! Note that the pronoun must agree in gender and number with the noun to which it refers back. In the following example, whose is **deren** because **die Frau** is feminine.

the woman whose house I am buying = die Frau, deren Haus ich kaufe

why adverb
= warum
why not? = warum nicht?
that's why I can't stand him = darum kann ich ihn nicht ausstehen

wide
1 adjective
* (broad) = breit
the room is 5 metres wide = das Zimmer ist fünf Meter breit
* (large) = groß
a wide range of games = eine große Auswahl an Spielen
* (extensive) = weit
2 adverb = weit
to open the window wide = das Fenster weit aufmachen

wife noun
= (die) Ehefrau

wild adjective
* (not tame) = wild
* (out of control) = verrückt
* (furious) = wütend, = wild✶
to go wild = wild werden✶ (**!** sein)

wildlife noun
(animals) = (die) Tierwelt
(animals and plants) = (die) Tier- und Pflanzenwelt

! A hyphen is used to represent the second part of the compound noun **Tierwelt** and avoid repetition.

will verb

! Note that will is normally translated by **werden**, since in German the future tense is formed by **werden** and the infinitive of the main verb. However, the present tense and verbs implying the future, such as **können** (= can), **sollen** (= should) and **müssen** (= must), are often used to express the future tense.

* **it will be sunny tomorrow** = morgen wird die Sonne scheinen
what will we do? = was machen wir?

! Note that **werden** is always used when some doubt is expressed about the future.

they will probably leave tomorrow = sie werden wahrscheinlich morgen abfahren
* (expressing intentions, making assumptions)
she'll be there by now = sie wird jetzt schon da sein

! Note that in the following two examples the present tense is used.

we won't stay long = wir bleiben nicht lange
I'll wait for you at the airport = ich warte am Flughafen auf dich
* (expressing willingness) = wollen
he won't help me = er will mir nicht helfen
* (in invitations, requests, short questions and answers)
will you have some more coffee? = möchten Sie noch Kaffee?
he will be there, won't he? = er wird doch da sein?
will you please be quiet! = sei bitte ruhig!
he won't be ready yet—yes he will = er wird noch nicht fertig sein—doch

win verb
= gewinnen

wind noun
= (der) Wind

window noun
= (das) Fenster

windscreen noun
= (die) Windschutzscheibe

windscreen wiper noun
(der) Scheibenwischer

windsurfing noun
= (das) Windsurfen

windy adjective
= windig

wine noun
= (der) Wein

wing noun
= (der) Flügel

winter noun
= (der) Winter
in winter = im Winter

wipe verb
= abwischen
to wipe one's mouth = sich (dative) den Mund abwischen
to wipe one's feet = sich (dative) die Schuhe abtreten
to wipe the floor = den Boden aufwischen
wipe up
= aufwischen
(dry dishes) = abtrocknen

wise adjective
= weise
(of a decision) = klug

wish
1 noun = (der) Wunsch
best wishes = alles Gute, (in a letter) = mit freundlichen Grüßen ▶**Letter-writing p. 262**

W

2 *verb*
= wünschen
to wish for something = sich (*dative*) etwas wünschen
to wish someone a happy birthday = jemandem alles Gute zum Geburtstag wünschen

with *preposition*
* = mit (+ *dative*)
to go away with friends = mit Freunden wegfahren (**!** *sein*)
* (*at the house of*) = bei (+ *dative*)
I stayed the night with friends = ich habe bei Freunden übernachtet
* (*showing emotion*) = vor (+ *dative*)
to tremble with fear = vor Angst zittern

> **!** *Note that* with *is often used after adjectives—*to be angry *or* happy with someone, *etc. You will find translations for these under the entries* angry, happy, *etc.*

without *preposition*
= ohne (+ *accusative*)

wolf *noun*
= (der) Wolf

woman *noun*
= (die) Frau

wonder
1 *verb*
* (*ask oneself*) = sich fragen
I wonder if I should do it? = ich frage mich, ob ich es tun soll?
I wonder [who | why | what …]? = [wer | warum | was …] wohl?
* (*in polite requests*)
I wonder if you could help me? = könntest du mir vielleicht helfen?
I wonder if I could ask you a favour? = könnte ich Sie vielleicht um einen Gefallen bitten?
2 *noun* = (das) Wunder

wonderful *adjective*
= wunderbar

wood *noun*
* (*timber*) = (das) Holz
made of wood = aus Holz
* (*forest*) = (der) Wald

wool *noun*
= (die) Wolle

word *noun*
= (das) Wort
I didn't say a word = ich habe kein Wort gesagt
to have a word with someone = mit jemandem sprechen

> **!** *Note that* Wort *has two plurals:* Worte *is used when the words are connected in a text or conversation, and* Wörter *when the words are unrelated.*

in other words = mit anderen Worten
words in the dictionary = Wörter im Wörterbuch

word processor *noun*
= (das) Textverarbeitungssystem

work
1 *verb*
* = arbeiten
to work at home = zu Hause arbeiten
to work as a doctor = Arzt/Ärztin sein
▶**Professions p. 298**
* (*function*) = funktionieren
the TV isn't working = der Fernseher funktioniert nicht
it's not working = es funktioniert nicht, = es geht nicht✗
* (*to be successful*)
(*of an idea*) = klappen
(*of medicine*) = wirken
* (*use, operate*) = bedienen
to work the brake = die Bremse betätigen
2 *noun*
* = (die) Arbeit
to be out of work = arbeitslos sein
to be off work = nicht arbeiten
it's hard work learning German = Deutsch zu lernen ist schwer
* (*for building, repairs*)
work(s) = Arbeiten (*plural*)
* (*by an artist*) = (das) Werk
work out
* (*solve*) = lösen
to work out the answer = die Antwort herausfinden
* (*understand*) = verstehen
* (*with figures*) = ausrechnen
* (*go well*) = klappen
* (*take exercise*) = trainieren
work up
to get worked up = sich aufregen

worker *noun*
(*in a factory*) = (der) Arbeiter/(die) Arbeiterin
(*in an office*) = (der/die) Angestellte

working-class *adjective*
= der Arbeiterklasse
a working-class family = eine Familie der Arbeiterklasse
to be working-class = zur Arbeiterklasse gehören

world *noun*
= (die) Welt
the biggest city in the world = die größte Stadt auf der Welt
all over the world = in der ganzen Welt

worm *noun*
= (der) Wurm

worried *adjective*
= besorgt

✗ in informal situations

worry *verb*
* (*be worried*) = sich (*dative*) Sorgen machen
  don't worry about it = mach dir darum keine Sorgen
* (*make worried*) = beunruhigen

worse *adjective*
* = schlechter
  he's getting worse (*in health*) = es geht ihm schlechter
* (*more serious*) = schlimmer
  there's nothing worse = es gibt nichts Schlimmeres

worst
1 *noun*
  the worst = das Schlimmste
  that's the worst of all = das ist das Allerschlimmste
  he/she is the worst at French = er ist der Schlechteste/sie ist die Schlechteste in Französisch
2 *adjective* = schlechtester/schlechteste/ schlechtestes
  (*most serious*) = schlimmster/ schlimmste/schlimmstes
  the worst film I've ever seen = der schlechteste Film, den ich je gesehen habe
  his worst enemy = sein schlimmster Feind

worth *adjective*
  to be worth £100 = hundert Pfund wert sein
  it isn't worth it = es lohnt sich nicht

would *verb*

> ! Note that would *is usually translated by the imperfect subjunctive of* werden, *to form the conditional tense.*

I would do it = ich würde es tun
I would pay, but I haven't got any money on me = ich würde zahlen, aber ich habe kein Geld dabei
he wouldn't talk to me = er wollte nicht mit mir sprechen

> ! The imperfect subjunctive, especially of haben *or* sein, *can be used instead of the conditional tense.*

we would have missed the train if we had left later = wir hätten den Zug verpasst, wenn wir später weggegangen wären
* (*in reported speech*)
  he said he'd come = er sagte, er würde kommen
* (*when talking about one's wishes, asking*)
  what would you like? = was möchten Sie?
  we would like to stay another night = wir möchten noch eine Nacht bleiben

wrap *verb*
  = einwickeln

wreck
1 *verb* = zerstören
2 *noun* = (das) Wrack

wrestling *noun*
  = (das) Ringen

wrist *noun*
  = (das) Handgelenk

write *verb*
  = schreiben
  to write to someone, (*US*) **to write someone** = jemandem schreiben
  to write to a company = an eine Firma schreiben
  to write a letter = einen Brief schreiben
  to write a cheque = einen Scheck ausschreiben
write back
  = zurückschreiben
write down
  = aufschreiben
write out
  to write out a list = eine Liste aufstellen
  to write out a cheque = einen Scheck ausstellen

writing pad *noun*
  = (der) Schreibblock

wrong
1 *adjective*
* (*not correct*) = falsch
  that's wrong = das ist falsch
  to say the wrong thing = das Falsche sagen
  to be wrong (*make a mistake*) = sich irren
* (*not as it should be*)
  to be wrong = nicht stimmen
  there's something wrong = etwas stimmt nicht
  what's wrong? = was ist los?
  what's wrong with you? (*if ill*) = was fehlt dir?, (*if behaving oddly*) = was hast du?
* (*dishonest*) = unrecht
  it's wrong to steal = es ist unrecht zu stehlen
  she hasn't done anything wrong = sie hat nichts Unrechtes getan
2 *adverb*
  to get something wrong = etwas falsch machen
  the radio has gone wrong = das Radio ist kaputtgegangen**✱**

X-ray
1 *noun* = (das) Röntgenbild
  to have an X-ray = sich röntgen lassen
2 *verb* = röntgen

yacht *noun*
= (die) Jacht

yard *noun*
* (*of a building*) = (der) Hof
  (*for storage*) = (das) Lager
* (*measure*) = (das) Yard
* (*US: garden*) = (der) Garten

yawn *verb*
= gähnen

year *noun*
* = (das) Jahr
  last year = voriges Jahr
  he's lived there for years = er wohnt seit
  Jahren da
  18 years old = achtzehn Jahre alt
  a 4-year-old = ein Vierjähriger/eine
  Vierjährige
  to work all year round = das ganze Jahr
  über arbeiten
  that'll take years = das dauert ewig
* (*group of students, vintage*) =
  (der) Jahrgang
  which year are you in? (*at school*) = in
  welche Klasse gehst du?
  a first-year student = ein Student/eine
  Studentin im ersten Jahr

yell
1 *verb* = schreien
2 *noun* = (der) Schrei

yellow
adjective = gelb ▶ Colours p. 204

yes *adverb*
* = ja
  are you coming with us?—yes I am =
  kommst du mit?—ja
* (*when contradicting*) = doch
  they don't know each other—yes they do
  = sie kennen sich nicht—doch

yesterday *adverb*
= gestern

yet
1 *adverb*
* = noch
  it's not ready yet = es ist noch nicht fertig
* (*in questions*) = schon
  have they arrived yet? = sind sie schon
  angekommen?
2 *conjunction* = doch
  and yet = und doch

yoghurt *noun*
= (der) *or* (das) Joghurt

you *pronoun*

> ❗ *In German* **you** *has two forms,* **du** *and*
> **Sie**. *Note that* **du** *is less formal and is*
> *used when speaking to someone you*
> *know well, a child or a family member.*
> *Young people always address each other*
> *as* **du**. *When speaking to a person or a*
> *group of people you do not know very*
> *well, use the polite form,* **Sie**.

* (*as the subject of a sentence, in the*
  nominative)
  (*informal*) = du, (*plural*) = ihr
  (*polite*) = Sie
  it was you = du warst es/ihr wart es/Sie
  waren es
  you two are annoying me = ihr zwei ärgert
  mich/Sie zwei ärgern mich
* (*as the object of a sentence, in the*
  accusative)
  (*informal*) = dich, (*plural*) = euch
  (*polite*) = Sie
  he knows you = er kennt dich/euch/Sie
* (*as an indirect object, in the dative*)
  (*informal*) = dir, (*plural*) = euch
  (*polite*) = Ihnen
  I'll give you my address = ich gebe
  dir/euch/Ihnen meine Adresse
* (*indefinite use*) = man

> ❗ *Note that* **man** *can only be used as the*
> *subject of a sentence. The direct-object*
> *form in the accusative is* **einen**. *The dative*
> *is* **einem**.

  you never know = man kann nie wissen
  he can make you angry = er kann einen
  ärgern
  she helps you if she can = sie hilft einem,
  wenn sie kann
  smoking is bad for you = Rauchen ist
  ungesund

young
1 *adjective* = jung
  young people = junge Leute
2 *noun*
* (*young animal*) = (das) Junge
* **the young** (*young people*) = die Jugend

your *adjective*
* (*informal*) = dein, (*plural*) = euer
  (*polite*) = Ihr

> ❗ *Note that* **dein, euer** *and* **Ihr** *change their*
> *endings in the same way as* **ein**. *The*
> *informal and polite forms follow the same*
> *rules as for* **you**.

  I hate your dog = ich hasse
  deinen/euren/Ihren Hund

> ❗ *Note that the second e is dropped in*
> **euren**.

* (*indefinite use*) = sein

> ❗ *Note that* **sein** *is used when* **you** *would*
> *be translated by* **man**.

  you buy your ticket at the door = man
  kauft seine Karte an der Tür
  smoking is bad for your health = Rauchen
  ist schlecht für die Gesundheit

yours *pronoun*
* (*informal*) = deiner/deine/deins, (*plural*) = eurer/eure/eures

> **!** *Note that the pronoun agrees in number and gender with the noun it stands for:*
> yours (*meaning the pencil*) is red = deiner (*der Bleistift*) ist rot; yours (*meaning the shoes*) are new = deine (*die Schuhe*) sind neu.

a friend of yours = ein Freund von dir/euch
these books are yours = diese Bücher gehören dir/euch

> **!** *This pronoun has informal and polite forms that follow the same rules as for* you.

* (*polite*) = Ihrer/Ihre/Ihrs
my garden is bigger than yours = mein Garten ist größer als Ihrer
she is a friend of yours = sie ist eine Freundin von Ihnen

yourself *pronoun*

> **!** *This pronoun has informal and polite forms that follow the same rules as for* you.

* (*when translated by a reflexive verb in German*)
(*informal*) = dich, (*polite*) = sich
calm yourself = beruhige dich/beruhigen Sie sich
(*reflexive dative pronoun*) = dir, (*polite*) = sich
did you hurt yourself? = hast du dir wehgetan?/haben Sie sich wehgetan?
* (*used for emphasis*) = selbst
you said it yourself = du hast es selbst gesagt/Sie haben es selbst gesagt
* **by yourself** = allein

yourselves *pronoun*

> **!** *This pronoun has informal and polite forms that follow the same rules as for* you.

* (*when translated by a reflexive verb in German*)
(*informal*) = euch, (*polite*) = sich
calm yourselves = beruhigt euch/beruhigen Sie sich

(*reflexive dative pronoun*) = euch, (*polite*) = sich
did you hurt yourselves? = habt ihr euch wehgetan?/haben Sie sich wehgetan?
* (*used for emphasis*) = selbst
are you going to organize it yourselves? = organisiert ihr das selbst?/organisieren Sie das selbst?
* **by yourselves** = allein

youth *noun*
* (die) Jugend
* (*young man*) = (der) Jugendliche

youth hostel *noun*
= (die) Jugendherberge

Zz

zap *verb*
* (*kill*) = abknallen✗
* (*switch channels*) = umschalten
* (*remove from a computer screen*) = löschen

zapper *noun*
= (die) Fernbedienung

zebra *noun*
= (das) Zebra

zebra crossing *noun* (*British*)
= (der) Zebrastreifen

zero *noun*
= (die) Null

zip *noun* (*British*)
= (der) Reißverschluss
to undo the zip = den Reißverschluss aufmachen

Zip code *noun* (*US*)
= (die) Postleitzahl

zipper *noun* (*US*) ▶ zip

zodiac *noun*
= (der) Tierkreis

zone *noun*
= (die) Zone

zoo *noun*
= (der) Zoo

Z

German in use

German in use

Regular verbs

Most German verbs are regular and add the same endings to their stem. You find the stem by taking away the **-en** (or sometimes just **-n**) from the end of the infinitive. The infinitive of the verb, for example **machen**, is the form you look up in the dictionary. The stem of **machen** is **mach-**. There are six endings for each tense, to go with the different pronouns:

ich = *I*   du = *you*   er/sie/es = *he/she/it*
wir = *we*   ihr = *you*   sie/Sie = *they/you* (*polite form*).

Present tense

For example, *I make, I am making* or *I do make*:

infinitive	ich	du	er/sie/es	wir	ihr	sie/Sie
machen	mache	machst	macht	machen	macht	machen

Imperfect tense

For example, *I made, I was making* or *I used to make*:

infinitive	ich	du	er/sie/es	wir	ihr	sie/Sie
machen	machte	machtest	machte	machten	machtet	machten

Future tense

For example, *I will make* or *I shall make*. This is formed by using the present tense of **werden**, which is the equivalent of *will* or *shall*, with the infinitive verb: **ich werde machen**.

infinitive	ich	du	er/sie/es	wir	ihr	sie/Sie
werden	werde	wirst	wird	werden	werdet	werden

Perfect tense

For example, *I made* or *I have made*. For most German verbs the perfect is formed by using the present tense of **haben**, which is the equivalent of *have*, with the past participle: **ich habe gemacht**. Some verbs take **sein** instead of **haben**, and these are all marked (**! sein**) in the dictionary. They are mainly verbs expressing motion and involving a change of place:

he drove to Berlin today = er ist heute nach Berlin gefahren

Or they express a change of state, and this includes verbs meaning to happen (**geschehen**, **passieren**, **vorkommen**):

he woke up = er ist aufgewacht

infinitive	ich	du	er/sie/es	wir	ihr	sie/Sie
haben	habe	hast	hat	haben	habt	haben
sein	bin	bist	ist	sind	seid	sind

Irregular verbs and other forms

Some German verbs are irregular and change their stem or add different endings. All the irregular verbs that appear in the dictionary are given in the *List of irregular verbs* on page 361.

The subjunctive

This is a form of the verb that is used to express speculation, doubt or unlikelihood. It is rarely used in English (*if I were you* instead of *if I was you* is an exceptional example), but is still used in both written and spoken German.

Present tense

infinitive	ich	du	er/sie/es	wir	ihr	sie/Sie
machen	mache	machest	mache	machen	machet	machen
sein	sei	sei(e)st	sei	seien	seid	seien

Imperfect tense

For regular verbs this is the same as the normal imperfect forms, but irregular verbs vary.

infinitive	ich	du	er/sie/es	wir	ihr	sie/Sie
machen	machte	machtest	machte	machten	machtet	machten
werden	würde	würdest	würde	würden	würdet	würden
sein	wäre	wär(e)st	wäre	wären	wär(e)t	wären

The imperfect subjunctive of werden is used with an infinitive to form the conditional tense. This tense expresses what might happen if something else occurred.

he would go = er würde gehen
I wouldn't do that = das würde ich nicht machen

Reflexive verbs

The object of a reflexive verb is the same as its subject. In German, the object is a reflexive pronoun. This is usually in the accusative (I wash = **ich wasche mich**). The reflexive pronouns of some verbs are in the dative (I imagine = **ich stelle mir vor**), and these are marked in the English–German part of the dictionary with (*dative*).

infinitive	ich	du	er/sie/es	wir	ihr	sie/Sie
sich	wasche	wäschst	wäscht	waschen	wascht	waschen
waschen	mich	dich	sich	uns	euch	sich
sich	stelle	stellst	stellt	stellen	stellt	stellen
vorstellen	mir vor	dir vor	sich vor	uns vor	euch vor	sich vor

The passive

In the passive form, the subject of the verb experiences the action rather than performs it: he was asked = **er wurde gefragt**. In German, the passive is formed using parts of **werden** with the past participle:

present passive	*it is done*	es wird gemacht
imperfect passive	*it was done*	es wurde gemacht
future passive	*it will be done*	es wird gemacht werden
perfect passive	*it has been done*	es ist gemacht worden

When forming the perfect passive, note that the past participle of **werden** becomes **worden** rather than **geworden**.

Separable verbs

Separable verbs are marked in the German-English part of the dictionary, with a vertical bar after the prefix: **an|fangen**. In the perfect tense, the **ge-** of the past participle comes between the prefix and the verb, for example **er/sie/es hat an*ge*fangen**.

Articles

There are two articles in English, the definite article *the* and the indefinite article *a/an*. The way these are translated into German depends on the gender, number and case of the noun with which the article goes.

There are three genders of nouns in German: masculine (**der Mann** = the man), feminine (**die Frau** = the woman) and neuter (**das Buch** = the book). There are two forms of number: singular (**der Baum** = the tree) and plural (**die Bäume** = the trees). And there are four cases, which show the part a noun plays in a sentence: nominative, accusative, genitive and dative.

Definite article

the = der/die/das, (*plural*) = die

	SINGULAR masculine	feminine	neuter	PLURAL all genders
nominative	**der** Mann	**die** Frau	**das** Buch	**die** Bäume
accusative	**den** Mann	**die** Frau	**das** Buch	**die** Bäume
genitive	**des** Mannes	**der** Frau	**des** Buches	**der** Bäume
dative	**dem** Mann	**der** Frau	**dem** Buch	**den** Bäumen

Indefinite article

a/an = ein/eine/ein. This article can only be singular.

	masculine	feminine	neuter
nominative	**ein** Mann	**eine** Frau	**ein** Buch
accusative	**einen** Mann	**eine** Frau	**ein** Buch
genitive	**eines** Mannes	**einer** Frau	**eines** Buches
dative	**einem** Mann	**einer** Frau	**einem** Buch

Nouns

In German, all nouns start with a capital letter: **das Buch** = the book.

Gender

There are three genders of nouns in German: masculine (**der Mann** = the man), feminine (**die Frau** = the woman) and neuter (**das Buch** = the book). These three examples are logical, with masculine for a male person, feminine for a female person and neuter for an object. But it is not always like this with German nouns. Gender is sometimes determined by a noun's ending. For example, **das Mädchen** (= the girl) is neuter rather than feminine, simply because the ending **-chen** is always neuter.

The gender of German nouns is given in the dictionary. There are some general rules regarding the gender of groups of nouns, but individual genders must be checked by looking them up.

Masculine nouns

* male persons and animals: **der Arbeiter** = worker; **der Bär** = bear
* 'doers' and 'doing' instruments ending in **-er** in German: **der Gärtner** = gardener; **der Computer** = computer
* days, months and seasons: (**der**) **Montag** = Monday
* words ending in **-ich**, **-ig** and **-ling**: **der Honig** = honey; **der Lehrling** = apprentice
* words ending in **-ismus**, **-ist** and **-ant**.

Feminine nouns

* female persons and animals: **die Schauspielerin** = actress; **die Henne** = hen; the feminine form of professions and animals is made by adding **-in** to the masculine (**der Schauspieler/die Schauspielerin** = actor/actress)
* nouns ending in **-ei**, **-ie**, **-ik**, **-in**, **-ion**, **-heit**, **-keit**, **-schaft**, **-tät**, **-ung**, **-ur**: **die Gärtnerei** = gardening; **die Energie** = energy
* most nouns ending in **-e**: **die Blume** = flower; note that there are many exceptions, including **der Name** = name, **der Käse** = cheese, **das Ende** = end.

Neuter nouns

* names of continents, most countries and towns (see page 208): (**das**) **Deutschland** = Germany; (**das**) **Köln** = Cologne
* nouns ending in **-chen** and **-lein** (indicating *small*): **das Mädchen**, **das Fräulein** = girl.
* most (but not all!) nouns beginning with **Ge-** or ending in **-nis**, **-tel** or **-um**: **das Geheimnis** = secret; **das Zentrum** = centre
* infinitives of verbs used as nouns: **das Lachen** = laughter; **das Essen** = food

Compound nouns

When two nouns are put together to make one compound noun, it takes the gender of the second noun:

der Brief + die Marke = die Briefmarke.

Plural

There are no absolutely definitive rules for the plural forms of German nouns. Plurals generally add an ending (**der Freund, die Freunde**), and change a vowel to an umlaut (**der Gast, die Gäste**; **das Haus, die Häuser**). Feminine words ending in **-heit**, **-keit** and **-ung** add **-en** to make the plural (**die Abbildung, die Abbildungen**).

The plurals of all nouns are given in the German–English part of the dictionary.

Case

There are four cases, which show the part a noun plays in a sentence: nominative, accusative, genitive and dative. The noun's article changes according to the case, and the ending of the noun changes in some cases:

	SINGULAR masculine	feminine	neuter
nominative	der Mann	die Frau	das Buch
accusative	den Mann	die Frau	das Buch
genitive	des **Mannes**	der Frau	des **Buches**
dative	dem Mann	der Frau	dem Buch

	PLURAL masculine	feminine	neuter
nominative	die Männer	die Frauen	die Bücher
accusative	die Männer	die Frauen	die Bücher
genitive	der Männer	der Frauen	der Bücher
dative	den **Männern**	den Frauen	den **Büchern**

The nominative is used for the subject of a sentence; in sentences with **sein** (to be) and **werden** (to become), the noun after the verb is in the nominative.

the dog barked = der Hund bellte
that is my car = das ist mein Wagen

The accusative is used for the direct object and after some prepositions (listed on page 358):

she has a son = sie hat einen Sohn

The genitive shows possession, and is also used after some prepositions (listed on page 358):

my husband's dog = der Hund meines Mannes

The dative is used for the indirect object. Some German verbs, such as **helfen**, take only the dative. They are marked (+ *dative*) in the English–German part of the dictionary. The dative is also used after some prepositions (listed on page 358):

she gave the books to the children = sie gab den Kindern die Bücher

The following sentence combines all four cases:

der Mann gibt der Frau den Bleistift des Mädchens = *the man gives the woman the girl's pencil*
der Mann *is the subject* (*in the nominative*)
gibt *is the verb*
der Frau *is the indirect object* (*in the dative*)
den Bleistift *is the direct object* (*in the accusative*)
des Mädchens *is in the genitive* (*showing possession*).

Adjectives

An adjective is a word describing a noun. In German, an adjective in front of a noun adds endings that vary with the noun's gender, number and case. Adjectives that come after a noun do not add endings.

With the definite article

Adjectives following **der/die/das** take these endings:

	SINGULAR			PLURAL
	masculine	feminine	neuter	all genders
nominative	der rote Hut	die rote Lampe	das rote Buch	die roten Autos
accusative	den roten Hut	die rote Lampe	das rote Buch	die roten Autos
genitive	des roten Hutes	der roten Lampe	des roten Buches	der roten Autos
dative	dem roten Hut	der roten Lampe	dem roten Buch	den roten Autos

Some German adjectives follow the pattern of the definite article, and adjectives after them change their endings in the same way as after **der/die/das**. For example, **dieser/diese/dieses** (= this):

	SINGULAR			PLURAL
	masculine	feminine	neuter	all genders
nominative	dieser	diese	dieses	diese
accusative	diesen	diese	dieses	diese
genitive	dieses	dieser	dieses	dieser
dative	diesem	dieser	diesem	diesen

Other common examples are:

jeder/jede/jedes = *every, each*
jener/jene/jenes = *that*
mancher/manche/manches = *many a, some*

solcher/solche/solches = *such*
welcher/welche/welches = *which*

These adjectives appear in this way, with their masculine/feminine/neuter forms throughout the dictionary.

With the indefinite article

Adjectives following **ein/eine/ein** take these endings:

	SINGULAR		
	masculine	**feminine**	**neuter**
nominative	ein rot**er** Hut	eine rot**e** Lampe	ein rot**es** Buch
accusative	einen rot**en** Hut	eine rot**e** Lampe	ein rot**es** Buch
genitive	eines rot**en** Hutes	einer rot**en** Lampe	eines rot**en** Buches
dative	einem rot**en** Hut	einer rot**en** Lampe	einem rot**en** Buch

Some German adjectives follow the pattern of the indefinite article, and adjectives after them change their endings in the same way as after **ein/eine/ein**. They are:

dein = *your*	kein = *no*
euer = *your*	mein = *my*
Ihr = *your*	sein = *his/its*
ihr = *her/their*	unser = *our*

These adjectives can also go with plural nouns: no cars = **keine Autos**. All genders take the same endings in the plural:

	PLURAL
	all genders
nominative	kein**e** roten Autos
accusative	kein**e** roten Autos
genitive	kein**er** roten Autos
dative	kein**en** roten Autos

Without an article

Adjectives in front of a noun on their own, without an article, take the following endings:

	SINGULAR			PLURAL
	masculine	**feminine**	**neuter**	**all genders**
nominative	gut**er** Wein	frisch**e** Milch	kalt**es** Bier	alt**e** Leute
accusative	gut**en** Wein	frisch**e** Milch	kalt**es** Bier	alt**e** Leute
genitive	gut**en** Weins	frisch**er** Milch	kalt**en** Biers	alt**er** Leute
dative	gut**em** Wein	frisch**er** Milch	kalt**em** Bier	alt**en** Leuten

Adjectives as nouns

In German, adjectives can be used as nouns, spelt with a capital letter: **alt** = old, **ein Alter** = an old man, **eine Alte** = an old woman.

With the definite article (**der/die/das**), these nouns take the following endings:

	SINGULAR		PLURAL
	masculine	**feminine**	**both genders**
nominative	der Fremde	die Fremde	die Fremden
accusative	den Fremden	die Fremde	die Fremden
genitive	des Fremden	der Fremden	der Fremden
dative	dem Fremden	der Fremden	den Fremden

The feminine noun refers to a female stranger or foreigner. In the dictionary, this noun appears as:

der/die **Fremde**, *plural* **Fremden**.

With the indefinite article (**ein/eine/ein**), these nouns take the following endings:

	SINGULAR		PLURAL
	masculine	**feminine**	**both genders, without an article**
nominative	ein Fremder	eine Fremde	Fremde
accusative	einen Fremden	eine Fremde	Fremde
genitive	eines Fremden	einer Fremden	Fremder
dative	einem Fremden	einer Fremden	Fremden

Comparative and superlative

In English, the comparative of the adjective *small* is *smaller*, and of *difficult* is *more difficult*. The superlatives are *smallest* and *most difficult*. In German, there is just one way to form the comparative and superlative: by adding the endings **-er** and **-(e)st**:

small, smaller, smallest	= klein, kleiner, der/die/das kleinste

Many adjectives change their vowel to an umlaut in the comparative and superlative:

cold, colder, coldest	= kalt, kälter, der/die/das kälteste

Some important adjectives are irregular:

big, bigger, biggest	= groß, größer, der/die/das größte
good, better, best	= gut, besser, der/die/das beste
high, higher, highest	= hoch, höher, der/die/das höchste
much, more, most	= viel, mehr, der/die/das meiste
near, nearer, nearest	= nah, näher, der/die/das nächste

Comparative and superlative adjectives take the same endings as basic adjectives:

a smaller child	= ein kleineres Kind
the coldest month	= der kälteste Monat

Adverbs

In German almost all adjectives can also be used as adverbs, describing a verb, an adjective or another adverb.

she sings beautifully = sie singt schön

In the dictionary, most adjectives are not listed as adverbs as well. The adverb is only given if it has special importance, a different meaning, or if it is formed differently in German.

Some words, such as **auch** (= also), **fast** (= almost), **immer** (= always) and **leider** (= unfortunately) are used only as adverbs:

she is very clever = sie ist sehr klug

Comparative and superlative

The comparative is formed by adding **-er** to the basic adverb, and the superlative by putting **am** in front of the basic adverb and adding the ending **-(e)sten**:

clearly, more clearly, most clearly	= klar, klarer, am klarsten

Some important adverbs are irregular:

soon, earlier, at the earliest	= bald, früher, am frühesten
well, better, best	= gut, besser, am besten
willingly, more willingly, most willingly	= gern, lieber, am liebsten

Pronouns

Pronouns are words—such as *he*, *which* and *mine* in English—that stand instead of a noun.

Personal pronouns

These pronouns, such as he/she/it = **er/sie/es**, refer to people or things.

	I	you	he/it	she/it	it	we	you	they	you
nominative	ich	du	er	sie	es	wir	ihr	sie	Sie
accusative	mich	dich	ihn	sie	es	uns	euch	sie	Sie
dative	mir	dir	ihm	ihr	ihm	uns	euch	ihnen	Ihnen
	me	*you*	*him/it*	*her/it*	*it*	*us*	*you*	*them*	*you*

The genitive form is not given, because it is so rarely used.

In German there are two forms for you, **du** and **Sie**. **Du** is less formal and is used when speaking to someone you know well, a child or a family member. When speaking to a person or a group of people you do not know very well, use the polite form, **Sie**.

German pronouns agree in gender with the noun they refer to. In the nominative case, *it* might be translated by **er** or **sie**, as well as **es**:

it (the pencil) is red = er (der Bleistift) ist rot
it (the rose) is beautiful = sie (die Rose) ist schön
it (the car) is expensive = es (das Auto) ist teuer

Possessive pronouns

The possessive pronouns are:

mine = meiner/meine/mein(e)s
yours (informal singular) = deiner/deine/dein(e)s
his = seiner/seine/sein(e)s
hers = ihrer/ihre/ihr(e)s
its = seiner/seine/sein(e)s

ours = unserer/unsere/unser(e)s
yours (informal plural) = eurer/eure/eures
theirs = ihrer/ihre/ihr(e)s
yours (polite) = Ihrer, Ihre, Ihr(e)s

They all take endings like **meiner/meine/mein(e)s**, as follows:

	SINGULAR			PLURAL
	masculine	feminine	neuter	all genders
nominative	meiner	meine	mein(e)s	meine
accusative	meinen	meine	mein(e)s	meine
genitive	meines	meiner	meines	meiner
dative	meinem	meiner	meinem	meinen

Throughout the dictionary, these pronouns are given in their three nominative singular forms, in the order masculine/feminine/neuter: **meiner/meine/meins**. As can be seen in the table, in the neuter form an **-e-** can be added (making **meines**). This applies to all the possessive pronouns, but the extra **-e-** is rare.

Relative pronouns

These pronouns are used to introduce and link a new clause. In English they are *who*, *which*, *that* and *what*. In German they are **der**, **die** or **das**, depending on the noun referred to:

	SINGULAR			PLURAL
	masculine	feminine	neuter	all genders
nominative	der	die	das	die
accusative	den	die	das	die
genitive	dessen	deren	dessen	deren
dative	dem	der	dem	denen

Relative pronouns can be left out in English, but never in German:

the book (that) I'm reading = das Buch, das ich lese

They agree in gender and number with the noun they refer back to:

the man who visited us = der Mann, der uns besucht hat (**der** is masculine singular)

But the case of the pronoun depends on its function in the clause it introduces:

the pencil I bought yesterday = der Bleistift, den ich gestern gekauft habe

(**den** is masculine singular, but accusative because it is the object of the clause it introduces)

Interrogative pronouns

These pronouns are used to ask questions:

who? = wer?
what? = was?
which? = welcher/welche/welches?

Wer changes as follows:

nominative	wer?
accusative	wen?
genitive	wessen?
dative	wem?

Reflexive pronouns

The object of a reflexive verb is the same as its subject. In German, the object is a reflexive pronoun. This is usually in the accusative (I wash = **ich wasche *mich***). The reflexive pronouns of some verbs are in the dative (I imagine = **ich stelle *mir* vor**).

Indefinite pronouns

These pronouns do not refer to identifiable people or objects. In German, many indefinite pronouns, such as **etwas** (= something) and **nichts** (= nothing) never change. But some do take endings:

	someone	no one
nominative	jemand	niemand
accusative	jemanden	niemanden
dative	jemandem	niemandem

The genitive case is rarely used.

Prepositions

Prepositions are small words like *in*, that stand in front of a noun or pronoun. In German, the noun following a preposition always has to be in one of three cases—dative, accusative or genitive.

Prepositions can be prefixes and form separable verbs:

to walk along the street = die Straße entlanggehen
he is walking along the street = er geht die Straße entlang

In the dictionary, the case governed by a preposition is given:

mit (+ *dative*) means *mit always takes the dative case.*

The most common case used after prepositions is the dative. The following prepositions always take the dative:

aus	nach
außer	seit
bei	von
mit	zu

Some prepositions always take the accusative:

bis	gegen
durch	ohne
entlang	um
für	

Some prepositions always take the genitive:

anstatt
trotz
während
wegen

There is a group of prepositions that can take the dative or the accusative, depending on the sentence. They are:

an	über
auf	unter
hinter	vor
in	zwischen
neben	

If the phrase containing one of these prepositions describes position—where something is happening—the dative case is used:

she sat in the kitchen = sie saß in der Küche

But if the phrase containing the preposition describes movement—motion towards something—the accusative follows:

she went into the kitchen = sie ging in die Küche

Some forms of the definite article are usually shortened when used with prepositions:

am (an dem); **ans** (an das); **aufs** (auf das); **beim** (bei dem); **durchs** (durch das); **fürs** (für das); **im** (in dem); **ins** (in das); **ums** (um das); **vom** (von dem); **zum** (zu dem); **zur** (zu der).

Conjunctions

Conjunctions are small words, such as *and* = **und**, which join clauses together in a sentence. These common conjunctions link clauses together:

aber = *but*
denn = *for*
oder = *or*
sondern = *but* (*on the contrary*)
und = *and*

The conjunctions do not change normal word order in the two clauses:

ich gehe, und er kommt auch = *I am going, and he is coming too*

But there are many other conjunctions that send the verb to the end of the second clause:

als = *when*, = *as*   ob = *whether*
bevor = *before*   während = *while*
bis = *until*   wenn = *when*, = *if*
da = *since*   weil = *because*
dass = *that*

er konnte nicht in die Schule gehen, *weil* er krank *war* = *he couldn't go to school, because he was ill*

Word order

The basic rule for German word order is that the verb comes second in a sentence. The subject of the sentence usually comes before the verb:

meine Mutter fährt am Freitag nach Köln = *my mother is going to Cologne on Friday*

When the verb is made up of two parts, such as in the perfect and the future tenses, the auxiliary verb comes second in the sentence, while the past participle (in the perfect) or infinitive (in the future tense) goes to the end:

wir haben sehr lang gewartet = *we waited a very long time*
sie wird sicher bald kommen = *she is sure to turn up soon*

Past participles and infinitives go to the end in other sentences too:

ich kann dieses Lied nicht leiden = *I can't stand this song*
du musst hier bleiben = *you must stay here*

When a sentence starts with a clause, the verb stays in second place:

da ich kein Geld hatte, blieb ich zu Hause = *since I had no money, I stayed at home*

In the clause itself, the verb goes to the end:

er konnte nicht in die Schule gehen, weil er krank war

The relative pronouns **der**, **die** and **das**, as well as a number of conjunctions, send the verb to the end of the clause:

der Junge, der hier wohnt = *the boy who lives here*

When separable verbs separate, the prefix goes to the end:

der Film fängt um acht Uhr an = *the film starts at 8 o'clock*

In questions and commands, the verb is usually first in the sentence:

kommst du heute Abend? = *are you coming this evening?*
komm schnell rein! = *come in quickly!*

When there are a number of phrases in a sentence, the usual order for the different elements is 1 time, 2 manner, 3 place:

wir fahren heute mit dem Auto nach München = *we are driving to Munich today*
(*time* = heute; *manner* = mit dem Auto; *place* = nach München)

German irregular verbs

Present tense

In the present tense, the stem often changes in the **du** and **er/sie/es** forms. For example, **befehl-** becomes **befiehl-** and **fahr-** becomes **fähr-**. The other forms add regular endings to the stem. Some examples:

infinitive	ich	du	er/sie/es	wir	ihr	sie/Sie
befehlen	befehle	befiehlst	befiehlt	befehlen	befehlt	befehlen
fahren	fahre	fährst	fährt	fahren	fahrt	fahren

Imperfect tense

In the imperfect tense, the stem usually changes. The same endings are added to the changed stem in many cases. Some examples:

infinitive	ich	du	er/sie/es	wir	ihr	sie/Sie
befehlen	befahl	befahlst	befahl	befahlen	befahlt	befahlen
fahren	fuhr	fuhrst	fuhr	fuhren	fuhrt	fuhren

Future tense

This is formed using **werden** and the infinitive, as with regular verbs: **ich werde fahren**.

Perfect tense

The stem often changes in the perfect tense, making an irregular past participle:

befehlen—ich habe befohlen;
gehen—ich bin gegangen.

Auxiliary verbs

There are three verbs in German that help to make a compound tense, such as the future and imperfect. They are also used as verbs in their own right: to have = **haben**; to be = **sein**; to become = **werden**. Their present tenses are given on page 351.

haben	ich	du	er/sie/es	wir	ihr	sie/Sie
imperfect	hatte	hattest	hatte	hatten	hattet	hatten
perfect	habe gehabt	hast gehabt	hat gehabt	haben gehabt	habt gehabt	haben gehabt

sein	ich	du	er/sie/es	wir	ihr	sie/Sie
imperfect	war	warst	war	waren	wart	waren
perfect	bin gewesen	bist gewesen	ist gewesen	sind gewesen	seid gewesen	sind gewesen

werden	ich	du	er/sie/es	wir	ihr	sie/Sie
imperfect	wurde	wurdest	wurde	wurden	wurdet	wurden
perfect	bin geworden	bist geworden	ist geworden	sind geworden	seid geworden	sind geworden

List of irregular verbs

In this list of irregular verbs, the 1st, 2nd and 3rd persons singular of the present tense (**ich**, **du**, **er/sie/es**) are given.

The 1st and 3rd persons singular of the imperfect are always identical:

ich backte, er/sie/es backte

The other forms add regular endings to the stem.

Separable verbs, such as **anfangen**, are not listed. You can look them up in the table under the simple verb without the prefix, such as **fangen**.

infinitive	present tense ich, du, er/sie/es	imperfect tense er/sie/es	perfect tense er/sie/es
backen	backe, bäckst, bäckt	backte	hat gebacken
befehlen	befehle, befiehlst, befiehlt	befahl	hat befohlen
beginnen	beginne, beginnst, beginnt	begann	hat begonnen
beißen	beiße, beißt, beißt	biss	hat gebissen

infinitive	present tense ich, du, er/sie/es	imperfect tense er/sie/es	perfect tense er/sie/es
bekommen	bekomme, bekommst, bekommt	bekam	hat bekommen
bergen	berge, birgst, birgt	barg	hat geborgen
besitzen	besitze, besitzt, besitzt	besaß	hat besessen
betrügen	betrüge, betrügst, betrügt	betrog	hat betrogen
biegen	biege, biegst, biegt	bog	hat or ist gebogen
bieten	biete, bietest, bietet	bot	hat geboten
binden	binde, bindest, bindet	band	hat gebunden
bitten	bitte, bittest, bittet	bat	hat gebeten
blasen	blase, bläst, bläst	blies	hat geblasen
bleiben	bleibe, bleibst, bleibt	blieb	ist geblieben
braten	brate, brätst, brät	briet	hat gebraten
brechen	breche, brichst, bricht	brach	hat gebrochen
brennen	brenne, brennst, brennt	brannte	hat gebrannt
bringen	bringe, bringst, bringt	brachte	hat gebracht
denken	denke, denkst, denkt	dachte	hat gedacht
dürfen	darf, darfst, darf	durfte	hat gedurft
einladen	lade ein, lädst ein, lädt ein	lud ein	hat eingeladen
einweisen	weise ein, weist ein, weist ein	wies ein	hat eingewiesen
empfangen	empfange, empfängst, empfängt	empfing	hat empfangen
empfehlen	empfehle, empfiehlst, empfiehlt	empfahl	hat empfohlen
entscheiden	entscheide, entscheidest, entscheidet	entschied	hat entschieden
erfahren	erfahre, erfährst, erfährt	erfuhr	hat erfahren
erfinden	erfinde, erfindest, erfindet	erfand	hat erfunden
erschrecken	erschrecke, erschrickst, erschrickt	erschrak	ist erschrocken
ertrinken	ertrinke, ertrinkst, ertrinkt	ertrank	ist ertrunken
essen	esse, isst, isst	aß	hat gegessen
fahren	fahre, fährst, fährt	fuhr	ist gefahren
fallen	falle, fällst, fällt	fiel	ist gefallen
fangen	fange, fängst, fängt	fing	hat gefangen
fechten	fechte, fichtst, ficht	focht	hat gefochten
finden	finde, findest, findet	fand	hat gefunden
flechten	flechte, flichtst, flicht	flocht	hat geflochten
fliegen	fliege, fliegst, fliegt	flog	ist geflogen
fliehen	fliehe, fliehst, flieht	floh	ist geflohen
fließen	fließe, fließt, fließt	floss	ist geflossen
fressen	fresse, frisst, frisst	fraß	hat gefressen
frieren	friere, frierst, friert	fror	hat or ist gefroren
geben	gebe, gibst, gibt	gab	hat gegeben
gefallen	gefalle, gefällst, gefällt	gefiel	hat gefallen
gehen	gehe, gehst, geht	ging	ist gegangen
gelingen	es gelingt mir/dir/ihm/ihr/ihm	gelang	ist gelungen
gelten	gelte, giltst, gilt	galt	hat gegolten
genießen	genieße, genießt, genießt	genoss	hat genossen
geraten	gerate, gerätst, gerät	geriet	ist geraten
geschehen	es geschieht	geschah	ist geschehen
gewinnen	gewinne, gewinnst, gewinnt	gewann	hat gewonnen
gießen	gieße, gießt, gießt	goss	hat gegossen
gleichen	gleiche, gleichst, gleicht	glich	hat geglichen
graben	grabe, gräbst, gräbt	grub	hat gegraben
greifen	greife, greifst, greift	griff	hat gegriffen
haben	habe, hast, hat	hatte	hat gehabt
halten	halte, hältst, hält	hielt	hat gehalten

infinitive	present tense ich, du, er/sie/es	imperfect tense er/sie/es	perfect tense er/sie/es
hängen	hänge, hängst, hängt	hing	hat gehangen
heben	hebe, hebst, hebt	hob	hat gehoben
heißen	heiße, heißt, heißt	hieß	hat geheißen
helfen	helfe, hilfst, hilft	half	hat geholfen
hinweisen	weise hin, weist hin, weist hin	wies hin	hat hingewiesen
kennen	kenne, kennst, kennt	kannte	hat gekannt
klingen	klinge, klingst, klingt	klang	hat geklungen
kneifen	kneife, kneifst, kneift	kniff	hat gekniffen
kommen	komme, kommst, kommt	kam	ist gekommen
können	kann, kannst, kann	konnte	hat gekonnt
kriechen	krieche, kriechst, kriecht	kroch	ist gekrochen
lassen	lasse, lässt, lässt	ließ	hat gelassen
laufen	laufe, läufst, läuft	lief	ist gelaufen
leiden	leide, leidest, leidet	litt	hat gelitten
leihen	leihe, leihst, leiht	lieh	hat geliehen
lesen	lese, liest, liest	las	hat gelesen
liegen	liege, liegst, liegt	lag	hat gelegen
lügen	lüge, lügst, lügt	log	hat gelogen
mahlen	mahle, mahlst, mahlt	mahlte	hat gemahlen
meiden	meide, meidest, meidet	mied	hat gemieden
melken	melke, melkst, melkt	melkte	hat gemolken
messen	messe, misst, misst	maß	hat gemessen
misslingen	misslinge, misslingst, misslingt	misslang	ist misslungen
mögen	mag, magst, mag	mochte	hat gemocht
müssen	muss, musst, muss	musste	hat gemusst
nehmen	nehme, nimmst, nimmt	nahm	hat genommen
nennen	nenne, nennst, nennt	nannte	hat genannt
pfeifen	pfeife, pfeifst, pfeift	pfiff	hat gepfiffen
quellen	quelle, quillst, quillt	quoll	ist gequollen
raten	rate, rätst, rät	riet	hat geraten
reiben	reibe, reibst, reibt	rieb	hat gerieben
reißen	reiße, reißt, reißt	riss	hat gerissen
reiten	reite, reitest, reitet	ritt	ist geritten
rennen	renne, rennst, rennt	rannte	ist gerannt
riechen	rieche, riechst, riecht	roch	hat gerochen
rufen	rufe, rufst, ruft	rief	hat gerufen
saufen	saufe, säufst, säuft	soff	hat gesoffen
schaffen	schaffe, schaffst, schafft	schuf	hat geschaffen
scheiden	scheide, scheidest, scheidet	schied	hat or ist geschieden
scheinen	scheine, scheinst, scheint	schien	hat geschienen
schieben	schiebe, schiebst, schiebt	schob	hat geschoben
schießen	schieße, schießt, schießt	schoss	hat geschossen
schlafen	schlafe, schläfst, schläft	schlief	hat geschlafen
schlagen	schlage, schlägst, schlägt	schlug	hat geschlagen
schleichen	schleiche, schleichst, schleicht	schlich	ist geschlichen
schleifen	schleife, schleifst, schleift	schliff	hat geschliffen
schließen	schließe, schließt, schließt	schloss	hat geschlossen
schmeißen	schmeiße, schmeißt, schmeißt	schmiss	hat geschmissen
schmelzen	schmelze, schmilzt, schmilzt	schmolz	ist geschmolzen
schneiden	schneide, schneidest, schneidet	schnitt	hat geschnitten
schreiben	schreibe, schreibst, schreibt	schrieb	hat geschrieben

infinitive	present tense ich, du, er/sie/es	imperfect tense er/sie/es	perfect tense er/sie/es
schreien	schreie, schreist, schreit	schrie	hat geschrien
schweigen	schweige, schweigst, schweigt	schwieg	hat geschwiegen
schwimmen	schwimme, schwimmst, schwimmt	schwamm	ist geschwommen
schwören	schwöre, schwörst, schwört	schwor	hat geschworen
sehen	sehe, siehst, sieht	sah	hat gesehen
sein	bin, bist, ist	war	ist gewesen
singen	singe, singst, singt	sang	hat gesungen
sinken	sinke, sinkst, sinkt	sank	ist gesunken
sitzen	sitze, sitzt, sitzt	saß	hat gesessen
sollen	soll, sollst, soll	sollte	hat gesollt
spinnen	spinne, spinnst, spinnt	spann	hat gesponnen
sprechen	spreche, sprichst, spricht	sprach	hat gesprochen
springen	springe, springst, springt	sprang	ist gesprungen
stechen	steche, stichst, sticht	stach	hat gestochen
stehen	stehe, stehst, steht	stand	hat gestanden
stehlen	stehle, stiehlst, stiehlt	stahl	hat gestohlen
steigen	steige, steigst, steigt	stieg	ist gestiegen
sterben	sterbe, stirbst, stirbt	starb	ist gestorben
stinken	stinke, stinkst, stinkt	stank	hat gestunken
stoßen	stoße, stößt, stößt	stieß	hat gestoßen
streichen	streiche, streichst, streicht	strich	hat gestrichen
streiten	streite, streitest, streitet	stritt	hat gestritten
tragen	trage, trägst, trägt	trug	hat getragen
treffen	treffe, triffst, trifft	traf	hat getroffen
treiben	treibe, treibst, treibt	trieb	hat getrieben
treten	trete, trittst, tritt	trat	ist getreten
trinken	trinke, trinkst, trinkt	trank	hat getrunken
tun	tue, tust, tut	tat	hat getan
überweisen	überweise, überweist, überweist	überwies	hat überwiesen
umziehen	ziehe um, ziehst um, zieht um	zog um	ist or hat umgezogen
verbieten	verbiete, verbietest, verbietet	verbot	hat verboten
verderben	verderbe, verdirbst, verdirbt	verdarb	hat or ist verdorben
vergessen	vergesse, vergisst, vergisst	vergaß	hat vergessen
verlieren	verliere, verlierst, verliert	verlor	hat verloren
verschwinden	verschwinde, verschwindest, verschwindet	verschwand	ist verschwunden
verstehen	verstehe, verstehst, versteht	verstand	hat verstanden
verzeihen	verzeihe, verzeihst, verzeiht	verzieh	hat verziehen
wachsen	wachse, wächst, wächst	wuchs	ist gewachsen
waschen	wasche, wäschst, wäscht	wusch	hat gewaschen
wenden	wende, wendest, wendet	wandte or wendete	hat gewandt or gewendet
werben	werbe, wirbst, wirbt	warb	hat geworben
werden	werde, wirst, wird	wurde	ist geworden
werfen	werfe, wirfst, wirft	warf	hat geworfen
wiegen	wiege, wiegst, wiegt	wog	hat gewogen
wissen	weiß, weißt, weiß	wusste	hat gewusst
wollen	will, willst, will	wollte	hat gewollt
ziehen	ziehe, ziehst, zieht	zog	hat gezogen
zwingen	zwinge, zwingst, zwingt	zwang	hat gezwungen